Life of

Napoleon Bonaparte

By Sir Walter Scott

Volume V

OMNIA VERITAS

SIR WALTER SCOTT

LIFE OF
NAPOLEON BONAPARTE
VOLUME V
1827

PUBLISHED BY
OMNIA VERITAS LTD

www.omnia-veritas.com

Hougoumont

CHAPTER LXXV **19**

Buonaparte marches upon Blucher, who is in possession of Soissons—Attacks the place without success—Battle of Craonne—Blucher retreats on Laon—Battle of Laon—Napoleon is compelled to withdraw on the 11th—He attacks Rheims, which is evacuated by the Russians—Defeat at Bar-sur-Aube of Oudinot and Gerard, who, with Macdonald, are forced to retreat towards Paris—Schwartzenberg wishes to retreat behind the Aube—but the Emperor Alexander and Lord Castlereagh opposing the measure, it is determined to proceed upon Paris—Napoleon occupies Arcis—Battle of Arcis—Napoleon is joined, in the night after the battle, by Macdonald, Oudinot, and Gerard—and retreats along the Aube. 19

BATTLE OF CRAONNE. 21
BATTLE OF LAON—RHEIMS. 23
OUDINOT AND GERARD. 26
THE MARCH UPON PARIS. 28

CHAPTER LXXVI **33**

Plans of Buonaparte—Military and Political Questions regarding Paris—Napoleon crosses the Marne on 22d March—Retrospect of Events in the vicinity of Lyons, &c.—Defeats of the French in various quarters—Marmont and Mortier retreat under the walls of Paris—Joseph Buonaparte—Maria Louisa, with the Civil Authorities, leave the City—Attack of Paris on the 30th—A Truce accorded—Joseph flies.. 33

PLANS OF BUONAPARTE. 33
PARIS. 35
THE ALLIES ADVANCE. 40
ALLIES APPROACH PARIS. 43
PARIS. 44
BELLEVILLE—MESNILMONTANT. 50
FALL OF PARIS. 53

CHAPTER LXXVII **57**

State of Parties in Paris—Royalists—Revolutionists—Buonapartists—Talleyrand—Chateaubriand—Mission to the Allied Sovereigns—Their answer—Efforts of the Buonapartists—Feelings of the lowest classes—of the middling ranks—Neutrality of the National Guard—Growing confidence of the Royalists—Proclamations and White Cockades—Crowds assemble at the Boulevards—The Allies are received with shouts of welcome—Their Army retires to quarters—and the Cossacks bivouac in the Champs Elysées... 57

PARTIES IN PARIS. 58
PROCLAMATION OF THE ALLIES. 60
ENTRANCE OF THE ALLIES. 63

CHAPTER LXXVIII 67

Fears of the Parisians—Proceedings of Napoleon—Operations of the French Cavalry in rear of the Allies—Capture of Weissemberg—The Emperor Francis is nearly surprised—Napoleon reaches Troyes on the night of the 29th March—Opinion of Macdonald as to the possibility of relieving Paris—Napoleon leaves Troyes, on the 30th, and meets Belliard, a few miles from Paris, in full retreat—Conversation betwixt them—He determines to proceed to Paris, but is at length dissuaded—and despatches Caulaincourt to receive terms from the Allied Sovereigns—He himself returns to Fontainbleau. 67

FEARS OF THE PARISIANS. 67
DOULANCOURT—TROYES. 69
CONVERSATION WITH BELLIARD. 71

CHAPTER LXXIX 75

The Allied Sovereigns issue a Proclamation that they will not treat with Buonaparte—A Provisional Government is named by the Conservative Senate, who also decree the forfeiture of Napoleon—This decree is sanctioned by all the Public Bodies in Paris—The legality of these proceedings discussed—Feelings towards Napoleon, of the Lower Classes, and of the Military—On 4th April, Buonaparte issues a document abdicating the Throne of France—His subsequent agitation, and wish to continue the war—The deed is finally despatched. 75

PROCLAMATION OF THE ALLIES. 76
DECREE OF FORFEITURE. 78
DECLARATIONS OF PUBLIC BODIES. 79
THE MILITARY—FONTAINBLEAU. 86
FONTAINBLEAU. 88

CHAPTER LXXX 93

Victor, and other Maréchals give in their adhesion to the Provisional Government—Marmont enters into a separate Convention; but assists at the Conferences held at Paris, leaving Souham second in command of his Army—The Commanders have an interview with the Emperor Alexander—Souham enters with his Army, into the lines of the Allies; in consequence, the Allied Sovereigns insist upon the unconditional Submission of Napoleon—His reluctant acquiescence—The Terms granted to him—Disapprobation of Lord Castlereagh—General Desertion of Napoleon—Death of Josephine—Singular

Statement made by Baron Fain, Napoleon's Secretary, of the Emperor's attempt to commit Suicide—After this he becomes more resigned—Leaves Fontainbleau, 28th April. 93

MARMONT'S CONVENTION. 94
CONFERENCES AT PARIS. 97
FINAL ACT OF ABDICATION. 99
TREATY OF FONTAINBLEAU. 100
GENERAL DESERTION. 103
DEATH OF JOSEPHINE—FONTAINBLEAU. 106
LEAVES FONTAINBLEAU. 110

CHAPTER LXXXI 113

Commissioners appointed to escort Napoleon—He leaves Fontainbleau on the 20th April—His interview with Augereau at Valence—Expressions of popular dislike towards Napoleon in the South of France—Fears for his personal safety—His own agitation and precautions—He arrives at Frejus, and embarks on board the Undaunted, with the British and Austrian Commissioners—Arrives at Elba on 4th May.................... 113

LEAVES FONTAINBLEAU—AUGEREAU. 114
FREJUS—VOYAGE TO ELBA. 116
LANDS AT PORTO FERRAJO. 120

CHAPTER LXXXII 123

Elba—Napoleon's mode of Life and occupation there—Effects of his residence at Elba upon the adjoining Kingdom of Italy—He is visited by his Mother and the Princess Pauline—and by a Polish lady—Sir Niel Campbell the only Commissioner left at Elba—Napoleon's Conversations on the State of Europe—His pecuniary Difficulties—and fears of Assassination—Symptoms of some approaching crisis—A part of the Old Guard disbanded—Napoleon escapes from Elba—Fruitless pursuit by Sir Niel Campbell.................... 123

ELBA. 123
PECUNIARY DIFFICULTIES. 134
ESCAPES FROM ELBA. 140

CHAPTER LXXXIII 141

Retrospect—Restoration of the Bourbons displeasing to the Soldiery, but satisfactory to the People—Terms favourable to France granted by the Allies—Discontent about the manner of conceding the Charter—Other grounds of dissatisfaction—Apprehensions lest the Church and Crown Lands should be resumed—Resuscitation of the Jacobin faction—Increased Dissatisfaction in the Army—The Claims of the Emigrants mooted in the Chamber of Delegates—Maréchal Macdonald's Proposal—Financial Difficulties—Restriction on the Press—Reflections on this subject. 141

THE RESTORATION. *143*
MINISTRY OF LOUIS XVIII. *145*
TERMS OF THE TREATY. *147*
PARTIES IN FRANCE. *151*
THE CLERGY. *153*
THE JACOBINS. *156*
BUONAPARTISTS—THE ARMY. *158*
THE ARMY—STATE OF PARTIES. *160*
EMIGRANT-CLAIMS. *164*
FRENCH FINANCE. *166*
THE PRESS. *168*

CHAPTER LXXXIV 173

Carnot's Memorial on Public Affairs—Fouché joins the Jacobins—Projects of that Party; which finally joins the Buonapartists—Active Intrigues—Congress of Vienna—Murat, alarmed at its proceedings, opens an intercourse with Napoleon—Plans of the Conspirators—Buonaparte's Escape from Elba—He lands at Cannes—Is joined at Grenoble, by 3000 Troops—Halts at Lyons, appoints a Ministry, and issues several Decrees—Dismay of the Government—Intrigues of Fouché—Treachery of Ney—Revolt of the Royal Army at Melun—The King leaves Paris and Buonaparte arrives there—His Reception.. 173

CARNOT'S MEMORIAL. *174*
CARNOT'S MEMORIAL—FOUCHÉ. *176*
PROJECTS OF THE JACOBINS. *179*
JACOBINS—BUONAPARTISTS. *181*
RICHARD LE NOIR. *184*
CONGRESS OF VIENNA. *187*
ESCAPE FROM ELBA. *189*
GRENOBLE. *192*
MELUN—LYONS. *194*
DECREES—AUXERRE. *196*
FOUCHÉ—NEY. *199*
TREASON OF NEY—MELUN. *202*
RE-ENTERS PARIS. *205*

CHAPTER LXXXV 209

Various attempts to organise a defence for the Bourbons fail—Buonaparte, again reinstated on the throne of France, is desirous of continuing the peace with the Allies—but no answer is returned to his letters—Treaty of Vienna—Grievances alleged by Buonaparte in justification of the step he had taken—Debates in the British House of Commons, on the renewal of War—Murat occupies Rome with 50,000 men—his Proclamation summoning all Italians to arms—He advances against the Austrians—is repulsed at Occhio-Bello—defeated at Tolentino—flies to Naples, and thence, in disguise, to France—where Napoleon refuses to receive him. 209

DUCHESS D'ANGOULÊME. 210
DECLARATION AND TREATY OF VIENNA. 212
ALLEGED GRIEVANCES. 214
MURAT. 217

CHAPTER LXXXVI 223

Buonaparte's attempts to conciliate Britain—Plot to carry off Maria Louisa fails—State of feeling in France—The Army—The Jacobins—The Constitutionalists—Fouché and Siêyes made Peers—Freedom of the Press granted, and outraged—Independent conduct of Comté, editor of Le Censeur—Disaffections among the lower orders—Part of these assemble before the Tuileries, and applaud the Emperor—Festival of the Federates—New Constitution—It is received with dissatisfaction—Meeting of the Champ de Mai to ratify it—Buonaparte's Address to the Chambers of Peers and Deputies—The spirit of Jacobinism predominant in the latter. 223

MARIA LOUISA. 223
STATE OF PARTIES. 225
LIBERTY OF THE PRESS. 228
FESTIVAL OF THE FEDERATES. 231
ADDITIONAL ACT. 234
CHAMBER OF DEPUTIES. 236

CHAPTER LXXXVII 241

Preparations for War—Positions of the Allied Forces, amounting in whole to One Million of Men—Buonaparte's Force not more than 200,000—Conscription not ventured upon—National Guard—their reluctance to serve—Many Provinces hostile to Napoleon—Fouché's Report makes known the Disaffection—Insurrection in La Vendée—quelled—Military Resources—Plan of Campaign—Paris Placed in a Complete State of Defence—Frontier Passes and Towns fortified—Generals who accept Command under Napoleon—He Announces his Purpose to measure himself with Wellington. 241

PREPARATIONS FOR WAR. 241
DISAFFECTION. 243
PLAN OF THE CAMPAIGN. 246
PREPARATIONS OF WAR. 247

CHAPTER LXXXVIII **251**

Army of Wellington covers Brussels—that of Blucher on the Sambre and Meuse—Napoleon reviews his Grand Army on 14th June—Advances upon Charleroi—His plan to separate the Armies of the two opposing Generals fails—Interview of Wellington and Blucher at Bric—British Army concentrated at Quatre-bras—Napoleon's plan of attack—Battle of Ligny, and defeat of Blucher on 16th June—Action at Quatre-bras on the same day—The British retain possession of the field—Blucher eludes the French pursuit—Napoleon joins Ney—Retreat of the British upon Waterloo. 251

BLUCHER'S ARMY. 252
FRASNES AND QUATRE-BRAS. 255
LIGNY. 257
QUATRE-BRAS. 259
GENAPPE—WATERLOO. 262

CHAPTER LXXXIX **265**

Strength of the two armies—Plans of their Generals—The Battle of Waterloo commenced on the forenoon of the 18th June—French attack directed against the British centre—shifted to their right—Charges of the Cuirassiers—and their reception—Advance of the Prussians—Ney's charge at the head of the Guards—His repulse—and Napoleon's orders for retreat—The victorious Generals meet at La Belle Alliance—Behaviour of Napoleon during the engagement—Blucher's pursuit of the French—Loss of the British—of the French—Napoleon's subsequent attempts to undervalue the military skill of the Duke of Wellington answered—His unjust censures of Grouchy—The notion that the British were on the point of losing the battle when the Prussians came up, shown to be erroneous. 265

WATERLOO. 265
PLANS OF ATTACK. 269
PICTON—PONSONBY. 271
WATERLOO. 274
LOSSES ON BOTH SIDES. 279

CHAPTER XC **293**

Buonaparte's arrival at Paris—The Chambers assemble, and adopt Resolutions, indicating a wish for Napoleon's Abdication—Fouché presents Napoleon's Abdication, which stipulates that his Son shall succeed him—Carnot's Report to the Peers, of the means of defence—Contradicted by Ney—Stormy Debate on the Abdication Act—Both Chambers evade formally recognising Napoleon II.—Provisional Government—Napoleon at Malmaison—His offer of his services in the defence of Paris rejected—Surveillance of General Beker—Means provided at Rochefort for his departure to the United States—He arrives at Rochefort on 3d July—The Provisional Government attempt in vain to treat with the Allies—The Allies advance to Paris—Chamber of Peers disperse—Louis XVIII. re-enters Paris on 8th July. 293

PARIS. 293
CHAMBER OF DEPUTIES. 294
GENERAL COUNCIL. 298
PROVISIONAL GOVERNMENT. 301
ACT OF ABDICATION. 303
MALMAISON. 307
ARRIVES AT ROCHEFORT. 310
LOUIS RE-ENTERS PARIS. 312
THE CHAMBERS. 314
LEGITIMACY. 315
SECOND RESTORATION. 320

CHAPTER XCI. 325

Disposition of the British Fleet along the Western Coast of France, in order to prevent Buonaparte's Escape—The Bellerophon off Rochefort—Orders under which Captain Maitland acted—Plans agitated for Napoleon's Escape—Savary and Las Cases open a Negotiation with Captain Maitland—Captain Maitland's Account of what passed at their Interviews—Las Cases' Account—The Statements compared—Napoleon's Letter to the Prince Regent—He surrenders himself on board the Bellerophon, on 15th July—His arrival off Plymouth—All approach to the Ship prohibited—Final determination of the English Government that Buonaparte shall be sent to St. Helena—His Protest. 325

LORD KEITH—CAPTAIN MAITLAND. 325
PROPOSALS FROM THE ARMY. 328
NEGOTIATION WITH MAITLAND. 330
THE BELLEROPHON. 333
PLYMOUTH SOUND. 340
SIR HENRY BUNBURY'S MINUTES. 341
INTERVIEW WITH LORD KEITH, ETC. 345

CHAPTER XCII 347

Napoleon's real view of the measure of sending him to St. Helena—Allegation that Captain Maitland made terms with him—disproved—Probability that the insinuation arose with Las Cases—Scheme of removing Napoleon from the Bellerophon, by citing him as a witness in a case of libel—Threats of self-destruction—Napoleon goes on board the Northumberland, which sails for St. Helena—His behaviour on the voyage—He arrives at St. Helena, 16th October. 347

THE BELLEROPHON. 347
CAPTAIN MAITLAND. 349
THE BELLEROPHON. 353
O'MEARA—THE NORTHUMBERLAND. 356
VOYAGE TO ST. HELENA. 357
ST. HELENA. 360

CHAPTER XCIII 361

Causes which justify the English Government in the measure of Napoleon's Banishment—Napoleon's wish to retire to England, in order that, being near France, he might again interfere in her affairs—Reasons for withholding from him the title of Emperor—Sir George Cockburn's Instructions—Temporary Accommodation at Briars—Napoleon removes to Longwood—Precautions taken for the safe custody of the Prisoner. 361

LONGWOOD—BRIARS. 368
LONGWOOD. 371

CHAPTER XCIV 375

Buonaparte's alleged grievances considered—Right to restrict his Liberty—Limits allowed Napoleon—Complaints urged by Las Cases against Sir George Cockburn—Sir Hudson Lowe appointed Governor of St. Helena—Information given by General Gourgaud to Government—Agitation of various Plans for Buonaparte's Escape—Writers on the subject of Napoleon's Residence at St. Helena—Napoleon's irritating Treatment of Sir Hudson Lowe—Interviews between them. 375

ALLEGED GRIEVANCES. 378
COCKBURN'S INSTRUCTIONS. 383
RECAPITULATION. 389
SIR HUDSON LOWE. 393
GOURGAUD. 395
WARDEN—O'MEARA, ETC. 398
ANTOMMARCHI. 401
RUPTURE WITH SIR H. LOWE. 404

CHAPTER XCV. 407

Instructions to Sir Hudson Lowe—Sum allowed for the Ex-Emperor's Expenses—Napoleon's proposal to defray his own Expenses—Sale of his Plate—made in order to produce a false impression: he had at that time a large sum of Money in his strong-box—Wooden-House constructed in London, and transported to St. Helena—Interview between Sir H. Lowe and Napoleon—Delays in the Erection of the House—The Regulation that a British Officer should attend Napoleon in his Rides—Communication with Europe carried on by the Inmates of Longwood—Regulation respecting Napoleon's Intercourse with the Inhabitants of St. Helena—General Reflections on the Disputes between him and Sir H. Lowe...407

LOWE'S INSTRUCTIONS. 407
HOUSEHOLD EXPENSES. 408
INSTRUCTIONS TO THE GOVERNOR.. 416
INTERVIEW WITH SIR H. LOWE. 418
LONGWOOD. 422
GOURGAUD—LONGWOOD. 428

CHAPTER XCVI 435

Napoleon's Domestic Habits—Manner in which he spent the day—his Dress—Nature of the Fragments of Memoirs he dictated to Gourgaud and Montholon—His admiration of Ossian—He prefers Racine and Corneille to Voltaire—Dislike of Tacitus—His Vindication of the Character of Cæsar—His Behaviour towards the Persons of his Household—Amusements and Exercises—His Character of Sir Pulteney Malcolm—Degree of his Intercourse with the Islanders, and with Visitors to the Island—Interview with Captain Basil Hall—with Lord Amherst and the Gentlemen attached to the Chinese Embassy. 435

DOMESTIC HABITS. 435
HIS MEMOIRS. 437
OSSIAN... 440
CONDUCT TOWARDS HIS HOUSEHOLD. 443
AMUSEMENTS. 444
SOCIETY AT LONGWOOD. 446
CAPTAIN BASIL HALL. 450
LORD AMHERST. 453

CHAPTER XCVII 457

Napoleon's Illness—viz. Cancer in the Stomach—Removal of Las Cases—Montholon's Complaints brought forward by Lord Holland—and replied to by Lord Bathurst—Effect of the failure of Lord Holland's motion—Removal of Dr. O'Meara from his attendance on Buonaparte—who refuses to permit the visits of any other English Physician—Two Priests sent to St. Helena at his desire—Dr. Antommarchi—Continued Disputes with Sir Hudson Lowe—Plans for Effecting Buonaparte's Escape—Scheme of a Smuggler to approach St. Helena in a Submarine Vessel—Seizure of the Vessel—Letter expressing the King of England's interest in the Illness of Napoleon—Consent of the latter to admit the visits of Dr. Arnott—Napoleon employs himself in making his Will—and gives other directions connected with his Decease—Extreme Unction administered to him—His Death, on 5th May, 1821—Anatomization of the Body—His Funeral. 457

ILLNESS. 457
LAS CASES. 462
LORD HOLLAND'S MOTION. 464
REMOVAL OF O'MEARA. 471
RELIGIOUS OPINIONS. 473
PLANS OF ESCAPE. 476
INCREASED ILLNESS. 478
LAST ILLNESS. 481
DEATH. 484
FUNERAL. 487

CONCLUSION 489

CONCLUSION 489

APPENDIX. 511

No. I. 511

REMARKS ON THE CAMPAIGN OF 1815, BY CAPTAIN JOHN W. PRINGLE, OF THE ROYAL ENGINEERS. 511

No. II. 551

BUONAPARTE'S PROTEST. 551

No. III. 559
No. IV. 561

INTERVIEW BETWIXT NAPOLEON BUONAPARTE AND HENRY ELLIS, ESQ., THIRD COMMISSIONER OF LORD AMHERST'S EMBASSY TO CHINA. 561

No. V. 569

MEMORANDUM OF THE ESTABLISHMENT AT LONGWOOD. 569

No. VI. 572

INTERVIEW BETWEEN BUONAPARTE AND THE WIDOW OF THEOBALD WOLFE TONE. 572

No. VII. 575

BUONAPARTE'S LAST WILL AND TESTAMENT. 575
I. 575
II. 576
III. 577

Chapter LXXV

Buonaparte marches upon Blucher, who is in possession of Soissons—Attacks the place without success—Battle of Craonne—Blucher retreats on Laon—Battle of Laon—Napoleon is compelled to withdraw on the 11th—He attacks Rheims, which is evacuated by the Russians—Defeat at Bar-sur-Aube of Oudinot and Gerard, who, with Macdonald, are forced to retreat towards Paris—Schwartzenberg wishes to retreat behind the Aube—but the Emperor Alexander and Lord Castlereagh opposing the measure, it is determined to proceed upon Paris—Napoleon occupies Arcis—Battle of Arcis—Napoleon is joined, in the night after the battle, by Macdonald, Oudinot, and Gerard—and retreats along the Aube.

The sword was now again brandished, not to be sheathed or reposed, until the one party or the other should be irretrievably defeated.

The situation of Buonaparte, even after the victory of Montereau, and capture of Troyes, was most discouraging. If he advanced on the grand army of the allies which he had in front, there was every likelihood that they would retire before him, wasting his force in skirmishes, without a possibility of his being able to force them to a general action; while, in the meantime, it might be reckoned for certain that Blucher, master of the Marne, would march upon Paris. On the contrary, if Napoleon moved with his chief force against Blucher, he had, in like manner, to apprehend that Schwartzenberg would resume the route upon Paris by way of the valley of the Seine. Thus, he could make no exertion upon the one side, without exposing the capital to danger on the other.

After weighing all the disadvantages on either side, Napoleon determined to turn his arms against Blucher, as most hostile to his person, most rapid in his movements, and most persevering in his purposes. He left Oudinot, Macdonald, and Gerard in front of the grand army, in hopes that, however inferior in numbers, they might be able to impose upon Schwartzenberg a belief that Napoleon was present in person, and thus either induce the Austrian to continue his retreat, or at least prevent him from resuming the offensive. For this purpose the French troops were to move on Bar-sur-Aube, and occupy, if practicable, the heights in that neighbourhood. The soldiers were also to use the cry of *Vive l'Empereur*, as if Napoleon had been present. It was afterwards seen, that as the maréchals did not command 40,000 men in all, including a force under Macdonald, it was impossible for them to discharge effectually the part assigned them. In the meanwhile, Napoleon himself continued his lateral march on Blucher, supposing it possible for him, as formerly, to surprise his flank, as the Prussians marched upon Paris. For this purpose he moved as speedily as possible to La Ferté-Gauchère, where he arrived 1st March; but Sacken and D'Yorck, who would have been the first victims of this manœuvre, as their divisions were on the left bank of the Marne, near to Meaux, crossed the river at La Ferté Jouarre, and formed a junction with Blucher, who now resolved to fall back on the troops of Bulow and Winzengerode. These generals were, it will be remembered, advancing from the frontiers of Belgium.

A sudden hard frost rendered the country passable, which had before been in so swampy a condition as to render marching very difficult. This was much to the advantage of the Prussians. Napoleon detached the forces under Marmont and Mortier, whom he had united with his own, to press upon and harass the retreat of the Prussian field-maréchal; while he himself, pushing on by a shorter line, possessed himself of the town of Fismes, about half way betwixt Rheims and Soissons. The occupation of this last place was now a matter of the last consequence. If Blucher should find Soissons open to him, he might cross the Marne, extricate himself from his pursuers without difficulty, and form his junction with the army of the North. But if excluded from this town and bridge, Blucher must have hazarded a battle on the most disadvantageous terms, having Mortier and Marmont on his front, Napoleon on his left flank, and in his rear, a town, with a hostile garrison and a deep river.

It was almost a chance, like that of the dice, which party possessed this important place. The Russians had taken it on 15th February;[1] but, being immediately evacuated by them, it was on the 19th occupied by Mortier, and garrisoned by 500 Poles, who were imagined capable of the most determined defence. On the 2d March, however, the commandant, intimidated by the advance of Bulow's army of 30,000 men, yielded up Soissons to that general, upon a threat of an instant storm, and no quarter allowed. The Russian standards then waved on the ramparts of Soissons, and Blucher, arriving under its walls, acquired the full power of uniting himself with his rear-guard, and giving or refusing battle at his pleasure, on the very moment when Buonaparte, having turned his flank, expected to have forced on him a most disadvantageous action.

The Emperor's wrath exhaled in a bulletin against the inconceivable baseness of the commandant of Soissons, who was said to have given up so important a place when he was within hearing of the cannonade on the 2d and 3d, and must thereby have known the approach of the Emperor.[2] In the heat of his wrath, he ordered Soissons to be assaulted and carried by storm at all risks; but it was defended by General Langeron with 10,000 Russians. A desperate conflict ensued, but Langeron retained possession of the town.

BATTLE OF CRAONNE

Abandoning this project, Napoleon crossed the Aisne at Béry-au-Bac, with the purpose of attacking the left wing of Blucher's army, which, being now concentrated, was strongly posted betwixt the village of Craonne and the town of Laon, in such a manner as to secure a retreat upon the very strong position which the latter town affords. Blucher imagined a manœuvre, designed to show

---

[1] See *ante*, vol. iv.
[2] Moniteur, March 11.

Buonaparte that his favourite system of turning an enemy's flank had its risks and inconveniences. He detached ten thousand horse under Winzengerode, by a circuitous route, with orders that when the French commenced their march on Craonne, they should move round and act upon their flank and rear. But the state of the roads, and other impediments, prevented this body of cavalry from getting up in time to execute the intended manœuvre.

Meanwhile, at eleven in the morning of the 7th March, the French began their attack with the utmost bravery. Ney assaulted the position on the right flank, which was defended by a ravine, and Victor, burning to show the zeal which he had been accused of wanting, made incredible exertions in front. But the assault was met by a defence equally obstinate, and the contest became one of the most bloody and best-sustained during the war. It was four in the afternoon, and the French had not yet been able to dislodge the Russians on any point, when the latter received orders from Blucher to withdraw from the disputed ground, and unite with the Prussian army on the splendid position of Laon, which the maréchal considered as a more favourable scene of action. There were no guns lost, or prisoners made. The Russians, in despite of a general charge of the French cavalry, retreated as on the parade. As the armies, considering the absence of Winzengerode with the detachment of cavalry, and of Langeron with the garrison of Soissons, were nearly equal, the indecisive event of the battle was the more ominous. The slain and wounded were about the same number on both sides, and the French only retained as a mark of victory the possession of the field of battle.[3]

Napoleon himself followed the retreat of the Russians as far as an inn between Craonne and Laon, called L'Ange Gardien, where he reposed for the night. He, indeed, never more needed the assistance of a guardian angel, and his own appears to have deserted his charge. It was here that Rumigny found him when he presented the letter of Caulaincourt, praying for final instructions from the Emperor; and it was here he could only extract the ambiguous reply,

---

[3] "This was the best fought action during the campaign: the numbers engaged on both sides were nearly equal; the superiority, if any, being on the side of the French."—Lord Burghersh, *Operations*, &c., p. 196.

that if he must submit to the bastinado, it should be only by force. At this cabaret, also, he regulated his plan for attacking the position of Blucher on the next morning; and thus ridding himself finally, if possible, of that Silesian army, which had been his object of disquietude for forty-two days, during the course of which, scarce two days had passed without their being engaged in serious conflict, either in front or rear. He received valuable information for enabling him to make the projected attack, from a retired officer, M. Bussy de Bellay, who had been his schoolfellow at Brienne, who lived in the neighbourhood, and was well acquainted with the ground, and whom he instantly rewarded with the situation of an aide-de-camp, and a large appointment. When his plan for the attack was finished, he is said to have exclaimed, "I see this war is an abyss without a bottom, but I am resolved to be the last whom it shall devour."

The town of Laon is situated upon a table-land, or eminence, flattened on the top, which rises very abruptly above a plain extending about a league in length. The face of the declivity is steep, shelving, almost precipitous, and occupied by terraces serving as vineyards. Bulow defended this town and bank. The rest of the Silesian army was placed on the plain below; the left wing, composed of Prussians, extending to the village of Athies; the right, consisting of Russians, resting on the hills between Thiers and Semonville.

BATTLE OF LAON—RHEIMS

Only the interval of one day elapsed between the bloody battle of Craonne and that of Laon. On the 9th, availing himself of a thick mist, Napoleon pushed his columns of attack to the very foot of the eminence on which Laon is situated, possessed himself of two of the villages, termed Semilly and Ardon, and prepared to force his way up the hill towards the town. The weather cleared, the French attack was repelled by a tremendous fire from terraces, vineyards, windmills, and every point of advantage. Two battalions of Yagers, the impetus of their attack increased by the rapidity of the descent, recovered the villages, and the attack of Laon in front seemed to be abandoned. The French, however, continued to retain possession, in that quarter, of a part of the village of Clacy. Thus stood the action on the right and centre. The French had been repulsed all along the line. On the left Maréchal Marmont had advanced upon the village of Athies, which was the key of Blucher's position in that point. It was gallantly defended by D'Yorck and Kleist, supported by Sacken and Langeron. Marmont made some progress, notwithstanding this resistance, and night found him bivouacking in front of the enemy, and in possession of part of the disputed village of Athies. But he was not destined to remain there till daybreak.

Upon the 10th, at four in the morning, just as Buonaparte, arising before daybreak, was calling for his horse, two dismounted dragoons were brought before him, with the unpleasing intelligence that the enemy had made a *hourra* upon Marmont, surprised him in his bivouac, and cut to pieces, taken, or dispersed his whole division, and they alone had escaped to bring the tidings. All the maréchal's guns were lost, and they believed he was himself either killed or prisoner. Officers sent to reconnoitre, brought back a confirmation of the truth of this intelligence, excepting as to the situation of the maréchal. He was on the road to Rheims, near Corbeny, endeavouring to rally the fugitives. Notwithstanding this great loss, and as if in defiance of bad fortune, Napoleon renewed the attack upon Clacy and Semilly; but all his attempts being fruitless, he was induced to relinquish the undertaking, under the excuse that the position was found impregnable. On the 11th, he withdrew from before Laon, having been foiled in all his attempts, and having lost thirty guns, and nearly 10,000 men. The allies suffered comparatively little, as they fought under cover.

Napoleon halted at Soissons, which, evacuated by Langeron when Blucher concentrated his army, was now again occupied by the French. Napoleon directed its defences to be strengthened, designing to leave Mortier to defend the place against the advance of Blucher, which, victorious as he was, might be instantly expected.

While at Soissons, Napoleon learned that Saint Priest, a French emigrant, and a general in the Russian service, had occupied Rheims, remarkable for the venerable cathedral in which the kings of France were crowned. Napoleon instantly saw that the possession of Rheims would renew the communication betwixt Schwartzenberg and Blucher, besides neutralizing the advantages which he himself expected from the possession of Soissons. He moved from Soissons to Rheims, where, after an attack which lasted till late in the night, the Russian general being wounded, his followers were discouraged, and evacuated the place. The utmost horrors might have been expected during a night attack, when one army forced another from a considerable town. But in this instance we have the satisfaction to record, that the troops on both sides behaved in a most orderly manner.[4] In his account of the previous action, Napoleon threw in one of those strokes of fatality which he loved to introduce. He endeavoured to persuade the public, or perhaps he himself believed, that Saint Priest was shot by a ball from the same cannon which killed Moreau.[5]

During the attack upon Rheims, Marmont came up with such forces as he had been able to rally after his defeat at Athies, and contributed to the success of the assault. He was, nevertheless, received by Napoleon with bitter reproaches, felt severely by a chief, of whose honour and talents no doubt had been expressed through a long life of soldiership.

Napoleon remained at Rheims three days, to repose and recruit his shattered army, which was reinforced from every quarter where men could be collected. Janssens, a Dutch officer, displayed a particular degree of military talent in bringing a body of about 4000 men, draughted from the garrisons of the places on the Moselle, to join the army at Rheims; a movement of great difficulty, considering he had to penetrate through a country which was in a great measure possessed by the enemy's troops.[6]

The halt of Napoleon at Rheims was remarkable, as affording the last means of transacting business with his civil ministers. Hitherto, an auditor of the council of state had weekly brought to the Imperial headquarters the report of the ministers, and received

---

[4] Baron Fain, p. 193.
[5] Moniteur, March 14.
[6] Baron Fain, p. 194.

the orders of the Emperor.[7] But a variety of causes rendered this regular communication during the rest of the campaign, a matter of impossibility. At Rheims, also, Napoleon addressed to Caulaincourt, a letter, dated 17th March, by which he seems to have placed it in the power of that plenipotentiary to comply in full with the terms of the allies. But the language in which it is couched is so far from bearing the precise warrant necessary for so important a concession, that there must remain a doubt whether Caulaincourt would have felt justified in acting upon it, or whether so acting, Napoleon would have recognised his doing so, if circumstances had made it convenient for him to disown the treaty.[8]

OUDINOT AND GERARD

While Napoleon was pursuing, fighting with, and finally defeated by Blucher, his lieutenant-generals were not more fortunate in front of the allied grand army. It will be recollected that the Maréchals Oudinot and Gerard were left at the head of 25,000 men exclusive of the separate corps under Macdonald, with orders to possess themselves of the heights of Bar-sur-Aube, and prevent Schwartzenberg from crossing that river. They made the movement in advance accordingly, and after a sharp action, which left the town in their possession, they were so nigh to the allied troops, who still held the suburbs, that a battle became unavoidable, and the maréchals had no choice save of making the attack, or of receiving it. They chose the former, and gained at first some advantages from the very audacity of their attempt; but the allies had now been long accustomed to stand their ground under greater disasters. Their

---

[7] "Whatever might have been the hardships of the campaign, and the importance of occasional circumstances, Napoleon superintended and regularly provided for everything; and, up to the present moment, showed himself adequate to direct the affairs of the interior, as well as the complicated movements of the army."—Baron Fain, p. 195.

[8] The words alleged to convey such extensive powers as totally to recall and alter every former restriction upon Caulaincourt's exercise of his own opinion, are contained, as above stated, in a letter from Rheims, dated 17th March, 1814. "I have charged the Duke of Bassano to answer your letter in detail. I give you directly the authority to make such concessions as shall be indispensable to maintain the continuance (*activité*) of the negotiations, and to arrive at a knowledge of the ultimatum of the allies; it being distinctly understood that the treaty shall have for its immediate result the evacuation of our territory, and the restoring prisoners on both sides."—Napoleon, *Mémoires*, tom. ii., p. 399.

numerous reserves were brought up, and their long train of artillery got into line. The French, after obtaining a temporary footing on the heights of Vernonfait, were charged and driven back in disorder. Some fine cavalry, which had been brought from the armies in Spain, was destroyed by the overpowering cannonade. The French were driven across the Aube, the town of Bar-sur-Aube was taken, and the defeated maréchals could only rally their forces at the village of Vandœuvres, about half-way between Bar and Troyes.

The defeat of Oudinot and Gerard obliged Maréchal Macdonald, who defended the line of the river above Bar, to retreat to Troyes, from his strong position at La Ferté-sur-Aube. He therefore fell back towards Vandœuvres. But though these three distinguished generals, Macdonald, Oudinot, and Gerard, had combined their talents, and united their forces, it was impossible for them to defend Troyes, and they were compelled to retreat upon the great road to Paris. Thus, the headquarters of the allied monarchs were, for the second time during this changeful war, established in the ancient capital of Champagne; and the allied grand army recovered, by the victory of Bar-sur-Aube, all the territory which they had yielded up in consequence of Buonaparte's success at Montereau. They once more threatened to descend the Seine upon Paris, being entitled to despise any opposition offered by a feeble line, which Macdonald, Oudinot, and Gerard, endeavoured to defend on the left bank.

But Schwartzenberg's confidence in his position was lowered, when he heard that Napoleon had taken Rheims; and that, on the evening of the 17th, Ney, with a large division, had occupied Chalons-sur-Marne. This intelligence made a deep impression on the Austrian council of war. Their tactics being rigidly those of the old school of war, they esteemed their army turned whenever a French division occupied such a post as interposed betwixt them and their allies. This, indeed, is in one sense true; but it is equally true, that every division so interposed is itself liable to be turned, if the hostile divisions betwixt which it is interposed take combined measures for attacking it. The catching, therefore, too prompt an alarm, or considering the consequences of such a movement as irretrievable, belongs to the pedantry of war, and not to its science.

At midnight a council was held for the purpose of determining the future motions of the allies. The generalissimo recommended a retreat behind the line of the Aube. The Emperor Alexander opposed this with great steadiness. He observed, with justice, that the protracted war was driving the country people to despair, and that the peasantry were already taking up arms, while the allies only wanted resolution, certainly neither opportunity nor numbers, to decide the affair by a single blow.

So many were the objections stated, and so difficult was it to bring the various views and interests of so many powers to coincide in the same general plan, that the Emperor informed one of his attendants, he thought the anxiety of the night must have turned half his hair grey. Lord Castlereagh was against the opinion of Schwartzenberg, the rather that he concluded that a retreat behind the Aube would be a preface to one behind the Rhine. Taking it upon him, as became the Minister of Britain at such a crisis, he announced to the allied powers, that, so soon as they should commence the proposed retreat, the subsidies of England would cease to be paid to them.[9]

THE MARCH UPON PARIS

It was, therefore, finally agreed to resume offensive operations, for which purpose they proposed to diminish the distance betwixt the allied grand army and that of Silesia, and resume such a communication with Blucher as might prevent the repetition of such disasters as those of Montmirail and Montereau. With this view it was determined to descend the Aube, unite their army at Arcis, offer Napoleon battle, should he desire to accept it, or move boldly on Paris if he should refuse the proffered action. What determined them more resolutely, from this moment, to approach the capital as soon as possible, was the intelligence which

---

[9] Lord Burghersh, in his memoranda previously quoted, states that Lord Castlereagh was not at Troyes upon this occasion, that he made no such declaration as Sir Walter Scott ascribes to him: and that any such declaration would have been uncalled for, as Prince Schwartzenberg was bent on concentrating his forces at Arcis—which he did. Compare *"Operations,"* &c., p. 179.—Ed. (1842.)

arrived at the headquarters by Messieurs de Polignac.[10] These gentlemen brought an encouraging account of the progress of the Royalists in the metropolis, and of the general arrangements which were actively pursued for uniting with the interests of the Bourbons that of all others, who, from dislike to Buonaparte's person and government, or fear that the country, and they themselves, must share in his approaching ruin, were desirous to get rid of the Imperial government. Talleyrand was at the head of the confederacy, and all were resolved to embrace the first opportunity of showing themselves, which the progress of the allies should permit. This important intelligence, coming from such unquestionable authority, strengthened the allies in their resolution to march upon Paris.

In the meantime, Napoleon being at Rheims, as stated, on the 15th and 16th March, was alarmed by the news of the loss of the battle of Bar, the retreat of the three maréchals beyond the Seine, and the demonstrations of the grand army to cross that river once more. He broke up, as we have seen, from Rheims on the 17th, and sending Ney to take possession of Chalons, marched himself to Epernay, with the purpose of placing himself on the right flank, and in the rear of Schwartzenberg, in case he should advance on the road to Paris. At Epernay, he learned that the allies, alarmed by his movements, had retired to Troyes, and that they were about to retreat upon the Aube, and probably to Langres. He also learned that the maréchals, Macdonald and Oudinot, had resumed their advance so soon as their adversaries began to retreat. He hastened to form a junction with these persevering leaders, and proceeded to ascend the Aube as high as Bar, where he expected to throw himself into Schwartzenberg's rear, having no doubt that his army was retiring from the banks of the Aube.

In these calculations, accurate as far as the information permitted, Buonaparte was greatly misled. He conceived himself to be acting upon the retreat of the allies, and expected only to find a rear-guard at Arcis; he was even talking jocularly of making his father-in-law prisoner during his retreat. If, contrary to his expectation, he should find the enemy, or any considerable part of

---

[10] For *Messieurs de Polignac*, we should read *Monsieur de Vitrolles*.—See Lord Burghersh's "Operations," p. 266. *Note*.—Ed. (1842.)

them, still upon the Aube, it was, from all he had heard, to be supposed his appearance would precipitate their retreat towards the frontier. It has also been asserted, that he expected Maréchal Macdonald to make a corresponding advance from the banks of the Seine to those of the Aube; but the orders had been received too late to admit of the necessary space being traversed so as to arrive on the morning of the day of battle.

Napoleon easily drove before him such bodies of light cavalry, and sharp-shooters, as had been left by the allies, rather for the purpose of reconnoitring than of making serious opposition. He crossed the Aube at Plancey, and moved upwards along the left bank of the river, with Ney's corps, and his whole cavalry, while the infantry of his guard advanced upon the right; his army being thus, according to the French military phrase, *à cheval* upon the Aube. The town of Arcis had been evacuated by the allies upon his approach, and was occupied by the French on the morning of the 20th March. That town forms the outlet of a sort of defile, where a succession of narrow bridges cross a number of drains, brooks, and streamlets, the feeders of the river Aube, and a bridge in the town crosses the river itself. On the other side of Arcis is a plain, in which some few squadrons of cavalry, resembling a reconnoitring party, were observed manœuvring.

Behind these horse, at a place called Clermont, the Prince Royal of Wirtemberg, whose name has been so often honourably mentioned, was posted with his division, while the elite of the allied army was drawn up on a chain of heights still farther in the rear, called Mesnil la Comtesse. But these forces were not apparent to the vanguard of Napoleon's army. The French cavalry had orders to attack the light troops of the allies; but these were instantly supported by whole regiments, and by cannon, so that the attack was unsuccessful; and the squadrons of the French were repulsed and driven back on Arcis at a moment, when, from the impediments in the town and its environs, the infantry could with difficulty debouche from the town to support them. Napoleon showed, as he always did in extremity, the same heroic courage which he had exhibited at Lodi and Brienne. He drew his sword, threw himself among the broken cavalry, called on them to remember their former victories, and checked the enemy by an impetuous charge, in which he and his staff-officers fought hand to hand with their opponents, so that he was in personal danger from the lance of a Cossack, the thrust of which was averted by his aide-de-camp, Girardin. His Mameluke Rustan fought stoutly by his side, and received a gratuity for his bravery. These desperate exertions afforded time for the infantry to debouche from the town. The Imperial Guards came up, and the combat waxed very warm. The superior numbers of the allies rendered them the assailants on all points. A strongly situated village in front, and somewhat to the left of Arcis, called Grand Torcy, had been occupied by the French. This place was repeatedly and desperately attacked by the allies, but the French made good their position. Arcis itself was set on fire by the shells of the assailants, and night alone separated the combatants, by inducing the allies to desist from the attack.

In the course of the night, Buonaparte was joined by Macdonald, Oudinot, and Gerard, with the forces with which they had lately held the defensive upon the Seine; and the anxious question remained, whether, thus reinforced, he should venture an action with the grand army, to which he was still much inferior in numbers. Schwartzenberg, agreeably to the last resolution of the allies, drew up on the heights of Mesnil la Comtesse, prepared to receive battle. On consideration of the superior strength of the enemy, and of the absence of some troops not yet come up, Napoleon finally determined not to accept a battle under such disadvantageous circumstances. He therefore commenced a retreat, the direction of which was doomed to prove the crisis of his fate. He retired as he had advanced, along both sides of the Aube; and though pursued and annoyed in this movement (which was necessarily executed through Arcis and all its defiles,) his rear-guard was so well conducted, that he sustained little loss. A late author,[11] who has composed an excellent and scientific work on this campaign, has remarked—"In concluding the account of the two days thus spent by the contending armies in presence of each other, it is equally worthy of remark, that Buonaparte, with a force not exceeding 25,000 or 30,000 men, should have risked himself in such a position in front of 80,000 of the allies, as that the latter should

---

[11] Memoir of the Operations of the Allied Armies in 1813 and 1814. By Lord Burghersh.

have allowed him to escape them with impunity." The permitting him to retreat with so little annoyance has been censured in general by all who have written on this campaign.[12]

---

[12] Jomini, tom. iv., 564.

Chapter LXXVI

Plans of Buonaparte—Military and Political Questions regarding Paris—Napoleon crosses the Marne on 22d March—Retrospect of Events in the vicinity of Lyons, &c.—Defeats of the French in various quarters—Marmont and Mortier retreat under the walls of Paris—Joseph Buonaparte—Maria Louisa, with the Civil Authorities, leave the City—Attack of Paris on the 30th—A Truce accorded—Joseph flies.

PLANS OF BUONAPARTE

The decline of Napoleon's waning fortunes having been such, as to turn him aside from an offered field of battle, and to place him betwixt two armies, each superior in number to his own, called now for a speedy and decisive resolution.

The manœuvres of Schwartzenberg and Blucher tended evidently to form a junction; and when it is considered that Buonaparte had felt it necessary to retreat from the army of Silesia before Laon, and from the grand army before Arcis, it would have been frenzy to wait till they both closed upon him. Two courses, therefore, remained;—either to draw back within the closing circle which his enemies were about to form around him, and, retreating before them until he had collected his whole forces, make a stand under the walls of Paris, aided by whatever strength that capital possessed, and which his energies could have called out; or, on the contrary, to march eastward, and breaking through the same circle, to operate on the rear of the allies, and on their lines of communication. This last was a subject on which the Austrians had expressed such feverish anxiety, as would probably immediately induce them to give up all thoughts of advancing, and march back to the frontier. Such a result was the rather to be hoped, because the continued stay of the allies, and the passage and repassage of troops through an exhausted country, had worn out the patience of the hardy peasantry of Alsace and Franche Comté, whom the exactions and rapine, inseparable from the movements of a hostile soldiery, had now roused from the apathy with which they had at first witnessed the invasion of their territory. Before Lyons, Napoleon might reckon on being reinforced by the veteran army of Suchet, arrived from Catalonia; and he would be within reach of the numerous chain of fortresses, which had garrisons strong enough to form an army, if drawn together.

The preparations for arranging such a force, and for arming the peasantry, had been in progress for some time. Trusty agents, bearing orders concealed in the sheaths of their knives, the collars of their dogs, or about their persons, had been detached to warn the various commandants of the Emperor's pleasure. Several were taken by the blockading troops of the allies, and hanged as spies, but others made their way. While at Rheims, Buonaparte had issued an order for rousing the peasantry, in which he not only declared their arising in arms was an act of patriotic duty, but denounced as traitors the mayors of the districts who should throw obstructions in the way of a general levy. The allies, on the contrary, threatened the extremity of military execution on all the peasantry who should obey Napoleon's call to arms. It was, as we formerly observed, an excellent exemplification, how much political opinions depend on circumstances; for, after the second capture of Vienna, the Austrians were calling out the levy-en-masse, and Napoleon, in his turn, was threatening to burn the villages, and execute the peasants, who should dare to obey.

While Napoleon was at Rheims, the affairs of the north-east frontier seemed so promising, that Ney offered to take the command of the insurrectionary army; and, as he was reckoned the best officer of light troops in Europe, it is not improbable he might have brought the levies-en-masse on that warlike border, to have fought like the French national forces in the beginning of the Revolution. Buonaparte did not yield to this proposal. Perhaps he thought so bold a movement could only succeed under his own eye.

PARIS

But there were two especial considerations which must have made Napoleon hesitate in adopting this species of back-game, designed to redeem the stake which it was impossible to save by the ordinary means of carrying on the bloody play. The one was the military question, whether Paris could be defended, if Napoleon was to move to the rear of the allied army, instead of falling back upon the city with the army which he commanded. The other question was of yet deeper import, and of a political nature. The means of the capital for defence being supposed adequate, was it likely that Paris, a town of 700,000 inhabitants, divided into factions unaccustomed to the near voice of war, and startled by the dreadful novelty of their situation, would submit to the sacrifices which a successful defence of the city must in every event have required? Was, in short, their love and fear of Buonaparte so great, that without his personal presence, and that of his army, to encourage, and at the same time overawe them, they would willingly incur the risk of seeing their beautiful metropolis destroyed, and all the horrors of a sack inflicted by the mass of nations whom Napoleon's ambition had been the means of combining against them, and who proclaimed themselves the enemies, not of France, but of Buonaparte?

Neither of these questions could be answered with confidence. Napoleon, although he had embodied 30,000 national guards, had not provided arms for a third part of the number. This is hinted at by some authors, as if the want of these arms ought to be imputed to some secret treason. But this accusation has never been put in any tangible shape. The arms never existed, and never were ordered; and although Napoleon had nearly three months' time allowed him, after his return to Paris, yet he never thought of arming the Parisians in general. Perhaps he doubted their fidelity to his cause. He ordered, it is said, 200 cannon to be provided for the defence of the northern and eastern line of the city, but neither were these obtained in sufficient quantity. The number of individuals who could be safely intrusted with arms, was also much limited. Whether, therefore, Paris was, in a military point of view, capable of defence or not, must have, in every event, depended much on the strength of the military force left to protect it. This Napoleon knew must be very moderate. His hopes were therefore necessarily limited by circumstances, to the belief that Paris, though incapable of a protracted defence, might yet hold out for such a space as might enable him to move to its relief.

But, secondly, as the means of holding out Paris were very imperfect, so the inclination of the citizens to defend themselves at the expense of any considerable sacrifice, was much doubted. It was not in reason to be expected that the Parisians should imitate the devotion of Zaragossa. Each Spanish citizen, on that memorable occasion, had his share of interest in the war which all maintained—a portion, namely, of that liberty and independence for which it was waged. But the Parisians were very differently situated. They were not called on to barricade their streets, destroy their suburbs, turn their houses into fortresses, and themselves into soldiers, and expose their property and families to the horrors of a storm; and this not for any advantage to France or themselves, but merely that they might maintain Napoleon on the throne. The ceaseless, and of late the losing wars, in which he seemed irretrievably engaged, had rendered his government unpopular; and it was plain to all, except perhaps himself, that he did not stand in that relation to the people of Paris, when citizens are prepared to die for their sovereign. It might have been as well expected that the frogs in the fable would, in case of invasion, have risen in a mass to defend King Serpent. It is probable that Buonaparte did not see this in the true point of view; but that, with the feelings of self-importance which sovereigns must naturally acquire from their situation, and which, from his high actions and distinguished talents, he of all sovereigns, was peculiarly entitled to indulge—it is probable that he lost sight of the great disproportion betwixt the nation and an individual; and forgot, amid the hundreds of thousands which Paris contains, what small relation the number of his own faithful and devoted followers bore, not only to those who were perilously engaged in factions hostile to him, but to the great mass, who, in Hotspur's phrase, loved their own shops or barns better than his house.[13]

Thirdly, the consequences of Paris being lost, either from not possessing, or not employing, the means of defence, were sure to be

---

[13] Henry IV., act ii., scene ii.

productive of irretrievable calamity. Russia, as had been shown, could survive the destruction of its capital, and perhaps Great Britain's fate might not be decided by the capture of London. But the government of France had, during all the phases of the Revolution, depended upon the possession of Paris—a capital which has at all times directed the public opinion of that country. Should the military occupation of this most influential of all capitals, bring about, as was most likely, a political and internal revolution, it was greatly to be doubted, whether the Emperor could make an effectual stand in any other part of his dominions.

It must be candidly admitted, that this reasoning, as being subsequent to the fact, has a much more decisive appearance than it could have had when subjected to the consideration of Napoleon. He was entitled, from the feverish anxiety hitherto shown by the Austrians, upon any approach to flank movements, and by the caution of their general proceedings, to think, that they would be greatly too timorous to adopt the bold step of pressing onward to Paris. It was more likely that they would follow him to the frontier, with the purpose of preserving their communications. Besides, Napoleon at this crisis had but a very slender choice of measures. To remain where he was, between Blucher and Schwartzenberg, was not possible; and, in advancing to either flank, he must have fought with a superior enemy. To retreat upon Paris, was sure to induce the whole allies to pursue in the same direction; and the encouragement which such a retreat must have given to his opponents, might have had the most fatal consequences. Perhaps his partisans might have taken more courage during his absence, from the idea that he was at the head of a conquering army, in the rear of the allies, than during his actual presence, if he had arrived in Paris in consequence of a compulsory retreat.

Buonaparte seems, as much from a sort of necessity as from choice, to have preferred breaking through the circle of hunters which hemmed him in, trusting to strengthen his army with the garrisons drawn from the frontier fortresses, and with the warlike peasantry of Alsace and Franche Comté, and, thus reinforced, to advance with rapidity on the rear of his enemies, ere they had time to execute, or perhaps to arrange, any system of offensive operations. The scheme appeared the more hopeful, as he was peremptory in his belief that his march could not fail to draw after him, in pursuit, or observation at least, the grand army of Schwartzenberg; the general maxim, that the war could only be decided where he was present in person, being, as he conceived, as deeply impressed by experience upon his enemies as upon his own soldiers.

Napoleon could not disguise from himself, what indeed he had told the French public, that a march, or, as he termed it, a *hourra* upon Paris, was the principal purpose of the allies. Every movement made in advance, whether by Blucher or Schwartzenberg, had this for its object. But they had uniformly relinquished the undertaking, upon his making any demonstration to prevent it; and therefore he did not suspect them of a resolution so venturous as to move directly upon Paris, leaving the French army unbroken in their rear, to act upon their line of communication with Germany. It is remarked, that those chess-players who deal in the most venturous gambits are least capable of defending themselves when attacked in the same audacious manner; and that, in war, the generals whose usual and favourite tactics are those of advance and attack, have been most frequently surprised by the unexpected adoption of offensive operations on the part of their enemy. Napoleon had been so much accustomed to see his antagonists bend their attention rather to parry blows than to aim them, and was so confident in the dread impressed by his rapidity of movement, his energy of assault, and the terrors of his reputation, that he seems to have entertained little apprehension of the allies adopting a plan of operations which had no reference to his own, and which, instead of attempting to watch or counteract his movements in the rear of their army, should lead them straight forward to take possession of his capital. Besides, notwithstanding objections have been stated, which seemed to render a *permanent* defence impossible, there were other considerations to be taken into view. The ground to the north of Paris is very strong, the national guard was numerous, the lower part of the population of a military character, and favourable to his cause. A defence, if resolute, however brief, would have the double effect of damping the ardour of the assailants, and of detaining them before the walls of the capital, until Buonaparte should advance to its relief, and thus place the allies between two fires. It was not to be supposed that the surrender of Paris would be the work of a single day. The unanimous voice of the journals, of the ministers of the police, and of the thousands whose interest was radically and deeply entwisted with that of Buonaparte, assured their master on that point. The movement to the rear, therefore, though removing him from Paris, which it might expose to temporary alarm, might not, in Buonaparte's apprehension, seriously compromise the security of the capital.

The French Emperor, in executing this decisive movement, was extremely desirous to have possessed himself of Vitry, which lay in the line of his advance. But as this town contained a garrison of about 5000 men, commanded by an officer of resolution, he returned a negative to the summons; and Napoleon, in no condition to attempt a *coup-de-main* on a place of some strength, passed the Marne on the 22d of March, over a bridge of rafts constructed at Frigincour, and continued his movement towards the eastern frontier, increasing the distance at every step betwixt him and his capital, and at the same time betwixt him and his enemies.

In the meantime, events had taken place in the vicinity of Lyons, tending greatly to limit any advantages which Napoleon might have expected to reap on the south-eastern part of the frontier towards Switzerland, and also to give spirits to the numerous enemies of his government in Provence, where the Royalists always possessed a considerable party.

The reinforcements despatched by the Austrians under General Bianchi, and their reserves, brought forward by the Prince of Hesse-Homberg, had restored their superiority over Augereau's army. He was defeated at Macon on the 11th of March, in a battle which he had given for the purpose of maintaining his line on the Saone. A second time, he was defeated on the 18th at St. George, and obliged to retire in great disorder, with scarce even the means of defending the Isère, up which river he retreated. Lyons, thus uncovered, opened its gates to Bianchi; and, after all that they had heard concerning the losses of the allies, the citizens saw with astonishment and alarm an untouched body of their troops, amounting to 60,000 men, defile through their streets. This defeat of Augereau was probably unknown to Napoleon, when he determined to march to the frontiers, and thought he might reckon on co-operation with the Lyonnese army. Though, therefore, the Emperor's movement to St. Dizier was out of the rules of ordinary war, and though it enabled the allies to conceive and execute the daring scheme which put an end to the campaign, yet it was by no means hopeless in its outset; or, we would rather say, was one of the few alternatives which the crisis of his affairs left to Buonaparte, and which, judging from the previous vacillation and cautious timidity displayed in the councils of the allies, he had no reason to apprehend would have given rise to the consequences that actually followed.

THE ALLIES ADVANCE

The allies, who had in their latest councils wound up their resolution to the decisive experiment of marching on Paris, were at first at a loss to account for Napoleon's disappearance, or to guess whither he had gone. This occasioned some hesitation and loss of time. At length, by the interception of a French courier, they found despatches addressed by Buonaparte to his government at Paris, from which they were enabled to conjecture the real purpose and direction of his march. A letter,[14] in the Emperor's own hand, to Maria Louisa, confirmed the certainty of the information.[15] The allies resolved to adhere, under this unexpected change of circumstances, to the bold resolution they had already formed. To conceal the real direction of his march, as well as to open communications with the Silesian army, Schwartzenberg, moving

---

[14] "Mon Amie, j'ai été tous les jours à cheval; le 20 j'ai pris Arcis-sur-Aube. L'ennemi m'y attaqua à 8 heures du soir: le même soir je l'ai battu, et lui ai fait 4000 morts: je lui ai pris 2 pieces de canon et même repris 2: ayant quitté le 21, l'armée ennemie s'est mise, en bataille pour protéger la marche de ses armées, sur Brienne, et sur Bar-sur-Aube, j'ai décidé de me porter sur la Marne et ses environs afin de la pousser plus loin de Paris, en me rapprochant de mes *places*. Je serai ce soir à St. Dizier. Adieu, mon amie, embrassez mon fils."

[15] "General Muffling told me that the word *St. Dizier*, of so much importance, was so badly written, that they were several hours in making it out. Blucher forwarded the letter to Maria Louisa, with a letter in German, saying, that as she was the daughter of a *respectable* sovereign, who was fighting in the same cause with himself, he had sent it to her."—*Memorable Events*, p. 98.

laterally, transferred his headquarters to Vitry, where he arrived on the 24th, two days after it had been summoned by Napoleon. Blucher, in the meantime, approached his army from Laon to Chalons, now entirely re-organised after the two bloody battles which it had sustained. As a necessary preparation for the advance, General Ducca was left on the Aube, with a division of Austrians, for the purpose of defending their depôts, keeping open their communications, and guarding the person of the Emperor Francis, who did not perhaps judge it delicate to approach Paris in arms, with the rest of the sovereigns, while the city was nominally governed by his own daughter as Regent. Ducca had also in charge, if pressed, to retreat upon the Prince of Hesse-Homberg's army, which was in triumphant possession of Lyons.

This important arrangement being made, another was adopted equally necessary to deceive and observe Napoleon. Ten thousand cavalry were selected, under the enterprising generals, Winzengerode and Czernicheff, who, with fifty pieces of cannon, were despatched to hang on Buonaparte's march, to obstruct his communications with the country he had left, intercept couriers from Paris, or information respecting the motions of the allied armies, and to present on all occasions such a front, as, if possible, might impress him with the belief, that their corps formed the vanguard of the whole army of Schwartzenberg. The Russian and Prussian light troops meanwhile scoured the roads, and intercepted, near Sommepuix, a convoy of artillery and ammunition belonging to Napoleon's rear-guard, when twenty pieces of cannon, with a strong escort, fell into their hands. They also cut off several couriers, bringing important despatches to Napoleon from Paris. One of these was loaded with as heavy tidings as ever were destined to afflict falling greatness. This packet informed Napoleon of the descent of the English in Italy; of the entry of the Austrians into Lyons, and the critical state of Augereau; of the declaration of Bourdeaux in favour of Louis; of the demonstrations of Wellington towards Toulouse; of the disaffected state of the public mind, and the exhausted condition of the national resources. Much of these tidings was new to the allied sovereigns and generals; but it was received by them with very different sensations from those which the intelligence was calculated to inflict upon him for whom the packet was intended.

Blucher, in the meantime, so soon as he felt the opposition to his movements diminished by the march of Buonaparte from Chalons to Arcis, had instantly resumed the offensive, and driven the corps of Mortier and Marmont, left to observe his motions, over the Marne. He passed the Aisne, near Béry-le-Bac, repossessed himself of Rheims by blowing open the gates and storming the place, and, having gained these successes, moved towards Chalons and Vitry. His course had hitherto been south-eastward, in order to join with Schwartzenberg; but he now received from the King of Prussia the welcome order to turn his march westward, and move straight upon Paris. The grand army adopted the same direction, and thus they moved on in corresponding lines, and in communication with each other.

While Buonaparte, retiring to the east, prepared for throwing himself on the rear of the allies, he was necessarily, in person, exposed to the same risk of having his communications cut off, and his supplies intercepted, which it was the object of his movement to inflict upon his enemy. Marmont and Mortier, who retreated before Blucher over the Marne, had orders to move upon Vitry, probably because that movement would have placed them in the rear of Schwartzenberg, had he been induced to retreat from the line of the Aube, as Napoleon expected he would. But as a very different course had been adopted by the allies, from that which Napoleon had anticipated, the two maréchals found themselves unexpectedly in front of their grand army near Fère-Champenoise. They were compelled to attempt a retreat to Sezanne, in which, harassed by the numerous cavalry of the allies, they sustained heavy loss.

While the cavalry were engaged in pursuit of the maréchals, the infantry of the allies were approaching the town of Fère-Champenoise, when a heavy fire was heard in the vicinity, and presently appeared a large column of infantry, advancing checker-wise and by intervals, followed and repeatedly charged by several squadrons of cavalry, who were speedily recognised as belonging to the Silesian army. The infantry, about 5000 in number, had left Paris with a large convoy of provisions and ammunition. They were proceeding towards Montmirail, when they were discovered and attacked by the cavalry of Blucher's army. Unable to make a stand, they endeavoured, by an alteration of their march, to reach Fère-Champenoise, where they expected to find either the Emperor, or Marmont and Mortier. It was thus their misfortune to fall upon Scylla in seeking to avoid Charybdis. The column consisted entirely of young men, conscripts, or national guards, who had never before been in action. Yet, neither the necessity of their condition, nor their unexpected surprise in meeting first one, and then a second army of enemies, where they looked only for friends, could induce these spirited young men to surrender. Rappatel, the aide-de-camp of Moreau, and entertained in the same capacity by the Emperor Alexander, was shot, while attempting, by the orders of the Emperor, to explain to them the impossibility of resistance. The French say, that the brother of Rappatel served in the company from which the shot came which killed the unfortunate officer. The artillery at length opened on the French on every side; they were charged by squadron after squadron; the whole convoy was taken, and the escort were killed, wounded, or made prisoners.[16]

ALLIES APPROACH PARIS

Thus the allies continued to advance upon Paris, while the shattered divisions of Mortier and Marmont, hard pressed by the cavalry, lost a rear-guard of 1500 men near Ferté Gauchère. At Crecy they parted into two bodies, one retreating on Meaux, the other on Lagny. They were still pursued and harassed; and at length, the soldiers becoming desperate, could hardly be kept together, while the artillerymen cut the traces of their guns, and mounted their draught-horses, to effect their escape. It is computed that the French divisions, between Fère-Champenoise and Lagny, lost 8000 men, and eighty guns, besides immense quantities of baggage and ammunition. Indeed, surrounded as they were by overpowering numbers, it required no little skill in the generals, as well as bravery and devotion in the soldiers, to keep the army from dissolving entirely. The allies, gaining advantages at every step, moved on with

---

[16] Lord Burghersh, Observations, &c., p. 232; Baron Fain, p. 222.

such expedition, that when, on the 27th March, they took up their headquarters at Collomiers, they had marched upwards of seventy miles in three days.

An effort was made, by about 10,000 men of the national guards, to stop a column of the army of Silesia, but it totally failed; General Horne galloping into the very centre of the French mass of infantry, and making prisoner the general who commanded them with his own hand. When Blucher approached Meaux, the garrison (a part of Mortier's army) retreated, blowing up a large powder magazine. This was on the 28th of March, and on the evening of the same day, the vanguard of the Silesian army pushed on as far as Claye, from whence, not without a sharp action, they dislodged a part of the divisions of Marmont and Mortier. These maréchals now retreated under the walls of Paris, their discouraged and broken forces forming the only regular troops, excepting those of the garrison, which could be reckoned on for the defence of the capital.

The allied armies moved onward, on the same grand point, leaving, however, Generals Wrede and Sacken, with a corps d'armée of 30,000 men, upon the line of the Marne, to oppose any attempt which might be made for annoying the rear of the army, and thus relieving the metropolis.

Deducing this covering army, the rest of the allied forces moved in columns along the three grand routes of Meaux, Lagny, and Soissons, thus threatening Paris along all its north-eastern quarter. The military sovereigns and their victorious armies were now in sight of that metropolis, whose ruler and his soldiers had so often and so long lorded it in theirs; of that Paris, which, unsatisfied with her high rank among the cities of Europe, had fomented constant war until all should be subjugated to her empire; of that proud city, who boasted herself the first in arms and in science, the mistress and example of the civilized world, the depositary of all that is wonderful in the fine arts, and the dictatress as well of taste as of law to continental Europe.

PARIS

The position of Paris, on the north-eastern frontier, which was thus approached, is as strongly defensible, perhaps, as can be said of any unfortified town in the world. Art, however, had added little to the defence of the city itself, except a few wretched redoubts (called by the French *tambours*,) erected for protection of the barriers. But the external line was very strong, as will appear from the following sketch. The heights which environ the city on the eastern side, rise abruptly from an extensive plain, and form a steep and narrow ridge, which sinks again as suddenly upon the eastern quarter of the town, which it seems to screen as with a natural bulwark. The line of defence which they afford is extremely strong. The southern extremity of the ridge, which rests upon the wood of Vincennes, extending southward to the banks of the river Marne, is called the heights of Belleville and Romainville, taking its name from two delightful villages which occupy it, Belleville being nearest, and Romainville most distant from Paris. The heights are covered with romantic groves, and decorated by many pleasant villas, with gardens, orchards, vineyards, and plantations. These, which, in peaceful times, are a favourite resort of the gay Parisians, on their parties of pleasure, were now to be occupied by other guests, and for far different purposes. In advance of these heights, and protected by them, is the village of Pantin, situated on the great road from Bondy. To the left of Romainville, and more in front of Belleville, is a projecting eminence, termed the Butte de Saint Chaumont. The ridge there sinks, and admits a half-finished aqueduct, called the canal de l'Ourcq. The ground then again rises into the bold and steep eminence, called Montmartre, from being the supposed place of the martyrdom of St. Denis, the patron of France. From the declivity of this steep hill is a level plain, extending to the river Seine, through which runs the principal northern approach to Paris, from the town of Saint Denis. The most formidable preparations had been made for maintaining this strong line of defence, behind which the city lay sheltered. The extreme right of the French forces occupied the wood of Vincennes, and the village of Charenton upon the Marne, and was supported by the troops stationed on the heights of Belleville, Romainville, and on the Butte de Chaumont, which composed the right wing. Their centre occupied the line formed by the half-finished canal de l'Ourcq, was defended by the village of La Villette, and a strong redoubt on the farm of Rouvroi, mounted with eighteen heavy guns, and by the embankments of the canal, and still farther protected by a powerful artillery planted in the rear, on the heights of Montmartre. The left wing was thrown back from the village called Monceaux, near the north-western extremity of the heights, and prolonged itself to that of Neuilly, on the Seine, which was strongly occupied by the extreme left of their army. Thus, with the right extremity of the army resting upon the river Marne, and the left upon the Seine, the French occupied a defensive semicircular line, which could not be turned, the greater part of which was posted on heights of uncommon steepness, and the whole defended by cannon, placed with the utmost science and judgment, but very deficient in point of numbers.

The other side of Paris is almost defenceless; but, in order to have attacked it on that side, the allies must have previously crossed the Seine; an operation successfully practised in the following year, but which at that period, when their work, to be executed at all, must be done suddenly, they had no leisure to attempt, considering the great probability of Napoleon's coming up in their rear, recalled by the danger of the capital. They were therefore compelled to prefer a sudden and desperate attack upon the strongest side of the city, to the slower, though more secure measure of turning the formidable line of defence which we have endeavoured to describe.

Three times, since the allies crossed the Rhine, the capital of France had been menaced by the approach of troops within twenty miles of the city, but it had uniformly been delivered by the active and rapid movements of Napoleon. Encouraged by this recollection, the citizens, without much alarm, heard, for the fourth time, that the Cossacks had been seen at Meaux. Stifled rumours, however, began to circulate, that the divisions of Marmont and Mortier had sustained severe loss, and were in full retreat on the capital; a fact speedily confirmed by the long train of wounded who entered the barriers of the city, with looks of consternation and words of discouragement. Then came crowds of peasants, flying they knew not whither, before an enemy whose barbarous rapacity had been so long the theme of every tongue, bringing with them their half-naked and half-starved families, their teams, their carts, and such of their herds and household goods as they could remove in haste. These unfortunate fugitives crowded the Boulevards of Paris, the usual resort of the gay world, adding, by exaggerated and contradictory reports, to the dreadful ideas which the Parisians already conceived of the approaching storm.

The government, chiefly directed by Joseph Buonaparte, in the name of his sister-in-law Maria Louisa, did all they could to encourage the people, by exaggerating their means of defence, and maintaining with effrontery, that the troops which approached the capital, composed but some isolated column which by accident straggled towards Paris, while the Emperor was breaking, dividing, and slaughtering, the gross of the confederated army. The light could not be totally shut out, but such rays as were admitted were highly coloured with hope, having been made to pass through the medium of the police and public papers. A grand review of the troops destined for the defence of the capital was held upon the Sunday preceding the assault. Eight thousand troops of the line, being the garrison of Paris, under Gerard, and 30,000 national guards, commanded by Hulin, governor of the city, passed in order through the stately court of the Tuileries, followed by their trains of artillery, their corps of pioneers, and their carriages for baggage and ammunition. This was an imposing and encouraging spectacle, until it was remembered that these forces were not designed to move out to distant conquest, the destination of many hundreds of thousands which in other days had been paraded before that palace; but that they were the last hope of Paris, who must defend all that she contained by a battle under her walls. The remnants of Marmont and Mortier's corps d'armée made no part of this parade. Their diminished battalions, and disordered state of equipment, were ill calculated to inspire courage into the public mind. They were concentrated and stationed on the line of defence already described, beyond the barriers of the city. But the maréchals themselves entered Paris, and gave their assistance to the military councils of Joseph Buonaparte.

Preparations were made by the government to remove beyond the Loire, or at least in that direction. Maria Louisa had none of the spirit of an Amazon, though graced with all the domestic virtues. She was also placed painfully in the course of a war betwixt her husband and father. Besides, she obeyed, and probably with no lack of will, Napoleon's injunctions to leave the capital, if danger should approach. She left Paris,[17] therefore, with her son, who is said to have shown an unwillingness to depart, which, in a child, seemed to have something ominous in it.[18] Almost all the civil authorities of Buonaparte's government left the city at the same time, after destroying the private records of the high police, and carrying with them the crown jewels, and much of the public treasure. Joseph Buonaparte remained, detaining with him, somewhat, it is said, against his inclination, Cambacérès, the chancellor of the Emperor, whom, though somewhat too unwieldy for the character, Napoleon had, in one of his latest councils, threatened with the honours and dangers of the Colonelcy of a battalion. Joseph himself had the talents of an accomplished man, and an amiable member of society, but they do not seem to have been of a military description. He saw his sister-in-law depart, attended by a regiment of seven hundred men, whom some writers have alleged had been better employed in the defence of the city; forgetting of what importance it was to Napoleon, that the person of the Empress should be protected alike against a roving band of Hulans, or Cossacks, or the chance of some civic mutiny. These arrangements being made, Joseph published, on the morning of the 29th, a proclamation, assuring the citizens of Paris, that "he would remain with them;" he described the enemy as a single straggling column which had approached from Meaux, and required them by a brief and valorous resistance to sustain the honour of the French name, until the arrival of the Emperor, who, he assured the Parisians, was on full march to their succour.[19]

---

[17] "At half past ten on the morning of the 29th, the Empress, in a brown cloth riding-habit, with the King of Rome, in one coach, surrounded by guards, and followed by several other coaches, with attendants, quitted the palace; the spectators observing the most profound silence."—*Memorable Events in Paris in 1814*, p. 50.

[18] Souvenirs de Mad. Durand, tom. i., p. 205.

[19] "I saw the proclamation of *Roi Joseph* selling for a sous, on the Boulevards, where groups of people were assembled. The flight of the Empress caused considerable alarm. Many loudly expressed their discontent at the national guard, for permitting her to leave Paris, as they entertained a dastardly hope that her presence would preserve them from the vengeance of the allies. For the first time I heard the people openly dare to vent complaints against the Emperor, as the sole cause of their impending calamity; but I witnessed no patriotic feeling to repulse the enemy."—*Memorable Events*, p. 53.

Between three and four o'clock on the next eventful morning, the drums beat to arms, and the national guards assembled in force. But of the thousands which obeyed the call, a great part were, from age, habits, and want of inclination, unfit for the service demanded from them. We have also already alluded to the scarcity of arms, and certainly there were very many of those citizen-soldiers, whom, had weapons been more plenty, the government of Buonaparte would not have intrusted with them.

Most of the national guards, who were suitably armed, were kept within the barrier until about eleven o'clock, and then, as their presence became necessary, were marched to the scene of action, and arrayed in a second line behind the regular troops, so as rather to impose upon the enemy, by an appearance of numbers, than to take a very active share in the contest. The most serviceable were, however, draughted to act as sharp-shooters, and several battalions were stationed to strengthen particular points of the line. The whole of the troops, including many volunteers, who actively engaged in the defence of the city, might be between 10,000 and 20,000.

The proposed assault of the allies was to be general and simultaneous, along the whole line of defence. The Prince Royal of Wirtemberg was to attack the extreme right of the French, in the wood of Vincennes, drive them from the banks of the Marne and the village of Charenton, and thus turn the heights of Belleville. The Russian general, Rayefski, making a flank movement from the public road to Meaux, was to direct three strong columns, with their artillery and powerful reserves, in order to attack in front the important heights of Belleville and Romainville, and the villages which give name to them. The Russian and Prussian body-guards had charge to attack the centre of the enemy, posted upon the canal de l'Ourcq, the reserves of which occupied the eminence called Montmartre. The army of Silesia was to assail the left of the French line, so as to turn and carry the heights of Montmartre from the north-east. The third division of the allied army, and a strong body of cavalry, were kept in reserve. Before the attack commenced, two successive flags of truce were despatched to summon the city to capitulate. Both were refused admittance; so that the intention of the defenders of Paris appeared fixed to hazard an engagement.

It was about eight o'clock, when the Parisians, who had assembled in anxious crowds at the barriers of St. Denis and of Vincennes, the outlets from Paris, corresponding with the two extremities of the line, became sensible, from the dropping succession of musket shots, which sounded like the detached pattering of large drops of rain before a thunder-storm, that the work of destruction was already commenced. Presently platoons of musketry, with a close and heavy fire of cannon, from the direction of Belleville, announced that the engagement had become general on that part of the line.

BELLEVILLE—MESNILMONTANT

General Rayefski had begun the attack by pushing forward a column, with the purpose of turning the heights of Romainville on the right; but its progress having been arrested by a heavy fire of artillery, the French suddenly became the assailants, and under the command of Marmont, rushed forward and possessed themselves of the village of Pantin,[20] in advance of their line; an important post, which they had abandoned on the preceding evening, at the approach of the allied army. It was instantly recovered by the Russian grenadiers, at the point of the bayonet; and the French, although they several times attempted to resume the offensive, were driven back by the Russians on the villages of Belleville and Mesnilmontant, while the allies pushed forward through the wood of Romainville, under the acclivity of the heights. The most determined and sustained fire was directed upon them from the French batteries along the whole line. Several of these were served by the youths of the Polytechnic school, boys from twelve to sixteen years of age, who showed the greatest activity and the most devoted courage. The French infantry rushed repeatedly in columns from the heights, where opportunities occurred to check the progress of the allies. They were as often repulsed by the Russians, each new attempt giving rise to fresh conflicts and more general slaughter, while a continued and dispersed combat of sharpshooters took place among the groves, vineyards, and gardens of the villas, with which

---

[20] Lord Burghersh's account states, that the village of Pantin was attacked, but never retaken by the French.—"Operations," p. 240.—Ed. (1842.)

the heights are covered. At length, by order of General de Tolli, the Russian commander-in-chief, the front attack on the heights was suspended until the operations of the allies on the other points should permit it to be resumed at a cheaper risk of loss. The Russian regiments which had been dispersed as sharpshooters, were withdrawn, and again formed in rank, and it would seem that the French seized this opportunity to repossess themselves of the village of Pantin, and to assume a momentary superiority in the contest.

Blucher had received his orders late in the morning, and could not commence the attack so early as that upon the left. About eleven o'clock, having contented himself with observing and blockading a body of French troops, who occupied the village of St. Denis, he directed the columns of General Langeron against the village of Aubervilliers, and, having surmounted the obstinate opposition which was there made, moved them by the road of Clichy, right against the extremity of the heights of Montmartre, whilst the division of Kleist and D'Yorck marched to attack in flank the villages of La Villette and Pantin, and thus sustain the attack on the centre and right of the French. The defenders, strongly intrenched and protected by powerful batteries, opposed the most formidable resistance, and, as the ground was broken and impracticable for cavalry, many of the attacking columns suffered severely. When the divisions of the Silesian army, commanded by Prince William of Prussia, first came to the assistance of the original assailants upon the centre, the French concentrated themselves on the strong post of La Villette, and the farm of Rouvroy, and continued to offer the most desperate resistance in defence of these points. Upon the allied left wing the Prussian guards, and those of Baden, threw themselves with rival impetuosity into the village of Pantin, and carried it at the point of the bayonet. During these advantages, the Prince Royal of Wirtemberg, on the extreme left of the allies, had forced his way to Vincennes, and threatened the right of the French battalions posted at Belleville, as had been projected in the plan of the attack. General Rayefski renewed the suspended assault upon these heights in front, when he learned that they were thus in some measure turned in flank, and succeeded in carrying those of Romainville, with the village. Marmont and Oudinot in vain attempted a charge upon the allied troops, who had thus established themselves on the French line of defence. They were repulsed and pursued by the victors, who, following up their advantage, possessed themselves successively of the villages of Belleville and Mesnilmontant, the Butte de St. Chaumont, and the fine artillery which defended this line.

About the same time the village of Charonne, on the right extremity of the heights, was also carried, and the whole line of defence occupied by the right wing of the French fell into possession of the allies. Their light horse began to penetrate from Vincennes as far as the barriers of Paris, and their guns and mortars upon the heights were turned upon the city. The centre of the French army, stationed upon the canal de l'Ourcq, had hitherto stood firm, protected by the redoubt at Rouvroy, with eighteen heavy pieces of cannon, and by the village of La Villette, which formed the key of the position. But the right flank of their line being turned by those troops who had become possessed of Romainville, the allies overwhelmed this part of the line also; and, carrying by assault the farm of Rouvroy, with its strong redoubt, and the village of La Villette, drove the centre of the French back upon the city. A body of French cavalry attempted to check the advance of the allied columns, but were repulsed and destroyed by a brilliant charge of the black hussars of Brandenburgh. Meanwhile, the right wing of the Silesian army approached close to the foot of Montmartre, and Count Langeron's corps were preparing to storm this last remaining defensible post, when a flag of truce appeared, to demand a cessation of hostilities.

It appears that, in the morning, Joseph Buonaparte had shown himself to the defenders riding along the lines, accompanied by his staff, and had repeated to all the corps engaged, the assurance that he would live and die with them. There is reason to think, that if he did not quite credit that such extensive preparations for assault were made by a single division of the allies, yet he believed he had to do with only one of their two armies, and not with their united force. He was undeceived by a person named Peyre, called, by some, an engineer officer attached to the staff of the Governor of Paris, and, by others, a superintendent belonging to the corps of firemen in that city. Peyre, it seems, had fallen into the hands of a party of Cossacks the night before, and was carried in the morning to the presence of the Emperor Alexander, at Bondy. In his route, he had an opportunity of calculating the immense force of the armies now under the walls of Paris. Through the medium of this officer, the Emperor Alexander explained the intentions of the allied sovereigns, to allow fair terms to the city of Paris, provided it was proposed to capitulate ere the barriers were forced; with the corresponding intimation, that if the defence were prolonged beyond that period, it would not be in the power either of the Emperor, the King of Prussia, or the allied generals, to prevent the total destruction of the town.

FALL OF PARIS

Mons. Peyre, thus erected into a commissioner and envoy of crowned heads, was set at liberty, and with danger and difficulty found his way into the French lines, through the fire which was maintained in every direction. He was introduced to Joseph, to whom he delivered his message, and showed proclamations to the city of Paris, with which the Emperor Alexander had intrusted him. Joseph hesitated, at first inclining to capitulate, then pulling up resolution, and determining to abide the chance of arms. He continued irresolute, blood flowing fast around him, until about noon, when the enemy's columns, threatening an attack on Montmartre, and the shells and bullets from the artillery, which was in position to cover the attempt, flying fast over the heads of himself and his staff, he sent Peyre to General Marmont, who acted as commander-in-chief, with permission to the maréchal to demand a cessation of arms. At the same time, Joseph himself fled with his whole attendants; thus abandoning the troops, whom his exhortations had engaged, in the bloody and hopeless resistance of which he had solemnly promised to partake the dangers.[21] Marmont, with Moncey, and the other generals who conducted the defence, now saw all hopes of making it good at an end. The whole line was

---

[21] "Prince Joseph, observing the vast number of the enemy's troops that had arrived at the foot of Montmartre, was convinced that the capitulation could be no longer delayed. He gave the necessary powers to the Duke of Ragusa; and immediately proceeded to join the government at Blois."—Baron Fain, p. 232.

carried, excepting the single post of Montmartre, which was turned, and on the point of being stormed on both flanks, as well as in front; the Prince Royal of Wirtemberg had occupied Charenton, with its bridge over the Marne, and pushing forward on the high-road from thence to Paris, his advanced posts were already skirmishing at the barriers called the Trône; and a party of Cossacks had been with difficulty repulsed from the faubourg St. Antoine, on which they made a *Hourra*. The city of Paris is merely surrounded by an ordinary wall, to prevent smuggling. The barriers are not much stronger than any ordinary turnpike gate, and the stockade with which they had been barricaded, could have been cleared away by a few blows of the pioneers' axes. Add to this, that the heights commanding the city, Montmartre excepted, were in complete possession of the enemy; that a bomb or two, thrown probably to intimidate the citizens, had already fallen in the faubourg Montmartre, and the chaussée d'Antin; and that it was evident that any attempt to protract the defence of Paris, must be attended with utter ruin to the town and its inhabitants. Marshal Marmont, influenced by these considerations, despatched a flag of truce to General Barclay de Tolli, requesting a suspension of hostilities, to arrange the terms on which Paris was to be surrendered. The armistice was granted, on condition that Montmartre, the only defensible part of the line which the French still continued to occupy, should be delivered up to the allies. Deputies were appointed on both sides, to adjust the terms of surrender. These were speedily settled. The French regular troops were permitted to retire from Paris unmolested, and the metropolis was next day to be delivered up to the allied sovereigns, to whose generosity it was recommended.

Thus ended the assault of Paris, after a bloody action, in which the defenders lost upwards of 4000 in killed and wounded; and the allies, who had to storm well-defended batteries, redoubts, and intrenchments, perhaps about twice the number. They remained masters of the line at all points, and took nearly one hundred pieces of cannon. When night fell, the multiplied and crowded watch-fires that occupied the whole chain of heights on which the victors now bivouacked, indicated to the astonished inhabitants of the French metropolis, how numerous and how powerful were the armies into whose hands the fate of war had surrendered them.[22]

---

[22] "During the battle, the Boulevards des Italiens, and the Caffé Tortoni, were thronged with fashionable loungers of both sexes, sitting as usual on the chairs placed there, and appearing almost uninterested spectators of the number of wounded French, and prisoners of the allies which were brought in. About two o'clock, a general cry of *sauve qui peut* was heard on the Boulevards; this caused a general and confused flight, which spread like the undulations of a wave, even beyond the Pont Neuf. During the whole of the battle, wounded soldiers crawled into the streets, and lay down to die on the pavement. The *Moniteur* of this day was a full sheet; but no notice was taken of the war or the army. Four columns were occupied by an article on the dramatic works of Denis, and three with a dissertation on the existence of Troy."—*Memorable Events*, pp. 90-93.

Chapter LXXVII

State of Parties in Paris—Royalists—Revolutionists—Buonapartists—Talleyrand—Chateaubriand—Mission to the Allied Sovereigns—Their answer—Efforts of the Buonapartists—Feelings of the lowest classes—of the middling ranks—Neutrality of the National Guard—Growing confidence of the Royalists—Proclamations and White Cockades—Crowds assemble at the Boulevards—The Allies are received with shouts of welcome—Their Army retires to quarters—and the Cossacks bivouac in the Champs Elysées.

The battle was fought and won; but it remained a high and doubtful question in what way the victory was to be improved, so as to produce results of far greater consequence than usually follow from the mere military occupation of an enemy's capital. While the mass of the inhabitants were at rest, exhausted by the fatigues and anxieties of the day, many secret conclaves, on different principles, were held in the city of Paris, upon the night after the assault. Some of these even yet endeavoured to organise the means of resistance, and some to find out what modern policy has called a *Mezzo-termine*, some third expedient, between the risk of standing by Napoleon, and that of recalling the banished family.

The only middle mode which could have succeeded, would have been a regency under the Empress; and Fouché's Memoirs state, that if he had been in Paris at the time, he might have succeeded in establishing a new order of things upon such a basis. The assertion may be safely disputed. To Austria such a plan might have had some recommendations; but to the sovereigns and statesmen of the other allied nations, the proposal would only have appeared a device to obtain immediate peace, and keep the throne, as it were, in commission, that Buonaparte might ascend it at his pleasure.[23]

PARTIES IN PARIS

We have the greatest doubts whether, among the ancient chiefs of the Revolution, most of whom had, as hackneyed tools, lost credit in the public eye, both by want of principle and political inconsistency, there remained any who could have maintained a popular interest in opposition to that of the Royalists on the one hand, and the Buonapartists on the other. The few who remained steady to their democratic principles, Napoleon had discredited and thrown into the shade; and he had rendered many of the others still more inefficient, by showing that they were accessible to bribery and to ambition, and that ancient demagogues could, without much trouble, be transmuted into supple and obsequious courtiers. Their day of power and interest was past, and the exaggerated vehemence of their democratic opinions had no longer any effect on the lower classes, who were in a great proportion attached to the empire.

The Royalists, on the other hand, had been long combining and extending their efforts and opinions, which gained, chiefly among the higher orders, a sort of fashion which those of the democrats had lost. Talleyrand was acceptable to them as himself noble by birth; and he knew better than any one how to apply the

---

[23] The passage is curious, whether we regard it as really emanating from Fouché, or placed in the mouth of that active revolutionist by some one who well understood the genius of the party. "Had I been at Paris at that time," (the period of the siege, namely,) "the weight of my influence, doubtless, and my perfect acquaintance with the secrets of every party, would have enabled me to give these extraordinary events a very different direction. My preponderance, and the promptness of my decision, would have predominated over the more slow and mysterious influence of Talleyrand. That elevated personage could not have made his way unless we had been harnessed to the same car. I would have revealed to him the ramifications of my political plan, and, in spite of the odious policy of Savary, the ridiculous government of Cambacérès, the lieutenancy of the puppet Joseph, and the base spirit of the Senate, we would have breathed new life into the carcase of the Revolution, and these degraded patricians would not have thought of acting exclusively for their own interests. By our united impulse, we would have pronounced before the interference of any foreign influence, the dethronement of Napoleon, and proclaimed the Regency, of which I had already traced the basis. This conclusion was the only one which could have preserved the Revolution and its principles."—*Mémoires*, tom. ii., p. 229.

lever to unfasten the deep foundations of Napoleon's power. Of his address, though not successful in the particular instance, Las Cases gives us a curious specimen. Talleyrand desired to sound the opinion of Decrès, about the time of the crisis of which we are treating. He drew that minister towards the chimney, and opening a volume of Montesquieu, said, as if in the tone of an ordinary conversation, "I found a passage here this morning, which struck me in an extraordinary manner. Here it is, in such a book and chapter, page so and so: *When a prince has raised himself above all laws, when his tyranny becomes insupportable, there remains nothing to the oppressed subject except——*"

"It is quite enough," said Decrès, placing his hand upon Talleyrand's mouth, "I will hear no more. Shut your book." And Talleyrand closed the book, as if nothing remarkable had happened.[24]

An agent of such extraordinary tact was not frequently baffled, in a city, and at a time, when so many were, from hope, fear, love, hatred, and all the other strongest passions, desirous, according to the Roman phrase, of a new state of things. He had been unceasingly active, and eminently successful, in convincing the Royalists, that the King must purchase the recovery of his authority by consenting to place the monarchy on a constitutional footing; and in persuading another class, that the restoration of the Bourbons was the most favourable chance for the settlement of a free system of government. Nor did this accomplished politician limit his efforts to those who had loyalty to be awakened, and a love of liberty to be rekindled, but extended them through a thousand ramifications, through every class of persons. To the bold he offered an enterprise requiring courage; to the timid (a numerous class at the time) he showed the road of safety; to the ambitious, the prospect of gaining power; to the guilty, the assurance of indemnity and safety. He had inspired resolution even into the councils of the allies. A note from him to the Emperor Alexander, in the following words, is said to have determined that prince to persevere in the march upon Paris. "You venture nothing," said this laconic billet, "when you may safely venture every thing—Venture once more."

---

[24] Las Cases, tom. ii., p. 251.

It is not to be supposed that Talleyrand wrought in this deep intrigue without active coadjutors. The Abbé de Pradt, whose lively works have so often given some interest to our pages, was deeply involved in the transactions of that busy period, and advocated the cause of the Bourbons against that of his former master. Bournonville and other senators were engaged in the same cabals.

PROCLAMATION OF THE ALLIES

The Royalists, on their own part, were in the highest state of activity, and prepared to use their utmost exertions to obtain the mastery of the public spirit. At this most critical moment all was done, by Monsieur de Chateaubriand, which eloquence could effect, to appeal to the affections, perhaps even the prejudices of the people, in his celebrated pamphlet, entitled, "Of Buonaparte and the Bourbons." This vigorous and affecting comparison between the days when France was in peace and honour under her own monarchs, contrasted with those in which Europe appeared in arms under her walls, had been written above a month, and the manuscript was concealed by Madame de Chateaubriand in her bosom. It was now privately printed. So was a proclamation by Monsieur, made in the name of his brother, the late King of France. Finally, in a private assembly of the principal Royalists, amongst whom were the illustrious names of Rohan, Rochefoucault, Montmorency, and Noailles, it was resolved to send a deputation to the allied sovereigns, to learn, if possible, their intention. Monsieur Douhet, the gentleman intrusted with this communication, executed his mission at the expense of considerable personal danger, and returned into Paris with the answer, that the allies had determined to avoid all appearance of dictating to France respecting any family or mode of government, and that although they would most joyfully and willingly acknowledge the Bourbons, yet it could only be in consequence of a public declaration in their favour. At the same time Monsieur Douhet was furnished with a proclamation of the allies, signed Schwartzenberg, which, without mentioning the Bourbons, was powerfully calculated to serve their cause. It declared the friendly intention of the allies towards France, and represented the power of the government which now oppressed them, as the only obstacle to instant peace. The allied sovereigns, it was stated, sought but to see a salutary government in France, who would cement the friendly union of all nations. It belonged to the city of Paris to pronounce their opinion, and accelerate the peace of the world.[25]

Furnished with this important document, which plainly indicated the private wishes of the allies, the Royalists resolved to make an effort on the morning of March 31st. It was at first designed they should assemble five hundred gentlemen in arms; but this plan was prudently laid aside, and they determined to relinquish all appearance of force, and address the citizens only by means of persuasion.

In the meantime, the friends of the imperial government were not idle. The conduct of the lower classes, during the battle on the heights, had assumed an alarming character. For a time they had listened with a sort of stupified terror to the distant thunders of the fight, beheld the wounded and fugitives crowd in at the barriers, and gazed in useless wonder on the hurried march of troops moving out in haste to reinforce the lines. At length, the numerous crowds which assembled in the Boulevards and, particularly in the streets near the Palais Royal, assumed a more active appearance. There began to emerge from the suburbs and lanes those degraded members of the community, whose slavish labour is only relieved by coarse debauchery, invisible for the most part to the more decent classes of society, but whom periods of public calamity or agitation bring into view, to add to the general confusion and terror. They gather in times of public danger, as birds of ill omen and noxious reptiles are said to do at the rising of a tropical hurricane; and their fellow-citizens look with equal disgust and dread upon faces and figures, as strange to them as if they had issued from some distant and savage land. Paris, like every great metropolis, has her share, and more than her share, of this unwholesome population. It was the frantic convocations of this class which had at once instigated and

---

[25] London Gazette, April 5.—"Early in the morning of the 31st March, before the barriers, were open, the soldiers of the allied army climbed up the pallisades of the barrier Rochechouard to look into Paris. They threw this proclamation over the wall, and through the iron gates."—*Memorable Events*, p. 124.

carried into effect the principal horrors of the Revolution, and they seemed now resolved to signalize its conclusion by the destruction of the capital. Most of these banditti were under the influence of Buonaparte's police, and were stimulated by the various arts which his emissaries employed. At one time horsemen galloped through the crowd, exhorting them to take arms, and assuring them that Buonaparte had already attacked the rear of the allies. Again they were told that the King of Prussia was made prisoner, with a column of 10,000 men. At other times, similar emissaries, announcing that the allies had entered the suburbs, and were sparing neither sex nor age, exhorting the citizens, by placards pasted on the walls, to shut their shops, and prepare to defend their houses.

This invitation to make the last earthly sacrifices in behalf of a military despot, to which Zaragossa had submitted in defence of her national independence, was ill received by the inhabitants. A free state has millions of necks, but a despotic government is in the situation desired by the Imperial tyrant—it has but one. When it was obvious that the Emperor Napoleon had lost his ascendency, no shop-keeper in Paris was fool enough to risk, in his cause, his shop, his family, and his life, or to consent to measures for preserving the capital, which were to commence by abandoning to the allied troops, and the scum of their own population, all that was, to him individually, worth fighting for. The placards we have mentioned were pulled down, therefore, as fast as they were pasted up; and there was an evident disposition, on the part of the better class of citizens and the national guards, to discourage all counsels which tended to stimulate resistance to the desperate extremity therein recommended.

Nevertheless, the state of the capital continued very alarming, the lower classes exhibiting alternately the symptoms of panic terror, of fury, and of despair. They demanded arms, of which a few were distributed to them; and there is no doubt, that had Napoleon arrived among them in the struggle, there would have been a dreadful battle, in which Paris, in all probability, would have shared the fate of Moscow. But when the cannonade ceased, when the flight of Joseph, and the capitulation of the city became publicly known, this conflict of jarring passions died away into silence, and the imperturbable and impassive composure of the national guard maintained the absolute tranquillity of the metropolis.

On the morning of the 31st, the Royalists were seen in groups in the Place Louis Quinze, the Garden of the Tuileries, the Boulevards, and other public places. They distributed the proclamations of the allies, and raised the long-forgotten cry of *Vive le Roi!* At first, none save those engaged in the perilous experiment, durst echo back a signal so dangerous; but by degrees the crowds increased, the leaders got on horseback, and distributed white cockades, lilies, and other emblems of loyalty, displaying banners, at the same time, made out of their own handkerchiefs. The ladies of their party came to their assistance. The Princess of Leon, Vicomtesse of Chateaubriand, Comtesse of Choiseuil, and other women of rank, joined the procession, distributing on all hands the emblems of their party, and tearing their dress to make white cockades, when the regular stock was exhausted. The better class of the bourgeois began to catch the flame, and remembered their old royalist opinions, and by whom they were defeated on the celebrated day of the Sections, when Buonaparte laid the foundation of his fame in the discomfiture of the national guard. Whole pickets began to adopt the white, instead of the three-coloured cockade; yet the voices were far from unanimous, and, on many points, parties of different principles met and skirmished together in the streets. But the tendency to discord was diverted, and the attention of the Parisians, of all classes and opinions, suddenly fixed upon the imposing and terrible spectacle of the army of the allies, which now began to enter the city.

ENTRANCE OF THE ALLIES

The sovereigns had previously received, at the village of Pantin, the magistrates of Paris, and Alexander had expressed himself in language still more explicit than that of their proclamation. He made war, he said, on Napoleon alone; one who had been his friend, but relinquished that character to become his enemy, and inflict on his empire great evils. He was not, however, come to retaliate those injuries, but to make a secure peace with any government which France might select for herself. "I am at peace," said the Emperor, "with France, and at war with Napoleon alone."

These gracious expressions were received with the more gratitude by the citizens of Paris, that they had been taught to consider the Russian prince as a barbarous and vindictive enemy. The measure of restoring the Bourbons seemed now to be regarded by almost every one, not particularly connected with the dynasty of Napoleon, like a haven on the leeward, unexpectedly open to a tempest-tossed and endangered vessel. There was no loss of honour in adopting it, since the French received back their own royal family—there was no compulsion, since they received them upon their own free choice. They escaped from a great and imminent danger, as if it had been by a bridge of gold.

An immense crowd filled the Boulevards (a large wide open promenade, which, under a variety of distinctive names, forms a circuit round the city,) in order to witness the entrance of the allied sovereigns and their army, whom, in the succession of four-and-twenty hours, this mutable people were disposed to regard as friends rather than enemies—a disposition which increased until it amounted to enthusiasm for the persons of those princes, against whom a bloody battle had been fought yesterday under the walls of Paris, in evidence of which mortal strife, there still remained blackening in the sun the unburied thousands who had fallen on both sides. There was in this a trait of national character. A Frenchman submits with a good grace, and apparent or real complaisance, to that which he cannot help; and it is not the least advantage of his philosophy, that it entitles him afterwards to plead, that his submission flowed entirely from good-will, and not from constraint. Many of those who, on the preceding day, were forced to fly from the heights which defend Paris, thought themselves at liberty next morning to maintain, that the allies had entered the capital only by their consent and permission, because they had joined in the plaudits which accompanied their arrival. To vindicate, therefore, their city from the disgrace of being entered by force, as well as giving way to the real enthusiasm which was suddenly inspired by the exchange of the worst evils which a conquered people have to dread for the promised blessings of an honourable peace and internal concord, the Parisians received the Emperor Alexander and the King of Prussia with such general and unremitting plaudits, as might have accompanied their triumphal entrance into their own capitals. Even at their first entrance within the barriers, we learn from Sir Charles Stewart's official despatch,[26] the crowd was already so enormous, as well as the acclamations so great, that it was difficult to move forward; but before the monarchs had reached the porte St. Martin to turn on the Boulevards, there was a moral impossibility of proceeding; all Paris seemed to be assembled and concentrated in one spot—one spring evidently directed all their movements. They thronged around the monarchs, with the most unanimous shouts of "*Vive l'Empereur Alexandre!—Vive le Roi de Prusse!*" mingled with the loyal exclamations, "*Vive le Roi!—Vive Louis XVIII.!—Vivent les Bourbons!*" To such unexpected unanimity might be applied the words of Scripture, quoted by Clarendon on a similar occasion—"God had prepared the people, for the thing was done suddenly." The procession lasted several hours, during which 50,000 chosen troops of the Silesian and grand army filed along the Boulevards in broad and deep columns, exhibiting a whole forest of bayonets, mingled with long trains of artillery, and preceded by numerous regiments of cavalry of every description. Nothing surprised those who witnessed this magnificent spectacle, more than the high state of good order and regular equipment in which the men and horses appeared. They seemed rather to resemble troops drawn from peaceful quarters to some grand or solemn festival, than regiments engaged during a long winter campaign in constant marches and countermarches, as well as in a succession of the fiercest and most sanguinary conflicts, and who had fought a general action but the day before.[27] After making the circuit of half of Paris by the interior Boulevards, the monarchs halted in the Champs Elysées, and the troops passed in review before them as they were dismissed to their quarters in the city. The Cossacks of the guard established their bivouac in the Champs

---

[26] London Gazette Extraordinary, April 9.
[27] "This magnificent pageant far surpassed any idea I had formed of military pomp. The cavalry were fifteen abreast, the artillery five, and the infantry thirty. All the men were remarkably clean, healthy, and well clothed. The bands of music were very fine. The people, astonished at the prodigious number of troops, repeatedly exclaimed, 'Oh! how we have been deceived.'"—*Memorable Events*, p. 106.

Elysées themselves, which may be termed the Hyde Park of Paris, and which was thus converted into a Scythian encampment.

Chapter LXXVIII

Fears of the Parisians—Proceedings of Napoleon—Operations of the French Cavalry in rear of the Allies—Capture of Weissemberg—The Emperor Francis is nearly surprised—Napoleon reaches Troyes on the night of the 29th March—Opinion of Macdonald as to the possibility of relieving Paris—Napoleon leaves Troyes, on the 30th, and meets Belliard, a few miles from Paris, in full retreat—Conversation betwixt them—He determines to proceed to Paris, but is at length dissuaded—and despatches Caulaincourt to receive terms from the Allied Sovereigns—He himself returns to Fontainbleau.

FEARS OF THE PARISIANS

When the enthusiasm attending the entrance of the allies, which had converted a day of degradation into one of joy and festivity, began to subside, the perilous question occurred to those who found themselves suddenly embarked in a new revolution, Where were Napoleon and his army, and what means did his active and enterprising genius possess of still re-establishing his affairs, and taking vengeance on his revolted capital? That terrible and evil spirit, who had so long haunted their very dreams, and who had been well termed the nightmare of Europe, was not yet conjured down, though for the present he exercised his ministry elsewhere. All trembled for the consequence of his suddenly returning in full force, combined either with the troops of Augereau, or with the garrisons withdrawn from the frontier fortresses. But their fears were without foundation; for, though he was not personally distant, his powers of inflicting vengeance were now limited. We proceed to trace his progress after his movement eastward, from the neighbourhood of Vitry to St. Dizier, which had permitted the union of the two allied armies.

Here he was joined by Caulaincourt, who had to inform him of the dissolution of the Congress at Chatillon, with the addition, that he had not received his instructions from Rheims, until the diplomatists had departed. Those subsequently despatched by Count Frochot, he had not received at all.

Meanwhile, Napoleon's cavalry commenced the proposed operations in the rear of the allies, and made prisoners some persons of consequence, who were travelling, as they supposed, in perfect security, between Troyes and Dijon. Among these was Baron Weissemberg, who had long been the Austrian envoy at the court of London. The Emperor Francis was nearly surprised in person by the French light troops. He was obliged to fly in a *drosky*, a Russian carriage, attended only by two domestics, from Bar-sur-Aube to Chatillon, and from thence he retreated to Dijon![28] Napoleon showed every civility to his prisoner, Weissemberg, and despatched him to the Emperor of Austria, to solicit once more his favourable interference. The person of the present King of France[29] (then Monsieur) would have been a yet more important capture, but the forays of the light cavalry did not penetrate so far as to endanger him.

On the 24th March, Napoleon halted at Doulevent, to concentrate his forces, and gain intelligence. He remained there also on the 25th, and employed his time in consulting his maps, and dictating new instructions for Caulaincourt, by which he empowered him to make every cession. But the hour of safety was past. Upon the morning of the 26th, Napoleon was roused by the intelligence, that the allies had attacked the rear of his army under Macdonald, near St. Dizier. He instantly hastened to the support of the maréchal, concluding that his own scheme had been successful, and that his retreat to the eastward had drawn after him the grand army of the allies. The allies showed a great number of cavalry with flying guns, but no infantry. Napoleon ordered an attack on them, in

---

[28] Sir Robert Wilson, Sketch of the Military and Political Power of Russia, p. 90.
[29] Charles X.

which the French were successful, the allies falling back after slight opposition. He learned from the prisoners, that he had been engaged, not with Schwartzenberg, but with Blucher's troops. This was strange intelligence. He had left Blucher threatening Meaux, and now he found his army on the verge of Lorraine.

On the 27th, by pushing a reconnoitring party as far west as Vitry, Napoleon learned the real state of the case; that both the allied armies had marched upon Paris; and that the cavalry with which he had skirmished were 10,000 men, under Winzengerode, left behind by the allies as a curtain to screen their motions, and engage his attention. Every word in this news had a sting in it. To hasten after the allies, to surprise them, if possible, ere the cannon on Montmartre were yet silenced, was the most urgent thought that ever actuated the mind even of Napoleon, so accustomed to high and desperate risks. But the direct route on Paris had been totally exhausted of provision, by the march and countermarch of such large armies. It was necessary to go round by Troyes, and, for that purpose, to retrograde as far as Doulevent. Here he received a small billet in cipher, from the postmaster-general, La Valette, the first official communication he had got from the capital during ten days. "The partisans of the stranger," these were the contents, "are making head, seconded by secret intrigues. The presence of Napoleon is indispensable, if he desires to prevent his capital from being delivered to the enemy. There is not a moment to be lost."[30] The march was precipitated accordingly.

DOULANCOURT—TROYES

At the bridge of Doulancourt, on the banks of the Aube, the Emperor received despatches, informing him that an assault on Paris was hourly be expected. Napoleon dismissed his aide-de-camp, Dejean, to ride post to Paris, and spread the news of his speedy arrival. He gave him two bulletins, describing in extravagant colours a pretended victory at Arcis, and the skirmish at St. Dizier. He then advanced to Troyes, which he reached on that same night (29th March,) the imperial guard marching fifteen leagues in one day. On

---
[30] Baron Fain, p. 227.

the 30th, Maréchal Macdonald gave to Berthier the following sound and striking opinion:—"It is too late," he said, "to relieve Paris; at least by the route we follow. The distance is fifty leagues; to be accomplished by forced marches, it will require at least four days; and then in what condition for combat is the army like to arrive, for there are no depôts, or magazines, after leaving Bar-sur-Seine. The allies being yesterday at Meaux, must have pushed their advanced guards up to the barriers by this time. There is no good reason to hope that the united corps of the Dukes of Treviso and Ragusa could check them long enough to allow us to come up. Besides, at our approach, the allies will not fail to defend the passage of the Marne. I am then of opinion, that if Paris fall under the power of the enemy, the Emperor should direct his march on Sens, in order to retreat upon Augereau, unite our forces with his, and, after having reposed our troops, give the enemy battle on a chosen field. If Providence has then decreed our last hour, we will at least die with honour, instead of being dispersed, pillaged, taken, and slaughtered by Cossacks." Napoleon's anxiety for the fate of his capital, did not permit him to hearken to this advice; though it seems the best calculated to have placed him in a condition, either to make a composition with the allies, or to carry on a formidable war in their rear.

From Troyes, Napoleon despatched to Paris another aide-de-camp, General Girardin, who is said to have carried orders for defending the city to the last, and at all risks—an accusation, however, which, considering the mass of unimaginable mischief that such an order must have involved, is not to be received without more proof than we have been able to obtain.

On the 30th March, Napoleon left Troyes, and, finding the road entirely unoccupied by the enemy, threw himself into a post-carriage, and travelled on at full speed before his army, with a very slight attendance. Having in this way reached Villeneuve L'Archeveque, he rode to Fontainbleau on horseback, and though it was then night, took a carriage for Paris, Berthier and Caulaincourt accompanying him. On reaching an inn, called La Cour de France, at a few miles' distance from Paris, he at length met ample proof of his misfortune in the person of General Belliard, with his cavalry. The fatal intelligence was communicated.

CONVERSATION WITH BELLIARD

Leaping from his carriage, Napoleon turned back with Belliard, exclaiming—"What means this? Why here with your cavalry, Belliard? And where are the enemy?"—"At the gates of Paris."—"And the army?"—"It is following me."—"Where are my wife and son?—Where Marmont?—Where Mortier?"—"The Empress set out for Rambouillet, and thence for Orleans. The maréchals are busy completing their arrangements at Paris." He then gave an account of the battle; and Napoleon instantly ordered his carriage for Paris. They had already proceeded a mile and a half on the road. The same conversation proceeded, and we give it as preserved, because it marks the character of the principal personage, and the tone of his feeling, much better than these can be collected from his expressions upon more formal occasions, and when he had in view some particular purpose.[31]

General Belliard reminded him there were no longer any troops in Paris. "It matters not," said Napoleon; "I will find the national guard there. The army will join me to-morrow, or the day after, and I will put things on a proper footing."—"But I must repeat to your Majesty, you cannot go to Paris. The national guard, in virtue of the treaty, mount guard at the barriers, and though the allies are not to enter till seven o'clock in the morning, it is possible they may have found their way to the outposts, and that your Majesty may find Russian or Prussian parties at the gates, or on the Boulevards."—"It is all one—I am determined to go there—My carriage!—Follow me with your cavalry."—"But, Sire, your Majesty will expose Paris to the risk of storm or pillage. More than 20,000 men are in possession of the heights—for myself, I have left the city in consequence of a convention, and cannot therefore return."—"What is that convention? who has concluded it?"—"I cannot tell,

---

[31] It is taken from a work which has remarkable traces of authenticity, General Koch's *Mémoires, pour servir à l'Histoire de la Campagne de 1814*. See also, *Memoirs of the Operations of the Allied Armies*, already quoted, p. 208.—S.

Sire; I only know from the Duke of Treviso that such exists, and that I must march to Fontainbleau."—"What is Joseph about?—Where is the minister at war?"—"I do not know; we have received orders from neither of them during the whole day. Each maréchal acted on his own responsibility. They have not been seen to-day with the army—At least not with the Duke of Treviso's corps."—"Come, we must to Paris—nothing goes right when I am absent—they do nothing but make blunders."

Berthier and Caulaincourt joined in trying to divert the Emperor from his purpose. He never ceased demanding his carriage. Caulaincourt announced it, but it did not come up. Napoleon strode on with hurried and unequal steps, asking repeated questions concerning what had been already explained. "You should have held out longer," he said, "and tried to wait for the arrival of the army. You should have raised Paris, which cannot surely like the entrance of the Russians. You should have put in motion the national guard, whose disposition is good, and intrusted to them the defence of the fortifications which the minister has caused to be erected, and which are well furnished with artillery. Surely the citizens could have defended these, while the troops of the line fought upon the heights and in the plain?"—"I repeat to you, Sire, that it was impossible. The army of 15,000 or 18,000 men has resisted one of 100,000 for four hours, expecting your arrival. There was a report of it in the city, which spread to the troops. They redoubled their exertions. The national guard has behaved extremely well, both as sharpshooters and in defence of the wretched redoubts which protected the barriers."—"It is astonishing. How many cavalry had you?"—"Eighteen hundred horse, Sire, including the brigade of Dautencour."—"Montmartre, well fortified and defended by heavy cannon, should have been impregnable."—"Luckily, Sire, the enemy were of your opinion, and approached the heights with much caution. But there was no occasion, we had not above seven six-pounders."—"What can they have made of my artillery? I ought to have had more than two hundred guns, and ammunition to serve them for a month."—"The truth is, Sire, that we had only field-artillery, and at two o'clock we were obliged to slacken our fire for want of ammunition."—"Go, go—I see every one has lost their senses. This comes of employing people who have neither common sense nor energy. Well! Joseph imagines himself capable of conducting an army; and Clarke, a mere piece of routine, gives himself the airs of a great minister; but the one is no better than a fool, and the other a —— ——, or a traitor, for I begin to believe what Savary said of him."—The conversation going on in this manner, they had advanced a mile farther from the Cour de France, when they met a body of infantry under General Curial. Napoleon inquired after the Duke of Treviso, to whose corps d'armée they belonged, and was informed he was still at Paris.

It was then, that on the pressing remonstrances of his officers, who saw that in going on to Paris he was only rushing on death or captivity, Napoleon at length turned back; and having abandoned the strong inflexible impulse which would have carried him thither at all adventures, he seems to have considered his fate as decided, or at least to have relaxed considerably in the original vehemence which he opposed to adversity.

He returned to the Cour de France, and gave orders for disposing the forces, as they should come up, on the heights of Longjumeau, behind the little river of Essonne. Desirous at the same time of renewing the negotiation for peace, which, on successes of an ephemeral description, he had broken off at Chatillon, Napoleon despatched Caulaincourt to Paris, no longer to negotiate, but to receive and submit to such terms as the allied sovereigns might be inclined to impose upon him. He returned to Fontainbleau the same night. He did not take possession of any of the rooms of state, but chose a private and more retired apartment. Among the many strange transactions which had taken place in that venerable and ancient palace, its halls were now to witness one the most extraordinary.

Chapter LXXIX

The Allied Sovereigns issue a Proclamation that they will not treat with Buonaparte—A Provisional Government is named by the Conservative Senate, who also decree the forfeiture of Napoleon—This decree is sanctioned by all the Public Bodies in Paris—The legality of these proceedings discussed—Feelings towards Napoleon, of the Lower Classes, and of the Military—On 4th April, Buonaparte issues a document abdicating the Throne of France—His subsequent agitation, and wish to continue the war—The deed is finally despatched.

While Napoleon breathed nothing save the desire of recovering by war what war had taken from him, or at least that of making such a peace as should leave him at the head of the French government, political events were taking place in Paris which pointed directly at the overthrow of his power.

His great military talents, together with his extreme inflexibility of temper, had firmly impressed the allied monarchs with the belief, that no lasting peace could be made in Europe while he remained at the head of the French nation. Every concession which he had seemed willing to make at different times, had been wrung from him by increasing difficulties, and was yielded with such extreme reluctance, as to infer the strongest suspicion that they would all be again resumed, should the league of the allies be dissolved, or their means of opposing his purposes become weaker. When, therefore, Caulaincourt came to Paris on the part of his master, with power to subscribe to all and each of the demands made by the allies, he was not indeed explicitly refused audience; but, before he was admitted to a conference with the Emperor Alexander, to whom his mission was addressed, the sovereigns had come under engagements which precluded them altogether from treating with Napoleon.[32]

When the Emperor of Russia halted, after the progress of the allied sovereigns through the city, it was at the hotel of Talleyrand. He was scarcely arrived there ere the principal Royalists, and those who had acted with them, waited on him to crave an audience. Besides the Emperor Alexander, the King of Prussia, and Prince Schwartzenberg, were present General Pozzo di Borgo, Nesselrode, Lichtenstein, the Duke Dalberg, Baron Louis, the Abbé de Pradt, and others. Three points were discussed, 1st, The possibility of a peace with Napoleon, upon sufficient guarantees; 2d, The plan of a regency; 3d, The restoration of the Bourbons.

PROCLAMATION OF THE ALLIES

The first proposition seemed inadmissible. The second was carefully considered. It was particularly urged that the French were indifferent to the cause of the Bourbons—that the allied monarchs would observe no mark of recollection of them exhibited by the people of France—and that the army seemed particularly averse to them. The united testimony of the French gentlemen present was offered to repel these doubts; and it was at length agreed, that the third proposition—the restoration of the ancient family, and the ancient limits—should be the terms adopted for the settlement of France.[33] A proclamation was immediately dispersed, by which the sovereigns made known their determination not to treat with Buonaparte or any of his family.[34]

---

[32] According to Lord Burghersh, (Operations, p. 249,) Caulaincourt saw the Emperor Alexander at his headquarters, *before* he entered Paris.—Ed. (1842.)

[33] De Pradt, Précis Hist. de la Restauration, p. 54.

[34] Dated Paris, March 31, three o'clock in the afternoon. "After some discussion, the Emperor of Russia agreed not to treat with Napoleon, and, at the suggestion of Abbé Louis, nor with any of his family. De Pradt told me he retired into a corner of the apartment, with Roux Laborie, to whom he dictated the Emperor's declaration, which was hastily written with a pencil, and shown to Alexander, who approved of it. Michaud, who was in waiting, caused it immediately to be printed, putting, under the name of the Emperor, '*Michaud, Imprimeur du Roi,*' and two hours afterwards it was stuck up in Paris. It

But more formal evidence, in the shape of legal procedure, was necessary to establish the desire of the French people to coincide in the proposed change of government. The public body which ought naturally to have taken the lead on such an important affair, was the Legislative Assembly, in whom Napoleon's constitution vested some ostensible right of interference when the state was in danger; but so far had the Emperor been from recognising such a power in practice, that the instant when the Assembly assumed the right of remonstrating with him, though in the most respectful terms, he suspended their functions, and spurned them from the footstool of his throne, informing them, that not they, but He, was the representative of the people, from whom there lay no appeal, and besides whom, no body in the state possessed power and efficacy. This legislative council, therefore, being dispersed and prorogued, could not take the initiative upon the present occasion.

The searching genius of Talleyrand sought an organ of public opinion where few would have looked for it—in the Conservative Senate, namely, whose members had been so long the tools of Buonaparte's wildest projects, and the echoes of his most despotic decrees—that very body, of which he himself said, with equal bitterness and truth, that they were more eager to yield up national rights than he had been to demand the surrender, and that a sign from him had always been an order for the Senate, who hastened uniformly to anticipate and exceed his demands. Yet when, on the summons of Talleyrand, who knew well with whom he was dealing, this Senate was convoked, in a meeting attended by sixty-six of their number, forming a majority of the body, they at once, and without hesitation, named a Provisional Government, consisting of Talleyrand, Bournonville, Jaucourt, Dalberg, and the Abbé de Montesquieu; men recommended by talents and moderation, and whose names, known in the Revolution, might, at the same time, be a guarantee to those who dreaded a renovation of the old despotic government with the restoration of the ancient race of kings.

---

was read by the people with great eagerness, and I saw many of them copying it."—*Memorable Events*, p. 128.

DECREE OF FORFEITURE

On the 2d and 3d of April the axe was laid to the roots. A decree of the Senate sent forth the following statement:—1st, That Napoleon, after governing for some time with prudence and wisdom, had violated the constitution, by raising taxes in an arbitrary and lawless manner, contrary to the tenor of his oath.—2d, That he had adjourned without necessity the Legislative Body, and suppressed a report of that assembly, besides disowning its right to represent the people.—3d, That he had published several unconstitutional decrees, particularly those of 5th March last, by which he endeavoured to render national a war, in which his own ambition alone was interested.—4th, That he had violated the constitution by his decrees respecting state prisons.—5th, That he had abolished the responsibility of ministers, confounded together the different powers of the state, and destroyed the independence of judicial authorities.—6th, That the liberty of the press, constituting one of the rights of the nation, had been uniformly subjected to the arbitrary censure of his police; while, at the same time, he himself had made use of the same engine to fill the public ear with invented fictions, false maxims, doctrines favourable to despotism, and insults upon foreign governments.—7th, That he had caused acts and reports, adopted by the Senate, to be altered by his own authority, before publication.—8th, That instead of reigning, according to his oath, for the honour, happiness, and glory of the French nation, he had put the finishing stroke to the distresses of the country, by a refusal to treat on honourable conditions—by the abuse which he had made of the means intrusted to him, in men and money—by abandoning the wounded, without dressing or sustenance—and by pursuing measures of which the consequences have been the ruin of towns, the depopulation of the country, famine and pestilence. From all these inductive causes, the Senate, considering that the Imperial government, established by the decree of 28th Floreal, in the year XII., had ceased to exist, and that the manifest desire of all Frenchmen was to obtain an order of things, of which the first result should be peace and concord among the great members of the European family: Therefore, the Senate declared and decreed, 1st, That Napoleon Buonaparte had forfeited the throne, and the right of inheritance established in his family.—2d, That the people and army of France were disengaged and freed from the oath of fidelity, which they had taken to Napoleon and his constitution.[35]

DECLARATIONS OF PUBLIC BODIES

About eighty members of the Legislative Body, at the summons of the Provisional Government, assembled on the 3d April, and formally adhered to the above decree of forfeiture. The consequences of these bold measures showed, either that Napoleon had in reality never had more than a slight hold on the affections of the people of France, or that the interest they took in his fortunes had been in a great degree destroyed by the fears and passions excited by the immediate crisis. Even before the Senate could reduce its decree into form, the council-general of the department of the Seine had renounced Napoleon's authority, and imputed to him alone the present disastrous state of the country. The decree of the Senate was followed by declarations from all the public bodies in and around Paris, that they adhered to the Provisional Government, and acquiesced in the decree of forfeiture. Numerous individuals, who had been favoured and enriched by Buonaparte, were among the first to join the tide when it set against him. But it had been always his policy to acquire adherents, by addressing himself rather to men's interests than to their principles; and many of his friends so gained, naturally became examples of the politic observation, "that if a prince places men in wealthy circumstances, the first thing they think of, in danger, is how to preserve the advantages they have obtained, without regard to his fate to whom they owe them."

We do not believe that it occurred to any person while these events were passing, to question either the formality or the justice of the doom of forfeiture against Napoleon; but Time has called out many authors, who, gained by the brilliancy of Napoleon's reputation, and some of them bound to him by ties of gratitude or friendship, have impugned, more or less directly, the formality of the Senate's procedure, as well as the justice of their sentence. We,

---

[35] On the 3d of April, the *Moniteur*, in which these documents are given, was declared, by the provisional government, the only official journal.

therefore, feel it our duty to bestow some consideration upon this remarkable event in both points of view.

The objection proposed against the legality of the Senate's acting as the organ of the people, in pronouncing the doom of forfeiture, rests upon the idea, that the right of dethroning the sovereign, who shall be guilty of oppression beyond endurance, can only be exercised in a peculiar and formal manner, or, as our law-phrase goes, "according to the statute made and provided in that case." This seems to take a narrow view of the subject. The right of redressing themselves under such circumstances, does not belong to, and is not limited by, any peculiar forms of civil government. It is a right which belongs to human nature under all systems whatever. It exists in every government under the sun, from that of the Dey of Algiers to the most free republic that ever was constructed. There is, indeed, much greater latitude for the exercise of arbitrary authority in some governments than in others. An Emperor of Morocco may, with impunity, bathe his hands to the elbows in the blood of his subjects shed by his own hand; but even in this the most absolute of despotisms, there are peculiar limits which cannot be passed by the sovereign without the exercise of the natural right of resistance on the part of his subjects, although their system of government be as arbitrary as words can declare it to be, and the Emperor is frequently dethroned and slain by his own guards.

In limited governments, on the other hand, like that of Great Britain, the law imposes bounds, beyond which the royal authority shall not pass; but it makes no provision for what shall take place, should a monarch, as in the case of James II., transgress the social compact. The constitution averts its eyes from contemplating such an event—indeed it is pronounced impossible; and when the emergency did arrive, and its extrication became a matter of indispensable necessity, it was met and dealt with as a concurrence of circumstances which had not happened before, and ought never to be regarded as being possible to occur again. The foreigner who peruses our constitution for the forms of procedure competent in such an event as the Revolution, might as well look in a turnpike act for directions how to proceed in a case resembling that of Phaeton.

If the mode of shaking off an oppressive yoke, by declaring the monarchy abdicated or forfeited, be not a fixed form in a regular government, but left to be provided for by a convention or otherwise, as a case so calamitous and so anomalous should demand, far less was it to be supposed that a constitution like that of France, which Buonaparte had studiously deprived of every power and means of checking the executive, should contain a regular form of process for declaring the crown forfeited. He had been as careful as despot could, to leave no bar in existence before which the public might arraign him; but will it be contended, that the public had therefore forfeited its natural right of accusing and of obtaining redress? If he had rendered the Senate the tame drudges which we have described, and prorogued the Legislative Body by an arbitrary *coup d'état*, was he therefore to escape the penalty of his misgovernment? On the contrary, the nation of France, like Great Britain at the time of the Revolution 1688, was to proceed as it best could in taking care, *Ne quid detrimenti respublica capiat*. The Senate was not, perhaps, the best organ for expressing public opinion, but it was the only one Napoleon had left within reach, and therefore it was seized upon and made use of. That it was composed of men who had so long gone on with Napoleon's interest, and now were able to keep up in course with him no longer, made his misrule even yet more glaring, and the necessity of the case more evident.

It is of far more importance to be enabled to form an accurate judgment respecting the *justice* of the sentence of forfeiture pronounced against this eminent man, than upon its mere formality. That we may examine this question with the impartiality it deserves, we must look upon it not only divested of our feelings as Britons, but as unconnected with the partisans either of the Bourbons or of Buonaparte. With these last there could be no room either for inquiry or conviction. The Royalist must have been convinced that Napoleon deserved, not deprivation only, but death also, for usurping the throne of his rightful sovereign; and the Buonapartist, on the other hand, would hold it cowardly treason to desert the valiant Emperor, who had raised France to such a state of splendour by his victories, more especially to forsake him in the instant when Fortune was looking black upon his cause. There could be no argument between these men, save with their good swords in a fair field.

But such decided sentiments were not entertained upon the part of the great bulk of the French nation. A large number of the middle classes, in particular, remembering the first terrors of the Revolution, had showed their willingness to submit to the yoke which gradually assumed a despotic character, rather than, by a renewed struggle for their liberties, to run the risk of reviving the days of Terror and Proscription. It is in the person of such an individual, desirous of the honour and advantage of his country, and anxious at the same time for the protection of his own family and property, that we now endeavour to consider the question of Napoleon's forfeiture.

The mind of such a person would naturally revert to the period when Buonaparte, just returned from Egypt, appeared on the stage like a deity descending to unloose a perplexing knot, which no human ingenuity could extricate. Our citizen would probably admit, that Napoleon used the sword a little too freely in severing the intricacies of the noose; or, in plain words, that the cashiering the Council of Five Hundred, at the head of his grenadiers, was an awkward mode of ascending to power in a country which still called itself free. This feeling, however, would be greatly overbalanced by recollecting the use which was made of the power thus acquired; the subjugation, to wit, of foreign enemies, the extinction of civil dissensions, the protection of property, and, for a time, of personal liberty also. Napoleon's having elevated France from the condition of a divided and depressed country, in the immediate apprehension of invasion, into that of arbitress of Europe, would at once justify committing the chief authority to such able hands, and excuse the means he had used for attaining it; especially in times when the violent and successive changes under which they had long suffered, had made the nation insensible to irregularities like those attached to the revolution of the 18th Brumaire. Neither would our citizens probably be much shocked at Napoleon's assuming the crown. Monarchy was the ancient government of France, and successive changes had served to show that they could not fix on any other form of constitution, labour how they would, which was endowed with the same degree of permanence. The Bourbons had, indeed, the claim by birth to mount that throne, were it to be again erected. But they were in exile, separated by civil war, party prejudices, the risk of reaction, and a thousand other difficulties, which seemed at the time absolutely insurmountable. Buonaparte was standing under the canopy, he grasped the regal sceptre in his hand, his assuming the royal seat passed almost as a matter of course.

Our supposed Parisian has next to review a course of years of such brilliancy as to baffle criticism, and charm reason to silence, till the undertakings of the Emperor seem to rise above each other in wonder, each being a step towards the completion of that stupendous pyramid, of which the gradations were to be formed by conquered provinces, until the refractory and contumacious isle of Britain should be added to complete the pile, on the top of which was destined to stand the armed form of Napoleon, trampling the world under his foot. This is the noble work which France and her monarch were in the act of achieving. It requires the sacrifice of children or relatives to fill their ranks; they go where Honour calls, and Victory awaits them. These times, however, are overclouded; there come tidings that the stone heaved by such portentous exertion so high up the hill, has at length recoiled on him who laboured to give it a course contrary to nature. It is then that the real quality of the fetters, hitherto gilded over by success, begins to be felt, and the iron enters into the soul. The parent must not weep aloud for the child—the Emperor required his service;—the patriot must not speak a word on public affairs—the dungeon waits for him.

While news of fresh disasters from Spain and Moscow were every day arriving, what comfort could a citizen of France find in adverting to past victories? These had brought on France the hatred of Europe, the tears of families, the ruin of fortunes, general invasion, and wellnigh national bankruptcy. Every year had the children of France undergone decimation—taxes to the amount of fifteen hundred millions of francs yearly, had succeeded to the four hundred millions imposed under the reign of the Bourbons—the few remaining ships of France rotted in her harbours—her bravest children were slaughtered on their native soil—a civil war was on the point of breaking out—one half of France was overrun by the foreign enemy. Was this most melancholy state of the country brought about in defending strongly, but unfortunately, any of the rights of France? No—she might have enjoyed her triumphs in the most profound peace. Two wars with Spain and Russia, which gave fire to this dreadful train of calamities, were waged for no national or reasonable object, but merely because one half of Europe could not satisfy the ambition of one man. Again, our citizen inquires, whether, having committed the dreadful error of commencing these wars, the Emperor has endeavoured to make peace with the parties injured? He is answered, that repeated terms of peace have been offered to Napoleon, upon condition of ceding his conquests, but that he had preferred hazarding the kingdom of France, to yielding up that which he termed his *glory*, a term which he successively conferred on whatever possession he was required to surrender; that even at Chatillon, many days passed when he might have redeemed himself by consenting that France should be reduced within the limits which she enjoyed under the Bourbons; but that the proposal when half admitted, had been retracted by him in consequence of some transient success; and finally, that in consequence of his intractability and obstinacy, the allied sovereigns had solemnly declared they would not enter into treaty with him, or those who acted with him. Our citizen would naturally look about for some means of escaping the impending danger, and would be informed that the peace which the allied princes refused to Buonaparte, they held out with ready hand to the kingdom of France under any other government. He would learn that if these terms were accepted, there was every prospect that a secure and lasting peace would ensue; if refused, the inevitable consequence would be a battle between two large armies fought under the walls of Paris, which city was almost certain to be burnt, whichever party got the advantage.

In consequence of this information, the citizen of Paris would probably be able to decide for himself. But if he inquired at a jurist, he would be informed that Napoleon held the crown not by right of blood, but by the choice, or rather permission of the people, as an administrator bound to manage for their best advantage.

Now, every legal obligation may be unloosed in the same way in which it is formed. If, therefore, Napoleon's government was no longer for the advantage of France, but, on the contrary, tended plainly to her ruin, she had a right to rid herself of him, as of a servant unfit for duty, or as if mariners had taken aboard their vessel a comrade intended to act as pilot, but who had proved a second Jonas, whom it was necessary to sacrifice to appease a storm which had come upon them through his misconduct. Upon such reasoning, certainly neither unwise nor unpatriotic, the burghers of Paris, as well as all those who had any thing to lose in the struggle, may be supposed to have acted.

The lower, or rather the lowest class of inhabitants, were not accessible to the same arguments. They had been bequeathed to Buonaparte as an heir-loom of the Republic, of which he has been truly called the heir. His police had industriously maintained connexions amongst them, and retained in pay and in dependence on the government, their principal leaders. Names had changed around men of that ignorant condition, without their feeling their situation much altered. The Glory of France was to them as inspiring a watchword as the Rights of Man had been; and their quantum of sous per day, when employed, as they frequently were, upon the public works, was no bad exchange for Liberty and Equality, after they had arrived at the discovery of the poor cobbler, who exclaimed—"Fine Liberty, indeed, that leaves me cobbling shoes as she found me!" Bulletins and Moniteurs, which trumpeted the victories of Napoleon, were as animating and entertaining to the inhabitants of the suburbs as the speeches of republican orators; for in such triumphs of a nation, the poor have a share as ample as their wealthier neighbours. The evils of the war were also less felt by the poor. Their very poverty placed them beneath taxation, and the children, of whom they were bereaved by the conscription, they must otherwise have parted with, in all probability, that they might seek subsistence elsewhere. In the present circumstances the hatred to foreigners, proper to persons of their class, came to aid their admiration of Buonaparte. In a battle, they had something to gain and nothing to lose, saving their lives, of which their national gallantry induced them to take small heed. Had Napoleon been in Paris, he might have made much use of this force. But in his absence, the weight of property, prudently directed, naturally bore down the ebullitions of those who had only brute strength to throw into the balance, and the overwhelming force of the allied army kept the suburbs in subjection.

THE MILITARY—FONTAINBLEAU

The disposition of the military was a question of deep importance. Accustomed to follow Napoleon through every climate, and every description of danger, unquestionably their attachment to his person was of the most devoted and enthusiastic kind. But this can only be said in general of the regimental officers, and the soldiers. The maréchals, and many of the generals, were tired of this losing war. These, with many also of the inferior officers, and even of the soldiers, began to consider the interest of their general, and that of France, as having become separated from each other. It was from Paris that the changes had emanated by which the army was governed during every revolutionary crisis; and they were now required to engage in an undertaking which was likely to be fatal to that metropolis. To advance upon the allies, and fight a battle under the capital, was to expose to destruction the city, whose name to every Frenchman has a sacred and inviolable sound. The maréchals, in particular, were disgusted with a contest, in which each of them had been left successively without adequate means of resistance, to stem, or attempt to stem, a superior force of the enemy; with the certainty, at the same time, to be held up to public censure in the next bulletin, in case of failure, though placed in circumstances which rendered success impossible. These generals were more capable than the army at large of comprehending the nature of the war in which they were likely to be engaged, and of appreciating the difficulties of a contest which was to be maintained in future without money, ammunition, or supplies, excepting such as should be extorted from that part of the country over which they held military possession; and this, not only against all the allies now in France, and the insurgent corps of Royalists in the west, but also against a second, or reserved line of three or four hundred thousand Russians, Austrians, and other allied troops which had not yet crossed the frontier.

Besides, the soldiers with which an attack upon the allied army must have been undertaken, were reduced to a disastrous condition, by their late forced marches, and the want of succours and supplies of every description; the cavalry were in a great measure dismounted; the regiments not half complete; the horses unshod; the physical condition of the army bad, and its moral feelings depressed, and unfit for enterprise. The period seemed to have arrived, beyond which Napoleon could not maintain his struggle, without destruction to himself, to Paris, and to France. These sentiments were commonly entertained among the French general officers. They felt their attachment to Napoleon placed in opposition to the duty they owed their country by the late decree of the Senate, and they considered the cause of France as the most sacred. They had received intelligence from Bournonville of what had passed at Paris, and considering the large proportion of the capital which had declared against Buonaparte, and that an assault on Paris must have occasioned much effusion of French blood, and have become the signal of civil war, the maréchals and principal general officers agreed they could not follow Napoleon in such an attack on the city, or against the allies' line of defence around it, both because, in a military point of view, they thought the attempt desperate, considering the state of the army, and because, in a political position, they regarded it as contrary to their duty as citizens.[36]

---

[36] "Napoleon reached Fontainebleau at six in the morning of the 31st March. The large rooms of the castle were shut up, and he repaired to his little apartment on the first storey, parallel with the gallery of Francis I. There he shut himself up for the remainder of the day. Maret was the only one of his ministers who was with him. In the course of that evening, and the following morning, arrived the heads of the columns which Napoleon had brought from Champagne, and the advanced guard of the troops from Paris. These wrecks of the army assembled round Fontainebleau. Moncey, who commanded the national guard of Paris, Lafebvre, Ney, Macdonald, Oudinot, Berthier, Mortier, and Marmont, arrived at Napoleon's headquarters; so that he still had an army at his disposal."—Baron Fain, p. 355. "Marmont arrived at Fontainebleau, at three in the morning of the 1st of April, and gave Napoleon a detailed account of what had passed at Paris. The maréchal told me he appeared undetermined whether to retire on the banks of the Loire, or give battle to the allies near Paris. In the afternoon he went to inspect the position of Marmont's army at Essonne, with which he appeared to be satisfied, and determined to remain there and manœuvre, with a view to disengage Paris and give battle. With the greatest coolness he formed plans for the execution of these objects; but, while thus employed, the officers, whom the maréchal had left at Paris to deliver up that city to the allies, arrived, and informed them of the events of the day. Napoleon, hearing this, became furious: He raved

In the night betwixt the 2d and 3d of April, Caulaincourt returned from his mission to Paris. He reported, that the allies persisted in their determination to entertain no treaty with Buonaparte; but he was of opinion, that the scheme of a regency by the Empress, as the guardian of their son, might even yet be granted. Austria, he stated, was favourable to such an arrangement, and Russia seemed not irreconcilably averse to it. But the abdication of Buonaparte was a preliminary condition. As this news circulated among the maréchals, it fixed them in their resolution not to march against Paris, as, in their opinion, the war ought to be ended by this personal sacrifice on the part of Napoleon.

FONTAINBLEAU

Buonaparte had not, probably, expected this separation between the duties of a soldier and of a citizen. On the 4th April, he reviewed a part of his troops, addressed them on the display of the white colours in France by some factious persons, reminded them that the three-coloured cockade was that of victory and honour, and that he intended to march on the capital, to punish the traitors by whom it had been vilified.[37] He was answered by shouts of "Paris, Paris!" and had no reason to fear that the troops would hesitate to follow him in his effort. The orders were given to advance the imperial quarters from Fontainbleau to Essonne.

But after the review was over, Berthier, Ney, Macdonald, Caulaincourt, Oudinot, Bertrand, and other officers of the highest rank, followed the Emperor into his apartment, and explained to him the sentiments which they entertained on the subject of the proposed movement, their opinion that he ought to negotiate on the principle of personal abdication, and the positive determination

---

about punishing the rebellious city, and giving it up to pillage. With this resolution he separated from Marmont, and returned to Fontainbleau."—*Memorable Events*, p. 201.

[37] "Soldiers! the enemy has stolen three marches upon us, and has made himself master of Paris. He must be driven out of it. Unworthy Frenchmen, emigrants, whom we had pardoned, have adopted the white cockade, and have joined our enemies. Wretches! they shall receive the reward of this new crime. Let us swear to conquer or to die, and to cause to be respected that tri-coloured cockade, which, during twenty years, has found us in the paths of glory and of honour."—Lord Burghersh, *Observations, &c.*, p. 274.

which most of them had formed, on no account to follow him in an attack upon Paris.[38]

There is no doubt that, by an appeal to officers of an inferior rank and consideration, young Seids, who knew no other virtue than a determined attachment to their chief, through good or evil, Napoleon might have filled up, in a military point of view, the vacancy which the resignation of the maréchals must have created in his list of generals. But those who urged to him this unpleasant proposal, were the fathers of the war, the well-known brave and beloved leaders of large armies. Their names might be individually inferior to his own; but with what feelings would the public hear that he was deprived of those men, who had been so long the pride and dread of war? and what were likely to be the sentiments of the soldiery, upon whom the names of Ney, Macdonald, Oudinot, and others, operated like a war-trumpet.

With considerable reluctance, and after long debate, Napoleon assumed the pen, and acquiescing in the reasoning pressed upon him, wrote the following words, which we translate as literally as possible, as showing Napoleon's power of dignity of expression, when deep feeling predominated over his affectation of antithesis and Orientalism of composition:

"The allied powers having proclaimed that the Emperor Napoleon is the sole obstacle to the re-establishment of peace in Europe, the Emperor Napoleon, faithful to his oath, declares that he is ready to descend from the throne, to quit France, and even to relinquish life, for the good of the country, which is inseparable from the rights of his son, from those of the Regency in the person

---

[38] "Ney produced the *Moniteur*, containing the decree of forfeiture, and advised him to acquiesce and abdicate. Napoleon feigned to read, turned pale, and appeared much agitated; but did not shed tears, as the newspapers reported. He seemed not to know in what manner to act. He then asked, 'Que voulez vous?' Ney answered, 'Il n'y a que l'abdication qui puisse vous tirer de là.' During this conference, Lefebvre came in; and upon Napoleon expressing astonishment at what had been announced to him, said, in his blunt manner, 'You see what has resulted from not listening to the advice of your friends to make peace: you remember the communication I made to you lately, therefore you may think yourself well off that affairs have terminated as they have.'"—*Memorable Events*, p. 206.

of the Empress, and from the maintenance of the laws of the empire. Done at our Palace of Fontainbleau, 4th April, 1814."

Caulaincourt and Ney were appointed to be bearers of this important document, and commissioners to negotiate with the allies, concerning the terms of accommodation to which it might be supposed to lead. Caulaincourt was the personal representative of Napoleon; and Ney, who had all along been zealous for the abdication, was a plenipotentiary proposed by the rest of the maréchals. Napoleon, it is said, wished to add Marmont; but he was absent with the troops quartered at Essonne, who, having been withdrawn in consequence of the treaty of Paris, were disposed of in that position. Macdonald was suggested as the third plenipotentiary, as an officer whose high character best qualified him to represent the army. Napoleon hesitated; for though he had employed Macdonald's talents on the most important occasions, he knew that the maréchal disliked, upon principle, the arbitrary character of his government; and they had never stood to each other in any intimate or confidential relation. He consulted his minister, Maret. "Send the Duke of Tarentum," replied the minister. "He is too much a man of honour not to discharge, with religious fidelity, any trust which he undertakes." Marshal Macdonald's name was added to the commission accordingly.[39]

When the terms were in the act of being adjusted, the maréchals desired to know upon what stipulations they were to insist on Napoleon's personal behalf. "Upon none,"—said Buonaparte. "Do what you can to obtain the best terms for France: for myself, I ask nothing." They were instructed particularly to obtain an armistice until the treaty should be adjusted. Through the whole scene Buonaparte conducted himself with firmness, but he gave way to a natural emotion when he had finally signed the abdication. He threw himself on a sofa, hid his face for a few minutes, and then looking up, with that smile of persuasion which he had so often found irresistible, he implored his brethren of the field to annul the resolutions they had adopted, to destroy the papers, and follow him yet again to the contest. "Let us march," he said; "let us take the field once more! We are sure to beat them, and

---

[39] Baron Fain, p. 373.

to have peace on our own terms."[40] The moment would have been invaluable to a historical painter. The maréchals were deeply affected, but could not give way. They renewed their arguments on the wretched state of the army—on the reluctance with which the soldiers would move against the Senate—on the certainty of a destructive civil war—and on the probability that Paris would be destroyed. He acquiesced once more in their reasoning, and permitted them to depart on their embassy.[41]

---

[40] "He threw himself on a small yellow sofa, placed near the window, and striking his thigh with a sort of convulsive action, exclaimed, 'No, gentlemen, no! No regency! With my guard and Marmont's corps, I shall be in Paris to-morrow.'"—Bourrienne, tom. i., p. 87.— On the day of the entrance of the allies into Paris, Bourrienne, Napoleon's ex-private secretary, was appointed to the important office of Postmaster-General; a situation from which he was dismissed at the end of three weeks.

[41] "Immediately after their departure, Napoleon despatched a courier to the Empress, from whom he had received letters, dated Vendome. He authorised her to despatch to her father, the Duke of Cadore (Champagny,) to solicit his intercession in favour of herself and her son. Overpowered by the events of the day, he shut himself up in his chamber."—Baron Fain, p. 374.

Chapter LXXX

Victor, and other Maréchals give in their adhesion to the Provisional Government—Marmont enters into a separate Convention; but assists at the Conferences held at Paris, leaving Souham second in command of his Army—The Commanders have an interview with the Emperor Alexander—Souham enters with his Army, into the lines of the Allies; in consequence, the Allied Sovereigns insist upon the unconditional Submission of Napoleon—His reluctant acquiescence—The Terms granted to him—Disapprobation of Lord Castlereagh—General Desertion of Napoleon—Death of Josephine—Singular Statement made by Baron Fain, Napoleon's Secretary, of the Emperor's attempt to commit Suicide—After this he becomes more resigned—Leaves Fontainbleau, 28th April.

The plenipotentiaries of Napoleon had been directed to confer with Marmont at Essonne, in their road to the capital. They did so, and obtained information there, which rendered their negotiation more pressing. Several of the generals who had not been at Fontainbleau, and had not had an opportunity of acting in conjunction with the military council which assembled there, had viewed the act of the Senate, adhered to by the other public bodies, as decisively closing the reign of Buonaparte, or as indicating the commencement of a civil war. Most of them were of opinion, that the interest of an individual, whose talents had been as dangerous to France as the virtues of Cæsar had been to Rome, ought not to be weighed against the welfare of the capital and the whole nation. Victor, Duke of Belluno, had upon these principles given in his personal adhesion to the Provisional Government, and his example was followed by many others.

MARMONT'S CONVENTION

But the most important proselyte to the royal cause was the Maréchal Marmont, Duke of Ragusa, who, lying at Essonne with ten or twelve thousand men, formed the advance of the French army. Conceiving himself to have the liberty of other Frenchmen to attend at this crisis to the weal of France, rather than to the interest of Napoleon alone, and with the purpose of saving France from the joint evils of a civil and domestic war, he made use of the position in which he was placed, to give a weight to his opinion, which that of no other individual could have possessed at the moment. Maréchal Marmont, after negotiation with the Provisional Government on the one hand, and Prince Schwartzenberg on the other, had entered into a convention on his own account, and that of his corps d'armée, by which he agreed to march the division which he commanded within the lines of cantonment held by the allies, and thus renounced all idea of further prosecuting the war. On the other hand, the maréchal stipulated for the freedom and honourable usage of Napoleon's person, should he fall into the hands of the allies. He obtained also a guarantee, that his corps d'armée should be permitted to retreat into Normandy. This convention was signed at Chevilly, upon 3d April.[42]

This step has been considered as a defection on the part of Marmont;[43] but why is the choice of a side, betwixt the Provisional Government and the Emperor, more a desertion in that general than in any other of the maréchals or authorities who presently after took the very same step? And if the Duke of Ragusa by that means put further bloodshed out of question, ought it not to be matter of rejoicing (to borrow an expression of Talleyrand's on a similar occasion) that the maréchal's watch went a few minutes faster than those of his colleagues?

---

[42] "Marmont was not guilty of treachery in defending Paris; but history will say, that had it not been for the defection of the sixth corps, after the allies had entered Paris, they would have been forced to evacuate that great capital; for they would never have given battle on the left bank of the Seine, with Paris in their rear, which they had only occupied for two days; they would never have thus violated every rule and principle of the art of war."—Napoleon, *Montholon*, tom. ii., p. 265.

[43] Lord Burghersh, Observations, p. 296; Savary, tom. iv., p. 76.

When Macdonald and Ney communicated to Marmont that they were bearers of Napoleon's abdication, and that he was joined with them in commission, that maréchal asked why he had not been summoned to attend with the others at Fontainbleau, and mentioned the convention which he had entered into, as acting for himself.[44] The Duke of Tarentum expostulated with him on the disadvantage which must arise from any disunion on the part of the principal officers of the army. Respecting the council at Fontainbleau, he stated it had been convened under circumstances of such sudden emergency, that there was no time to summon any other than those maréchals who were close at hand, lest Napoleon had in the meanwhile moved forward the army. The commissioners entreated Marmont to suspend the execution of the separate convention, and to come with them, to assist at the conferences to be held at Paris. He consented, and mounted into Maréchal Ney's carriage, leaving General Souham, who, with all the other generals of his division, two excepted, were privy to the convention, in command of his corps d'armée, which he gave orders should remain stationary.

When the maréchals arrived in Paris, they found the popular tide had set strongly in favour of the Bourbons; their emblems were everywhere adopted; and the streets resounded with *Vive le Roi!* The populace seemed as enthusiastic in their favour as they had been indifferent a few days before. All boded an unfavourable termination for their mission, so far as respected the proposed regency.

The names and characters of the commissioners instantly obtained their introduction to the Emperor Alexander, who received them with his natural courtesy. "On the general subject of their mission," he said, "he could not treat but in concert with his allies." But he enlarged on the subject of Napoleon personally. "He was my friend," he said, "I loved and honoured him. His ambition forced me into a dreadful war, in which my capital was burnt, and the greatest evils inflicted on my dominions. But he is unfortunate, and

---

[44] There are some slight discrepancies between the account of Marmont's proceedings in the text, and that given by Lord Burghersh in his "Memoir on the Operations," pp. 298, 299.—Ed. (1842.)

these wrongs are forgotten. Have you nothing to propose on his personal account? I will be his willing advocate." The maréchals replied, that Napoleon had made no conditions for himself whatever. The Emperor would hardly believe this until they showed him their instructions, which entirely related to public affairs. The Emperor then asked if they would hear a proposal from him. They replied with suitable respect and gratitude. He then mentioned the plan, which was afterwards adopted, that Buonaparte should retain the imperial title over a small territory, with an ample revenue, guards, and other emblems of dignity. "The place," continued the Emperor of Russia, "may be Elba, or some other island." With this annunciation the commissioners of Buonaparte were dismissed for the evening.

Maréchal Marmont had done all in his power to stop the military movement which he had undertaken to execute, thinking it better, doubtless, to move hand in hand with his brethren, than to act singly in a matter of such responsibility; but accident precipitated what he desired to delay. Napoleon had summoned to his presence Count Souham, who commanded the division at Essonne in Marmont's absence. No reason was given for this command, nor could any thing be extracted from the messenger, which indicated the purpose of the order. Souham was therefore induced to suspect that Napoleon had gained intelligence of the Convention of Chevilly. Under this apprehension, he called the other generals who were in the secret to a midnight council, in which it was determined to execute the convention instantly, by passing over with the troops within the lines of the allies, without awaiting any farther orders from Maréchal Marmont. The division was put in movement upon the 5th of April, about five o'clock, and marched for some time with much steadiness, the movement being, as they supposed, designed for a flank attack on the position of the allies, but when they perceived that their progress was watched, without being interrupted, by a column of Bavarian troops,[45] they began to suspect the real purpose. When this became known, a kind of mutiny took place, and some Polish lancers broke off from the main body, and rode back to Fontainebleau; but the instinct of discipline prevailed,

---

[45] Lord Burghersh's Memorandum says these were Wurtemberg and Austrian troops, commanded by the Prince Royal of Wurtemberg.—Ed. (1842.)

and the officers were able to bring the soldiery into their new quarters at Versailles. They were not, however, reconciled to the measure in which they had been made partakers, and in a few days afterwards broke out into an actual mutiny, which was not appeased without considerable difficulty.[46]

CONFERENCES AT PARIS

Meanwhile, the commissioners of Buonaparte were admitted to a conference with the allied sovereigns and ministers in full council, but which, it may be conjectured, was indulged to them more as a form, that the allies might treat with due respect the representatives of the French army, than with any purpose on the part of the sovereigns of altering the plan to which they had pledged themselves by a proclamation, upon the faith of which thousands had already acted. However, the question, whether to adopt the projected regency, or the restoration of the Bourbons, as a basis of agreement, was announced as a subject of consideration to the meeting. The maréchals pleaded the cause of the Regency. The Generals Bournonville and Dessolles, were heard in reply to the commissioners from Fontainbleau, when, ere the debate had terminated, news arrived of the march of Marmont's division to Versailles. The commissioners were astounded with this unexpected intelligence; and the Emperor took the opportunity to determine, that the allies would not treat with Buonaparte save on the footing of unconditional abdication. With this answer, mitigated with the offer of an independent principality for their ancient commander, the maréchals returned to Fontainbleau, while the Senate busied themselves to arrange the plan of a free constitution, under which the Bourbons were to be called to the throne.

Napoleon, in the retirement of Fontainbleau, mused on the future with little hope of advantage from the mission of the maréchals. He judged that the sovereigns, if they listened to the proposal of a regency, would exact the most formidable guarantees against his own interference with the government; and that under his wife, Maria Louisa, who had no talent for public business,

---

[46] Lord Burghersh, Observations, &c., p. 301.

France would probably be managed by an Austrian committee. He again thought of trying the chance of war, and might probably have settled on the purpose most congenial to his nature, had not Colonel Gourgaud brought him the news, that the division of Marmont had passed into the enemy's cantonments on the morning of the 5th April. "The ungrateful man!" he said, "But he is more to be pitied than I am."[47] He ought to have been contented with this reflection, for which, even if unjust to the maréchal, every one must have had sympathy and excuse. But the next day he published a sort of appeal to the army on the solemnity of a military engagement, as more sacred than the duty of a patriot to his country; which he might more gracefully have abstained from, since all knew already to what height he carried the sentiments of arbitrary power.

When the maréchals returned, he listened to the news of the failure of their negotiation, as a termination which he had expected. But to their surprise, recollecting his disinterested behaviour when they parted, he almost instantly demanded what provision had been made for him personally, and how he was to be disposed of? They informed him that it was proposed he should reside as an independent sovereign, "in Elba, or somewhere else." Napoleon paused for a moment. "Somewhere else!" he exclaimed. "That must be Corsica. No, no.—I will have nothing to do with Corsica.[48]— Elba? Who knows any thing of Elba! Seek out some officer who is acquainted with Elba. Look out what books or charts can inform us about Elba."

In a moment he was as deeply interested in the position and capabilities of this little islet, as if he had never been Emperor of France, nay, almost of the world. But Buonaparte's nature was egotistical. He well knew how little it would become an Emperor resigning his crown, to be stipulating for his future course of life; and had reason to conclude, that by playing his part with magnanimity he might best excite a corresponding liberality in those with whom he treated. But when the die was cast, when his fate

---

[47] Baron Fain, p. 375.
[48] "From the way in which this is related, it would be thought that Napoleon despised his native country; but I must suggest a more natural interpretation, and one more conformable to the character of Napoleon, namely, that after his abdication he had no desire to remain in the French territories."—Louis Buonaparte.

seemed fixed, he examined with minuteness what he must afterwards consider as his sole fortune. To turn his thoughts from France to Elba, was like the elephant, which can transport artillery, applying his trunk to gather pins. But Napoleon could do both easily, because he regarded these two objects not as they differed from each other, but as they belonged, or did not belong, to himself.

FINAL ACT OF ABDICATION

After a night's consideration, the fallen Chief took his resolution, and despatched Caulaincourt and Macdonald once more to Paris, to treat with the allies upon the footing of an unconditional abdication of the empire. The document was couched in these words:—

"The allied powers having proclaimed that the Emperor was the sole obstacle to the re-establishment of peace in Europe, the Emperor, faithful to his oath, declares that he renounces for himself and his heirs the thrones of France and Italy, and that there is no personal sacrifice, not even that of life, which he is not ready to make to the interests of France."

Notwithstanding his having adopted this course, Napoleon, until the final adjustment of the treaty, continued to nourish thoughts of breaking it off. He formed plans for carrying on the war beyond the Loire—for marching to join Augereau—for penetrating into Italy, and uniting with Prince Eugene. At one time he was very near again summoning his troops to arms, in consequence of a report too hastily transmitted by a general much attached to him (General Alix, we believe,) stating that the Emperor of Austria was displeased at the extremities to which they urged his son-in-law, and was resolved to support him. On this report, which proved afterwards totally unfounded, Napoleon required the maréchals to give him back his letter of abdication. But the deed having been formally executed, and duly registered and delivered, the maréchals held themselves bound to retain it in their own hands, and to act upon it as the only means of saving France at this dreadful crisis.

Buonaparte reviewed his Old Guard in the courtyard of the castle; for their numbers were so diminished that there was space for them in that narrow circuit. Their zealous acclamations gratified his ears as much as ever; but when he looked on their diminished ranks, his heart failed; he retired into the palace, and summoned Oudinot before him. "May I depend on the adhesion of the troops?" he said—Oudinot replied in the negative, and reminded Napoleon that he had abdicated.—"Ay, but under conditions," said Napoleon.—"Soldiers do not understand conditions," said the maréchal: "they look upon your power as terminated."—"Then on that side all is over," said Napoleon; "let us wait the news from Paris."

TREATY OF FONTAINBLEAU

Macdonald, Caulaincourt, and Ney, soon afterwards arrived at Fontainbleau, with the treaty which they had concluded on the basis already announced by the Emperor of Russia, who had taken the principal share in drawing it up. Under his sanction the commissioners had obtained such terms as never before were granted to a dethroned monarch, and which have little chance to be conceded to such a one in future, while the portentous consequences are preserved by history. By these conditions, Buonaparte was to remain Emperor, but his sway was to be limited to the island of Elba, in the Mediterranean, in extent twenty leagues, and containing about twelve thousand inhabitants. He was to be recognised as one of the crowned heads of Europe—was to be allowed body-guards, and a navy on a scale suitable to the limits of his dominions; and, to maintain this state, a revenue of six millions of francs, over and above the revenues of the isle of Elba, were settled on him. Two millions and a half were also assigned in pensions to his brothers, Josephine, and the other members of his family—a revenue more splendid than ever King of England had at his personal disposal. It was well argued, that if Buonaparte deserved such advantageous terms of retirement, it was injustice to dethrone him. In other points the terms of this treaty seemed as irreconcilable with sound policy as they are with all former precedents. The name, dignity, military authority, and absolute power of an Emperor, conferred on the potentate of such Liliputian domains, were ludicrous, if it was supposed that Napoleon would remain quiet in his retreat, and hazardous if he should seek the means of again agitating Europe.

It was no compliment to Buonaparte's taste to invest him with the poor shadow of his former fortune, since for him the most honourable retirement would have been one which united privacy with safety and competence, not that which maintained a vain parade around him, as if in mockery of what he had formerly been. But time fatally showed, what many augured from the beginning, that so soon as his spirit should soar beyond the narrow circle into which it had been conjured, the imperial title and authority, the assistance of devoted body-guards and experienced counsellors, formed a stake with which, however small, the venturous gamester might again enter upon the hazardous game of playing for the kingdoms he had lost. The situation of Elba, too, as the seat of his new sovereignty, so near to Italy, and so little removed from France, seemed calculated on purpose to favour his resurrection at some future period as a political character.

The other stipulations of this extraordinary treaty divided a portion of revenue secured to Napoleon among the members of his family. The most rational was that which settled upon Maria Louisa and her son the duchies of Parma, Placentia, and Guastalla, in full sovereignty. Except this, all the other stipulations were to be made good at the expense of France, whose Provisional Government were never consulted upon the terms granted.[49]

It was not till the bad effects of this singular treaty had been experienced, that men inquired why and on what principle it was first conceded. A great personage has been mentioned as its original author. Possessed of many good and highly honourable qualities, and a steady and most important member of the great European confederacy, it is doing the memory of the Emperor Alexander no injury to suppose, that he remembered his education under his French tutor La Harpe, and was not altogether free from its effects. With these there always mingles that sort of showy sensibility which delights in making theatrical scenes out of acts of beneficence, and

---

[49] For the Treaty of Fontainbleau, see Parl. Debates, vol. xxviii., p. 201.

enjoying in full draughts the popular applause which they are calculated to excite. The contagious air of Paris—the shouts—the flattery—the success to a point hitherto unhoped for—the wish to drown unkindness of every sort, and to spread a feast from which no one should rise discontented—the desire to sum up all in one word, to show MAGNANIMITY in the hour of success, seems to have laid Alexander's heart more open than the rules of wisdom or of prudence ought to have permitted. It is generous to give, and more generous to pardon; but to bestow favours and forgiveness at the same moment, to secure the future fortune of a rival who lies prostrate at his feet, to hear thanks and compliments on every hand, and from the mouths even of the vanquished, is the most fascinating triumph of a victorious sovereign. It is only the consequences which teach him how thriftless and unprofitable a prodigality of beneficence often proves, and that in the attempt so to conduct great national measures that they shall please and satisfy every one, he must necessarily encroach on the rules both of justice and wisdom, and may occasion, by a thoughtless indulgence of romantic sensibility, new trains of misfortune to the whole civilized world. The other active parties in the treaty were the King of Prussia, who had no motive to scan with peculiar scrutiny a treaty planned by his ally the Emperor Alexander, and the Emperor of Austria, who could not in delicacy object to stipulations in favour of his son-in-law.

The maréchals, on the other hand, gladly received what probably they never would have stipulated. They were aware that the army would be conciliated with every mark of respect, however incongruous, which could be paid to their late Emperor, and perhaps knew Buonaparte so well as to believe that he might be gratified by preserving the external marks of imperial honour, though upon so limited a scale. There was one power whose representative foresaw the evils which such a treaty might occasion, and remonstrated against them. But the evil was done, and the particulars of the treaty adjusted, before Lord Castlereagh came to Paris. Finding that the Emperor of Russia had acted for the best, in the name of the other allies, the English minister refrained from risking the peace which had been made in such urgent circumstances, by insisting upon his objections. He refused, however, on the part of his government, to become a party to the treaty farther than by acceding to it so far as the territorial arrangements were concerned; but he particularly declined to acknowledge, on the part of England, the title of Emperor, which the treaty conferred on Napoleon.[50]

Yet when we have expressed with freedom all the objections to which the treaty of Fontainbleau seems liable, it must be owned, that the allied sovereigns showed policy in obtaining an accommodation on almost any terms, rather than renewing the war, by driving Napoleon to despair, and inducing the maréchals, from a sense of honour, again to unite themselves with his cause.

When the treaty was read over to Napoleon, he made a last appeal to his maréchals, inviting them to follow him to the Loire or to the Alps, where they would avoid what he felt an ignominious composition. But he was answered by a general silence. The generals whom he addressed, knew but too well that any efforts which he could make, must be rather in the character of a roving chieftain, supporting his condottieri by the plunder of the country, and that country their own, than that of a warlike monarch, waging war for a specific purpose, and at the head of a regular army. Napoleon saw their determination in their looks, and dismissed the council, promising an answer on an early day, but in the meantime declining to ratify the treaty, and demanding back his abdication from Caulaincourt; a request which that minister again declined to comply with.

Misfortunes were now accumulating so fast around Napoleon, that they seemed of force sufficient to break the most stubborn spirit.

GENERAL DESERTION

Gradually the troops of the allies had spread as far as the banks of the Loire. Fontainbleau was surrounded by their

---

[50] See Dispatch from Lord Castlereagh to Earl Bathurst, dated Paris, April 13, 1814, Parl. Papers, 1814.

detachments; on every side the French officers, as well as soldiers, were leaving his service; he had no longer the power of departing from the palace in safety.

Paris, so late the capital in which his will was law, and where to have uttered a word in his disparagement would have been thought worse than blasphemy, was become the scene of his rival's triumph and his own disgrace. The shouts which used to wait on the Emperor, were now welcoming to the Tuileries Monsieur, the brother of the restored King, who came in character of Lieutenant-general of the kingdom;—the presses, which had so long laboured in disseminating the praises of the Emperor, were now exerting all their art and malice in exposing his real faults, and imputing to him such as had no existence. He was in the condition of the huntsman who was devoured by his own hounds.

It was yet more affecting to see courtiers, dependents, and even domestics, who had lived in his smiles, dropping off under different pretexts to give in their adhesion to the Bourbons, and provide for their own fortune in the new world which had commenced at Paris. It is perhaps in such moments, that human nature is seen in its very worst point of view; since the basest and most selfish points of the character, which, in the train of ordinary life, may never be awakened into existence, show themselves, and become the ruling principle, in such revolutions. Men are then in the condition of well-bred and decorous persons, transferred from an ordinary place of meeting to the whirlpool of a crowd, in which they soon demean themselves with all the selfish desire of their own safety or convenience, and all the total disregard for that of others, which the conscious habits of politeness have suppressed but not eradicated.

Friends and retainers dropt from the unfortunate Napoleon, like leaves from the fading tree; and those whom shame or commiseration yet detained near his person, waited but some decent pretexts, like a rising breath of wind, to sweep them also away.

The defection included all ranks, from Berthier, who shared his bosom councils, and seldom was absent from his side, to the

Mameluke Roustan, who slept across the door of his apartment, and acted as a body guard. It would be absurd to criticise the conduct of the poor African,[51] but the fact and mode of Berthier's departure must not escape notice. He asked permission to go to Paris about some business, saying he would return next day. "He will *not* return," said Napoleon, calmly, to the Duke of Bassano.—"What!" said the minister, "can these be the adieus of Berthier?"—"I tell you, yes—he will return no more."[52] The abdicated sovereign had, however, the consolation of seeing that the attachment of several faithful servants was only tried and purified by adversity, as gold is by fire.[53]

The family connexions, and relatives of Napoleon, as well as his familiar friends, were separated from him in the general wreck. It will not be forgotten, that on the day before the battle of Paris, several members of Napoleon's administration set out with the Empress Maria Louisa, to escape from the approaching action. They halted at Blois, where they were joined by Joseph, and other members of the Buonaparte family. For some time this reunion maintained the character and language of a council of regency, dispersed proclamations, and endeavoured to act as a government. The news of the taking of Paris, and the subsequent events, disposed Joseph and Jerome Buonaparte to remove themselves to the provinces beyond the Loire. But Maria Louisa refused to accompany them, and while the point was yet contested, Count Schouwalow, one of the Austrian ministers,[54] arrived to take her under his protection. The ephemeral regency then broke up, and fled in different directions; the brothers of Buonaparte taking the direction of Switzerland, while Cardinal Fesch, and the mother of Napoleon retreated to Rome.

---

[51] The man had to plead his desire to remain with his wife and family, rather than return to a severe personal thraldom.—S.—"I was by no means astonished at Roustan's conduct he was imbued with the sentiments of a slave, and finding me no longer the master, he imagined that his services might be dispensed with."—Napoleon, *Las Cases*, tom. i., p. 336.
[52] Baron Fain, p. 400.
[53] The faithful few were, the Duke of Bassano, the Duke of Vicenza, Generals Bertrand, Flahaut, Belliard, Fouler; Colonels Bassy, Anatole de Montesquiou, Gourgaud, Count de Turenne; Barons Fain, Mesgrigny, De la Place, and Lelorgne d'Ideville; the Chevalier Jouanne, General Kosakowski, and Colonel Vensowitch. The two last were Poles.
[54] Count Schouwalow was a Russian, not an Austrian minister. Prince Esterhazy, however, was there.—*From Lord Burghersh.*—Ed. (1842.)

Maria Louisa made more than one effort to join her husband, but they were discouraged on the part of Napoleon himself, who, while he continued to ruminate on renewing the war, could not desire to have the Empress along with him in such an adventure.[55] Shortly afterwards, the Emperor of Austria visited his daughter and her son, then at Rambouillet, and gave her to understand that she was, for some time at least, to remain separate from her husband, and that her son and she were to return to Vienna along with him. She returned, therefore, to her father's protection.

DEATH OF JOSEPHINE—FONTAINBLEAU

It must be also here mentioned, as an extraordinary addition to this tale of calamity, that Josephine, the former wife of Buonaparte, did not long survive his downfall. It seemed as if the Obi-woman of Martinico had spoke truth; for, at the time when Napoleon parted from the sharer of his early fortunes, his grandeur was on the wane, and her death took place but a few weeks subsequent to his being dethroned and exiled. The Emperor of Russia had visited this lady, and showed her some attention, with which Napoleon, for reasons we cannot conjecture, was extremely displeased. She was amply provided for by the treaty of Fontainbleau, but did not survive to reap any benefit from the provision, as she shortly after sickened and died at her beautiful villa of Malmaison. She was buried on the 3d of June, at the village of Ruel. A vast number of the lower class attended the obsequies; for she had well deserved the title of patroness of the poor.[56]

While we endeavour to sum the mass of misfortunes with which Buonaparte was overwhelmed at this crisis, it seems as if Fortune had been determined to show that she did not intend to reverse the lot of humanity, even in the case of one who had been so long her favourite, but that she retained the power of depressing

---

[55] Savary, tom. iv., pp. 118-132.
[56] Her two grandsons walked as chief mourners; and in the procession were Prince Nesselrode, General Sacken and Czernicheffe, besides several other generals of the allied army, and some of the French maréchals and generals. The body has since been placed in a magnificent tomb of white marble, erected by her two children, with this inscription—"EUGENE ET HORTENSE A JOSEPHINE."—S.

the obscure soldier, whom she had raised to be almost king of Europe, in a degree as humiliating as his exaltation had been splendid. All that three years before seemed inalienable from his person, was now reversed. The victor was defeated, the monarch was dethroned, the ransomer of prisoners was in captivity, the general was deserted by his soldiers, the master abandoned by his domestics, the brother parted from his brethren, the husband severed from the wife, and the father torn from his only child. To console him for the fairest and largest empire that ambition ever lorded it over, he had, with the mock name of emperor, a petty isle to which he was to retire, accompanied by the pity of such friends as dared express their feelings, the unrepressed execrations of many of his former subjects, who refused to regard his present humiliation as an amends for what he had made them suffer during his power, and the ill-concealed triumph of the enemies into whose hands he had been delivered.

A Roman would have seen, in these accumulated disasters, a hint to direct his sword's point against his breast; a man of better faith would have turned his eye back on his own conduct, and having read, in his misuse of prosperity, the original source of those calamities, would have remained patient and contrite under the consequences of his ambition. Napoleon belonged to the Roman school of philosophy; and it is confidently reported, especially by Baron Fain, his secretary, though it has not been universally believed, that he designed, at this extremity, to escape from life by an act of suicide.

The Emperor, according to this account, had carried with him, ever since the retreat from Moscow, a packet containing a preparation of opium, made up in the same manner with that used by Condorcet for self-destruction. His valet-de-chambre, in the night betwixt the 12th and 13th of April, heard him arise and pour something into a glass of water, drink, and return to bed. In a short time afterwards, the man's attention was called by sobs and stifled groans—an alarm took place in the chateau—some of the principal persons were roused, and repaired to Napoleon's chamber. Yvan, the surgeon, who had procured him the poison, was also summoned; but hearing the Emperor complain that the operation of the potion was not quick enough, he was seized with a panic terror, and fled from the palace at full gallop. Napoleon took the remedies recommended, and a long fit of stupor ensued, with profuse perspiration. He awakened much exhausted, and surprised at finding himself still alive; he said aloud, after a few moments' reflection, "Fate will not have it so," and afterwards appeared reconciled to undergo his destiny, without similar attempts at personal violence.[57] There is, as we have already hinted, a difference of opinion concerning the cause of Napoleon's illness, some imputing it to indigestion. The fact of his having been very much indisposed is, however, indisputable. A general of the highest distinction transacted business with Napoleon on the morning of the 13th April. He seemed pale and dejected, as from recent and exhausting illness. His only dress was a night-gown and slippers, and he drank from time to time a quantity of tisan, or some such liquid, which was placed beside him, saying he had suffered severely during the night, but that his complaint had left him.

After this crisis, and having ratified the treaty which his maréchals had made for him, Napoleon appeared more at his ease than he had been for some time before, and conversed frankly with his attendants upon the affairs of France.

He owned, that, after all, the Government of the Bourbons would best suit France, as tending to reconcile all parties. "Louis," he said, "has talents and means; he is old and infirm; he will not, I think, choose to give his name to a bad reign. If he is wise, he will occupy my bed, and content himself with changing the sheets. But," he continued, "he must treat the army well, and take care not to look back on the past, otherwise his reign will be of brief endurance."

He also mentioned the inviolability of the sale of the national domains, as the woof upon which the whole web depended; cut one thread of it, he said, and the whole will be unravelled. Of the ancient

---

[57] "Dieu ne le veut pas."—*Manuscript de 1814*, p. 395. "Colonel Sir Niel Campbell told me, that in the course of conversation with him, on the 17th, Napoleon remarked—though many considered he ought to commit suicide, yet he thought it was more magnanimous to live."—*Memorable Events*, p. 235.

noblesse and people of fashion, he spoke in embittered language, saying they were an English colony in the midst of France, who desired only their own privileges, and would act as readily for as against him.

"If I were in Louis's situation," he said, "I would not keep up the Imperial Guard. I myself have treated them too well not to have insured their attachment; and it will be *his* policy to dismiss them, giving good pensions to such officers and soldiers as choose to retire from service, and preferment in the line to others who incline to remain. This done, he should choose another guard from the army at large."

After these remarkable observations, which, in fact, contained an anticipation of much that afterwards took place, Napoleon looked round upon his officers, and made them the following exhortation:—"Gentlemen, when I remain no longer with you, and when you have another government, it will become you to attach yourselves to it frankly, and serve it as faithfully as you have served me. I request, and even command you to do this; therefore, all who desire leave to go to Paris have my permission to do so, and those who remain here will do well to send in their adhesion to the government of the Bourbons." Yet while Napoleon used this manful and becoming language to his followers, on the subject of the change of government, it is clear that there lurked in his bosom a persuasion that the Bourbons were surrounded with too many difficulties to be able to surmount them, and that Destiny had still in reserve for him a distinguished part in the annals of Europe.

In a private interview with Macdonald, whose part in the abdication we have mentioned, he expressed himself warmly satisfied with his conduct, regretting that he had not more early known his value, and proposed he should accept a parting gift. "It is only," he said, anticipating the maréchal's objections, "the present of a soldier to his comrade." And indeed it was chosen with great delicacy, being a beautiful Turkish sabre, which Napoleon had himself received from Ibrahim Bey while in Egypt.[58]

LEAVES FONTAINBLEAU

Napoleon having now resigned himself entirely to his fate, whether for good or evil, prepared, on the 20th April, to depart for his place of retreat. But first he had the painful task of bidding farewell to the body in the universe most attached to him, and to which he was probably most attached—his celebrated Imperial Guard. Such of them as could be collected were drawn out before him in review. Some natural tears dropped from his eyes, and his features had the marks of strong emotion, while reviewing for the last time, as he must then have thought likely, the companions of so many victories. He advanced to them on horseback, dismounted, and took his solemn leave. "All Europe," he said, "had armed against him; France herself had deserted him, and chosen another dynasty. He might," he said, "have maintained with his soldiers a civil war of years, but it would have rendered France unhappy. Be faithful," he continued (and the words were remarkable,) "to the new sovereign whom France has chosen. Do not lament my fate; I will always be happy while I know you are so. I could have died—nothing was easier—but I will always follow the road of honour. I will record with my pen the deeds we have done together.[59] I cannot embrace you all, but I embrace your general,"—(he pressed the general to his bosom.)—"Bring hither the eagle,"—(he embraced the standard, and concluded,)—"Beloved eagle, may the kisses I bestow on you long resound in the hearts of the brave!—Adieu, my children—Adieu, my brave companions—Surround me once more—Adieu." Drowned in grief, the veteran soldiers heard the farewell of their dethroned leader; sighs and murmurs broke from their ranks, but the emotion burst out in no threats or remonstrances. They appeared resigned to the loss of their general, and to yield, like him, to necessity.

---

[58] The following words were engraven on the blade: "Sabre que portait l'Empereur le jour de la bataille du Mont Thabor."—Bourrienne.
[59] "He told M. de Caraman, that he had never had time to study; but that he now should, and meant to write his own memoirs."—*Memorable Events*, p. 232.

CHAPTER LXXXI

Commissioners appointed to escort Napoleon—He leaves Fontainbleau on the 20th April—His interview with Augereau at Valence—Expressions of popular dislike towards Napoleon in the South of France—Fears for his personal safety—His own agitation and precautions—He arrives at Frejus, and embarks on board the Undaunted, with the British and Austrian Commissioners—Arrives at Elba on 4th May.

Upon his unpleasant journey, Napoleon was attended by Bertrand and Drouet, honourably faithful to the adverse fortunes of the master who had been their benefactor when in prosperity. Four delegates from the allied powers accompanied him to his new dominions. Their names were—General Schouwaloff, on the part of Russia; the Austrian General, Kohler; Colonel Sir Niel Campbell, as representing Great Britain; and the General Baron Truchsess Waldbourg, as the commissioner of Prussia. Napoleon received the three first with much personal civility, but seemed to resent the presence of the representative of Prussia, a country which had been at one time the subject of his scorn, and always of his hatred. It galled him that she should assume an immediate share in deciding upon his fate.

He received the English commissioner with particular expressions of esteem, saying he desired to pass to Elba in an English vessel, and was pleased to have the escort of an English officer, "Your nation," he said, "has an elevated character, for which I have the highest esteem. I desired to raise the French people to such a pitch of sentiment, but——." He stopt, and seemed affected. He spoke with much civility to the Austrian General Kohler, but expressed himself somewhat bitterly on the subject of Russia. He even hinted to the Austrian, that should he not be satisfied with his reception in Elba, he might possibly choose to retire to Great

Britain;[60] and asked General Kohler, whether he thought he would not receive protection from them. "Yes, sire," replied the Austrian, "the more readily, that your Majesty has never made war in that country."

Napoleon proceeded to give a farewell audience to the Duke of Bassano, and seemed nettled when an aide-de-camp, on the part of General Bertrand, announced that the hour fixed for departing was arrived. "Good," he said. "This is something new. Since when is it that my motions have been regulated by the watch of the grand maréchal? I will not depart till it is my pleasure—perhaps I will not depart at all."[61] This, however, was only a momentary sally of impatience.

LEAVES FONTAINBLEAU—AUGEREAU

Napoleon left Fontainbleau the 20th April, 1814, at eleven o'clock in the morning. His retinue occupied fourteen carriages, and required relays of thirty pairs of post horses. On the journey, at least during its commencement, he affected a sort of publicity, sending for the public authorities of towns, and investigating into the state of the place, as he was wont to do on former occasions. The cries of *Vive l'Empereur* were frequently heard, and seemed to give him fresh spirits. On the other hand, the mayors, and sub-prefects, whom he interrogated concerning the decay of many of the towns, displeased him, by ascribing the symptoms of dilapidation to the war, or the conscription; and in several places the people wore the white cockade, and insulted his passage with shouts of *Vive le Roi*.

In a small barrack, near Valence, Napoleon, upon 24th April, met Augereau, his old companion in the campaigns of Italy, and in some degree his tutor in the art of war. The maréchal had resented some of the reflections which occurred in the bulletins, censuring his operations for the protection of Lyons. When, therefore, he

---

[60] General Sir Edward Paget and Lord Louvain, both informed me that Lord Castlereagh told them, that Napoleon had written to him for permission to retire to England, "it being the only country possessing great and liberal ideas."—*Memorable Events*, p. 232.
[61] Memorable Events, p. 326; Bourrienne, tom. x., p. 217.

issued a proclamation to his army, on the recent change, he announced Napoleon as one who had brought on his own ruin, and yet dared not die. An angry interview took place, and the following words are said to have been exchanged between them:—"I have thy proclamation," said Napoleon. "Thou hast betrayed me."—"Sire," replied the maréchal, "it is you who have betrayed France and the army, by sacrificing both to a frantic spirit of ambition."—"Thou hast chosen thyself a new master," said Napoleon.—"I have no account to render to you on that score," replied the general.—"Thou hast no courage," replied Buonaparte.—"'Tis thou hast none," replied the general, and turned his back, without any mark of respect, on his late master.[62]

At Montelimart, the exiled Emperor heard the last expressions of regard and sympathy. He was now approaching Provence, a region of which he had never possessed the affections, and was greeted with execrations and cries of—"Perish the Tyrant!"—"Down with the butcher of our children!" Matters looked worse as they advanced. On Monday, 25th April, when Sir Niel Campbell, having set out before Napoleon, arrived at Avignon, the officer upon guard anxiously inquired if the escort attending the Emperor was of strength sufficient to resist a popular disturbance, which was already on foot at the news of his arrival. The English commissioner entreated him to protect the passage of Napoleon by every means possible. It was agreed that the fresh horses should be posted at a different quarter of the town from that where it was natural to have expected the change. Yet the mob discovered and surrounded them, and it was with difficulty that Napoleon was saved from popular fury. Similar dangers attended him elsewhere; and, in order to avoid assassination, the Ex-Emperor of France was obliged to disguise himself as a postilion, or a domestic, anxiously altering from time to time the mode of his dress; ordering the servants to smoke in his presence; and inviting the commissioners, who travelled with him, to whistle or sing, that the incensed people might not be aware who was in the carriage. At Orgon, the mob brought before him his own

---

[62] Itineraire de Buonaparte, p. 235.—Augereau was an old republican, and had been ready to oppose Buonaparte on the day he dissolved the Legislative Body. He submitted to him during his reign, but was a severe censurer of his excessive love of conquest.—See *ante*, vol. iv.—S.

effigy dabbled with blood, and stopped his carriage till they displayed it before his eyes; and, in short, from Avignon to La Calade, he was grossly insulted in every town and village, and, but for the anxious interference of the commissioners, he would probably have been torn to pieces. The unkindness of the people seemed to make much impression on him. He even shed tears. He showed also, more fear of assassination than seemed consistent with his approved courage; but it must be recollected, that the danger was of a new and peculiarly horrible description, and calculated to appal many to whom the terrors of a field of battle were familiar. The bravest soldier might shudder at a death like that of the De Witts. At La Calade he was equally nervous, and exhibited great fear of poison. When he reached Aix, precautions were taken by detachments of gendarmes, as well as by parties of the allied troops, to ensure his personal safety.[63] At a chateau called Bouillidou, he had an interview with his sister Pauline. The curiosity of the lady of the house, and two or three females, made them also find their way to his presence. They saw a gentleman in an Austrian uniform. "Whom do you wish to see, ladies?"—"The Emperor Napoleon."—"I am Napoleon."—"You jest, sir," replied the ladies.—"What! I suppose you expected to see me look more mischievous? O yes—confess that, since fortune is adverse to me, I must look like a rascal, a miscreant, a brigand. But do you know how all this has happened? Merely because I wished to place France above England."

FREJUS—VOYAGE TO ELBA

At length he arrived at Frejus, the very port that received him, when, coming from Egypt, he was on the verge of commencing that astonishing career, now about to terminate, to all earthly appearance, at the very point from which he had started. He shut himself up in a solitary apartment, which he traversed with impatient and hasty steps, sometimes pausing to watch from the window the arrival of the vessels, one of which was to transport him from France, as it

---

[63] This, indeed, had been previously arranged, as troops in considerable numbers were posted for his protection at Grenoble, Gap, and Sisteron, being the road by which he was expected to have travelled; but, perhaps with a view to try an experiment on his popularity, he took the route we have detailed.—S.

then seemed, for ever. The French frigate, the Dryade, and a brig called the Inconstant, had come from Toulon to Frejus, and lay ready to perform this duty. But, reluctant perhaps to sail under the Bourbon flag, Napoleon preferred embarking on board his Britannic Majesty's ship the Undaunted, commanded by Captain Usher.[64] This vessel being placed at the direction of the British commissioner, Sir Niel Campbell, he readily acquiesced in Napoleon's wish to have his passage in her to Elba. It was eleven at night on the 28th ere he finally embarked, under a salute of twenty-one guns. "Adieu, Cæsar, and his fortune," said the Russian envoy. The Austrian and British commissioners accompanied him on his voyage.[65]

During the passage, Buonaparte seemed to recover his spirits, and conversed with great frankness and ease with Captain Usher and Sir Niel Campbell. The subject chiefly led to high-coloured statements of the schemes which he had been compelled to leave unexecuted, with severe strictures on his enemies, and much contempt for their means of opposition. The following particulars are amusing, and, so far as we know, have never appeared:

He was inquisitive about the discipline of the vessel, which he commended highly, but assured Captain Usher, that had his power lasted for five years longer, he would have had three hundred sail of the line. Captain Usher naturally asked how they were to be manned. Napoleon replied, that he had resolved on a naval conscription in all the seaports and sea-coast frontier of France, which would man his fleet, which was to be exercised in the Zuyder Zee, until fit for going to the open sea. The British officer scarce suppressed a smile as he

---

[64] When they came alongside of the Undaunted, Napoleon desired the captain to ascend, and then followed; the officers were on deck to receive him; they mutually bowed, and the Emperor instantly went forward alone among the men, most of whom spoke French, having been on this station for some years. They all kept their hats on; but he so fascinated them by his manner, that in a few minutes they, of their own accord, took them off. Captain Usher was very glad of this, as he was apprehensive the sailors might have thrown him overboard.—*Memorable Events*, p. 254.

[65] The Prussian commissioner wrote an account of their journey, called "Itineraire de Buonaparte, jusqu'à son embarquement à Frejus, Paris, 1815." The facts are amply confirmed by the accounts of his fellow-travellers. Napoleon always reckoned the pamphlet of General Truchsess Waldbourg, together with the account of De Pradt's Embassy to Poland, as the works calculated to do him most injury. Perhaps he was sensible that during this journey he had behaved beneath the character of a hero, or perhaps he disliked the publication of details which inferred his extreme unpopularity in the south of France.—S.

replied, that the marine conscripts would make a sorry figure in a gale of wind.

To the Austrian envoy, Napoleon's constant subject was the enlarged power of Russia, which, if she could by any means unite Poland into a healthful and integral part of her army, would, he stated, overwhelm Europe.

On a subsequent occasion, the Emperor favoured his auditors with a new and curious history of the renewal of the war with England. According to this edition, the isle of Malta was a mere pretext. Shortly after the peace of Amiens, he said, Mr. Addington, then the English Prime Minister, proposed to him a renewal of Mr. Pitt's commercial treaty with France; but that he, Napoleon, desirous to encourage the interior industry of France, had refused to enter into such a treaty, excepting upon terms of reciprocity; namely, that if France received so many millions of English import, England was to be obliged to take in return the same quantity of French productions. These terms were declined by Mr. Addington, on which Napoleon declared there should be no treaty at all, unless his principles were adopted. "Then," replied Mr. Addington, as quoted by Buonaparte, "there must be hostilities; for, unless the people of England have the advantages of commerce on the terms they are accustomed to, they will force me to declare war."—And the war took place accordingly, of which, he again averred, England's determination to recover the advantages of the treaty of commerce between Vergennes and Pitt, was the real cause.

"*Now*," he continued, kindling as he spoke, "England has no power which can oppose her system. She can pursue it without limits. There will be a treaty on very unequal terms, which will not afford due encouragement to the manufactures of France. The Bourbons are poor devils"——he checked himself—"they are grand seigneurs, content to return to their estates and draw their rents; but if the people of France see that, and become discontented, the Bourbons will be turned off in six months." He seemed again to recollect himself, like one who thinks he has spoken too much, and was perceptibly more reserved for the rest of the day.

This curious ebullition was concocted according to Napoleon's peculiar manner of blending what might be true in his narrative, with what was intended to forward his own purpose, and mingling it with so much falsehood and delusion, that it resembled what the English poet says of the Catholic Plot,

"Some truth there was, but mix'd and dash'd with lies."

It is probable that, after the peace of Amiens, Lord Sidmouth might have wished to renew the commercial treaty; but it is absolutely false that Napoleon's declining to do so had any effect upon the renewal of hostilities. His prophecy that his own downfall would be followed by the English urging upon France a disadvantageous commercial treaty, has proved equally false; and it is singular enough that he who, on board the Undaunted, declared that entering into such a measure would be the destruction of the Bourbons, should, while at St. Helena, ridicule and censure Lord Castlereagh for not having secured to Britain that commercial supremacy, the granting of which he had represented as the probable cause of such a result.[66] Thus did his colouring, if not his facts, change according to the mood of the moment.

While on board the Undaunted, Napoleon spoke with great freedom of the facility with which he had outwitted and defeated the allies during the last campaign. "The Silesian army," he said, "had given him most trouble. The old devil, Blucher, was no sooner defeated than he was willing to fight again." But he considered his victory over Schwartzenberg as certain, save for the defection of Marmont. Much more he said, with great apparent frankness, and seemed desirous to make himself in every respect agreeable to his companions on board. Even the seamen, who at first regarded him with wonder, mixed with suspicion, did not escape the charm of his affability, by which they were soon won over, all excepting the boatswain Hinton, a tar of the old school, who could never hear the

---

[66] Las Cases, tom. iii., p. 92.

Emperor's praises without muttering the vulgar, but expressive phrase—"*Humbug.*"[67]

With the same good-humour, Napoleon admitted any slight jest which might be passed, even at his own expense. When off Corsica, he proposed that Captain Usher should fire a gun to bring-to a fishing-boat, from which he hoped to hear some news. Captain Usher excused himself, saying, such an act of hostility towards a neutral would *denationalize* her, in direct contradiction of Napoleon's doctrine concerning the rights of nations. The Emperor laughed heartily. At another time he amused himself by supposing what admirable caricatures his voyage would give rise to in London. He seemed wonderfully familiar with that species of satire, though so peculiarly English.

LANDS AT PORTO FERRAJO

Upon the 4th of May, when they arrived within sight of Porto Ferrajo, the principal town of Elba, which has a very fine harbour, they found the island in some confusion. The inhabitants had been recently in a state of insurrection against the French, which had been quieted by the governor and the troops giving in their adhesion to the Bourbon government. This state of things naturally increased Napoleon's apprehensions, which had never entirely subsided since the dangers he underwent in Provence. Even on board the Undaunted, he had requested that a sergeant of marines might sleep each night on the outside of his cabin-door, a trusty domestic also mounting guard within. He now showed some unwillingness, when they made the island, to the ship running right under the batteries; and when he first landed in the morning, it was at an early hour, and in disguise, having previously obtained from Captain Usher, a sergeant's party of marines to attend him.

---

[67] The honest boatswain, however, could understand and value what was solid in Napoleon's merits. As he had to return thanks in name of the ship's company, for 200 louis with which the Emperor presented them, he wished "his honour good health, and better luck the next time."—S.

Having returned on board to breakfast, after his incognito visit to his island, the Emperor of Elba, as he may now be styled, went on shore in form, about two o'clock, with the commissioners, receiving, at leaving the Undaunted, a royal salute. On the beach, he was received by the governor, prefect, and other official persons, with such means of honour as they possessed, who conducted him to the Hôtel-de-Ville, in procession, preceded by a wretched band of fiddlers. The people welcomed him with many shouts. The name of Buonaparte had been unpopular among them as Emperor of France, but they anticipated considerable advantages from his residing among them as their own particular sovereign.

Chapter LXXXII

Elba—Napoleon's mode of Life and occupation there—Effects of his residence at Elba upon the adjoining Kingdom of Italy—He is visited by his Mother and the Princess Pauline—and by a Polish lady—Sir Niel Campbell the only Commissioner left at Elba—Napoleon's Conversations on the State of Europe—His pecuniary Difficulties—and fears of Assassination—Symptoms of some approaching crisis—A part of the Old Guard disbanded—Napoleon escapes from Elba—Fruitless pursuit by Sir Niel Campbell.

ELBA

Elba, to the limits of which the mighty empire of Napoleon was now contracted, is an island opposite to the coast of Tuscany, about sixty miles in circumference. The air is healthy, excepting in the neighbourhood of the salt marshes. The country is mountainous, and, having all the florid vegetation of Italy, is, in general, of a romantic character. It produces little grain, but exports a considerable quantity of wines; and its iron ore has been famous since the days of Virgil, who describes Elba as,

"Insula inexhaustis chalybum generosa metallis."

There are also other mineral productions. The island boasts two good harbours, and is liberally productive of vines, olives, fruits and maize. Perhaps, if an empire could be supposed to exist within such a brief space, Elba possesses so much both of beauty and variety, as might constitute the scene of a summer night's dream of sovereignty. Buonaparte seemed to lend himself to the illusion, as, accompanied by Sir Niel Campbell, he rode in his usual exploring mood, around the shores of his little state. He did not fail to visit the iron mines, and being informed the annual produce was 500,000 francs, "These, then," he said, "are mine." But being reminded that he had conferred that revenue on the Legion of Honour, he exclaimed, "Where was my head when I gave such a grant! But I have made many foolish decrees of that sort."

One or two of the poorer class of inhabitants, knelt, and even prostrated themselves when they met him. He seemed disgusted, and imputed this humiliating degree of abasement to the wretchedness of their education, under the auspices of the monks. On these excursions he showed the same apprehension of assassination which had marked his journey to Frejus. Two couriers, well armed, rode before him, and examined every suspicious spot. But as he climbed a mountain above Ferrajo, and saw the ocean approach its feet in almost every direction, the expression broke from him, accompanied with a good-humoured smile, "It must be confessed my isle is very little."

He professed, however, to be perfectly resigned to his fate; often spoke of himself as a man politically dead, and claimed credit for what he said upon public affairs, as having no remaining interest in them. He professed his intentions were to devote himself exclusively to science and literature. At other times, he said he would live in his little island, like a justice of peace in a country town in England.

The character of Napoleon, however, was little known to himself, if he seriously thought that his restless and powerful mind could be satisfied with the investigation of abstract truths, or amused by the leisure of literary research. He compared his abdication to that of Charles V., forgetting that the Austrian Emperor's retreat was voluntary, that he had a turn towards mechanical pursuits, and that even with these means of solace, Charles became discontented with his retirement. The character of Buonaparte was, on the contrary, singularly opposed to a state of seclusion. His propensities continued to be exactly of the same description at Elba, which had so long terrified and disquieted Europe. To change the external face of what was around him; to imagine extensive alterations, without accurately considering the means by which they were to be accomplished; to work within his petty province such alterations as its limits permitted; to resume, in short, upon a small scale, those changes which he had attempted upon that which was most magnificent; to apply to Elba the system of policy which he had exercised so long in Europe, was the only mode in which he seems to have found amusement and exercise for the impatient energies of a temper, accustomed from his early youth to work upon others, but apt to become lethargic, sullen, and discontented, when it was compelled, for want of other exercise, to recoil upon itself.

During the first two or three weeks of his residence in the island of Elba, Napoleon had already planned improvements, or alterations and innovations at least, which, had they been to be carried into execution with the means which he possessed, would have perhaps taken his lifetime to execute. It was no wonder, indeed, accustomed as he had been to speak the word, and to be obeyed, and to consider the improvements which he meditated as those which became the head of a great empire, that he should not have been able to recollect that his present operations respected a petty islet, where magnificence was to be limited, not only by utility, but by the want of funds.

In the course of two or three days' travelling, with the same rapidity which characterised his movements in his frequent progresses through France, and showing the same impatience of rest or delay, Napoleon had visited every spot in his little island, mines, woods, salt-marshes, harbours, fortifications, and whatever was worthy of an instant's consideration, and had meditated improvements and innovations respecting every one of them. Till he had done this he was impatient of rest, and having done so, he lacked occupation.

One of his first, and perhaps most characteristic proposals, was to aggrandize and extend his Liliputian dominions by occupation of an uninhabited island, called Rianosa, which had been left desolate on account of the frequent descents of the corsairs. He sent thirty of his guards, with ten of the independent company belonging to the island, upon this expedition—(what a contrast to those which he had formerly directed!)—sketched out a plan of fortifications, and remarked, with complacency, "Europe will say that I have already made a conquest."

In an incredibly short time Napoleon had also planned several roads, had contrived means to convey water from the mountains to Porto Ferrajo,[68] designed two palaces, one for the country, the other in the city, a separate mansion for his sister Pauline, stables for one hundred and fifty horses, a lazaretto, buildings for accommodation of the tunny fishery, and salt-works on a new construction, at Porto Longone. The Emperor of Elba proposed, also, purchasing various domains, and had the price estimated; for the inclination of the proprietor was not reckoned essential to the transaction. He ended by establishing four places of residence in the different quarters of the island; and his amusement consisted in constant change and alteration. He travelled from one to another with the restlessness of a bird in a cage, which springs from perch to perch, since it is prevented from winging the air, its natural element. It seemed as if the magnitude of the object was not so much the subject of his consideration, providing it afforded immediate scope for employing his constant and stimulated desire of activity. He was like the thorough-bred gamester, who, deprived of the means of depositing large stakes, will rather play at small game than leave the table.

Napoleon placed his court also upon an ambitious scale, having more reference to what he had so long been, than to what he actually now had been reduced to, while, at the same time, the furniture and internal accommodations of the imperial palace were meaner by far than those of an English gentleman of ordinary rank. The proclamation of the French governor on resigning his authority to Napoleon, was well and becomingly expressed; but the spiritual mandate of the Vicar-general Arrighi, a relation of Buonaparte's, which was designed to congratulate the people of Elba on becoming the subjects of the Great Napoleon, was extremely ludicrous. "Elevated to the sublime honour of receiving the anointed of the

---

[68] "One of Napoleon's first cares was to obtain a supply of water for the town of Porto-Ferrajo. Captain Usher accompanied him in a boat round the bay; they sailed every creek, and tasted the different rills. Seeing the English sailors watering, he said, 'Let us go to them; I am sure they will choose the best.' Napoleon made a sailor dip his hat into the water, and hold it for him to drink. 'It is excellent: I knew they would find it out.'"—*Memorable Events*, p. 259.

Lord," he described the exhaustless wealth which was to flow in upon the people, from the strangers who came to look upon the hero. The exhortation sounded as if the isle had become the residence of some nondescript animal, which was to be shown for money.

The interior of Napoleon's household, though reduced to thirty-five persons, still held the titles, and affected the rank, proper to an imperial court, of which it will be presently seen the petty sovereign made a political use. He displayed a national flag, having a red bend dexter in a white field, the bend bearing three bees. To dignify his capital, having discovered that the ancient name of Porto Ferrajo, was Comopoli (*i. e.* the city of Como,) he commanded it to be called Cosmopoli, or the city of all nations.

His body-guard, of about 700 infantry, and 80 cavalry, seemed to occupy as much of Napoleon's attention as the grand army did formerly. They were constantly exercised, especially in throwing shot and shells; and, in a short time, he was observed to be anxious about obtaining recruits for them. This was no difficult matter, where all the world had so lately been in arms, and engaged in a profession which many, doubtless, for whom a peaceful life had few charms, laid aside with regret, and longed to resume.

As early as the month of July 1814, there was a considerable degree of fermentation in Italy, to which the neighbourhood of Elba, the residence of several members of the Buonaparte family, and the sovereignty of Murat, occasioned a general resort of Buonaparte's friends and admirers. Every day this agitation increased, and various arts were resorted to for disseminating a prospect of Napoleon's future return to power. Sundry parties of recruits came over to Elba from Italy to enlist in his guards, and two persons employed in this service were arrested at Leghorn, in whose possession were found written lists, containing the names of several hundred persons willing to serve Napoleon. The species of ferment and discontent thus produced in Italy, was much increased by the impolitic conduct of Prince Rospigliosi, the civil governor of Tuscany, who re-established in their full force every form and regulation formerly practised under the Dukes of Tuscany, broke up the establishment of the museum, which had been instituted by Buonaparte's sister, and, while he returned to all the absurdities of the old government, relaxed none of the imposts which the French had laid on.

Napoleon's conduct towards the refugees who found their way to Elba, may be judged from the following sketch. On the 11th of July, Colomboni, commandant of a battalion of the 4th regiment of the line in Italy, was presented to the Emperor as newly arrived. "Well, Colomboni, your business in Elba?"—"First, to pay my duty to your Majesty; secondly, to offer myself to carry a musket among your guards."—"That is too low a situation, you must have something better," said Napoleon; and instantly named him to an appointment of 1200 francs yearly, though it appears the Emperor himself was then in great distress for money.

About the middle of summer, Napoleon was visited by his mother, and his sister the Princess Pauline.[69] At this time, too, he seems to have expected to be rejoined by his wife Maria Louisa, who, it was said, was coming to take possession of her Italian dominions. Their separation, with the incidents which happened before Paris, was the only subject on which he appeared to lose temper. Upon these topics he used strong and violent language. He said, that interdicting him intercourse with his wife and son, excited universal reprobation at Vienna—that no such instance of inhumanity and injustice could be pointed out in modern times—that the Empress was detained a prisoner, an orderly officer constantly attending upon her—finally, that she had been given to understand before she left Orleans, that she was to obtain permission to join him at the island of Elba, though it was now denied her. It was possible, he proceeded, to see a shade of policy, though none whatever of justice, in this separation. Austria had meant to unite the child of her sovereign with the Emperor of France, but was desirous of breaking off the connexion with the Emperor of Elba, as it might be apprehended that the respect due to the daughter of the House of Hapsburg would, had she resided with

---

[69] Napoleon's mother arrived on the 2d of August, and occupied a house on the quay at Porto Ferrajo. Pauline landed in October. She lived in the palace with her brother; who had a room built for her in the garden, in which she gave public balls every Sunday evening.

her husband, have reflected too much lustre on the abdicated sovereign.

The Austrian commissioner, General Kohler, on the other hand, insisted that the separation took place by the Empress Maria Louisa's consent, and even at her request; and hinted, that Napoleon's desire to have her society was dictated by other feelings than those of domestic affection. But allowing that Napoleon's views in so earnestly desiring the company of his wife might be political, we can see neither justice nor reason in refusing a request, which would have been granted to a felon condemned to transportation.

We have not thought it necessary to disturb the narrative of important events by noticing details which belong rather to romance; but as we are now treating of Napoleon in his more private character, a mysterious circumstance may be mentioned. About the end of August 1814, a lady arrived at the Isle of Elba, from Leghorn, with a boy about five or six years old. She was received by Napoleon with great attention, but at the same time with an air of much secrecy, and was lodged in a small and very retired villa, in the most remote corner of the island; from whence, after remaining two days, she re-embarked for Naples. The Elbese naturally concluded that this must have been the Empress Maria Louisa and her son. But the individual was known by those near Napoleon's person to be a Polish lady from Warsaw, and the boy was the offspring of an intrigue betwixt her and Napoleon several years before.[70] The cause of her speedy departure might be delicacy towards Maria Louisa, and the fear of affording the Court of Vienna a pretext for continuing the separation, of which Napoleon complained. In fact, the Austrians, in defence of their own conduct, imputed irregularities to that of Buonaparte; but the truth of these charges would be no edifying subject of investigation.

---

[70] "Our halt at Warsaw, in January 1807, was delightful. The Emperor and all the French officers paid their tribute of admiration to the charms of the fair Poles. There was one whose powerful fascinations made a deep impression on Napoleon's heart. He conceived an ardent affection for her, which she cordially returned. It is needless to name her, when I observe that her attachment remained unshaken amidst every danger, and that, at the period of Napoleon's reverses, she continued his faithful friend."—Savary, tom. iii., p. 16.

About the middle of May, Baron Kohler took farewell of Napoleon, to return to Vienna. He was an Austrian general of rank and reputation; a particular friend and old schoolfellow of Prince Schwartzenberg. The scene of Napoleon's parting with this gentleman was quite pathetic on the Emperor's side. He wept as he embraced General Kohler, and entreated him to procure, if possible, his re-union with his wife and child—calling him the preserver of his life—regretted his poverty, which prevented his bestowing on him some valuable token of remembrance—finally, folding the Austrian general in his arms, he held him there for some time, repeating expressions of the warmest attachment. This sensibility existed all upon one side; for an English gentleman who witnessed the scene, having asked Kohler afterwards what he was thinking of while locked in the Emperor's embraces—"of Judas Iscariot," answered the Austrian.

After the departure of Baron Kohler, Colonel Sir Niel Campbell was the only one of the four commissioners who continued to remain at Elba by orders of the British Cabinet. It was difficult to say what his office really was, or what were his instructions. He had neither power, title, nor means, to interfere with Napoleon's motions. The Emperor had been recognised by a treaty—wise or foolish, it was too late to ask—as an independent sovereign. It was therefore only as an envoy that Sir Niel Campbell could be permitted to reside at his court; and as an envoy also, not of the usual character, for settling affairs concerning the court from which he was despatched, but in a capacity not generally avowed—the office, namely, of observing the conduct of that at which he was sent to reside. In fact, Sir Niel Campbell had no direct or ostensible situation whatever, and of this the French minister of Elba soon took advantage. Drouet, the governor of Porto Ferrajo, made such particular inquiries into the character assumed by the British envoy, and the length of his stay, as obliged the latter to say that his orders were to remain in Elba till the breaking up of the Congress, which was now settling the affairs of Europe; but if his orders should direct him to continue there after that period, he would apply to have his situation placed on some recognised public footing, which he did not doubt would be respectable.

Napoleon did not oppose or murmur at the continued, though equivocal residence of Sir Niel Campbell at Elba; he affected, on the contrary, to be pleased with it. For a considerable time, he even seemed to seek the society of the British envoy, held frequent intercourse with him, and conversed with apparent confidence upon public affairs. The notes of such conversations are now before us; and though it is, on the one hand, evident that Napoleon's expressions were arranged, generally speaking, on a premeditated plan, yet, on the other, it is equally certain, that his ardent temperament, when once engaged in discourse, led him to discover more of his own private thoughts than he would, on cool reflection, have suffered to escape him.

On the 16th September 1814, for example, Sir Niel Campbell had an audience of three hours, during which, Napoleon, with his habitual impatience of a sedentary posture, walked from one end of the room to the other, and talked incessantly. He was happy, he said, that Sir Niel remained in Elba, *pour rompre la chimère*, (to destroy, namely, the idea, that he, Buonaparte, had further intention of disturbing the peace of Europe.) "I think," he continued, "of nothing beyond the verge of my little isles. I could have supported the war for twenty years, if I had chosen. I am now a deceased person, occupied with nothing but my family, my retreat, my house, my cows, and my poultry." He then spoke in the highest terms of the English character, protesting it had always had his sincere admiration, notwithstanding the abuse directed against it in his name. He requested the British envoy to lose no time in procuring him an English grammar. It is a pity Mr. Hinton, the boatswain, was not present, to have accompanied this eulogy with his favourite ejaculation.

In the rest of the conversation, the Elbese Emperor was probably more serious. He inquired with eagerness after the real state of France. Sir Niel Campbell informed him, that all the information he had been able to collect, ascribed great wisdom and moderation to the sovereign and government; but allowed that those who had lost good appointments, the prisoners of war who had returned from abroad, and great part of the army who remained embodied, were still attached to Napoleon. In answer, Buonaparte seemed to admit the stability of the throne, supported as it was by the maréchals and great officers; but he derided the idea of affording France the benefit of a free constitution. He said, the attempt to imitate that of Great Britain was a farce, a caricature. It was impossible, he observed, to imitate the two Houses of Parliament, for that respectable families like those composing the aristocracy of England, did not now exist in France. He talked with bitterness of the cession of Belgium, and of France being deprived of Antwerp. He himself spoke, he observed, as a spectator, without hopes or interest, for he had none; but thus to have mortified the French, showed an ignorance of the national character. Their chief feeling was for pride and glory, and the allies need not look forward to a state of satisfaction and tranquillity under such circumstances as France was now placed in. "The French," he said, "were conquered only by a great superiority of number, therefore were not humiliated; and the population had not suffered to the extent alleged, for he had always spared their lives, and exposed those of Italians, Germans, and other foreigners." He remarked that the gratitude of Louis XVIII. to Great Britain was offensive to France, and that he was called in derision the King of England's Viceroy.

In the latter months of 1814, Sir Niel Campbell began to become sensible that Napoleon desired to exclude him from his presence as much as he possibly could, without positive rudeness. He rather suddenly intrenched himself within all the forms of an imperial court; and without affording the British envoy any absolute cause of complaint, or even any title to require explanation, he contrived, in a great measure, to debar him from opportunities of conversation. His only opportunity of obtaining access to Napoleon, was on his return from short absences to Leghorn and Florence, when his attendance on the levee was matter of etiquette.

On such occasions, the tenor of Napoleon's prophecies was minatory of the peace of Europe. He spoke perpetually of the humiliation inflicted upon France, by taking from her Belgium and his favourite object Antwerp. On the 30th of October, while enlarging on these topics, he described the irritable feelings of the nation, saying, every man in France considered the Rhine to be their natural boundary, and nothing could alter this opinion. There was no want, he said, of a population in France, martial beyond any other nation, by natural disposition, by the consequences of the Revolution, and by the idea of glory. Louis XIV., according to his account, notwithstanding all the misfortunes he had brought upon the nation, was still beloved on account of the eclat of his victories, and the magnificence of his court. The battle of Rosbach had brought about the Revolution. Louis XVIII. totally mistook the character of the French in supposing, that either by argument or by reasoning, or indulging them with a free constitution, he could induce them to sink into a state of peaceful industry. He insisted that the Duke of Wellington's presence at Paris was an insult on the French nation; that very strong discord prevailed in the country, and that the king had but few friends, either in the army or among the people. Perhaps the King might try to get rid of a part of the army by sending them to St. Domingo, but that, he observed, would be soon seen through; he himself had made a melancholy trial, with the loss of 30,000 men, which had proved the inutility of such expeditions.

He then checked himself, and endeavoured to show that he had no personal feeling or expectation from the revolutions he foretold. "I am a deceased man," he said; "I was born a soldier; I have mounted a throne; I have descended from it; I am prepared for any fate. They may transport me to a distant shore, or they may put me to death here; I will spread my bosom open to the poniard. When merely General Buonaparte, I had property of my own acquiring—I am now deprived of all."

On another occasion he described the ferment in France, which he said he had learned from the correspondence of his guards with their native country, and so far forgot the character of a defunct person, as to say plainly, that the present disaffection would break out with all the fury of the former revolution, and require his own resurrection. "For *then*," he added, "the sovereigns of Europe will soon find it necessary, for their own repose, to call on ME to tranquillize matters."

This species of conversation was perhaps the best which could have been adopted, to conceal his secret purpose from the

British commissioner. Sir Niel Campbell, though not without entertaining suspicions, judged it, upon the whole unlikely that he meditated any thing eccentric, unless a tempting opening should present itself on the part of France or Italy.

Napoleon held the same species of language to others as well as the British resident. He was affable, and even cordial (in appearance,) to the numerous strangers whom curiosity led to visit him; spoke of his retirement as Dioclesian might have done in the gardens of Salonica; seemed to consider his political career as ended, and to be now chiefly anxious to explain such passages of his life as met the harsh construction of the world. In giving free and easy answers to those who conversed with him, and especially to Englishmen of rank, Buonaparte found a ready means of communicating to the public such explanations concerning his past life, as were best calculated to serve his wishes. In these he palliated, instead of denying, the scheme of poisoning his prisoners in Syria, the massacre at Jaffa, the murder of the Duke d'Enghien, and other enormities. An emperor, a conqueror, retired from war, and sequestered from power, must be favourably listened to by those who have the romantic pleasure of hearing him plead his own cause. Milder editions of his measures began to be circulated in Europe, and, in the curiosity to see and admire the captive sovereign, men forgot the ravages which he had committed while at liberty.

As the winter approached, a change was discernible in Napoleon's manners and habits. The alterations which he had planned in the island no longer gave him the same interest; he renounced, from time to time, the severe exercise in which he had at first indulged, used a carriage rather than his horse, and sunk occasionally into fits of deep contemplation, mingled with gloomy anxiety.

PECUNIARY DIFFICULTIES

He became also subjected to uneasiness, to which he had hitherto been a stranger, being that arising from pecuniary inconveniences. He had plunged into expenses with imprudent eagerness, and without weighing the amount of his resources against the cost of the proposed alterations. The ready money which he brought from France seems to have been soon exhausted, and to raise supplies, he commanded the inhabitants of his island to pay up, in the month of June, the contributions of the last year. This produced petitions, personal solicitations, and discontent. It was represented to him, that so poor were the inhabitants of the island, in consequence of want of sale for their wine for months past, that they would be driven to the most extreme straits if the requisition should be persisted in. In some of the villages, the tax-gatherers of the Emperor were resisted and insulted. Napoleon, on his side, sent part of his troops to quarter upon the insurgent peasantry, and to be supported by them at free cost, till the contributions should be paid up.

Thus, we recognise, in the government of this miniature state, the same wisdom, and the same errors, by which Buonaparte won and lost the empire of the world. The plans of improvements and internal ameliorations which he formed, were probably very good in themselves, but he proceeded to the execution of that which he had resolved with too much and too reckless precipitation; too much of a determination to work his own pleasure, and too little concern for the feelings of others.

The compositions proving a weak resource, as they were scarce to be extracted from the miserable islanders, Napoleon had recourse to others, which must have been peculiarly galling to a man of his haughty spirit. But as his revenue, so far as tangible, did not exceed 300,000 francs, and his expenditure amounted to at least a million, he was compelled to lower the allowances of most of his retinue; to reduce the wages of the miners to one-fourth; to raise money by the sale of the provisions laid up for the garrisons; nay, even by selling a train of brass artillery to the Duke of Tuscany. He disposed also of some property—a large house which had been used as a barrack, and he went the length of meditating the sale of the Town-house at Porto Ferrajo.

We have said, that Napoleon's impatience to execute whatever plans occurred to his fertile imagination, was the original cause of these pecuniary distresses. But they are not less to be imputed to the unfair and unworthy conduct of the French ministry. The French administration were, of all others, most intimately bound in conscience, honour, and policy, to see the treaty of Fontainbleau, as forming the footstool by which Louis XVIII. mounted his restored throne, distinctly observed towards Napoleon. The sixth article of that treaty provides an annuity, or revenue of two millions five hundred thousand francs, to be registered on the Great Book of France, and paid without abatement or deduction to Napoleon Buonaparte. This annual provision was stipulated by the maréchals, Macdonald and Ney, as the price of Napoleon's resignation, and the French ministers could not refuse a declaration of payment without gross injustice to Buonaparte, and at the same time a severe insult to the allied powers. Nevertheless, so far from this pension being paid with regularity, we have seen no evidence that Napoleon ever received a single remittance to account of it. The British resident observing how much the Ex-Emperor was harassed by pecuniary straits, gave it, not once but repeatedly, as his opinion, "that if these difficulties pressed upon him much longer, so as to prevent him from continuing the external show of a court, he was perfectly capable of crossing over to Piombino with his troops, or committing any other extravagance." This was Sir Niel Campbell's opinion on 31st October, 1814, and Lord Castlereagh made strong remonstrances on the subject, although Great Britain was the only power among the allies, who, being no principal party to the treaty of Fontainbleau, might safely have left it to those states who were. The French were not ashamed to defend their conduct on the technical objection, that the pension was not due until the year was elapsed; a defence which we must consider as evasive, since such a pension is of an alimentary nature, the termly payments of which ought to be made in advance. The subject was mentioned again and again by Sir Niel Campbell, but it does not appear that the French administration desisted from a course, which, whether arising from a spirit of mean revenge, or from avarice, or from being themselves embarrassed, was at once dishonourable and impolitic.

Other apprehensions agitated Buonaparte's mind. He feared the Algerine pirates, and requested the interference of England in his behalf. He believed, or affected to believe, that Brulart, the governor of Corsica, who had been a captain of Chouans, the friend of Georges, Pichegru, &c., was sent thither by Louis XVIII.th's administration for the purpose of having him assassinated, and that fitting agents were despatched from Corsica to Elba for that purpose.[71] Above all, he pretended to be informed of a design to dispense with the treaty of Fontainbleau, and to remove him from his place of refuge, to be imprisoned at St. Helena, or St. Lucie. It is not impossible that these fears were not altogether feigned; for though there is not an iota of evidence tending to show that there was reason for believing the allies entertained such an unworthy thought, yet the report was spread very generally through France, Italy, and the Mediterranean, and was encouraged, doubtless, by those who desired once more to place Buonaparte in action.[72] He certainly expressed great anxiety on the subject, sometimes declaring he would defend his batteries to the last; sometimes affecting to believe that he was to be sent to reside in England, a prospect which he pretended not to dislike personally, while he held out sufficient reasons to prevent the course from being adopted. "He concluded," he said, "he should have personal liberty, and the means of removing prejudices entertained against his character, which had not yet been fully cleared up;" but ended with the insinuation, that, by residing in England he would have easier communication with France, where there were four of his party to every single Bourbonist. And when he had exhausted these topics, he returned to the complaints of the hardship and cruelty of depriving him of the society of his wife and child.

While Buonaparte, chafed by poverty, and these other subjects of complaint, tormented too by the restlessness of a mind impatient

---

[71] Buonaparte had particular reason to dread Brulart. This Chouan chief had been one of the numbers who laid down their arms on Napoleon assuming the Consulate, and who had been permitted to reside at Paris. A friend of Brulart, still more obnoxious than himself, was desirous of being permitted to return from England, to which he had emigrated. He applied to Napoleon through Brulart, who was directed by the Emperor to encourage his friend to come over. Immediately on his landing in France, he was seized and executed. Brulart fled to England in grief and rage, at being made the means of decoying his friend to death. In the height of his resentment he wrote to Napoleon, threatening him with death by his hand. The recollection of this menace alarmed Buonaparte, when he found Brulart so near him as Corsica.

[72] Even Sir Niel Campbell said to Napoleon, "The newspapers say you are to be sent to St. Helena."—"Nous verrons cela," was the reply.—*Memorable Events*, p. 268.

of restraint, gave vent to expressions which excited suspicion, and ought to have recommended precaution, his court began to assume a very singular appearance, quite the opposite of that usually exhibited in the courts of petty sovereigns upon the continent. In the latter there is an air of antiquated gravity, which pervades the whole establishment, and endeavours to supply the want of splendour, and of real power. The heavy apparatus designed for the government of an independent state, is applied to the management of a fortune not equal to that of many private gentlemen; the whole course of business goes slowly and cumbrously on, and so that appearances are maintained in the old style of formal grandeur, the sovereign and his counsellors dream neither of expeditions, conquest, nor any other political object.

The Court of Porto Ferrajo was the reverse of all this. Indeed, the whole place was, in one sense, deserving of the name of Cosmopoli, which Napoleon wished to impose on it. It was like the court of a great barrack, filled with military, gendarmes, police officers of all sorts, refugees of every nation, expectants and dependents upon the court, domestics and adventurers, all connected with Buonaparte, and holding or expecting some benefit at his hand. Rumours of every kind were buzzed about through this miscellaneous crowd, as thick as motes in the sunshine. Suspicious characters appeared and disappeared again, without affording any trace of their journey or object. The port was filled with ships from all parts of Italy. This indeed was necessary to supply the island with provisions, when crowded with such an unusual degree of population; and, besides, vessels of all nations visited Porto Ferrajo, from the various motives of curiosity or speculation, or being compelled by contrary winds. The four armed vessels of Napoleon, and seventeen belonging to the service of the miners, were constantly engaged in voyages to every part of Italy, and brought over or returned to the continent, Italians, Sicilians, Frenchmen, and Greeks, who seemed all active, yet gave no reason for their coming or departure. Dominico Ettori, a monk who had escaped from his convent, and one Theologos, a Greek, were considered as agents of some consequence among this group.

The situation of Sir Niel Campbell was now very embarrassing. Napoleon, affecting to be more tenacious than ever of his dignity, not only excluded the British envoy from his own presence, but even threw obstacles in the way of his visiting his mother and sister. It was, therefore, only from interviews with Napoleon himself that he could hope to get any information, and to obtain these Sir Niel was, as already noticed, obliged to absent himself from the island of Elba occasionally, which gave him an opportunity of desiring an audience, as he went away and returned. At such times as he remained on the island he was discountenanced, and all attention withdrawn from him; but in a way so artful, as to render it impossible for him to make a formal complaint, especially as he had no avowed official character, and was something in the situation of a guest, whose uninvited intrusion has placed him at his landlord's mercy.

Symptoms of some approaching catastrophe could not, however, be concealed from the British resident. Napoleon had interviews with his mother, after which she appeared deeply distressed. She was heard also to talk of three deputations which he had received from France. It was besides accounted a circumstance of strong suspicion, that discharges and furloughs were granted to two or three hundred of Napoleon's Old Guard, by the medium of whom, as was too late discovered, the allegiance of the military in France was corrupted and seduced, and their minds prepared for what was to ensue. We cannot suppose that such a number of persons were positively intrusted with the secret; but every one of them was prepared to sound forth the praises of the Emperor in his exile, and all entertained and disseminated the persuasion, that he would soon appear to reclaim his rights.

At length Mariotti, the French consul at Leghorn, and Spannoki, the Tuscan governor of that town, informed Sir Niel Campbell that it was certainly determined at Elba, that Buonaparte, with his guards, should embark for the continent. Sir Niel was at Leghorn when he received this intelligence, and had left the Partridge sloop of war to cruize round Elba. It was naturally concluded that Italy was the object of Napoleon, to join with his brother-in-law Murat, who was at that time, fatally for himself, raising his banner.

ESCAPES FROM ELBA

On the 25th of February [1815,] the Partridge having come to Leghorn, and fetched off Sir Niel Campbell, the appearance, as the vessel approached Porto Ferrajo on her return, of the national guard on the batteries, instead of the crested grenadiers of the Imperial guard, at once apprized the British resident of what had happened. When he landed, he found the mother and sister of Buonaparte in a well-assumed agony of anxiety about the fate of their Emperor, of whom they affected to know nothing, except that he had steered towards the coast of Barbary. They appeared extremely desirous to detain Sir Niel Campbell on shore. Resisting their entreaties, and repelling the more pressing arguments of the governor, who seemed somewhat disposed to use force to prevent him from re-embarking, the British envoy regained his vessel, and set sail in pursuit of the adventurer. But it was too late; the Partridge only obtained a distant sight of the flotilla, after Buonaparte and his forces had landed.

The changes which had taken place in France, and had encouraged the present most daring action, form the subject of the next chapter.

Chapter LXXXIII

Retrospect—Restoration of the Bourbons displeasing to the Soldiery, but satisfactory to the People—Terms favourable to France granted by the Allies—Discontent about the manner of conceding the Charter—Other grounds of dissatisfaction—Apprehensions lest the Church and Crown Lands should be resumed—Resuscitation of the Jacobin faction—Increased Dissatisfaction in the Army—The Claims of the Emigrants mooted in the Chamber of Delegates—Maréchal Macdonald's Proposal—Financial Difficulties—Restriction on the Press—Reflections on this subject.

We must now look back to the re-establishment of the Bourbons upon the throne in 1814, an event which took place under circumstances so uncommon as to excite extravagant expectations of national felicity; expectations, which, like a premature and profuse display of blossom, diminished the chance of the fruit ripening, and exasperated the disappointment of over sanguine hopes. For a certain time all had been gay and rose-coloured. The French possess more than other nations the art of enjoying the present, without looking back with regret on the past, or forward to the future with unfavourable anticipations. Louis XVIII., respectable for his literary acquirements, and the practice of domestic virtues, amiable also from a mixture of *bonhommie*, and a talent for saying witty things, was received in the capital of his kingdom with acclamations, in which the soldiers alone did not cordially join. They indeed appeared with gloomy, sullen, and discontented looks. The late imperial, now royal guard, seemed, from the dark ferocity of their aspect, to consider themselves rather as the captives who were led in triumph, than the soldiers who partook of it.

But the higher and middling classes in general, excepting those who were direct losers by the dethronement of Napoleon, hailed with sincere satisfaction the prospect of peace, tranquillity, and freedom from vexatious exactions. If they had not, as they could hardly be supposed to have, any personal zeal for the representatives of a family so long strangers to France, it was fondly hoped the absence of this might be supplied by the unwonted prospect of ease and security which their accession promised. The allied monarchs, on their part, did every thing to favour the Bourbon family, and relaxed most of the harsh and unpalatable conditions which they had annexed to their proposed treaty with Buonaparte; as if to allow the legitimate heir the credit with his people of having at once saved their honour, and obtained for them the most advantageous terms.

The French readily caught at these indulgences, and, with the aptitude they possess of accommodating their feelings to the moment, for a time seemed to intimate that they were sensible of the full advantage of the change, and were desirous to make as much of it as they possibly could. There is a story of a French soldier in former times, who, having insulted his general in a fit of intoxication, was brought before him next morning, and interrogated, whether he was the person who had committed the offence. The accused replied *he* was not, for that the impudent rascal had gone away before four in the morning—at which hour the culprit had awaked in a state of sobriety. The French people, like the arch rogue in question, drew distinctions between their present and former selves, and seemed very willing to deny their identity. They were no longer, they said, either the Republican French, who had committed so many atrocities in their own country, or the Imperial French, who had made such devastation in other nations; and God forbid that the sins of either should be visited upon the present regenerate race of royalist Frenchmen, loyal to their native princes, and faithful to their allies, who desired only to enjoy peace abroad and tranquillity at home.

These professions, which were probably serious for the time, backed by the natural anxiety of the monarch to make, through his interest with the allied powers, the best terms he could for his country, were received as current without strict examination. It seemed that Buonaparte on his retirement to Elba, had carried away with him all the offences of the French people, like the scapegoat, which the Levitical law directed to be driven into the wilderness, loaded with the sins of the children of Israel. There was, in all the proceedings of the allied powers, not only moderation, but a studied delicacy, observed towards the feelings of the French, which almost savoured of romantic generosity. They seemed as desirous to disguise their conquest, as the Parisians were to conceal their defeat. The treasures of art, those spoils of foreign countries, which justice loudly demanded should be restored to their true owners, were confirmed to the French nation, in order to gratify the vanity of the metropolis. By a boon yet more fatal, announced to the public in one of those moments of romantic, and more than questionable generosity, which we have alluded to, the whole French prisoners of war in the mass, and without inquiry concerning their principles, or the part they were likely to take in future internal divisions, were at once restored to the bosom of their country. This was in fact treating the French nation as a heedless nurse does a spoiled child, when she puts into its hands the knife which it cries for. The fatal consequences of this improvident indulgence appeared early in the subsequent year.

THE RESTORATION

The Senate of Napoleon, when they called the Bourbons to the throne, had not done so without making stipulations on the part of the nation, and also upon their own. For the first purpose they framed a decree, under which they "called to the throne Louis Stanislaus Xavier, brother of the last King," but upon condition of his accepting a constitution of their framing. This assumed right of dictating a constitution, and naming a king for the nation, was accompanied by another provision, declaring the Senate hereditary, and confirming to themselves, and their heirs for ever, the rank, honours, and emoluments, which in Napoleon's time they only enjoyed for life.

The King refused to acknowledge the right of the Senate, either to dictate the terms on which he should ascend a throne, his own by hereditary descent, and to which he had never forfeited his claim; or to engross, as their own exclusive property, the endowments provided to their order by Buonaparte. He, therefore, assumed the crown as the lineal and true representative of him by whom it was last worn; and issued his own constitutional charter as a concession which the spirit of the times demanded, and which he had himself no desire to withhold.

    The objections to this mode of proceeding were, practically speaking, of no consequence. It signified nothing to the people of France, whether the constitution was proposed to the King by the national representatives, or by the King to them, so that it contained, in an irrevocable form, a full ratification of the national liberties. But for the King to have acknowledged himself the creature of the Senate's election would have been at once to recognise every ephemeral tyranny which had started up and fretted its part on the revolutionary stage; and to have sanctioned all subsequent attempts at innovation, since they who make kings and authorities must have the inherent right to dethrone and annul them. It should not be forgotten how the British nation acted on the great occasions of the Restoration and Revolution; recognising, at either crisis, the right of blood to succeed to the crown, whether vacant by the murder of Charles I., or the abdication of James II. In principle, too, it may be observed, that in all modern European nations, the king is nominally the source both of law and justice; and that statutes are promulgated, and sentences executed in his name, without inferring that he has the despotic right either to make the one, or to alter the other. Although, therefore, the constitution of France emanated in the usual form of a royal charter, the King was no more empowered to recall or innovate its provisions, than King John to abrogate those of the English Magna Charta. Monsieur, the King's brother, had promised in his name, upon his solemn entrance to Paris, that Louis would recognise the basis of the constitution prepared by the Senate. This pledge was fully redeemed by the charter, and wise men would have been more anxious to secure the benefits which it bestowed, than scrupulously to cavil on the mode in which they had been conferred.

In fact, Louis had adopted not only the form most consonant to ancient usage, but that which he thought most likely to satisfy both the royalists and the revolutionary party. He ascended the throne as his natural right; and, having done so, he willingly granted to the people, in an irrevocable form, the substantial principles of a free constitution. But both parties were rather displeased at what they considered as lost, than gratified at what they gained by this arrangement. The royalists regarded the constitution, with its concessions, as a voluntary abandonment of the royal prerogative; while the revolutionary party exclaimed, that the receiving the charter from the King as an act of his will was in itself a badge of servitude; and that the same royal prerogative which had granted these privileges, might, if recognised, be supposed to reserve the power of diminishing or resuming them at pleasure. And thus it is, that folly, party-spirit, pride, and passion, can misrepresent the best measures, and so far poison the public mind, that the very granting the object of their desires shall be made the subject of new complaints.

MINISTRY OF LOUIS XVIII

The formation of the ministry gave rise to more serious grounds of apprehension and censure. The various offices of administration were, upon the restoration, left in possession of persons selected from those who had been named by the Provisional Government. All the members of the Provisional State Council were called to be royal ministers of the State. Many of these, though possessed of reputed talents, were men hackneyed in the changes of the Revolution; and were not, and could not be, intrusted with the King's confidence beyond the bounds of the province which each administered.

Talleyrand, minister for foreign affairs, whose talents and experience might have given him claim to the situation of prime minister, was unpopular from his political versatility; and it was judged, after a time, most expedient to send him to the Congress at Vienna, that his diplomatic skill might be employed in arranging the exterior relations of France with the other powers of Europe. Yet the absence of this consummate statesman was of great prejudice to the King's affairs. His having preserved life, distinction, and frequently power, during so many revolutionary changes, proved, according to the phrase of the old Earl of Pembroke, that "he was born of the willow, not of the oak." But it was the opinion of the wisest men in France, that it was not fair, considering the times in which he lived, to speak of his attachment to, or defection from, individuals; but to consider the general conduct and maxims which he recommended relative to the interests of France. It has been truly said, that, after the first errors and ebullitions of republican zeal, if he were measured by this standard, he must be judged favourably. The councils which he gave to Napoleon were all calculated, it was said, for the good of the nation, and so were the measures which he recommended to the King. Much of this is really true; yet, when we think of the political consistency of the Prince of Beneventum, we cannot help recollecting the personal virtue of a female follower of the camp, which consisted in strict fidelity to the grenadier company.

Dupont was promoted to the situation of minister at war, owing, perhaps, to the persecution he had undergone from Buonaparte, in consequence of his surrender at Baylen to the Spaniards. Soult was afterwards called to this important office; how recommended, it would be vain to inquire. When Napoleon heard of his appointment from the English resident, he observed that it would be a wise and good one, if no *patriotic* party should show itself in France; but, if such should arise, he intimated plainly that there would be no room for the Bourbons to rest faith upon Soult's adherence to their cause; and so it proved.

To add still farther to the inconveniences of this state of administration, Louis XVIII. had a favourite, although he had no prime minister. Count Blacas d'Aulps, minister of the household, an ancient and confidential attendant on the royal person during his exile, was understood to be the channel through which the King's wishes were communicated to the other ministers; and his protection was supposed to afford the surest access to the favours of the crown.

Without doing his master the service of a premier, or holding either the power or the responsibility of that high situation, De Blacas had the full share of odium usually attached to it. The royalists, who pressed on him for grants which were in the departments of other ministers, resented his declining to interfere in their favour, as if, having satisfied his own ambition, he had become indifferent to the interest of those with whom he had been a joint sufferer during the emigration. The opposite party, on the other hand, represented Count Blacas as an absolute minister, an emigrant himself, and the patron of emigrants; a royalist of the highest class, and an enemy, of course, to all the constitutional stipulations in favour of liberty. Thus far it is certain, that the unpopularity of M. de Blacas, with all ranks and parties in the state, had the worst possible influence on the King's affairs; and as his credit was ascribed to a blind as well as an obstinate attachment on the part of Louis, the monarch was of course involved in the unpopularity of the minister of the household.

TERMS OF THE TREATY

The terms of the peace, as we have already hinted, had been studiously calculated to recommend it to the feelings of the French people. France was, indeed, stripped of that extended sway which rendered her dangerous to the independence of other European nations, and reduced, generally speaking, to the boundaries which she occupied on the 1st of January 1792. Still the bargain was not harshly driven. Several small additions were left with her on the side of Germany and the Netherlands, and on that of Savoy she had the considerable towns of Chamberri, Annecy, Avignon, with the Venaisson and Mont Belliard, included in her territories.[73] But these concessions availed little; and looking upon what they had lost, many of the French people, after the recollections had subsided of their escape from a dreadful war, were naturally, however unreasonably, disposed to murmur against the reduction of their territories, and to insist that Belgium, at least, should have remained with them. This opinion was encouraged and pressed by the Buonapartists, who considered the cession of that country with the

---

[73] See Treaty of Paris, Art. III. Parl. Debates, vol. xxviii., p. 178.

more evil eye, because it was understood to have been a point urged by England.

Yet if England played a proud, it was also a generous part. She had nothing to stipulate, nothing of which to demand restitution, for she had sustained no territorial loss during the whole period of hostilities. The war, which had nearly ruined most other nations, had put Britain in possession of all the colonies of France, and left the latter country neither a ship nor a port in the East or West Indies; and, to sum the whole, it was not in the power of united Europe to take from England by force any one of the conquests which she had thus made. The question therefore, only was, what Britain was voluntarily to cede to an enemy who could give her no equivalent, excepting the pledge to adopt better principles, and to act no longer as the disturber of Europe. The cessions were such in number and amount, as to show that England was far above the mean and selfish purpose of seeking a colonial monopoly, or desiring to destroy the possibility of commercial rivalry. All was restored to France, excepting only Tobago and the Mauritius.

These sacrifices, made in the spirit of peace and moderation, were not made in vain. They secured to Britain the gratitude and respect of other states, and, giving to her councils that character of justice and impartiality which constitutes the best national strength, they placed her in a situation of more influence and eminence in the civilized world than the uncontrolled possession of all the cotton-fields and sugar-islands of the east and west could ever have raised her to. Still, with respect to France in particular, the peace was not recommended by the eminence to which it had raised England. The rivalry, so long termed national, and which had been so carefully fostered by every state paper or political statement which Buonaparte had permitted to be published, rankled even in generous and honourable minds; and so prejudiced are the views of passion, that by mistaking each other's national feelings, there were many Frenchmen induced to believe that the superiority attained by Great Britain was to a certain degree an insult and degradation to France.

Every thing, indeed, which ought to have soothed and gratified the French people, was at last, by irritated feelings and artful misrepresentation, converted into a subject of complaint and grievance.

The government of Napoleon had been as completely despotic as it could be rendered in a civilized country like France, where public opinion forbade its being carried to barbaric extreme. On the contrary, in the charter, France was endowed with most of the elementary principles of a free and liberal constitution. The King had adopted, in all points of a general and national tendency, the principles proposed in the rejected constitutional act of the Senate.

The Chamber of Peers and Chamber of Deputies were the titles applied to the aristocratical and popular branches of the constitution, instead of the Senate and Legislative body. Their public duties were divided something like those of the Houses of Peers and Commons in England. The independence of the judicial order was recognised, and the military were confirmed in their rank and revenues. The Chamber of Peers was to be nominated by the King, with power to his Majesty to create its members for life, or hereditary, at his pleasure. The income of the suppressed Senate was resumed, and vested in the crown, excepting confiscated property, which was restored to the lawful owners. The Catholic religion was declared to be that of the State, but all other Christian sects were to be protected. The King's authority was recognised as head of the army, and the power of making peace and war was vested in him exclusively. The liberty of the press was established, but under certain restraints. The conscription was abolished—the responsibility of ministers recognised; and it may be said, in general, that a constitution was traced out, good so far as it went, and susceptible of receiving the farther improvements which time and experience might recommend. The charter[74] was presented to the Legislative Body by the King in person, [June 4,] with a speech, which announced, that the principles which it recognised were such as had been adopted in the will of his unfortunate brother, Louis XVI.[75]

---

[74] See Annual Register, vol. lvi., p. 420.
[75] See *ante*, vol. i.

Yet, though this charter contained a free surrender of great part of the royal rights which the old race of Bourbons had enjoyed, as well as of all the arbitrary power which Napoleon had usurped, we have seen that it was unacceptable to an active and influential party in the state, who disdained to accept security for property and freedom under the ancient forms of a feudal charter, and contended that it ought to have emanated directly from the will of the Sovereign People. We have no hesitation in saying, that this was as reasonable as the conduct of a spoiled child, who refuses what is *given* to him, because he is not suffered to *take* it; or the wisdom of an hungry man, who should quarrel with his dinner, because he does not admire the shape of the dish in which it is served up.

This is the common-sense view of the subject. If the constitution contained the necessary guarantees of political freedom and security of life and property; if it was to be looked to as the permanent settlement and bulwark of the liberties of France, and considered as a final and decided arrangement, liable indeed to be improved by the joint consent of the sovereign, and the legal representatives of the subject, but not to be destroyed by any or all of these authorities, it was a matter of utter unimportance, whether the system was constructed in the form of a charter granted by the King, or that of conditions dictated to him by the subject. But if there was to be a retrospect to the ephemeral existence of all the French constitutions hitherto, excepting that under which Buonaparte had enthralled the people, then perhaps the question might be entertained, whether the feudal or the revolutionary form was most likely to be innovated; or, in other words, whether the conditions attached to the plan of government now adopted, was most likely to be innovated upon by the King, or by the body who represented the people.

Assuming the fatal doctrine, that the party in whose name the conditions of the constitution are expressed, is entitled to suspend, alter, or recall them, sound policy dictated, that the apparent power of granting should be ascribed to the party least able and willing to recall or innovate upon the grant which he had made. In this view of the case, it might be reckoned upon that the King, unsupported, unless by the Royalists, who were few in number, unpopular from circumstances, and for the present divested, excepting nominally, of the great instrument of achieving despotic power, the undisputed command, namely, of the army, would be naturally unwilling to risk the continuance of his authority by any attempt to innovate upon those conditions, which he had by his own charter assured to the people. On the contrary, conditions formed and decreed by the Senate of Buonaparte, might on the popular party's resuming the ascendency, be altered or recalled by the chambers with the same levity and fickleness which the people of France, or at least those acting as their representatives, had so often displayed. To give permanence to the constitution, therefore, it was best it should emanate from the party most interested in preserving it, and least able to infringe it; and that undoubtedly, as France stood at the time, was the sovereign. In Great Britain, the constitution is accounted more secure, because the King is the source of law, of honour, and of all ministerial and executive power; whilst he is responsible to the nation through his ministers, for the manner in which that power is exercised. An arrangement of a different kind would expose the branches of the legislature to a discordant struggle, which ought never to be contemplated as possible.

The zealous liberalists of France were induced, however, to mutiny against the name under which their free constitution was assigned them, and to call back Buonaparte, who had abolished the very semblance of freedom, rather than to accept at the hands of a peaceful monarch, the degree of liberty which they themselves had acquired. The advantages which they gained will appear in the sequel.

Thus setting out with varying and contradictory opinions of the nature and origin of the new constitution, the parties in the state regarded it rather as a fortress to be attacked and defended, than as a temple in which all men were called to worship.

PARTIES IN FRANCE

The French of this period might be divided into three distinct and active parties—Royalists; Liberals of every shade, down to

Republicans; and Buonapartists. And it becomes our duty to say a few words concerning each of these.

The Royalists, while they added little real strength to the King by their numbers, attracted much jealous observation from their high birth and equally high pretensions; embroiled his affairs by their imprudent zeal; embittered his peace by their just and natural complaints; and drew suspicion on his government at every effort which he made to serve and relieve them. They consisted chiefly of the emigrant nobles and clergy.

The former class were greatly reduced in number by war and exile; insomuch, that to the House of Peers, consisting of one hundred and seventy, and upwards, the ancient nobles of France supplied only thirty. The rest were the fortunate maréchals and generals, whom the wars of the Revolution had raised to rank and wealth; and the statesmen, many of whom had attained the same station by less honourable means of elevation. The old noblesse, after their youth had been exhausted, their fortunes destroyed, and their spirits broken, while following through foreign countries the adverse fortunes of the exiled Bourbons, beheld the restoration, indeed, of the monarchy, but were themselves recalled to France only to see their estates occupied, and their hereditary offices around the person of the monarch filled, by the fortunate children of the Revolution. Like the disappointed English cavaliers, they might well complain that though none had wished more earnestly for the return of the legitimate prince, yet none had shared so little in the benefits attending it. By a natural, and yet a perverse mode of reasoning, the very injuries which the nobility had sustained, rendered them the objects of suspicion to the other ranks and parties of the state. They had been the companions of the King's exile, were connected with him by the ties of friendship, and had near access to his person by the right of blood. Could it be in nature, it was asked, that Louis could see their sufferings without attempting to relieve them; and how could he do so in the present state of France, unless at the expense of those who occupied or aspired to civil and military preferment, or of those who had acquired during the Revolution the national domains which those nobles once possessed? Yet the alarm was founded rather on suspicion than on facts. Of the preferment of emigrants in the army, we shall speak hereafter; but in the civil departments of the state, few of the old noblesse obtained office. To take a single example, in the course of eleven months there were thirty-seven prefects nominated to the departments, and the list did not comprehend a single one of those emigrants who returned to France with Louis; and but very few of those whose exile had terminated more early. The nobles felt this exclusion from royal favour, and expressed their complaints, which some, yet more imprudently, mingled with threatening hints, that their day of triumph might yet arrive. This language, as well as the air of exclusive dignity and distance which they affected, as if, the distinction of their birth being all that they had left to them, they were determined to enforce the most punctilious deference to that, was carefully remarked and recorded against the King.

The noblesse were supposed to receive particular encouragement from the princes of the blood, while, upon the whole, they were rather discouraged than brought forward or distinguished by Louis, who, as many of them spared not to say, was disposed to act upon the ungenerous maxim of courting his enemies, and neglecting those who could not upon principle become any thing save his friends. They did not, perhaps, make sufficient allowance for the great difficulties which the King incurred in governing France at so critical a period.

THE CLERGY

The state of the Clergy is next to be considered. They were, generally speaking, sincerely attached to the King; and had they been in possession of their revenues, and of their natural influence upon the public mind, their attachment would have been of the utmost consequence. But without this influence, and without the wealth, or at least the independence, on which it partly rests, they were as useless, politically speaking, as a key which does not fit the lock to which it is applied. This state of things, unfortunate in many respects, flowed from a maxim adopted during the Revolution, and followed by Buonaparte, who had his reasons for fearing the influence of the clergy. "We will not put down the ecclesiastical establishment by force; we will starve it to death." Accordingly, all grants and bequests to the Church had been limited and qualified by so many conditions and restrictions, as to intercept that mode of acquisition so fruitful in a Catholic country; while, on the other hand, the salary allowed by the State to each officiating curate was only five hundred livres (£26, 16s. 8d.) yearly. No doubt each community were permitted to subscribe what they pleased in addition to this miserable pittance; but in France, when the number of those who care for no religion at all, and of those whose zeal will not lead them the length of paying for it, is deduced, the remainder will afford but a small list of subscribers. The consequence was, that at the period of the restoration, many parishes were, and had been for years, without any public worship. Ignorance had increased in an incalculable degree. "We are informed," was the communication from Buonaparte to one of his prefects, "that dangerous books are distributed in your department."—"Were the roads sown with them," was the answer returned by the prefect, "your Majesty need not fear their influence; we have not a man who would or could read them."—When we add to this the relaxed state of public morals, the pains taken in the beginning of the Revolution to eradicate the sentiments of religion, and render its professors ridiculous, and the prevalence of the military character, so conspicuous through France, and so unfavourable to devotion; and when it is further remembered that all the wealth of the Church had fallen into the hands of the laity, which were fast clenched to retain it, and trembling at the same time lest it should be wrested from them—the reader may, from all these causes, form some notion of the low ebb of religion and of the Church in France.

The disposition of the King and Royal Family to restore the formal observances of the Romish Church, as well as to provide the suitable means of educating in future those designed for the ministry, and other religious institutions, excited among the Parisians a feeling of hatred and contempt. It must be owned, also, that though the abstract motive was excellent, there was little wisdom in attempting to bring back the nation to all those mummeries of Popish ceremonial, which, long before the Revolution, only subsisted through inveterate custom, having lost all influence on the public mind.

This general feeling was increased by particular events. Alarming tumults took place, on the subject of enforcing a rule unworthy of Christianity and civilisation, by which theatrical performers are declared in a constant state of excommunication. The rites of sepulture being refused to Mademoiselle Raucour, an actress, but a person of decent character and morals, occasioned a species of insurrection, which compelled from the government an order for interring her with the usual forms.[76]

The enforcing of the more regular observation of the Sabbath, an order warranted alike by religion and good morals, gave also great offence to the inhabitants of the capital. The solemn obsequies performed for the death of Louis XVI. and his unfortunate queen, when their remains were transferred from their hasty grave to the royal mausoleum at Saint Denis, a fraternal action, and connected with the forms of the Catholic Church—was also construed to the King's prejudice, as if, by the honour paid to these poor relics, he had intended to mark his hatred of the Revolution, and his recollection of the injuries he had sustained from it.[77] Some honours and attention bestowed on the few surviving chiefs of La Vendée, were equally the subject of misrepresentation. In short, whatever Louis XVIII. did, which had the least appearance of gratifying those who had lost all for his sake, was accounted an act of treason against freedom and the principles of the Revolution.

None of the circumstances we have noticed had, however, so much effect upon the public feeling as the fear which prevailed, that Louis, in his veneration for religion and its members, might be led to form some scheme of resuming the Church lands, which, having been confiscated by the decrees of the National Assembly, were now occupied by a host of proprietors, who watched, with vigilant jealousy, incipient measures, which they feared might end in resumption of their property. Imprudent priests added to this distrust and jealousy, by denunciations against those who held Church lands, and by refusing to grant them absolution unless they made restitution or compensation for them. This distrust spread far wider than among the actual proprietors of national domains. For if

---

[76] Savary, tom. iv., p. 235.
[77] Annual Register, vol. lvi., p. 51.

these were threatened with resumption of the property they had acquired under authority of the existing government for the time, it was most probable that the divine right of the clergy to a tithe of the produce of the earth, might next have been brought forward—a claim involving the interest of every landholder and farmer in France to a degree almost incalculable.

It is plain, from what we have stated, that the Royalist party, whether lay or clerical, were so little in a condition to be effectually serviceable to the King in the event of a struggle, that while their adherence and their sufferings claimed his attachment and gratitude, every mark which he afforded them of those feelings was calculated to render his government suspected and unpopular.

THE JACOBINS

Whilst the Royalists rather sapped and encumbered than supported the throne to which they adhered, their errors were carefully pointed out, circulated, and exaggerated, by the Jacobin, or as they called themselves, the Patriotic party. This faction, small in numbers, but formidable from their audacity, their union, and the dreadful recollection of their former power and principles, consisted of ex-generals, whose laurels had faded with the Republic; ex-ministers and functionaries, whose appointments and influence had not survived the downfall of the Directory; men of letters, who hoped again to rule the state by means of proclamations and journals; and philosophers, to whose vanity or enthusiasm abstract principles of unattainable liberty, and undesirable equality, were dearer than all the oceans of blood, and extent of guilt and misery, which they had already cost, and were likely again to occasion. It cannot be denied, that, in the discussion of the original rights of humanity, and constitutions of society, several of this party showed distinguished talent, and that their labours were calculated to keep up a general love of liberty, and to promote inquiry into the principles upon which it is founded. Unfortunately, however, their theoretical labours in framing constitutions diverted their attention from the essential points of government, to its mere external form, and led them, for example, to prefer a republic, where every species of violence was practised by the little dictator of the day, to a limited monarchy, under which life, person, and property, were protected. The chiefs of this party were men of that presumptuous and undoubting class, who, after having failed repeatedly in political experiments, were as ready as ever again to undertake them, with the same unhesitating and self-deceptive confidence of success. They were never satisfied even with what they themselves had done; for as there is no end of aiming at an ideal perfection in any human establishment, they proceeded with alterations on their own work, as if what Butler says of religion had been true in politics, and that a form of government

"was intended For nothing else but to be mended."

Danger did not appal the sages of this school. Many of them had been familiar with, and hardened to the perils of the most desperate revolutionary intrigues, by their familiar acquaintance with the springs which set each in motion, and were ready to recommence their desperate labours with as little forethought as belongs to the labourers in a powder-mill, which has exploded ten times during their remembrance, and destroyed the greater number of their comrades. In the character of these self-entitled philosophers and busy agitators, vanity as well as egotism were leading principles. The one quality persuaded them, that they might be able, by dint of management, to avert danger from themselves; and the other rendered them indifferent respecting the safety of others.

During the government of Buonaparte, this Jacobinical party was repressed by a strong hand. He knew, by experience of every sort, their restless, intriguing, and dangerous disposition. They also knew and feared his strength, and his unscrupulous use of it. The return of the Bourbons called them into life, like the sun which thaws the frozen adder; but it was only to show how they hated the beams which revived them. The Bourbon dynasty, with all the remembrances it combined, seemed to this faction the very opposite to their favourite Revolution; and they studied with malignant assiduity the degree of liberty afforded by the national charter, not in order to defend or to enjoy it, but to discover how it might be made the vantage-ground for overthrowing both the throne and the constitution.

Carnot and Fouché, formidable names, and revolutionists from their youth upward, were the ostensible leaders of this active party, and most of the surviving revolutionists rallied under their standards. These agitators had preserved some influence over the lees of the people, and were sure to find the means of augmenting it in the moment of popular commotion. The rabble of a great town is democratical and revolutionary by nature; for their vanity is captivated with such phrases as the sovereignty of the people, their sense of poverty and licentious fury tempted by occasion for uproar, and they regard the restraints of laws and good order as their constant and natural enemies. It is upon this envenomed and corrupted mass of evil passions that the experimental philosophers of the Revolution have always exercised their chemical skill. Of late, however, the intercourse between the philosophers of the Revolution and this class of apt and docile scholars had been considerably interrupted. Buonaparte, as we have hinted, restrained with a strong hand the teachers of the Revolutionary school; while, by the eclat of his victories, his largesses, and his expensive undertakings, in which many workmen were employed, he debauched from them great part of their popular disciples, who may be said, with the inconsequence and mutability belonging to their habits, principles, and temper, to have turned imperialists, without losing their natural aptitude to become Jacobins again on the next tempting opportunity.

BUONAPARTISTS—THE ARMY

The party of Imperialists or Buonapartists, if we lay the army out of view, was small and unimportant. The public functionaries, whom the King had displaced from the situations of emolument which they held under the Emperor—courtiers, prefects, commissioners, clerks, and commissaries—whose present means and future hopes were cut off, were of course disobliged and discontented men, who looked with a languishing eye towards the island of Elba. The immediate family connexions, favourites, and ministers of the late Emperor, confident in the wealth which most of them had acquired, and resenting the insignificance to which they were reduced by the restoration of the Bourbons, lent to this party the activity which money, and the habit of political intrigue, can at all times communicate. But the real and tremendous strength of the Buonapartists lay in the attachment of the existing army to its abdicated general. This was the more formidable, as the circumstances of the times, and the prevailing military character of the French nation, had raised the soldiers from their proper and natural character of servants of the state, into a distinct deliberative body, having interests of their own, which were in their nature incompatible with those of the commonwealth; since the very profession of arms implies an aptitude to a state of war, which, to all other ranks in the state, the army itself excepted, may indeed be a necessary and unavoidable evil, but never can be a real advantage.

The King could not be accused of neglecting to cultivate the affections, soothe the prejudices, and gratify the wishes of the army. The fact is, that the unprecedented difficulties of his situation forced him to study how to manage by flattery, and by the most imprudent indulgences and favours, the only part of his subjects, who, according to the rules of all well-governed states, ought to be subjected to absolute authority. Every effort was made to gratify the feelings of the troops, and the utmost exertions were made to remount, re-establish, and re-clothe them. Their ranks were augmented by upwards of 150,000 prisoners of war, whose minds were in general actuated by the desire of avenging the dishonour and hardship of their defeat and captivity, and whose presence greatly increased the discontent as well as the strength of the French army.

While the King cultivated the affections of the common soldiers with very imperfect success, he was more fortunate in attaching to himself the maréchals, whom he treated with the utmost respect and kindness. They were gratified by his attentions, and, having most of them some recent reason to complain of Napoleon, it is possible, that had they possessed absolute, or even very extensive interest with the army, that disturbance in the state of the nation which ensued, could not possibly have taken place. But while Napoleon had preserved towards the maréchals the distance at which a sovereign keeps subjects, he was often familiar with the inferior officers and soldiers, and took care to keep himself in their eye, and occupy their attention personally. He desired that his generals should resemble the hilt of the sword, which may be changed at pleasure, while the army was the blade itself, and retained the same temper, notwithstanding such partial alteration. Thus, the direct and personal interest of the Emperor superseded, in the soldier's bosom, all attachment to his lieutenants.

THE ARMY—STATE OF PARTIES

It would be wasting time to show reasons, why the French army should have been attached to Napoleon. They could not be supposed to forget the long career of success which they had pursued under his banner, the pensions granted in foreign countries which were now retrenched, and the licensed plunder of their Emperor's unceasing campaigns. At present, they conceived the King proposed to reduce their numbers so soon as he could with safety, and imagined their very existence was about to be at stake.

Nor was it only the selfish interests of the army which rendered them discontented. The sense of honour, as it was called, or rather the vanity of military ascendency and national aggrandisement, had been inspired by Buonaparte into all classes of his subjects, though they were chiefly cherished by his companions in arms. According to their opinion, the glory of France had risen with Buonaparte, and sunk with him for ever; not, as they fondly contended, through the superior force of the enemy, but by the treachery of Marmont, and the other generals whom Napoleon trusted. This sentiment passed from the ranks of the soldiers into other classes of society, all of which are in France deeply susceptible of what is represented to them as national glory; and it was again echoed back to the soldiers from fields, from workshops, from manufactories. All began to agree, that they had received the Bourbons from the hands of foreign conquerors; and that the King's reign had only commenced, because France had been conquered, and Paris surrendered. They remembered that the allies had declared the restoration of the ancient family was combined with the restriction of France within the ancient limits; and that, accordingly, the first act of Monsieur, as lieutenant of the kingdom, had been to order the surrender of upwards of fifty fortresses beyond the frontiers, which Buonaparte, it was supposed, would have rendered the means of re-acquiring the conquests, of which fortune or treachery had for a time bereft him. The meanest follower of the camp affected to feel his share in the national disgrace of losing provinces, to which France had no title save that of military usurpation. The hope that the government would at least endeavour to reconquer Belgium, so convenient for France, and which, as they contended, fell within her natural boundaries, served for a time to combat these feelings; but when it was perceived plainly that the government of France neither could nor would engage in external war, for this or any other object, the discontent of the army became universal, and they might be pronounced ripe for any desperate enterprise.

Among the soldiers, the late Imperial Guards were distinguished for their sullen enmity to the new order of things, and deemed themselves insulted at the guard of the King's person being committed to a body of household troops, selected as approved loyalists. The army were also much disgusted, that the decorations of the Legion of Honour had been distributed with a profusion, which seemed intended to diminish its value. But the course of promotion was the deepest source of discontent. The princes of the blood-royal had been early declared colonels-general by the King; and the army soon discovered, or supposed they discovered, that under their auspices the superior ranks of the army were likely to be filled by the emigrant nobility, whose military service was considered as having been continued, while they were in attendance upon the King during his exile. The most indecent competition was thus excited between those whose claims were founded on their devoted attachment to the House of Bourbon, and those who had borne arms against that family, but still in the service of France. The truth is, that the derangement of the finances, and the jealousy of the ministers, each of whom claimed the exclusive patronage of his own department, left the King no means so ready for discharging his debts of gratitude, and affording the means of subsistence to his ancient friends and adherents, as by providing for them in the army.

The measure, though perhaps unavoidable, was in many respects undesirable. Old men, past the age of service, or young men who had never known it, were, in virtue of these claims, placed in situations, to which the actual warriors conceived they had bought a title by their laurels and their scars. The appearance of the superannuated emigrants, who were thus promoted to situations ill-suited to age and infirmity, raised the ridicule and contempt of Buonaparte's soldiers, while the patrician haughtiness, and youthful presumption, of the younger nobles, excited their indignation. The agents and friends of Buonaparte suffered not these passions to cool. "There is a plot of the royalists against you," was incessantly repeated to the regiments upon which these new officers were imposed. "The Bourbons cannot think themselves safe while those who shared the triumphs of Napoleon have either honour or existence. Your ranks are subjected to the command of dotards, who have never drawn a sword in battle, or who have served only in the emigrant bands of Condé, or among the insurgent Chouans and Vendéans. What security have you against being disbanded on a day's notice? And if the obligations of the government to you bind them, as it would seem, so slightly, will you consider yours to them as of a stricter description?" Such insinuations, and such reasoning, inflamed the prejudices of the army. Disaffection spread generally through their ranks; and, long before the bold attempt of Napoleon, his former soldiery were almost universally prepared to aid him in the recovery of his power.

The state of active political parties in France, we have thus described; but, as is usual, the mass of the population were somewhat indifferent to their principles, unless in moments of excitation. Parties in a state are to the people at large what the winds are to the ocean. That which predominates for the time, rolls the tide in its own direction; the next day it is hushed, and the waves are under a different influence. The people of France at large were averse to the Republicans or Jacobins. They retained too awful an impression of the horrors of the tyranny exercised by these political fanatics, to regard them otherwise than with terror. They were as little Buonapartists; because they dreaded the restless temper of him who gave name to this faction, and saw that while he was at the head of the French government, the state of war must be perpetual.

They could not be termed Royalists, for they comprehended many with whom the name of Bourbon had lost its charms; and a very large proportion of the country had their fortune and prosperity so intimately connected with the Revolution, that they were not disposed to afford any countenance to the re-establishment of the monarchy on its ancient footing.

Upon the whole, this class of Frenchmen who may be called moderates, or constitutionalists, and who contained the great bulk of the men of property, substance, and education, hoped well of the King's government. His good sense, humanity, love of justice, moderation, and other valuable qualities, recommended him to their esteem, and they thought his restoration might be considered as the guarantee of a lasting peace with the other nations of Europe. But they dreaded and deprecated that counter revolutionary *reaction*, as the established phrase was, which was regarded as the object of the princes of the blood, the nobility, and the clergy. The property of many of the constitutionalists was vested in national domains, and they watched with doubt and fear every step which the emigrant nobility and clergy seemed disposed to take for recovery of their former rights.

On this subject the moderate party were sensitively jealous, and the proceedings which took place in the Chamber of Deputies threw striking light on the state of the public mind. We must, therefore, turn the reader's attention in that direction.

A petty riot, concerning precedence, had arisen in a church called Durnac, between the seigneur of the parish, and the mayor of the commune. The mayor brought the affair before the Chamber of Deputies by a violent petition, in which he generalized his complaint against the whole body of emigrants, whom he accused of desiring to place themselves above the constituted authorities, and to treat France as a conquered country. The Chamber, 20th November, 1814, treated the language of the petition as calumnious, and the squabble as unworthy of their notice. But the debate called forth expressions which intimated a suspicion that there existed a dark and secret system, which tended to sow the seeds of discord and anarchy among the citizens, and to resuscitate pretensions incompatible with the laws. "It was," said the member[78] who made this statement, "important to impress every class of Frenchmen with the great idea, that there was no safety for France, for the King, for every member of society, but in the maintenance of those constitutional principles on which were founded the laws for protecting the whole."

EMIGRANT-CLAIMS

The claims of the emigrants for restoration of their forfeited property, were, abstractedly, as just and indubitable as that of the King to the throne. But the political considerations in which they were involved, rendered any general attempt to enforce those claims the sure signal of civil war; a civil war almost certain to end in a second expatriation, both of the royal family and their followers. In this dilemma, government seems to have looked anxiously for some means of compromise which might afford relief to the emigrants, without innovating on that article of the charter which ratified the sale of national domains. M. Ferrand brought forward in the Chamber of Delegates, a motion [Dec. 3] for the restoration of such estates of emigrants as yet remained unsold. But this involved a question respecting the rights of the much more numerous class whose property had been seized upon by the state, and disposed of to third parties, to whom it was guaranteed by the charter. Since these gentlemen could not be restored *ex jure*, to their estates, as was proposed towards their more fortunate brethren, they had at least a title to the price which had been surrogated in place of the property, of which price the nation had still possession.

These proposals called forward M. Durbach, who charged Ferrand with the fatal purpose of opening the door on the vast subject of national domains. "Already," continued the orator, "the two extremities of the kingdom have resounded with the words of the minister, as with the claps which precede the thunderbolt. The effect which they have produced has been so rapid and so general, that all civil transactions have been at once suspended. A general distrust and excessive fear have caused a stagnation, the effects of

---

[78] M. Dumolard. See Moniteur, Nov. 24.

which even the royal treasury has felt. The proprietors of national property can no longer sell or mortgage their estates. They are suddenly reduced to poverty in the very bosom of wealth. Whence arises this calamity? The cause of it is the declaration of the minister, that the property they possess does not legally belong to them. For this is, in fact, the consequence of his assertion, that 'the law recognises in the emigrants a right to property which always existed.'"

The celebrated Maréchal Macdonald, a friend at once of monarchy and freedom, of France and the Bourbons, undertook to bring forward a plan for satisfying the emigrants, as far as the condition of the nation permitted; and giving, at the same time, some indemnity for the pensions assigned by Buonaparte to his veteran soldiers, which, during his reign, had been paid from countries beyond the verge of France, until after the retreat from Moscow, when they ceased to be paid at all. The maréchal's statement of the extent of the sale of the national domains, shows how formidable the task of undoing that extensive transference of property must necessarily have been; the number of persons directly or indirectly interested in the question of their security, amounting to nine or ten millions. "Against this Colossus," continued the maréchal, "whose height the eye cannot measure, some impotent efforts would affect to direct themselves; but the wisdom of the King has foreseen this danger, even for the sake of those imprudent persons who might have exposed themselves to it." He proceeded, in a very eloquent strain, to eulogize the conduct of the emigrants, to express respect for their persons, compassion for their misfortunes, honour for their fidelity, and proceeded to observe, that the existence of these old proprietors, as having claims on the estates which had been acquired by others, placed them in a situation which ought not to exist. He therefore proposed that the nation should satisfy the claims of these unfortunate gentlemen, if not in full, at least upon such terms of composition as had been applied to other national obligations. Upon this footing, he calculated that an annuity of twelve millions of livres yearly, would pay off the claims of the various emigrants of all descriptions. He next drew a picture of the distressed veteran soldiers; pensioners of the state who had been reduced to distress by the discontinuance of their pensions, bought with their blood in a thousand battles. Three millions more of livres he computed as necessary to discharge this sacred obligation.[79]

There was wisdom, manliness, and generosity in the plan of Maréchal Macdonald; and, could it have been carried into decisive execution, it would have greatly appeased the fears and jealousies of the proprietors of national domains, and shown an impartiality betwixt the claims of the emigrants and those of the army, which ought to have conciliated both. Unhappily, funds were awanting, and the royal government, so far from being able to incur a new expense of fifteen millions yearly, was not in a condition to discharge the various demands upon them, without continuing the oppressive tax of *Les droits réunis*.

It is, indeed, on the subject of finance and taxation, that almost all revolutions among civilized nations have been found to hinge; and there is scarce any judging how long actual oppression may be endured, so long as it spares the purse of individuals, or how early a heavy tax, even for the most necessary objects, will excite insurrection. Without the heavy taxation of the Spaniards, the Dutch would scarcely have rebelled against them; it was imposts which fired the blood of the Swiss against the Austrians; without the stamp-act the American Revolution might have been long postponed; and but for the disorder of the French finances, Louis XVI. need never have summoned together the National Assembly. France was now again agitated by one of those fever fits, which arise from the sensitiveness of the subject's purse.

FRENCH FINANCE

A report on the state of the public finances, by the Abbé de Montesquieu, had given a singular instance of Buonaparte's deceptive policy. Annual expositions of national receipt and expenditure had been periodically published since he assumed the reins of government, which were, to outward appearance,

---

[79] Moniteur, Dec. 7 and 10; Montgaillard, tom. viii., p. 84; Annual Register, vol. lvi., p. 63.

unchallengeably accurate; and as they seemed to balance each other, afforded the fair prospect that, the revenues of the state being realized, the expenses could not fall into arrear. But in reality, a number of extraordinary expenses were withheld from the view of the public, while, on the other hand, the produce of the taxes was over-estimated. Thus the two budgets of 1812, and 1813, upon close examination, exhibited a deficit of upwards of 312 millions of livres,[80] or thirteen millions sterling. Buonaparte was not ignorant of this fact, but concealed it from the eyes of the nation, in hopes of replacing it, as in his more successful days, by foreign tribute, and, in the meantime, supplied himself by the anticipation of other funds; as an unfaithful book-keeper makes up a plausible balance to meet the eye of his master, and covers his peculations by his dexterity in the use of ciphers. Upon the whole, the debts of France appeared to have increased in the course of thirteen years to the extent of 1,645,469,000 francs, or more than sixty-eight millions and a half of sterling money.

These financial involvements accorded ill with the accomplishment of an unfortunate and hasty promise of Monsieur,[81] that the severe and pressing taxes called *les droits réunis* should be abolished, which had been made when he first entered France, and while, betwixt hope and despair, he essayed every inducement for the purpose of drawing adherents to the royal cause. On the other hand, the King, upon ascending the throne, had engaged himself, with perhaps too much latitude, to pay all the engagements which the state had contracted under the preceding government. To redeem both these pledges was impossible, for without continuing this very obnoxious and oppressive tax, the crown could not have the means of discharging the national debt. A plan was in vain proposed by Jalabert to replace this oppressive excise by a duty on wines; the motion was referred to a committee of the Chamber of Representatives, but the substitution seems to have been found impossible. Louis naturally made the promise of his brother give way to his own more deliberate engagement. But it is not the less true, that by continuing to levy *les droits réunis*, many, not otherwise

---

[80] Moniteur, July 13; Montgaillard, tom. viii., p. 52.
[81] "No conqueror, no war, no conscription, no consolidated taxes!"—*Proclamation on entering France.*

disinclined to the royal government than as it affected their purses, were enabled to charge the King with breach of faith towards his subjects, and would listen to no defence upon a topic on which few people are disposed to hear reason against their own interest.

THE PRESS

There remained yet another subject of alarm and dread, to excite the minds not only of those who were desirous of revolution, or, according to the Roman phrase, *cupidi novarum rerum*; but of others, who, devotedly attached to the welfare of France, desired to see her enjoy, under the sway of a legitimate monarch, the exercise of national liberty. They had the misfortune to see that liberty attacked in the point where it is most sensitive, namely, by imposing restraints upon the public press.

Buonaparte had made it part of his system to keep this powerful engine in his own iron hand, well aware that his system of despotism could not have subsisted for six months, if his actions had been exposed to the censure of the public, and his statements to contradiction and to argument. The Bourbons having unloosed the chain by which the liberty of the press was confined, the spirit of literary and political controversy rushed out with such demoniacal violence, as astonished and terrified those who had released it from confinement. The quantity of furious abuse poured out against the Bourbons, might have authorised the authors to use the words of Caliban—

"You taught me language, and my profit on't Is—I know how to curse."[82]

Eager to repress the spirit which displayed itself so unequivocally, a motion was made on the 4th of July, 1814,[83] for establishing a censorship upon pamphlets under a certain length, and placing all journals and newspapers under the direction of government.

---

[82] Tempest, act i., scene ii.
[83] Moniteur, July 6; Annual Register, vol. lxvi., p. 56.

This important subject was discussed with great manliness and talent in the Assembly; but it is one of the many political maxims which the British receive as theorems, that, without absolute freedom of the public press (to be exercised always on the peril of such as misuse it,) there can neither be enlightened patriotism nor liberal discussion; and that, although the forms of a free constitution may be preserved where this liberty is restricted, they will soon fail to have the necessary beneficial effects in protecting the rights of the community and the safety of individuals. The liberty of the press affords a channel through which the injured may challenge his oppressor at the bar of the nation; it is the means by which public men may, in case of misconduct, be arraigned before their own and succeeding ages; it is the only mode in which bold and undisguised truth can press its way into the cabinets of monarchs; and it is the privilege, by means of which he, who vainly lifts his voice against the corruptions or prejudices of his own time, may leave his counsels upon record as a legacy to impartial posterity. The cruelty which would deafen the ear and extinguish the sight of an individual, resembles, in some similar degree, his guilt, who, by restricting the freedom of the press, would reduce a nation to the deafness of prejudice, and the blindness of ignorance. The downfall of this species of freedom, as it is the first symptom of the decay of national liberty, has been in all ages followed by its total destruction, and it may be justly pronounced that they cannot exist separately; or, as the elegiac poet has said of his hero and the country to which he belonged—

"Ille tibi superesse negat; tu non potes illi."

We must own, at the same time, that as no good comes to us unmixed with evil, the unlimited freedom of the press is attended with obvious inconveniencies, which, when a nation is in a certain state of excitation, render the exercise of it peculiarly dangerous. This is especially the case when a people, as then in France, are suddenly released from a state of bondage, and disposed, "like youthful colts broke loose," to make the most extravagant use of their liberty. With minds unprepared for discussion; with that degree of political misinformation which has done this age more dire mischief than absolute ignorance itself could have effected; subject to be influenced by the dashing pamphleteer, who soothes their prevailing passions, as the orations of their popular demagogues soothed those of the Athenians—it has been the opinion of many statesmen, that to withhold from such a nation the freedom of the press, is a measure justifiable alike by reason and necessity. "We proportion," say these reasoners, "liberty to the power of enjoying it. The considerate and the peaceful we suffer to walk at liberty, and armed, if their occasions require it; but we restrain the child, we withhold weapons from the ruffian, and we fetter the maniac. Why, therefore," they ask, "should a nation, when in a state of fever, be supplied, without restriction, with the indulgences which must necessarily increase the disorder?" Our answer is ready—that, granting the abuse of the liberty of the press to exist in the most fearful latitude (and we need not look to France for examples,) the advantages derived from it are so inestimable, that, to deprive us of them, would be as if an architect should shut up the windows which supply light and air to a mansion, because a certain proportion of cold, and perhaps of rain, may force their way in at the aperture. Besides, we acknowledge ourselves peculiarly jealous of the sentiments of the members of every government on this delicate subject. Their situation renders them doubtful friends to a privilege, through which alone they can be rendered amenable to the public for the abuse of their power, and through which also they often see their just and temperate exercise of authority maligned and misconstrued. To princes, also, the license of the press is, for many reasons distasteful. To put it under regulation, seems easy and desirable, and the hardship on the community not greater (in their account) than the enforcing of decent respect and subordination— of the sort of etiquette, in short, which is established in all courts, and which forbids the saving, under any pretext, what may be rude or disagreeable to a sovereign, or even unpleasing to be heard. Under these circumstances, and in the present state of France, men rather regretted than wondered that the ministers of Louis XVIII. were disposed to place restrictions on the freedom of the press, or that they effected their purpose of placing the light of nations under a censorial bushel.

But the victory thus obtained brought additional evils on the government. The law was evaded under various devices; the works which it was intended to intercept, acquired circulation and importance from the very circumstance of their being prohibited; while the whole tenor of the measure impressed many who had otherwise been friendly to the Bourbon family, with distrust respecting their designs upon the national liberty.[84]

Thus split into parties, oppressed with taxes, vexed with those nameless and mysterious jealousies and fears which form the most dangerous subjects of disagreement, because alike incapable of being explained and confuted, France was full of inflammable materials; and the next chapter will show that there was not wanting a torch to give kindling to them.

---

[84] Montgaillard, tom. viii., pp. 65, 79; Mad. de Staël, tom. iii., p. 70.

Chapter LXXXIV

Carnot's Memorial on Public Affairs—Fouché joins the Jacobins—Projects of that Party; which finally joins the Buonapartists—Active Intrigues—Congress of Vienna—Murat, alarmed at its proceedings, opens an intercourse with Napoleon—Plans of the Conspirators—Buonaparte's Escape from Elba—He lands at Cannes—Is joined at Grenoble, by 3000 Troops—Halts at Lyons, appoints a Ministry, and issues several Decrees—Dismay of the Government—Intrigues of Fouché—Treachery of Ney—Revolt of the Royal Army at Melun—The King leaves Paris and Buonaparte arrives there—His Reception.

Carnot has been repeatedly mentioned in this history as having been the associate and colleague of Robespierre during the whole Reign of Terror. His admirers pretend, that charging himself only with the conduct of the foreign war, he left to his brethren of the Committee of Public Safety the sole charge of those measures, for which no human language affords epithets of sufficient horror, through which they originally rose to power, and by which they maintained it. According to these fond advocates, their hero held his course through the Reign of Terror, unsullied by a bloody spot, as Arethusa rolled her waters through the ocean without mingling with its waves; and the faith of most readers will swallow the ancient miracle as easily as the modern. Carnot, however, had the independence of spirit to oppose Napoleon's seizure of the throne, and remained in obscurity until 1814, when he employed his talents as an engineer in defence of Antwerp. He gave in, late and reluctantly, his adherence to the restoration, and was confirmed in his rank of inspector-general of engineers. But this did not prevent him from being extremely active in conspiring the downfall of the monarch to whose allegiance he had submitted himself, and who afforded him subsistence and rank.

CARNOT'S MEMORIAL

Carnot gave his opinion upon public affairs in a "Memorial to his most Christian Majesty," made public in October, 1814, which was at once an apology for the Jacobin party, and a direct attack on the reigning dynasty. This document we must necessarily consider at some length, as it conveys the ostensible reasons on which the author, and many thousands besides, having in their anxious consideration the interests of the freedom of France, thought these interests would be best provided for by destroying the sway of a mild and somewhat feeble monarch, whose reign was identified with peace and tranquillity, in order to recall to the throne an absolute sovereign, ruling on military principles only, and whose first step under the canopy of state must necessarily be followed by war with all Europe.

In this singular, and, as it proved, too effective production, every fault committed by the restored family is exaggerated; and they, with the nobles, their personal adherents, are, under a thin and contemptuous veil of assumed respect towards the King, treated alike as fools, who did not understand how to govern France, and as villains, who meditated her ruin. The murder of the King is, with irony as envenomed as unjust, stated to have been occasioned, not by the violence and cruelty of his persecutors, but by the pusillanimity of his nobility, who first provoked the resentment of the nation, and then fled from the kingdom, when, if they had loved their sovereign, they should have rallied around him.[85] This plea, in the mouth of a regicide, is as if one of a band of robbers should impute an assassination not to their own guilty violence, but to the cowardice of the domestics of the murdered, by whom that violence might have been resisted.

No one also knew better than Carnot by what arts Louis XVI. was induced by degrees to abandon all means of defence which his situation afforded him, and to throw himself upon the sworn faith

---

[85] "Did you not abandon him in the most cowardly manner, when you saw him in that danger into which you had precipitated him? Was it not your duty to form a rampart round him with your bodies? Was it the business of Republicans to defend with their tongues him whom you had not the courage to defend with your swords?"—*Memorial*, pp. 11-14.

and allegiance of those by whom he was condemned to death. As whimsical and unlogical were the examples and arguments referred to by Carnot in support of the condemnation of Louis. Cicero, it seems, says in his Offices, "We hate all those we fear, and we wish for the death of those we hate." On this comprehensive ground, Carnot vindicates the orator's approbation of the death of Cæsar, notwithstanding the clemency of the usurper; "and Cato, indeed" (continues the colleague of Robespierre,) "went farther, and did not think it possible there should be a good king." Of course, not Louis XVI. alone, but all monarchs, might be justly put to death in Carnot's estimation; because they are naturally the objects of fear to their subjects—because we hate those we fear—and because, according to the kindred authority of Shylock, no man "hates the thing he would not kill."[86] The doctrine of regicide is said to be confirmed in the Old Testament; families were massacred—monarchs proscribed—intolerance promulgated, by the ministers of a merciful deity: Wherefore, then, should not the Jacobins put Louis XVI. to death? If it was alleged, that the persons of Kings were inviolable by the laws of all civil governments, those of usurpers certainly were not so protected; and what means were there, said Carnot, for positively distinguishing between an usurper and a legitimate king?—The difficulty of making such a distinction was no doubt a sufficient vindication of the judges of Louis XVI.

Trash like this had scarce been written since the club-room of the Jacobins was closed. But the object of Carnot's pamphlet was not to excuse a deed (which he would probably have rather boasted of as laudable,) but by the exaggerations of his eloquence, and the weight of his influence with the public, to animate the fury of the other parties against the Bourbons and their adherents. The King was charged with having been ungrateful to the call of the nation—(a call which assuredly he would never have heard but for the cannon of the allies,)—with having termed himself King by the grace of God—with resigning Belgium when Carnot was actually governor of Antwerp—with preferring Chouans, Vendéans, emigrants, Cossacks, or Englishmen, to the soldiers whose victories had kept him in exile, and in consequence of whose defeat alone he had regained the throne of his fathers. The emigrants are

---

[86] Merchant of Venice, act iv., scene i.

represented as an exasperated, yet a contemptible faction. The people, it is said, care little about the right of their rulers—about their quarrels—their private life, or even their political crimes, unless as they affect themselves. All government, of course, has its basis in popular opinion; but, alas! in actual history, "the people are only regarded," says M. Carnot, "as the victims of their chiefs; we witness nothing but the contest of subjects for the private interest of their princes—kings, who are themselves regicides and parricides—and priests who incite mankind to mutual slaughter. The eye can but repose on the generous efforts of some brave men who consecrate themselves to the deliverance of their fellow-countrymen; if they succeed, they are called heroes—if they fail, they are traitors and demagogues." In this and other passages, the author plainly intimated what spirits were at work, and what was the object of their machinations. The whole pamphlet was designed as a manifesto to the French public, darkly, yet distinctly, announcing the existence of a formidable conspiracy, the principles on which its members proceeded, and their grounds for expecting success.

CARNOT'S MEMORIAL—FOUCHÉ

Carnot himself affected to say, that the Memorial was only designed for circulation among his private connexions.[87] But it would not have answered the intended purpose had it not been printed and dispersed with the most uncommon assiduity. Small carts traversed the *boulevards,* from which it was hawked about among the people, in order to avoid the penalties which booksellers and stationers might have incurred by dealing in an article so inflammatory. Notwithstanding these evasions, the printers and retailers of this diatribe were prosecuted by government; but the *Cour d'Instruction* refused to confirm the bill of indictment, and this failure served to encourage the Jacobin faction. The official proceedings, by which the ministers endeavoured to suppress the

---

[87] The following letter appeared in the Journal des Débats of the 7th October:—"Sir, I have been for more than a month in the country, eleven leagues from Paris. On my return to the capital, I learn that there has been circulated, in my name, a pamphlet, entitled, 'Memorial addressed to the King,' &c. I declare, that the Memorial has become printed without my consent, and contrary to my intention.—Carnot." This statement is gravely repeated in the Edinburgh Review, vol. xxiv., p. 187.

publication, irritated rather than intimidated those who took interest in it. It argued, they said, at once a timorous and a vindictive spirit to oppress the inferior agents in an alleged libel, while the ministers dared not bring to trial the avowed author.[88] In this unquestionably they argued justly; for the measures corresponded with that paltry policy, which would rather assail the liberty of the press, than bring to fair trial and open punishment those by whom it is misused.

It would have been as impossible for Fouché to have lived amid such a complicated scene of political intrigue, without mingling in it, as for the sparks to resist flying upwards. He was, however, ill-placed for the character he desired to act. After having lent Buonaparte his aid to betray and dethrone the Directors, he had long meditated how to dethrone and betray Buonaparte, and substitute in his place a regency, or some form of government under which he might expect to act as prime minister. In this undertaking, he more than once ran the peril of life, and was glad to escape with an honourable exile. We have already stated that he had missed the most favourable opportunity for availing himself of his political knowledge, by his absence from Paris when it was taken by the allies. Fouché endeavoured, however, to obtain the notice of the restored monarch and his government, and to render his services acceptable to Louis. When the celebrated Revolutionist appeared in the antechamber on his first attendance at court, he observed a sneer on the countenance of some Royalists who were in waiting, and took the hint to read them a lesson, showing, that a minister of police, even when he has lost his office, is not a person to be jested with. "You, sir," said he to a gentleman, "seem proud of the lilies with which you are adorned. Do you recollect the language you held respecting the Bourbon family some time since in such a company?—And you, madam," he continued, addressing a lady, "to whom I gave a passport to England, may perhaps wish to be reminded of what then passed betwixt us on the subject of Louis XVIII." The laughers were conscience-struck, and Fouché was introduced into the cabinet.

The plan which Fouché recommended to the King was, as might have been expected, astucious and artificial in a high degree.

---

[88] Journal des Débats, Oct. 11.

He advised the King to assume the national cockade and three-coloured flag; to occupy the situation of chief of the Revolution. This, he said, would be the same sacrifice by Louis XVIII. as the attending on the mass by Henry IV.—He might have added, it was the sacrifice actually made by Louis XVI., who lost his life in requital.—What Fouché aimed at by this action is evident. He desired to place the King in a situation where he must have relied exclusively on the men of the Revolution, with whom he could not have communicated save by the medium of the Duc d'Otranto, who thus would become prime minister at the first step. But in every other point of view, the following that advice must have placed the King in a mean and hypocritical attitude, which must have disgusted even those whom it was adopted to conciliate.

By assuming the colours of the Revolution, the King of France must necessarily have stained himself with the variation of each of its numerous changes. It is true that the Revolution had produced many excellent improvements in France, affecting both the theory and the practice of government. These the sovereign was bound carefully to preserve for the advantage of the nation. But while we are grateful for the advantages of increased health and fertility that may follow a tornado, and treasure up the valuable things which an angry ocean may cast upon the shore, none but a blinded heathen worships the tempest, or sacrifices to the furious waves. The King, courting the murderers of his brother, could inspire, even in them, nothing save disgust at his hypocrisy, while it would justly have forfeited the esteem and affection, not of the royalists alone, but of all honest men.

Further to recommend himself to the Bourbons, Fouché addressed a singular epistle to Napoleon, in which he endeavoured to convince him, that the title of sovereign, in the paltry islet of Elba, did not become him who had possessed an immense empire. He remarked to Napoleon, that the situation of the island was not suitable to his purpose of retirement, being near so many points where his presence might produce dangerous agitation. He observed that he might be accused, although he was not criminal, and do evil without intending it, by spreading alarm. He hinted that the King of France, however determined to act with justice, yet might be instigated by the passions of others to break through that rule. He told the Ex-Emperor of France, that the titles which he retained were only calculated to augment his regret for the loss of real sovereignty. Nay, that they were attended with positive danger, since it might be thought they were retained only to keep alive his pretensions. Lastly, he exhorted Napoleon to assume the character of a private individual, and retire to the United States of America, the country of Franklin, Washington, and Jefferson.[89]

Fouché could scarcely expect that this monitory epistle should have much effect upon his once imperial master; he knew human nature and Buonaparte too well. But as it might tell to advantage with the royal family, he sent a copy of it to Monsieur, with a corresponding commentary, the object of which was to point out (what, indeed, circumstances had made evident,) that the tranquillity of the countries and sovereigns of Europe could never be secured while Napoleon remained in his present condition, and that his residence in the isle of Elba was to France what Vesuvius is to Naples.[90] The practical inference to be derived from this was, that a gentle degree of violence to remove the person of Napoleon would have been a stroke of state policy, in case the Ex-Emperor of France should not himself have the patriotic virtue to remove himself to America. The honourable and generous prince, to whom Fouché had addressed himself, had too noble a mind to adopt the hint; and this attempt to ingratiate himself with the Bourbon family entirely failed. But plotting was Fouché's element; and it seems to have signified little to him whom he had for partners, providing he had a stake in the political game. He retired to his country-house, and engaged himself with his old friends of the Jacobin party, who were not a little glad to avail themselves of his extensive acquaintance with all the ramifications of political intrigue.

PROJECTS OF THE JACOBINS

It was the policy of this party to insist upon the faults of the royal family, and enlarge on their prejudices against the men and

---

[89] Fouché, tom. ii., p. 232.
[90] Fouché, tom. ii., p. 235.

measures of that period when France was successful in foreign war, against the statesman who directed, and the soldiers who achieved her gigantic enterprises. The King, they said, had suffered misfortune without having learned wisdom; he was incapable of stepping beyond the circle of his Gothic prejudices; France had received him from the hand of foreign conquerors, surrounded by an emaciated group of mendicant nobles, whose pretensions were as antiquated and absurd as their decorations and manners. His government went to divide, they alleged, the French into two classes, opposed to each other in merits as in interests;—the emigrants, who alone were regarded by Louis as faithful and willing subjects; and the rest of the nation, in whom the Bourbons saw, at best, but repentant rebels. They asserted, that, too timid as yet to strike an open blow, the King and his ministers sought every means to disqualify and displace all who had taken any active share in the events of the Revolution, and to evade the general promise of amnesty. Under pretext of national economy, they were disbanding the army, and removing the officers of government—depriving thus the military and civil servants of France of the provision which their long services had earned. Louis, they said, had insulted the glory of France, and humiliated her heroes, by renouncing the colours and symbols under which twenty-five years had seen her victorious; he had rudely refused a crown offered to him by the people, and snatched it as his own right by inheritance, as if the dominion of men could be transferred from father to son like the property of a flock of sheep. The right of Frenchmen to choose their own ruler was hereditary and imprescriptible; and the nation, they said, must assert it, or sink to be the contempt, instead of being the pride at once and dread of Europe.

Such was the language which nettled, while it alarmed, the idle Parisians, who forgot at the moment that they had seen Napoleon take the crown from the altar at Notre Dame, and place it on his own head, with scarcely an acknowledgment to God, and not the shadow of any towards the nation. The departments were assailed by other arts of instigation. The chief of these was directed to excite the jealousy, so often alluded to, concerning the security of the property of national domains. Not content with urging everywhere that a revocation of the lands of the Church and emigrants was impending over the present proprietors, and that the clergy and nobles did not even deign to conceal their hopes and designs, a singular device was in many instances practised to enforce the belief of such assertions. Secret agents were despatched into the departments where property was advertised for sale. These emissaries made inquiries as if in the character of intending purchasers, and where the property appeared to have been derived from revolutionary confiscation, instantly objected to the security as good for nothing, and withdrew their pretended offers;—thus impressing the proprietor, and all in the same situation, with the unavoidable belief, that such title was considered as invalid, owing to the expected and menaced revocation of the Bourbon government.

It is generally believed that Buonaparte was not originally the object designed to profit by these intrigues. He was feared and hated by the Jacobin party, who knew what a slender chance his iron government afforded of their again attempting to rear their fantastic fabrics, whether of a pure republic, or a republican monarchy. It is supposed their eyes were turned in preference towards the Duke of Orleans. They reckoned probably on the strength of the temptation, and they thought, that in supplanting Louis XVIII., and placing his kinsman in his room, they would obtain, on the one hand, a king who should hold his power by and through the Revolution, and, on the other, that they would conciliate both foreign powers and the constitutionalists at home, by choosing their sovereign out of the family of Bourbon. The more cautious of those concerned in the intrigue, recommended that nothing should be attempted during the life of the reigning monarch; others were more impatient and less cautious; and the prince alluded to received an intimation of their plan in an unsigned billet, containing only these words—"We will act it without you; we will act it in spite of you; we will act it FOR you;"[91] as if putting it in his choice to be the leader or victim of the intended revolution.

JACOBINS—BUONAPARTISTS

---

[91] "Nous le ferons sans vous; nous le ferons malgré vous; nous le ferons pour vous."—S.

The Duke of Orleans was too upright and honourable to be involved in this dark and mysterious scheme; he put the letter which he had received into the hands of the King, and acted otherwise with so much prudence, as to destroy all the hopes which the revolutionary party had founded upon him. It was necessary to find out some other central point. Some proposed Eugene Beauharnois as the hero of the projected movement;[92] some projected a provisional government; and others desired that the republican model should be once more adopted. But none of these plans were likely to be favoured by the army. The cry of *Vive la Republique* had become antiquated; the power once possessed by the Jacobins of creating popular commotion was greatly diminished; and although the army was devoted to Buonaparte, yet it was probable that in a civil commotion in which he had no interest, they would follow the maréchals or generals who commanded them, in opposition to any insurrection merely revolutionary. If, on the contrary, the interests of Napoleon were put in the van, there was no fear of securing the irresistible assistance of the standing army. If he came back with the same principles of absolute power which he had formerly entertained, still the Jacobins would get rid of Louis and the charter, the two chief objects of their hatred; the former as a King given by the law, the latter as a law given by the King.

These considerations speedily determined the Jacobin party on a union with the Buonapartists. The former were in the condition of a band of housebreakers, who, unable to force an entrance into the house which they have the purpose to break into, renew their undertaking, and place at their head a brother of the same profession, because he has the advantage of having a crow-bar in his hand. When and how this league was formed—what sanction the Jacobin party obtained that Buonaparte, dethroned as a military despot, was to resume his dignity under constitutional restrictions, we have no opportunity of knowing. But so soon as the coalition was formed, his praises were sung forth on all sides, especially by many who had been, as Jacobins, his most decided enemies; and a

---

[92] "A military party made me a proposal of offering the dictatorship to Eugene Beauharnois. I wrote to him, under the impression that the matter had already assumed a substantial form; but I only received a vague answer. In the interim, all the interests of the Revolution congregated round myself and Carnot, whose memorial to the King had produced a general sensation."—Fouché, tom. i., p. 244.

great part of the French public were disposed to think of Buonaparte at Elba more favourably than Napoleon in the Tuileries. Gradually, even from the novelty and peculiarity of his situation, he began to excite a very different interest from that which attached to the despot who levied so many conscriptions, and sacrificed to his ambition so many millions of victims. Every instance of his activity, within the little circle of his dominions, was contrasted by his admirers with the constitutional inertness of the restored monarch. Excelling as much in the arts of peace as in those of war, it wanted but (they said) the fostering hand and unwearied eye of Napoleon to have rendered France the envy of the universe, had his military affairs permitted the leisure and opportunity which the Bourbons now enjoyed. These allegations, secretly insinuated, and at length loudly murmured, had their usual effects upon the fickle temper of the public; and, as the temporary enthusiasm in favour of the Bourbons faded into indifference and aversion, the general horror of Buonaparte's ambitious and tyrannical disposition began to give way to the recollection of his active, energetic, and enterprising qualities.

This change must soon have been known to him who was its object. An expression is said to have escaped from him during his passage to Elba, which marked at least a secret feeling that he might one day recover the high dignity from which he had fallen. "If Marius," he observed, "had slain himself in the marshes of Minturnæ, he would never have enjoyed his seventh consulate." What was perhaps originally but the vague aspirations of an ardent spirit striving against adversity, became, from the circumstances of France, a plausible and well-grounded hope. It required but to establish communications among his numerous and zealous partisans, with instructions to hold out such hopes as might lure the Jacobins to his standard, and to profit by and inflame the growing discontents and divisions of France; and a conspiracy was almost ready formed, with little exertion on the part of him who soon became its object and its centre.

Various affiliations and points of rendezvous were now arranged to recruit for partisans. The ladies of the Ex-Emperor's court, who found themselves humiliated at that of the King by the preference assigned to noble birth, were zealous agents in these political intrigues, for offended pride hesitates at no measures for obtaining vengeance. The purses of their husbands and lovers were of course open to these fair intriguers, and many of them devoted their jewels to forward the cause of Revolution. The chief of these female conspirators was Hortensia Beauharnois, wife of Louis Buonaparte, but now separated from her husband, and bearing the title of the Duchess of Saint Leu. She was a person of considerable talents, and of great activity and address. At Nanterre, Neuilly, and Saint Leu, meetings of the conspirators were held, and Madame Hamelin, the confidant of the duchess, is said to have assisted in concealing some of the principal agents.

The Duchess of Bassano, and the Duchess of Montebello (widow of Maréchal Lannes,) were warmly engaged in the same cause. At the meetings held in the houses of these intriguing females, the whole artillery of conspiracy was forged and put in order, from the political lie, which does its work if believed but for an hour, to the political song or squib, which, like the fire-work from which it derives its name, expresses love of frolic or of mischief, according to the nature of the materials amongst which it is thrown. From these places of rendezvous the agents of the plot sallied out upon their respective rounds, furnished with every lure that could rouse the suspicious landholder, attract the idle Parisian, seduce the *Ideologue*, who longed to try the experiments of his Utopian theories upon real government, and above all, secure the military—from the officer, before whose eyes truncheons, coronets, and even crowns, were disposed in ideal prospect, to the grenadier, whose hopes only aimed at blood, brandy, and free quarters.

RICHARD LE NOIR

The lower orders of the populace, particularly those inhabiting the two great suburbs of Saint Marceau and Saint Antoine, were disposed to the cause from their natural restlessness and desire of change; from the apprehension that the King would discontinue the expensive buildings in which Buonaparte was wont to employ them; from a Jacobinical dislike to the lawful title of Louis, joined to some tender aspirations after the happy days of liberty and equality; and lastly, from the disposition which the lees of society every where manifest to get rid of the law, their natural curb and enemy. The influence of Richard le Noir was particularly useful to the conspirators. He was a wealthy cotton-manufacturer, who combined and disciplined no less than three thousand workmen in his employment, so as to be ready at the first signal of the conspirators. Le Noir was called by the Royalists Santerre the Second; being said to aspire, like that celebrated suburban brewer, to become a general of Sans Culottes. He was bound to Buonaparte's interest by his daughter having married General Lefebvre Desnouettes, who was not the less the favourite of Napoleon that he had broken his parole, and fled from England when a prisoner of war. Thus agitated like a lake by a subterranean earthquake, revolutionary movements began to show themselves amongst the populace. At times, under pretence of scarcity of bread or employment, tumultuous groups assembled on the terrace of the Tuileries, with clamours which reminded the Duchess D'Angoulême of those that preceded the imprisonment and death of her parents. The police dispersed them for the moment; but if any arrests were made, it was only of such wretches as shouted when they heard others shout, and no efforts were made to ascertain the real cause of symptoms so alarming.

The police of Paris was at this time under the direction of M. D'André, formerly a financier. His loyalty does not seem to have been doubted, but his prudence and activity are very questionable; nor does he seem ever to have been completely master either of the duties of his office, or the tools by which it was to be performed. These tools, in other words, the subordinate agents and officers and clerks, the whole machinery as it were of the police, had remained unchanged since that dreadful power was administered by Savary, Buonaparte's head spy and confidential minister. This body, as well as the army, felt that their honourable occupation was declined in emolument and importance since the fall of Buonaparte, and looked back with regret to the days when they were employed in agencies, dark, secret, and well-recompensed, unknown to a peaceful and constitutional administration. Like evil spirits employed by the spells of a benevolent enchanter, these police officers seem to have served the King grudgingly and unwillingly; to have neglected their duty, when that could be done with impunity; and to have shown that they had lost their activity and omniscience, so soon as embarked in the service of legitimate monarchy.

Under the connivance, therefore, if not with the approbation of the police, conspiracy assumed a more open and daring aspect. Several houses of dubious fame, but especially the Café Montaussier, in the Palais Royal, were chosen as places of rendezvous for the subordinate satellites of the cause, where the toasts given, the songs sung, the tunes performed, and the language held, all bore allusion to Buonaparte's glories, his regretted absence, and his desired return. To express their hopes that this event would take place in the spring, the conspirators adopted for their symbol the violet; and afterwards applied to Buonaparte himself the name of Corporal Violet. The flower and the colour were publicly worn as a party distinction, before it would seem the court had taken the least alarm; and the health of Buonaparte, under the name of Corporal Violet, or Jean d'Epée, was pledged by many a Royalist without suspicion of the concealed meaning.

Paris was the centre of the conspiracy; but its ramifications extended through France. Clubs were formed in the chief provincial towns. Regular correspondences were established between them and the capital—an intercourse much favoured, it has been asserted, by Lavalette, who, having been long director-general of the posts under Buonaparte, retained considerable influence over the subordinate agents of that department, none of whom had been displaced upon the King's return. It appears from the evidence of M. Ferrand, director-general under the King, that the couriers, who, like the soldiers and police officers, had found more advantage under the imperial than under the royal government, were several of them in the interest of their old master. And it is averred, that the correspondence relating to the conspiracy was carried on through the royal post-office, contained in letters sealed with the King's seal, and despatched by public messengers wearing his livery.

Such open demonstrations of treasonable practices did not escape the observation of the Royalists, and they appear to have been communicated to the ministers from different quarters. Nay, it has been confidently stated, that letters, containing information of Napoleon's intended escape, were actually found in the bureau of one minister, unopened and unread. Indeed, each of these official personages seems scrupulously to have intrenched himself within the routine of his own particular department, so that what was only of general import to the whole, was not considered as the business of any one in particular. Thus, when the stunning catastrophe had happened, each endeavoured to shift the blame from himself, like the domestics in a large and ill-regulated family; and although all acknowledged that gross negligence had existed elsewhere, no one admitted that the fault lay with himself. This general infatuation surprises us upon retrospect; but Heaven, who frequently punishes mankind by the indulgence of their own foolish or wicked desires, had decreed that peace was to be restored to Europe, by the extermination of that army to whom peace was a state so odious; and for that purpose it was necessary that they should be successful in their desperate attempt to dethrone their peaceful and constitutional sovereign, and to reinstate the despotic leader, who was soon to lead them to the completion of their destiny, and of his own.

While the royal government in France was thus gradually undermined and prepared for an explosion, the rest of Europe resembled an ocean in the act of settling after a mighty storm, when the partial wrecks are visible, heaving on the subsiding swell, which threatens yet farther damage ere it be entirely lulled to rest.

CONGRESS OF VIENNA

The Congress of representatives of the principal states of Europe had met at Vienna, in order to arrange the confused and complicated interests which had arisen out of so prolonged a period of war and alteration. The lapse of twenty-five years of constant war and general change had made so total an alteration, not merely in the social relations and relative powers of the states of Europe, but in the habits, sentiments, and principles of the inhabitants, that it appeared altogether impossible to restore the original system as it existed before 1792. The continent resembled the wrecks of the city of London after the great conflagration in 1666, when the boundaries of individual property were so completely obliterated and confounded, that the king found himself obliged, by the urgency of the occasion, to make new, and in some degree arbitrary, distributions of the ground, in order to rebuild the streets upon a plan more regular, and better fitted to the improved condition of the age. That which proved ultimately an advantage to London, may perhaps produce similar good consequences to the civilized world, and a better and more permanent order of things may be expected to arise out of that which has been destroyed. In that case, the next generation may reap the advantages of the storms with which their fathers had to contend. We are, however, far from approving of some of the unceremonious appropriations of territory which were made upon this occasion, which, did our limits admit of entering into the discussion, carried, we think, the use of superior force to a much greater extent than could be justified on the principles upon which the allies acted.

Amid the labours of the Congress, their attention was turned on the condition of the kingdom of Naples; and it was urged by Talleyrand, in particular, that allowing the existence of the sovereignty of Murat in that beautiful kingdom, was preserving, at the risk of future danger to Europe, an empire, founded on Napoleon's principles, and governed by his brother-in-law. It was answered truly, that it was too late to challenge the foundation of Murat's right of sovereignty, after having gladly accepted and availed themselves of his assistance, in the war against Buonaparte. Talleyrand, by exhibiting to the Duke of Wellington a train of correspondence[93] between Buonaparte, his sister Caroline, and Murat, endeavoured to show that the latter was insincere, when seeming to act in concert with the allies. The Duke was of opinion, that the letters did not prove treachery, though they indicated what was to be expected, that Murat took part against his brother-in-law and benefactor, with considerable reluctance. The matter was now in agitation before the Congress; and Murat, conceiving his power in danger, seems to have adopted the rash expedient of changing sides once more, and again to have renewed his intercourse with

---

[93] See Parliamentary Debates, vol. xxxi., 1815.

Napoleon. The contiguity of Elba to Naples rendered this a matter of little difficulty; and they had, besides, the active assistance of Pauline, who went and came between Italy and her brother's little court. Napoleon, however, at all times resolutely denied that he had any precise share or knowledge of the enterprise which Murat meditated.

The King of France, in the meanwhile, recalled by proclamation all Frenchmen who were in the Neapolitan service, and directed the title of King Joachim to be omitted in the royal almanack.

Murat, alarmed at this indication of hostile intentions, carried on a secret correspondence with France, in the course of which a letter was intercepted, directed to the King of Naples, from General Excelsman, professing, in his own name and that of others, devoted attachment, and assuring him that thousands of officers, formed in his school and under his eye, would have been ready at his call, had not matters taken a satisfactory turn. In consequence of this letter, Excelsman was in the first place put on half-pay and sent from Paris, which order he refused to obey. Next he was tried before a court-martial, and triumphantly acquitted. He was admitted to kiss the king's hand, and swear to him fidelity *à toutes épreuves*. How he kept his word will presently appear. In the meantime the King had need of faithful adherents, for the nets of conspiracy were closing fast around him.

ESCAPE FROM ELBA

The plot formed against Louis XVIII. comprehended two enterprises. The first was to be achieved by the landing of Napoleon from Elba, when the universal good-will of the soldiers, the awe inspired by his name and character, and the suspicions and insinuations spread widely against the Bourbons, together with the hope of recovering what the nation considered as the lost glory of France, were certain to insure him a general good reception. A second, or subordinate branch of the conspiracy, concerned the insurrection of a body of troops under General L'Allemand, who were quartered in the north-east of France, and to whom was committed the charge of intercepting the retreat of the King and royal family from Paris, and, seizing them, to detain them as hostages at the restored Emperor's pleasure.

It is impossible to know at what particular period of his residence in Elba, Napoleon gave an express consent to what was proposed, and disposed himself to assume the part destined for him in the extraordinary drama. We should suppose, however, his resolution was adopted about that time when his manner changed completely towards the British envoy residing at his little court, and when he assumed the airs of inaccessible and imperial state, to keep at a distance, as an inconvenient observer, Sir Niel Campbell, to whom he had before seemed rather partial. His motions after that time have been described, so far as we have access to know them. It was on Sunday, 26th February, that Napoleon embarked with his guards on board the flotilla, consisting of the Inconstant brig, and six other small vessels, upon one of the most extraordinary and adventurous expeditions that was ever attempted.[94] The force, with which he was once more to change the fortunes of France, amounted but to about a thousand men. To keep the undertaking secret, his sister Pauline gave a ball on the night of his departure, and the officers were unexpectedly summoned, after leaving the entertainment, to go on board the little squadron.

In his passage Napoleon encountered two great risks. The first was from meeting a royal French frigate,[95] who hailed the Inconstant. The guards were ordered to put off their caps, and go down below, or lie upon the deck, while the captain of the Inconstant exchanged some civilities[96] with the commander of the

---

[94] "At this time there was a very pretty cunning little French actress at Elba. Napoleon pretended to be very angry with her, saying she was a spy of the Bourbons, and ordered her out of the island in twenty-four hours. Captain Adye took her in his vessel to Leghorn: Sir Niel Campbell went at the same time; and during this absence, on Sunday the 26th February, a signal gun was fired at four in the afternoon, the drums beat to arms, the officers tumbled what they could of their effects into flour sacks, the men arranged their knapsacks, the embarkation began, and at eight in the evening they were under weigh."—*Memorable Events*, p. 271.
[95] The Zephyr, Captain Andrieu.
[96] "He asked how the Emperor did. Napoleon replied through the speaking trumpet, 'Il se porte à merveille.'"—*Memorable Events*, p. 271.

frigate, with whom he chanced to be acquainted; and being well known in these seas, was permitted to pass on without farther inquiry. The second danger was caused by the pursuit of Sir Niel Campbell, in the Partridge sloop of war, who, following from Elba, where he had learned Napoleon's escape, with the determination to capture or sink the flotilla, could but obtain a distant view of the vessels as they landed their passengers.[97]

This was on the first of March, when Napoleon, causing his followers once more to assume the three-coloured cockade, disembarked at Cannes, a small seaport in the gulf of Saint Juan, not far from Frejus, which had seen him land, a single individual, returned from Egypt, to conquer a mighty empire; had beheld him set sail, a terrified exile, to occupy the place of his banishment; and now again witnessed his return, a daring adventurer, to throw the dice once more for a throne or a grave. A small party of his guard presented themselves before Antibes, but were made prisoners by General Corsin the governor of the place.

Undismayed by a circumstance so unfavourable, Napoleon instantly began his march at the head of scarce a thousand men, towards the centre of a kingdom from which he had been expelled with execrations, and where his rival now occupied in peace an hereditary throne. For some time the inhabitants gazed on them with doubtful and astonished eyes, as if uncertain whether to assist them as friends, or to oppose them as invaders. A few peasants cried *Vive l'Empereur!* but the adventurers received neither countenance nor opposition from those of the higher ranks. On the evening of 2d March, a day and a half after landing, the little band of invaders reached Ceremin, having left behind them their small train of artillery, in order to enable them to make forced marches. As Napoleon approached Dauphiné, called the cradle of the Revolution, the peasants greeted him with more general welcome, but still no proprietors appeared, no clergy, no public functionaries. But they were now near to those by whom the success or ruin of the expedition must be decided.

---

[97] Lord Castlereagh stated, in the House of Commons, 7th April, 1815, that Napoleon was not considered as a prisoner at Elba, and that if he should leave it the allies had no right to arrest him.—*Parl. Deb.*, vol. xxx., p. 426.

GRENOBLE

Soult, the minister at war, had ordered some large bodies of troops to be moved into the country betwixt Lyons and Chamberri, to support, as he afterwards alleged, the high language which Talleyrand had been of late holding at the Congress, by showing that France was in readiness for war. If the maréchal acted with good faith in this measure, he was at least most unfortunate; for, as he himself admits, even in his attempt at exculpation, the troops were so placed as if they had been purposely thrown in Buonaparte's way, and proved unhappily to consist of corps peculiarly devoted to the Ex-Emperor's person.[98] On the 7th of March, the seventh regiment of the line, commanded by Colonel Labédoyère, arrived at Grenoble. He was young, nobly born, handsome, and distinguished as a military man. His marriage having connected him with the noble and loyal family of Damas, he procured preferment and active employment from Louis XVIII. through their interest, and they were induced even to pledge themselves for his fidelity. Yet Labédoyère had been engaged by Cambrone deep in the conspiracy of Elba, and used the command thus obtained for the destruction of the monarch by whom he was trusted.

As Napoleon approached Grenoble, he came into contact with the outposts of the garrison, who drew out, but seemed irresolute. Buonaparte halted his own little party, and advanced almost alone, exposing his breast, as he exclaimed, "He who will kill his Emperor, let him now work his pleasure." The appeal was irresistible—the soldiers threw down their arms, crowded round the general who had so often led them to victory, and shouted *Vive l'Empereur!* In the meanwhile, Labédoyère, at the head of two battalions, was sallying from the gates of Grenoble. As they advanced he displayed an eagle, which, like that of Marius, worshipped by the Roman conspirator, had been carefully preserved

---

[98] "Soult did not betray Louis, nor was he privy to my return and landing in France. For some days, he thought that I was *mad*, and that I must certainly be lost. Notwithstanding this, appearances were so much against him, and without intending it, his acts turned out to be so favourable to my projects, that, were I on his jury, and ignorant of what I know, I should condemn him for having betrayed Louis. But he really was not privy to it."—Napoleon, *Las Cases*, tom. i., p. 343; *O'Meara*, vol. i., p. 386.

to be the type of civil war; at the same time he distributed among the soldiers the three-coloured cockades, which he had concealed in the hollow of a drum. They were received with enthusiasm. It was in this moment that Maréchal de Camp Des Villiers, the superior officer of Labédoyère, arrived on the spot, alarmed at what was taking place, and expostulated with the young military fanatic and the soldiers. He was compelled to retire. General Marchand, the loyal commandant of Grenoble, had as little influence on the troops remaining in the place: they made him prisoner, and delivered up the city to Buonaparte. Napoleon was thus at the head of nearly three thousand soldiers, with a suitable train of artillery, and a corresponding quantity of ammunition. He acted with a moderation which his success could well afford, and dismissed General Marchand uninjured.

When the first news of Napoleon's arrival reached Paris, it excited surprise rather than alarm;[99] but when he was found to traverse the country without opposition, some strange and combined treason began to be generally apprehended. That the Bourbons might not be wanting to their own cause, Monsieur, with the Duke of Orleans, set out for Lyons, and the Duke D'Angoulême repaired to Nismes. The Legislative Bodies, and most of the better classes, declared for the royal cause. The residents of the various powers hastened to assure Louis of the support of their sovereigns. Corps of volunteers were raised both among the Royalists and the Constitutional or moderate party. The most animating proclamations called the people to arms. An address by the celebrated Benjamin Constant, one of the most distinguished of the moderate party, was remarkable for its eloquence. It placed in the most striking light the contrast between the lawful government of a constitutional monarch, and the usurpation of an Attila, or Genghis, who governed only by the sword of his Mamelukes. It reminded

---

[99] "The Royalists made a mockery of this terror: it was strange to hear them say that this event was the most fortunate thing possible, because we should be relieved from Buonaparte; for the two Chambers would feel the necessity of giving the king absolute power—as if absolute power was a thing to be given."—Mad. de Staël, tom. iii., p. 138. "Yesterday the King received the diplomatic corps. His majesty said to the ambassadors, 'write to your respective courts that I am well, and that the foolish enterprise of *that man* shall as little disturb the tranquillity of Europe, as it has disturbed mine.'"—*Moniteur*, March 8.

France of the general detestation with which Buonaparte had been expelled from the kingdom, and proclaimed Frenchmen to be the scorn of Europe, should they again stretch their hands voluntarily to the shackles which they had burst and hurled from them. All were summoned to arms, more especially those to whom liberty was dear; for in the triumph of Buonaparte, it must find its grave for ever.— "With Louis," said the address, "was peace and happiness; with Buonaparte, war, misery, and desolation." Even a more animating appeal to popular feeling was made by a female on the staircase of the Tuileries, who exclaimed, "If Louis has not men enough to fight for him, let him call on the widows and childless mothers who have been rendered such by Napoleon."

MELUN—LYONS

Notwithstanding all these demonstrations of zeal, the public mind had been much influenced by the causes of discontent which had been so artfully enlarged upon for many months past. The decided Royalists were few, the Constitutionalists lukewarm. It became every moment more likely that not the voice of the people, but the sword of the army, must determine the controversy. Soult, whose conduct had given much cause for suspicion,[100] which was augmented by his proposal to call out the officers who since the restoration had been placed on half-pay, resigned his office, and was succeeded by Clarke, Duke of Feltre, less renowned as a soldier, but more trustworthy as a subject. A camp was established at Melun— troops were assembled there—and as much care as possible was used in selecting the troops to whom the royal cause was to be intrusted.

In the meantime, Fortune had not entirely abandoned the Bourbons. That part of the Buonapartist conspiracy which was to have been executed in the north was discovered and disconcerted. Lefebvre Desnouettes, discreditably known in England by his breach of parole, with the two Generals Lallemand, were the agents in this plot. On the 10th March, Lefebvre marched forward his

---

[100] "I am persuaded that the suspicion of his acting a treacherous part is groundless."— Mad. de Staël, tom. iii., p. 87.

regiment to join Buonaparte; but the officers having discovered his purpose, he was obliged to make his escape from the arrest with which he was threatened. The two Lallemands put the garrison of Lisle, to the number of 6000 men, in motion, by means of forged orders, declaring there was an insurrection in Paris. But Maréchal Mortier, meeting the troops on the march, detected and defeated the conspiracy, by which, had it taken effect, the King and Royal Family must have been made prisoners. The Lallemands were taken, and to have executed them on the spot as traitors, might have struck a wholesome terror into such officers as still hesitated; but the ministers of the King did not possess energy enough for such a crisis.[101]

The progress of Buonaparte, in the meantime, was uninterrupted. It was in vain that, at Lyons, Monsieur and the Duke of Orleans, with the assistance of the advice and influence of Maréchal Macdonald, endeavoured to retain the troops in their duty, and the inhabitants in their allegiance to the King. The latter, chiefly manufacturers, afraid of being undersold by those of England in their own market, shouted openly, "*Vive l'Empereur!*" The troops of the line remained silent and gloomy. "How will your soldiers behave?" said Monsieur to the colonel of the 13th Dragoons. The colonel referred him to the men themselves. They answered candidly, that they would fight for Napoleon alone. Monsieur dismounted, and addressed the soldiers individually. To one veteran, covered with scars, and decorated with medals, the prince said, "A brave soldier like you, at least, will cry, *Vive le Roi!*"—"You deceive yourself," answered the soldier. "No one here will fight against his father—I will cry, *Vive Napoleon!*" The efforts of Macdonald were equally vain. He endeavoured to move two battalions to oppose the entry of Buonaparte's advanced guard. So soon as the troops came in presence of each other, they broke their ranks, and mingled together in the general cry of "*Vive l'Empereur!*" Macdonald would have been made prisoner, but the forces whom he had just commanded would not permit this consummation of revolt. Monsieur was obliged to escape from Lyons, almost alone. The guard of honour formed by the citizens, to attend the person of the

---

[101] "General Lallemand would have been infallibly shot, had not Napoleon reached Paris with such extraordinary rapidity."—Savary, tom. iv., p. 256.

second of the Bourbon family, offered their services to Napoleon; but he refused them with contempt, while he sent a cross of honour to a single dragoon, who had the loyalty and devotion to attend Monsieur in his retreat.

Buonaparte, now master of the ancient capital of the Gauls, and at the head of 7000 men, was acknowledged by Mâcon, Chalons, Dijon, and almost all Burgundy. Marseilles, on the contrary, and all Provence, declared against the invader, and the former city set a price upon his head.

Napoleon found it necessary to halt at Lyons for the refreshment of his forces; and, being joined by some of the civilians of his party, he needed time also to organise his government and administration. Hitherto, the addresses which he had published had been of a military character, abounding with the Oriental imagery which Buonaparte regarded as essential to eloquence, promising that victory should move at the charging step, and that the eagle should fly with the national colours from steeple to steeple, till she perched on the towers of Notre Dame. The present decrees were of a different character, and related to the internal arrangement of his projected administration.

DECREES—AUXERRE

Cambacérès was named his minister of justice; Fouché, that of police (a boon to the revolutionists;) Davoust was made minister of war. Decrees upon decrees issued forth, with a rapidity which showed how Buonaparte had employed those studious hours at Elba, which he was supposed to have dedicated to the composition of his Memoirs. They ran in the name of Napoleon, by the grace of God, Emperor of the French, and were dated on the 13th of March, although not promulgated until the 21st of that month. The first of these decrees abrogated all changes in the courts of justice and tribunals which had taken place during the absence of Napoleon. The second displaced all officers belonging to the class of emigrants, and introduced into the army by the King. The third suppressed the order of St. Louis, the white flag and cockade, and other royal emblems, and restored the three-coloured banner and the imperial symbols of Buonaparte's authority. The same decree abolished the Swiss Guard, and the household troops of the King. The fourth sequestered the effects of the Bourbons. A similar ordinance sequestered the restored property of emigrant families, and was so artfully worded as to represent great changes of property having taken place in this manner. The fifth decree of Lyons suppressed the ancient nobility and feudal titles, and formally confirmed proprietors of national domains in their possessions. The sixth, declared sentence of banishment against all emigrants not erased from the list previous to the accession of the Bourbons, to which was added confiscation of their property. The seventh restored the Legion of Honour, in every respect as it had existed under the Emperor, uniting to its funds the confiscated revenues of the order of St. Louis. The eighth and last decree was the most important of all. Under pretence that emigrants who had borne arms against France, had been introduced into the body of the Peers, and that the Chamber of Deputies had already sat for the legal time, it dissolved both Chambers, and convoked the Electoral Colleges of the empire, in order that they might hold, in the ensuing month of May, an extraordinary assembly of the *Champ-de-Mai*. This convocation, for which the inventor found a name in the history of the ancient Franks, was to have two objects: *First*, to make such alterations and reformations in the constitution of the empire as circumstances should render advisable; *secondly*, to assist at the coronation of the Empress and of the King of Rome.

We cannot pause to criticise these various enactments. In general, however, it may be remarked, that they were admirably calculated to serve Napoleon's cause. They flattered the army, and at the same time heated their resentment against the emigrants, by insinuating that they had been sacrificed by Louis to the interest of these his followers. They held out to the Republicans a speedy prospect of confiscations, proscriptions, and revolutions of government; while the Imperialists were gratified with a view of ample funds for pensions, offices, and honorary decorations. To the proprietors of national domains was promised security; to the Parisians, the spectacle of the *Champ-de-Mai*; and to all France, peace and tranquillity, since the arrival of the Empress and her son, so confidently asserted to be at hand, must be considered as a pledge of the friendship of Austria. Russia was also said to be friendly to Napoleon, and the conduct of Alexander toward the members of Buonaparte's family, was boldly appealed to as evidence of the fact. England, it was averred, befriended him, else how could he have escaped from an isle surrounded by her naval force? Prussia, therefore, alone, might be hostile and unappeased; but, unsupported by the other belligerent powers, Prussia must remain passive, or would soon be reduced to reason. The very pleasure in mortifying one, at least, of the late victors of Paris, gave a zest and poignancy to the revolution, which the concurrence of the other great states would, according to Buonaparte, render easy and peaceful. Such news were carefully disseminated through France by Napoleon's adherents. They preceded his march, and prepared the minds of men to receive him as their destined master.

On the 13th, Buonaparte recommenced his journey, and, advancing through Mâcon, Chalons, and Dijon, he reached Auxerre on the 17th March. His own mode of travelling rather resembled that of a prince, who, weary of the fatigue of state, wishes to extricate himself, as much as possible, from its trammels, than that of an adventurer coming at the head of an army of insurgents, to snatch a crown from the head of the lawful monarch who wore it. He travelled several hours in advance of his army, often without any guard, or, at most, attended only by a few Polish lancers. The country through which he journeyed was favourable to his pretensions. It had been severely treated by the allies during the military manœuvres of the last campaign, and the dislike of the suffering inhabitants extended itself to the family who had mounted the throne by the influence of these strangers. When, therefore, they saw the late Emperor among them alone, without guards, inquiring, with his usual appearance of active interest, into the extent of their losses, and making liberal promises to repair them, it is no wonder that they should rather remember the battles he had fought in their behalf against the foreigners, than think on the probability that his presence among them might be the precursor of a second invasion.

The revolutionary fever preceded Buonaparte like an epidemic disorder. The 14th regiment of lancers, quartered at Auxerre, trampled under foot the white cockade at the first signal; the sixth regiment of lancers declared also for Napoleon, and without waiting for orders, drove a few soldiers of the household troops from Montereau, and secured that important post, which commands the passage of the Seine.

The dismay of the royal government at the revolt of Lyons, was much increased by false tidings which had been previously circulated, giving an account of a pretended victory obtained by the Royalist party in front of that town. The conspiracy was laid so deep, and extended so widely through every branch of the government, that those concerned contrived to send this false report to Paris in a demi-official form, by means of the telegraph. It had the expected effect, first, in suspending the preparations of the loyal party, and afterwards in deepening the anxiety which overwhelmed them, when Monsieur, returning almost unattended, brought the news of his bad success.

FOUCHÉ—NEY

At this moment of all but desperation, Fouché offered his assistance to the almost defenceless King. It is probable, that the more he reflected on the character of his old master, Napoleon, the deeper became his conviction, that they knew each other too well ever to resume an attitude of mutual confidence. Nothing deterred, therefore, by the communications which he had opened with the Imperialists, he now demanded a secret audience of the King. It was refused, but his communications were received through the medium of two confidential persons deputed by Louis. Fouché's language to them was that of a bold empiric, to whom patients have recourse in a moment of despair, and who confidently undertake the most utterly hopeless cases. Like such, he exacted absolute reliance on his skill—the most scrupulous attention to his injunctions—the most ample reward for his promised services; and as such, too, he spoke with the utmost confidence in the certainty of his remedy, whilst observing a vague yet studious mystery about the ingredients of which it was composed, and the mode in which it would operate. He required of Louis XVIII. that he should surrender all the executive authority to the Duke of Orleans, and all the ministerial Offices to himself and those whom he should appoint; which two conditions being granted, he undertook to put a period to Buonaparte's expedition. The Memoirs of this bold intriguer affirm, that he meant to assemble all that remained of the revolutionary party, and oppose the doctrines of Liberty and Equality to those of the glory of France, in the sense understood by Buonaparte.[102] What were the means that such politicians, so united, had to oppose to the army of France, Fouché has not informed us;[103] but it is probable, that, to stop the advance of 10,000 armed men, against whom the revolutionists could now scarce even array the mob of the suburbs, the ex-minister of police must have meditated the short sharp remedy of Napoleon's assassination, for accomplishing which, he, if any man, could have found trusty agents.

The King having refused proposals, which went to preserve his sceptre by taking it out of his hands, and by further unexplained means, the morality of which was liable to just suspicion, Fouché saw himself obliged to carry his intrigues to the service of his old master. He became, in consequence, so much an object of suspicion to the Royalists, that an order was issued for his arrest.[104] To the police agents, his own old dependents, who came to execute the order, he objected against the informality of their warrant, and stepping into his closet, as if to draw a protest, he descended by a secret stair into his garden, of which he scaled the wall. His next neighbour, into whose garden he escaped, was the Duchess de St. Leu; so that the fugitive arrived, as if by a trick of the stage, in the very midst of a circle of chosen Buonapartists, who received him

---

[102] Fouché, tom. ii., p. 249.

[103] "When the king's ministers desired to know what were the means which I proposed to employ, in order to prevent Napoleon from reaching Paris, I refused to communicate them, being determined to disclose them to no person but the King himself; but I protested that I was sure of success."—Fouché, p. 250.

[104] In the Memoirs of Fouché, it is avowed, that this order of arrest was upon no political ground, but arose from the envy of Savary, who, foreseeing that Fouché would be restored to the situation of minister of police, which he himself desired, on account of the large sums which were placed at the disposal of that functionary, hoped, in this manner, to put his rival out of his road.—S.

with triumph, and considered the mode of his coming among them as a full warrant for his fidelity.[105]

Louis XVIII. in his distress, had recourse to the assistance of another man of the Revolution, who, without possessing the abilities of Fouché, was perhaps, had he been disposed to do so, better qualified than he to have served the King's cause. Maréchal Ney was called forth to take the command of an army destined to attack Napoleon in the flank and rear as he marched towards Paris, while the forces at Melun opposed him in front. He had an audience of the King on the 9th of March, when he accepted his appointment with expressions of the most devoted faith to the King, and declared his resolution to bring Buonaparte to Paris like a wild beast in an iron cage. The maréchal went to Besançon, where, on the 11th of March, he learned that Buonaparte was in possession of Lyons. But he continued to make preparations for resistance, and collected all the troops he could from the adjoining garrisons. To those who objected to the bad disposition of the soldiers, and remarked that he would have difficulty in inducing them to fight, Ney answered determinedly, "They *shall* fight; I will take a musket from a grenadier and begin the action myself;—I will run my sword to the hilt in the first who hesitates to follow my example." To the minister at war he wrote, that all were dazzled by the activity and rapid progress of the invader; that Napoleon was favoured by the common people and the soldiers; but that the officers and civil authorities were loyal, and he still hoped "to see a fortunate close of this mad enterprise."

In these dispositions, Ney advanced to Lons-le-Saulnier. Here, on the night betwixt the 13th and 14th March, he received a letter from Napoleon, summoning him to join his standard, as "bravest of the brave," a name which could not but awake a thousand remembrances. He had already sounded both his officers and soldiers, and discovered their unalterable determination to join Buonaparte. He therefore had it only in his choice to retain his command by passing over to the Emperor, or else to return to the

---

[105] "Hortense received me with open arms; and as in a wonderful Arabian tale, I suddenly found myself in the midst of the *élite* of the Buonapartists, in the headquarters of the party, where I found mirth, and where my presence caused an intoxication of joy."—Fouché, p. 253.

King without executing any thing which might seem even an effort at realizing his boast, and also without the army over which he had asserted his possession of such influence.

Maréchal Ney was a man of mean birth, who, by the most desperate valour, had risen to the highest ranks in the army. His early education had not endowed him with a delicate sense of honour or a high feeling of principle, and he had not learned either as he advanced in life. He appears to have been a weak man, with more vanity than pride, and who, therefore, was likely to feel the loss of power more than the loss of character. He accordingly resolved upon adhering to Napoleon. Sensible of the incongruity of changing his side so suddenly, he affected to be a deliberate knave, rather than he would content himself with being viewed in his real character, of a volatile, light-principled, and inconsiderate fool. He pretended that the expedition of Napoleon had been long arranged between himself and the other maréchals. But we are willing rather to suppose that this was matter of mere invention, than to think that the protestations poured out at the Tuileries, only five days before, were, on the part of this unfortunate man, the effusions of premeditated treachery.

The maréchal now published an order of the day, declaring that the cause of the Bourbons was lost for ever. It was received by the soldiers with rapture, and Buonaparte's standard and colours were instantly displayed. Many of the officers, however, remonstrated, and left their commands. One, before he went away, broke his sword in two, and threw the pieces at Ney's feet, saying, "It is easier for a man of honour to break iron than to infringe his word."

TREASON OF NEY—MELUN

Ney was received by Napoleon with open arms.[106] His defection did incalculable damage to the King's cause, tending to

---

[106] "It is impossible not to condemn Ney's conduct. It behoved him to imitate Macdonald and to withdraw. It ought, however, to be added, that Generals Lecourbe and Bourmont were with him when he consented to be led astray. But, after committing this error, he fell

show that the spirit of treason which possessed the common soldiers, had ascended to and affected the officers of the highest rank in the army.

The King, in the meanwhile, notwithstanding these unpromising circumstances, used every exertion to induce his subjects to continue in their allegiance. He attended in person the sitting of the Chamber of Deputies, and was received with such enthusiastic marks of applause, that one would have thought the most active exertions must have followed. Louis next reviewed the national guards, about 25,000 men, who made a similar display of loyalty. He also inspected the troops of the line, 6000 in number, but his reception was equivocal. They placed their caps on their bayonets in token of respect, but they raised no shout.

Some of those about Louis's person continued to believe that these men were still attached to the King, or that at any rate, they ought to be sent to the camp at Melun, which was the last remaining point upon which the royal party could hope to make a stand.

As a last resource, Louis convoked a general council at the Tuileries on the 18th March. The generals present declared there could be no effectual opposition offered to Buonaparte. The royalist nobles contradicted them, and, after some expressions of violence had been uttered, much misbecoming the royal presence, Louis was obliged to break up the meeting, and prepare himself to abandon a capital, which the prevalence of his enemies, and the disunion of his friends, left him no longer any chance of defending.

Meantime, the two armies approached each other at Melun; that of the King was commanded by the faithful Macdonald. On the 20th, his troops were drawn up in three lines to receive the invaders, who were said to be advancing from Fontainbleau. There was a long pause of suspense, of a nature which seldom fails to render men more accessible to strong and sudden emotion. The glades of the forest, and the acclivity which ascends to it, were full in view of the

---

into a still greater one. He wrote to Napoleon to acquaint him with what he had done, announcing to him at the same time, that he was about to proceed to Auxerre, where he expected the honour of seeing him."—Savary, tom. iv., p. 252.

royal army, but presented the appearance of a deep solitude. All was silence, except when the regimental bands of music, at the command of the officers, who remained generally faithful, played the airs of *Vive Henri Quatre—O, Richard—La Belle Gabrielle*, and other tunes connected with the cause and family of the Bourbons. The sounds excited no corresponding sentiments among the soldiers. At length, about noon, the galloping of horse was heard. An open carriage appeared, surrounded by a few hussars, and drawn by four horses. It came on at full speed; and Napoleon, jumping from the vehicle, was in the midst of the ranks which had been formed to oppose him. His escort threw themselves from their horses, mingled with their ancient comrades, and the effect of their exhortations was instantaneous on men, whose minds were already half made up to the purpose which they now accomplished. There was a general shout of *Vive Napoleon!*—The last army of the Bourbons passed from their side, and no farther obstruction existed betwixt Napoleon and the capital, which he was once more—but for a brief space—to inhabit as a sovereign.

Louis XVIII. had anticipated too surely the defection which took place, to await the consequence of its actual arrival. The King departed from Paris, escorted by his household, at one in the morning of the 20th March. Even at that untimely hour, the palace was surrounded by the national guards, and many citizens, who wept and entreated him to remain, offering to spend the last drop of their blood for him. But Louis wisely declined accepting of sacrifices, which could now have availed nothing. Escorted by his household troops, he took the way to Lisle. Maréchal Macdonald, returning from the fatal position of Melun, assumed the command of this small body, which was indeed augmented by many volunteers, but such as considered their zealous wishes, rather than their power of rendering assistance. The King's condition was, however, pitied and respected, and he passed through Abbeville, and other garrison towns, where the soldiers received him with sullen respect; and though indicating that they intended to join his rival, would neither violate his person nor insult his misfortunes. At Lisle he had hoped to make a stand, but Maréchal Mortier, insisting upon the dissatisfied and tumultuary state of the garrison, urged him to proceed, for the safety of his life; and, compelled to a second exile, he departed to Ostend, and from thence to Ghent, where he established his exiled court. Maréchal Macdonald took leave of his Majesty on the frontiers, conscious that by emigrating he must lose every prospect of serving in future either France or her monarch. The household troops, about two hundred excepted, were also disbanded on the frontiers. They had been harassed in their march thither by some light horse, and in their attempt to regain their homes in a state of dispersion, some were slain, and almost all were plundered and insulted.

In the meanwhile, the Revolution took full effect at Paris. Lavalette, one of Buonaparte's most decided adherents, hastened from a place of concealment to assume the management of the post-office in the name of Napoleon, an office which he had enjoyed during his former reign. He was thus enabled to intercept the royal proclamations, and to announce to every department officially the restoration of the Emperor. Excelsman, the oath of fealty to the king, *à toutes épreuves*, scarce dry upon his lips, took down the white flag, which floated on the Tuileries, and replaced the three-coloured banner.

RE-ENTERS PARIS

It was late in the evening ere Napoleon arrived in the same open carriage, which he had used since his landing. There was a singular contrast betwixt his entry and the departure of the King. The latter was accompanied by the sobs, tears, and kind wishes of those citizens who desired peace and tranquillity, by the wailing of the defenceless, and the anxious fears of the wise and prudent. The former entered amid the shouts of armed columns, who, existing by war and desolation, welcomed with military acclamations the chief who was to restore them to their element. The inhabitants of the suburbs cheered in expectation of employment and gratuities, or by instigation of their ringleaders, who were chiefly under the management of the police, and well prepared for the event. But among the immense crowds of the citizens of Paris, who turned out to see this extraordinary spectacle, few or none joined in the gratulation. The soldiers of the guard resented their silence, commanded the spectators to shout, struck with the flat of their swords, and pointed their pistols at the multitude, but could not, even by these military means, extort the expected cry of Liberty and Napoleon, though making it plain by their demeanour, that the last, if not the first, was returned to the Parisians. In the court of the Carousel, and before the Tuileries, all the adherents of the old Imperial government, and those who, having deserted Napoleon, were eager to expiate their fault, by now being first to acknowledge him, were assembled to give voice to their welcome, which atoned in some degree for the silence of the streets. They crowded around him so closely, that he was compelled to exclaim—"My friends, you stifle me!" and his adjutants were obliged to support him in their arms up the grand staircase, and thence into the royal apartments, where he received the all-hail of the principal devisers and abettors of this singular undertaking.

Never, in his bloodiest and most triumphant field of battle, had the terrible ascendency of Napoleon's genius appeared half so predominant as during his march, or rather his journey, from Cannes to Paris. He who left the same coast disguised like a slave, and weeping like a woman, for fear of assassination, reappeared in grandeur like that of the returning wave, which, the farther it has retreated, is rolled back on the shore with the more terrific and overwhelming violence. His looks seemed to possess the pretended power of northern magicians, and blunted swords and spears. The Bravest of the Brave, who came determined to oppose him as he would a wild beast, recognised his superiority when confronted with him, and sunk again into his satellite. Yet the lustre with which Napoleon shone was not that of a planet duly moving in its regular sphere, but that of a comet, inspiring forebodings of pestilence and death, and

> "with fear of change, Perplexing nations."

The result of his expedition was thus summed by one of the most eloquent and best-informed British statesmen.[107]

---

[107] Sir James Mackintosh. See Debate on Mr. Abercrombie's Motion respecting Buonaparte's Escape from Elba.—*Parl. Deb.*, vol. xxx., p. 738.

"Was it," said the accomplished orator, "in the power of language to describe the evil? Wars which had raged for twenty-five years throughout Europe; which had spread blood and desolation from Cadiz to Moscow, and from Naples to Copenhagen; which had wasted the means of human enjoyment, and destroyed the instruments of social improvement; which threatened to diffuse among the European nations the dissolute and ferocious habits of a predatory soldiery—at length by one of those vicissitudes which bid defiance to the foresight of man, had been brought to a close, upon the whole happy beyond all reasonable expectation, with no violent shock to national independence, with some tolerable compromise between the opinions of the age and the reverence due to ancient institutions; with no too signal or mortifying triumph over the legitimate interests or avowable feelings of any numerous body of men, and, above all, without those retaliations against nations or parties which beget new convulsions, often as horrible as those which they close, and perpetuate revenge and hatred and blood from age to age. Europe seemed to breathe after her sufferings. In the midst of this fair prospect, and of these consolatory hopes, Napoleon Buonaparte escaped from Elba; three small vessels reached the coast of Provence; their hopes are instantly dispelled; the work of our toil and fortitude is undone; the blood of Europe is spilt in vain—

"Ibi omnis effusus labor!"

Chapter LXXXV

Various attempts to organise a defence for the Bourbons fail—Buonaparte, again reinstated on the throne of France, is desirous of continuing the peace with the Allies—but no answer is returned to his letters—Treaty of Vienna—Grievances alleged by Buonaparte in justification of the step he had taken—Debates in the British House of Commons, on the renewal of War—Murat occupies Rome with 50,000 men—his Proclamation summoning all Italians to arms—He advances against the Austrians—is repulsed at Occhio-Bello—defeated at Tolentino—flies to Naples, and thence, in disguise, to France—where Napoleon refuses to receive him.

When Paris was lost, the bow of the Bourbons was effectually broken; and the attempts of individuals of the family to make a stand against the evil hour, was honourable indeed to their own gallantry, but of no advantage to their cause.

The Duke d'Angoulême placed himself at the head of a considerable body of troops, raised by the town of Marseilles, and the royalists of Provence. But being surrounded by General Gilly, he was obliged to lay down his arms, on condition of amnesty to his followers, and free permission to himself to leave France. General Grouchy refused to confirm this capitulation, till Buonaparte's pleasure was known. But the restored Emperor, not displeased, it may be, to make a display of generosity, permitted the Duke d'Angoulême to depart by sea from Cette, only requiring his interference with Louis XVIII. for returning the crown jewels which the King had removed with him to Ghent.[108]

---

[108] Napoleon to Grouchy.

The Duke of Bourbon had retired to La Vendée to raise the warlike royalists of that faithful province. But it had been previously occupied by soldiers attached to Buonaparte, so judiciously posted as to render an insurrection impossible; and the duke found himself obliged to escape by sea from Nantes.

DUCHESS D'ANGOULÊME

The Duchess d'Angoulême, the only remaining daughter of Louis XVI., whose childhood and youth had suffered with patient firmness such storms of adversity, showed on this trying occasion that she had the active as well as passive courage becoming the descendant of a long line of princes. She threw herself into Bourdeaux, where the loyalty of Count Lynch, the mayor, and of the citizens in general, promised her determined aid, and the princess herself stood forth amongst them, like one of those heroic women of the age of chivalry, whose looks and words were able in moments of peril to give double edge to men's swords, and double constancy to their hearts. But unhappily there was a considerable garrison of troops of the line in Bourdeaux, who had caught the general spirit of revolt. General Clausel also advanced on the city with a force of the same description. The duchess made a last effort, assembled around her the officers, and laid their duty before them in the most touching and pathetic manner. But when she saw their coldness, and heard their faltering excuses, she turned from them in disdain:—"You fear," she said—"I pity you, and release you from your oaths." She embarked on board an English frigate, and Bourdeaux opened its gates to Clausel, and declared for the Emperor. Thus, notwithstanding the return of Napoleon was far from being acceptable to the French universally, or even generally, all open opposition to his government ceased, and he was acknowledged as Emperor within about twenty days after he landed on the beach at Cannes, with a thousand followers.[109]

---

[109] "The result of the royalist enterprise rather contributed to tranquillise Napoleon. He was astonished by the courage which the Duke d'Angoulême exhibited in La Drôme, and especially Madame at Bourdeaux. He admired the intrepidity of this heroic princess, whom the desertion of an entire army had not been able to dispirit. It was proposed in council to obtain the crown diamonds for the Duke d'Angoulême. I recommended the Emperor to

But though he was thus replaced on the throne, Napoleon's seat was by no means secure, unless he could prevail upon the confederated sovereigns of Europe to acknowledge him in the capacity of which their united arms had so lately deprived him. It is true, he had indirectly promised war to his soldiers, by stigmatizing the cessions made by the Bourbons of what he called the territory of France. It is true, also, that then, and till his death's-day, he continued to entertain the rooted idea that Belgium, a possession which France had acquired within twenty years, was an integral portion of that kingdom. It is true, Antwerp and the five hundred sail of the line which were to be built there, continued through his whole life to be the very Delilah of his imagination. The cause of future war was, therefore, blazing in his bosom. But yet at present he felt it necessary for his interest to assure the people of France, that his return to the empire would not disturb the treaty of Paris, though it had given the Low Countries to Holland. He spared no device to spread reports of a pacific tendency.

From the commencement of his march, it was affirmed by his creatures that he brought with him a treaty concluded with all the powers of Europe for twenty years. It was repeatedly averred, that Maria Louisa and her son were on the point of arriving in France, dismissed by her father as a pledge of reconciliation; and when she did not appear, it was insinuated that she was detained by the Emperor Francis, as a pledge that Buonaparte should observe his promise of giving the French a free constitution. To such bare-faced assertions he was reduced, rather than admit that his return was to be the signal for renewing hostilities with all Europe.

Meantime, Napoleon hesitated not to offer to the allied ministers his willingness to acquiesce in the treaty of Paris; although, according to his uniform reasoning, it involved the humiliation and disgrace of France. He sent a letter to each of the sovereigns, expressing his desire to make peace on the same principles which had been arranged with the Bourbons. To these letters no answers were returned. The decision of the allies had already been adopted.

---

throw M. de Vitrolles into the bargain; but he would not consent."—Fouché, tom. ii., p. 261.

DECLARATION AND TREATY OF VIENNA

The Congress at Vienna happened fortunately not to be dissolved, when the news of Buonaparte's escape from Elba was laid before them by Talleyrand, on the 11th March. The astonishing, as well as the sublime, approaches to the ludicrous, and it is a curious physiological fact, that the first news of an event which threatened to abolish all their labours, seemed so like a trick in a pantomime, that laughter was the first emotion it excited from almost every one. The merry mood did not last long; for the jest was neither a sound nor safe one. It was necessary for the Congress, by an unequivocal declaration, to express their sentiments, upon this extraordinary occasion. This declaration appeared on the 13th March, and after giving an account of the fact, bore the following denunciation:—

"By thus breaking the convention which had established him in the island of Elba, Buonaparte destroys the only legal title on which his existence depended; and, by appearing again in France with projects of confusion and disorder, he has deprived himself of the protection of the law, and has manifested to the universe, that there can be neither peace nor truce with him.

"The powers consequently declare, that Napoleon Buonaparte has placed himself without the pale of civil and social relations, and that, as an enemy and disturber of the tranquillity of the world, he has rendered himself liable to public vengeance. They declare at the same time, that, firmly resolved to maintain entire the treaty of Paris of the 30th of May, 1814, and the dispositions sanctioned by that treaty, and those which they have resolved on, or shall hereafter resolve on, to complete and to consolidate it, they will employ all their means, and will unite all their efforts, that the general peace, the object of the wishes of Europe, and the constant purpose of their labours, may not again be troubled; and to provide against every attempt which shall threaten to replunge the world into the disorders of revolution."[110]

---

[110] Parl. Debates, vol. xxx., p. 373.

This manifesto was instantly followed by a treaty betwixt Great Britain, Austria, Prussia, and Russia, renewing and confirming the league entered into at Chaumont. The first article declared the resolution of the high contracting parties to maintain and enforce the treaty of Paris, which excluded Buonaparte from the throne of France, and to enforce the decree of outlawry issued against him as above mentioned. 2. Each of the contracting parties agreed to keep constantly in the field an army of 150,000 men complete, with the due proportion of cavalry and artillery. 3. They agreed not to lay down their arms but by common consent, until either the purpose of the war should have been attained, or Buonaparte should be rendered incapable of disturbing the peace of Europe. After other subordinate articles, the 7th provided, that the other powers of Europe should be invited to accede to the treaty; and the 8th, that the King of France should be particularly called upon to become a party to it. A separate article provided, that the King of Great Britain should have the option of furnishing his contingent in men, or of paying, instead, at the rate of L.30 sterling per annum for each cavalry soldier, and L.20 per annum for each infantry soldier, which should be wanting to make up his complement. To this treaty a declaration was subjoined, when it was ratified by the Prince Regent, referring to the eighth article of the treaty, and declaring that it should not be understood as binding his Britannic Majesty to prosecute the war, with the view of forcibly imposing on France any particular government. The other contracting powers agreed to accept of the accession of his Royal Highness, under this explanation and limitation.[111]

The treaty of Vienna may be considered in a double point of view, first, upon principle, and, secondly, as to its mode of expression; and it was commented upon in both respects in the British House of Commons. The expediency of the war was denied by several of the Opposition members, on account of the exhausted state of Great Britain, but they generally admitted that the escape of Buonaparte gave a just cause for the declaration of hostilities. The great statesman and jurisconsult, whom we have already quoted, delivered an opinion for himself, and those with whom he acted, couched in the most positive terms.

---

[111] Parl. Debates, vol. xxx.; Ann. Reg., vol. lvii.

"Some insinuations," said Sir James Mackintosh, "had been thrown out, of differences of opinion on his side of the house, respecting the evils of this escape. He utterly denied them. All agreed in lamenting the occurrence which rendered the renewal of war so probable, not to say certain. All his friends, with whose sentiments he was acquainted, were of opinion, that, in the theory of public law, the assumption of power by Napoleon had given to the allies a just cause of war against France. It was perfectly obvious, that the abdication of Napoleon, and his perpetual renunciation of the supreme authority, was a condition, and the most important condition, on which the allies had granted peace to France. The convention of Fontainbleau, and the treaty of Paris, were equally parts of the great compact which re-established friendship between France and Europe. In consideration of the safer and more inoffensive state of France when separated from her terrible leader, confederated Europe had granted moderate and favourable terms of peace. As soon as France had violated this important condition, by again submitting to the authority of Napoleon, the allies were doubtless released from their part of the compact, and re-entered into their belligerent rights."[112]

ALLEGED GRIEVANCES

The provocations pleaded by Buonaparte (which seem to have been entirely fanciful, so far as respects any design on his freedom,) were, first, the separation from his family. But this was a question with Austria exclusively; for what power was to compel the Emperor Francis to restore his daughter, after the fate of war had flung her again under his paternal protection? Napoleon's feelings in his situation were extremely natural, but those of the Emperor cannot be blamed, who considered his daughter's honour and happiness as interested in separating her from a man, who was capable of attempting to redeem his broken fortunes by the most desperate means. Much would depend upon the inclination of the illustrious person herself; but even if some degree of paternal restraint had been exerted, could Napoleon really feel himself justified in renewing a sort of Trojan war with all the powers in

---

[112] Parl. Debates, vol. xxx., p. 378.

Europe, in order to recover his wife, or think, because he was separated from her society by a flinty-hearted father, that he was therefore warranted in invading and subduing the kingdom of France? The second article of provocation, and we admit it as a just one, was, that Napoleon was left to necessities to which he ought not to have been subjected, by France withholding his pension till the year should elapse. This was a ground of complaint, and a deep one; but against whom? Surely not against the allies, unless Buonaparte had called upon them to make good their treaty; and had stated, that France had failed to make good those obligations, for which he had their guarantee. England, who was only an accessory to the treaty, had nevertheless already interfered in Buonaparte's behalf, and there can be no doubt that redress would have been granted by the contracting parties, who could not in decency avoid enforcing a treaty, which had been of their own forming. That this guarantee gave Napoleon a right to appeal and to complain, cannot be denied; but that it gave him a right to proceed by violence, without any expostulation previously made, is contrary to all ideas of the law of nations, which enacts, that no aggression can constitute a legitimate cause of war, until redress has been refused. This, however, is all mere legal argument. Buonaparte did NOT invade France, because she was deficient in paying his pension. He invaded her, because he saw a strong prospect of regaining the throne; nor do we believe that millions of gold would have prevailed on him to forego the opportunity.

His more available ground of defence, however, was, that he was recalled by the general voice of the nation of France; but the whole facts of the case contradicted this statement. His league with the Revolutionists was made reluctantly on their part, nor did that party form any very considerable portion of the nation. "His election," according to Grattan, "was a military election; and when the army disposed of the civil government, it was the march of a military chief over a conquered nation. The nation did not rise to assist Louis, or resist Buonaparte, because the nation could not rise against the army. The mind of France, as well as her constitution, had completely lost, for the present, the power of resistance. They passively yielded to superior force."[113]

In short, the opinion of the House of Commons was so unanimous on the disastrous consequences of Napoleon's quitting Elba, that the minority brought charges against Ministers for not having provided more effectual means to prevent his escape. To these charges it was replied, that Britain was not his keeper; that it was impossible to maintain a line of blockade around Elba; and if it had been otherwise, that Britain had no right to interfere with Buonaparte's motions, so far as concerned short expeditions unconnected with the purpose of escape; although it was avowed, that if a British vessel had detected him in the act of going to France with an armed force, for the purpose of invasion, the right of stopping his progress would have been exercised at every hazard. Still it was urged, they had no title either to establish a police upon the island, the object of which should be to watch its acknowledged Emperor, or to maintain a naval force around it, to apprehend him in case he should attempt an escape. Both would have been in direct contradiction of the treaty of Fontainbleau, to which Britain had acceded, though she was not of the contracting parties.[114]

The style of the declaration of the allies was more generally censured in the British Parliament than its warlike tone. It was contended that, by declaring Napoleon an outlaw, it invoked against him the daggers of individuals, as well as the sword of justice. This charge of encouraging assassination was warmly repelled by the supporters of Ministry.[115] The purpose of the proclamation, it was said, was merely to point out Napoleon to the French nation, as a person who had forfeited his civil rights, by the act of resuming, contrary to treaty, a position in which, from his temper, habits, and talents, he must again become an object of suspicion and terror to all Europe. His inflexible resolution, his unbounded ambition, his own genius, his power over the mind of others—those great military talents, in short, which, so valuable in war, are in peace so

---

[113] See debate, May 25, 1815, on the Prince Regent's message relating to France. Parl. Debates, vol. xxxii., p. 424.
[114] See Parl. Debates, vol. xxx., p. 726.
[115] See Parl. Debates, vol. xxx., p. 338.

dangerous, had afforded reasons for making the peace of Paris, by which Napoleon was personally excluded from the throne. When Napoleon broke that peace, solemnly concluded with Europe, he forfeited his political rights, and in that view alone the outlawry was to be construed. In consequence of these resolutions, adopted at Vienna and London, all Europe rang with the preparations for war; and the number of troops with which the allies proposed to invade France were rated at no less than one million and eleven thousand soldiers.[116]

Before proceeding farther, it is requisite to say a few words on the subject of Murat. He had been for some time agitated by fears naturally arising from the attack made upon his government at the Congress by Talleyrand. The effect had not, it was true, induced the other powers to decide against him; but he seems to have been conscious that the reports of General Nugent and Lord William Bentinck concurred in representing him as having acted in the last campaign rather the part of a trimmer betwixt two parties, than that of a confederate, sincere, as he professed to be, in favour of the allies. Perhaps his conscience acknowledged this truth, for it certainly seems as if Eugene might have been more hardly pressed, had Murat been disposed to act with energy in behalf of the allies. He felt, therefore, that the throne of Tancred tottered under him, and rashly determined that it was better to brave a danger than to allow time to see whether it might not pass away. Murat had held intercourse with the isle of Elba, and cannot but have known Buonaparte's purpose when he left it; but he ought, at the same time, to have considered, that if his brother-in-law met with any success, his own alliance would become essential to Austria, who had such anxiety to retain the north of Italy, and must have been purchased on his own terms.

MURAT

---

[116] The contingents of the various powers were as follows:—Austria 300,000 men; Russia 225,000; Prussia 236,000; States of Germany 150,000; Great Britain 50,000; Holland 50,000; in all, 1,011,000 soldiers.—S.

Instead, however, of waiting for an opportunity of profiting by Napoleon's attempt, which could not have failed to arrive, Murat resolved to throw himself into the fray, and carve for himself. He placed himself at the head of an army of 50,000 men, and without explaining his intentions, occupied Rome, the Pope and cardinals flying before him; threatened the whole line of the Po, which the Austrian force was inadequate to maintain; and, on 31st of March, addressed a proclamation to all Italians, summoning them to rise in arms for the liberation of their country.[117] It seemed now clear, that the purpose of this son of a pastry-cook amounted to nothing else than the formation of Italy into one state, and the placing himself on the throne of the Cæsars. The proclamation was signed Joachim Napoleon, which last name, formerly laid aside, he reassumed at this critical period. The appeal to the Italians was in vain. The feuds among the petty states are so numerous, their pretensions so irreconcilable, and their weakness has made them so often the prey of successive conquerors, that they found little inviting in the proposal of union, little arousing in the sound of independence. The proclamation, therefore, had small effect, except upon some of the students at Bologna. Murat marched northward, however, and being much superior in numbers, defeated the Austrian general Bianchi, and occupied Modena and Florence.

Murat's attitude was now an alarming one to Europe. If he should press forward into Lombardy, he might co-operate with Buonaparte, now restored to his crown, and would probably be reinforced by thousands of the veterans of the Viceroy Eugene's army. Austria, therefore, became desirous of peace, and offered to guarantee to him the possession of the kingdom of Naples, with an addition he had long coveted, the marches, namely, of the Roman See. Britain, at the same time, intimated, that having made truce with Joachim at the instance of Austria, it was to last no longer than his good intelligence with her ally. Murat refused the conditions of the one power, and neglected the remonstrances of the other. "It was too late," he said; "Italy deserves freedom, and she shall be free." Here closed all hopes of peace; Austria declared war against Murat, and expedited the reinforcements sent into Italy; and Britain

---

[117] Mémoires de Fleury de Chamboullon, tom. i., p. 397.

prepared a descent upon his Neapolitan dominions, where Ferdinand still continued to have many adherents.[118]

Murat's character as a tactician was far inferior to that which he deservedly bore as a soldier in the field of battle, and he was still a worse politician than a general. A repulse sustained in an attempt to pass the Po near Occhio-bello, seems to have disconcerted the plan of his whole campaign, nor did he find himself able to renew the negotiations which he had rashly broken off. He seemed to acknowledge, by his military movements, that he had attempted a scheme far beyond his strength and understanding. He retreated upon his whole line, abandoning Parma, Reggio, Modena, Florence, and all Tuscany, by which last movement he put the Austrians in possession of the best and shortest road to Rome. In consequence, he was pressed on his retreat in front and rear, and compelled to give battle near Tolentino. It was sustained for two days, (2d and 3d of May,) but the Neapolitans could not be brought into close action with the iron-nerved Austrians. It was in vain that Murat placed field-pieces in the rear of his attacking columns, with orders to fire grape on them should they retreat; in vain that he himself set the example of the most desperate courage. The Neapolitan army fled in dispersion and discomfiture. Their guns, ammunition, treasure, and baggage, became the spoil of the Austrians; and in traversing the mountains of Abruzzo, Murat lost half his army without stroke of sword.

The defeated prince was pursued into his Neapolitan dominions, where he learned that the Calabrians were in insurrection, and that an English fleet, escorting an invading army from Sicily, had appeared in the Bay of Naples. His army, reduced to a handful by repeated skirmishes, in which he had behaved with such temerity as to make his followers think he desired death, was directed to throw itself into Capua. He himself, who had left Naples splendidly apparelled, according to his custom, and at the head of a gallant army, now entered its gates, attended only by four lancers, alighted at the palace, and appeared before the Queen, pale, haggard, dishevelled, with all the signs of extreme fatigue and dejection. His salutation was in the affecting words, "Madam, I have not been able

---

[118] See papers relating to Maréchal Murat.—Parl. Debates, vol. xxxi., pp. 59-153.

to find death." He presently found, that remaining at Naples, which was about to fall into other hands, would compromise his liberty, perhaps his life. He took leave of his Queen, whom circumstances were about to deprive of that title, cut off his hair, and disguising himself in a grey frock, escaped to the little island of Ischia, and reached on 25th May, Cannes, which had received Napoleon a few weeks before. His wife, immediately afterwards, alarmed by the tendency of the Neapolitan mob to insurrection, surrendered herself to Commodore Campbell of the Tremendous, and was received on board his vessel.[119]

A courier announced Murat's arrival in France to Buonaparte, who, instead of sending consolation to his unhappy relative, is said to have asked with bitter scorn, "Whether Naples and France had made peace since the war of 1814!" The answer seems to imply, that although the attempts of Joachim and Napoleon coincided in time, and in other circumstances, so punctually as to make it evident they had been undertaken in concert, yet that there had been no precise correspondence, far less any formal treaty, betwixt the adventurous brothers. Indeed, Napoleon at all times positively denied that he had the least accession to Murat's wildly-concerted project (*levée des boucliers,*) and affirmed that it was essentially injurious to him. Napoleon's account was, that when he retired to Elba, he took farewell of Murat by letter, forgiving all that had passed between them, and recommending to his brother-in-law to keep on good terms with the Austrians, and only to check them if he saw them likely to advance on France. He offered also to guarantee his kingdom. Murat returned an affectionate answer, engaging to prove himself, in his conduct towards Napoleon, more an object of pity than resentment, declining any other guarantee than the word of the Emperor, and declaring that the attachment of his future life was to make amends for the past defection. "But it was Murat's fate to ruin us every way," continued Napoleon; "once by declaring against us, and again by unadvisedly taking our part."[120] He encountered

---

[119] Commodore Campbell had promised Caroline a free passage to France; but, on the declaration of Lord Exmouth, that the commodore had exceeded his instructions, fresh negotiations were entered into with Austria; the result being that the ex-queen accepted the protection of the Emperor Francis, and has since resided, as Countess of Lipano, in his dominions.
[120] Las Cases, tom. ii., p. 355.

Austria without sufficient means, and being ruined, left her without any counterbalancing power in Italy. From that time it became impossible for Napoleon to negotiate with her.

Receiving the Emperor's account as correct, and allowing that the brothers-in-law played each his own part, it was not to be supposed that they acted entirely without a mutual understanding. Each, indeed, was willing to rest on his own fortunes, well knowing that his claim to the other's assistance would depend chiefly upon his success, and unwilling, besides, to relinquish the privilege of making peace, should it be necessary, at the expense of disowning the kindred enterprise of his brother-in-law. Notwithstanding the splendid details which the *Moniteur* gave of Murat's undertaking, while it yet seemed to promise success, it is certain that Buonaparte endeavoured to propitiate Austria, by the offer of abandoning Murat; and that Murat, could his offers have obtained a hearing after the repulse of Occhio-bello, was ready once more to have deserted Napoleon, whose name he had so lately reassumed. Involved in this maze of selfish policy, Murat had now the mortification to find himself contemned by Napoleon, when he might, indeed, be a burden, but could afford him no aid. Had he arrived at Milan as a victor, and extended a friendly hand across the Alps, how different would have been his reception! But Buonaparte refused to see him in his distress, or to permit him to come to Paris, satisfied that the sight of his misery would be a bitter contradiction to the fables which the French journals had, for some time, published of his success. Fouché sent him a message, much like that which enjoined the dishonoured ambassadors of Solomon to tarry at Jericho till their beards grew. It recommended to Murat to remain in seclusion, till the recollection of his disgrace should be abated by newer objects of general interest.

Buonaparte had sometimes entertained thoughts of bringing Murat to the army, but was afraid of shocking the French soldiers, who would have felt disgust and horror at seeing the man who had betrayed France. "I did not," he said to his followers at St. Helena, "think I could carry him through, and yet he might have gained us the victory; for there were moments during the battle (of Waterloo) when to have forced two or three of the English squares might have insured it, and Murat was just the man for the work. In leading a charge of cavalry, never was there an officer more determined, more brave, and more brilliant."[121]

Murat was thus prohibited to come to the court of the Tuileries, where his defection might have been forgiven, but his defeat was an inexpiable offence. He remained in obscurity near Toulon, till his fate called him elsewhere, after the decisive battle of Waterloo.[122] From this episode, for such, however important, it is in the present history, we return to France and our immediate subject.

---

[121] O'Meara, vol. ii., p. 95.

[122] It is well known that Joachim Murat, escaping with difficulty from France, fled to Corsica, and might have obtained permission to reside upon parole in the Austrian territories, safe and unmolested. He nourished a wild idea, however, of recovering his crown, which induced him to reject these terms of safety, and invade the Neapolitan territories at the head of about two hundred men. That his whole expedition might be an accurate parody on that of Buonaparte to Cannes, he published swaggering proclamations, mingled with a proper quantum of falsehood. A storm dispersed his flotilla. He himself, October 8th, landed at a little fishing town near Monte Leone. He was attacked by the country people, fought as he was wont, but was defeated and made prisoner, tried by martial law, and condemned. The Sicilian royal family have shown themselves no forgiving race, otherwise mercy might have been extended to one, who, though now a private person, had been so lately a king, that he might be pardoned for forgetting that he had no longer the power of making peace and war without personal responsibility. Murat met his fate as became *Le Beau Sabreur*. He fastened his wife's picture on his breast, refused to have his eyes bandaged, or to use a seat, received six balls through his heart, and met the death which he had braved with impunity in the thick of many conflicts, and sought in vain in so many others.—S.

Chapter LXXXVI

Buonaparte's attempts to conciliate Britain—Plot to carry off Maria Louisa fails—State of feeling in France—The Army—The Jacobins—The Constitutionalists—Fouché and Siêyes made Peers—Freedom of the Press granted, and outraged—Independent conduct of Comté, editor of Le Censeur—Disaffections among the lower orders—Part of these assemble before the Tuileries, and applaud the Emperor—Festival of the Federates—New Constitution—It is received with dissatisfaction—Meeting of the Champ de Mai to ratify it—Buonaparte's Address to the Chambers of Peers and Deputies—The spirit of Jacobinism predominant in the latter.

MARIA LOUISA

While Murat was struggling and sinking under his evil fate, Buonaparte was actively preparing for the approaching contest. His first attempt, as we have already seen, was to conciliate the allied powers. To satisfy Great Britain, he passed an act abolishing the slave trade, and made some regulations concerning national education, in which he spoke highly of the systems of Bell and Lancaster. These measures were favourably construed by some of our legislators; and that they were so, is a complete proof that Buonaparte understood the temper of our nation. To suppose that, during his ten months of retirement, his mind was actively employed upon the miseries of the negroes, or the deplorable state of ignorance to which his own measures, and the want of early instruction, had reduced the youth of France, would argue but little acquaintance with his habits of ambition. To believe, on the contrary, that he would, at his first arrival in France, make any apparent sacrifices which might attract the good-will of his powerful and dangerous neighbours, is more consonant with his schemes, his interest, and his character. The path which he chose to gain the esteem of Britain, was by no means injudicious. The abolition of negro slavery, and the instruction of the poor, have (to the honour of our legislature) been frequent and anxious subjects of deliberation in the House of Commons; and to mankind, whether individually or collectively, no species of flattery is more pleasing than that of assent and imitation. It is not a little to the credit of our country, that the most avowed enemy of Britain strove to cultivate our good opinion, not by any offers of national advantage but by appearing to concur in general measures of benevolence, and attention to the benefit of society. Yet, upon the whole, the character of Napoleon was too generally understood, and the purpose of his apparent approximation to British sentiments, too obviously affected, for serving to make any general or serious impression in his favour.

With Austria, Napoleon acted differently. He was aware that no impression could be made on the Emperor Francis, or his minister Metternich, and that it had become impossible, with their consent, that he should fulfil his promise of presenting his wife and son to the people on the Champ de Mai. Stratagem remained the only resource; and some Frenchmen at Vienna, with those in Maria Louisa's train, formed a scheme of carrying off the Empress of France and her child. The plot was discovered and prevented, and the most public steps were immediately taken, to show that Austria considered all ties with Buonaparte as dissolved for ever. Maria Louisa, by her father's commands, laid aside the arms and liveries of her husband, hitherto displayed by her attendants and carriages, and assumed those of the house of Austria. This decisive event put an end to every hope so long cherished by Napoleon, that he might find some means of regaining the friendship of his father-in-law.

Nor did the other powers in Europe show themselves more accessible to his advances. He was, therefore, reduced to his own partisans in the French nation, and those won over from other parties, whom he might be able to add to them.

The army had sufficiently shown themselves to be his own, upon grounds which are easily appreciated. The host of public official persons, to whom the name under which they exercised their offices was indifferent, provided the salary continued to be attached to them, formed a large and influential body. And although we, who have never, by such mutations of our political system, been put to the trial of either abandoning our means of living, or submitting to a change of government, may, on hearing quoted names of respectability and celebrity who adopted the latter alternative, exclaim against French versatility, a glance at Britain during the frequent changes of the 17th century, may induce us to exchange the exclamation of poor France! for that of poor human nature! The professors of Cromwell's days, who piously termed themselves followers of Providence, because they complied with every change that came uppermost; and the sect of time-servers, including the honest patriot, who complained at the Restoration that he had complied with seven forms of government during the year, but lost his office by being too late of adhering to the last—would have made in their day a list equally long, and as entertaining, as the celebrated *Dictionnaire de Girouettes*. In matters dependent upon a sudden breeze of sentiment, the mercurial Frenchman is more apt to tack about than the phlegmatic and slowly-moved native of Britain; but when the steady trade-wind of interest prevails for a long season, men in all nations and countries show the same irresistible disposition to trim their sails by it; and in politics as in morals, it will be well to pray against being led into temptation.

STATE OF PARTIES

Besides those attached to him by mere interest, or from gratitude and respect for his talents, Napoleon had now among his adherents, or rather allies, not as a matter of choice, but of necessity, the Jacobin party, who had been obliged, though unwillingly, to adopt him as the head of a government, which they hoped to regenerate. To these were to be added a much larger and more respectable body, who, far from encouraging his attempt, had testified themselves anxious to oppose it to the last, but who, conceiving the cause of the Bourbons entirely lost, were willing to adhere to Buonaparte, on condition of obtaining a free constitution for France. Many of these acted, of course, on mixed motives; but if we were asked to form a definition of them, we should be induced to give the same, which, laying aside party spirit, we should ascribe to a right English Whig, whom we conceive to be a man of sense and moderation, a lover of laws and liberty, whose chief regard to particular princes and families is founded on what he apprehends to be the public good; and who differs from a sensible Tory so little, that there is no great chance of their disputing upon any important constitutional question, if it is fairly stated to both. Such, we believe, is the difference betwixt rational Constitutionalists and Royalists in France; and, undoubtedly, while all the feelings of the latter induced them to eye with abhorrence the domination of a usurper, there must have been many of the former, who, fearing danger to the independence of France from the intervention of foreign powers, conceived, that by advocating the cause of Napoleon, they were in some degree making a virtue of necessity, and playing an indifferent game with as much skill as the cards they held would permit. Many patriotic and sensible men, who had retained a regard for liberty during all the governments and all the anarchies which had subsisted for twenty years, endeavoured now to frame a system of government, grounded upon something like freedom, upon the difficulties of Buonaparte. Pressed as he was from abroad, and unsupported at home, save by the soldiery, he would, they conceived, be thrown by necessity under the protection of the nation, and obliged to recruit his adherents by complying with public opinion, and adopting a free government. Under this persuasion a great number of such characters, more or less shaded by attachment to a moderate and limited monarchy, were prepared to acknowledge Buonaparte's re-established authority, in so far as he should be found to deserve it, by concessions on his part.

The conduct and arguments of another portion of the friends of the constitution, rather resembled that which might have been adopted in England by moderate and intelligent Tories. Such men were not prepared to resign the cause of their lawful monarch, because fortune had for a time declared against him. They were of opinion, that to make a constitution permanent, the monarch must have his rights ascertained and vindicated, as well as those of the people; and that if a usurper were to be acknowledged upon any terms, however plausible, so soon as he had cut his way to success by his sword, the nation would be exposed to perpetual revolutions. Louis, these men might argue, had committed no crime whatever; he was only placed in circumstances which made some persons suppose he might possibly be tempted to meditate changes on the constitution, and on the charter which confirmed it. There was meanness in deserting a good and peaceable king at the command of a revolted army, and a discarded usurper. They regretted that their prince must be replaced by foreign bayonets; yet it was perhaps better that a moderate and peaceful government should be restored even thus, than that the French nation should continue to suffer under the despotic tyranny of their own soldiery. Those reasoners ridiculed the idea of a free constitution, which was to be generated betwixt Buonaparte, who, in his former reign, never allowed freedom of thought, word, or action, to exist unrepressed, and the old Revolutionists, who, during their period of power, could be satisfied with no degree of liberty until they destroyed every compact which holds civil society together, and made the country resemble one great bedlam, set on fire by the patients, who remained dancing in the midst of the flames.

Such we conceive to have been the principles on which wise and moderate men on either side acted during this distracted period. It is easy to suppose, that their opinions must have been varied by many more and less minute shades, arising from temperament, predilections, prejudices, passions, and feelings of self-interest, and that they were on either side liable to be pushed into exaggeration, or, according to the word which was formed to express that exaggeration—into Ultraism.

Meantime, Napoleon did all that was possible to conciliate the people's affection, and to show himself sincerely desirous of giving France the free constitution which he had promised. He used the advice of Carnot, Siêyes, and Fouché, and certainly profited by several of their lessons. He made it, notwithstanding, a condition, that Carnot and Siêyes should accept each a title and a seat in his House of Peers, to show that they were completely reconciled to the Imperial government; and both the ancient republicans condescended to exchange the *bonnet rouge*, for a coronet, which, considering their former opinions, sate somewhat awkwardly upon their brows.

But although the union of the Imperialists and popular party had been cemented by mutual hatred of the Bourbons, and was still kept together by apprehension of the King's adherents within, and his allies on the exterior, seeds of discord were soon visible between the Emperor and the popular leaders. While the former was eager once more to wield with full energy the sceptre he had recovered, the latter were continually reminding him, that he had only assumed it in a limited and restricted capacity, as the head of a free government, exercising, indeed, its executive power, but under the restraint of a popular constitution. Napoleon, in the frequent disputes which arose on these important points, was obliged to concede to the demagogues the principles which they insisted upon. But then, for the safety of the state, involved in foreign and domestic dangers, he contended it was necessary to invest the chief magistrate with a vigour beyond the law, a dictatorial authority, temporary in its duration, but nearly absolute in its extent, as had been the manner in the free states of antiquity, when the republic was in imminent danger. Carnot and Fouché, on the other hand, considered, that although it seemed natural, and might be easy, to confer such power at the present moment, the resumption of it by the nation, when it was once vested in the hands of Buonaparte, would be a hopeless experiment. The Emperor, therefore, and his ministers, proceeded to their mutual tasks with no mutual confidence; but, on the contrary, with jealousy, thinly veiled by an affectation of deference on the side of Buonaparte, and respect on that of his counsellors.

LIBERTY OF THE PRESS

The very first sacrifice which the Emperor gave to freedom proved an inconvenient one to his government. This was nothing less than the freedom of the press. It is true, that the influence of his minister of police managed by indirect means to get possession of most of the journals; so that of sixty writers, employed generally, if not constantly, in periodical composition, five only were now found friendly to the royal cause. The other pens, which a few days before described Napoleon as a species of Ogre, who had devoured the youth of France, now wrote him down a hero and a liberator. Still, when the liberty of the press was once established, it was soon found impossible to prevent it from asserting its right of utterance; and there were found authors to advocate the cause of the Bourbons, from principle, from caprice, from the love of contradiction.

Napoleon, who always showed himself sensitively alive to the public censure, established inspectors of the booksellers. The minister of police, a friend of liberty, but, as Compte, the editor of *Le Censeur*, neatly observed, only of liberty after the fashion of M. Fouché, used every art in his power to prevent the contagion of freedom from spreading too widely. This M. Compte was a loud, and probably a sincere advocate of freedom, and had been a promoter of Buonaparte's return, as likely to advance the good cause. Seeing the prevailing influence of the military, he published some severe remarks on the undue weight the army assumed in public affairs, which, he hesitated not to say, was bringing France to the condition of Rome, when the empire was disposed of by the Prætorian guards. This stung to the quick—the journal was seized by the police, and the minister endeavoured to palliate the fact in the *Moniteur*, by saying, that, though seized, it had been instantly restored. But Compte was not a man to be so silenced; he published a contradiction of the official statement, and declared that his journal had not been restored. He was summoned the next day before the prefect, alternately threatened and wheedled, upbraided at one moment with ungrateful resistance to the cause of the Emperor, and requested at the next to think of something in which government might serve him. Steeled against every proffer and entreaty, Compte only required to be permitted to profit by the restored liberty of the press; nor could the worthy magistrate make him rightly understand that when the Emperor gave all men liberty to publish what pleased themselves, it was under the tacit condition that it should also please the prefect and minister of police. Compte had the spirit to publish the whole affair.

In the meanwhile, proclamations of Louis, forbidding the payment of taxes, and announcing the arrival of 1,200,000 men under the walls of Paris, covered these walls every night in spite of the police. A newspaper, called the *Lily*, was also secretly, but generally circulated, which advocated the royal cause. In the better classes of society, where Buonaparte was feared and hated, lampoons, satires, pasquinades, glided from hand to hand, turning his person, ministers, and government, into the most bitter ridicule. Others attacked him with eloquent invective, and demanded what he had in common with the word Liberty, which he now pretended to connect with his reign. He was, they said, the sworn enemy of liberty, the assassin of the Republic, the destroyer of French freedom, which had been so dearly bought; the show of liberty which he held, was a trick of legerdemain, executed under protection of his bayonets. Such was his notion of liberty when it destroyed the national representation at St. Cloud—Such was the freedom he gave when he established an Oriental despotism in the enlightened kingdom at France. Such, when abolishing all free communication of sentiments among citizens, and proscribing every liberal and philosophical idea under the nickname of Ideology. "Can it be forgotten," they continued, "that Heaven and Hell are not more irreconcilable ideas, than Buonaparte and Liberty?—The very word Freedom," they said, "was proscribed under his iron reign, and only first gladdened the ears of Frenchmen after twelve years of humiliation and despair, on the happy restoration of Louis XVIII.— Ah, miserable impostor!" they exclaimed, "when would he have spoke of liberty, had not the return of Louis familiarized us with freedom and peace." The spirit of disaffection spread among certain classes of the lower ranks. The market-women (*dames des halles,*) so formidable during the time of the Fronde, and in the early years of the Revolution, for their opposition to the court, were now royalists, and, of course, clamorous on the side of the party they espoused. They invented, or some loyal rhymer composed for them, a song,[123] the burden of which demanded back the King, as their father of Ghent. They ridiculed, scolded, and mobbed the commissaries of police, who endeavoured to stop these musical expressions of disaffection; surrounded the chief of their number, danced around him, and chanted the obnoxious burden, until Fouché being

---

[123] *Donnez nous nôtre paire de gants,* equivalent in pronunciation to *nôtre Père de Ghent.*—S.

ashamed to belie the new doctrines of liberty of thought, speech, and publication, his agents were instructed to leave these Amazons undisturbed on account of their political sentiments.

While Buonaparte was unable to form an interest in the saloons, and found that even the *dames des halles* were becoming discontented, he had upon his side the militia of the suburbs; those columns of pikemen so famous in the Revolution, whose furious and rude character added to the terrors, if not to the dignity, of his reign. Let us not be accused of a wish to depreciate honest industry, or hold up to contempt the miseries of poverty. It is not the poverty, but the ignorance and the vice of the rabble of great cities, which render them always disagreeable, and sometimes terrible. They are entitled to protection from the laws, and kindness from the government; but he who would use them as political engines, invokes the assistance of a blatant beast with a thousand heads, well furnished with fangs to tear and throats to roar, but devoid of tongues to speak reason, ears to hear it, eyes to see it, or judgment to comprehend it.

For a little time after Buonaparte's return, crowds of artisans of the lowest order assembled under the windows of the Tuileries, and demanded to see the Emperor, whom, on his appearance, they greeted with shouts, as *le Grand Entrepreneur*, or general employer of the class of artisans, in language where the coarse phraseology of their rank was adorned with such flowers of rhetoric as the times of terror had coined. Latterly, the numbers of this assembly were maintained by a distribution of a few *sous* to the shouters.

However disgusted with these degrading exhibitions, Buonaparte felt he could not dispense with this species of force, and was compelled to institute a day of procession, and a solemn festival, in favour of this description of persons, who, from the mode in which they were enrolled, were termed Federates.

FESTIVAL OF THE FEDERATES

On 14th May, the motley and ill-arranged ranks which assembled on this memorable occasion, exhibited, in the eyes of the disgusted and frightened spectators, all that is degraded by habitual vice, and hardened by stupidity and profligacy. The portentous procession moved on along the Boulevards to the court of the Tuileries, with shouts, in which the praises of the Emperor were mingled with imprecations, and with the Revolutionary songs (long silenced in Paris,)—the Marseilloise Hymn, the Carmagnole, and the Day of Departure. The appearance of the men, the refuse of manufactories, of work-houses, of jails; their rags, their filth, their drunkenness; their ecstacies of blasphemous rage, and no less blasphemous joy, stamped them with the character of the willing perpetrators of the worst horrors of the Revolution. Buonaparte himself was judged, by close observers, to shrink with abhorrence from the assembly he himself had convoked. His guards were under arms, and the field artillery loaded, and turned on the Place de Carrousel, filled with the motley crowd, who, from the contrasted colour of the corn porters and charcoal-men, distinguished in the group, were facetiously called his Grey and Black Mousquetaires. He hasted to dismiss his hideous minions, with a sufficient distribution of praises and of liquor. The national guards conceived themselves insulted on this occasion, because compelled to give their attendance along with the Federates. The troops of the line felt for the degraded character of the Emperor. The haughty character of the French soldiers had kept them from fraternizing with the rabble, even in the cause of Napoleon. They had been observed, on the march from Cannes, to cease their cries of *Vive l'Empereur*, when, upon entering any considerable town, the shout was taken up by the mob of the place, and to suspend their acclamations, rather than mingle them with those of the *pequins*, whom they despised. They now muttered to each other, on seeing the court which Buonaparte seemed compelled to bestow on these degraded artisans, that the conqueror of Marengo and Wagram had sunk into the mere captain of a rabble. In short, the disgraceful character of the alliance thus formed between Buonaparte and the lees of the people, was of a nature incapable of being glossed over even in the flattering pages of the *Moniteur*, which, amidst a flourishing description of this memorable procession, was compelled to admit, that, in some places, the name of the Emperor was incongruously mingled with expressions and songs, which recalled an era *unfortunately too famous*.

Fretted by external dangers, and internal disturbances, and by the degrading necessity of appearing every night before a mob, who familiarly hailed him as *Père le Violette*, and, above all, galled by the suggestions of his philosophical counsellors, who, among other innovations, wished him to lay aside the style of Emperor for that of President, or Grand General of the Republic, Napoleon, to rid himself at once of occupations offensive to his haughty disposition, withdrew from the Tuileries to the more retired palace of the Elysée Bourbon, and seemed on a sudden to become once more the Emperor he had been before his abdication. Here he took into his own hands, with the assistance of Benjamin Constant, and other statesmen, the construction of a new constitution. Their system included all those checks and regulations which are understood to form the essence of a free government, and greatly resembled that granted by the Royal Charter.[124] Nevertheless, it was extremely ill received by all parties, but especially by those who expected from Napoleon a constitution more free than that which they had dissolved by driving Louis XVIII. from the throne. There were other grave exceptions stated against the scheme of government.

First, The same objection was stated against this Imperial grant which had been urged with so much vehemence against the royal charter, namely, that it was not a compact between the people and the sovereign, in which the former called the latter to the throne under certain conditions, but a recognition by the sovereign of the liberties of the people. The meeting of the Champ de Mai had indeed been summoned, (as intimated in the decrees from Lyons,)

---

[124] The following is an abridgment of its declarations:—The legislative power resides in the Emperor and two Chambers. The Chamber of Peers is hereditary, and the Emperor names them. Their number is unlimited. The Second Chamber is elected by the people, and is to consist of 629 members—none are to be under twenty-five years. The President is appointed by the members, but approved of by the Emperor. Members to be paid at the rate settled by the Constituent Assembly. It is to be renewed every five years. The Emperor may prorogue, adjourn, or dissolve the House of Representatives. Sittings to be public. The Electoral Colleges are maintained. Land-tax and direct taxes to be voted only for a year; indirect may be for several years. No levy of men for the army, nor any exchange of territory, but by a law. Taxes to be proposed by the Chamber of Representatives. Ministers to be responsible. Judges to be irremovable. Juries to be established. Right of petition is established—freedom of worship—inviolability of property. The last article says, that "the French people declare that they do not mean to delegate the power of restoring the Bourbons, or any prince of that family, even in case of the exclusion of the Imperial dynasty."—S.

chiefly with the purpose of forming and adopting the new constitution; but, according to the present system, they were only to have the choice of adopting or rejecting that which Napoleon had prepared for them. The disappointment was great among those philosophers who desired "better bread than is made of wheat;" and could not enjoy liberty itself, unless it emanated directly from the will of the people, and was sanctioned by popular discussion. But Napoleon was determined that the convention of the 10th May should have no other concern in the constitution, save to accept it when offered. He would not intrust such an assembly with the revision of the laws by which he was to govern.

ADDITIONAL ACT

Secondly, This new constitution, though presenting an entirely new basis of government, was published under the singular title of an "Additional[125] Act to the Constitutions of the Emperor," and thereby constituted a sort of appendix to a huge mass of unrepealed organic laws, many of them inconsistent with the Additional Act in tenor and in spirit.

Those who had enjoyed the direct confidence of the Emperor while the treaty was framing, endeavoured to persuade themselves that Napoleon meant fairly by France, yet confessed they had found it difficult to enlighten his ideas on the subject of a limited monarchy. They felt, that though the Emperor might be induced to contract his authority, yet what remained in his own hand would be wielded as arbitrarily as ever; and likewise that he would never regard his ministers otherwise than as the immediate executors of his pleasure, and responsible to himself alone. He would still continue to transport his whole chancery at his stirrup, and transmit

---

[125] "The word *additional* disenchanted the friends of liberty. They recognised in it the ill-disguised continuation of the chief institutions created in favour of absolute power. From that moment Napoleon to their view became an incurable despot, and I, for my part, regarded him in the light of a madman delivered, bound hand and foot, to the mercy of Europe."—Fouché, tom. ii., p. 276.

sealed orders to be executed by a minister whom he had not consulted on their import.[126]

The Royalists triumphed on the publication of this Additional Act: "Was it for this," they said, "you broke your oaths, and banished your monarch, to get the same, or nearly similar laws, imposed on you by a Russian ukase or a Turkish firman, which you heretofore enjoyed by charter, in the same manner as your ancestors, called freemen by excellence, held their rights from their limited sovereigns; and for this have you exchanged a peaceful prince, whose very weakness was your security, for an ambitious warrior, whose strength is your weakness? For this have you a second time gone to war with all Europe—for the Additional Act and the Champ de Mai?"

The more determined Republicans, besides their particular objections to an Upper House, which the Emperor could fill with his own minions, so as effectually to control the representatives of the people, found the proposed constitution utterly devoid of the salt which should savour it. There was no acknowledgment of abstract principles; no dissertation concerning the rights of government and the governed; no metaphysical discussions on the origin of laws; and they were as much mortified and disappointed as the zealot who hears a discourse on practical morality, when he expected a sermon on the doctrinal points of theology. The unfortunate Additional Act became the subject of attack and raillery on all sides; and was esteemed to possess in so slight a degree the principles of durability, that a bookseller being asked for a copy by a customer, replied, He did not deal in *periodical publications*.[127]

Under these auspices the Champ de Mai was opened, and that it might be in all respects incongruous, it was held on the 1st of June.[128] Deputies were supposed to attend from all departments,

---

[126] Letters from Paris, written during the last reign of Napoleon, vol. i., p. 197 [By John Cam Hobhouse, Esq.; now Sir J. C. Hobhouse.]
[127] It was subjected, notwithstanding, with the usual success, to the electoral bodies, whose good-nature never refused a constitution which was recommended by the existing government. The number of those who gave their votes were more than a million; being scarce a tenth part, however, of those who had qualifications.
[128] Moniteur, June 2; Savary, tom. iv., p. 34; Fouché, tom. ii., p. 277.

not, as it had been latterly arranged, to canvass the new constitution, but to swear to observe it; and not to receive the Empress Maria Louisa and her son as the pledge of twenty years peace, but to behold the fatal eagles, the signal of instant and bloody war, distributed by the Emperor to the soldiers.

Napoleon and his brothers, whom he had once more collected around him, figured, in quaint and fantastic robes, in the Champ de Mai; he as Emperor, and they as princes of the blood—another subject of discontent to the Republicans. The report of the votes was made, the electors swore to the Additional Act, the drums rolled, the trumpets flourished, the cannon thundered. But the acclamations were few and forced. The Emperor seemed to view the scene as an empty pageant, until he was summoned to the delivery of the eagles to the various new-raised regiments; and then, amid the emblems of past, and, as might be hoped, the auguries of future victories, he was himself again. But, on the whole, the Champ de Mai, was, in the language of Paris, *une pièce tombée*, a condemned farce, which was soon to be succeeded by a bloody tragedy.

CHAMBER OF DEPUTIES

The meeting of the Chambers was the next subject of interest. The Chamber of Peers did not present, like the corresponding assembly in Britain, members of long descent, ample fortunes, independence of principle, and education corresponding to their rank of hereditary legislators. It consisted in the princes of Napoleon's blood royal, to whom was added Lucien, long estranged from his brother's councils, but who now, instigated by fraternal affection, or tired of literary leisure, having presented his epic poem to a thankless and regardless public, endeavoured to save his brother in his present difficulties, as by his courage and presence of mind he had assisted him during the revolution of Brumaire. There were about one hundred other dignitaries, more than one half of whom were military men, including two or three old Jacobins, such as Siêyes and Carnot, who had taken titles, decorations, and rank, inconsistently with the tenor of their whole life. The rest had been the creatures of Buonaparte's former reign, with some men of letters devoted to his cause, and recently ennobled. This body, which could have no other will than that of the Emperor, was regarded by the Republicans and Constitutionalists with jealousy, and by the citizens with contempt. Buonaparte himself expressed his opinion of it with something approaching the latter sentiment. He had scarce formed his tools, before he seems to have been convinced of their inefficacy, and of the little influence which they could exercise on the public mind.[129]

It was very different with the second Chamber, in which were posted the ancient men of the Revolution, and their newer associates, who looked forward with hope that Buonaparte might yet assume the character of a patriot sovereign, and by his military talents save France for her sake, not for his own. The latter class comprehended many men, not only of talent, but of virtue and public spirit; with too large a proportion, certainly, of those who vainly desired a system of Republican liberty, which so many years of bloody and fruitless experiment should have led even the most extravagant to abandon, as inconsistent with the situation of the country, and the genius of the French nation.

The disputes of the Chamber of Representatives with the executive government commenced on June 4th, the first day of their sitting; and, like those of their predecessors, upon points of idle etiquette. They chose Lanjuinais for their president; a preferment which, alighting on one who had been the defender of Louis XVI., the active and determined resister of the power of Robespierre, and especially, the statesman who drew up the list of crimes in consequence of which Napoleon's forfeiture had been declared in 1814, could not be acceptable to the Emperor. Napoleon being applied to for confirmation of the election, referred the committee for his answer to the chamberlain, who, he stated, would deliver it the next day by the page in waiting. The Chamber took fire, and Napoleon was compelled to return an immediate though reluctant approval of their choice. The next remarkable indication of the temper of the Chamber, was the *extempore* effusion of a deputy named Sibuet, against the use of the epithets of duke, count, and

---

[129] The punsters of Paris selected Labédoyère, Drouot, Ney, and L'Allemand, as the *Quatre pairs fides (perfides.)* while Vandamme and others were termed the *Pairs sifflés.*—S.

other titles of honour, in the Chamber of Representatives. Being observed to read his invective from notes, which was contrary to the form of the Chamber, Sibuet was silenced for the moment as out of order; but the next day, or soon afterwards, having got his speech by heart, the Chamber was under the necessity of listening to him, and his motion was got rid of with difficulty.[130] On the same day, a list of the persons appointed to the peerage was demanded from Carnot, in his capacity of minister, which he declined to render till the session had commenced. This also occasioned much uproar and violence, which the president could scarce silence by the incessant peal of his bell. The oath to be taken by the deputies was next severely scrutinized, and the Imperialists carried with difficulty a resolution, that it should be taken to the Emperor and the constitution, without mention of the nation.

The second meeting, on June 7th, was as tumultuous as the first. A motion was made by Felix Lepelletier, that the Chamber should decree to Napoleon the title of Saviour of his Country. This was resisted on the satisfactory ground, that the country was not yet saved; and the Chamber passed to the order of the day by acclamation.[131]

Notwithstanding these open intimations of the reviving spirit of Jacobinism, or at least of opposition to the Imperial sway, Napoleon's situation obliged him for the time to address the unruly spirits which he had called together, with the confidence which it was said necromancers found it needful to use towards the dangerous fiends whom they had evoked. His address to both Chambers was sensible, manly, and becoming his situation. He surrendered, in their presence, all his pretensions to absolute power, and professed himself a friend to liberty; demanded the assistance of the Chambers in matters of finance, intimated a desire of some regulations to check the license of the press, and required from the representatives an example of confidence, energy, and patriotism, to encounter the dangers to which the country was exposed. The Peers replied in corresponding terms. Not so the second Chamber; for, notwithstanding the utmost efforts of the Imperialists, their reply

---

[130] See Moniteur, June 6.
[131] Moniteur, June 9.

bore a strong tincture of the sentiments of the opposite party. The Chamber promised, indeed, their unanimous support in repelling the foreign enemy; but they announced their intention to take under their consideration the constitution, as recognised by the Additional Act, and to point out its defects and imperfections, with the necessary remedies. They also added a moderating hint, directed against the fervour of Napoleon's ambition. "The nation," they said, "nourishes no plans of aggrandisement. Not even the will of a victorious prince will lead them beyond the boundaries of self-defence." In his rejoinder, Napoleon did not suffer these obnoxious hints to escape his notice. He endeavoured to school this refractory assembly into veneration for the constitution, which he declared to be "the pole-star in the tempest;" and judiciously observed, "there was little cause to provide against the intoxications of triumph, when they were about to contend for existence. He stated the crisis to be imminent, and cautioned the Chamber to avoid the conduct of the Roman people in the latter ages of the empire, who could not resist the temptation of engaging furiously in abstract discussions, even while the battering-rams of the common enemy were shaking the gates of the capitol."

Thus parted Buonaparte and his Chambers of Legislature; he to try his fortune in the field of battle, they to their task of altering and modifying the laws, and inspiring a more popular spirit and air into the enactments he had made, in hopes that the dictatorship of the Jacobins might be once again substituted for the dictatorship of the Emperor. All men saw that the Imperialists and Republicans only waited till the field was won, that they might contend for the booty; and so little was the nation disposed to sympathize with the active, turbulent, and bustling demagogues by whom the contest was to be maintained against the Emperor, that almost all predicted with great unconcern their probable expulsion, either by the sword of Buonaparte or the Bourbons.

Chapter LXXXVII

Preparations for War—Positions of the Allied Forces, amounting in whole to One Million of Men—Buonaparte's Force not more than 200,000—Conscription not ventured upon—National Guard—their reluctance to serve—Many Provinces hostile to Napoleon—Fouché's Report makes known the Disaffection—Insurrection in La Vendée—quelled—Military Resources—Plan of Campaign—Paris Placed in a Complete State of Defence—Frontier Passes and Towns fortified—Generals who accept Command under Napoleon—He Announces his Purpose to measure himself with Wellington.

PREPARATIONS FOR WAR

We are now to consider the preparations made for the invasion of France along the whole eastern frontier—the means of resistance which the talents of the Emperor presented to his numerous enemies—and the internal situation of the country itself.

While the events now commemorated were passing in France, the allies made the most gigantic preparations for the renewal of war. The Chancellor of the Exchequer of England had achieved a loan of thirty-six millions, upon terms surprisingly moderate, and the command of this treasure had put the whole troops of the coalition into the most active advance.

The seat of the Congress had been removed from Vienna to Frankfort, to be near the theatre of war. The Emperors of Russia and Austria, with the King of Prussia, had once more placed themselves at the head of their respective armies. The whole eastern frontier was menaced by immense forces. One hundred and fifty thousand Austrians, disengaged from Murat, might enter France through Switzerland, the Cantons having acceded to the coalition. An army equal in strength menaced the higher Rhine. Schwartzenberg commanded the Austrians in chief, having under him Bellegarde, and Frimont, Bianchi, and Vincent. Two hundred thousand Russians were pressing towards the frontiers of Alsace. The Archduke Constantine was nominated generalissimo, but Barclay de Tolly, Sacken, Langeron, &c. were the efficient commanders. One hundred and fifty thousand Prussians, under Blucher, occupied Flanders, and were united with about eighty thousand troops, British, or in British pay, under the Duke of Wellington. There were also to be reckoned the contingents of the different princes of Germany, so that the allied forces were computed grossly to amount to upwards of one million of men. The reader must not, however, suppose that such an immense force was, or could be, brought forward at once. They were necessarily disposed on various lines for the convenience of subsistence, and were to be brought up successively in support of each other.

To meet this immense array, Napoleon, with his usual talent and celerity, had brought forward means of surprising extent. The regular army, diminished by the Bourbons, had been, by calling out the retired officers and disbanded soldiers, increased from something rather under 100,000 men, to double that number of experienced troops, of the first quality. But this was dust in the balance; and the mode of conscription was so intimately connected with Napoleon's wars of conquest and disaster, that he dared not propose, nor would the Chamber of Representatives have agreed, to have recourse to the old and odious resource of conscription, which, however, Buonaparte trusted he might still find effectual in the month of June, to the number of 300,000. In the meantime, it was proposed to render moveable, for active service, two hundred battalions of the national guard, choosing those most fit for duty, which would make a force of 112,000 men. It was also proposed to levy as many Federates, that is, volunteers of the lower orders, as could be brought together in the different departments. The levy of the national guards was ordered by an Imperial decree of 5th April, 1815, and commissioners, chiefly of the Jacobin faction, were sent down into the different departments, Buonaparte being well pleased at once to employ them in their own sphere, and to get rid of their presence at Paris. Their efforts were, however, unable to excite the spirit of the country; for they had either survived their own energies, or the nation had been too long accustomed to their mode of oratory, to feel any responsive impulse. Liberty and fraternity was no longer a rallying sound, and the summons to arms, by decrees as peremptory as those relating to the conscription, though bearing another name, spread a general spirit of disgust through many departments in the north of France. There and in Brittany the disaffection of the inhabitants appeared in a sullen, dogged stubbornness, rather than in the form of active resistance to Napoleon's decrees. The national guards refused to parade, and, if compelled to do so, took every opportunity to desert and return home; so that it often happened that a battalion, which had mustered six hundred men, dwindled down to a fifth before they had marched two leagues.

In the departments of La Garde, of the Marne, and the Nether Loire, the white flag was displayed, and the tree of liberty, which had been replanted in many places after the political regeneration of Buonaparte, was cut down. The public mind in many provinces displayed itself as highly unfavourable to Napoleon.

DISAFFECTION

A report drawn up by Fouché, stated in high-coloured language the general disaffection. Napoleon always considered this communication as published with a view of prejudicing his affairs; and as that versatile statesman was already in secret correspondence with the allies, it was probably intended as much to encourage the Royalists, as to dismay the adherents of Napoleon. This arch-intriguer, whom, to use an expression of Junius, treachery itself could not trust, was at one moment nearly caught in his own toils; and although he carried the matter with infinite address, Napoleon would have made him a prisoner, or caused him to be shot, but for the intimation of Carnot, that, if he did so, his own reign would not last an hour longer.[132]

Thus Buonaparte was already, in a great measure, reduced to the office of Generalissimo of the State; and there were not wanting

---

[132] The particulars of this intrigue show with what audacity, and at what risk, Fouché waded, swam, or dived, among the troubled waters which were his element. An agent of Prince Metternich had been despatched to Paris, to open a communication with Fouché on the part of the Austrian government. Falling under suspicion, from some banking transaction, this person was denounced to Buonaparte as a suspicious person, and arrested by his interior police, which, as there cannot be too much precaution in a well-managed state, watched, and were spies upon, the general police under Fouché. The agent was brought before Buonaparte, who threatened to cause him be shot to death on the very spot, unless he told him the whole truth. The man then confessed that Metternich sent him to Fouché, to request the latter to send a secure agent to Bâle, to meet with a confidential person on the part of the Austrian minister, whom Fouché's envoy was to recognise by a peculiar sign, which the informer also made known. "Have you fulfilled your commission so far as concerns Fouché?" said the Emperor.—"I have," answered the Austrian agent.—"And has he despatched any one to Bâle?"—"That I cannot tell." The agent was detained in a secret prison. Baron Fleury de Chamboullon, an auditor, was instantly despatched to Bâle, to represent the agent whom Fouché should have sent thither, and fathom the depth and character of the intrigue betwixt the French and Austrian ministers. Fouché soon discovered that the agent sent to him by Metternich was missing, conjectured his fate, and instantly went to seek an audience of the Emperor. Having mentioned other matters, he seemed to recollect himself, and begged pardon, with affected unconcern, for not having previously mentioned an affair of some consequence, which, nevertheless, he had forgotten amid the hurry of business. "An agent had come to him from the Austrian government," he said, "requesting him to send a confidential person to Bâle, to a correspondent of Metternich, and he now came to ask whether it would be his Majesty's pleasure that he should avail himself of the opening, in order to learn the secret purposes of the enemy?" Napoleon was not deceived by this trick. There were several mirrors in the room, by which he could perceive and enjoy his perfidious minister's ill-concealed embarrassment. "Monsieur Fouché," he said, "it may be dangerous to treat me as a fool: I have your agent in safe custody, and penetrate your whole intrigue. Have you sent to Bâle?"—"No, Sire."—"The happier for you: had you done so, you should have died." Fleury was unable to extract any thing of consequence from Werner, the confidant of Metternich, who met him at Bâle. The Austrian seemed to expect communications from Fouché, without being prepared to make them. Fleury touched on the plan of assassinating Buonaparte, which Werner rejected with horror, as a thing not to be thought of by Metternich or the allies. They appointed a second meeting, but in the interim Fouché made the Austrian aware of the discovery, and Baron Fleury, on his second journey to Bâle, found no Mr. Werner to meet him.—See Fleury de Chamboullon, tom. ii., p. 6.

Buonaparte gives almost the same account of this intrigue in his St. Helena Conversations as Fouché in his Memoirs. But Napoleon does not mention Carnot's interposition to prevent Fouché from being put to death without process of law. "You may shoot Fouché to-day," said the old Jacobin, "but to-morrow you will cease to reign. The people of the Revolution permit you to retain the throne only on condition you respect their liberties. They account Fouché one of their strongest guarantees. If he is guilty, he must be legally proceeded against." Buonaparte, therefore, gaining no proof against Fouché by the mission of Fleury, was fain to shut his eyes on what he saw but too well.—S.

many, who dared to entreat him to heal the wounds of the country by a second abdication in favour of his son—a measure which the popular party conceived might avert the impending danger of invasion.

In the meantime, about the middle of May, a short insurrection broke out in La Vendée, under De Autechamp, Suzannet, Sapineau, and especially the brave La Rochejacquelein. The war was neither long nor bloody, for an overpowering force was directed against the insurgents, under Generals Lamarque and Travot. The people were ill prepared for resistance, and the government menaced them with the greatest severities, the instructions of Carnot to the military having a strong tincture of his ancient education in the school of terror. Yet the Chamber of Deputies did not in all respects sanction the severities of the government. When a member, called Leguevel, made a motion for punishing with pains and penalties the Royalists of the west, the assembly heard him with patience and approbation, propose that the goods and estates of the revolters (whom he qualified as brigands, priests, and Royalists) should be confiscated; but when he added, that not only the insurgents themselves, but their relations in the direct line, whether ascendants or descendants, should be declared outlaws, a general exclamation of horror drove the orator from the tribune.

After a battle near La Roche Servière, which cost the brave La Rochejacquelein his life, the remaining chiefs signed a capitulation, by which they disbanded their followers, and laid down their arms, at the very time when holding out a few days would have made them acquainted with the battle of Waterloo. Released from actual civil war, Napoleon now had leisure to prepare for the external conflict.

The means resorted to by the French government, which we have already alluded to, had enabled Carnot to represent the national means in a most respectable point of view. By his report to the two Chambers, he stated, that on 1st April 1814, the army had consisted of 450,000 men, who had been reduced by the Bourbons to 175,000. Since the return of Napoleon, the number had been increased to 375,000 combatants of every kind; and before the 1st of August, was expected to amount to half a million. The Imperial Guards, who were termed the country's brightest ornament in time of peace, and its best bulwark in time of war, were recruited to the number of 40,000 men.

Stupendous efforts had repaired, the report stated, the losses of the artillery during the three disastrous years of 1812, 1813, 1814. Stores, ammunition, arms of every kind, were said to be provided in abundance. The remounting of the cavalry had been accomplished in such a manner as to excite the surprise of every one. Finally, there was, as a body in reserve, the whole mass of sedentary national guards, so called, because they were not among the chosen bands which had been declared moveable. But the bulk of these were either unfit for service, or unwilling to serve, and could only be relied on for securing the public tranquillity. Corps of Federates had been formed in all the districts where materials could be found of which to compose them.

From these forces Napoleon selected a grand army to act under his personal orders. They were chosen with great care, and the preparation of their *matériel* was of the most extensive and complete description. The numbers in gross might amount to 150,000; as great a number of troops, perhaps, as can conveniently move upon one plan of operations, or be subjected to one generalissimo. A large deduction is to be made to attain the exact amount of his effective force.

PLAN OF THE CAMPAIGN

Thus prepared for action, no doubt was made that Buonaparte would open the campaign, by assuming offensive operations. To wait till the enemy had assembled their full force on his frontier, would have suited neither the man nor the moment. It was most agreeable to his system, his disposition, and his interest, to rush upon some separate army of the allies, surprise them, according to his own phrase, in delict, and, by its dispersion or annihilation, give courage to France, animate her to fresh exertions in his cause, intimidate the confederated powers, and gain time for sowing in their league the seeds of disunion. Even the Royalists, whose interest was so immediately connected with the defeat of Buonaparte, were dismayed by witnessing his gigantic preparations, and sadly anticipated victories as the first result, though they trusted that, as in 1814, he would be at length worn out by force of numbers and reiterated exertions.

But though all guessed at the mode of tactics which Napoleon would employ, there was a difference of opinion respecting the point on which his first exertions would be made; and in general it was augured, that, trusting to the strength of Lisle, Valenciennes, and other fortified places on the frontiers of Flanders, his first real attack, whatever diversion might be made elsewhere, would take place upon Manheim, with the view of breaking asunder the Austrian and Russian armies as they were forming, or rather of attacking them separately, to prevent their communication in line. If he should succeed in thus overwhelming the advance of the Austrians and Russians, by directing his main force to this one point, before they were fully prepared, it was supposed he might break up the plan of the allies for this campaign.

But Buonaparte was desirous to aim a decisive blow at the most enterprising and venturous of the invading armies. He knew Blucher, and had heard of Wellington; he therefore resolved to move against those generals, while he opposed walls and fortified places to the more slow and cautious advance of the Austrian general, Schwartzenberg, and trusted that distance might render ineffectual the progress of the Russians.

PREPARATIONS OF WAR

According to this general system, Paris, under the direction of General Haxo, was, on the northern side, placed in a complete state of defence, by a double line of fortifications, so that, if the first were forced, the defenders might retire within the second, instead of being compelled, as in the preceding year, to quit the heights and fall back upon the city. Montmartre was very strongly fortified. The southern part of the city on the opposite side of the Seine was only covered with a few field-works; time, and the open character of the ground, permitting no more. But the Seine itself was relied upon as a barrier, having proved such in 1814.

On the frontiers, similar precautions were observed. Intrenchments were constructed in the five principal passes of the Vosgesian mountains, and all the natural passes and strongholds of Lorraine were put in the best possible state of defence. The posts on the inner line were strengthened with the greatest care. The fine military position under the walls of Lyons was improved with great expense and labour. A *tête-de-pont* was erected at Brotteau; a drawbridge and barricade protected the suburb la Guillotière; redoubts were erected between the Saonne and Rhine, and upon the heights of Pierre Encise and the Quarter of Saint John. Guise, Vitri, Soissons, Chauteau-Thierry, Langres, and all the towns capable of any defence, were rendered as strong as posts, palisades, redoubts, and field-works could make them. The Russian armies, though pressing fast forward, were not as yet arrived upon the line of operations; and Napoleon doubtless trusted that these impediments, in front of the Austrian line, would arrest any hasty advance on their part, since the well-known tactics of that school declare against leaving in their rear fortresses or towns possessed by the enemy, however insignificant or slightly garrisoned, or however completely they might be masked.

About now to commence his operations, Napoleon summoned round him his best and most experienced generals. Soult, late minister of war for Louis XVIII., was named major-general. He obeyed, he says, not in any respect as an enemy of the King, but as a citizen and soldier, whose duty it was to obey whomsoever was at the head of the government, as that of the Vicar of Bray subjected him in ghostly submission to each head of the Church *pro tempore*. Ney was ordered to repair to the army at Lisle, "if he wished," so the command was expressed, "to witness the first battle." Macdonald was strongly solicited to accept a command, but declined it with disdain. Davoust, the minister-at-war, undertook to remove his scruples, and spoke to him of what his honour required. "It is not from you," replied the maréchal, "that I am to learn sentiments of honour," and persisted in his refusal. D'Erlon, Reille, Vandamme, Gerard, and Mouton de Lobau, acted as lieutenant-generals. The cavalry was placed under the command of Grouchy (whom Napoleon had created a maréchal.) Pajol, Excelmans, Milhaud, and Kellerman, were his seconds in command. Flahault, Dejean, Labédoyère, and other officers of distinction, acted as the Emperor's aides-de-camp. The artillery were three hundred pieces; the cavalry approached to twenty-five thousand men; the guard to the same number; and there is little doubt that the whole army amounted in effective force to nearly 130,000 soldiers, in the most complete state as to arms and equipment, who now marched to a war which they themselves had occasioned, under an Emperor of their own making, and bore both in their hearts and on their tongues the sentiments of death or victory.

For the protection of the rest of the frontier, during Napoleon's campaign in Flanders, Suchet was intrusted with the command on the frontiers of Switzerland, with directions to attack Montmellian as soon as possible after the 14th of June, which day Buonaparte had fixed for the commencement of hostilities. Massena was ordered to repair to Metz, to assume the government of that important fortress, and the command of the 3d and 4th divisions. All preparations being thus made, Napoleon at length announced what had long occupied his secret thoughts. "I go," he said, as he threw himself into his carriage to join his army, "I go to measure myself with Wellington."

But although Napoleon's expressions were those of confidence and defiance, his internal feelings were of a different complexion. "I no longer felt," as he afterwards expressed himself in his exile, "that complete confidence in final success, which accompanied me on former undertakings. Whether it was that I was getting beyond the period of life when men are usually favoured by fortune, or whether the impulse of my career seemed impeded in my own eyes, and to my own imagination, it is certain that I felt a depression of spirit. Fortune, which used to follow my steps to load me with her bounties, was now a severe deity, from whom I might snatch a few favours, but for which she exacted severe retribution. I had no sooner gained an advantage than it was followed by a reverse."[133] With such feelings, not certainly unwarranted by the circumstances under which the campaign was undertaken, nor disproved by the event, Napoleon undertook his shortest and last campaign.

---

[133] Las Cases, tom. ii., p. 276.

Chapter LXXXVIII

Army of Wellington covers Brussels—that of Blucher on the Sambre and Meuse—Napoleon reviews his Grand Army on 14th June—Advances upon Charleroi—His plan to separate the Armies of the two opposing Generals fails—Interview of Wellington and Blucher at Bric—British Army concentrated at Quatre-bras—Napoleon's plan of attack—Battle of Ligny, and defeat of Blucher on 16th June—Action at Quatre-bras on the same day—The British retain possession of the field—Blucher eludes the French pursuit—Napoleon joins Ney—Retreat of the British upon Waterloo.

The triple line of strong fortresses possessed by the French on the borders of Belgium served Napoleon as a curtain, behind which he could prepare his levies and unite his forces at pleasure, without any possibility of the allies or their generals being able to observe his motions, or prepare for the attack which such motions indicated. On the other hand, the frontier of Belgium was open to his observation, and he knew perfectly the general disposal of the allied force.

If the French had been prepared to make their meditated attack upon Flanders in the month of May, they would have found no formidable force to oppose them, as at that time the armies of the Prussian general Kleist, and the hereditary Prince of Orange, did not, in all, exceed 50,000 men. But the return of Napoleon, which again awakened the war, was an event as totally unexpected in France as in Flanders, and, therefore, that nation was as much unprepared to make an attack as the allies to repel one. Thus it happened, that while Napoleon was exerting himself to collect a sufficient army by the means we have mentioned, the Duke of Wellington, who arrived at Brussels from Vienna in the beginning of April, had leisure to garrison and supply the strong places of

Ostend, Antwerp, and Nieuport, which the French had not dismantled, and to fortify Ypres, Tournay, Mons, and Ath. He had also leisure to receive his reinforcements from England, and to collect the German, Dutch, and Belgian contingents.

Thus collected and reinforced, the Duke of Wellington's army might contain about 30,000 English troops. They were not, however, those veteran soldiers who had served under him during the Peninsular war; the flower of which had been despatched upon the American expedition. Most were second battalions, or regiments which had been lately filled up with new recruits. The foreigners were 15,000 Hanoverians, with the celebrated German Legion, 8000 strong, which had so often distinguished itself in Spain; 5000 Brunswickers, under their gallant duke; and about 17,000 Belgians, Dutch, and Nassau troops, commanded by the Prince of Orange.

Great and just reliance was placed upon the Germans; but some apprehensions were entertained for the steadiness of the Belgian troops. Discontents had prevailed among them, which, at one period, had broken out in open mutiny, and was not subdued without bloodshed. Most of them had served in the French ranks, and it was feared some of them might preserve predilections and correspondences dangerous to the general cause. Buonaparte was under the same belief. He brought in his train several Belgian officers, believing there would be a movement in his favour so soon as he entered the Netherlands. But the Flemings are a people of sound sense and feeling. Whatever jealousies might have been instilled into them for their religion and privileges under the reign of a Protestant and a Dutch sovereign, these were swallowed up in their apprehensions for the returning tyranny of Napoleon. Some of these troops behaved with distinguished valour; and most of them supported the ancient military character of the Walloons. The Dutch corps were in general enthusiastically attached to the Prince of Orange, and the cause of independence.

BLUCHER'S ARMY

The Prussian army had been recruited to its highest war-establishment, within an incredibly short space of time after Buonaparte's return had been made public, and was reinforced in a manner surprising to those who do not reflect, how much the resources of a state depend on the zeal of the inhabitants. Their enthusiastic hatred to France, founded partly on the recollection of former injuries, partly on that of recent success, was animated at once by feelings of triumph and of revenge, and they marched to this new war, as to a national crusade against an inveterate enemy, whom, when at their feet, they had treated with injudicious clemency. Blucher was, however, deprived of a valuable part of his army by the discontent of the Saxon troops. A mutiny had broken out among them, when the Congress announced their intention of transferring part of the Saxon dominions to Prussia; much bloodshed had ensued, and it was judged most prudent that the troops of Saxony should remain in garrison in the German fortresses.

Prince Blucher arrived at Liege, with the Prussian army, which was concentrated on the Sambre and Meuse rivers, occupying Charleroi, Namur, Givet, and Liege. The Duke of Wellington covered Brussels, where he had fixed his headquarters, communicating by his left with the right of the Prussians. There was a general idea that Napoleon's threatened advance would take place on Namur, as he was likely to find least opposition at that dismantled city.

The Duke of Wellington's first corps, under the Prince of Orange, with two divisions of British, two of Hanoverians, and two of Belgians, occupied Enghien, Brain le Comte, and Nivelles, and served as a reserve to the Prussian division under Ziethen, which was at Charleroi. The second division, commanded by Lord Hill, included two British, two Hanoverian, and one Belgian divisions. It was cantoned at Halle, Oudenarde, and Grammont. The reserve, under Picton, who, at Lord Wellington's special request, had accepted of the situation of second in command, consisted of the remaining two British divisions, with three of the Hanoverians, and was stationed at Brussels and Ghent. The cavalry occupied Grammont and Nieve.

The Anglo-Belgic army was so disposed, therefore, as might enable the divisions to combine with each other, and with the Prussians, upon the earliest authentic intelligence of the enemy's being put in motion. At the same time, the various corps were necessarily, to a certain degree, detached, both for the purpose of being more easily maintained (especially the cavalry,) and also because, from the impossibility of foreseeing in what direction the French Emperor might make his attack, it was necessary to maintain such an extensive line of defence as to be prepared for his arrival upon any given point. This is the necessary inconvenience attached to a defensive position, where, if the resisting general should concentrate his whole forces upon any one point of the line to be defended, the enemy would, of course, choose to make their assault on some of the other points, which such concentration must necessarily leave comparatively open.

In the meantime, Napoleon in person advanced to Vervins on 12th June, with his Guard, who had marched from Paris. The other divisions of his selected grand army had been assembled on the frontier, and the whole, consisting of five divisions of infantry, and four of cavalry, were combined at Beaumont on the 14th of the same month, with a degree of secrecy and expedition which showed the usual genius of their commander. Napoleon reviewed the troops in person, reminded them that the day was the anniversary of the great victories of Marengo and Friedland, and called on them to remember that the enemies whom they had then defeated, were the same which were now arrayed against them. "Are they and we," he asked, "no longer the same men?"[134] The address produced the strongest effect on the minds of the French soldiery, always sensitively alive to military and national glory.

Upon the 15th June, the French army was in motion in every direction. Their advanced-guard of light troops swept the western bank of the Sambre clear of all the allied corps of observation. They

---

[134] "The madmen! a moment of prosperity has blinded them. The oppression and humiliation of the French people are beyond their power: if they enter France, they will there find their tomb. Soldiers! we have forced marches to make, battles to fight, hazards to run; but, with firmness, victory will be ours: the rights, honour, and happiness of our country will be reconquered. To every Frenchman who has any heart, the moment is arrived—to conquer or to die!"—*Moniteur, June 17.*

then advanced upon Charleroi, which was well defended by the Prussians under General Ziethen, who was at length compelled to retire on the large village of Gosselies. Here his retreat was cut off by the second division of the French army, and Ziethen was compelled to take the route of Fleurus, by which he united himself with the Prussian force, which lay about the villages of Ligny and St. Amand. The Prussian general had, however, obeyed his orders, by making such protracted resistance as gave time for the alarm being taken. In the attack and retreat, he lost four or five guns, and a considerable number in killed and wounded.

By this movement the plan of Napoleon was made manifest. It was at once most scientific and adventurous. His numbers were unequal to sustain a conflict with the armies of Blucher and Wellington united, but by forcing his way so as to separate the one enemy from the other, he would gain the advantage of acting against either individually with the gross of his forces, while he could spare enough of detached troops to keep the other in check. To accomplish this masterly manœuvre, it was necessary to push onwards upon a part of the British advance, which occupied the position of Quatre-bras, and the yet more advanced post of Frasnes, where some of the Nassau troops were stationed. But the extreme rapidity of Napoleon's forced marches had in some measure prevented the execution of his plan, by dispersing his forces so much, that at a time when every hour was of consequence, he was compelled to remain at Charleroi until his wearied and over-marched army had collected.

FRASNES AND QUATRE-BRAS

In the meantime, Ney was detached against Frasnes and Quatre-bras, but the troops of Namur kept their post on the evening of the 15th. It is possible the French maréchal might have succeeded had he attacked at Frasnes with his whole force; but hearing a cannonade in the direction of Fleurus (which was that of Ziethen's action,) he detached a division to support the French in that quarter. For this exercise of his own judgment, instead of yielding precise obedience to his orders, Ney was reprimanded; a circumstance curiously contrasted with the case of Grouchy, upon whom Napoleon laid the whole blame of the defeat at Waterloo, because he *did* follow his orders precisely, and press the Prussians at Wavre, instead of being diverted from that object by the cannonade on his left.

The manœuvre meditated by Napoleon thus failed, though it had nearly been successful. He continued, however, to entertain the same purpose of dividing, if possible, the British army from the Prussians.

The British general received intelligence of the advance of the French, at Brussels, at six o'clock on the evening of the 15th,[135] but it was not of sufficient certainty to enable him to put his army in motion, on an occasion when a false movement might have been irretrievable ruin. About eleven of the same night, the certain accounts reached Brussels that the advance of the French was upon the line of the Sambre. Reinforcements were hastily moved on Quatre-bras, and the Duke of Wellington arrived there in person at an early hour on the 16th, and instantly rode from that position to Bric, where he had a meeting with Blucher. It appeared at this time that the whole French force was about to be directed against the Prussians.

Blucher was prepared to receive them. Three of his divisions, to the number of 80,000 men, had been got into position on a chain of gentle heights, running from Bric to Sombref; in front of their line lay the villages of the Greater and Lesser St. Amand, as also that of Ligny, all of which were strongly occupied. From the extremity of his right, Blucher could communicate with the British at Quatre-bras, upon which the Duke of Wellington was, as fast as distance would permit, concentrating his army. The fourth Prussian division, being that of Bulow, stationed between Liege and Hainault, was at too great a distance to be brought up, though every effort was made for the purpose. Blucher undertook, however, notwithstanding the absence of Bulow, to receive a battle in this position, trusting to the

---

[135] The reader will find this statement corrected, on some points, in a note of chap. lxxxix., *post.*

support of the English army, who, by a flank movement to the left, were to march to his assistance.

Napoleon had, in the meantime, settled his own plan of battle. He determined to leave Ney with a division of 45,000 men, with instructions to drive the English from Quatre-bras, ere their army was concentrated and reinforced, and thus prevent their co-operating with Blucher, while he himself, with the main body of his army, attacked the Prussian position at Ligny. Ney being thus on the French left wing at Frasnes and Quatre-bras, and Buonaparte on the right at Ligny, a division under D'Erlon, amounting to 10,000 men, served as a centre of the army, and was placed near Marchiennes, from which it might march laterally either to support Ney or Napoleon, whichever might require assistance. As two battles thus took place on the 16th June, it is necessary to take distinct notice of both.

LIGNY

That of Ligny was the principal action. The French Emperor was unable to concentrate his forces, so as to commence the attack upon the Prussians, until three o'clock in the afternoon, at which hour it began with uncommon fury all along the Prussian line. After a continued attack of two hours, the French had only obtained possession of a part of the village of St. Amand. The position of the Prussians, however, was thus far defective, that the main part of their army being drawn up on the heights, and the remainder occupying villages which lay at their foot, the reinforcements despatched to the latter were necessarily exposed during their descent to the fire from the French artillery, placed on the meadows below. Notwithstanding this disadvantage, by which the Prussians suffered much, Napoleon thought the issue of the contest so doubtful, that he sent for D'Erlon's division, which, as we have mentioned, was stationed near Marchiennes, half-way betwixt Quatre-bras and Ligny. In the meanwhile, observing that Blucher drew his reserves together on St. Amand, he changed his point of attack, and directed all his force against Ligny, of which, after a desperate resistance, he at length obtained possession. The French

Guards, supported by their heavy cavalry, ascended the heights, and attacked the Prussian position in the rear of Ligny. The reserves of the Prussian infantry having been despatched to St. Amand, Blucher had no means of repelling this attack, save by his cavalry. He placed himself at their head, and charged in the most determined manner, but without success. The cavalry of Blucher were forced back in disorder.

The prince maréchal, as he directed the retreat, was involved in one of the charges of cavalry, his horse struck down by a cannon-shot, and he himself prostrated on the ground. His aide-de-camp threw himself beside the veteran, determined to share his fate, and had the precaution to fling a cloak over him, to prevent his being recognised by the French. The enemy's cuirassiers passed over him, and it was not until they were repulsed, and in their turn pursued by the Prussian cavalry, that the gallant veteran was raised and remounted.[136] Blucher's death, or captivity, at that eventful moment, might have had most sinister effects on the event of the campaign, as it may be fairly doubted whether any thing short of his personal influence and exertion could, after this hard-fought and unfortunate day, have again brought the Prussian army into action on the eventful 18th of June. When relieved, and again mounted, Blucher directed the retreat upon Tilly, and achieved it unmolested by the enemy, who did not continue their pursuit beyond the heights which the Prussians had been constrained to abandon.

Such was the battle of Ligny, in which the Prussians, as Blucher truly said, "lost the field, but not their honour."[137] The victory was attended with none of those decisive consequences which were wont to mark the successes of Buonaparte. There were no corps cut off or dispersed, no regiments which fled or flung down their arms, no line of defence forced, and no permanent advantage gained. Above all, there was not a man who lost heart or courage. The Prussians are believed to have lost in this bloody action at least 10,000 men; the *Moniteur* makes the number of the killed and wounded 15,000, and General Gourgaud, dissatisfied with this liberal allowance, rates them afterwards at no less than 25,000

---

[136] Blucher's Official Report.
[137] Blucher's Official Report.

men, while writing under Napoleon's dictation. The loss of the victors was, by the official accounts, estimated at 3000 men,[138] which ought to have been more than tripled. Still, the French Emperor had struck a great blow—overpowered a stubborn and inveterate enemy, and opened the campaign with favourable auspices. The degree of advantage, however, which Napoleon might have derived from the Prussian retreat was greatly limited by the indifferent success of Ney against the forces of Lord Wellington. Of this second action we have now to give some account.

QUATRE-BRAS

Frasnes had been evacuated by the British, who, on the morning of the 16th, were in position at Quatre-bras, a point of importance, as four roads diverge from it in different directions; so that the British general might communicate from his left with the Prussian right at St. Amand, besides having in his rear a causeway open for his retreat. On the left of the causeway, leading from Charleroi to Brussels, is a wood, called Bois de Bossu, which, during the early part of the day, was strongly contested by the sharpshooters on both sides, but at length carried by the French, and maintained for a time. About three o'clock in the afternoon, the main attack commenced, but was repulsed. The British infantry, however, and particularly the 42d Highlanders, suffered severely from an unexpected charge of lancers, whose approach was hid from them by the character of the ground, intersected with hedges, and covered with heavy crops of rye. Two companies of the Highlanders were cut off, not having time to form the square; the other succeeded in getting into order, and beating off the lancers. Ney then attempted a general charge of heavy cavalry; but they were received with such a galling fire from the British infantry, joined to a battery of two guns, that it could not be sustained; the whole causeway was strewed with men and horses, and the fugitives, who escaped to the rear, announced the loss of an action which was far from being decided, considering that the British had few infantry

---

[138] Bulletin, Moniteur, June 21. Gourgaud, however, states the actual loss, on the part of the French, to have been 7000.

and artillery, though reinforcements of both were coming fast forward.

The French, as already noticed, had, about three o'clock, obtained possession of the Bois de Bossu and driven out the Belgians. They were in return themselves expelled by the British guards, who successfully resisted every attempt made by the French to penetrate into the wood during the day.

As the English reinforcements arrived in succession, Maréchal Ney became desirous of an addition of numbers, and sent to procure the assistance of D'Erlon's division, posted, as has been said, near Marchiennes. But these troops had been previously ordered to succour Buonaparte's own army. As the affair of Ligny was, however, over before they arrived, the division was again sent back towards Frasnes to assist Ney; but his battle was also by this time over, and thus D'Erlon's troops marched from one flank to the other, without firing a musket in the course of the day. The battle of Quatre-bras terminated with the light. The British retained possession of the field, which they had maintained with so much obstinacy, because the Duke of Wellington conceived that Blucher would be able to make his ground good at Ligny, and was consequently desirous that the armies should retain the line of communication which they had occupied in the morning.

But the Prussians, evacuating all the villages which they held in the neighbourhood of Ligny, had concentrated their forces to retreat upon the river Dyle, in the vicinity of Wavre. By this retrograde movement, they were placed about six leagues to the rear of their former position, and had united themselves to Bulow's division, which had not been engaged in the affair at Ligny. Blucher had effected this retreat, not only without pursuit by the French, but without their knowing for some time in what direction he had gone.

This doubt respecting Blucher's movements, occasioned an uncertainty and delay in those of the French, which were afterwards attended with the very worst consequences. Napoleon, or General Gourgaud in his name, does not hesitate to assert, that the cause of this delay rested with Maréchal Grouchy, on whom was devolved the duty of following up the Prussian retreat. "If Maréchal Grouchy," says the accusation, "had been at Wavre on the 17th, and in communication with *my* (Napoleon's) right, Blucher would not have dared to send any detachment of his army against me on the 18th; or if he had, I would have destroyed them."[139] But the maréchal appears to make a victorious defence. Grouchy says, that he sought out the Emperor on the night of the 16th, so soon as the Prussian retreat commenced, but that he could not see him till he returned to Fleurus; nor did he obtain any answer to his request of obtaining some infantry to assist his cavalry in following Blucher and his retreating army, excepting an intimation that he would receive orders next day. He states, that he went again to headquarters in the morning of the 17th, aware of the full importance of following the Prussians closely up, but that he could not see Buonaparte till half-past seven, and then was obliged to follow him to the field of battle of the preceding day, previous to receiving his commands. Napoleon talked with various persons on different subjects, without giving Grouchy any orders until near noon, when he suddenly resolved to send the maréchal with an army of 32,000 men, not upon Wavre, for he did not know that the Prussians had taken that direction, but to follow Blucher wherever he might have gone. Lastly, Grouchy affirms that the troops of Gérard and Vandamme, who were placed under his command, were not ready to move until three o'clock. Thus, according to the maréchal's very distinct narrative, the first orders for the pursuit were not given till about noon on the 17th, and the troops were not in a capacity to obey them until three hours after they were received. For this delay Grouchy blames Excelmans and Gérard, who commanded under him. His corps, at any rate, was not in motion until three o'clock upon the 17th.[140]

Neither could his march, when begun, be directed with certainty on Wavre. The first traces of the Prussians which he could receive, seemed to intimate, on the contrary, that they were retiring towards Namur, which induced Grouchy to push the pursuit in the latter direction, and occasioned the loss of some hours. From all these concurring reasons, the maréchal shows distinctly, that he

---

[139] Gourgaud, Campaign de 1815, ou Relation des Opérations, &c.
[140] Grouchy, Observations sur la Relation de Gourgaud.

could not have attained Wavre on the evening of the 17th June, because he had no orders to go there till noon, nor troops ready to march till three o'clock; nor had either Napoleon or his general any foreknowledge of the motions of Blucher, which might induce them to believe Wavre was the true point of his retreat. It was not till he found the English resolved to make a stand at Waterloo, and the Prussians determined to communicate with them, that Napoleon became aware of the plan arranged betwixt Wellington and Blucher, to concentrate the Prussian and English armies at Waterloo. This was the enigma on which his fate depended, and he failed to solve it. But it was more agreeable, and much more convenient, for Napoleon to blame Grouchy, than to acknowledge that he himself had been surprised by the circumstances in which he unexpectedly found himself on the 18th.

Meantime, having detached Grouchy to pursue the Prussians, Napoleon himself moved laterally towards Frasnes, and there united himself with the body commanded by Maréchal Ney. His purpose was to attack the Duke of Wellington, whom he expected still to find in the position of Quatre-bras.

But about seven in the morning, the duke, having received intelligence of the Prince Maréchal Blucher's retreat to Wavre, commenced a retreat on his part towards Waterloo, in order to recover his communication with the Prussians, and resume the execution of the plan of co-operation, which had been in some degree disconcerted by the sudden irruption of the French, and the loss of the battle of Ligny by the Prussians. The retreat was conducted with the greatest regularity, though it was as usual unpleasant to the feelings of the soldier. The news of the battle of Ligny spread through the ranks, and even the most sanguine did not venture to hope that the Prussians would be soon able to renew the engagement. The weather was dreadful, as the rain fell in torrents; but this so far favoured the British, by rendering the ploughed fields impracticable for horse, so that their march was covered from the attacks of the French cavalry on the flanks, and the operations of those by whom they were pursued were confined to the causeway.

GENAPPE—WATERLOO

At Genappe, however, a small town, where a narrow bridge over the river Dyle can only be approached by a confined street, there was an attack on the British rear, which the English light cavalry were unable to repel; but the heavy cavalry being brought up, repulsed the French, who gave the rear of the army no farther disturbance for the day.

At five in the evening, the Duke of Wellington arrived on the memorable field of Waterloo, which he had long before fixed as the position in which he had, in certain events, determined to make a stand for covering Brussels.

The scene of this celebrated action must be familiar to most readers, either from description or recollection. The English army occupied a chain of heights, extending from a ravine and village, termed Merke Braine, on the right, to a hamlet called Ter la Haye, on the left. Corresponding to this chain of heights there runs one somewhat parallel to them, on which the French were posted. A small valley winds between them of various breadth at different points, but not generally exceeding half a mile. The declivity on either side into the valley has a varied, but on the whole a gentle slope, diversified by a number of undulating irregularities of ground. The field is crossed by two highroads, or causeways, both leading to Brussels—one from Charleroi through Quatre-bras and Genappe, by which the British army had just retreated, and another from Nivelles. These roads traverse the valley, and meet behind the village of Mont St. Jean, which was in the rear of the British army. The farm-house of Mont St. Jean, which must be carefully distinguished from the hamlet, was much closer to the rear of the British than the latter. On the Charleroi causeway in front of the line, there is another farm-house, called La Haye Sainte, situated nearly at the foot of the declivity leading into the valley. On the opposite chain of eminences, a village called La Belle Alliance gives name to the range of heights. It exactly fronts Mont St. Jean, and these two points formed the respective centres of the French and English positions.

An old-fashioned Flemish villa, called Goumont, or Hougomont, stood in the midst of the valley, surrounded with gardens, offices, and a wood, about two acres in extent, of tall beech-trees. Behind the heights of Mont St. Jean, the ground again sinks into a hollow, which served to afford some sort of shelter to the second line of the British. In the rear of this second valley, is the great and extensive forest of Soignies, through which runs the causeway to Brussels. On that road, two miles in the rear of the British army, is placed the small town of Waterloo.

CHAPTER LXXXIX

Strength of the two armies—Plans of their Generals—The Battle of Waterloo commenced on the forenoon of the 18th June—French attack directed against the British centre—shifted to their right—Charges of the Cuirassiers—and their reception—Advance of the Prussians—Ney's charge at the head of the Guards—His repulse—and Napoleon's orders for retreat—The victorious Generals meet at La Belle Alliance—Behaviour of Napoleon during the engagement—Blucher's pursuit of the French—Loss of the British—of the French—Napoleon's subsequent attempts to undervalue the military skill of the Duke of Wellington answered—His unjust censures of Grouchy—The notion that the British were on the point of losing the battle when the Prussians came up, shown to be erroneous.

WATERLOO

There might be a difference of opinion in a mere military question, whether the English general ought to have hazarded a battle for the defence of Brussels, or whether, falling back on the strong city of Antwerp, it might have been safer to wait the arrival of the reinforcements which were in expectation. But in a moral and political point of view, the protecting Brussels was of the last importance. Napoleon has declared, that, had he gained the battle of Waterloo, he had the means of revolutionizing Belgium;[141] and although he was doubtless too sanguine in this declaration, yet unquestionably the French had many partisans in a country which they had so long possessed. The gaining of the battle of Ligny had no marked results, still less had the indecisive action at

---

[141] Montholon, tom. ii., p. 283.

Quatre-bras; but had these been followed by the retreat of the English army to Antwerp, and the capture of Brussels, the capital city of the Netherlands, they would then have attained the rank of great and decisive victories.

Napoleon, indeed, pretended to look to still more triumphant results from such a victory, and to expect nothing less than the dissolution of the European Alliance as the reward of a decided defeat of the English in Belgium. So long as it was not mentioned by what means this was to be accomplished, those who had no less confidence in Napoleon's intrigues than his military talents, must have supposed that he had already in preparation among the foreign powers some deep scheme, tending to sap the foundation of their alliance, and ready to be carried into action when he should attain a certain point of success. But when it is explained that these extensive expectations rested on Napoleon's belief that a single defeat of the Duke of Wellington would occasion a total change of government in England; that the statesmen of the Opposition would enter into office as a thing of course, and instantly conclude a peace with him;[142] and that the coalition, thus deprived of subsidies, must therefore instantly withdraw the armies which were touching the French frontier on its whole northern and eastern line—Napoleon's extravagant speculations can only serve to show how very little he must have known of the English nation, with which he had been fighting so long. The war with France had been prosecuted more than twenty years, and though many of these were years of bad success and defeat, the nation had persevered in a resistance which terminated at last in complete triumph. The national opinion of the great general who led the British troops, was too strongly rooted to give way upon a single misfortune; and the event of the campaign of 1814, in which Napoleon, repeatedly victorious, was at length totally defeated and dethroned, would have encouraged a more fickle people than the English to continue the war notwithstanding a single defeat, if such an event had unhappily occurred. The Duke had the almost impregnable fortress and seaport of Antwerp in his

---

[142] "My intentions were, to attack and to destroy the English. This, I knew, would produce an immediate change of ministry. The indignation against them would have excited such a popular commotion, that they would have been turned out; and peace would have been the result."—Napoleon, *Voice*, &c., vol. i., p. 176.

rear, and might have waited there the reinforcements from America. Blucher had often shown how little he was disheartened by defeat; at worst, he would have fallen back on a Russian army of 200,000 men, who were advancing on the Rhine. The hopes, therefore, that the battle of Waterloo, if gained by the French, would have finished the war, must be abandoned as visionary, whether we regard the firm and manly character of the great personage at the head of the British monarchy, the state of parties in the House of Commons, where many distinguished members of the Opposition had joined the Ministry on the question of the war, or the general feeling of the country, who saw with resentment the new irruption of Napoleon. It cannot, however, be denied, that any success gained by Napoleon in this first campaign, would have greatly added to his influence both in France and other countries, and might have endangered the possession of Flanders. The Duke of Wellington resolved, therefore, to protect Brussels, if possible, even by the risk of a general action.

By the march from Quatre-bras to Waterloo, the Duke had restored his communication with Blucher, which had been dislocated by the retreat of the Prussians to Wavre. When established there, Blucher was once more upon the same line with the British, the distance between the Prussian right flank, and the British left, being about five leagues, or five leagues and a half. The ground which lay between the two extreme points, called the heights of St. Lambert, was exceedingly rugged and wooded; and the cross-roads which traversed it, forming the sole means of communication between the English and Prussians, were dreadfully broken up by the late tempestuous weather.

The duke despatched intelligence of his position in front of Waterloo to Prince Blucher, acquainting him at the same time with his resolution to give Napoleon the battle which he seemed to desire, providing the prince would afford him the support of two divisions of the Prussian army. The answer was worthy of the indefatigable and indomitable old man, who was never so much disconcerted by defeat as to prevent his being willing and ready for combat on the succeeding day. He sent for reply, that he would move to the Duke of Wellington's support, not with two divisions only, but with his whole army; and that he asked no time to prepare for the movement, longer than was necessary to supply food and serve out cartridges to his soldiers.

It was three o'clock on the afternoon of the 17th,[143] when the British came on the field, and took up their bivouac for the night in the order of battle in which they were to fight the next day. It was much later before Napoleon reached the heights of Belle Alliance in person, and his army did not come up in full force till the morning of the 18th. Great part of the French had passed the night in the little village of Genappe, and Napoleon's own quarters had been at the farm-house called Caillou, about a mile in the rear of La Belle Alliance.

In the morning, when Napoleon had formed his line of battle, his brother Jerome, to whom he ascribed the possession of very considerable military talents, commanded on the left—Counts Reille and D'Erlon the centre—and Count Lobau on the right. Maréchals Soult and Ney acted as lieutenant-generals to the Emperor. The French force on the field consisted probably of about 75,000 men. The English army did not exceed that number, at the highest computation. Each army was commanded by the chief, under whom they had offered to defy the world. So far the forces were equal. But the French had the very great advantage of being trained and experienced soldiers of the same nation, whereas the English, in the Duke of Wellington's army, did not exceed 35,000; and although the German Legion were veteran troops, the other soldiers under his command were those of the German contingents, lately levied, unaccustomed to act together, and in some instances suspected to be lukewarm to the cause in which they were engaged; so that it

---

[143] "All his arrangements having been effected early in the evening of the 17th, the Duke of Wellington rode across the country to Blucher, to inform him personally that he had thus far effected the plan agreed on at Bry, and express his hope to be supported on the morrow by two Prussian divisions. The veteran replied, that he would leave a single corps to hold Grouchy at bay as well as they could, and march himself with the rest of his army upon Waterloo; and Wellington immediately returned to his post. The fact of the duke and Blucher having met between the battles of Ligny and Waterloo, is well known to many of the superior officers then in the Netherlands; but the writer of this compendium has never happened to see it mentioned in print. The horse that carried the Duke of Wellington through this long night's journey, so important to the decisive battle of the 18th, remained till lately—if does not still remain—a free pensioner in the best paddock of Strathfield-saye."—*Hist. of Nap. Buonaparte*, Family Library, vol. ii., p. 313.

would have been imprudent to trust more to their assistance and co-operation than could possibly be avoided. In Buonaparte's mode of calculating, allowing one Frenchman to stand as equal to one Englishman, and one Englishman or Frenchman against two of any other nation, the inequality of force on the Duke of Wellington's side was very considerable.

The British army thus composed, was divided into two lines. The right of the first line consisted of the second and fourth English divisions, the third and sixth Hanoverians, and the first corps of Belgians, under Lord Hill. The centre was composed of the corps of the Prince of Orange, with the Brunswickers and troops of Nassau, having the guards, under General Cooke, on the right, and the division of General Alten on the left. The left wing consisted of the divisions of Picton, Lambert, and Kempt. The second line was in most instances formed of the troops deemed least worthy of confidence, or which had suffered too severely in the action of the 16th to be again exposed until extremity. It was placed behind the declivity of the heights to the rear, in order to be sheltered from the cannonade, but sustained much loss from shells during the action. The cavalry were stationed in the rear, distributed all along the line, but chiefly posted on the left of the centre, to the east of the Charleroi causeway. The farm-house of La Haye Sainte, in the front of the centre, was garrisoned, but there was not time to prepare it effectually for defence. The villa, gardens, and farm-yard of Hougomont formed a strong advanced post towards the centre of the right. The whole British position formed a sort of curve, the centre of which was nearest to the enemy, and the extremities, particularly on their right, drawn considerably backward.

PLANS OF ATTACK

The plans of these two great generals were extremely simple. The object of the Duke of Wellington was to maintain his line of defence, until the Prussians coming up, should give him a decided superiority of force. They were expected about eleven or twelve o'clock; but the extreme badness of the roads, owing to the violence of the storm, detained them several hours later.

Napoleon's scheme was equally plain and decided. He trusted by his usual rapidity of attack, to break and destroy the British army before the Prussians should arrive in the field; after which, he calculated to have an opportunity of destroying the Prussians, by attacking them on their march through the broken ground interposed betwixt them and the British. In these expectations he was the more confident, that he believed Grouchy's force, detached on the 17th in pursuit of Blucher, was sufficient to retard, if not altogether to check, the march of the Prussians. His grounds for entertaining this latter opinion, were, as we shall afterwards show, too hastily adopted.

Commencing the action according to his usual system, Napoleon kept his guard in reserve, in order to take opportunity of charging with them, when repeated attacks of column after column, and squadron after squadron, should induce his wearied enemy to show some symptoms of irresolution. But Napoleon's movements were not very rapid. His army had suffered by the storm even more than the English, who were in bivouac at three in the afternoon of the 17th June; while the French were still under march, and could not get into line on the heights of La Belle Alliance until ten or eleven o'clock of the 18th. The English army had thus some leisure to take food, and to prepare their arms before the action; and Napoleon lost several hours ere he could commence the attack. Time was, indeed, inestimably precious for both parties, and hours, nay, minutes, were of importance. But of this Napoleon was less aware than was the Duke of Wellington.

The tempest which had raged with tropical violence all night, abated in the morning; but the weather continued gusty and stormy during the whole day. Betwixt eleven and twelve, before noon, on the memorable 18th June, this dreadful and decisive action commenced, with a cannonade on the part of the French, instantly followed by an attack, commanded by Jerome, on the advanced post of Hougomont. The troops of Nassau, which occupied the wood around the chateau, were driven out by the French, but the utmost efforts of the assailants were unable to force the house, garden, and farm offices, which a party of the guards sustained with the most dauntless resolution. The French redoubled their efforts, and precipitated themselves in numbers on the exterior hedge, which screens the garden-wall, not perhaps aware of the internal defence afforded by the latter. They fell in great numbers on this point by the fire of the defenders, to which they were exposed in every direction. The number of their troops, however, enabled them, by possession of the wood, to mask Hougomont for a time, and to push on with their cavalry and artillery against the British right, which formed in squares to receive them. The fire was incessant, but without apparent advantage on either side. The attack was at length repelled so far, that the British again opened their communication with Hougomont, and that important garrison was reinforced by Colonel Hepburn and a body of the guards.

Meantime, the fire of artillery having become general along the line, the force of the French attack was transferred to the British centre. It was made with the most desperate fury, and received with the most stubborn resolution. The assault was here made upon the farm-house of Saint Jean by four columns of infantry, and a large mass of cuirassiers, who took the advance. The cuirassiers came with the utmost intrepidity along the Genappe causeway, where they were encountered and charged by the English heavy cavalry; and a combat was maintained at the sword's point, till the French were driven back on their own position, where they were protected by their artillery. The four columns of French infantry, engaged in the same attack, forced their way forward beyond the farm of La Haye Sainte, and dispersing a Belgian regiment, were in the act of establishing themselves in the centre of the British position, when they were attacked by the brigade of General Pack, brought up from the second line by General Picton, while, at the same time, a brigade of British heavy cavalry wheeled round their own infantry, and attacked the French charging columns in flank, at the moment when they were checked by the fire of the musketry. The results were decisive. The French columns were broken with great slaughter, and two eagles, with more than 2000 men, were made prisoners. The latter were sent instantly off for Brussels.

PICTON—PONSONBY

The British cavalry, however, followed their success too far. They got involved amongst the French infantry and some hostile cavalry which were detached to support them, and were obliged to retire with considerable loss. In this part of the action, the gallant General Picton, so distinguished for enterprise and bravery, met his death, as did General Ponsonby, who commanded the cavalry.

About this period the French made themselves masters of the farm of La Haye Sainte, cutting to pieces about two hundred Hanoverian sharpshooters, by whom it was most gallantly defended. The French retained this post for some time, till they were at last driven out of it by shells.

Shortly after this event, the scene of conflict again shifted to the right, where a general attack of French cavalry was made on the squares, chiefly towards the centre of the British right, or between that and the causeway. They came up with the most dauntless resolution, in despite of the continued fire of thirty pieces of artillery, placed in front of the line, and compelled the artillerymen, by whom they were served, to retreat within the squares. The enemy had no means, however, to secure the guns, or even to spike them, and at every favourable moment the British artillerymen sallied from their place of refuge, again manned their pieces, and fired on the assailants—a manœuvre which seems peculiar to the British service.[144] The cuirassiers, however, continued their dreadful onset, and rode up to the squares in the full confidence, apparently, of sweeping them before the impetuosity of their charge. Their onset and reception was like a furious ocean pouring itself against a chain of insulated rocks. The British squares stood unmoved, and never gave fire until the cavalry were within ten yards, when men rolled one way, horses galloped another, and the cuirassiers were in every instance driven back.

---

[144] Baron Muffling, speaking of this peculiarity, says—"The English artillery have a rule not to remove their guns, when attacked by cavalry in a defensive position. The field pieces are worked till the last moment, and the men then throw themselves into the nearest square, bearing off the implements they use for serving the guns. If the attack is repulsed, the artillerymen hurry back to their pieces, to fire on the retreating enemy. This is an extremely laudable practice, if the infantry be properly arranged to correspond with it."—S.

The French authors have pretended that squares were broken, and colours taken; but this assertion, upon the united testimony of every British officer present, is a positive untruth. This was not, however, the fault of the cuirassiers, who displayed an almost frantic valour. They rallied again and again, and returned to the onset, till the British could recognise even the faces of individuals among their enemies. Some rode close up to the bayonets, fired their pistols, and cut with their swords with reckless and useless valour. Some stood at gaze, and were destroyed by the musketry and artillery. Some squadrons, passing through the intervals of the first line, charged the squares of Belgians posted there, with as little success. At length the cuirassiers suffered so severely on every hand, that they were compelled to abandon the attempt, which they had made with such intrepid and desperate courage. In this unheard-of struggle, the greater part of the French heavy cavalry were absolutely destroyed. Buonaparte hints at it in his bulletin as an attempt made without orders, and continued only by the desperate courage of the soldiers and their officers.[145] It is certain that, in the destruction of this noble body of cuirassiers, he lost the corps which might have been most effectual in covering his retreat. After the broken remains of this fine cavalry were drawn off, the French confined themselves for a time to a heavy cannonade, from which the British sheltered themselves in part by lying down on the ground, while the enemy prepared for an attack on another quarter, and to be conducted in a different manner.

It was now about six o'clock, and during this long succession of the most furious attacks, the French had gained no success save occupying for a time the wood around Hougomont, from which they had been expelled, and the farm house of La Haye Sainte, which had been also recovered. The British, on the other hand, had suffered very severely, but had not lost one inch of ground, save the two posts, now regained. Ten thousand men were, however, killed and wounded; some of the foreign regiments had given way, though

---

[145] "By a movement of impatience, which has often been so fatal to us, the cavalry of reserve having perceived a retrograde movement made by the English to shelter themselves from our batteries, crowned the heights of Mount St. Jean, and charged the infantry. This movement, which, made in time, and supported by the reserves, must have decided the day, made in an isolated manner, and before affairs on the right were terminated, became fatal."—*Bulletin, Moniteur,* June 21.

others had shown the most desperate valour. And the ranks were thinned both by the actual fugitives, and by the absence of individuals, who left the bloody field for the purpose of carrying off the wounded, and some of whom might naturally be in no hurry to return to so fatal a scene.

WATERLOO

But the French, besides losing about 15,000 men, together with a column of prisoners more than 2000 in number, began now to be disturbed by the operations of the Prussians on their right flank; and the secret of the Duke of Wellington was disclosing itself by its consequences. Blucher, faithful to his engagement, had, early in the morning, put in motion Bulow's division, which had not been engaged at Ligny, to communicate with the English army, and operate a diversion on the right flank and rear of the French. But although there were only about twelve or fourteen miles between Wavre and the field of Waterloo, yet the march was, by unavoidable circumstances, much delayed. The rugged face of the country, together with the state of the roads, so often referred to, offered the most serious obstacles to the progress of the Prussians, especially as they moved with an unusually large train of artillery. A fire, also, which broke out in Wavre, on the morning of the 18th, prevented Bulow's corps from marching through that town, and obliged them to pursue a circuitous and inconvenient route. After traversing, with great difficulty, the cross-roads by Chapelle Lambert, Bulow, with the 4th Prussian corps, who had been expected by the Duke of Wellington about eleven o'clock, announced his arrival by a distant fire, about half-past four. The first Prussian corps, following the same route with Bulow, was yet later in coming up. The second division made a lateral movement in the same direction as the fourth and first, but by the hamlet of Ohain, nearer to the English flank. The Emperor instantly opposed to Bulow, who appeared long before the others, the 6th French corps, which he had kept in reserve for that service; and, as only the advanced guard was come up, they succeeded in keeping the Prussians in check for the moment. The first and second Prussian corps appeared on the field still later than the fourth. The third corps had put themselves in motion to follow in the same direction, when they were furiously attacked by the French under Maréchal Grouchy, who, as already stated, was detached to engage the attention of Blucher, whose whole force he believed he had before him.

Instead of being surprised, as an ordinary general might have been, with this attack upon his rear, Blucher contented himself with sending back orders to Thielman, who commanded the third corps, to defend himself as well as he could upon the line of the Dyle. In the meantime, without weakening the army under his own command, by detaching any part of it to support Thielman, the veteran rather hastened than suspended his march towards the field of battle, where he was aware that the war was likely to be decided in a manner so complete, as would leave victory or defeat on every other point a matter of subordinate consideration.

At half-past six, or thereabouts, the second grand division of the Prussian army began to enter into communication with the British left, by the village of Ohain, while Bulow pressed forward from Chapelle Lambert on the French right and rear, by a hollow, or valley, called Frischemont. It became now evident that the Prussians were to enter seriously into the battle, and with great force. Napoleon had still the means of opposing them, and of achieving a retreat, at the certainty, however, of being attacked upon the ensuing day by the combined armies of Britain and Prussia. His celebrated Guard had not yet taken any part in the conflict, and would now have been capable of affording him protection after a battle which, hitherto, he had fought at disadvantage, but without being defeated. But the circumstances by which he was surrounded must have pressed on his mind at once. He had no succours to look for; a reunion with Grouchy was the only resource which could strengthen his forces; the Russians were advancing upon the Rhine with forced marches; the Republicans at Paris were agitating schemes against his authority. It seemed as if all must be decided on that day, and on that field. Surrounded by these ill-omened circumstances, a desperate effort for victory, ere the Prussians could act effectually, might perhaps yet drive the English from their position; and he determined to venture on this daring experiment.

About seven o'clock, Napoleon's Guard were formed in two columns, under his own eye, near the bottom of the declivity of La Belle Alliance. They were put under command of the dauntless Ney. Buonaparte told the soldiers, and, indeed, imposed the same fiction on their commander, that the Prussians whom they saw on the right were retreating before Grouchy. Perhaps he might himself believe that this was true. The Guard answered, for the last time, with shouts of *Vive l'Empereur*, and moved resolutely forward, having, for their support, four battalions of the Old Guard in reserve, who stood prepared to protect the advance of their comrades. A gradual change had taken place in the English line of battle, in consequence of the repeated repulse of the French. Advancing by slow degrees, the right, which at the beginning of the conflict, presented a segment of a convex circle, now resembled one that was concave, the extreme right, which had been thrown back, being now rather brought forward, so that their fire both of artillery and infantry fell upon the flank of the French, who had also to sustain that which was poured on their front from the heights. The British were arranged in a line of four men deep, to meet the advancing columns of the French Guard, and poured upon them a storm of musketry which never ceased an instant. The soldiers fired independently, as it is called; each man loading and discharging his piece as fast as he could. At length the British moved forward, as if to close round the heads of the columns, and at the same time continued to pour their shot upon the enemy's flanks. The French gallantly attempted to deploy, for the purpose of returning the discharge; but in their effort to do so, under so dreadful a fire, they stopt, staggered, became disordered, were blended into one mass, and at length gave way, retiring, or rather flying, in the utmost confusion. This was the last effort of the enemy, and Napoleon gave orders for the retreat; to protect which, he had now no troops left, save the last four battalions of the Old Guard, which had been stationed in the rear of the attacking columns. These threw themselves into squares, and stood firm. But at this moment the Duke of Wellington commanded the whole British line to advance, so that whatever the bravery and skill of these gallant veterans, they also were thrown into disorder, and swept away in the general rout, in spite of the efforts of Ney, who, having had his horse killed, fought sword in hand, and on foot, in the front of the battle, till the very last.[146] That maréchal, whose military virtues at least cannot be challenged, bore personal evidence against two circumstances, industriously circulated by the friends of Napoleon. One of these fictions occurs in his own bulletin, which charges the loss of the battle to a panic fear, brought about by the treachery of some unknown persons, who raised the cry of "*Sauve qui peut.*"[147] Another figment, greedily credited at Paris, bore, that the four battalions of Old Guard, the last who maintained the semblance of order, answered a summons to surrender, by the magnanimous reply, "The Guard can die, but cannot yield." And one edition of the story adds, that thereupon the battalions made a half wheel inwards, and discharged their muskets into each other's bosoms, to save themselves from dying by the hands of the English. Neither the original reply, nor the pretended self-sacrifice of the Guard, have the slightest foundation. Cambrone, in whose mouth the speech was placed, gave up his sword, and remained prisoner; and the military conduct of the French Guard is better eulogised by the undisputed truth, that they fought to extremity, with the most unyielding constancy, than by imputing to them an act of regimental suicide upon the lost field of battle.[148] Every attribute of brave men they have a just right to claim. It is no compliment to ascribe to them that of madmen. Whether the words were used by Cambrone or no, the Guard well deserved to have them inscribed on their monument.

Whilst this decisive movement took place, Bulow, who had concentrated his troops, and was at length qualified to act in force,

---

[146] "I had my horse killed and fell under it. The brave men who will return from this terrible battle, will, I hope, do me the justice to say, that they saw me on foot with sword in hand during the whole of the evening; and that I only quitted the scene of carnage among the last, and at the moment when retreat could no longer be prevented."—*Ney's Letter to the Duke of Otranto.*

[147] "Cries of *all is lost, the Guard is driven back*, were heard on every side. The soldiers pretend even that on many points ill-disposed persons cried out *sauve qui peut*. However this may be, a complete panic at once spread itself throughout the whole field. The Old Guard was infected, and was itself hurried along. In an instant, the whole army was nothing but a mass of confusion; all the soldiers of all arms were mixed *pel-mel*, and it was utterly impossible to rally a single corps."—*Bulletin, Moniteur,* June 21. "A retrograde movement was declared, and the army formed nothing but a confused mass. There was not, however, a total rout, nor the cry of *sauve qui peut*, as has been calumniously stated in the official bulletin."—*Ney to the Duke of Otranto.*

[148] Fleury de Chamboullon, tom. ii., p. 187.

carried the village of Planchenois in the French rear, and was now firing so close on their right wing, that the cannonade annoyed the British who were in pursuit, and was suspended in consequence. Moving in oblique lines, the British and Prussian armies came into contact with each other on the heights so lately occupied by the French, and celebrated the victory with loud shouts of mutual congratulation.

The French army was now in total and inextricable confusion and rout; and when the victorious generals met at the farm-house of La Belle Alliance, it was agreed that the Prussians, who were fresh in comparison, should follow up the chase, a duty for which the British, exhausted by the fatigues of a battle of eight hours, were totally inadequate.

During the whole action, Napoleon maintained the utmost serenity. He remained on the heights of La Belle Alliance, keeping pretty near the centre, from which he had a full view of the field, which does not exceed a mile and a half in length. He expressed no solicitude on the fate of the battle for a long time, noticed the behaviour of particular regiments, and praised the English several times, always, however, talking of them as an assured prey. When forming his guard for the last fatal effort, he descended near them, half down the causeway from La Belle Alliance, to bestow upon them what proved his parting exhortation. He watched intently their progress with a spyglass, and refused to listen to one or two aides-de-camp, who at that moment came from the right to inform him of the appearance of the Prussians. At length, on seeing the attacking columns stagger and become confused, his countenance, said our informer, became pale as that of a corpse, and muttering to himself, "They are mingled together," he said to his attendants, "All is lost for the present," and rode off the field; not stopping or taking refreshment till he reached Charleroi, where he paused for a moment in a meadow, and occupied a tent which had been pitched for his accommodation.[149]

---

[149] Our informant on these points, was Lacoste, a Flemish peasant, who was compelled to act as Buonaparte's guide, remained with him during the whole action, and accompanied him to Charleroi. He seemed a shrewd sensible man in his way, and told his story with the

Meantime, the pursuit of his discomfited army was followed up by Blucher with the most determined perseverance. He accelerated the march of the Prussian advanced guard, and despatched every man and horse of his cavalry upon the pursuit of the fugitive French. At Genappe they attempted something like defence, by barricading the bridge and streets; but the Prussians forced them in a moment, and although the French were sufficiently numerous for resistance, their disorder was so irremediable, and their moral courage was so absolutely quelled for the moment, that in many cases they were slaughtered like sheep. They were driven from bivouac to bivouac, without exhibiting even the shadow of their usual courage. One hundred and fifty guns were left in the hands of the English, and a like number taken by the Prussians in course of the pursuit. The latter obtained possession also of all Napoleon's baggage, and of his carriage, where, amongst many articles of curiosity, was found a proclamation intended to be made public at Brussels the next day.

LOSSES ON BOTH SIDES

The loss on the British side during this dreadful battle was, as the Duke of Wellington, no user of exaggerated expressions, truly termed it, *immense*. One hundred officers slain, five hundred wounded, many of them to death, fifteen thousand men killed and wounded, (independent of the Prussian loss at Wavre,) threw half Britain into mourning. Many officers of distinction fell. It required all the glory, and all the solid advantages, of this immortal day, to reconcile the mind to the high price at which it was purchased. The commander-in-chief, compelled to be on every point of danger, was repeatedly in the greatest jeopardy. Only the Duke himself, and one gentleman, of his numerous staff, escaped unwounded in horse and person.

It would be difficult to form a guess at the extent of the French loss. Besides those who fell in the battle and flight, great

---

utmost simplicity. The author saw him, and heard his narrative, very shortly after the action.—S.

numbers deserted. We do not believe, that of 75,000 men, the half were ever again collected under arms.[150]

Having finished our account of this memorable action, we are led to notice the communications and criticisms of Napoleon himself on the subject, partly as illustrative of the narrative, but much more as indicating his own character.

The account of the battle of Waterloo, dictated by Napoleon to Gourgaud, so severely exposed by General Grouchy[151] as a mere military romance, full of gratuitous suppositions, misrepresentations, and absolute falsehoods, accuses the subordinate generals who fought under Buonaparte of having greatly degenerated from their original character. Ney and Grouchy are particularly aimed at; the former by name, the latter by obvious implication. It is said they had lost that energy and enterprising genius by which they had formerly been distinguished, and to which France owed her triumphs. They had become timorous and circumspect in all their operations; and although their personal bravery remains, their greatest object was to compromise themselves as little as possible. This general remark, intended, of course, to pave the way for transferring from the Emperor to his lieutenants the blame of the miscarriage of the campaign, is both unjust and ungrateful. Had they lost energy, who struggled to the very last in the field of Waterloo, long after the Emperor had left the field? Was Grouchy undecided in his operations, who brought his own division safe to Paris, in spite of all the obstacles opposed to him by a victorious army, three times the amount of his own in numbers? Both these officers had given up, for the sake of Napoleon, the rank and appointments which they might have peacefully borne under the Bourbons. Did it indicate the reluctance to commit themselves, with which they are charged, that they ventured on the decided step of joining his desperate career, not only abandoning all regard to their interest and their safety, but compromising their character as men of loyalty in the face of all Europe, and exposing themselves to certain death, if the Bourbons should be successful? Those who fight with the cord around their neck, which was decidedly the case with Grouchy and Ney, must

---

[150] See Captain Pringle's Remarks on the Campaign of 1815, Appendix, No. I.
[151] "Observations sur 'Le Campagne de 1815,' par Le Général Grouchy, 1819."

have headed the forlorn hope; and is it consistent with human nature, in such circumstances, to believe that they, whose fortune and safety depended on the victory, personally brave as they are admitted to be, should have loitered in the rear, when their fate was in the balance?

He who was unjust to his own followers, can scarce be expected to be candid towards an enemy. The Duke of Wellington has, upon all occasions, been willing to render the military character of Napoleon that justice which a generous mind is scrupulously accurate in dispensing to an adversary, and has readily admitted that the conduct of Buonaparte and his army on this memorable occasion, was fully adequate to the support of their high reputation. It may be said that the victor can afford to bestow praise on the vanquished, but that it requires a superior degree of candour in the vanquished to do justice to the conqueror. Napoleon, at any rate, does not seem to have attained, in this particular, to the pitch of a great or exalted mind, since both he and the various persons whom he employed as the means of circulating his statements, concur in a very futile attempt to excuse the defeat at Waterloo, by a set of apologies founded in a great degree upon misrepresentation. The reader will find these scientifically discussed in a valuable article in the Appendix.[152] But it may be necessary, at the risk of some repetition, to take some notice of them here in a popular form. The allegations, which are designed to prove the incapacity of the British general, and to show that the battle of Waterloo was only lost by a combination of extraordinary fatalities, may be considered in their order.

The first, and most frequently repeated, is the charge, that the Duke of Wellington, on the 15th, was surprised in his cantonments, and could not collect his army fast enough at Quatre-bras. In this his Grace would have been doubtless highly censurable, if Napoleon had, by express information, or any distinct movement indicative of his purpose, shown upon which point he meant to advance. But the chivalrous practice of fixing a field of combat has been long out of

---

[152] See an account of the action of Waterloo, equally intelligible and scientific, drawn up by Captain Pringle of the artillery, which will amply supply the deficiencies of our narrative—Appendix, No. I.

date; and Napoleon, beyond all generals, possessed the art of masking his own movements, and misleading his enemy concerning the actual point on which he meditated an attack. The Duke and Prince Blucher were, therefore, obliged to provide for the concentration of their forces upon different points, according as Buonaparte's selection should be manifested; and in order to be ready to assemble their forces upon any one position, they must, by spreading their cantonments, in some degree delay the movement upon all. The Duke could not stir from Brussels, or concentrate his forces, until he had certain information of those of the enemy; and it is said that a French statesman, who had promised to send him a copy of the plan of Buonaparte's campaign, contrived, by a trick of policy, to evade keeping his word.[153] We do not mean to deny the talent and activity displayed by Buonaparte, who, if he could have brought forward his whole army upon the evening of the 15th of June, might probably have succeeded in preventing the meditated junction of Blucher and Wellington. But the celebrated prayer for annihilation of time and space would be as little reasonable in the mouth of a general as of a lover, and, fettered by the limitations against which that modest petition is directed, Buonaparte failed in bringing forward in due time a sufficient body of forces to carry all before him at Quatre-bras; while, on the other hand, the Duke of Wellington, from the same obstacles of time and space, could not

---

[153] This was Fouché, who seems to have been engaged in secret correspondence with all and sundry of the belligerent powers, while he was minister of police under Napoleon. In his Memoirs [vol. ii., p. 279] he is made to boast that he contrived to keep his word to the Duke of Wellington, by sending the plan of Buonaparte's campaign by a female, a Flemish postmistress, whom he laid wait for on the frontier, and caused to be arrested. Thus he "kept the word of promise to the ear, And broke it to the sense."

This story, we have some reason to believe, is true. One of the marvels of our times is how Fouché, after having been the mainspring of such a complication of plots and counterplots, revolutionary and counter-revolutionary intrigues, contrived after all *to die in his bed!*—S.— On the second restoration, Louis XVIII. saw himself reduced to the sad necessity of admitting Fouché to his counsels. But the clamours raised against his profligacy and treachery convincing him that it would be dangerous to continue in France, he resigned in September, and was sent ambassador to Dresden. In January, 1816, he was denounced as a regicide by both Chambers, and condemned to death, in case he re-entered the French territory. He died at Trieste, December 26, 1820, in his sixty-seventh year, leaving behind him an immense fortune.

assemble a force sufficient to drive Ney before him, and enable him to advance to the support of Blucher during the action of Ligny.[154]

The choice of the field of Waterloo is also charged against the Duke of Wellington as an act of weak judgment; because, although possessed of all the requisites for maintaining battle or pursuing victory, and, above all, of the facilities for communicating with the Prussian army, it had not, according to the imperial critic, the means of affording security in case of a retreat, since there was only one communication to the rear—that by the causeway of Brussels, the rest of the position being screened by the forest of Soignies, in front of which the British army was formed, and through which, it is assumed, retreat was impossible.

Taking the principle of this criticism as accurate, it may be answered, that a general would never halt or fight at all, if he were to refuse combat on every other save a field of battle which possessed all the various excellences which may be predicated of one in theory. The commander must consider whether the ground suits his present

---

[154] Some people have been silly enough to consider the Duke of Wellington's being surprised as a thing indisputable, because the news of the French advance first reached him in a ball-room. It must be supposed that these good men's idea of war is, that a general should sit sentinel with his truncheon in his hand, like a statue in the midst of a city market-place, until the tidings come which call him to the field.
"Free is his heart who for his country fights; He on the eve of battle may resign Himself to social pleasure—sweetest then, When danger to the soldier's soul endears The human joy that never may return." Home's *Douglas*.—S.
"The fiction of the Duke of Wellington having been *surprised* on this great occasion, has maintained its place in almost all narratives of the war for fifteen years. The duke's magnanimous silence under such treatment, for so long a period, will be appreciated by posterity. The facts of the case are now given from the most unquestionable authority. At half-past one o'clock, P.M., of Thursday the 15th, a Prussian officer of high rank arrived at Wellington's headquarters in Brussels, with the intelligence of Napoleon's decisive operations. By two o'clock, orders were despatched to all the cantonments of the duke's army, for the divisions to break up and concentrate on the left of Quatre-bras his grace's design being that his whole force should be assembled there by eleven o'clock on the next night, Friday the 16th. It was at first intended, to put off a ball announced for the evening of Thursday, at the Duchess of Richmond's hotel in Brussels; but on reflection it seemed highly important that the population of that city should be kept, as far as possible, in ignorance as to the course of events, and the Duke of Wellington desired that the ball should proceed accordingly; nay, the general officers received his commands to appear in the ball room, each taking care to quit the apartment as quietly as possible at ten o'clock, and proceed to join his respective division *en route*. This arrangement was carried into strict execution. The duke himself retired at twelve o'clock, and left Brussels at six o'clock next morning for Quatre-bras."—*Hist. of Nap. Buonaparte*, Family Library, vol. ii., p. 309.

exigencies, without looking at other circumstances which may be less pressing at the time. Generals have been known to choose by preference the ground from which there could be no retiring; like invaders who burn their ships, as a pledge that they will follow their enterprise to the last. And although provision for a safe retreat is certainly in most cases a desirable circumstance, yet it has been dispensed with by good generals, and by none more frequently than by Napoleon himself. Was not the battle of Essling fought without any possible mode of retreat save the frail bridges over the Danube? Was not that of Wagram debated under similar circumstances? And, to complete the whole, did not Napoleon, while censuring the Duke of Wellington for fighting in front of a forest, himself enter upon conflict with a defile in his rear, formed by the narrow streets and narrower bridge of Genappe, by which alone, if defeated, he could cross the Dyle?—It might, therefore, be presumed, that if the Duke of Wellington chose a position from which retreat was difficult, he must have considered the necessity of retreat as unlikely, and reckoned with confidence on being able to make good his stand until the Prussians should come up to join him.

Even this does not exhaust the question; for the English general-officers unite in considering the forest of Soignies as a very advantageous feature in the field; and, far from apprehending the least inconvenience from its existence, the Duke of Wellington regarded it as affording a position, which, if his first and second line had been unhappily forced, he might have nevertheless made good against the whole French army. The hamlet of Mont Saint Jean, in front, affords an excellent key to the position of an army compelled to occupy the forest. The wood itself is every where passable for men and horses, the trees being tall, and without either low boughs or underwood; and, singular as the discrepancy between the opinions of distinguished soldiers may seem, we have never met an English officer who did not look on the forest of Soignies as affording an admirable position for making a final stand. In support of their opinion they refer to the defence of the Bois de Bossu, near Quatre-bras, against the reiterated attacks of Maréchal Ney. This impeachment of the Duke of Wellington may therefore be set aside, as inconsistent with the principles of British warfare. All that can be added is, that there are cases in which national habits and manners may render a position advantageous to soldiers of one country, which is perilous or destructive to those of another.

The next subject of invidious criticism, is of a nature so singular, that, did it not originate with a great man, in peculiar circumstances of adversity, it might be almost termed ludicrous. Napoleon expresses himself as dissatisfied, because he was defeated in the common and vulgar proceeding of downright fighting, and by no special manœuvres or peculiar display of military art on the part of the victor. But if it can afford any consolation to those who cherish his fame, it is easy to show that Napoleon fell a victim to a scheme of tactics early conceived, and persevered in under circumstances which, in the case of ordinary men, would have occasioned its being abandoned; resumed after events which seemed so adverse, that nothing save dauntless courage and unlimited confidence could have enabled the chiefs to proceed in their purpose; and carried into execution, without Napoleon's being able to penetrate the purpose of the allied generals, until it was impossible to prevent the annihilation of his army;—that he fell, in short, by a grand plan of strategie, worthy of being compared to that of any of his own admirable campaigns.

To prove what we have said, it is only necessary to remark, that the natural bases and points of retreat of the Prussian and English armies were different; the former being directed on Maestricht, the other on Antwerp, where each expected their reinforcements. Regardless of this, and with full confidence in each other, the Prince Maréchal Blucher, and the Duke of Wellington, agreed to act in conjunction against the French army. The union of their forces, for which both were prepared, was destined to have taken place at Ligny, where the duke designed to have supported the Prussians, and where Blucher hazarded an action in expectation of his ally's assistance. The active movements of Napoleon, and the impossibility of the English force being sufficiently concentrated at Quatre-bras to afford the means of overpowering Ney and the force in their front, prevented their making a lateral march to relieve Blucher at that critical period. Otherwise, the parts of the bloody drama, as afterwards acted, would have been reversed, and the

British army would have moved to support the Prussians at Ligny, as the Prussians came to the aid of the British at Waterloo.

Napoleon had the merit of disconcerting this plan for the time; but he did not, and could not, discover that the allied generals retained, after the loss of the battle of Ligny, the same purpose which they had adopted on the commencement of the campaign. He imagined, as did all around him, that Blucher must retreat on Namur, or in such a direction as would effectually accomplish a separation betwixt him and the English, as it was natural to think a defeated army should approach towards its own resources, instead of attempting further offensive operations. At all events, Napoleon was in this respect so much mistaken, as to believe that if Blucher did retire on the same line with the English, the means which the Prussian retained for co-operating with his allies were so limited, and (perhaps he might think) the spirit of the general so subdued, that Maréchal Grouchy, with 32,000 men, would be sufficient to keep the whole Prussian force in check. The maréchal was accordingly, as we have seen, despatched much too late, without any other instructions than to follow and engage the attention of the Prussians. Misled by the demonstration of Blucher, he at first took the road to Namur, and thus, without any fault on his part, lost time, which was inconceivably precious.

Buonaparte's subsequent accounts of this action blame Maréchal Grouchy for not discovering Blucher's real direction, which he had no means of ascertaining, and for not obeying orders which were never given to him, and which could not be given, because Napoleon was as ignorant as the maréchal, that Blucher had formed the determination, at all events, to unite himself with Wellington. This purpose of acting in co-operation, formed and persevered in, was to the French Emperor the riddle of the Sphinx, and he was destroyed because he could not discover it. Indeed, he ridiculed even the idea of such an event. One of his officers, according to Baron Muffling, having hinted at the mere possibility of a junction between the Prussian army and that of Wellington, he smiled contemptuously at the thought. "The Prussian army," he said, "is defeated—It cannot rally for three days—I have 75,000 men, the English only 50,000. The town of Brussels awaits me with open arms. The English Opposition waits but for my success to raise their heads. Then adieu subsidies, and farewell coalition!" In like manner, Napoleon frankly acknowledged, while on board the Northumberland, that he had no idea that the Duke of Wellington meant to fight, and therefore omitted to reconnoitre the ground with sufficient accuracy. It is well known, that when he observed them still in their position on the morning of the 18th, he exclaimed, "I have them, then, these English!"

It was half past eleven, just about the time that the battle of Waterloo commenced, that Grouchy, as already hinted, overtook the rear of the Prussians. A strong force, appearing to be the whole of the Prussian army, lay before the French maréchal, who, from the character of the ground, had no means of ascertaining their numbers, or of discovering the fact, that three divisions of Blucher's army were already on the march to their right, through the passes of Saint Lambert; and that it was only Thielman's division which remained upon the Dyle. Still less could he know, what could only be known to the duke and Blucher, that the English were determined to give battle in the position at Waterloo. He heard, indeed, a heavy cannonade in that direction, but that might have proceeded from an attack on the British rear-guard, the duke being, in the general opinion of the French army, in full retreat upon Antwerp. At any rate, the maréchal's orders were to attack the enemy which he found before him. He could not but remember, that Ney had been reprimanded for detaching a part of his force on the 16th, in consequence of a distant cannonade; and he was naturally desirous to avoid censure for the self-same cause. Even if Napoleon was seriously engaged with the English, it seemed the business of Grouchy to occupy the large force which he observed at Wavre, and disposed along the Dyle, to prevent their attempting any thing against Napoleon, if, contrary to probability, the Emperor should be engaged in a general battle. Lastly, as Grouchy was to form his resolution under the idea of having the whole Prussian force before him, which was estimated at 80,000 men, it would have been impossible for him to detach from an army of 32,000 any considerable body, to the assistance of Napoleon; and in attacking with such inadequate numbers, he showed his devotion, at the risk of being totally destroyed.

He engaged, however, in battle without any hesitation, and attacked the line of the Prussians along the Dyle on every accessible point; to wit, at Wavre, at the mill of Bielge, and at the village of Limale. The points of attack were desperately defended by the Prussians under Thielman, so that Grouchy could only occupy that part of Wavre which was on his own side of the Dyle. About four o'clock, and consequently when the fate of the battle of Waterloo was nearly decided, Grouchy received from Maréchal Soult the only order which reached him during the day, requiring him to manœuvre so as to unite himself to the right flank of the Emperor, but at the same time acquainting him with the (false) intelligence, that the battle was gained upon the line of Waterloo. A postscript informed Grouchy, that Bulow was appearing upon Napoleon's right flank, and that if he could come up with speed, he would take the Prussian *flagrante delicto*.[155]

These orders were quite intelligible. But two things were necessary to their being carried into execution. First, that Grouchy should get clear of Thielman, the enemy with whom he was closely engaged, and who would not fail to pursue the French maréchal if he retreated or moved to his left flank, without having repulsed him. Secondly, it was indispensable he should pass the small river Dyle, defended by Thielman's division, since the road leading through the woods of Chapelle Lambert, was that by which he could best execute his march towards Waterloo. Grouchy redoubled his efforts to force the Dyle, but he could not succeed till night, and then but partially; for the Prussians continued to hold the mill of Bielge, and remained in force within a cannon-shot of Grouchy's position.

In the morning, the maréchal, anxious to learn with certainty the fate of Napoleon, though believing, according to Soult's letter, that he was victorious, sent out reconnoitring parties. When he learned the truth, he commenced a retreat, which he conducted with such talent, that though closely pursued by the Prussians, then in all the animation of triumph, and though sustaining considerable loss, he was enabled to bring his corps unbroken under the walls of Paris. Weighing all these circumstances, it appears that Buonaparte had no right to count upon the assistance of Grouchy, far less to throw

---

[155] Savary, tom. iv., p. 75.

censure on that general for not coming to his assistance, since he scrupulously obeyed the orders he received; and when at four o'clock, that of attacking and pressing the Prussian rear was qualified by the directions of Soult, to close up to Buonaparte's right wing, Grouchy was engaged in an obstinate engagement with Thielman, whom he must necessarily defeat before he could cross the Dyle, to accomplish the junction proposed.

The movement of Blucher, therefore, was a masterpiece of courage and judgment, since the prince maréchal left one division of his army to maintain a doubtful onset against Grouchy, and involved himself with the other three in that flank movement through the woods of Saint Lambert, by which he paid with interest the debt which he owed Napoleon for a similar movement, previous to the affairs of Champ-Aubert and Montmirail, in 1814.

The same system which placed Blucher in motion, required that the Duke of Wellington should maintain his position, by confining himself to a strictly defensive contest. The British, as they were to keep their place at all risks, so on no temptation of partial success were they to be induced to advance. Every step which they might have driven the French backward, before the coming up of the Prussians, would have been a disadvantage as far as it went, since the object was not to beat the enemy by the efforts of the English only, which, in the state of the two armies, might only have amounted to a repulse, but to detain them in the position of La Belle Alliance, until the army of Blucher should come up. When Napoleon, therefore, objects to the conduct of the Duke of Wellington on the 18th, that he did not manœuvre in the time of action, he objects to the very circumstance which rendered the victory of the day so decisive. He was himself decoyed into, and detained in a position, until his destruction was rendered inevitable.

It has been a favourite assertion with almost all the French, and some English writers, that the English were on the point of being defeated, when the Prussian force came up. The contrary is the truth. The French had attacked, and the British had resisted, from past eleven until near seven o'clock; and though the battle was most bloody, the former had gained no advantage save at the wood of Hougomont, and the farm-house of La Haye Sainte; both they gained, but speedily lost. Baron Muffling has given the most explicit testimony, "that the battle could have afforded no favourable result to the enemy, even if the Prussians had never come up." He was an eyewitness, and an unquestionable judge, and willing, doubtless, to carry the immediate glory acquired by his countrymen on this memorable occasion, and in which he had a large personal stake, as high as truth and honour will permit. At the time when Napoleon made the last effort, Bulow's troops were indeed upon the field, but had not made any physical impression by their weapons, or excited any moral dread by their appearance. Napoleon announced to all his Guard, whom he collected and formed for that final exertion, that the Prussians whom they saw were closely pursued by the French of Grouchy's army. He himself, perhaps, had that persuasion; for the fire of Grouchy's artillery, supposed to be a league and a half, but in reality nearly three leagues distant, was distinctly heard; and some one of Napoleon's suite saw the smoke from the heights above Wavre. "The battle," he said, "is won; we must force the English position, and throw them upon the defiles.—*Allons! La Garde en avant!*"[156] Accordingly, they then made the attack in the evening, when they were totally repulsed, and chased back upon, and beyond, their own position. Thus, before the Prussians came into serious action, Napoleon had done his utmost, and had not a corps remaining in order, excepting four battalions of the Old Guard. It cannot be therefore said, that our allies afforded the British army protection from any enemy that was totally disorganised; but that for which the Prussians do deserve the gratitude of Britain and of Europe, is the generous and courageous confidence with which they marched at so many risks to assist in the action, and the activity and zeal with which they completed the victory. It is universally acknowledged, that the British army, exhausted by so long a conflict, could not have availed themselves of the disorder of their enemy at its conclusion; while, on the contrary, nothing could exceed the dexterity and rapidity with which the Prussians conducted the pursuit. The laurels of Waterloo must be divided—the British won

---

[156] He gave the same explanation when on board of the Northumberland. General Gourgaud had inaccurately stated that the Emperor had mistaken the corps of Bulow for that of Grouchy. Napoleon explained, that this was not the case, but that he had opposed a sufficient force to those Prussians whom he saw in the field, and concluded that Grouchy was closing up on their flank and rear.—S.

the battle, the Prussians achieved and rendered available the victory.[157]

---

[157] Baron Muffling's account of the British army must interest our readers:—"There is not, perhaps, in all Europe, an army superior to the English in the actual field of battle. That is to say, an army in which military instruction is entirely directed to that point, as its exclusive object. The English soldier is strongly formed and well fed, and nature has endowed him with much courage and intrepidity. He is accustomed to severe discipline, and is very well armed. The infantry opposes with confidence the attack of cavalry, and shows more indifference than any other European army when attacked in the flank or rear. These qualities explain why the English have never been defeated in a pitched field since they were commanded by the Duke of Wellington.
"On the other hand, there are no troops in Europe less experienced than the English in the light service and in skirmishes; accordingly, they do not practise that service themselves. The English army in Spain formed the standing force round which the Spaniards and Portuguese rallied. The Duke of Wellington acted wisely in reserving his English troops for regular battles, and in keeping up that idea in his army.
"If, on the one hand, a country is worthy of envy which possesses an army consisting entirely of grenadiers, that army might, on the other hand, experience great disadvantage if forced to combat unassisted against an able general, who understands their peculiarities, and can avoid giving them battle excepting on advantageous ground. However, it is to be supposed that the English will seldom make war on the Continent without allies, and it appears their system is established on that principle. Besides, such an army as the English is most precious for those they may act with, as the most difficult task of the modern art of war is to form an army for pitched battles." The Baron adds, in a note upon the last sentence,—"The people who inhabit other quarters of the world, and are not come to the same state of civilisation with us, afford a proof of this. Most of them know better than Europeans how to fight man to man, but can never attain the point of gaining a battle over us. Discipline, in the full extent of the word, is the fruit of moral and religious instruction."—*Histoire de la Campagne de l'Armée Angloise, &c., sous les ordres du Duc de Wellington, et de l'Armée Prussienne, sous les ordres du Prince Blucher de Wahlstadt, 1815, Par 6 de 10. Stutgart et Tubingue. 1817.*—S.

CHAPTER XC

Buonaparte's arrival at Paris—The Chambers assemble, and adopt Resolutions, indicating a wish for Napoleon's Abdication—Fouché presents Napoleon's Abdication, which stipulates that his Son shall succeed him—Carnot's Report to the Peers, of the means of defence—Contradicted by Ney—Stormy Debate on the Abdication Act—Both Chambers evade formally recognising Napoleon II.—Provisional Government—Napoleon at Malmaison—His offer of his services in the defence of Paris rejected—Surveillance of General Beker—Means provided at Rochefort for his departure to the United States—He arrives at Rochefort on 3d July—The Provisional Government attempt in vain to treat with the Allies—The Allies advance to Paris—Chamber of Peers disperse—Louis XVIII. re-enters Paris on 8th July.

Immense as the direct and immediate consequences of the battle of Waterloo certainly were, being the total loss of the campaign, and the entire destruction of Napoleon's fine army, the more remote contingencies to which it gave rise were so much more important, that it may be doubted whether there was ever in the civilized world a great battle followed by so many and such extraordinary results.

PARIS

That part of the French army which escaped from the field of Waterloo, fled in the most terrible disorder towards the frontiers of France. Napoleon himself continued his flight from Charleroi, in the neighbourhood of which was his first place of halting, and hurried on to Philippeville. From this point, he designed, it was said, to have marched to place himself at the head of Grouchy's army. But no troops of any kind having been rallied, and Charleroi having been almost instantly occupied by the Prussian pursuers, a report became current that the division was destroyed, and Grouchy himself made prisoner. Napoleon, therefore, pursued his own retreat, leaving orders, which were not attended to, that the relics of the army should be rallied at Avesnes. Soult could only succeed in gathering together a few thousands, as far within the French territory as Laon. Meanwhile, Buonaparte, travelling post, had reached Paris, and brought thither the news of his own defeat.

On the 19th of June the public ear of the capital had been stunned by the report of a hundred pieces of cannon, which announced the victory at Ligny, and the public prints had contained the most gasconading accounts of that action; of the forcing the passage of the Sambre, the action at Charleroi, and the battle of Quatre-bras. The Imperialists were in the highest state of exultation, the Republicans doubtful, and the Royalists dejected. On the morning of the 21st, the third day after the fatal action, it was at first whispered, and then openly said, that Napoleon had returned alone from the army on the preceding night, and was now in the palace of Bourbon-Elysée. The fatal truth was not long in transpiring—he had lost a dreadful and decisive pitched battle, and the French army, which had left the capital so confident, so full of hope, pride, and determination, was totally destroyed.

CHAMBER OF DEPUTIES

Many reasons have been given for Napoleon's not remaining with his army on this occasion, and endeavouring at least to bring it into a state of reorganisation; but the secret seems to be explained by his apprehension of the faction of Republicans and Constitutionalists in Paris. He must have remembered that Fouché, and others of that party, had advised him to end the distresses of France by his abdication of the crown, even before he placed himself at the head of his army. He was aware, that what they had ventured to suggest in his moment of strength, they would not hesitate to demand and extort from him in the hour of his weakness, and that the Chamber of Representatives would endeavour to obtain peace for themselves by sacrificing him. "He is known," says an author already quoted, friendly to his fame, "to have said, after the disasters of the Russian campaign, that he would confound the Parisians by his presence, and fall among them like a thunderbolt. But there are things which succeed only because they have never been done before, and for that reason ought never to be attempted again. His fifth flight from his army occasioned the entire abandonment of himself and his cause by all who might have forgiven him his misfortune, but required that he should be the first to arise from the blow."[158]

It was a curious indication of public spirit in Paris, that, upon the news of this appalling misfortune, the national funds rose, immediately after the first shock of the tidings was past; so soon, that is, as men had time to consider the probable consequence of the success of the allies. It seemed as if public credit revived upon any intelligence, however disastrous otherwise, which promised to abridge the reign of Buonaparte.

The anticipations of Napoleon did not deceive him. It was plain, that, whatever deference the Jacobins had for him in his hour of strength, they had no compassion for his period of weakness. They felt the opportunity favourable to get rid of him, and did not disguise their purpose to do so.

The two Chambers hastily assembled. La Fayette addressed that of the Representatives in the character of an old friend of freedom, spoke of the sinister reports that were spread abroad, and invited the members to rally under the three-coloured banner of liberty, equality, and public order, by adopting five resolutions. The first declared, that the independence of the nation was menaced; the second declared the sittings of the Chambers permanent, and denounced the pains of treason against whomever should attempt to dissolve them; the third announced that the troops had deserved

---

[158] Hobhouse's Letters from Paris, written during the Last Reign of Napoleon.—S.

well of their country; the fourth called out the national guard; the fifth invited the ministers to repair to the Assembly.[159]

These propositions intimated the apprehensions of the Chamber of Representatives, that they might be a second time dissolved by an armed force, and, at the same time, announced their purpose to place themselves at the head of affairs, without farther respect to the Emperor. They were adopted, all but the fourth concerning the national guard, which was considered as premature. Regnault de St. Jean d'Angely attempted to read a bulletin, giving an imperfect and inconsistent account of what had passed on the frontiers; but the representatives became clamorous, and demanded the attendance of the ministers. At length, after a delay of three or four hours, Carnot, Caulaincourt, Davoust, and Fouché, entered the hall with Lucien Buonaparte.

The Chamber formed itself into a secret committee, before which the ministers laid the full extent of the disaster, and announced that the Emperor had named Caulaincourt, Fouché, and Carnot, as commissioners to treat of peace with the allies. The ministers were bluntly reminded by the Republican members, and particularly by Henry Lacoste, that they had no basis for any negotiations which could be proposed in the Emperor's name, since the allied powers had declared war against Napoleon, who was now in plain terms pronounced, by more than one member, the sole obstacle betwixt the nation and peace. Universal applause followed from all parts of the hall, and left Lucien no longer in doubt, that the representatives intended to separate their cause from that of his brother. He omitted no art of conciliation or entreaty, and—more eloquent probably in prose than in poetry—appealed to their love of glory, their generosity, their fidelity, and the oaths which they had so lately sworn. "We *have* been faithful," replied Fayette; "we have followed your brother to the sands of Egypt—to the snows of Russia. The bones of Frenchmen, scattered in every region, attest our fidelity."[160] All seemed to unite in one sentiment, that the abdication of Buonaparte was a measure absolutely necessary. Davoust, the minister at war, arose, and disclaimed, with

---

[159] Moniteur, June 22; Montgaillard, tom. viii., p. 220.
[160] Montgaillard, tom. viii., p. 222.

protestations, any intention of acting against the freedom or independence of the Chamber. This was, in fact, to espouse their cause. A committee of five members was appointed to concert measures with Ministers. Even the latter official persons, though named by the Emperor, were not supposed to be warmly attached to him. Carnot and Fouché were the natural leaders of the popular party, and Caulaincourt was supposed to be on indifferent terms with Napoleon, whose Ministers, therefore, seemed to adopt the interest of the Chamber in preference to his. Lucien saw that his brother's authority was ended, unless it could be maintained by violence. The Chamber of Peers might have been more friendly to the Imperial cause, but their constitution gave them as little confidence in themselves as weight with the public. They adopted the three first resolutions of the Lower Chamber, and named a committee of public safety.

The line of conduct which the Representatives meant to pursue was now obvious; they had spoken out, and named the sacrifice which they exacted from Buonaparte, being nothing less than abdication. It remained to be known whether the Emperor would adopt measures of resistance, or submit to this encroachment. If there could be a point of right, where both were so far wrong, it certainly lay with Napoleon. These very Representatives were, by voluntary consent, as far as oaths and engagements can bind men, his subjects, convoked in his name, and having no political existence excepting as a part of his new constitutional government. However great his faults to the people of France, he had committed none towards these accomplices of his usurpation, nor were they legislators otherwise than as he was their Emperor. Their right to discard and trample upon him in his adversity, consisted only in their having the power to do so; and the readiness which they showed to exercise that power, spoke as little for their faith as for their generosity. At the same time, our commiseration for fallen greatness is lost in our sense of that justice, which makes the associates and tools of a usurper the readiest implements of his ruin.

When Buonaparte returned to Paris, his first interview was with Carnot, of whom he demanded, in his usual tone of authority, an instant supply of treasure, and a levy of 300,000 men. The minister replied, that he could have neither the one nor the other. Napoleon then summoned Maret, Duke of Bassano, and other confidential persons of his court. But when his civil counsellors talked of defence, the word wrung from him the bitter ejaculation, "Ah, my old guard, could they but defend themselves like you!" A sad confession, that the military truncheon, his best emblem of command, was broken in his gripe. Lucien urged his brother to maintain his authority, and dissolve the Chambers by force; but Napoleon, aware that the national guard might take the part of the representatives, declined an action so full of hazard. Davoust, was, however, sounded concerning his willingness to act against the Chambers, but he positively refused to do so. Some idea was held out by Fouché to Napoleon, of his being admitted to the powers of a dictator; but this could be only thrown out as a proposal for the purpose of amusing him. In the meantime, arrived the news of the result of the meeting of the Representatives in secret committee.

The gauntlet was now thrown down, and it was necessary that Napoleon should resist or yield; declare himself absolute, and dissolve the Chambers by violence; or abdicate the authority he had so lately resumed. Lucien finding him still undetermined, hesitated not to say, that the smoke of the battle of Mont Saint Jean had turned his brain.[161] In fact, his conduct at this crisis was not that of a great man. He dared neither venture on the desperate measures which might, for a short time, have preserved his power, nor could he bring himself to the dignified step of an apparently voluntary resignation. He clung to what could no longer avail him, like the distracted criminal, who, wanting resolution to meet his fate by a voluntary effort, must be pushed from the scaffold by the hand of the executioner.

GENERAL COUNCIL

Buonaparte held, upon the night of the 21st, a sort of general council, comprehending the ministers of every description; the president and four members of the Chamber of Peers, the president,

---

[161] Fleury de Chamboullon, tom. ii., p. 296; Miss Williams' Narrative.

and four vice-presidents, of the Representatives, with other official persons and counsellors of state. The Emperor laid before this assembly the state of the nation, and required their advice. Regnault (who was the Imperial orator in ordinary) seconded the statement with a proposal, that measures be taken to recruit with heroes the heroic army, and bring succours to what, by a happily selected phrase, he termed the "astonished eagle." He opined, therefore, that the Chambers should make an appeal to French valour, while the Emperor was treating of peace "in the most steady and dignified manner." Fayette stated, that resistance would but aggravate the calamities of France. The allies stood pledged to demand a particular sacrifice when they first engaged in the war; they were not likely to recede from it after this decisive victory. One measure alone he saw betwixt the country and a bloody and ruinous conflict, and he referred to the great and generous spirit of the Emperor to discover its nature. Maret, Duke of Bassano, long Buonaparte's most confidential friend, and fatally so, because (more a courtier than a statesman) he attended rather to soothe his humour than to guide his councils, took fire at this suggestion. He called for severe measures against the Royalists and the disaffected; a revolutionary police, and revolutionary punishments. "Had such," he said, "been earlier resorted to, a person" (meaning probably Fouché) "who now hears me, would not be now smiling at the misfortunes of his country, and Wellington would not be marching upon Paris." This speech was received with a burst of disapprobation, which even the presence of the Emperor, in whose cause Maret was thus vehement, proved unable to restrain; hisses and clamour drowned the voice of the speaker. Carnot, who had juster views of the military strength, or rather weakness of France at the moment, was desirous, democrat as he was, to retain the advantage of Napoleon's talents. He is said to have wept when the abdication was insisted upon. Lanjuinais and Constant supported the sentiments of Fayette. But the Emperor appeared gloomy, dissatisfied, and uncertain, and the council broke up without coming to any determination.[162]

For another anxious night the decision of Buonaparte was suspended. Had the nation, or even the ministers, been unanimous

---

[162] Montgaillard, tom. viii., p. 223; Fouché, tom. ii., p. 282; Las Cases, tom. i., p. 10; Savary, tom. iv., p. 98.

in a resolution to defend themselves, unquestionably France might have been exposed to the final chance of war, with some prospect of a struggle on Napoleon's part; though, when it is considered within how short a time the allies introduced, within the limits of France, an armed force amounting to 800,000 effective men, it does not appear how his resistance could have eventually proved successful. It would be injustice to deny Napoleon a natural feeling of the evils which must have been endured by the nation in such a protracted contest, and we readily suppose him unwilling to have effected a brief continuation of his reign, by becoming the cause of so much misery to the fine country which he had so long ruled. Like most men in difficulties, he received much more advice than offers of assistance. The best counsel was, perhaps, that of an American gentleman, who advised him instantly to retreat to the North American States, where he could not indeed enjoy the royal privileges and ceremonial, to which he was more attached than philosophy warrants, but where that general respect would have been paid to him, which his splendid talents, and wonderful career of adventure, were so well calculated to enforce. But now, as at Moscow, he lingered too long in forming a decided opinion; for, though the importunity of friends and opponents wrung from him the resignation which was demanded at all hands, yet it was clogged by conditions which could only be made in the hope of retaining a predominant interest in the government by which his own was to be succeeded.

On the morning of the 22d June, only four days after the defeat at Waterloo, the Chamber of Representatives assembled at nine in the morning, and expressed the utmost impatience to receive the Act of Abdication. A motion was made by Duchesne, that it should be peremptorily demanded from the Emperor, when this degree of violence was rendered unnecessary by his compliance.[163] It

---

[163] "We all manœuvred to extort his abdication. There was a multitude of messages backwards and forwards, parleys, objections, replies—in a word, evolutions of every description: ground was taken, abandoned, and again retaken. At length, after a warm battle, Napoleon surrendered, in full council, under the conviction that longer resistance was useless; then turning to me, he said, with a sardonic smile, 'Write to those gentlemen to make themselves easy; they shall be satisfied.' Lucien took up the pen, and drew, under Napoleon's dictation, the act of abdication."—Fouché, tom. ii., p. 283.

was presented by Fouché, whose intrigues were thus far crowned with success, and was couched in the following terms:—

"Frenchmen!—In commencing war for maintaining the national independence, I relied on the union of all efforts, of all wills, and the concurrence of all the national authorities. I had reason to hope for success, and I braved all the declarations of the powers against me.

"Circumstances appear to me changed. I offer myself as a sacrifice to the hatred of the enemies of France. May they prove sincere in their declarations, and have really directed them only against my power! My political life is terminated, and I proclaim my son, under the title of Napoleon II., Emperor of the French.

"The present ministers will provisionally form the council of the government. The interest which I take in my son induces me to invite the Chambers to form, without delay, the regency by a law.

"Unite all for the public safety, in order to remain an independent nation.

(Signed) "Napoleon."[164]

PROVISIONAL GOVERNMENT

The Republican party having thus obtained a victory, proposed instantly several new models for settling the form of a constitution, in the room of that, which, exactly three weeks before, they had sworn to in the Champ de Mai. This was judged somewhat premature; and they resolved for the present to content themselves with nominating a Provisional Government, vesting the executive powers of the state in five persons—two to be chosen from Buonaparte's House of Peers, and three from that of the Representatives.

---

[164] Moniteur, June 23.

In the meanwhile, to preserve the decency due to the late Emperor, the Chamber named a committee to wait on him with an address of thanks, in which they carefully avoided all mention and recognition of his son. Napoleon, for the last time, received the committee delegated to present the address, in the imperial habit, and surrounded by his state-officers and guards. He seemed pale and pensive, but firm and collected, and heard with a steady indifference the praises which they bestowed on his patriotic sacrifice. His answer recommended unanimity, and the speedy preparation of means of defence; but at the conclusion he reminded them, that his abdication was conditional, and comprehended the interests of his son.

Lanjuinais, President of the Chamber, replied, with profound respect, that the Chamber had given him no directions respecting the subject which Napoleon pressed upon. "I told you," said he, turning to his brother Lucien, "they would not, could not do it.—Tell the Assembly," he said, again addressing the President, "that I recommend my son to their protection. It is in his favour I have abdicated."

Thus the succession of Napoleon II. came to be now the point of debate between the abdicated Emperor and the Legislative Bodies. It is certain the appointment could not have been rendered acceptable to the allies; and the influence which Buonaparte and his friends were likely to have in a regency, were strong arguments for all in France who had opposed him in the struggle, uniting to set aside his family and dynasty.

Upon the same 22d June, a strange scene took place in the Chamber of Peers. The government had received intelligence that Maréchal Grouchy, whom we left on the banks of the Dyle, near Wavre, and who continued his action with Thielman, to whom he was opposed, till deep in the night, had, on hearing the loss of the battle at Waterloo, effected a most able retreat through Namur, defended himself against several attacks, and finally made his way to Laon. This good news encouraged Carnot to render a brilliant account to the Chamber, of Grouchy being at the head of an untouched army of upwards of 60,000 men (Grouchy's whole force at Wavre having been only 32,000); of Soult collecting 20,000 of the old guard at Mezières; of 10,000 new levies despatched from the interior to join the rallied forces, with 200 pieces of cannon. Ney, half frantic at hearing these exaggerated statements, and his mind galled with the sense of Napoleon's injustice towards him, as expressed in the bulletins, started up, and spoke like a possessed person under the power of the exorcist. There was a reckless desperation in the manner of his contradicting the minister. It seemed as if he wished the state of the world undone in his own undoing. "The report," he said, "was false—false in every respect. Dare they tell eyewitnesses of the disastrous day of the 18th, that we have yet 60,000 soldiers embodied? Grouchy cannot have under him 20,000, or 25,000 soldiers, at the utmost. Had he possessed a greater force, he might have covered the retreat, and the Emperor would have been still in command of an army on the frontiers. Not a man of the guard," he said, "will ever rally more. I myself commanded them—I myself witnessed their total extermination, ere I left the field of battle. They are annihilated.—The enemy are at Nivelles with 80,000 men; they may, if they please, be at Paris in six days. There is no safety for France but in instant propositions of peace." On being contradicted by General Flahault, Ney resumed his sinister statement with even more vehemence; and at length striking at once into the topic which all felt, but none had ventured yet to name, he said in a low, but distinct voice—"Yes! I repeat it—your only course is by negotiation—you must recall the Bourbons;—and, for me, I will retire to the United States."

The most bitter reproaches were heaped on Ney for this last expression. Lavalette and Carnot especially appeared incensed against him. Ney replied with sullen contempt to those who blamed his conduct, "I am not one of those to whom their interest is every thing; what should I gain by the restoration of Louis, except being shot for desertion? but I must speak the truth, for the sake of the country." This strange scene sunk deep into the minds of thinking men, who were thenceforward induced to view the subsequent sounding resolutions, and bustling debates of the Chambers, as empty noise, unsupported by the state of the national resources.

ACT OF ABDICATION

After this debate on the state of the means of defence, there followed one scarce less stormy, in the House of Peers, upon the reading of the Act of Abdication. Lucien Buonaparte took up the question of the succession, and insisted upon the instant recognition of his nephew, according to the rules of the constitution. The Count de Pontecoulant interrupted the orator, demanding by what right Lucien, an Italian prince, and an alien, presumed to name a sovereign to the French empire, where he himself had not even the privileges of a denizen? To this objection—a strange one, certainly, coming from lips which had sworn faith but twenty-two days before to a constitution, recognising Lucien not only as a denizen, but as one of the blood-royal of France, the prince answered, that he was a Frenchman by his sentiments, and by virtue of the laws. Pontecoulant then objected to accept as sovereign a child residing in a different kingdom; and Labédoyère, observing the hesitation of the assembly, started up, and demeaning himself with unrestrained fury, exhibited the same blind and devoted attachment to Napoleon, which had prompted him to show the example of defection at Grenoble.

"The Emperor," he said, "had abdicated solely in behalf of his son. His resignation was null, if his son was not instantly proclaimed. And who were they who opposed this generous resolution? Those whose voices had been always at the sovereign's devotion while in prosperity; who had fled from him in adversity, and who were already hastening to receive the yoke of foreigners. Yes," continued this impetuous young man, aiding his speech with the most violent gestures, and overpowering, by the loudness of his tone, the murmurs of the assembly, "if you refuse to acknowledge the Imperial prince, I declare that Napoleon must again draw his sword—again shed blood. At the head of the brave Frenchmen who have bled in his cause, we will rally around him; and woe to the base generals who are perhaps even now meditating new treasons! I demand that they be impeached, and punished as deserters of the national standard—that their names be given to infamy, their houses razed, their families proscribed and exiled. We will endure no traitors amongst us. Napoleon, in resigning his power to save the nation, has done his duty to himself, but the nation is not worthy of him, since she has a second time compelled him to abdicate; she who vowed to abide by him in prosperity and reverses." The ravings of this daring enthusiast, who was, in fact, giving language to the feelings of a great part of the French army, were at length drowned in a general cry of order. "You forget yourself," exclaimed Massena. "You believe yourself still in the *corps de garde*," said Lameth. Labédoyère strove to go on, but was silenced by the general clamour, which at length put an end to this scandalous scene.[165]

The peers, like the deputies of the Lower Chamber, having eluded the express recognition of Napoleon II., the two chambers proceeded to name the members of the provisional government. These were Carnot, Fouché, Caulaincourt, Grenier, and Quinette.[166] In their proclamation they stated that Napoleon had resigned, and that his son had been *proclaimed*, (which, by the way, was not true;) calling on the nation for exertions, sacrifices, and unanimity, and promising, if not an actually new constitution, as had been usual on such occasions, yet such a complete revision and repair of that which was now three weeks old, as should make it in every respect as good as new.[167]

This address had little effect either on the troops or the Federates, who, like Labédoyère, were of opinion that Napoleon's abdication could only be received on his own terms. These men assembled in armed parties, and paraded under Buonaparte's windows, at the palace of Bourbon-Elysée. Money and liquor were delivered to them, which increased their cries of *Vive Napoleon! Vive l'Empereur!* They insulted the national guards, and seemed disposed to attack the residence of Fouché. On the other hand, the national guards were 30,000 men in number, disposed in general to support order, and many of them leaning to the side of Louis XVIII. A moment of internal convulsion seemed inevitable; for it was said,

---

[165] Moniteur, June 23.
[166] Carnot, Fouché, Grenier, and Quinette, had all voted for the death of Louis XVI.
[167] "I was present at the moment of abdication; and, when the question of Napoleon's removal was agitated, I requested permission to participate in his fate. Such had been till then the disinterestedness and simplicity, some will say folly, of my conduct, that, notwithstanding my daily intercourse as an officer of the household, and member of his council, the Emperor scarcely knew me. 'Do you know whither your offer may lead you?' said he, in his astonishment. 'I have made no calculation about it,' I replied. He accepted me, and here I am at St. Helena."—Las Cases, tom. i., part i., p. 9.

that if Napoleon II. was not instantly acknowledged, Buonaparte would come down and dissolve the Chamber with an armed force.

On the meeting of the 24th June, the important question of succession was decided, or rather evaded, as follows:—Manuel, generally understood to be the organ of Fouché in the House of Representatives, made a long speech to show that there was no occasion for a formal recognition of the succession of Napoleon II., since he was, by the terms of the constitution, already in possession of the throne. When the orator had given this deep reason that their sovereign should neither be acknowledged nor proclaimed, purely because he was their sovereign, all arose and shouted, *Vive Napoleon II.!* But when there was a proposal to swear allegiance to the new Emperor, there was a general cry of "No oaths! No oaths!" as if there existed a consciousness in the Chamber of having been too lavish of these ill-redeemed pledges, and a general disgust at commencing a new course of perjury.

The Chamber of Representatives thus silenced, if they did not satisfy, the Imperialist party, by a sort of incidental and ostensible acknowledgment of the young Napoleon's right to the crown; while at the same time, by declaring the Provisional Government to be a necessary guarantee for the liberties of the subject, they prevented the interference either of Napoleon himself, or any of his friends, in the administration of the country. Yet, notwithstanding the simulated nature of their compliance with the special condition of Napoleon's resignation, the Chambers and Provisional Government were as strict in exacting from the abdicated sovereign the terms of his bargain, as if they had paid him the stipulated value in sterling, instead of counterfeit coin. Thus they exacted from him a proclamation, addressed in his own name to the soldiers, in order to confirm the fact of his abdication, which the troops were unwilling to believe on any authority inferior to his own. In this address, there are, however, expressions which show his sense of the compulsion under which he acted. After an exhortation to the soldiers to continue in their career of honour, and an assurance of the interest which he should always take in their exploits, follows this passage:— "Both you and I have been calumniated. Men, very unfit to appreciate our labours, have seen in the marks of attachment which you have given me, a zeal of which I was the sole object. Let your future successes tell them, that it was the country, above all things, which you served in obeying me; and that, if I had any share in your affections, I owed it to my ardent love for France, our common mother."[168]

MALMAISON

These expressions were highly disagreeable to the Chamber of Representatives, who at the same time regarded the presence of Napoleon in the capital as dangerous to their own power, and to the public tranquillity. The suburbs, with their fierce inmates, continued to be agitated, and soldiers, the straggling relics of the field of Waterloo, were daily gathering under the walls of Paris, furious at their recent defeat, and calling on their Emperor to lead them to vengeance. There seems to have been little to prevent Napoleon from still placing himself at the head of a small but formidable army. To remove him from this temptation, the Provisional Government required him to retire to the palace of Malmaison, near St. Germains, so long the favourite abode of the discarded Josephine. Napoleon had not been within its walls a single day, before, surrounded by Fouché's police, he found that he, who, not a month since, had disposed of the fate of myriads, was no longer the free master of his own actions. He was watched and controlled, though without the use of actual force, and now, for the first time, felt what it was to lose that free agency, of which his despotism had for so many years deprived so large a portion of mankind. Yet he seemed to submit to his fate with indifference, or only expressed impatience when beset by his personal creditors, who, understanding that he was not likely to remain long in France, attempted to extort from him a settlement of their claims. This petty persecution was given way to by the government, as one of several expedients to abridge his residence in France; and they had the means of using force, if all should fail.

Short as was the time he lingered at Malmaison, incredible as it may be thought, Napoleon was almost forgotten in Paris. "No

---

[168] Dated Malmaison, June 25. See Fleury de Chamboullon, tom. ii., p. 294.

one," says a well-informed author, living in that city during the crisis, "except the immediate friends of government, pretends to know whether he is still at Malmaison, or seems to think it a question of importance to ask. On Saturday last, Count M—— saw him there; he was tranquil, but quite lost. His friends now pretend, that, since his return from Elba, he has never been quite the man he was."[169] There was, however, a reason for his protracting his residence at Malmaison, more honourable than mere human reluctance to submit to inevitable calamity.

The English and Prussian forces were now approaching Paris by rapid marches; every town falling before them which could have been reckoned upon as a bar to their progress. When Paris was again to be girt round with hostile armies, honourable as well as political feelings might lead Napoleon to hope that the Representatives might be inclined to wave all personal animosity, and, having recourse to his extraordinary talents and his influence over the minds of the army and federates, by which alone the capital could be defended, might permit him once more to assume the sword for protection of Paris. He offered to command the army as general in chief, in behalf of his son. He offered to take share in the defence, as an ordinary citizen. But the internal discord had gone too far. The popular party which then prevailed, saw more danger in the success of Napoleon, than in the superiority of the allies. The latter they hoped to conciliate by treaty. They doubted, with good reason, the power of resisting them by force; and if such resistance was, or could be maintained by Napoleon, they feared his supremacy, in a military command, at least as much as the predominance of the allies. His services were therefore declined by them.

Like skilful anglers, the Provisional Government had been gradually drawing their nets around Napoleon, and it was now time, as they thought, to drag him upon the shallows. They proceeded to place him under a sort of arrest, by directing General Beker, an officer with whom Napoleon had been on indifferent terms, to watch over, and, if necessary, to restrain his movements in such a manner, that it should be impossible for him to make his escape,

---

[169] Hobhouse's Letters from Paris, vol. ii.; Fleury de Chamboullon, tom. ii., p. 298.

and to use measures to induce him to leave Malmaison for Rochefort, where the means were provided for his departure out of France. Orders were at the same time given for two frigates to transport him to the United States of America; and the *surveillance* of General Beker and the police was to continue until the late Emperor was on board the vessels. This order was qualified by directions that all possible care should be taken to ensure the safety of Napoleon's person. A corresponding order was transmitted by Davoust, who, giving way to one of those equivocal bursts of feeling, by which men compromise a conflict between their sentiments and their duty or their interest, refused to sign it himself, but ordered his secretary to do so, which, as he observed, would be quite the same.[170]

Napoleon submitted to his destiny with resignation and dignity. He received General Beker with ease, and even cheerfulness; and the latter, with feelings which did him honour, felt the task committed to him the more painful, that he had experienced the personal enmity of the individual who was now intrusted to his custody.[171] About forty persons, of different ranks and degrees, honourably dedicated their services to the adversity of the Emperor, whom they had served in prosperity.

Yet, amid all these preparations for departure, a longing hope remained, that his exile might be dispensed with. He heard the distant cannonade as the war-horse hears the trumpet. Again he offered his services to march against Blucher as a simple volunteer, undertaking that, when he had repulsed the invaders, he would then proceed on his journey of expatriation.[172] He had such hopes of his request being granted as to have his horses brought out and in readiness to enable him to join the army. But the Provisional Government anew declined an offer, the acceptance of which would indeed have ruined all hopes of treating with the allies. Fouché, on

---

[170] "The secretary found himself equally incapable of putting his name to such a communication. Was it sent or not?—this is a point which I cannot decide."—Las Cases, tom. i., part i., pp. 17-20.
[171] "Fouché knew that General Beker had a private pique against the Emperor; and therefore did not doubt of finding in the former a man disposed to vengeance; but he was grossly deceived in his expectations, for Beker constantly showed a degree of respect and attachment to the Emperor highly honourable to his character."—Las Cases, tom. i., p. 17.
[172] Las Cases, tom. i., p. 20.

hearing Napoleon's proposal, is said to have exclaimed, "Is he laughing at us!" Indeed, his joining the troops would have soon made him master of the destiny of the Provisional Government, whatever might have been the final result.

ARRIVES AT ROCHEFORT

On the 29th of June, Napoleon departed from Malmaison; on the 3d of July he arrived at Rochefort. General Beker accompanied him, nor does his journey seem to have been marked by any circumstances worthy of remark. Wherever he came, the troops received him with acclamation; the citizens respected the misfortunes of one who had been wellnigh master of the world, and were silent where they could not applaud.

Thus, the reign of the Emperor Napoleon was completely ended. But, before adverting to his future fate, we must complete, in a few words, the consequences of his abdication, and offer some remarks on the circumstances by which it was extorted and enforced.

The Provisional Government had sent commissioners to the Duke of Wellington, to request passports for Napoleon to the States of America. The duke had no instructions from his government to grant them. The Prussian and English generals alike declined all overtures made for the establishment, or acknowledgment, either of the present Provisional Administration, or any plan which they endeavoured to suggest, short of the restoration of the Bourbons to the seat of government. The Provisional Commissioners endeavoured, with as little success, to awaken the spirit of national defence. They had lost the road to the soldiers' hearts. The thoughts of patriotism had in the army become indissolubly united with the person and the qualities of Napoleon. It was in vain that deputies, with scarfs, and proclamations of public right, and invocation of the ancient watchwords of the Revolution, endeavoured to awaken the spirit of 1794. The soldiers and federates answered sullenly, "Why should we fight any more? we have no longer an Emperor."

Meanwhile, the Royalist party assumed courage, and showed themselves in arms in several of the departments, directed the public opinion in many others, and gained great accessions from the Constitutionalists. Indeed, if any of the latter still continued to dread the restoration of the Bourbons, it was partly from the fear of reaction and retaliation on the side of the successful Royalists, and partly because it was apprehended that the late events might have made on the mind of Louis an impression unfavourable to constitutional limitations, a disgust to those by whom they were recommended and supported, and a propensity to resume the arbitrary measures by which his ancestors had governed their kingdom. Those who nourished those apprehensions could not but allow, that they were founded on the fickleness and ingratitude of the people, who had shown themselves unworthy of, and easily induced to conspire against, the mild and easy rule of a limited monarchy. But they involved, nevertheless, tremendous consequences, if the King should be disposed to act upon rigorous and vindictive principles; and it was such an apprehension on the part of some, joined to the fears of others for personal consequences, the sullen shame of a third party, and the hatred of the army to the princes whom they had betrayed, which procured for the Provisional Government a show of obedience.

It was thus that the Chambers continued their resistance to receiving their legitimate monarch, though unable to excite any enthusiasm save that expressed in the momentary explosions discharged within their own place of meeting, which gratified no ears, and heated no brains but their own. In the meanwhile, the armies of Soult and Grouchy were driven under the walls of Paris, where they were speedily followed by the English and the Prussians. The natural gallantry of the French then dictated a resistance, which was honourable to their arms, though totally unsuccessful. The allies, instead of renewing the doubtful attack on Montmartre, crossed the Seine, and attacked Paris on the undefended side. There was not, as in 1814, a hostile army to endanger the communications on their rear. The French, however, showed great bravery, both by an attempt to defend Versailles, and in a *coup-de-main* of General Excelmans, by which he attempted to recover that town. But at length, in consequence of the result of a council of war held in Paris, on the night betwixt the 2d and 3d of July, an armistice was concluded, by which the capital was surrendered to the allies, and the French army was drawn off behind the Loire.

The allies suspended their operations until the French troops should be brought to submit to their destined movement in retreat, against which they struggled with vain enthusiasm. Permitting their violence to subside, they delayed their own occupation of Paris until the 7th of July, when it had been completely evacuated. The British and Prussians then took military possession, in a manner strictly regular, but arguing a different state of feelings on both parts, from those exhibited in the joyous procession of the allies along the Boulevards in 1814. The Provisional Government continued their sittings, though Fouché, the chief among them, had been long intriguing (and ever since the battle of Waterloo, with apparent sincerity) for the second restoration of the Bourbon family, on such terms as should secure the liberties of France. They received, on the 6th of July, the final resolution of the allied sovereigns, that they considered all authority emanating from the usurped power of Napoleon Buonaparte as null, and of no effect; and that Louis XVIII., who was presently at Saint Denis, would on the next day, or day after at farthest, enter his capital, and resume his regal authority.

On the 7th of July, the Provisional Commission dissolved itself. The Chamber of Peers, when they heard the act of surrender, dispersed in silence; but that of the Representatives continued to sit, vote, and debate, for several hours. The president then prorogued the meeting till eight the next morning, in defiance of the cries of several members, who called on him to maintain the literal permanence of the sitting. The next morning, the members who attended found the hall sentinelled by the national guard, who refused them admittance, and heard the exclamations and complaints of the deputies with great disregard. Nay, the disappointed and indignant legislators were subjected to the ridicule of the idle spectators, who accompanied the arrival and retreat of each individual with laughter and acclamation, loud in proportion to the apparent excess of his mortification.

LOUIS RE-ENTERS PARIS

On the 8th of July, Louis re-entered his capital, attended by a very large body of the national guards and royal volunteers, as well as by his household troops. In the rear of these soldiers came a numerous état-major, among whom were distinguished the Maréchals Victor, Marmont, Macdonald, Oudinot, Gouvion, St. Cyr, Moncey, and Lefebvre. An immense concourse of citizens received, with acclamations, the legitimate monarch; and the females were observed to be particularly eager in their expressions of joy. Thus was Louis again installed in the palace of his ancestors, over which the white banner once more floated. Here, therefore, ended that short space, filled with so much that is wonderful, that period of an Hundred Days, in which the events of a century seemed to be contained. Before we proceed with the narrative, which must in future be the history of an individual, it may not be improper to cast a look back upon the events comprised within that extraordinary period, and offer a few remarks on their political nature and tendency.

It is unnecessary to remind the reader, that Napoleon's restoration to the throne was the combined work of two factions. One comprehended the army, who desired the recovery of their own honour, sullied by recent defeats, and the recalling of the Emperor to their head, that he might save them from being disbanded, and lead them to new victories. The other party was that which not only desired that the kingdom should possess a large share of practical freedom, but felt interested that the doctrines of the Revolution should be recognised, and particularly that which was held to entitle the people, or those who might contrive to assume the right of representing them, to alter the constitution of the government at pleasure, and to be, as was said of the great Earl of Warwick, the setters up and pullers down of kings. This party, availing themselves of some real errors of the reigning family, imagining more, and exciting a cloud of dark suspicions, had instigated a general feeling of dissatisfaction against the Bourbons. But though they probably might have had recourse to violence, nothing appears less probable than their success in totally overturning royalty, had they been unsupported by the soldiers. The army, which rose so readily at Buonaparte's summons, had no community of feeling with the Jacobins, as they were called; and but for his arrival upon the scene, would have acted, there can be little doubt, at the command of the maréchals, who were almost all attached to the royal family. It was, therefore, the attachment of the army to their ancient commander which gave success to the joint enterprise, which the Jacobinical party alone would have attempted in vain.

THE CHAMBERS

The Republican, or Jacobin party, closed with their powerful ally; their leaders accepted titles at his hands; undertook offices, and became members of a Chamber of Peers and of Representatives, summoned by his authority. They acknowledged him as their Emperor; received as his boon a new constitution; and swore in the face of all France the oath of fealty to it, and to him as their sovereign. On such terms the Emperor and his Legislative Body parted on the 7th of June. Suspicion there existed between them certainly, but, in all outward appearance, he departed a contented prince from a contented people. Eleven days brought the battle of Waterloo, with all its consequences. Policy of a sound and rational sort should have induced the Chambers to stand by the Emperor whom they had made, to arm him with the power which the occasion required, and avail themselves of his extraordinary military talent, to try some chance of arresting the invaders in their progress. Even shame might have prevented them from lending their shoulders to overthrow the tottering throne before which they had so lately kneeled. They determined otherwise. The instant he became unfortunate, Napoleon ceased to be their Emperor, the source of their power and authority. They could see nothing in him but the hurt deer, who is to be butted from the herd; the Jonas in the vessel, who is to be flung overboard. When Napoleon, therefore, talked to them of men and arms, they answered him, with "equality and the rights of man;" every chance of redeeming the consequences of Waterloo was lost, and the Emperor of their choice, if not ostensibly, was in effect at least arrested, and sent to the sea-coast, like a felon for deportation. Their conduct, however, went clearly to show, that Napoleon was not the free choice of the

French people, and especially that he was not the choice of those who termed themselves exclusively the friends of freedom.

Having thus shown how easily they could get rid of the monarch who had called them into political existence, the Chambers applied to the allies, inviting them to give their concurrence to the election of another sovereign, and assist them to build another throne on the quicksand which had just swallowed that of Napoleon. In one respect they were not unreasonably tenacious. They cared little who the sovereign should be, whether Orleans or Orange, the Englishman Wellington or the Cossack Platoff, providing only he should derive no right from any one but themselves; and that they should be at liberty to recall that right when it might please them to do so. And there can be little doubt, that any new sovereign and constitution which could have been made by the assistance of such men, would have again occasioned the commencement of the wild dance of revolution, till like so many mad Dervises, dizzy with the whirl, the French nation would once more have sunk to rest under the iron sway of despotism.

The allied sovereigns viewed these proposals with an evil eye, both in respect to their nature, and to those by whom they were proposed. Of the authorities, the most prudent was the Duke of Otranto, and he had been Fouché of Nantes. Carnot's name was to be found at all the bloody rescripts of Robespierre, in which the conscience of the old decemvir and young count had never found any thing to boggle at. There were many others, distinguished in the Revolutionary days. The language which they held was already assuming the cant of democracy, and though there was among them a large proportion of good and able men, it was not to be forgotten how many of such existed in the first Assembly, for no purpose but to seal the moderation and rationality of their political opinions with their blood. It was a matter of imperious necessity to avoid whatever might give occasion to renew those scenes of shameful recollections, and the sovereigns saw a guarantee against their return, in insisting that Louis XVIII. should remount the throne as its legitimate owner.

LEGITIMACY

The right of legitimacy, or the right of succession, a regulation adopted into the common law of most monarchical constitutions, is borrowed from the analogy of private life, where the eldest son becomes naturally the head and protector of the family upon the decease of the father. While states, indeed, are small—before laws are settled—and when much depends on the personal ability and talents of the monarch—the power, which, for aught we know, may exist among the abstract rights of man, of choosing each chief magistrate after the death of his predecessor, or perhaps more frequently, may be exercised without much inconvenience. But as states become extended, and their constitutions circumscribed and bounded by laws, which leaves less scope and less necessity for the exercise of the sovereign's magisterial functions, men become glad to exchange the licentious privilege of a Tartarian couroultai, or a Polish diet, for the principle of legitimacy; because the chance of a hereditary successor's proving adequate to the duties of his situation, is at least equal to that of a popular election lighting upon a worthy candidate; and because, in the former case, the nation is spared the convulsions occasioned by previous competition and solicitation, and succeeding heart-burnings, factions, civil war, and ruin, uniformly found at last to attend elective monarchies.

The doctrine of legitimacy is peculiarly valuable in a limited monarchy, because it affords a degree of stability otherwise unattainable. The principle of hereditary monarchy, joined to that which declares that the King can do no wrong, provides for the permanence of the executive government, and represses that ambition which would animate so many bosoms, were there a prospect of the supreme sway becoming vacant, or subject to election from time to time. The King's ministers, on the other hand, being responsible for his actions, remain a check, for their own sakes, upon the exercise of his power; and thus provision is made for the correction of all ordinary evils of administration, since, to use an expressive, though vulgar simile, it is better to rectify any occasional deviation from the regular course by changing the driver, than by overturning the carriage.

Such is the principle of legitimacy which was invoked by Louis XVIII., and recognised by the allied sovereigns. But it must not be confounded with the slavish doctrine, that the right thus vested is, by divine origin, indefeasible. The heir-at-law in private life may dissipate by his folly, or forfeit by his crimes, the patrimony which the law conveys to him; and the legitimate monarch may most unquestionably, by departing from the principles of the constitution under which he is called to reign, forfeit for himself, and for his heirs if the legislature shall judge it proper, that crown, which the principle of legitimacy bestowed on him as his birth-right. The penalty of forfeiture is an extreme case, provided, not in virtue of the constitution, which recognises no possible delinquency in the sovereign, but because the constitution has been attacked and infringed upon by the monarch, and therefore can no longer be permitted to afford him shelter. The crimes by which this high punishment is justly incurred, must therefore be of an extraordinary nature, and beyond the reach of those correctives for which the constitution provides, by the punishment of ministers and counsellors. The constitutional buckler of impeccability covers the monarch (personally) for all blameworthy use of his power, providing it is exercised within the limits of the constitution; it is when he stirs beyond it, and not sooner, that it affords no defence for the bosom of a tyrant. A King of Britain, for example, may wage a rash war, or make a disgraceful peace, in the lawful, though injudicious and blameworthy exercise of the power vested in him by the constitution. His advisers, not he himself, shall be called in such a case, to their responsibility. But if, like James II., the sovereign infringes upon, or endeavours to destroy, the constitution itself, it is then that resistance becomes lawful and honourable; and the King is justly held to have forfeited the right which descended to him from his forefathers, by his attempt to encroach on the rights of the subjects.

The principles of hereditary monarchy, of the inviolability of the person of the King, and of the responsibility of ministers, were recognised by the constitutional charter of France. Louis XVIII. was therefore, during the year previous to Buonaparte's return, the lawful sovereign of France, and it remains to be shown by what act of treason to the constitution he had forfeited his right of legitimacy. If the reader will turn back to vol. iv., p. 86, (and we are not conscious of having spared the conduct of the Bourbons,) he will probably be of opinion with us, that the errors of the restored King's government were not only fewer than might have been expected in circumstances so new and difficult, but were of such a nature as an honest, well-meaning, and upright Opposition would soon have checked; he will find that not one of them could be personally attributed to Louis XVIII., and that, far from having incurred the forfeiture of his legitimate rights, he had, during these few months, laid a strong claim to the love, veneration, and gratitude of his subjects. He had fallen a sacrifice, in some degree, to the humours and rashness of persons connected with his family and household—still more to causeless jealousies and unproved doubts, the water-colours which insurrection never lacks to paint her cause with; to the fickleness of the French people, who became tired of his simple, orderly, and peaceful government; but, above all, to the dissatisfaction of a licentious and licensed soldiery, and of clubs of moody banditti, panting for a time of pell-mell havoc and confusion. The forcible expulsion of Louis XVIII., arising from such motives, could not break the solemn compact entered into by France with all Europe, when she received her legitimate monarch from the hand of her clement conquerors, and with him, and for his sake, obtained such conditions of peace as she was in no condition to demand, and would never otherwise have been granted. The King's misfortune, as it arose from no fault of his own, could infer no forfeiture of his vested right. Europe, the virtual guarantee of the treaty of Paris, had also a title, leading back the lawful King in her armed and victorious hand, to require of France his reinstatement in his rights; and the termination which she thus offered to the war was as just and equitable as the conduct of the sovereigns during this brief campaign had been honourable and successful.

To these arguments, an unprejudiced eye could scarcely see any answer; yet the popular party endeavoured to found a pleading against the second restoration of Louis, upon the declaration of the allies. This manifesto had announced, they said, that the purpose of the war was directed against Buonaparte personally, and that it was the intention of the allied sovereigns, when he should be dethroned, to leave the French the free exercise of choice respecting their own internal government.[173] The Prince Regent's declaration, in

---

[173] Parl. Debates, vol. xxx., p. 373.

particular, was referred to, as announcing that the treaty of Vienna, which resolved on the dethronement of Napoleon, should not bind the British government to insist upon the restoration of the Bourbon family as an indispensable condition of peace.[174] Those who urged this objection did not, or would not consider the nature of the treaty which this explanatory clause referred to. That treaty of Vienna had for its express object the restoration of Louis XVIII., and the Prince Regent adhered to it with the same purpose of making every exertion for bringing about that event. The restrictive clause was only introduced, because his Royal Highness did not intend to bind himself to make that restoration *alone* the cause of continuing the war to extremity. Many things might have happened to render an absolute engagement of this nature highly inexpedient; but, since none of these did happen, and since the re-establishment of the throne of the Bourbons was, in consequence of the victory of Waterloo, a measure which could be easily accomplished, it necessarily followed, that it *was* to be accomplished according to the tenor of the treaty of Vienna.

But, even had the sovereigns positively announced in their manifestoes, that the will of the French people should be consulted exclusively, what right had the Legislative Body, assembled by Buonaparte, to assume the character of the French people? They had neither weight nor influence with any party in the state, except by the momentary possession of an authority, which was hardly acknowledged on any side. The fact, that Napoleon's power had ceased to exist, did not legitimate them. On the contrary, flowing from his commission, it must be held as having fallen with his authority. They were either the Chambers summoned by Napoleon, and bound to him as far as oaths and professions could bind them, or they were a body without any pretension whatever to a political character.

La Fayette, indeed, contended that the present representatives of France stood in the same situation as the convention parliaments of England, and the army encamped in Hounslow-heath, at the time of the English Revolution. To have rendered this parallel apt, it

---

[174] "It is not to be understood as binding his Britannic Majesty to prosecute the war with a view of imposing upon France any particular government."—*Parl. Debates*, vol. xxx., p. 798.

required all the peculiar circumstances of justice which attended the great event of 1688. The French should have been able to vindicate the reason of their proceedings by the aggressions of their exiled monarch, and by the will of the nation generally, nay, almost unanimously, expressed in consequence thereof. This, we need not say, they were wholly unable to do. But the English history *did* afford one example of an assembly, exactly resembling their own, in absence of right, and exuberance of pretension; and that precedent existed when the Rump Parliament contrived to shuffle the cards out of the hands of Richard Cromwell, as the Provisional Commissioners at Paris were endeavouring by legerdemain to convey the authority from Napoleon II. This Rump Parliament also sat for a little time as a government, and endeavoured to settle the constitution upon their own plan, in despite of the whole people of England, who were longing for the restoration of their lawful monarch, as speedily was shown to be the case, when Monk, with an armed force, appeared to protect them in the declaration of their real sentiments. This was the most exact parallel afforded by English history to the situation of the Provisional Commissioners of France; and both they and the Rump Parliament being equally intrusive occupants of the supreme authority, were alike justly deprived of it by the return of the legitimate monarch.

SECOND RESTORATION

While the allied powers were thus desirous that the King of France should obtain possession of a throne which he had never forfeited, they, and England in particular, saw at once the justice and the policy of securing to France every accession of well-regulated freedom, which she had obtained by and through the Revolution, as well as such additional improvements upon her constitution as experience had shown to be desirable. These were pointed out and stipulated for by the celebrated Fouché, who, on this occasion, did much service to his country. Yet he struggled hard, that while the King acknowledged, which he was ready to do, the several benefits, both in point of public feeling and public advantage, which France had derived from the Revolution, the sovereign should make some steps to acknowledge the Revolution itself.[175] He contended for the three-coloured banners being adopted, as a matter of the last importance;—in that, somewhat resembling the archfiend in the legends of necromancy, who, when the unhappy persons with whom he deals decline to make over their souls and bodies according to his first request, is humble enough to ask and accept the most petty sacrifices—the paring of the nails, or a single lock of hair, providing it is offered in symbol of homage and devotion. But Louis XVIII. was not thus to be drawn into an incidental and equivocal homologation, as civilians term it, of all the wild work of a period so horrible, which must have been by implication a species of ratification even of the death of his innocent and murdered brother. To preserve and cherish the good which had flowed from the Revolution, was a very different thing from a ratification of the Revolution itself. A tempest may cast rich treasures upon the beach, a tornado may clear the air; but while these benefits are suitably prized and enjoyed, it is surely not requisite that, like ignorant Indians, we should worship the wild surge, and erect altars to the howling of the wind.

The King of France having steadily refused all proposals which went to assign to the government an authority founded on the Revolution, the constitution of France is to be recognised as that of a hereditary monarchy, limited by the Royal Charter, and by the principles of freedom. It thus affords to the other existing monarchies of Europe a guarantee against sudden and dangerous commotion; while in favour of the subject, it extends all the necessary checks against arbitrary sway, and all the suitable provisions for ameliorating and extending the advantages of liberal institutions, as opportunity shall offer, and the expanding light of information shall recommend.

The allies, though their treaty with France was not made in the same humour of romantic generosity which dictated that of 1814, insisted upon no articles which could be considered as dishonourable to that nation. The disjoining from her empire three or four border fortresses was stipulated, in order to render a rapid and successful invasion of Germany or the Netherlands more

---

[175] Memoirs, tom. ii., p. 292.

difficult in future. Large sums of money were also exacted in recompense of the heavy expenses of the allies; but they were not beyond what the wealth of France could readily discharge. A part of her fortresses were also detained by the allies as a species of pledge for the peaceable behaviour of the kingdom; but these were to be restored after a season, and the armies of Europe, which for a time remained within the French territories, were at the same time to be withdrawn. Finally, that splendid Museum, which the right of conquest had collected by the stripping of so many states, was transferred by the same right of conquest, not to those of the allies who had great armies in the field, but to the poor and small states, who had resigned their property to the French under the influence of terror, and received it back from the confederates with wonder and gratitude.

These circumstances were indeed galling to France for the moment; but they were the necessary consequence of the position in which, perhaps rather passively than actively, she had been placed by the Revolution of the Hundred Days. All the prophecies which had been circulated to animate the people against the allies, of their seeking selfish and vindictive objects, or endeavouring to destroy the high national rank which that fair kingdom ought to hold in Europe, were proved to be utterly fallacious. The conquered provinces, as they are called, the acquisitions of Louis XIV., were not rent from the French empire—their colonies were left as at the peace of Paris. The English did not impose on them an unfavourable treaty of commerce, which Napoleon affirmed was their design, and the omission to insist on which he afterwards considered as a culpable neglect of British interests by the English ministers. France was left, as she ought to be, altogether independent, and splendidly powerful.

Neither were the predictions concerning the stability of the new royal government less false than had been the vaticinations respecting the purposes of the allies. Numbers prophesied the downfall of the Bourbon dynasty. It was with difficulty that the political augurs would allow that it might last as long as the life of Louis XVIII. He now sleeps with his fathers; and his successor, generally beloved for his courteous manners, and respected for his integrity and honour, reigns over a free and flourishing people. Time, that grand pacificator, is daily abating the rancour of party, and removing from the scene those of all sides, who, unaccustomed to the general and impartial exercise of the laws, were ready to improve every advantage, and debate every political question, sword in hand, or, as they themselves express it, *par voie du fait*. The guarantee for the permanence of their freedom, is the only subject on which reasonable Frenchmen of the present day are anxious. We trust there is no occasion for their solicitude. Fatal indeed would be the advice which should induce the French Government to give the slightest subject for just complaints. The ultra Royalist, the Jacobin *enragé*, are gradually cooled by age, or fate has removed them from the scene. Those who succeed, having never seen the sword drawn, will be less apt to hurry into civil strife; and the able and well-intentioned on either side, while they find room in the Chambers for expressing their difference of opinion, will acquire the habit of enduring contradiction with candour and good-humour, and be led to entertain the wholesome doubt, whether, in the imperfect state of the human intellect, it is possible for one class of statesmen to be absolutely and uniformly right, and their opponents, in all instances, decidedly wrong. The French will learn, that it is from freedom of debate—from an appeal, not to the arms, but to the understandings of the people—by the collision of intellect, not the strife of brutal violence, that the political institutions of this ingenious people are in future to be improved.

The aspirations of France after glory in the field had been indulged, during the period of which we have treated, dreadfully for other countries, and the requital to herself was sufficiently fearful. A sentiment friendly to peace and good order has of late years distinguished even those two nations, which, by a rash and wicked expression, have been sometimes termed natural enemies. The enlarged ideas of commerce, as they spread wider, and become better understood, will afford, perhaps, the strongest and most irresistible motive for amicable intercourse—that, namely, which arises from mutual advantage; for commerce keeps pace with civilisation, and a nation, as it becomes wealthy from its own industry, acquires more and more a taste for the conveniences and luxuries, which are the produce of the soil, or of the industry, of other countries. Britain, of whom all that was selfish was expected and predicated by Napoleon and his friends—Britain, who was said to meditate enchaining France by a commercial treaty (which would have ruined her own manufactures,) has, by opening her ports to the manufactures of her neighbour, had the honour to lead the way in a new and more honourable species of traffic, which has in some degree the property ascribed by the poet to Mercy—

"It blesseth him who gives, and him who takes."

To the eye of a stranger, the number of new buildings established in Paris, and indeed throughout France, are indications of capital and enterprise, of a nature much more satisfactory than the splendid but half-finished public edifices which Napoleon so hastily undertook, and so often left in an incomplete state. The general improvement of ideas may be also distinctly remarked, on comparing the French people of 1815 and 1826, and observing the gradual extinction of long-cherished prejudices and the no less gradual improvement and enlargement of ideas. This state of advancement cannot, indeed, be regular—it must have its ebbs and flows. But on the whole, there seems more reason than at any former period of the world, for hoping that there will be a general peace of some lengthened endurance; and that Britain and France, in particular, will satisfy themselves with enjoying in recollection the laurels each country has won in the field, and be contented to struggle for the palm of national superiority by the arts of peaceful and civilized industry.

Chapter XCI

Disposition of the British Fleet along the Western Coast of France, in order to prevent Buonaparte's Escape—The Bellerophon off Rochefort—Orders under which Captain Maitland acted—Plans agitated for Napoleon's Escape—Savary and Las Cases open a Negotiation with Captain Maitland—Captain Maitland's Account of what passed at their Interviews—Las Cases' Account—The Statements compared—Napoleon's Letter to the Prince Regent—He surrenders himself on board the Bellerophon, on 15th July—His arrival off Plymouth—All approach to the Ship prohibited—Final determination of the English Government that Buonaparte shall be sent to St. Helena—His Protest.

Our history returns to its principal object. Buonaparte arrived at Rochefort upon the 3d July; so short had been the space between the bloody cast of the die at Waterloo, and his finding himself an exile. Yet even this brief space of fifteen days had made his retreat difficult, if not impracticable. Means, indeed, were provided for his transportation. The two French frigates, the Saale and the Medusa, together with the Balladière, a corvette, and the Epervier, a large brig, waited Buonaparte's presence, and orders to sail for America from their station under the isle d'Aix. But, as Napoleon himself said shortly afterwards, wherever there was water to swim a ship, there he was sure to find the British flag.

LORD KEITH—CAPTAIN MAITLAND

The news of the defeat at Waterloo had been the signal to the Admiralty to cover the western coast of France with cruisers, in order to prevent the possibility of Napoleon's escaping by sea from any of the ports in that direction. Admiral Lord Keith, an officer of great experience and activity, then commander-in-chief of the Channel fleet, had made a most judicious disposition of the fleet under his command, by stationing an inner line of cruisers, of various descriptions, off the principal ports between Brest and Bayonne, with an exterior line, necessarily more widely extended, betwixt Ushant and Cape Finisterre. The commanders of these vessels had the strictest orders to suffer no vessel to pass unexamined. No less than thirty ships of different descriptions maintained this blockade. According to this arrangement, the British line-of-battle ship, the Bellerophon, cruised off Rochefort, with the occasional assistance of the Slaney, the Phœbe, and other small vessels, sometimes present, and sometimes detached, as the service might require. Captain Maitland, who commanded the Bellerophon, is a man of high character in his profession, of birth, of firmness of mind, and of the most indisputable honour. It is necessary to mention these circumstances, because the national character of England herself is deeply concerned and identified with that of Captain Maitland, in the narrative which follows.

The several orders under which this officer acted, expressed the utmost anxiety about intercepting Buonaparte's flight, and canvassed the different probabilities concerning its direction. His attention was at a later date particularly directed to the frigates in Aix roads, and the report concerning their destination. Admiral Hotham writes to Captain Maitland, 8th July, 1815, the following order:—

"The Lords Commissioners of the Admiralty having every reason to believe that Napoleon Buonaparte meditates his escape, with his family, from France to America, you are hereby required and directed, in pursuance of orders from their Lordships, signified to me by Admiral the Right Honourable Viscount Keith, to keep the most vigilant look-out, for the purpose of intercepting him; and to make the strictest search of any vessel you may fall in with; and if you should be so fortunate as to intercept him, you are to transfer him and his family to the ship you command, and, there keeping him in careful custody, return to the nearest port in England (going into Torbay in preference to Plymouth,) with all possible expedition; and, on your arrival, you are not to permit any communication whatever with the shore, except as hereinafter directed; and you will be held responsible for keeping the whole transaction a profound secret, until you receive their Lordships' further orders.

"In case you should arrive at a port where there is a flag officer, you are to send to acquaint him with the circumstances, strictly charging the officer sent on shore with your letter not to divulge its contents; and if there should be no flag-officer at the port where you arrive, you are to send one letter express to the Secretary of the Admiralty, and another to Admiral Lord Keith, with strict injunctions of secrecy to each officer who may be the bearer of them."

We give these orders at full length, to show that they left Captain Maitland no authority to make conditions or stipulations of surrender, or to treat Napoleon otherwise than as an ordinary prisoner of war.

Captain Maitland proceeded to exercise all the vigilance which an occasion so interesting demanded; and it was soon evident, that the presence of the Bellerophon was an absolute bar to Napoleon's escape by means of the frigates, unless it should be attempted by open force. In this latter case, the British officer had formed his plan of bearing down upon and disabling the one vessel, and throwing on board of her a hundred men selected for the purpose, while the Bellerophon set sail with all speed in pursuit of her consort, and thus made sure of both. He had also two small vessels, the Slaney and the Phœbe, which he could attach to the pursuit of the frigate, so as at least to keep her in view. This plan might have failed by accident, but it was so judiciously laid as to have every chance of being successful; and it seems that Napoleon received no encouragement from the commanders of the frigates to try the event of a forcible escape.

The scheme of a secret flight was next meditated. A chasse-marée, a peculiar species of vessel, used only in the coasting trade, was to be fitted up and manned with young probationers of the navy, equivalent to our midshipmen. This, it was thought, might elude the vigilance of such British cruisers as were in shore; but then it must have been a suspicious object at sea, and the possibility of its being able to make the voyage to America, was considered as precarious. A Danish corvette was next purchased, and as, in leaving the harbour, it was certain she would be brought to and examined by the English, a place of concealment was contrived, being a cask supplied with air-tubes, to be stowed in the hold of the vessel, in which it was intended Napoleon should lie concealed. But the extreme rigour with which the search was likely to be prosecuted, and the corpulence of Buonaparte, which would not permit him to remain long in a close or constrained position, made this as well as other hopeless contrivances be laid aside.[176]

PROPOSALS FROM THE ARMY

There were undoubtedly at this time many proposals made to the Ex-Emperor by the army, who, compelled to retreat behind the Loire, were still animated by a thirst of revenge, and a sense of injured honour. There is no doubt that they would have received Napoleon with acclamation; but if he could not, or would not, pursue a course so desperate in 1814, when he had still a considerable army, and a respectable extent of territory remaining, it must have seemed much more ineligible in 1815, when his numbers were so much more disproportioned than they had formerly been, and when his best generals had embraced the cause of the Bourbons, or fled out of France. Napoleon's condition, had he embraced this alternative, would have been that of the chief of a roving tribe of warriors, struggling for existence, with equal misery to themselves and the countries through which they wandered, until at length broken down and destroyed by superior force.

Rejecting this expedient, and all others having been found equally objectionable, the only alternative which remained was to surrender his person, either to the allied powers as a body, or to any one of them in particular. The former course would have been difficult, unless Napoleon had adopted the idea of resorting to it

---

[176] Savary, tom. iv., p. 149; Las Cases, tom. i., pp. 24-27.

earlier, which, in the view of his escape by sea, he had omitted to do. Neither had he time to negotiate with any of the allied sovereigns, or of travelling back to Paris for the purpose, with any chance of personal safety, for the Royalists were now every where holding the ascendency, and more than one of his generals had been attacked and killed by them.

He was cooped up, therefore, in Rochefort,[177] although the white flag was already about to be hoisted there, and the commandant respectfully hinted the necessity of his departure. It must have been anticipated by Napoleon, that he might be soon deprived of the cover of the batteries of the isle of Aix. The fact is (though we believe not generally known,) that on the 13th July, Lord Castlereagh wrote to Admiral Sir Henry Hotham, commanding off Cape Finisterre, suggesting to him the propriety of attacking, with a part of his force, the two frigates in the roads of the isle d'Aix, having first informed the commandant that they did so in the capacity of allies of the King of France, and placing it upon his responsibility if he fired on them from the batteries. Napoleon could not, indeed, know for certain that such a plan was actually in existence, and about to be attempted, but yet must have been aware of its probability, when the Royalist party were becoming every where superior, and their emblems were assumed in the neighbouring town of Rochelle. It is, therefore, in vain to state Buonaparte's subsequent conduct, as a voluntary confidence reposed by him in the honour of England. He was precisely in the condition of the commandant of a besieged town, who has the choice of surrendering, or encountering the risks of a storm. Neither was it open for him to contend, that he selected the British, out of all the other allied powers, with whom to treat upon this occasion. Like the commandant in the case above supposed, he was under the necessity of surrendering to those who were the immediate besiegers, and therefore he was compelled to apply for terms of safety to him who alone possessed the direct power of granting it, that is, to Captain Frederick Maitland, of the Bellerophon.

---

[177] "At Rochefort, the Emperor lived at the prefecture: numbers were constantly grouped round the house; and acclamations continued to be frequently repeated. He leads the same sort of life as if at the Tuileries: we do not approach his person more frequently; he scarcely receives any persons but Bertrand and Savary."—Las Cases, tom. i., p. 24.

NEGOTIATION WITH MAITLAND

Napoleon opened a communication with this officer on the 10th July, by two of his attendants, General Savary and Count Las Cases, under pretence of inquiring about a safe-conduct—a passport which Napoleon pretended to expect from England, and which, he said, had been promised to him, without stating by whom. Under this round assertion, for which, there was not the slightest ground, Messrs. Savary and Las Cases desired to know, whether Captain Maitland would permit the frigates to sail with him uninterrupted, or at least give him leave to proceed in a neutral vessel. Captain Maitland, without hesitation, declared that he would not permit any armed vessel to put to sea from the port of Rochefort. "It was equally out of his power," he stated, "to allow the Emperor to proceed in a neutral vessel, without the sanction of Admiral Hotham, his commanding officer." He offered to write to that officer, however, and the French gentlemen having assented, he wrote, in their presence, to the admiral, announcing the communication he had received, and requesting orders for his guidance. This was all but a prelude to the real subject of negotiation. The Duke of Rovigo (Savary) and Count Las Cases remained two or three hours on board, and said all they could to impress Captain Maitland with the idea, that Napoleon's retirement was a matter of choice, not of compulsion, and that it was the interest of Britain to consent to his going to America; a measure, they said, which was solely dictated to him by humanity, and a desire to save human blood. Captain Maitland asked the natural question, which we give in his own words:—

"'Supposing the British government should be induced to grant a passport for Buonaparte's going to America, what pledge could he give that he would not return, and put England, as well as all Europe, to the same expense of blood and treasure that has just been incurred?'

"General Savary made the following reply:—'When the Emperor first abdicated the throne of France, his removal was brought about by a faction, at the head of which was Talleyrand, and the sense of the nation was not consulted: but in the present instance he has voluntarily resigned the power. The influence he once had over the French people is past; a very considerable change has taken place in their sentiments towards him, since he went to Elba; and he could never regain the power he had over their minds; therefore, he would prefer retiring into obscurity, where he might end his days in peace and tranquillity; and were he solicited to ascend the throne again, he would decline it.'

"'If that is the case,' said Captain Maitland, 'why not ask an asylum in England?' Savary answered, 'There are many reasons for his not wishing to reside in England; the climate is too damp and cold; it is too near France; he would be, as it were, in the centre of every change and revolution that might take place there, and would be subject to suspicion; he has been accustomed to consider the English as his most inveterate enemies, and they have been induced to look upon him as a monster, without one of the virtues of a human being.'"

Captain Knight of the Falmouth was present during the whole of this conversation, from which Captain Maitland, like an able diplomatist, drew a conclusion respecting the affairs of Napoleon, exactly opposite from that which they endeavoured to impress upon him, and concluded that he must be in extremity.

On the 14th July, Count Las Cases again came on board the Bellerophon, now attended by General Count Lallemand. The pretext of the visit was, to learn whether Captain Maitland had received any answer from the admiral. Captain Maitland observed, the visit on that account was unnecessary, as he would have forwarded the answer so soon as received; and added, he did not approve of frequent communication by flags of truce; thus repelling rather than inviting them. The conference was resumed after breakfast, Captain Maitland having, in the meantime, sent for Captain Sartorius of the Slaney, to be witness of what passed. In this most important conference, we hold it unjust to Captain Maitland to use any other words than his own, copied from his Journal, the original of which we have ourselves had the advantage of seeing:—

"When breakfast was over, we retired to the after-cabin. Count Las Cases then said, 'The Emperor is so anxious to spare the further effusion of human blood, that he will proceed to America in any way the British Government chooses to sanction, either in a French ship of war, a vessel armed *en flute*, a merchant vessel, or even in a British ship of war.' To this I answered, 'I have no authority to agree to any arrangement of that sort, nor do I believe my Government would consent to it; but I think I may venture to receive him into this ship, and convey him to England; *if however,*' I added, '*he adopts that plan, I cannot enter into any promise, as to the reception he may meet with, as, even in the case I have mentioned, I shall be acting on my own responsibility, and cannot be sure that it would meet with the approbation of the British Government.*'

"There was a great deal of conversation on this subject, in the course of which Lucien Buonaparte's name was mentioned, and the manner in which he had lived in England alluded to; but I invariably assured Las Cases most explicitly, that I had no authority to make conditions of any sort, as to Napoleon's reception in England. In fact, I could not have done otherwise, since, with the exception of the order [inserted at page 220,] I had no instructions for my guidance, and was, of course, in total ignorance of the intention of his Majesty's ministers as to his future disposal. One of the last observations Las Cases made, before quitting the ship, was, 'Under all circumstances, I have little doubt that you will see the Emperor on board the Bellerophon;' and, in fact, Buonaparte must have determined on that step before Las Cases came on board, as his letter to his Royal Highness the Prince Regent is dated the 13th of July, the day before this conversation."

The Count Las Cases gives nearly a similar detail of circumstances, with a colouring which is exaggerated, and an arrangement of dates which is certainly inaccurate. It must be also noticed that Count Las Cases dissembled his acquaintance with the English language; and therefore, if any mistake had occurred betwixt him and Captain Maitland, who spoke French with difficulty, he had himself so far to blame for it.[178] Of the visit on board the

---

[178] "Our situation was quite sufficient to remove any scruples I might otherwise have entertained, and rendered this little deception pardonable."—Las Cases, tom. i., p. 26.

Bellerophon on the 10th, after giving the same statement as Captain Maitland, concerning the application for the passports, the count states, "It was suggested to us to go to England, and we were assured we had no room to fear any bad treatment."[179]

On the 14th, being the date of his second visit, he states that there was a repetition of the invitation to England, and the terms on which it was recommended. "Captain Maitland," he says, "told him, that if the Emperor chose immediately to embark, he had authority to receive him on board, and conduct him to England." This is so expressed as to lead the reader to believe that Captain Maitland spoke to the Count of some new directions or orders which he had received, or pretended to have received, concerning Buonaparte. Such an inference would be entirely erroneous; no new or extended authority was received by Captain Maitland, nor was he capable of insinuating the existence of such. His sole instructions were contained in the orders of Admiral Hotham, quoted at p. 220, directing him, should he be so fortunate as to intercept Buonaparte, to transfer him to the ship he commanded, to make sail for a British port, and, when arrived there, to communicate instantly with the port-admiral, or with the Admiralty.

THE BELLEROPHON

Count Las Cases makes Captain Maitland proceed to assure him and Savary, that, "in his own private opinion, Napoleon would find in England all the respect and good treatment to which he could make any pretension; that there, the princes and ministers did not exercise the absolute authority used on the continent, and that the English people had a liberality of opinion, and generosity of sentiment, superior to that entertained by sovereigns." Count Las Cases states himself to have replied to the panegyric on England, by an oration in praise of Buonaparte, in which he described him as retiring from a contest which he had yet the means of supporting, in order that his name and rights might not serve as a pretext to prolong civil war. The Count, according to his own narrative,

---

[179] "Il nous fut suggéré de nous rendre en Angleterre, et affirmé qu'on ne pouvait y craindre aucun mauvais traitement."—*Journal de Las Cases*, tom. i., part i., p. 28.—S.

concluded by saying, that, "under all the circumstances, he thought the Emperor might come on board the Bellerophon, and go to England with Captain Maitland, for the purpose of receiving passports for America." Captain Maitland desired it should be understood, that he by no means warranted that such would be granted.

"At the bottom of my heart," says Las Cases, "I never supposed the passports would be granted to us; but as the Emperor had resolved to remain in future a personal stranger to political events, we saw, without alarm, the probability that we might be prevented from leaving England; but to that point all our fears and suppositions were limited. Such, too, was doubtless the belief of Maitland. I do him, as well as the other officers, the justice to believe, that he was sincere, and of good faith, in the painting they drew us of the sentiments of the English nation."[180]

The envoys returned to Napoleon, who held, according to Las Cases, a sort of council, in which they considered all the chances. The plan of the Danish vessel, and that of the chasse-marée, were given up as too perilous; the British cruiser was pronounced too strong to be attacked; there remained only the alternative of Napoleon's joining the troops, and renewing the war, or accepting Captain Maitland's offer by going on board the Bellerophon. The former was rejected; the latter plan adopted, and "then," says M. Las Cases, "*Napoleon wrote to the Prince Regent.*"[181] The letter follows, but it is remarkable that the date is omitted. This is probably the reason why Count Las Cases did not discover that his memory was betraying him, since that date must have reminded him that the letter was written *before*, not *after*, the conference of the 14th July.

From this narrative two things are plain; I. That no terms of capitulation were made with Captain Maitland. II. That it is the object of Count Las Cases to insinuate the belief, that it was in consequence of the arguments used by Captain Maitland, supported by the British officers present, that Las Cases was induced to recommend, and Napoleon to adopt, the step of surrendering

---

[180] Las Cases, tom. i., p. 29.
[181] "*Alors* Napoléon écrivitu Prince Régent."—*Journal*, tom. i., p. 33.—S.

himself on board the Bellerophon. But this whole inference is disproved by two small ciphers; the date, namely, of *13th of July* on the letter addressed to the Prince Regent, which, therefore, could not, in the nature of things, have been written in consequence of a conference betwixt Las Cases and Captain Maitland, and a consultation betwixt Napoleon and his followers; which conference and consultation did not take place till the *14th of July*. The resolution was taken, and the letter written, the day before all those glowing descriptions of the English people put into the mouth of Captain Maitland; and the faith of Napoleon was grounded upon the impersonal suggestion to go to England,[182] made to Las Cases and Savary on their first visit to the Bellerophon. The visit of the 14th, doubtless, confirmed the resolution which had been adopted the preceding day.

No delay now intervened. On the same 14th of July, General Baron Gourgaud was sent off with the letter, so often mentioned, addressed to the Prince Regent, which was in these well-known terms:

"*Rochefort, July 13th, 1815.*

"Royal Highness,

"A victim to the factions which distract my country, and to the enmity of the greatest powers of Europe, I have terminated my political career, and I come, like Themistocles, to throw myself upon the hospitality of the British people. I put myself under the protection of their laws; which I claim from your Royal Highness, as the most powerful, the most constant, and the most generous of my enemies.

"Napoleon."

Captain Maitland informed Count Las Cases, that he would despatch General Gourgaud to England, by the Slaney, and himself prepare to receive Napoleon and his suite. General Gourgaud proposed to write to Count Bertrand instantly, when, in presence

---

[182] See p. 224, where Las Cases says, "*It was suggested* to us to go to England."—S.

and hearing of his brother officers, Captains Sartorius and Gambier, Captain Maitland gave another instance of his anxiety not to be misunderstood on this important occasion.

"When General Gourgaud was about to write the letter, to prevent any future misunderstanding, I said, 'M. Las Cases, you will recollect that I am not authorised to stipulate as to the reception of Buonaparte in England, but that he must consider himself entirely at the disposal of his Royal Highness the Prince Regent.' He answered, 'I am perfectly aware of that, and have already acquainted the Emperor with what you said on the subject.'"

Captain Maitland subjoins the following natural and just remark:—

"It might, perhaps, have been better if this declaration had been given in an official written form; and could I have foreseen the discussions which afterwards took place, and which will appear in the sequel, I undoubtedly should have done so; but as I repeatedly made it in the presence of witnesses, it did not occur to me as being necessary; and how could a stronger proof be adduced, that no stipulations were agreed to respecting the reception of Buonaparte in England, than the fact of their not being reduced to writing? which certainly would have been the case had any favourable terms been demanded on the part of M. Las Cases, and agreed to by me."

To conclude the evidence on this subject, we add Captain Maitland's letter, addressed to the Secretary of the Admiralty on 14th July:

"For the information of the Lords Commissioners of the Admiralty, I have to acquaint you that the Count Las Cases and General Lallemand this day came on board his Majesty's ship under my command, with a proposal from Count Bertrand for me to receive on board Napoleon Buonaparte, for the purpose of throwing himself on the generosity of the Prince Regent. Conceiving myself authorised by their lordships' secret order, I have acceded to the proposal, and he is to embark on board this ship to-morrow morning. That no misunderstanding might arise, I have explicitly and clearly explained to Count Las Cases, that I have no authority whatever for granting terms of any sort, but that all I can do is to carry him and his suite to England, to be received in such manner as his Royal Highness may deem expedient."

Is it in human nature to suppose, that a British officer, with two others of the same rank as witnesses of the whole negotiation, would have expressed himself otherwise than as truth warranted, in a case which was sure to be so strictly inquired into?

On the 15th July, 1815, Napoleon finally left France, to the history of which he had added so much of victory, and so much of defeat; the country which his rise had saved from civil discord and foreign invasion, and which his fall consigned to both; in a word, that fair land to which he had been so long as a Deity, and was in future to be of less import than the meanest peasant on the soil. He was accompanied by four of his generals—Bertrand, Savary, Lallemand, and Montholon, and by Count Las Cases, repeatedly mentioned as counsellor of state. Of these, Bertrand and Montholon had their ladies on board, with three children belonging to Count Bertrand, and one of Count Montholon's. The son of Las Cases accompanied the Emperor as a page. There were nine officers of inferior rank, and thirty-nine domestics. The principal persons were received on board the Bellerophon, the others in the corvette.

Buonaparte came out of Aix roads on board of the Epervier. Wind and tide being against the brig, Captain Maitland sent the barge of the Bellerophon to transport him to that ship. Most of the officers and crew of the Epervier had tears in their eyes, and they continued to cheer the Emperor while their voices could be heard. He was received on board the Bellerophon respectfully, but without any salute or distinguished honours.[183] As Captain Maitland

---

[183] "Buonaparte's dress was an olive-coloured great coat over a green uniform, with scarlet cape and cuffs, green lapels turned back and edged with scarlet, skirts hooked back with bugle horns embroidered in gold, plain sugar-loaf buttons and gold epaulettes; being the uniform of *chasseur à cheval* of the imperial guard. He wore the star, or grand cross of the legion of honour, and the small cross of that order; the iron crown; and the union, appended to the button-hole of his left lapel. He had a small cocked hat, with a tri-coloured cockade, plain gold-hilted sword, military boots, and white waistcoat and breeches. The following day he appeared in shoes, with gold buckles, and silk stockings—the dress he always wore afterwards while with me."—Maitland, p. 66.

advanced to meet him on the quarterdeck, Napoleon pulled off his hat, and, addressing him in a firm tone of voice, said, "I come to place myself under the protection of your prince and laws." His manner was uncommonly pleasing, and he displayed much address in seizing upon opportunities of saying things flattering to the hearers whom he wished to conciliate.[184]

As when formerly on board Captain Usher's vessel, Buonaparte showed great curiosity concerning the discipline of the ship, and expressed considerable surprise that the British vessels should so easily defeat the French ships, which were heavier, larger, and better manned than they. Captain Maitland accounted for this by the greater experience of the men and officers. The Ex-Emperor examined the marines also, and, pleased with their appearance, said to Bertrand, "How much might be done with an hundred thousand such men!" In the management of the vessel, he particularly admired the silence and good order of the crew while going through their manœuvres, in comparison to a French vessel, "where every one," he said, "talks and gives orders at once." When about to quit the Bellerophon, he adverted to the same subject, saying, there had been less noise on board that vessel, with six hundred men, in the whole passage from Rochefort, than the crew of the Epervier, with only one hundred, had contrived to make between the isle d'Aix and Basque roads.

He spoke, too, of the British army in an equal style of praise, and was joined by his officers in doing so. One of the French

---

[184] "Rear-Admiral Hotham came to visit the Emperor, and remained to dinner. From the questions asked by Napoleon relative to his ship, he expressed a wish to know whether his Majesty would condescend to go on board the following day; upon which the Emperor said he would breakfast with the admiral, accompanied by all his attendants. On the 16th, I attended him on board the Superb: all the honours, except those of firing cannon, were liberally done; we went round the ship, and examined the most trifling objects: every thing seemed to be in admirable order. Admiral Hotham evinced, throughout, all the refinement and grace of a man of rank and education. On our leaving the Bellerophon in the morning to visit the Superb, Napoleon stopped short in front of the guard drawn up on the quarterdeck to salute him. He made them perform several movements, giving them the word of command himself; having desired them to charge bayonets, and perceiving this motion was not performed altogether in the French manner, he advanced into the midst of the soldiers, put the weapons aside with his hands, and seized a musket from one of the rear rank, with which he went through the exercise himself, according to our method."—Las Cases, tom. i., p. 35.

officers observing that the English cavalry were superb, Captain Maitland observed, that in England, they had a higher opinion of the infantry. "You are right," said the French gentleman; "there is none such in the world; there is no making an impression on them; you might as well attempt to charge through a wall; and their fire is tremendous." Bertrand reported to Captain Maitland that Napoleon had communicated to him his opinion of the Duke of Wellington in the following words:—"The Duke of Wellington, in the management of an army, is fully equal to myself, with the advantage of possessing more prudence." This we conceive to be the genuine unbiassed opinion of one great soldier concerning another. It is a pity that Napoleon could on other occasions express himself in a strain of depreciation, which could only lower him who used it, towards a rival in the art of war.

During the whole passage, notwithstanding his situation, and the painful uncertainty under which he laboured, Napoleon seemed always tranquil, and in good temper;[185] at times, he even approached to cheerfulness. He spoke with tenderness of his wife and family, complained of being separated from them, and had tears in his eyes when he showed their portraits to Captain Maitland. His health seemed perfectly good; but he was occasionally subject to somnolency, proceeding, perhaps, from the exhaustion of a constitution which had gone through such severe service.

On 23d July, they passed Ushant. Napoleon remained long on deck, and cast many a melancholy look to the coast of France, but made no observations. At daybreak on 24th, the Bellerophon was off Dartmouth; and Buonaparte was struck, first with the boldness of the coast, and then, as he entered Torbay,[186] with the well-known beauty of the scenery. "It reminded him," he said, "of Porto Ferrajo,

---

[185] Some of the London newspapers having represented Napoleon "as taking possession of the chief cabin in a most brutal way, saying '*Tout ou rien pour moi.*'"—Captain Maitland makes this declaration—"I here, once for all, beg to state most distinctly, that from the time of his coming on board my ship, to the period of his quitting her, his conduct was invariably that of a gentleman; and in no instance do I recollect him to have made use of a rude expression, or to have been guilty of any kind of ill-breeding."—*Narrative*, p. 72.

[186] "July 24, we anchored at Torbay about eight in the morning: Napoleon had risen at six, and went on the poop, whence he surveyed the coast and anchorage. I remained by his side to give the explanations he required."—*Las Cases*, tom. i., p. 41.

in Elba;" an association which must at the moment have awakened strange remembrances in the mind of the deposed Emperor.

PLYMOUTH SOUND

The Bellerophon had hardly anchored, when orders came from the admiral, Lord Keith, which were soon after seconded by others from the Admiralty, enjoining that no one, of whatever rank or station, should be permitted to come on board the Bellerophon, excepting the officers and men belonging to the ship. On the 26th, the vessel received orders to move round to Plymouth Sound.

In the meantime, the newspapers which were brought on board tended to impress anxiety and consternation among the unhappy fugitives. The report was generally circulated by these periodical publications, that Buonaparte would not be permitted to land, but would be presently sent off to St. Helena, as the safest place for detaining him as a prisoner of war. Napoleon himself became alarmed, and anxiously desirous of seeing Lord Keith, who had expressed himself sensible of some kindness which his nephew, Captain Elphinstone of the 7th Hussars, had received from the Emperor, when wounded and made prisoner at Waterloo. Such an interview accordingly took place betwixt the noble admiral and the late Emperor, upon the 28th July, but without any results of importance, as Lord Keith was not then possessed of the decision of the British Government.

That frenzy of popular curiosity, which, predominating in all free states, seems to be carried to the utmost excess by the English nation, caused such numbers of boats to surround the Bellerophon, that, notwithstanding the peremptory orders of the Admiralty, and in spite of the efforts of the man-of-war's boats, which maintained constant guard round the vessel, it was almost impossible to keep them at the prescribed distance of a cable's length from the ship. They incurred the risk of being run down—of being, as they might apprehend, shot (for muskets were discharged for the purpose of intimidation,) of all the dangers of a naval combat, rather than lose the opportunity of seeing the Emperor whom they had heard so much of. When he appeared he was greeted with huzzas, which he returned with bows, but could not help expressing his wonder at the eagerness of popular curiosity, which he was not accustomed to see in such a pitch of excitation.

SIR HENRY BUNBURY'S MINUTES

On the evening of the 30th of July, Major-General Sir Henry Bunbury, one of the Under Secretaries of State, arrived, bringing with him the final intentions of the British Government, for the disposal of Buonaparte and his suite. Upon the 31st, Lord Keith and Sir Henry waited upon the Ex-Emperor, on board of the Bellerophon, to communicate to him the unpleasing tidings. They were accompanied by Mr. Meike, the secretary of Lord Keith, whose presence was deemed necessary as a witness to what passed. Napoleon received the admiral and under secretary of state with becoming dignity and calmness. The letter of Lord Melville (First Lord of the Admiralty) was read to the Ex-Emperor, announcing his future destination. It stated, that "it would be inconsistent with the duty of the British ministers to their sovereign and his allies, to leave *General Buonaparte* the means or opportunity of again disturbing the peace of Europe—announced that the island of St. Helena was selected for his future residence, and selected as such, because its local situation would permit his enjoying more freedom than could be compatible with adequate security elsewhere—that, with the exception of Generals Savary and Lallemand, the General might select three officers, together with his surgeon, to attend him to St. Helena—that twelve domestics would also be allowed." The same document stated, that "the persons who might attend upon him would be liable to a certain degree of restraint, and could not be permitted to leave the island without the sanction of the British Government." Lastly, it was announced that "Rear-Admiral Sir George Cockburn, appointed to the chief command of the Cape of Good Hope, would be presently ready to sail, for the purpose of conveying General Buonaparte to St. Helena, and therefore it was desirable that he should without delay make choice of the persons who were to form his suite."[187]

The letter was read in French to Buonaparte by Sir Henry Bunbury. He listened without impatience, interruption, or emotion of any kind. When he was requested to state if he had any reply, he began, with great calmness of manner and mildness of countenance, to declare that he solemnly protested against the orders which had been read—that the British Ministry had no right to dispose of him in the way proposed—that he appealed to the British people and the laws—and asked what was the tribunal which he ought to appeal to. "I am come," he continued, "voluntarily to throw myself on the hospitality of your nation—I am not a prisoner of war, and if I was, have a right to be treated according to the law of nations. But I am come to this country a passenger on board one of your vessels, after a previous negotiation with the commander. If he had told me I was to be a prisoner, I would not have come. I asked him if he was willing to receive me on board, and convey me to England. *Admiral* Maitland said he was, having received, or telling me he had received, special orders of government concerning me. It was a snare, then, that had been spread for me; I came on board a British vessel as I would have entered one of their towns—a vessel, a village, it is the same thing. As for the island of St. Helena, it would be my sentence of death. I demand to be received as an English citizen. How many years entitle me to be domiciliated?"

Sir Henry Bunbury answered, that he believed four were necessary. "Well, then," continued Napoleon, "let the Prince Regent during that time place me under any superintendence he thinks proper—let me be placed in a country-house in the centre of the island, thirty leagues from every seaport—place a commissioned officer about me, to examine my correspondence and superintend my actions; or if the Prince Regent should require my word of honour, perhaps I might give it. I might then enjoy a certain degree of personal liberty, and I should have the freedom of literature. In St. Helena I could not live three months; to my habits and constitution it would be death. I am used to ride twenty miles a-day—what am I to do on that little rock at the end of the world?

---

[187] Las Cases, tom. i., p. 50.

No! Botany Bay is better than St. Helena—I prefer death to St. Helena—And what good is my death to do you? I am no longer a sovereign. What danger could result from my living as a private person in the heart of England, and restricted in any way which the Government should think proper?"

He referred repeatedly to the manner of his coming on board the Bellerophon, insisting upon his being perfectly free in his choice, and that he had preferred confiding to the hospitality and generosity of the British nation.

"Otherwise," he said, "why should I not have gone to my father-in-law, or to the Emperor Alexander, who is my personal friend? We have become enemies, because he wanted to annex Poland to his dominions, and my popularity among the Poles was in his way. But otherwise he was my friend, and he would not have treated me in this way. If your Government act thus, it will disgrace you in the eyes of Europe. Even your own people will blame it. Besides, you do not know the feeling that my death will create both in France and Italy. There is, at present, a high opinion of England in these countries. If you kill me, it will be lost, and the lives of many English will be sacrificed. What was there to force me to the step I took? The tri-coloured flag was still flying at Bourdeaux, Nantes, and Rochefort.[188] The army has not even yet submitted. Or, if I had chosen to remain in France, what was there to prevent me from remaining concealed for years amongst a people so much attached to me?"

He then returned to his negotiation with Captain Maitland, and dwelt on the honours and attentions shown to him personally by that officer and Admiral Hotham. "And, after all, it was only a snare for me!"[189] He again enlarged on the disgrace to England

---

[188] The white flag was flying at Rochelle and the isle of Oleron. It was hoisted on the 12th, and hauled down afterwards; again hoisted on the 13th July, to the final exclusion of the three-coloured ensign.—S.
[189] Admiral Hotham and Captain Maitland had no particular orders how this uncommon person was to be treated, and were naturally desirous of showing respect under misfortunes to one who had been so great. Their civilities went no farther than manning the yards when he entered the Superb on a breakfast visit, and when he returned to the Bellerophon on the same occasion. Captain Maitland also permitted Napoleon to lead the way into the dining cabin, and seat himself in the centre of the table; an honour which it would have been both

which was impending. "I hold out to the Prince Regent," he said, "the brightest page in his history, in placing myself at his discretion. I have made war upon you for twenty years, and I give you the highest proof of confidence by voluntarily giving myself into the hands of my most inveterate and constant enemies. Remember," he continued, "what I have been, and how I stood among the sovereigns of Europe. *This* courted my protection—*that* gave me his daughter—all sought for my friendship. I was Emperor acknowledged by all the powers in Europe, except Great Britain, and she had acknowledged me as Chief Consul. Your Government has no right to term me *General Buonaparte*," he added, pointing with his finger to the offensive epithet in Lord Melville's letter. "I am Prince, or Consul, and ought to be treated as such, if treated with at all. When I was at Elba, I was at least as much a sovereign in that island as Louis on the throne of France. We had both our respective flags, our ships, our troops—Mine, to be sure," he said with a smile, "were rather on a small scale—I had six hundred soldiers, and he had two hundred thousand. At length, I made war upon him, defeated him, and dethroned him. But there was nothing in this to deprive me of my rank as one of the sovereigns of Europe."

During this interesting scene, Napoleon spoke with little interruption from Lord Keith and Sir Henry Bunbury, who declined replying to his remonstrances, stating themselves to be unauthorised to enter into discussions, as their only duty was to convey the intentions of Government to Napoleon, and transmit his answer, if he charged them with any. He repeated again and again his determination not to go to St. Helena, and his desire to be suffered to remain in Great Britain.

Sir Henry Bunbury then said, he was certain that St. Helena had been selected as the place of his residence, because its local

---

ungracious and uncalled for to have disputed. Even these civilities could not have been a portion of the snare of which Napoleon complains, or have had the least effect in inducing him to take his resolution of surrendering to the English, as the argument in the text infers; for that resolution had been taken, and the surrender made, before the attentions Napoleon founds upon could have been offered and received. This tends to confirm the opinion of Nelson, that the French, when treated with ceremonial politeness, are apt to form pretensions upon the concessions made to them in ordinary courtesy.—S.

situation allowed freer scope for exercise and indulgence than could have been permitted in any part of Great Britain.

"No, no," repeated Buonaparte, with animation, "I will not go there—You would not go there, sir, were it your own case—nor, my Lord, would you." Lord Keith bowed and answered—"He had been already at St. Helena four times." Napoleon went on reiterating his protestations against being imprisoned, or sent to St. Helena. "I *will not* go thither," he repeated; "I am not a Hercules," (with a smile,) "but you shall not conduct me to St. Helena. I prefer death in this place. You found me free, send me back again; replace me in the condition in which I was, or permit me to go to America."

He dwelt much on his resolution to die rather than to go to St. Helena; he had no great reason, he said, to wish for life. He urged the admiral to take no farther steps to remove him into the Northumberland, before Government should have been informed of what he had said, and have signified their final decision. He conjured Sir Henry Bunbury to use no delay in communicating his answer to Government, and referred himself to Sir Henry to put it into form. After some cursory questions and pauses, he again returned to the pressing subject, and urged the same arguments as before. "He had expected," he said, "to have had liberty to land, and settle himself in the country, some commissioner being named to attend him, who would be of great use for a year or two to teach him what he had to do. You could choose," he said, "some respectable man, for the English service must have officers distinguished for probity and honour; and do not put about me an intriguing person, who would only play the spy, and make cabals." He declared again his determination not to go to St. Helena; and this interesting interview was concluded.

INTERVIEW WITH LORD KEITH, ETC

After the admiral and Sir Henry Bunbury had left the cabin, Napoleon recalled Lord Keith, whom, in respect of his former attention to his lordship's relative, Captain Elphinstone, he might consider as more favourable to his person.

Napoleon, opened the conversation, by asking Lord Keith's advice how to conduct himself. Lord Keith replied, that he was an officer, and had discharged his duty, and left with him the heads of his instructions. If he considered it necessary to renew the discussion, Sir Henry Bunbury must be called in. Buonaparte said that was unnecessary. "Can you," said he, "after what is passed, detain me until I hear from London?" Lord Keith replied, that must depend on the instructions brought by the other admiral, with which he was unacquainted. "Was there any tribunal," he asked, "to which he could apply?" Lord Keith answered, that he was no civilian, but believed that there was none whatever. He added, that he was satisfied there was every disposition on the part of the British Government to render his situation as comfortable as prudence would permit. "How so?" said Napoleon, lifting the paper from the table, and speaking with animation. Upon Lord Keith's observing, that it was surely preferable to being confined to a smaller space in England, or being sent to France, or perhaps to Russia. "Russia!" exclaimed Buonaparte, "God preserve me from it!"[190]

During this remarkable scene, Napoleon's manner was perfectly calm and collected, his voice equal and firm, his tones very pleasing. Once or twice only he spoke more rapidly, and in a harsher key. He used little gesticulation, and his attitudes were ungraceful; but the action of the head was dignified, and the countenance remarkably soft and placid, without any marks of severity. He seemed to have made up his mind, anticipating what was to be announced, and perfectly prepared to reply. In expressing his positive determination not to go to St. Helena, he left it to his hearers to infer, whether he meant to prevent his removal by suicide, or to resist it by force.[191]

---

[190] Russie!—Dieu m'en garde.—S.
[191] Having had the inestimable advantage of comparing Sir Henry Bunbury's Minutes of this striking transaction with those of Mr. Meike, who accompanied Lord Keith in the capacity of secretary, the Author has been enabled to lay before the public the most ample and exact account of the interview of 31st July which has yet appeared.—S.

Chapter XCII

Napoleon's real view of the measure of sending him to St. Helena—Allegation that Captain Maitland made terms with him—disproved—Probability that the insinuation arose with Las Cases—Scheme of removing Napoleon from the Bellerophon, by citing him as a witness in a case of libel—Threats of self-destruction—Napoleon goes on board the Northumberland, which sails for St. Helena—His behaviour on the voyage—He arrives at St. Helena, 16th October.

The interest attaching to the foregoing interview betwixt Napoleon and the gentlemen sent to announce his doom, loses much, when we regard it in a great measure as an empty personification of feeling, a well-painted passion which was not in reality felt. Napoleon, as will presently appear, was not serious in averring that he had any encouragement from Captain Maitland to come on board his ship, save in the character of a prisoner, to be placed at the Prince Regent's discretion. Neither had he the most distant idea of preventing his removal to the Northumberland, either by violence to himself or any one else. Both topics of declamation were only used for show—the one to alarm the sense of honour entertained by the Prince Regent and the people of England, and the other to work upon their humanity.

THE BELLEROPHON

There is little doubt that Napoleon saw the probability of the St. Helena voyage, so soon as he surrendered himself to the captain of the Bellerophon.[192] He had affirmed, that there was a purpose of

---

[192] "Aug. 3. The Emperor said to me, 'after all, it is quite certain that I shall go to St. Helena; but what can we do in that desolate place?'—'Sire,' I replied, 'we will live on the

transferring him to St. Helena or St. Lucie, even before he left Elba; and if he thought the English capable of sending him to such banishment while he was under the protection of the treaty of Fontainbleau, he could hardly suppose that they would scruple to execute such a purpose, after his own conduct had deprived him of all the immunities with which that treaty had invested him.

Nevertheless, while aware that his experiment might possibly thus terminate, Napoleon may have hoped a better issue, and conceived himself capable of cajoling the Prince Regent[193] and his administration into hazarding the safety and the peace of Europe, in order to display a Quixotic generosity towards an individual, whose only plea for deserving it was that he had been for twenty years their mortal enemy. Such hopes he may have entertained; for it cannot be thought that he would acknowledge even to himself the personal disqualifications which rendered him, in the eyes of all Europe, unworthy of trust or confidence. His expectation of a favourable reception did not go so far, in all likelihood, as those of the individual among his followers, who believed that Napoleon would receive the Order of the Garter from the Prince Regent; but he might hope to be permitted to reside in Britain on the same terms as his brother Lucien had done.

Doubtless he calculated upon, and perhaps overrated, all these more favourable chances. Yet, if the worst should arrive, he saw even in that *worst*, that island of St. Helena itself, the certainty of personal safety, which he could not be assured of in any despotic country, where, as he himself must have known pretty well, an obnoxious prisoner, or *detenu*, may lose his life *par négligence*, without any bustle or alarm being excited upon the occasion. Upon the 16th August, while on his passage to St. Helena, he frankly acknowledged, that though he had been deceived in the reception he had expected from the English, still, harshly and unfairly as he

---

past; there is enough in it to satisfy us. Do we not enjoy the life of Cæsar and that of Alexander? We shall possess still more; you will reperuse yourself, Sire!'—'Be it so,' rejoined Napoleon, 'we will write our memoirs. Yes, we must be employed; for occupation is the scythe of time.'"—Las Cases, tom. i., p. 57.

[193] "Speaking of Napoleon's wish for an interview with the Prince Regent, Lord Keith said, 'D—n the fellow, if he had obtained an interview with his Royal Highness, in half an hour they would have been the best friends in England.'"—Maitland, p. 211.

thought himself treated, he found comfort from knowing that he was under the protection of British laws, which he could not have enjoyed had he gone to another country, where his fate would have depended upon the caprice of an individual. This we believe to be the real secret of his rendition to England, in preference to his father-in-law of Austria, or his friend in Russia. He might, in the first-named country, be kept in custody, more or less severe; but he would be at least secure from perishing of some political disease. Even while at St. Helena, he allowed, in an interval of good tempered candour, that comparing one place of exile to another, St. Helena was entitled to the preference. In higher latitudes, he observed, they would have suffered from cold, and in any other tropical island they would have been burned to death. At St. Helena the country was wild and savage, the climate monotonous, and unfavourable to health, but the temperature was mild and pleasing.[194]

CAPTAIN MAITLAND

The allegation on which Napoleon had insisted so much, namely, that Captain Maitland had pledged himself for his good reception in England, and received him on board his vessel, not as a prisoner, but as a guest, became now an important subject of investigation. All the while Napoleon had been on board the Bellerophon, he had expressed the greatest respect for Captain Maitland, and a sense of his civilities totally inconsistent with the idea that he conceived himself betrayed by him. He had even sounded that officer, by the means of Madame Bertrand, to know whether he would accept a present of his portrait set with diamonds, which Captain Maitland requested might not be offered, as he was determined to decline it.

On the 6th of August, Count Las Cases, for the first time, hinted to Captain Maitland, that he had understood him to have given an assurance, that Napoleon should be well received in England. Captain Maitland replied, it was impossible the count could mistake him so far, since he had expressly stated he could

---

[194] Las Cases, tom. i., part ii., p. 229.

make no promises; but that he thought his orders would bear him out in receiving Napoleon on board, and conveying him to England. He reminded the count, that he had questioned him (Captain Maitland) repeatedly, as to his private opinion, to which he could only answer, that he had no reason to think Napoleon would be ill received. Las Cases had nothing to offer in reply. Upon the same 6th August, Napoleon himself spoke upon the subject, and it will be observed how very different his language was to Captain Maitland, from that which he held in his absence. "They say," he remarked, "that I made no conditions. *Certainly I made no conditions.* How could an individual enter into terms with a nation? I wanted nothing of them but hospitality, or, as the ancients would express it, air and water. As for you, captain, I have no cause of complaint; your conduct has been that of a man of honour."

The investigation of this matter did not end here, for the ungrounded assertion that Captain Maitland had granted some conditions, expressed or implied, was no sooner repelled than it was again revived.

On the 7th, Count Las Cases having a parting interview with Lord Keith, for the purpose of delivering to him a protest on the part of Buonaparte, "I was in the act of telling him," said the count, "that Captain Maitland had said he was authorised to carry us to London, without letting us suspect that we were to be regarded as prisoners of war; and that the captain could not deny that we came freely and in good faith; that the letter from the Emperor to the Prince of Wales, of the existence of which I had given Captain Maitland information, must necessarily have created tacit conditions, since he had made no observation on it." Here the admiral's impatience, nay, anger, broke forth. He said to him sharply, that in that case Captain Maitland was a fool, since his instructions contained not a word to such a purpose; and this he should surely know, since it was he, Lord Keith, who issued them. Count Las Cases still persevered, stating that his lordship spoke with a hasty severity, for which he might be himself responsible; since the other officers, as well as Rear-Admiral Hotham, had expressed themselves to the same effect, which could not have been the case had the letter of instructions been so clearly expressed, and so positive, as his lordship seemed to think.[195]

Lord Keith, upon this statement of Count Las Cases, called upon Captain Maitland for the most ample account he could give of the communications which he had had with the count, previous to Napoleon's coming on board the Bellerophon. Captain Maitland of course obeyed, and stated at full length the manner in which the French frigates lay blockaded, the great improbability of their effecting an escape, and the considerable risk they would have run in attempting it; the application to him, first by Savary and Las Cases, afterwards by Las Cases and Gourgaud; his objecting to the frequent flags of truce; his refusal to allow Buonaparte to pass to sea, either in French ships of war, or in a neutral vessel; his consenting to carry to England the late Emperor and his suite, to be at the disposal of the Prince Regent, with his cautions to them, again and again renewed, in the presence of Captain Sartorius and Captain Gambier, that he could grant no stipulations or conditions whatever. These officers gave full evidence to the same effect, by their written attestations. If, therefore, the insinuation of Count Las Cases, for it amounts to no more, is to be placed against the express and explicit averment of Captain Maitland, the latter must preponderate, were it but by aid of the direct testimony of two other British officers. Finally, Captain Maitland mentioned Napoleon's acknowledgment, and that of his suite, that though their expectations had been disappointed, they imputed no blame to him, which he could not have escaped, had he used any unwarranted and fallacious proposals to entice them on board his vessel. As the last piece of evidence, he mentioned his taking farewell of Montholon, who again reverted to Napoleon's wish to make him a present, and expressed the Emperor's sense of his civilities, and his high and honourable deportment through the whole transaction.

Captain Maitland, to use his own words, then said, "'I feel much hurt that Count Las Cases should have stated to Lord Keith,

---

[195] Las Cases, tom. i., p. 69.—The reader may judge for himself, by turning to p. 220, where the instructions are printed, acting under which no man but a fool, as the admiral truly said, could have entered into such a treaty, as Count Las Cases pretends Captain Maitland to have engaged in.—S.

that I had promised Buonaparte should be well received in England, or indeed made promises of any sort. I have endeavoured to conduct myself with integrity and honour throughout the whole of this transaction, and therefore cannot allow such an assertion to go uncontradicted.'—'Oh!' said Count Montholon, 'Las Cases negotiated this business; it has turned out very differently from what he and all of us expected. He attributes the Emperor's situation to himself, and is therefore desirous of giving it the best countenance he can; but I assure you the Emperor is convinced your conduct has been most honourable;' then taking my hand, he pressed it, and added, 'and that is my opinion also.'"

Lord Keith was of course perfectly convinced that the charge against Captain Maitland was not only totally unsupported by testimony, but that it was disproved by the evidence of impartial witnesses, as well as by the conduct and public expression of sentiments of those who had the best right to complain of that officer's conduct, had it been really deserving of censure. The reason why Count Las Cases should persist in grounding hopes and wishes of his own framing, upon supposed expressions of encouragement from Captain Maitland, has been probably rightly treated by Count Montholon. Napoleon's conduct, in loading Captain Maitland with the charge of "laying snares for him," while his own conscience so far acquitted that brave officer, that he pressed upon him thanks, and yet more substantial evidence of his favourable opinion, can, we are afraid, only be imputed to a predominant sense of his own interest, to which he was not unwilling to have sacrificed the professional character and honourable name of an officer, to whom, on other occasions, he acknowledged himself obliged. As Captain Maitland's modest and manly Narrative[196] is now published, the figment, that Napoleon came on board the Bellerophon in any other character than as a prisoner of war, must be considered as silenced for ever.

Having prosecuted this interesting subject to a conclusion, we return to the train of circumstances attending Napoleon's departure from England, so far as they seem to contain historical interest.

---

[196] "Narrative of the surrender of Buonaparte, and of his residence on Board H.M.S. Bellerophon. By Captain F. L. Maitland, C. B. 1826."

THE BELLEROPHON

The inconvenient resort of immense numbers, sometimes not less than a thousand boats, scarce to be kept off by absolute force by those who rowed guard within the prescribed distance of 300 yards from the Bellerophon, was rendered a greater annoyance, when Napoleon's repeated expressions, that he would never go to St. Helena, occasioned some suspicions that he meant to attempt his escape. Two frigates were therefore appointed to lie as guards on the Bellerophon, and sentinels were doubled and trebled, both by night and day.

An odd incident, of a kind which could only have happened in England (for though as many bizarre whims may arise in the minds of foreigners, they are much more seldom ripened into action,) added to the cares of those who were to watch this important prisoner. Some newspaper, which was not possessed of a legal adviser to keep it right in point of form, had suggested (in tenderness, we suppose, to public curiosity,) that the person of Napoleon Buonaparte should be removed to shore by agency of a writ of Habeas Corpus. This magical rescript of the Old Bailey, as Smollett terms it, loses its influence over an alien and prisoner of war, and therefore such an absurd proposal was not acted upon. But an individual prosecuted for a libel upon a naval officer, conceived the idea of citing Napoleon as an evidence in a court of justice, to prove, as he pretended, the state of the French navy, which was necessary to his defence. The writ was to have been served on Lord Keith; but he disappointed the litigant, by keeping his boat off the ship while he was on board, and afterwards by the speed of his twelve-oared barge, which the attorney's panting rowers toiled after in vain. Although this was a mere absurdity, and only worthy of the laughter with which the anecdote of the attorney's pursuit and the admiral's flight was generally received, yet it might have given rise to inconvenience, by suggesting to Napoleon, that he was, by some process or other, entitled to redress by the common law of England, and might have encouraged him in resisting attempts to remove him from the Bellerophon. On the 4th of August, to end such inconvenient occurrences, the Bellerophon was appointed to put to sea and remain cruising off the Start, where she was to be joined by the squadron destined for St. Helena, when Napoleon was with his immediate attendants to be removed on board the Northumberland.

His spirit for some time seemed wound up to some desperate resolve, and though he gave no hint of suicide before Captain Maitland, otherwise than by expressing a dogged resolution not to go to St. Helena, yet to Las Cases he spoke in undisguised terms of a Roman death.[197] We own we are not afraid of such resolutions being executed by sane persons when they take the precaution of consulting an intelligent friend. It is quite astonishing how slight a backing will support the natural love of life, in minds the most courageous, and circumstances the most desperate. We are not, therefore, surprised to find that the philosophic arguments of Las Cases determined Napoleon to survive and write his history. Had he consulted his military attendants, he would have received other counsels, and assistance to execute them if necessary. Lallemand, Montholon, and Gourgaud, assured Captain Maitland, that the Emperor would sooner kill himself than go to St. Helena, and that even were he to consent, they three were determined themselves to put him to death, rather than he should so far degrade himself. Captain Maitland, in reply, gave some hints indicative of the gallows, in case such a scheme were prosecuted.

Savary and Lallemand, were, it must be owned, under circumstances peculiarly painful. They had been among the list of persons excluded from the amnesty by the royal government of France, and now they were prohibited by the British Ministry from accompanying Napoleon to St. Helena. They entertained, not unnaturally, the greatest anxiety about their fate, apprehensive, though entirely without reason, that they might be delivered up to the French Government. They resolved upon personal resistance to prevent their being separated from their Emperor, but fortunately were so considerate amid their wrath, as to take the opinion of the

---

[197] "'My friend,' said the Emperor to me, 'I have sometimes an idea of quitting you, and this would not be very difficult; it is only necessary to create a little mental excitement, and I shall soon have escaped. All will be over, and you can then quietly rejoin your families.' I remonstrated warmly against such notions. Poets and philosophers had said, that it was a spectacle worthy of the Divinity to see men struggling with fortune; reverses and constancy had their glory."—Las Cases, tom. i., p. 56.

late distinguished lawyer and statesman, Sir Samuel Romilly.[198] As the most effectual mode of serving these unfortunate gentlemen, Sir Samuel, by personal application to the Lord Chancellor, learned that there were no thoughts of delivering up his clients to the French government, and thus became able to put their hearts at ease upon that score. On the subject of the resistance, as to the legality of which they questioned him, Sir Samuel Romilly acquainted them, that life taken in an affray of the kind, would be construed into murder by the law of England. No greater danger, indeed, was to be expected from an assault, legalized upon the opinion of an eminent lawyer, than from a suicide adjusted with the advice of a counsellor of state; and we suppose neither Napoleon nor his followers were more serious in the violent projects which they announced, than they might think necessary to shake the purpose of the English Ministry. In this they were totally unsuccessful; and their intemperate threats only occasioned their being deprived of arms, excepting Napoleon, who was left in possession of his sword. Napoleon and his followers were greatly hurt at this marked expression of want of confidence, which must also have been painful to the English officers who executed the order, though it was explained to the French gentlemen, that the measure was only one of precaution, and that their weapons were to be carefully preserved and restored to them. During his last day on board the Bellerophon, Napoleon was employed in composing a Protest, which, as it contains nothing more than his address to Lord Keith and Sir Henry Bunbury, we have thrown into the Appendix.[199] He also wrote a second letter to the Prince Regent.

On the 4th of August, the Bellerophon set sail, and next morning fell in with the Northumberland, and the squadron destined for St. Helena, as also with the Tonnant, on board of which Lord Keith's flag was hoisted.

---

[198] Savary, tom. iv., p. 189.
[199] See Appendix, No. II.—"It occurred to me, that, in such a decisive moment, the Emperor was bound to show a formal opposition to this violence. I ventured, therefore, to read to him a paper which I had prepared, with the general sense of which he seemed pleased. After suppressing a few phrases, and correcting others, it was signed, and sent to Lord Keith."—Las Cases, tom. i., p. 59.

O'MEARA—THE NORTHUMBERLAND

It was now that Napoleon gave Captain Maitland the first intimation of his purpose to submit to his exile, by requesting that Mr. O'Meara, surgeon of the Bellerophon, might be permitted to attend him to St. Helena, instead of his own surgeon, whose health could not stand the voyage. This made it clear that no resistance was designed; and, indeed, so soon as Napoleon observed that his threats had produced no effect, he submitted with his usual equanimity. He also gave orders to deliver up his arms. His baggage was likewise subjected to a form of search, but without unpacking or disturbing any article. The treasure of Buonaparte, amounting only to 4000 gold Napoleons, was taken into custody, to abridge him of that powerful means of effecting his escape. Full receipts, of course, were given, rendering the British Government accountable for the same; and Marchand, the favourite valet-de-chambre of the Emperor, was permitted to take whatever money he thought might be immediately necessary.

About eleven o'clock on the morning of the 7th August, Lord Keith came in his barge to transfer Napoleon from the Bellerophon to the Northumberland. About one o'clock, when Buonaparte had announced that he was in full readiness, a captain's guard was turned out; Lord Keith's barge was prepared; and as Napoleon crossed the quarter-deck, the soldiers presented arms under three ruffles of the drum, being the salute paid to a general officer. His step was firm and steady; his farewell to Captain Maitland polite and friendly.[200] That officer had no doubt something to forgive to Napoleon, who had endeavoured to fix on him the stigma of having laid a snare for

---

[200] "Taking off his hat, he said, 'Captain Maitland, I take this last opportunity of once more returning you my thanks for the manner in which you have treated me while on board the Bellerophon, and also to request you will convey them to the officers and ship's company you command;' then turning to the officers, who were standing by me, he added, 'Gentlemen, I have requested your captain to express my gratitude to you for your attention to me, and to those who have followed my fortunes.' He then went forward to the gangway; and before he went down the ship's side, bowed two or three times to the ship's company. After the boat had shoved off, and got the distance of about thirty yards from the ship, he stood up, pulled his hat off, and bowed, first to the officers, and then to the men; and immediately sat down and entered into conversation with Lord Keith."—Maitland, p. 202.

him; yet the candid and manly avowal of the feelings which remained on his mind at parting with him, ought not to be suppressed. They add credit, were that required, to his plain, honest, and unvarnished narrative.

"It may appear surprising, that a possibility could exist of a British officer being prejudiced in favour of one who had caused so many calamities to his country; but to such an extent did he possess the power of pleasing, that there are few people who could have sat at the same table with him for nearly a month, as I did, without feeling a sensation of pity, allied perhaps to regret, that a man possessed of so many fascinating qualities, and who had held so high a station in life, should be reduced to the situation in which I saw him."[201]

VOYAGE TO ST. HELENA

Napoleon was received on board of the Northumberland with the same honours paid at leaving the Bellerophon. Sir George Cockburn, the British admiral, to whose charge the late Emperor was now committed, was in every respect a person highly qualified to discharge the task with delicacy towards Napoleon, yet with fidelity to the instructions he had received. Of good birth, accustomed to the first society, a handsome person, and an agreeable address, he had yet so much of the firmness of his profession as to be able to do unpleasing things when necessary. In every particular within the circle of his orders, he was kind, gentle, and accommodating; beyond them, he was inflexible. This mixture of courtesy and firmness was particularly necessary, since Napoleon, and still more his attendants on his behalf, were desirous upon several occasions to arrogate a degree of royal rank for the prisoner, which Sir George Cockburn's instructions, for reasons to be hereafter noticed, positively forbade him to concede. All that he

---

[201] "After Napoleon had quitted the ship, being desirous to know what were the feelings of the ship's company towards him, I asked my servant what the people said of him. 'Why, sir,' he answered, 'I heard several of them conversing together about him this morning; when one of them observed, "Well! they may abuse that man as much as they please, but if the people of England knew him as well as we do, they would not hurt a hair of his head;" in which the others agreed.'"—Maitland, p. 223.

could give, he gave with a readiness which showed kindness as well as courtesy; but aware that, beyond the fixed limit, each admitted claim would only form the foundation for another, he made his French guests sensible that ill-humour or anger could have no effect upon his conduct.

The consequence was, that though Napoleon, when transferred to the Northumberland, was, by the orders of the Admiralty, deprived of certain marks of deference which he received on board of the Bellerophon (where Captain Maitland had no precise orders on the subject, and the withholding of which in him would have been a gratuitous infliction of humiliation,) yet no positive quarrel, far less any rooted ill-will, took place betwixt Napoleon and the admiral. The latter remained at the principal place of his own table, was covered when on the quarterdeck, after the first salutations had passed, and disregarded other particulars of etiquette observed towards crowned heads; yet such circumstances only occasioned a little temporary coldness, which, as the admiral paid no attention to his guests' displeasure, soon gave way to a Frenchman's natural love of society; and Sir George Cockburn (ceasing to be the *Réquin*, as Las Cases says the French termed him when they were in the pet,) became that mixture of the obliging gentleman and strict officer, for which Napoleon held him whenever he spoke candidly on the subject.

It may be mentioned as no bad instance of this line of conduct, and its effects, that upon the Northumberland crossing the line, the Emperor desiring to exhibit his munificence to the seamen, by presenting them with a hundred louis-d'or, under pretext of paying the ordinary fine, Sir George Cockburn, considering this tribute to Neptune as too excessive in amount, would not permit the donative to exceed a tenth part of the sum; and Napoleon, offended by the restriction, paid nothing at all. Upon another occasion, early in the voyage, a difference in national manners gave rise to one of those slight misunderstandings which we have noticed. Napoleon was accustomed, like all Frenchmen, to leave the table immediately after dinner, and Sir George Cockburn, with the English officers, remained after him at table; for, in permitting his French guests their liberty, the admiral did not choose to admit the right of Napoleon to break up the party at his, Sir George's, own table. This gave some discontent.[202] Notwithstanding these trifling subjects of dissatisfaction, Las Cases informs us that the admiral, whom he took to be prepossessed against them at first, became every day more amicable. The Emperor used to take his arm every evening on the quarterdeck, and hold long conversations with him upon maritime subjects, as well as past events in general.[203]

While on board the Northumberland, the late Emperor spent his mornings in reading or writing;[204] his evenings in his exercise upon deck, and at cards. The game was generally *vingt un*. But when the play became rather deep, he discouraged that amusement, and substituted chess. Great tactician as he was, Napoleon did not play well at that military game, and it was with difficulty that his

---

[202] Las Cases [tom. i., p. 101,] gives somewhat a different account of this trifling matter, which appears to have been a misunderstanding. Las Cases supposes the admiral to have been offended at Napoleon's rising, whereas Sir George Cockburn was only desirous to show that he did not conceive himself obliged to break up the party because his French guests withdrew. It seems, however, to have dwelt on Napoleon's mind, and was always quoted when he desired to express dissatisfaction with the admiral.

[203] Las Cases, tom. i., p. 138.—"After dinner the grand maréchal and I always followed the Emperor to the quarterdeck. After the preliminary remarks on the weather, &c., Napoleon used to start a subject of conversation, and when he had taken eight or nine turns the whole length of the deck, he would seat himself on the second gun from the gangway, on the larboard side. The midshipmen soon observed this habitual predilection, so that the cannon was thenceforth called the *Emperor's gun*. It was there that Napoleon often conversed hours together, and that I learned, for the first time, a part of what I am about to relate."—Las Cases, p. 95.

[204] "Sept. 1-6.—The Emperor expressed a wish to learn English. I endeavoured to form a very simple plan for his instruction. This did very well for two or three days; but the *ennui* occasioned by the study was at least equal to that which it was intended to counteract, and the English was laid aside."—Las Cases, tom. i., p. 137. "Sept. 7. The Emperor observed that I was very much occupied, and he even suspected the subject on which I was engaged. He determined to ascertain the fact, and obtained sight of a few pages of my Journal; he was not displeased with it. He observed that such a work would be interesting rather than useful. The military events, for example, thus detailed, in the ordinary course of conversation, would be meagre, incomplete, and devoid of end or object. I eagerly seized the favourable opportunity, and ventured to suggest the idea of his dictating to me the campaigns in Italy. On the 9th, the Emperor called me into his cabin, and dictated to me, for the first time, some details respecting the siege of Toulon," &c.—Las Cases, p. 171. "Sept. 19-22. The Emperor now began regularly to dictate to me his campaigns of Italy. For the first few days he viewed this occupation with indifference; but the regularity and promptitude with which I presented to him my daily task, together with the progress we made, soon excited his interest; and at length the pleasure he derived from this dictation, rendered it absolutely necessary to him. He was sure to send for me about eleven o'clock every morning, and he seemed to wait the hour with impatience."—Las Cases, p. 187.

antagonist, Montholon, could avoid the solecism of beating the Emperor.

During this voyage, Napoleon's *jour de fête* occurred, which was also his birth-day. It was the 15th August; a day for which the Pope had expressly canonized a St. Napoleon to be the Emperor's patron. And now, strange revolution, it was celebrated by him on board of an English man-of-war, which was conducting him to his place of imprisonment, and, as it proved, his tomb. Yet Napoleon seemed cheerful and contented during the whole day, and was even pleased with being fortunate at play, which he received as a good omen.[205]

ST. HELENA

Upon the 15th October, 1815, the Northumberland reached St. Helena, which presents but an unpromising aspect to those who design it for a residence, though it may be a welcome sight to the sea-worn mariner. Its destined inhabitant, from the deck of the Northumberland, surveyed it with his spy-glass. St. James' Town, an inconsiderable village, was before him, enchased as it were in a valley, amid arid and scarped rocks of immense height; every platform, every opening, every gorge, was bristled with cannon. Las Cases, who stood by him, could not perceive the slightest alteration of his countenance.[206] The orders of Government had been that Napoleon should remain on board till a residence could be prepared suitable for the line of life he was to lead in future. But as this was likely to be a work of time, Sir George Cockburn readily undertook, on his own responsibility, to put his passengers on shore, and provide in some way for the security of Napoleon's person, until the necessary habitation should be fitted up. He was accordingly transferred to land upon the 16th October;[207] and thus the Emperor of France, nay, wellnigh of Europe, sunk into the Recluse of St. Helena.

---

[205] Las Cases, tom. i., p. 92.
[206] Las Cases, tom. i., p. 241.
[207] "Before Napoleon stepped into the boat, he sent for the captain of the Northumberland and took leave of him, desiring him, at the same time, to convey his thanks to the officers and crew."—Las Cases, tom. i., p. 243.

Chapter XCIII

Causes which justify the English Government in the measure of Napoleon's Banishment—Napoleon's wish to retire to England, in order that, being near France, he might again interfere in her affairs—Reasons for withholding from him the title of Emperor—Sir George Cockburn's Instructions—Temporary Accommodation at Briars—Napoleon removes to Longwood—Precautions taken for the safe custody of the Prisoner.

We are now to touch upon the arguments which seem to justify the Administration of England in the strict course which they adopted towards Napoleon Buonaparte, in restraining his person, and abating the privileges of rank which he tenaciously claimed. And here we are led to observe the change produced in men's feelings within the space of only twelve years. In 1816, when the present author, however inadequate to the task, attempted to treat of the same subject,[208] there existed a considerable party in Britain who were of opinion that the British government would best have discharged their duty to France and Europe, by delivering up Napoleon to Louis XVIII.'s government, to be treated as he himself had treated the Duke d'Enghien. It would be at this time of day needless to throw away argument upon the subject, or to show that Napoleon was at least entitled to security of life, by his surrender to the British flag.

As needless would it be to go over the frequently repeated ground, which proves so clearly that in other respects the transaction with Captain Maitland amounted to an unconditional surrender. Napoleon had considered every plan of escape by force or address, and none had seemed to him to present such chance of a favourable result, as that which upon full consideration he adopted.

---

[208] See the Edinburgh Annual Register for 1815.

A surrender to England ensured his life, and gave him the hope of taking further advantages from the generosity of the British nation; for an unconditional surrender, as it secures nothing, so it excludes nothing. General Bertrand, when on board the Northumberland, said that Napoleon had been much influenced in taking the step he had done by the Abbé Siêyes, who had strongly advised him to proceed at once to England, in preference to taking any other course, which proves that his resolution must of course have been formed long before he ever saw Captain Maitland. Even M. Las Cases, when closely examined, comes to the same result; for he admits that he never hoped that Napoleon would be considered as a free man, or receive passports for America; but only that he would be kept in custody under milder restrictions than were inflicted upon him. But as he made no stipulation of any kind concerning the nature of these restrictions, they must of course have been left to the option of the conquering party. The question, therefore, betwixt Napoleon and the British nation, was not one of *justice*, which has a right to its due, though the consequence should be destruction to the party by which it is to be rendered, but one of generosity and clemency, feelings which can only be wisely indulged with reference to the safety of those who act upon them.

Napoleon being thus a prisoner surrendered at discretion, became subjected to the common laws of war, which authorise belligerent powers to shut up prisoners of war in places of confinement, from which it is only usual to except such whose honour may be accounted as a sufficient guarantee for their good faith, or whose power of doing injury is so small that it might be accounted contemptible. But Buonaparte was neither in the one situation nor the other. His power was great; the temptation to use it strong; and the confidence to be placed in his resolution or promise to resist such temptation, very slight indeed.

There is an unauthorised report, that Lord Castlereagh, at the time of the treaty of Fontainbleau, asked Caulaincourt, why Napoleon did not choose to ask refuge in England, rather than accept the almost ridiculous title of Emperor of Elba. We doubt much if Lord Castlereagh did this. But if, either upon such a hint, or upon his own free motion, Napoleon had chosen in 1814, to repose his confidence in the British nation; or even had he fallen into our hands by chance of war, England ought certainly, on so extraordinary an occasion, to have behaved with magnanimity; and perhaps ought either to have permitted Napoleon to reside as an individual within her dominions, or suffered him to have departed to America. It might then have been urged (though cautious persons might even then hesitate,) that the pledged word of a soldier, who had been so lately a sovereign, ought to be received as a guarantee for his observance of treaty. Nay, it might then have been held, that the talents and activity of a single individual, supposing them as great as human powers can be carried, would not have enabled him, however desirous, to have again disturbed the peace of Europe. There would have been a natural desire, therefore, to grant so remarkable a person that liberty which a generous nation might have been willing to conceive would not, and could not, be abused. But the experiment of Elba gave too ample proof at once how little reliance was to be placed in Napoleon's engagement, and how much danger was to be apprehended from him, even when his fortunes were apparently at the lowest ebb. His breach of the treaty of Fontainbleau altered entirely his relations with England and with Europe; and placed him in the condition of one whose word could not be trusted, and whose personal freedom was inconsistent with the liberties of Europe. The experiment of trusting to his parole had been tried and failed. The wise may be deceived once; only fools are twice cheated in the same manner.

It may be pleaded and admitted for Napoleon, that he had, to instigate his returning from Elba, as strong a temptation as earth could hold out to an ambitious spirit like his own—the prospect of an extraordinary enterprise, with the imperial throne for its reward. It may be also allowed, that the Bourbons, delaying to pay his stipulated revenue, afforded him, so far as they were concerned, a certain degree of provocation. But all this would only argue against his being again trusted within the reach of such temptation. While France was in a state of such turmoil and vexation, with the remains of a disaffected army fermenting amid a fickle population—while the king (in order to make good his stipulated payments to the allies) was obliged to impose heavy taxes, and to raise them with some severity, many opportunities might arise, in which Napoleon, either complaining of some petty injuries of his own, or invited by the discontented state of the French nation, might renew his memorable attempt of 28th February. It was the business of the British Ministry to prevent all hazard of this. It was but on the 20th April before, that they were called upon by the Opposition to account to the House of Commons for not taking proper precautions to prevent Buonaparte's escape from Elba.[209] For what then would they have rendered themselves responsible, had they placed him in circumstances which admitted of a second escape?—at least for the full extent of all the confusion and bloodshed to which such an event must necessarily have given rise. The justice, as well as the necessity of the case, warranted the abridgement of Buonaparte's liberty, the extent of which had been made, by his surrender, dependent upon the will of Britain.

In deducing this conclusion, we have avoided having any recourse to the argument *ad hominem*. We have not mentioned the dungeon of Toussaint, on the frontier of the Alps, or the detention of Ferdinand, a confiding and circumvented ally, in the chateau of Valençay. We have not adverted to the instances of honours and appointments bestowed on officers who had broken their parole of honour, by escaping from England, yet were received in the Tuileries with favour and preferments. Neither have we alluded to the great state maxim, which erected political necessity, or expediency, into a power superior to moral law. Were Britain to vindicate her actions by such instances as the above, it would be reversing the blessed rule, acting towards our enemy, not according as we would have *desired* he should have done, but as he actually *had* done in regard to us, and observing a crooked and criminal line of policy, because our adversary had set us the example.

But Buonaparte's former actions must necessarily have been considered, so far as to ascertain what confidence was to be reposed in his personal character; and if that was found marked by gross instances of breach of faith to others, Ministers would surely have been inexcusable had they placed him in a situation where his fidelity was what the nation had principally to depend on for

---

[209] Mr. Abercrombie's motion respecting the escape of Buonaparte from Elba.—*Parl. Debates*, vol. xxx., p. 716.

tranquillity. The fact seems to be admitted by Las Cases, that while he proposed to retire to England, it was with the hope of again meddling in French affairs.[210] The example of Sir Niel Campbell had shown how little restraint the mere presence of a commissioner would have had over this extraordinary man; and his resurrection after leaving Elba, had distinctly demonstrated that nothing was to be trusted to the second political death which he proposed to submit to as a recluse in England.

It has, however, been urged, that if the character of the times and his own rendered it an act of stern necessity to take from Napoleon his personal freedom, his captivity ought to have been at least accompanied with all marks of honourable distinction; and that it was unnecessarily cruel to hurt the feelings of his followers and his own, by refusing him the Imperial title and personal observances, which he had enjoyed in his prosperity, and of which he was tenacious in adversity.

It will be agreed on all hands, that if any thing could have been done consistent with the main exigencies of the case, to save Napoleon a single pang in his unfortunate situation, that measure should have been resorted to. But there could be no reason why Britain, in compassionate courtesy, should give to her prisoner a title which she had refused to him *de jure*, even while he wielded the empire of France *de facto*; and there were arguments, to be hereafter

---

[210] This, to be sure, according to Las Cases, was only in order to carry through those great schemes of establishing the peace, the honour, and the union of the country. He had hoped to the last, it seems, in the critical moment, "That, at the sight of the public danger, the eyes of the people of France would be opened; that they would return to him, and enable him to save the country of France. It was this which made him prolong the time at Malmaison; it was this which induced him to tarry yet longer at Rochefort. If he is now at St. Helena, he owes it to that sentiment. It is a train of thought from which he could never be separated. Yet more lately, when there was no other resource than to accept the hospitality of the Bellerophon, perhaps it was not without a species of satisfaction that he found himself irresistibly drawn on by the course of events towards England, since being there was being near France. He knew well that he would not be free, but he hoped to make his opinion heard; and then how many chances would open themselves to the new direction which he wished to inspire."—*Journal*, tom. i., p. 334. We cannot understand the meaning of this, unless it implies that Napoleon, while retiring into England, on condition of abstaining from politics, entertained hopes of regaining his ascendency in French affairs, by and through the influence which he expected to exercise over those of Britain.—S.

stated, which weighed powerfully against granting such an indulgence.

The place of Napoleon's confinement, also, has been the subject of severe censure; but the question is entirely dependent upon the right of confining him at all. If that is denied, there needs no further argument; for a place of confinement, to be effectual, must connect several circumstances of safety and seclusion, each in its degree aggravating the sufferings of the person confined, and inflicting pain which ought only to be the portion of a legal prisoner. But if it be granted that a person so formidable as Napoleon should be debarred from the power of making a second avatar on the earth, there is perhaps no place in the world where so ample a degree of security could have been reconciled with the same degree of personal freedom to the captive, as St. Helena.

The healthfulness of the climate of that island will be best proved by the contents of a report annexed to a return made on 20th March, 1821, by Dr. Thomas Shortt, physician to the forces; from which it appears, that among the troops then stationed in St. Helena, constantly employed in ordinary or on fatigue duty, and always exposed to the atmosphere, the proportion of sick was only as one man to forty-two, even including casualties, and those sent to the hospital after punishment. This extraordinary degree of health, superior to that of most places in the world, Dr. Shortt imputes to the circumstance of the island being placed in the way of the trade-winds, where the continued steady breeze carries off the superfluous heat, and with it such effluvia noxious to the human constitution, as it may have generated. The same cause, bringing with it a succession of vapours from the ocean, affords a cloudy curtain to intercept the sun's rays, and prevents the occurrence of those violent and rapid forms of disease, which present themselves throughout the tropics in general. Checked perspiration is noticed as an occasional cause of disease, but which, if properly treated, is only fatal to those whose constitutions have been previously exhausted by long residence in a hot climate. It should also be observed, that the climate of the island is remarkably steady, not varying upon an average more than twenty degrees in the course of the year; which equality of temperature is another great cause of the general healthfulness.[211] The atmosphere is warm indeed; but, as Napoleon was himself born in a hot climate, and was stated to be afraid of the cold even of Britain, that could hardly in his case be considered as a disadvantageous circumstance.

In respect to Napoleon's personal treatment, Sir George Cockburn proceeded on his arrival to arrange this upon the system recommended by his final instructions, which run thus:

"In committing so important a trust to British officers, the Prince Regent is sensible that it is not necessary to impress upon them his anxious desire that no greater measure of severity with respect to confinement or restriction be imposed, than what is deemed necessary for the faithful discharge of that duty, which the admiral, as well as the Governor of St. Helena must ever keep in mind—the perfect security of General Buonaparte's person. Whatever, consistent with this great object, can be allowed in the shape of indulgence, his royal highness is confident will be willingly shown to the general; and he relies on Sir George Cockburn's known zeal and energy of character, that he will not allow himself to be betrayed into any improvident relaxation of his duty."[212]

It was in the spirit of these instructions that Sir George Cockburn acted, in selecting a place of residence for his important prisoner, while, at the same time, he consulted Napoleon's wishes as much as the case could possibly admit.

The accommodation upon the island was by no means such as could be desired in the circumstances. There were only three houses of a public character, which were in any degree adapted for such a guest. Two, the town residences of the governor and lieutenant-governor of the island, were unfit for the habitation of Napoleon, because they were within James' Town, a situation which, for obvious reasons, was not advisable. The third was Plantation-house, a villa in the country, belonging to the governor, which was the best dwelling in the island. The British Administration had prohibited the

---

[211] See Appendix, No. III.
[212] Extract of a despatch from Earl Bathurst, addressed to the Lords Commissioners of the Admiralty, dated 30th July 1815.

selection of this house for the residence of the late Imperial captive. We differ from their opinion in this particular, because the very best accommodation was due to fallen greatness; and, in his circumstances, Napoleon, with every respect to the authority of the governor, ought to have been the last person on the island subjected to inconvenience. We have little doubt that it would have been so arranged, but for the disposition of the late French Emperor and his followers to use every point of deference, or complaisance, exercised towards them, as an argument for pushing their pretensions farther. Thus the civility showed by Admiral Hotham and Captain Maitland, in manning the yards as Napoleon passed from one vessel to the other, was pleaded upon as a proof that his free and regal condition was acknowledged by these officers; and, no doubt, the assigning for his use the best house in the island, might, according to the same mode of logic, have been assumed to imply that Napoleon had no superior in St. Helena. Still there were means of repelling this spirit of encroachment, if it had shown itself; and we think it would have been better to risk the consequences indicated, and to have assigned Plantation-house for his residence, as that which was at least the best accommodation which the island afforded. Some circumstances about the locality, it is believed, had excited doubts whether the house could be completely guarded. But this, at any rate, was a question which had been considered at home, where, perhaps the actual state of the island was less perfectly understood; and Sir George Cockburn, fettered by his instructions, had no choice in the matter.

LONGWOOD—BRIARS

Besides Plantation-house, there was another residence situated in the country, and occupied by the lieutenant-governor, called Longwood, which, after all the different estates and residences in the island had been examined, was chosen by Sir George Cockburn as the future residence of Napoleon. It lies detached from the generally inhabited places of the island, consequently none were likely to frequent its neighbourhood, unless those who came there on business. It was also distant from those points which were most accessible to boats, which, until they should be sufficiently defended, it was not desirable to expose to the observation of Napoleon or his military companions. At Longwood, too, there was an extent of level ground, capable of being observed and secured by sentinels, presenting a space adapted for exercise, whether on horseback or in a carriage; and the situation, being high, was more cool than the confined valleys of the neighbourhood. The house itself was equal in accommodation (though that is not saying much) to any on the island, Plantation-house excepted.

To conclude, it was approved of by Napoleon, who visited it personally, and expressed himself so much satisfied, that it was difficult to prevail on him to leave the place. Immediate preparations were therefore made, for making such additions as should render the residence, if not such a one as could be wished, at least as commodious as the circumstances admitted. Indeed it was hoped, by assistance of artificers, and frames to be sent from England, to improve it to any extent required. In the meanwhile, until the repairs immediately necessary could be made at Longwood, General Bertrand, and the rest of Napoleon's suite, were quartered in a furnished house in James' Town, while he himself, at his own request, took up his abode at Briars, a small house or cottage, romantically situated, a little way from the town, in which he could only have one spare room for his own accommodation. Sir George Cockburn would have persuaded him rather to take up his temporary abode in the town, where the best house in the place was provided for him. Napoleon declined this proposal, pleading his natural aversion to expose himself to the public gaze. Besides the solitude, the pleasing landscape, agreeable especially to those whose persons have been lately confined to a ship, and whose eyes have long wandered over the waste of ocean, determined the Ex-Emperor in favour of Briars.

Whilst dwelling at Briars, Napoleon limited himself more than was necessary; for, taking exception at the sentinels, who were visible from the windows of the house, and objecting more reasonably to the resort of visitors, he sequestered himself in a small pavilion, consisting of one good room, and two small attic apartments, which stood about twenty yards from the house. Of course his freedom, unless when accompanied by a British field-officer, was limited to the small garden of the cottage, the rest of the precincts being watched by sentinels. Sir George Cockburn felt for the situation of his prisoner, and endeavoured to hurry forward the improvements at Longwood, in order that Napoleon might remove thither. He employed for this purpose the ship-carpenters of the squadron, and all the artificers the island could afford; "and Longwood," says Dr. O'Meara, "for nearly two months, exhibited as busy a scene as had ever been witnessed, during the war, in any of his Majesty's dock-yards, whilst a fleet was fitting out under the personal direction of some of our best naval commanders. The admiral, indefatigable in his exertions, was frequently seen to arrive at Longwood shortly after sunrise, stimulating by his presence the St. Helena workmen, who, in general lazy and indolent, beheld with astonishment the despatch and activity of a man-of-war succeed to the characteristic idleness, which until then they had been accustomed both to witness and to practise."[213]

During the Ex-Emperor's residence at Briars, he remained much secluded from society, spent his mornings in the garden, and in the evening played at whist for sugar-plums, with Mr. Balcombe, the proprietor, and the members of his family. The Count Las Cases, who seems, among those of his retinue, to have possessed the most various and extensive information, was naturally selected as the chief, if not the only companion of his studies and recreations in the morning.[214] On such occasions he was usually gentle, accessible, and captivating in his manners.

The exertions of Sir George Cockburn, struggling with every difficulty which want of building materials, means of transport, and every thing which facilitates such operations, could possibly

---

[213] Voice, &c., vol. i., p. 14.
[214] "*Briars, Oct. 28-31.* We had nearly arrived at the end of the campaign of Italy. The Emperor, however, did not yet find that he had sufficient occupation. Employment was his only resource, and the interest which his first dictations had assumed furnished an additional motive for proceeding with them. The campaign of Egypt was now about to be commenced. The Emperor had frequently talked of employing the grand mareschal on this subject. I suggested, that he should set us all to work at the same time, and proceed at once with the campaigns of Italy and Egypt—the history of the Consulate—the return from Elba, &c. The idea pleased the Emperor; and, from that time, one or two of his suite came regularly every day to write by his dictations, the transcript of which they brought to him next morning."—Las Cases, tom. i., p. 286.

interpose, at length enabled him to accomplish the transmutation of Longwood into such a dwelling-house, as, though it was far below the former dignity of its possessor, might sufficiently accommodate a captive of the rank at which Napoleon was rated by the British Government.[215]

LONGWOOD

On the 9th December, Longwood received Napoleon and part of his household; the Count and Countess of Montholon and their children; the Count Las Cases and his son. General Gourgaud, Doctor O'Meara, who had been received as his medical attendant, and such other of Napoleon's attendants as could not be lodged within the house, were, for the time, accommodated with tents; and the Count and Countess Bertrand were lodged in a small cottage at a place called Hut's-gate, just on the verge of what might be called the privileged grounds of Longwood, whilst a new house was building for their reception. Upon the whole, as it is scarcely denied, on the one hand, that every effort was made to render Longwood-house as commodious for the prisoner as time and means could possibly permit, so, on the other, it must in fairness be considered, that the delay, however inevitable, must have been painfully felt by the Ex-Emperor, confined to his hut at Briars; and that the house at Longwood, when finished as well as it could be in the circumstances, was far inferior in accommodation to that which every Englishman would have desired that the distinguished prisoner should have enjoyed whilst in English custody.

It had been proposed to remedy the deficiencies of Longwood by constructing a habitation of wood upon a suitable scale, and sending it out in pieces from England, to be put together on the spot; the only mode, as the island can scarce be said to afford any building-materials, by which the desired object of Napoleon's fitting accommodation could, it was thought, be duly attained.

---

[215] The suite of apartments, destined for his own peculiar use, consisted of a saloon, an eating-room, a library, a small study, and a sleeping apartment. This was a strange contrast with the palaces which Napoleon had lately inhabited; but it was preferable, in the same proportion, to the Tower of the Temple, and the dungeons of Vincennes.—S.

Circumstances, however, prevented this plan from being attempted to be carried into execution for several months; and a series of unhappy disputes betwixt the governor and his prisoner added years of delay; which leads us again to express our regret that Plantation-house had not been at once assigned to Napoleon for his residence.

We have already said, that around the house of Longwood lay the largest extent of open ground in the neighbourhood, fit for exercise either on foot or upon horseback. A space of twelve miles in circumference was traced off, within which Napoleon might take exercise without being attended by any one. A chain of sentinels surrounded this domain to prevent his passing, unless accompanied by a British officer. If he inclined to extend his excursions, he might go to any part of the island, providing the officer was in attendance, and near enough to observe his motions. Such an orderly officer was always in readiness to attend him when required. Within the limited space already mentioned, there were two camps, that of the 53d regiment at Deadwood, about a mile from Longwood; another at Hut's-gate, where an officer's guard was mounted, that being the principal access to Longwood.

We are now to consider the means resorted to for the safe custody of this important prisoner. The old poet has said, that "every island is a prison;"[216] but, in point of difficulty of escape, there is none which can compare with St. Helena; which was no doubt the chief reason for its being selected as the place of Napoleon's detention.

Dr. O'Meara, no friendly witness, informs us that the guards, with attention at once to Napoleon's feelings, and the security of his person, were posted in the following manner:

"A subaltern's guard was posted at the entrance of Longwood, about six hundred paces from the houses, and a cordon of sentinels and picquets was placed round the limits. At nine o'clock the sentinels were drawn in and stationed in communication with each other, surrounding the house in such positions, that no person could

---

[216] "Every island is a prison, Strongly guarded by the sea; Kings and princes, for that reason, Prisoners are, as well as we." Ritson's *Songs*, vol. ii., p. 105.

come in or go out without being seen and scrutinized by them. At the entrance of the house double sentinels were placed, and patrols were continually passing backward and forward. After nine, Napoleon was not at liberty to leave the house, unless in company with a field officer; and no person whatever was allowed to pass without the counter-sign. This state of affairs continued until daylight in the morning. Every landing-place in the island, and, indeed, every place which presented the semblance of one, was furnished with a picquet, and sentinels were even placed upon every goat-path leading to the sea: though in truth the obstacles presented by nature, in almost all the paths in that direction, would, of themselves, have proved insurmountable to so unwieldy a person as Napoleon."[217]

The precautions taken by Sir George Cockburn, to avail himself of the natural character and peculiarities of the island, and to prevent the possibility of its new inhabitant making his escape by sea, were so strict, as, even without the assistance of a more immediate guard upon his person, seemed to exclude the possibility, not only of an escape, but even an attempt to communicate with the prisoners from the sea-coast.

"From the various signal-posts on the island," continues the account of Dr. O'Meara, "ships are frequently discovered at twenty-four leagues' distance, and always long before they can approach the shore. Two ships of war continually cruised, one to windward, and the other to leeward, to whom signals were made, as soon as a vessel was discovered, from the posts on shore. Every ship, except a British man-of-war, was accompanied down to the road by one of the cruisers, who remained with her until she was either permitted to anchor, or was sent away. No foreign vessels were allowed to anchor, unless under circumstances of great distress; in which case, no person from them was permitted to land, and an officer and party from one of the ships of war was sent on board to take charge of them as long as they remained, as well as in order to prevent any improper communication. Every fishing-boat belonging to the island was numbered, and anchored every evening at sunset, under the superintendence of a lieutenant in the navy. No boats, excepting

---

[217] Voice from St. Helena, vol. i., p. 21.

guard-boats from the ships of war, which pulled about the island all night, were allowed to be down after sunset. The orderly officer was also instructed to ascertain the actual presence of Napoleon twice in the twenty-four hours, which was done with as much delicacy as possible. In fact, every human precaution to prevent escape, short of actually incarcerating or enchaining him, was adopted by Sir George Cockburn."[218]

---

[218] Voice from St. Helena, vol. i., p. 22.

Chapter XCIV

Buonaparte's alleged grievances considered—Right to restrict his Liberty—Limits allowed Napoleon—Complaints urged by Las Cases against Sir George Cockburn—Sir Hudson Lowe appointed Governor of St. Helena—Information given by General Gourgaud to Government—Agitation of various Plans for Buonaparte's Escape—Writers on the subject of Napoleon's Residence at St. Helena—Napoleon's irritating Treatment of Sir Hudson Lowe—Interviews between them.

Hitherto, as we have prosecuted our task, each year has been a history which we have found it difficult to contain within the limits of half a volume; remaining besides conscious, that, in the necessary compression, we have been obliged to do injustice to the importance of our theme. But the years of imprisonment which pass so much more slowly to the captive, occupy, with their melancholy monotony, only a small portion of the page of history; and the tale of five years of St. Helena, might, so far as events are concerned, be sooner told than the history of a single campaign, the shortest which was fought under Buonaparte's auspices. Yet these years were painfully marked, and indeed embittered, by a train of irritating disputes betwixt the prisoner and the officer to whom was committed the important, and yet most delicate, task of restraining his liberty, and cutting off all prospect of escape; and whose duty it was, at the same time, to mix the necessary degree of vigilance with as much courtesy, and we will add kindness, as Napoleon could be prevailed on to accept.

We have had considerable opportunity to collect information on this subject, the correspondence of Sir Hudson Lowe with his Majesty's Government having been opened to our researches by the liberality of Lord Bathurst, late secretary of state for the colonial department. This communication has enabled us to speak with confidence respecting the general principles by which the British Government were guided in their instructions to Sir Hudson Lowe, and the tenor of these instructions themselves. We therefore propose to discuss, in the first place, the alleged grievances of Napoleon, as they arose out of the instructions of the British Government; reserving as a second subject of discussion, the farther complaints of the aggravated mode in which these instructions are alleged to have been executed by the Governor of St. Helena. On the latter subject our information is less perfect, from the distance of Sir Hudson Lowe from Europe precluding personal inquiry, and the impossibility of producing impartial evidence on the subject of a long train of minute and petty incidents, each of which necessarily demands investigation, and is the subject of inculpation and defence. We have, however, the means of saying something upon this subject also.

We have already discussed the circumstances of Napoleon's surrender to the British, without reserve, qualification, or condition of any kind; and we have seen, that if he sustained any disappointment in being detained a prisoner, instead of being considered as a guest, or free inmate of Britain, it arose from the failure of hopes which he had adopted on his own calculation, without the slightest encouragement from Captain Maitland. We doubt greatly, indeed, if his most sanguine expectations ever seriously anticipated a reception very different from what he experienced; at least he testified little or no surprise when informed of his destiny. But, at any rate, he was a prisoner of war, having acquired by his surrender no right save to claim safety of life and limb. If the English nation had inveigled Napoleon into a capitulation, under conditions which they had subsequently broken, he would have been in the condition of Toussaint, whom, nevertheless, he immured in a dungeon. Or, if he had been invited to visit the Prince Regent of England in the character of an ally, had been at first received with courteous hospitality, and then committed to confinement as a prisoner, his case would have approached that of Prince Ferdinand of Spain, trepanned to Bayonne. But we should be ashamed to vindicate our country by quoting the evil example of our enemy. Truth and falsehood remain immutable and irreconcilable; and the worst criminal ought not to be proceeded against according to his own example, but according to the general rules of justice. Nevertheless, it greatly diminishes our interest in a complaint, if he who prefers it has himself been in the habit of meting to others with the same unfair weight and measure, which he complains of when used towards himself.

Napoleon, therefore, being a prisoner of war, and to be disposed of as such, (a point which admits of no dispute,) we have, we conceive, further proved, that his residence within the territories of Great Britain was what could hardly take place consistently with the safety of Europe. To have delivered him up to any of the other allied powers, whose government was of a character similar to his own, would certainly have been highly objectionable; since in doing so Britain would have so far broken faith with him, as to part with the power of protecting his personal safety, to which extent the country to which he surrendered himself stood undeniably pledged. It only remained to keep this important prisoner in such a state of restraint, as to ensure his not having the means of making a second escape, and again involving France and Europe in a bloody and doubtful war. St. Helena was selected as the place of his detention, and, we think, with much propriety; since the nature of that sequestered island afforded the means for the greatest certainty of security, with the least restriction on the personal liberty of the distinguished prisoner. Waves and rocks around its shores afforded the security of walls, ditches, bars, and bolts, in a citadel; and his hours of exercise might be safely extended over a space of many miles, instead of being restrained within the narrow and guarded limits of a fortress.

The right of imprisoning Napoleon being conceded, or at least proved, and the selection of St. Helena, as his place of residence, being vindicated, we have no hesitation in avowing the principle, that every thing possible ought to have been done to alleviate the painful feelings, to which, in every point of view, a person so distinguished as Napoleon must have been subjected by so heavy a change of fortune. We would not, at that moment, have remembered the lives lost, fortunes destroyed, and hopes blighted, of so many hundreds of our countrymen, civilians travelling in France, and detained there against every rule of civilized war; nor have thought ourselves entitled to avenge upon Napoleon, in his misfortunes, the cruel inflictions, which his policy, if not his inclination, prompted him to award against others. We would not have made his dungeon so wretched, as that of the unhappy Negro chief, starved to death amidst the Alpine snows. We would not have surrounded him, while a prisoner, with spies, as in the case of the Earl of Elgin; or, as in that of Prince Ferdinand, have spread a trap for him by means of an emissary like the false Baron Koli, who, in proffering to assist his escape, should have had it for an object to obtain a pretence for treating him more harshly. These things we would not then have remembered; or, if we could not banish them from our recollection, in considering how far fraud and ignoble violence can debase genius, and render power odious, we would have remembered them as examples, not to be followed, but shunned. To prevent the prisoner from resuming a power which he had used so fatally, we would have regarded as a duty not to Britain alone, but to Europe and to the world. To accompany his detention with every alleviation which attention to his safe custody would permit, was a debt due, if not to his personal deserts, at least to our own nobleness. With such feelings upon the subject in general, we proceed to consider the most prominent subjects of complaint, which Buonaparte and his advocates have brought against the Administration of Great Britain, for their treatment of the distinguished exile.

ALLEGED GRIEVANCES

The first loud subject of complaint has been already touched upon, that the imperial title was not given to Napoleon, and that he was only addressed and treated with the respect due to a general officer of the highest rank. On this subject Napoleon was particularly tenacious. He was not of the number of those persons mentioned by the Latin poet, who, in poverty and exile, suited their titles and their language to their condition.[219] On the contrary, he

---

[219] Et tragicus plerumque dolet sermone pedestri. Telephus et Peleus, cum pauper et exul uterque, Projicit ampullas et sesquipedalia verba. Hor. *Ars Poetica*. "Princes will sometimes mourn their lot in prose. Peleus and Telephus, broke down by woes, In indigence and exile forced to roam, Leave sounding phrase, and long-tail'd words, at home."—S.

contended with great obstinacy, from the time he came to Portsmouth, on his right to be treated as a crowned head; nor was there, as we have noticed, a more fertile source of discord betwixt him and the gentlemen of his suite on one side, and the Governor of St. Helena on the other, than the pertinacious claim, on Napoleon's part, for honours and forms of address, which the orders of the British Ministry had prohibited the governor from granting, and which, therefore, Napoleon's knowledge of a soldier's duty should have prevented his exacting. But, independently of the governor's instructions, Buonaparte's claim to the peculiar distinction of a sovereign prince was liable to question, both in respect of the party by whom it was insisted on, and in relation to the government from whom it was claimed.

Napoleon, it cannot be denied, had been not only an Emperor, but perhaps the most powerful that has ever existed; and he had been acknowledged as such by all the continental sovereigns. But he had been compelled, in 1814, to lay aside and abdicate the empire of France, and to receive in exchange the title of Emperor of Elba. His breach of the treaty of Paris was in essence a renunciation of the empire of Elba; and the reassumption of that of France was so far from being admitted by the allies, that he was declared an outlaw by the Congress at Vienna. Indeed, if this second occupation of the French throne were even to be admitted as in any respect re-establishing his forfeited claim to the Imperial dignity, it must be remembered that he himself a second time abdicated, and formally renounced a second time the dignity he had in an unhappy hour reassumed. But if Napoleon had no just pretension to the Imperial title or honours after his second abdication, even from those who had before acknowledged him as Emperor of France, still less had he any right to a title which he had laid down, from a nation who had never acquiesced in his taking it up. At no time had Great Britain recognised him as Emperor of France; and Lord Castlereagh had expressly declined to accede to the treaty of Paris, by which he was acknowledged as Emperor of Elba.[220] Napoleon, indeed, founded, or attempted to found, an argument upon the treaty of Amiens having been concluded with him, when he held the capacity of First Consul of France. But he had himself destroyed the

---

[220] Parl. Debates, vol. xxx., p. 377.

Consular Government, of which he then constituted the head; and his having been once First Consul gave him no more title to the dignity of Emperor, than the Directorship of Barras invested *him* with the same title. On no occasion whatever, whether directly or by implication, had Great Britain recognised the title of her prisoner to be considered as a sovereign prince; and it was surely too late to expect acquiescence in claims in his present situation, which had not been allowed when he was actually master of half the world.

But it may be urged that, admitting that Napoleon's claim to be treated with royal ceremonial was in itself groundless, yet since he had actually enjoyed the throne for so many years, the British ministers ought to have allowed to him that rank which he had certainly possessed *de facto*, though not *de jure*. The trifling points of rank and ceremonial ought, it may be thought, according to the principles which we have endeavoured to express, to have been conceded to eclipsed sovereignty and down-fallen greatness.

To this it may be replied, that if the concession recommended could have had no further consequences than to mitigate the repinings of Napoleon—if he could have found comfort in the empty sound of titles, or if the observance of formal etiquette could have reconciled his feelings to his melancholy and dethroned condition, without altering the relative state of the question in other respects—such concession ought not to have been refused to him.

But the real cause of his desiring to have, and of the British Government's persisting in refusing to him, the name and honours of a sovereign, lay a great deal deeper. It is true, that it was a foible of Buonaparte, incident, perhaps, to his situation as a *parvenu* amongst the crowned heads of Europe, to be at all times peculiarly and anxiously solicitous that the most strict etiquette and form should be observed about his person and court. But granting that his vanity, as well as his policy, was concerned in insisting upon such rigid ceremonial as is frequently dispensed with by sovereigns of ancient descent, and whose title is unquestionable, it will not follow that a person of his sense and capacity could have been gratified, even if indulged in all the marks of external influence paid to the Great Mogul, on condition that, like the later descendants of Timur, he was still to remain a close prisoner. His purpose in tenaciously claiming the name of a sovereign, was to establish his claim to the immunities belonging to that title. He had already experienced at Elba the use to be derived from erecting a barrier of etiquette betwixt his person and any inconvenient visitor. Once acknowledged as Emperor, it followed, of course, that he was to be treated as such in every particular; and thus it would have become impossible to enforce such regulations as were absolutely demanded for his safe custody. Such a *status*, once granted, would have furnished Napoleon with a general argument against every precaution which might be taken to prevent his escape. Who ever heard of an emperor restricted in his promenades, or subjected, in certain cases, to the surveillance of an officer, and the restraint of sentinels? Or how could these precautions against escape have been taken, without irreverence to the person of a crowned head, which, in the circumstances of Napoleon Buonaparte, were indispensably necessary? Those readers, therefore, who may be of opinion that it was necessary that Napoleon should be restrained of his liberty, must also allow that the British Government would have acted imprudently if they had gratuitously invested him with a character which they had hitherto refused him, and that at the very moment when their doing so was to add to the difficulties attending his safe custody.

The question, however, does not terminate even here; for not only was Great Britain at full liberty to refuse to Buonaparte a title which she had never recognised as his due—not only would her granting it have been attended with great practical inconvenience, but farther, she could not have complied with his wishes, without affording the most serious cause of complaint to her ally the King of France. If Napoleon was called emperor, his title could apply to France alone; and if he was acknowledged as Emperor of France, of what country was Louis XVIII. King? Many wars have arisen from no other cause than that the government of one country has given the title and ceremonial due to a sovereign, to a person pretending to the throne of the other, and it is a ground of quarrel recognised by the law of nations. It is true, circumstances might have prevented Louis from resenting the supposed recognition of a royal character in his rival, as severely as Britain did the acknowledgment of the exiled Stuarts by Louis XIV., yet it must have been the subject of serious complaint; the rather that a conduct tending to indicate England's acquiescence in the imperial title claimed by Napoleon, could not but keep alive dangerous recollections, and encourage a dangerous faction in the bosom of France.

Yet, notwithstanding all we have said, we feel there was an awkwardness in approaching the individual who had been so preeminently powerful, with the familiarity applicable to one who had never stood more high above others than he would have done merely as General Buonaparte. A compromise was accordingly offered by Sir Hudson Lowe, in proposing to make use of the word Napoleon, as a more dignified style of addressing his prisoner. But an easy and respectable alternative was in the prisoner's own power. Napoleon had but to imitate other sovereigns, who, either when upon foreign travel, or when other circumstances require it, usually adopt a conventional appellative, which, while their doing so waves no part of their own claim of right to royal honours, is equally far from a concession of that right on the part of those who may have occasion to transact with them. Louis XVIII. was not the less the legitimate King of France, that he was for many years, and in various countries, only known by the name of the Comte de Lille. The conveniency of the idea had struck Napoleon himself; for at one time, when talking of the conditions of his residence in England, he said he would have no objection to resume the name of Meuron, an aide-de-camp who had died by his side at the battle of Arcola.[221] But it seems that Napoleon, more tenacious of form than a prince who had been cradled in it, considered this vailing of his dignity as too great a concession on his part to be granted to the Governor of St. Helena. Sir Hudson Lowe, at one time desirous to compromise this silly subject of dispute, would have been contented to render Napoleon the title of Excellency, as due to a field-mareschal, but neither did this meet with acception. Napoleon was determined either to be acknowledged by the governor as Emperor, or to retain his grievance in its full extent. No modifications could be devised by which it could be rendered palatable.

---

[221] "In default of America, I prefer England to any other country. I shall take the name of Colonel Meuron, or of Duroc."—*Instructions to Gourgaud*, July 13, 1815; Savary, tom. iv., p. 162.

Whether this pertinacity in claiming a title which was rendered ridiculous by his situation, was the result of some feelings which led him to doubt his own title to greatness, when his ears were no longer flattered by the language of humility; or whether the political considerations just alluded to, rendered him obstinate to refuse all epithets, except one which might found him in claims to those indemnities and privileges with which so high a title is intimate, and from which it may be said to be inseparable, it is impossible for us to say; vanity and policy might combine in recommending to him perseverance in his claim. But the strife should certainly, for his own sake, have been abandoned, when the point remained at issue between the governor and him only, since even if the former had wished to comply with the prisoner's desires, his instructions forbade him to do so. To continue an unavailing struggle, was only to invite the mortification of defeat and repulse. Yet Napoleon and his followers retained so much sensibility on this subject, that though they must have been aware that Sir Hudson Lowe only used the language prescribed by his government, and indeed dared use no other, this unfortunate phrase of *General Buonaparte* occurring so often in their correspondence, seemed to render every attempt at conciliation a species of derogation and insult, and made such overtures resemble a coarse cloth tied over a raw wound, which it frets and injures more than it protects.

COCKBURN'S INSTRUCTIONS

Whatever might be the merits of the case, as between Napoleon and the British Ministry, it was clear that Sir George Cockburn and Sir Hudson Lowe were left by their instructions no option in the matter at issue. These instructions bore that Napoleon, their prisoner, was to receive the style and treatment due to General Buonaparte, a prisoner of war; and it was at their peril if they gave him a higher title, or a different style of attention from what that title implied. No one could know better than Napoleon how strictly a soldier is bound by his *consigne*; and to upbraid Sir Hudson Lowe as ungenerous, unmanly, and so forth, because he did not disobey the instructions of his government, was as unreasonable as to hope that his remonstrances could have any effect save those of irritation and annoyance. He ought to have been aware that persisting to resent, in rough and insulting terms, the deprivation of his title on the part of an officer who was prohibited from using it, might indeed fret and provoke one with whom it would have been best to keep upon civil terms, but could not bring him one inch nearer to the point which he so anxiously desired to attain.

In fact, this trivial but unhappy subject of dispute was of a character so subtle, that it penetrated into the whole correspondence between the Emperor and the governor, and tended to mix with gall and vinegar all attempts made by the latter to cultivate something like civil intercourse. This unlucky barrier of etiquette started up and poisoned the whole effect of any intended politeness. While Sir George Cockburn remained on the island, for example, he gave more than one ball, to which *General Buonaparte* and his suite were regularly invited. In similar circumstances, Henry IV. or Charles II. would have attended the ball, and to a certainty would have danced with the prettiest young woman present, without dreaming that, by so doing, they derogated from pretensions derived from a long line of royal ancestors. Buonaparte and Las Cases, on the contrary, took offence at the familiarity, and wrote it down as a wilful and flagrant affront on the part of the admiral. These were not the feelings of a man of conscious dignity of mind, but of an upstart, who conceives the honour of preferment not to consist in having enjoyed, or in still possessing, a high situation, gained by superiority of talent, so much as in wearing the robes or listening to the sounding titles, which are attached to it.

A subject, upon which we are called upon to express much more sympathy with the condition of Napoleon, than moves us upon the consideration of his abrogated title, is, the screen which was drawn betwixt him, and, it may be said, the living world, through which he was not permitted to penetrate, by letter, even to his dearest friends and relatives, unless such had been previously communicated to, and read by, the governor of the island.

It is no doubt true, that this is an inconvenience to which prisoners of war are, in all cases, subjected; nor do we know any country in which their parole is held so sacred as to induce the government to dispense with the right of inspecting their letters. Yet the high place so lately occupied by the fallen monarch might, we think, have claimed for him some dispensation from a restriction so humiliating. If a third person, cold-blooded at best, perhaps inclined to hold up to scorn the expressions of our grief or our affection, is permitted to have the review of the effusions of our heart towards a wife, a sister, a brother, or a bosom-friend, the correspondence loses half its value; and, forced as we are to keep it within the bounds of the most discreet caution, it becomes to us rather a new source of mortification, than the opening of a communion with those absent persons, whose friendship and attachment we hold to be the dearest possession of our lives. We the rather think that some exercise of this privilege might have been left to Napoleon, without any risk of endangering the safe custody of his person; because we are pretty well convinced that all efforts strictly to enforce this regulation did, and must have proved, ineffectual, and that in some cases by means of money, and at other times by the mere influence of compassion, he and his followers would always acquire the means of transmitting private letters from the island without regard to the restriction. Whatever, therefore, was to be apprehended of danger in this species of intercourse by letter, was much more likely to occur in a clandestine correspondence, than in one carried on even by sealed letters, openly and by permission of the government. We cannot help expressing our opinion, that, considering the accurate attention of the police, which would naturally have turned in foreign countries towards letters from St. Helena, there was little danger of the public post being made use of for any dangerous machinations. Supposing, therefore, that the Exile had been permitted to use it, it would have been too dangerous to have risked any proposal for his escape through that medium. A secret correspondence must have been resorted to for that purpose, and that under circumstances which would have put every well-meaning person, at least, upon his guard against being aiding in it; since, if the ordinary channels of communication were open to the prisoner, there could have been no justifiable reason for his resorting to private means of forwarding letters from the island. At the same time, while such is our opinion, it is founded upon reasoning totally unconnected with the claim of right urged by Napoleon; as his situation, considering him as a prisoner of war, and a most important one, unquestionably entitled the government of Britain to lay him under all the restrictions incident to persons in that situation.

Another especial subject of complaint pleaded upon by Napoleon and his advocates, arose from a regulation, which, we apprehend, was so essential to his safe custody, that we are rather surprised to find it was dispensed with upon any occasion, or to any extent; as, if fully and regularly complied with, it would have afforded the means of relaxing a considerable proportion of other restrictions of a harassing and irritating character, liable to be changed from time to time, and to be removed and replaced in some cases, without any very adequate or intelligible motive. The regulation which we allude to is that which required that Buonaparte should be visible twice, or at least once, in the day, to the British orderly officer. If this regulation had been submitted to with equanimity by the Ex-Emperor, it would have given the strongest possible guarantee against the possibility of his attempting an escape. From the hour at which he had been seen by the officer, until that at which he should again become visible, no vessel would have been permitted to leave the island; and supposing that he was missed by the officer at the regular hour, the alarm would have been general, and, whether concealed in the town, or on board any of the vessels in the roadstead, he must necessarily have been discovered. Indeed, the risk was too great to induce him to have tried an effort so dangerous. It might easily have been arranged, that the orderly officer should have the opportunity to execute his duty with every possible respect to Napoleon's privacy and convenience, and the latter might himself have chosen the time and manner of exhibiting himself for an instant. In this case, and considering how many other precautions were taken to prevent escape—that every accessible path to the beach was closely guarded—and that the island was very much in the situation of a citadel, of which soldiers are the principal inhabitants—the chance of Napoleon's attempting to fly, even if permitted the unlimited range of St. Helena, was highly improbable, and the chance of his effecting his purpose next to an impossibility. But this security depended upon his submitting to see a British officer at a fixed hour; and, resolute in his plan of yielding nothing to circumstances, Napoleon resisted, in every possible manner, the necessity of complying with this very important regulation. Indeed,

Sir Hudson Lowe, on his part, was on many occasions contented to wink at its being altogether neglected, when the orderly officer could not find the means of seeing Napoleon by stealth while engaged in a walk, or in a ride, or as it sometimes happened, through the casement. This was not the way in which this important regulation ought to have been acted upon and enforced, and the governor did not reap a great harvest of gratitude from his conduct in dispensing with this act of superintendence upon his own responsibility.

We have seen that a circuit of twelve miles and upwards was laid off for Buonaparte's private exercise. No strangers entered these precincts without a pass from Bertrand, and the Emperor had uninterrupted freedom to walk or ride within them, unaccompanied by any one save those in his own family. Beyond these privileged bounds, he was not permitted to move, without the attendance of a British officer; but under the escort of such a person he was at liberty to visit every part of the island. To this arrangement Napoleon was more averse, if possible, than to that which appointed that a British officer should see him once a-day.

Other subjects of complaint there were; but as they chiefly arose out of private discussions with Sir Hudson Lowe—out of by-laws enacted by that officer—and restrictions of a more petty description, we limit ourselves for the present to those of a general character, which, however inconvenient and distressing, were, it is to be observed, such as naturally attached to the condition of a prisoner; and which, like the fetters of a person actually in chains, are less annoying when submitted to with fortitude and equanimity, than when the captive struggles in vain to wrench himself out of their gripe. We are far, nevertheless, from saying, that the weight of the fetters in the one case, and the hardship of the personal restrictions in the other, are in themselves evils which can be easily endured by those who sustain them. We feel especially how painful the loss of liberty must have been to one who had not only enjoyed the freedom of his own actions, but the uncontrolled right of directing those of others. Impatience, however, in this, as in other instances, has only the prerogative of injuring its master. In the many hours of meditation which were afforded to Buonaparte by his residence in St. Helena, we can never perceive any traces of the reflection, that he owed his present unhappy situation less to the immediate influence of those who were agents in his defeat and imprisonment, than to that course of ambition, which, sparing neither the liberties of France, nor the independence of Europe, had at length rendered his personal freedom inconsistent with the rights of the world in general. He felt the distresses of his situation, but he did not, or could not, reason on their origin. It is impossible to reflect upon him without the idea being excited, of a noble lion imprisoned within a narrow and gloomy den, and venting the wrath which once made the forest tremble, upon the petty bolts and bars, which, insignificant as they are, defy his lordly strength, and detain him captive.

The situation was in every respect a painful one; nor is it possible to refuse our sympathy, not only to the prisoner, but to the person whose painful duty it became to be his superintendent. His duty of detaining Napoleon's person was to be done most strictly, and required a man of that extraordinary firmness of mind, who should never yield for one instant his judgment to his feelings, and should be able at once to detect and reply to all such false arguments, as might be used to deter him from the downright and manful discharge of his office. But, then, there ought to have been combined with those rare qualities a calmness of temper almost equally rare, and a generosity of mind, which, confident in its own honour and integrity, could look with serenity and compassion upon the daily and hourly effects of the maddening causes, which tortured into a state of constant and unendurable irritability the extraordinary being subjected to their influence. Buonaparte, indeed, and the followers who reflected his passions, were to be regarded on all occasions as men acting and speaking under the feverish and delirious influence of things long past, and altogether destitute of the power of cool or clear reasoning, on any grounds that exclusively referred to things present. The emperor could not forget his empire, the husband could not forget his wife, the father his child, the hero his triumphs, the legislator his power. It was scarce in nature, that a brain agitated by such recollections should remain composed under a change so fearful, or be able to reflect calmly on what he now was, when agitated by the extraordinary contrast of his present situation with what he had been. To have soothed him would have been a vain attempt; but the honour of England required that he should have no cause of irritation, beyond those which severely enough attached to his condition as a captive.

From the character we have given of Sir George Cockburn, it may be supposed that he was attentive, as far as his power extended, and his duty permitted, to do all that could render Napoleon's situation more easy. The various authors, Dr. O'Meara, Las Cases, Santini, and others, who have written with much violence concerning Sir Hudson Lowe's conduct, have mentioned that of Sir George as fair, honourable, and conciliatory. No doubt there were many occasions, as the actual inconveniences of the place were experienced, and as the rays of undefined hope vanished from their eyes, when Napoleon and his followers became unreasonably captious in their discussions with the admiral. On such occasions he pursued with professional bluntness the straightforward path of duty, leaving it to the French gentlemen to be sullen as long as they would, and entering into communication again with them whenever they appeared to desire it. It was probably this equanimity, which, notwithstanding various acknowledgments of his good and honourable conduct towards them, seemed to have drawn upon Sir George Cockburn the censure of M. Las Cases, and something that was meant as a species of insult from Napoleon himself. As Sir George Cockburn is acknowledged on the whole to have discharged his duty towards them with mildness and temper, we are the rather tempted to enter into their grounds of complaint against him, because they tend to show the exasperated and ulcerated state of mind with which these unfortunate gentlemen regarded those, who, in their present office, had no alternative but to discharge the duty which their sovereign and country had imposed upon them.

At the risk of being thought trifling with our readers' patience, we shall recapitulate the grievances complained of by Las Cases, who frankly admits, that the bad humour, arising out of his situation, may have in some degree influenced his mind in judging of Sir George Cockburn's conduct, and shall subjoin to each charge the answer which seems to correspond to it.

RECAPITULATION

1st, The admiral is accused of having called the Emperor Napoleon, *General Buonaparte*; and to have pronounced the words with an air of self-satisfaction, which showed that the expression gratified him. It is replied, that Sir George Cockburn's instructions were to address Napoleon by that epithet; and the commentary on the looks or tone with which he did so, is hypercritical.—2d, Napoleon was quartered in Briars for two months, while the admiral himself resided in Plantation-house. Answered, that the instructions of Government were, that Napoleon should remain on board till his abode was prepared; but finding that would occupy so much more time than was expected, Sir George Cockburn, on his own responsibility, placed him on shore, and at Briars, as being the residence which he himself preferred.—3d, The admiral placed sentinels under Napoleon's windows. Replied, it is the usual practice when prisoners of importance are to be secured, especially if they do not even offer their parole that they will make no attempt to escape.—4th, Sir George did not permit any one to visit Napoleon without his permission. Replied, it seemed a necessary consequence of his situation, until Sir George should be able to distinguish those visitors who might be with propriety admitted to an unlimited privilege of visiting the important prisoner.—5th, He invited Napoleon to a ball, by the title of General Buonaparte. The subject of the title has been already discussed; and it does not appear how its being used in sending an invitation to a convivial party, could render the name by which the admiral was instructed to address his prisoner more offensive than on other occasions.—6th, Sir George Cockburn, pressed by Bertrand's notes, in which he qualified the prisoner as an emperor, replied sarcastically, that he knew of no emperor at St. Helena, nor had heard that any European emperor was at present travelling abroad. Replied, by referring to the admiral's instructions, and by the fact, that if an emperor can abdicate his quality, certainly Napoleon was no longer one.—7th, Sir George Cockburn is said to have influenced the opinions of others upon this subject, and punished with arrest some subordinate persons, who used the phrase of emperor. Answered as before, he had orders from his government not to suffer Buonaparte to be addressed as emperor, and it was his duty to cause them to be obeyed. He could not, however, have been very rigorous, since Monsieur La Cases informs us that the officers of the 53d used the *mezzotermine* Napoleon, apparently without censure from the governor.—Lastly, There remains only to be added the complaint, that there was an orderly officer appointed to attend Napoleon when he went beyond certain limits, a point of precaution which must be very useful, if not indispensable, where vigilant custody is required.

From this summary of offences, it must be plain to the reader, that the resentment of Las Cases and his master was not so much against Sir George Cockburn personally, as against his office; and that the admiral would have been very acceptable, if he could have reconciled it to his duty to treat Napoleon as an emperor and a free man; suffered himself, like Sir Niel Campbell, to be admitted or excluded from his presence, as the etiquette of an imperial court might dictate; and run the risk of being rewarded for his complaisance by learning, when he least looked for it, that Napoleon had sailed for America, or perhaps for France. The question how far Britain, or rather Europe, had a right to keep Napoleon prisoner, has already been discussed. If they had no such right, and if a second insurrection in France, a second field of Waterloo, should be hazarded, rather than that Napoleon Buonaparte should suffer diminution of dignity, or restraint of freedom, then Napoleon had a right to complain of the ministry, but not of the officer, to whom his instructions were to be at once the guide and vindication of his conduct.

While these things passed at St. Helena, the ministry of Great Britain were employed in placing the detention of the Ex-Emperor under the regulation of an act of Parliament, which interdicted all intercourse and commerce with St. Helena, excepting by the East India Company's regular chartered vessels. Ships not so chartered, attempting to trade or touch at St. Helena, or hovering within eight leagues of the island, were declared subject to seizure and confiscation. The crews of the vessels who came on shore, or other persons visiting the island, were liable to be sent on board, at the governor's pleasure; and those who might attempt to conceal themselves on shore, were declared subject to punishment. Ships were permitted to approach upon stress of weather, but it was incumbent on them to prove the indispensable necessity, and while they remained at St. Helena, they were watched in the closest manner. A clause of indemnity protected the governor and commissioners from any act transgressing the letter of the law, which they might already have committed, while detaining Napoleon in custody. Such was the act 56 George III. ch. 23, which legalized the confinement of Napoleon at St. Helena.[222]

Another convention betwixt the principal powers of Europe, at Paris, 2d August, 1815, had been also entered into upon the subject of Napoleon, and the custody of his person. It set forth, I. That, in order to render impossible any further attempt on the part of Napoleon Buonaparte against the repose of the world, he should be considered as prisoner to the high contracting powers, the King of Great Britain and Ireland, the Emperor of Austria, the Emperor of Russia, and the King of Prussia. II. That the custody of his person was committed to the British Government, and it was remitted to them to choose the most secure place and mode of detaining him in security. III. That the courts of Austria, Russia, and Prussia, were to name commissioners who were to inhabit the same place which should be assigned for Napoleon Buonaparte's residence, and who, without being responsible for his detention, should certiorate themselves that he was actually present. IV. His Most Christian Majesty was also invited to send a commissioner. V. The King of Great Britain engaged faithfully to comply with the conditions assigned to him by this convention.[223]

Of these powers, only three availed themselves of the power, or privilege, of sending commissioners to St. Helena. These were Count Balmain, on the part of Russia, Baron Sturmer for Austria, and an old emigrant nobleman, the Marquis de Montchenu, for France. Prussia seems to have thought the expense of a resident commissioner at St. Helena unnecessary. Indeed, it does not appear that any of these gentlemen had an important part to play while at St. Helena, but yet their presence was necessary to place what should pass there under the vigilance of accredited representatives of the high powers who had engaged in the Convention of Paris. The imprisonment of Napoleon was now not the work of England

---

[222] Parl. Debates, vol. xxxiii., p. 213.
[223] Parl. Debates, vol. xxxiii., p. 235.

alone, but of Europe, adopted by her most powerful states, as a measure indispensable for public tranquillity.

SIR HUDSON LOWE

Several months before the arrival of the commissioners, Sir George Cockburn was superseded in his anxious and painful office by Sir Hudson Lowe, who remained Governor of St. Helena, and had the charge of Napoleon's person, until the death of that remarkable person. The conduct of this officer has been censured, in several of the writings which have treated of Napoleon's confinement, with such extremity of bitterness as in some measure defeats its own end, and leads us to doubt the truth of charges which are evidently brought forward under deep feelings of personal animosity to the late Governor of St. Helena. On the other hand, it would require a strong defence on the part of Sir Hudson Lowe himself, refuting or explaining many things which as yet have neither received contradiction nor commentary, to induce us to consider him as the very rare and highly exalted species of character, to whom, as we have already stated, this important charge ought to have been intrusted.

Sir Hudson Lowe had risen to rank in the army while serving chiefly in the Mediterranean, in a foreign corps in the pay of England. In this situation he became master of the French and Italian languages, circumstances which highly qualified him for the situation to which he was appointed. In the campaign of 1814, he had been attached to the army of the allies, and carried on a correspondence with the English Government, describing the events of the campaign, part of which was published, and intimates spirit and talent in the writer. Sir Hudson Lowe received from several of the allied sovereigns and generals the most honourable testimonies of his services that could be rendered. He had thus the opportunity and habit of mixing with persons of distinction in the discussion of affairs of importance; and his character as a gentleman and a man of honour was carefully inquired into, and highly vouched, ere his nomination was made out. These were points on which precise inquiries could be made, and distinct answers received, and they were all in favour of Sir Hudson Lowe.

But there were other qualifications, and those not less important, his possession of which could only be known by putting him upon trial. The indispensable attribute, for example, of an imperturbable temper, was scarce to be ascertained, until his proceedings in the office intrusted to him should show whether he possessed or wanted it. The same must be said of that firmness and decision, which dictate to an official person the exact line of his duty—prevent all hesitation or wavering in the exercise of his purpose—render him, when it is discharged, boldly and firmly confident that he has done exactly that which he ought—and enable him fearlessly to resist all importunity which can be used to induce him to change his conduct, and to contemn all misrepresentations and obloquy which may arise from his adhering to it.

Knowing nothing of Sir Hudson Lowe personally, and allowing him to possess the qualities of an honourable, and the accomplishments of a well-informed man, we are inclined, from a review of his conduct, divesting it so far as we can of the exaggerations of his personal enemies, to think there remain traces of a warm and irritable temper, which seems sometimes to have overborne his discretion, and induced him to forget that his prisoner was in a situation where he ought not, even when his conduct seemed most unreasonable and most provoking, to be considered as an object of resentment, or as being subject, like other men, to retort and retaliation. Napoleon's situation precluded the possibility of his inflicting an insult, and therefore the temper of the person to whom such was offered, ought, if possible, to have remained cool and unruffled. It does not seem to us that this was uniformly the case.

In like manner, Sir Hudson Lowe appears to have been agitated by an oppressive sense of the importance and the difficulties of his situation, to a nervous and irritating degree. This over-anxiety led to frequent changes of his regulations, and to the adoption of measures which were afterwards abandoned, and perhaps again resumed. All this uncertainty occasioned just subject of complaint to his prisoner; for, though a captive may become gradually accustomed to the fetters which he wears daily in the same manner, he must be driven to impatience if the mode of adjusting them be altered from day to day.

It is probable that the warm temper of Sir Hudson Lowe was in some degree convenient to Napoleon, as it afforded him the means of reprisals upon the immediate instrument of his confinement, by making the governor feel a part of the annoyance which he himself experienced. Sir George Cockburn had been *in seipso totus, teres, atque rotun dus.* He did what his duty directed, and cared little what Napoleon thought or said upon the subject. The new governor was vulnerable; he could be rendered angry, and might therefore be taken at advantage. Thus Napoleon might enjoy the vindictive pleasure, too natural to the human bosom, of giving pain to the person who was the agent, though not the author, in the restrictions to which he himself was subjected. But Napoleon's interest in provoking the governor did not rest upon the mere gratification of spleen. His views went far deeper, and were connected with the prospect of obtaining his liberty, and with the mode by which he hoped to accomplish it. And this leads us to inquire upon what these hopes were rested, and to place before our readers evidence of the most indisputable credit, concerning the line of policy adopted in the councils of Longwood.

GOURGAUD

It must be premised that the military gentlemen, who, so much to the honour of their own fidelity, had attended on Buonaparte, to soften his calamity by their society and sympathy, were connected by no other link than their mutual respect for the same unhappy master. Being unattached to each other by any ties of friendship, or community of feelings or pursuits, it is no wonder that these officers, given up to ennui, and feeling the acidity of temper which such a situation is sure to cause, should have had misunderstandings, nay, positive quarrels, not with the governor only, but with each other. In these circumstances, the conduct of General Gourgaud distinguished him from the rest. After the peace of Paris, this officer had been aide-de-camp to the Duke of Berri, a situation which he abandoned on Napoleon's return at the period of the Hundred Days. As he was in attendance upon the Ex-Emperor at the moment of his fall, he felt it his duty to accompany him to St. Helena. While upon that island, he took less share in Napoleon's complaints and quarrels with the governor, than either Generals Bertrand and Montholon, or Count Las Cases, avoided all appearance of intrigue with the inhabitants, and was regarded by Sir Hudson Lowe as a brave and loyal soldier, who followed his emperor in adversity, without taking any part in those proceedings which the governor considered as prejudicial to his own authority. As such, he is characterised uniformly in Sir Hudson's despatches to his Government.

This officer had left in France a mother and sister, to whom he was tenderly devoted, and who loved him with the fondest affection. From attachment to these beloved relatives, and their affecting desire that he should rejoin them, General Gourgaud became desirous of revisiting his native country; and his resolution was the stronger, that considerable jealousies and misunderstandings arose betwixt him and Count Bertrand. In these circumstances, he applied for and obtained permission from the governor, to return to London direct. Before leaving St. Helena, he was very communicative both to Sir Hudson Lowe and Baron Sturmer, the Austrian commissioner, respecting the secret hopes and plans which were carrying on at Longwood. When he arrived in Britain in the spring 1818, he was no less frank and open with the British Government; informing them of the various proposals for escape which had been laid before Napoleon; the facilities and difficulties which attended them, and the reasons why he preferred remaining on the island, to making the attempt. At this period it was supposed that General Gourgaud was desirous of making his peace with the King of France; but whatever might be his private views, the minutes of the information which he afforded to Sir Hudson Lowe and Baron Sturmer at St. Helena, and afterwards at London to the Under Secretary at War, are still preserved in the records of the Foreign Office. They agree entirely with each other, and their authenticity cannot be questioned. The communications are studiously made, with considerable reserve as to proper names, in order that no individual should be called in question for any thing which is there stated; and in general they bear, as was to be expected, an air of the utmost simplicity and veracity. We shall often have occasion to allude to these documents, that the reader may be enabled to place the real purposes of Napoleon in opposition to the language which he made use of for accomplishing them; but we have not thought it proper to quote the minutes at length, unless as far as Napoleon is concerned. We understand that General Gourgaud, on his return to the continent, has resumed that tenderness to Napoleon's memory, which may induce him to regret having communicated the secrets of his prison-house to less friendly ears. But this change of sentiments can neither diminish the truth of his evidence, nor affect our right to bring forward what we find recorded as communicated by him.

Having thus given an account of the evidence we mean to use, we resume the subject of Napoleon's quarrels with Sir Hudson Lowe.

It was not, according to General Gourgaud, for want of means of escape, that Napoleon continued to remain at St. Helena. There was one plan for carrying him out in a trunk with dirty linen; and so general was the opinion of the extreme stupidity of the English sentinels, that there was another by which it was proposed he should slip through the camp in disguise of a servant carrying a dish. When the Baron Sturmer represented the impossibility of such wild plans being in agitation, Gourgaud answered, "There was no impossibility to those who had millions at their command. Yes, I repeat it," he continued, "he can escape from hence, and go to America whenever he has a mind."[224]—"Why, then, should he remain here?" said Baron Sturmer. Gourgaud replied, "That all his followers had urged him to make the experiment of escape; but he preferred continuing on the island. He has a secret pride in the consequence attached to the custody of his person, and the interest generally taken in his fate. He has said repeatedly, 'I can no longer

---

[224] "*Je le répète, il peut s'évader seul, et aller en Amérique quand il le voudra.*" Taken from a report of Baron Sturmer to Prince Metternich, giving an account of General Gourgaud's communications, dated 14th March, 1818.—S.

live as a private person. I would rather be a prisoner on this rock, than a free but undistinguished individual in the United States."[225]

General Gourgaud said, therefore, that the event to which Napoleon trusted for liberty, was some change of politics in the court of Great Britain, which should bring into administration the party who were now in opposition, and who, he rather too rashly perhaps conceived, would at once restore to him his liberty. The British ministers received the same assurances from General Gourgaud with those given at St. Helena. These last are thus expressed in the original:—

"Upon the subject of General Buonaparte's escape, M. Gourgaud stated confidently, that although Longwood was, from its situation, capable of being well protected by sentries, yet he was certain that there would be no difficulty in eluding at any time the vigilance of the sentries posted round the house and grounds; and, in short, that escape from the island appeared to him in no degree impracticable. The subject, he confessed, had been discussed at Longwood amongst the individuals of the establishment, who were separately desired to give their plans for effecting it. But he expressed his belief to be, that General Buonaparte was so fully impressed with the opinion, that he would be permitted to leave St. Helena, either upon a change of ministry in England, or by the unwillingness of the English to bear the expense of detaining him, that he would not at present run the hazard to which an attempt to escape might expose him. It appeared, however, from the statement of General Gourgaud, and from other circumstances stated by him, that Buonaparte had always looked to the period of the removal of the allied armies from France as that most favourable for his return; and the probability of such an event, and the consequences which would flow from it, were urged by him as an argument to dissuade General Gourgaud from quitting him until after that period."

WARDEN—O'MEARA, ETC

---

[225] "*Je ne puis plus vivre en particulier. J'aime mieux être prisonnier ici, que abre aux Etats Unis.*"—S.

General Gourgaud's communications further bear, what, indeed, can be collected from many other circumstances, that as Napoleon hoped to obtain his liberty from the impression to be made on the minds of the English nation, he was careful not to suffer his condition to be forgotten, and most anxious that the public mind should be carefully kept alive to it, by a succession of publications coming out one after another, modified according to the different temper and information of the various authors, but bearing all of them the stamp of having issued in whole or in part from the interior of Longwood. Accordingly, the various works of Warden,[226] O'Meara,[227] Santini,[228] the letter of Montholon,[229] and other publications upon St. Helena,[230] appeared one after another, to keep the subject awake; which, although seemingly discharged by various hands, bear the strong peculiarity of being directed at identically the same mark, and of being arrows from the same quiver. Gourgaud mentioned this species of file-firing, and its purpose. Even the *Manuscrit de St. Hélène*, a tract, in which dates and facts were misplaced and confounded, was also, according to General Gourgaud, the work of Buonaparte, and composed to puzzle and *mystify* the British public. He told Sir Hudson Lowe that he was not to consider the abuse in these various pamphlets as levelled against him personally, but as written upon political calculation, with the view of extorting some relaxation of vigilance by the reiteration of complaints. The celebrated Letter of Montholon was, according to the same authority, written in a great measure by Napoleon; and the same was the case with Santini's, though so grossly over coloured that he himself afterwards disowned it.[231] Other papers, he said, would appear under the names of captains of merchantmen and the like, for Napoleon was possessed by a mania for scribbling, which had no interruption. It becomes the historian, therefore, to receive with caution the narratives of those who have thus taken a determinedly partial part in the controversy, and concocted their statements from the details

---

[226] Warden's Letters from St. Helena.
[227] Voice from St. Helena, &c.
[228] Appeal to the British Nation, &c. By M. Santini, Porter of the Emperor's closet.
[229] Official Memoir, dictated by Napoleon; being a Letter from Count de Montholon to Sir Hudson Lowe.
[230] Manuscrit venu de St. Hélène d'une manière inconnue, &c.
[231] "Santini has published a brochure full of trash. There are some truths in it; but every thing is exaggerated."—Napoleon, *Voice*, &c., vol. ii., p. 76.

afforded by the party principally concerned. If what General Gourgaud has said be accurate, it is Napoleon who is pleading his own cause under a borrowed name, in the pages of O'Meara, Santini, Montholon, &c. Even when the facts mentioned in these works, therefore, are undeniable, still it is necessary to strip them of exaggeration, and place them in a fair and just light before pronouncing on them.

The evidence of O'Meara, as contained in a *Voice from St. Helena*, is that of a disappointed man, bitterly incensed against Sir Hudson Lowe, as the cause of his disappointment. He had no need to kindle the flame of his own resentment, at that of Buonaparte. But it may be granted that their vindictive feelings must have strengthened each other. The quarrel was the more irreconcilable, as it appears that Dr. O'Meara was originally in great habits of intimacy with Sir Hudson Lowe, and in the custom of repeating at Plantation-house the gossip which he had heard at Longwood. Some proofs of this were laid before the public, in the *Quarterly Review*;[232] and Sir Hudson Lowe's correspondence with government contains various allusions to Mr. O'Meara's authority,[233] down to the period when their mutual confidence was terminated by a violent quarrel.[234]

---

[232] Vol. xxviii., p. 227.

[233] Sir Hudson Lowe writes, for example, to Lord Bathurst, 13th May, 1816:—"Having found Dr. O'Meara, who was attached to Buonaparte's family on the removal of his French physician, very useful in giving information in many instances, and as, if removed, it might be difficult to find another person who might be equally agreeable to General Buonaparte, I have deemed it advisable to suffer him to remain in the family on the same footing as before my arrival." On the 29th of March, 1817, Sir Hudson writes:—"Dr. O'Meara had informed me of the conversations that had occurred, and, with that readiness which he always manifests upon such occasions, immediately wrote them down for me."—S.

[234] "A catastrophe seemed inevitable. Napoleon indeed concluded that there was a determination to bring it about. On the 6th of May, he sent for O'Meara, in order that he might learn his personal position. He desired me to express to him in English, that he had hitherto no cause of complaint against him. It was necessary, he said, to come to an understanding. Was he to consider him as his own physician personally, or merely as a prison doctor, appointed by the English Government? Was he his confessor or his inspector? *Had he made reports respecting him*, or was it his intention to do so if called upon. The doctor replied with great firmness, and in a tone of feeling. He said he had made *no report* respecting the Emperor, and that he could not imagine any instance in which he might be induced to make a report, except in case of serious illness."—Las Cases, tom. i., p. 211.

Count Las Cases is not, in point of impartiality, to be ranked much above Dr. O'Meara. He was originally a French emigrant, a worshipper by profession of royalty, and therefore only changed his idol, not his religion, when he substituted the idol Napoleon for the idol Bourbon. He embraces with passive obedience the interests of his chief, real or supposed, and can see nothing wrong which Napoleon is disposed to think right. He was also the personal enemy of Sir Hudson Lowe. We have no idea that he would falsify the truth; but we cannot but suspect the accuracy of his recollection, when we find he inserts many expressions and incidents in his Journal, long after the period at which it was originally written, and it is to be presumed from memory. Sir Hudson Lowe had the original manuscript for some time in his possession, and we have at present before us a printed copy, in which Sir Hudson has, with his own hand, marked those additions which had been made to the Journal since he saw it in its primitive state. It is remarkable that all, or almost all, the additions which are made to the Journal, consist of passages highly injurious to Sir Hudson Lowe, which had no existence in the original manuscript. These additions must therefore have been made under the influence of recollection, sharpened by angry passions, since they did not at first seem important enough to be preserved. When memory is put on the rack by passion and prejudice, she will recollect strange things; and, like witnesses under the actual torture, sometimes avow what never took place.

ANTOMMARCHI

Of Dr. Antommarchi it is not necessary to say much; he was a legatee of Buonaparte, and an annuitant of his widow, besides being anxious to preserve the countenance of his very wealthy family. He never speaks of Sir Hudson Lowe without rancour. Sir Hudson's first offence against him was inquiring for clandestine correspondence;[235] his last was, preventing the crowd at Napoleon's funeral from pulling to pieces the willow-trees by which the grave was sheltered, besides placing a guard over the place of sepulture.[236] What truth is there, then, to be reposed in an author, who can thus

---

[235] Last Days of the Emperor Napoleon, vol. i., p. 60.
[236] Last Days of the Emperor Napoleon, vol. ii., p. 185.

misrepresent two circumstances—the one imposed on Sir Hudson Lowe by his instructions; the other being what decency and propriety, and respect to the deceased, imperatively demanded?

The mass of evidence shows, that to have remained upon good, or even on decent terms with the governor, would not have squared with the politics of one who desired to have grievances to complain of; and who, far from having the usual motives which may lead a captive and his keeper to a tolerable understanding, by a system of mutual accommodation, wished to provoke the governor, if possible, beyond the extent of human patience, even at the risk of subjecting himself to some new infliction, which might swell the list of wrongs which he was accumulating to lay before the public.

What we have stated above is exemplified by Napoleon's reception of Sir Hudson Lowe, against whom he appears to have adopted the most violent prejudices at the very first interview, and before the governor could have afforded him the slightest disrespect. We quote it, because it shows that the mind of the prisoner was made up to provoke and insult Sir Hudson, without waiting for any provocation on his part.

The governor's first aggression (so represented,) was his requiring permission of *General Buonaparte* to call together his domestics, with a view to their taking the declaration required by the British Government, binding themselves to abide by the rules laid down for the custody of Buonaparte's person. This permission was refused in very haughty terms. If Napoleon had been at the Tuileries, such a request could not have been more highly resented. The servants, however, appeared, and took the necessary declaration. But the affront was not cancelled; "Sir Hudson Lowe had put his finger betwixt Napoleon and his valet-de-chambre." This was on the 27th April, 1816.[237]

Upon the 30th, the governor again paid his respects at Longwood, and was received with one of those calculated bursts of furious passion with which Napoleon was wont to try the courage and shake the nerves of those over whom he desired to acquire

---

[237] Las Cases, tom. ii., p. 89.

influence. He spoke of protesting against the Convention of Paris, and demanded what right the sovereigns therein allied had to dispose of one, their equal always, and often their superior. He called upon the governor for death or liberty—as if it had been in Sir Hudson Lowe's power to give him either the one or the other. Sir Hudson enlarged on the conveniences of the building which was to be sent from England, to supply the present want of accommodation. Buonaparte repelled the proposed consolation with fury. It was not a house that he wanted, it was an executioner and a line. These he would esteem a favour; all the rest was but irony and insult. Sir Hudson Lowe could in reply only hope that he had given no personal offence, and was reminded of his review of the domestics; which reproach he listened to in silence.[238]

Presently afterwards, Napoleon fell on a new and cutting method of exercising Sir Hudson's patience. A book on the campaign of 1814,[239] lay on the table. Napoleon turned up some of the English bulletins, and asked, with a tone which was perfectly intelligible, whether the governor had not been the writer of these letters. Being answered in the affirmative, Napoleon, according to Dr. O'Meara, told Sir Hudson they were full of folly and falsehood; to which the governor, with more patience than most men could have commanded on such an occasion, replied, "I believe I saw what I have stated;"[240] an answer certainly as temperate as could be returned to so gratuitous an insult. After Sir Hudson left the room in which he had been received with so much unprovoked incivility, Napoleon is described as having harangued upon the sinister expression of his countenance, abused him in the coarsest manner, and even caused his valet-de-chambre throw a cup of coffee out of the window, because it had stood a moment on the table beside the governor.[241]

---

[238] Las Cases, tom. ii., p. 115-120.
[239] Hist. de la Campagne de 1814 par Alphonse de Beauchamp.
[240] "It appears that this governor was with Blucher, and is the writer of some official letters to your government, descriptive of part of the operations of 1814. I pointed them out to him, and asked him, 'Est-ce vous, Monsieur?' He replied, 'Yes.' I told him that they were *pleines de faussetés et de sottises*. He shrugged up his shoulders, and replied, '*J'ai cru voir cela*.'"—*Voice*, &c., vol. i., p. 49.
[241] Las Cases, tom. i., p. 121.

Every attempt at conciliation on the part of the governor, seemed always to furnish new subjects of irritation. He sent fowling-pieces to Longwood, and Napoleon returned for answer, it was an insult to give fowling-pieces where there is no game; though Santini, by the way, pretended to support the family in a great measure by his gun. Sir Hudson sent a variety of clothes and other articles from England, which it might be supposed the exiles were in want of. The thanks returned were, that the governor treated them like paupers, and that the articles ought, in due respect, to have been left at the store, or governor's house, while a list was sent to the Emperor's household, that such things were at their command if they had any occasion for them. On a third occasion, Sir Hudson resolved to be cautious. He had determined to give a ball; but he consulted Dr. O'Meara whether Napoleon would take it well to be invited. The doctor foresaw that the fatal address, *General Buonaparte*, would make shipwreck of the invitation. The governor proposed to avoid this stumbling-block, by asking Napoleon verbally and in person. But with no name which his civility could devise for the invitation, could it be rendered acceptable. A governor of St. Helena, as Napoleon himself observed, had need to be a person of great politeness, and at the same time of great firmness.

RUPTURE WITH SIR H. LOWE

At length, on 18th August, a decisive quarrel took place. Sir Hudson Lowe was admitted to an audience, at which was present Sir Pulteney Malcolm, the admiral who now commanded on the station. Dr. O'Meara has preserved the following account of the interview, as it was detailed by Napoleon to his suite, the day after it took place.

"'That governor,' said Napoleon, 'came here yesterday to annoy me. He saw me walking in the garden, and in consequence, I could not refuse to see him. He wanted to enter into some details with me about reducing the expenses of the establishment. He had the audacity to tell me that things were as he found them, and that he came up to justify himself; that he had come up two or three times before to do so, but that I was in a bath.' I replied, 'No, sir, I was not in a bath; but I ordered one on purpose not to see you. In endeavouring to justify yourself you make matters worse.' He said, that I did not know him; that, if I knew him, I should change my opinion. 'Know you, sir!' I answered, 'how could I know you? People make themselves known by their actions—by commanding in battles. You have never commanded in battle. You have never commanded any but vagabond Corsican deserters, Piedmontese and Neapolitan brigands. I know the name of every English general who has distinguished himself; but I never heard of you, except as a *scrivano* [clerk] to Blucher, or as a commandant of brigands. You have never commanded, or been accustomed to men of honour.' He said, that he had not sought for his present situation. I told him that such employments were not asked for; that they were given by governments to people who had dishonoured themselves. He said, that he only did his duty, and that I ought not to blame him, as he only acted according to his orders. I replied, 'So does the hangman; he acts according to his orders. But when he puts a rope about my neck to finish me, is that a reason that I should like that hangman, because he acts according to his orders? Besides, I do not believe that any government could be so mean as to give such orders as you cause to be executed.' I told him, that if he pleased, he need not send up any thing to eat; that I would go over and dine at the table of the brave officers of the 53d; that I was sure there was not one of them who would not be happy to give a plate at the table to an old soldier; that there was not a soldier in the regiment who had not more heart than he had; that in the iniquitous bill of Parliament, they had decreed that I was to be treated as a prisoner; but that he treated me worse than a condemned criminal or a galley slave, as they were permitted to receive newspapers and printed books, of which he deprived me.' I said, 'You have power over my body, but none over my soul. That soul is as proud, fierce, and determined at the present moment, as when it commanded Europe.' I told him that he was a *sbirro Siciliano* (Sicilian thief-taker,) and not an Englishman; and desired him not to let me see him again until he came with orders to despatch me, when he would find all the doors thrown open to admit him.'"[242]

---

[242] *Voice*, &c., vol. i., p. 93.—"The Emperor admitted that he had, during this conversation, seriously and repeatedly offended Sir Hudson Lowe; and he also did him the justice to

It is not surprising that this extreme violence met with some return on Sir Hudson's part. He told Napoleon that his language was uncivil and ungentlemanlike, and that he would not remain to listen to it. Accordingly, he left Longwood without even the usual salutation.

Upon these occasions, we think it is evident that Napoleon was the wilful and intentional aggressor, and that his conduct proceeded either from the stings of injured pride, or a calculated scheme, which made him prefer being on bad rather than good terms with Sir Hudson Lowe. On the other hand, we could wish that the governor had avoided entering upon the subject of the expenses of his detention with Napoleon in person. The subject was ill-chosen, and could produce no favourable result.

They never afterwards met in friendship, or even on terms of decent civility; and having given this account of their final quarrel, it only remains for us to classify, in a general manner, the various subjects of angry discussion which took place betwixt them, placed in such uncomfortable relative circumstances, and each determined not to give way to the other's arguments, or accommodate himself to the other's wishes or convenience.

---

acknowledge, that Sir Hudson had not precisely shown, in a single instance, any want of respect; he had contented himself with muttering, between his teeth, sentences which were not audible. The only failure, perhaps, on the part of the governor, and which was trifling, compared with the treatment he had received, was the abrupt way in which he retired, while the admiral withdrew slowly, and with numerous salutes."—Las Cases, tom. iii., p. 222.

CHAPTER XCV

Instructions to Sir Hudson Lowe—Sum allowed for the Ex-Emperor's Expenses—Napoleon's proposal to defray his own Expenses—Sale of his Plate—made in order to produce a false impression: he had at that time a large sum of Money in his strong-box—Wooden-House constructed in London, and transported to St. Helena—Interview between Sir H. Lowe and Napoleon—Delays in the Erection of the House—The Regulation that a British Officer should attend Napoleon in his Rides—Communication with Europe carried on by the Inmates of Longwood—Regulation respecting Napoleon's Intercourse with the Inhabitants of St. Helena—General Reflections on the Disputes between him and Sir H. Lowe.

LOWE'S INSTRUCTIONS

Before entering upon such brief inquiry as our bounds will permit, into the conduct of the new governor towards Napoleon, it may be necessary to show what were his, Sir Hudson Lowe's, instructions from the English Government on the subject of the custody of the Ex-Emperor:—

"*Downing Street, 12th September, 1816.*

"You will observe, that the desire of his Majesty's Government is, to allow every indulgence to General Buonaparte, which may be compatible with the entire security of his person. That he should not by any means escape, or hold communication with any person whatsoever, excepting through your agency, must be your unremitted care; and those points being made sure, every resource and amusement, which may serve to reconcile Buonaparte to his confinement, may be permitted."

A few weeks later, the Secretary of State wrote to Sir Hudson Lowe a letter to the same purpose with the former, 26th October, 1816:—

"With respect to General Buonaparte himself, I deem it unnecessary to give you any farther instructions. I am confident that your own disposition will prompt you to anticipate the wishes of his Royal Highness the Prince Regent, and make every allowance for the effect which so sudden a change of situation cannot fail to produce on a person of his irritable temper. You will, however, not permit your forbearance or generosity towards him to interfere with any regulations which may have been established for preventing his escape, or which you may hereafter consider necessary for the better security of his person."

The just and honourable principle avowed by Government is obvious. But it was an extraordinary and most delicate tax upon Sir Hudson Lowe, which enjoined him to keep fast prisoner an individual, who, of all others, was likely to be most impatient of restraint, and, at the same time, to treat him with such delicacy as might disguise his situation from himself, if it could not reconcile him to it. If Sir Hudson failed in doing so, he may be allowed to plead, that it was in a case in which few could have succeeded. Accordingly, Napoleon's complaints against the governor were bitter and clamorous.

HOUSEHOLD EXPENSES

The first point of complaint on the part of the family at Longwood, respected the allowance assigned by the British Government for their support, which they alleged to be insufficient to their wants. This was not a point on which Napoleon thought it proper to express his feelings in his own person. *His* attention was apparently fixed upon obtaining concessions in certain points of etiquette, which might take him from under the condition in which he was most unwilling to allow himself to be placed, in the rank, namely, of a prisoner of war. The theme, of the inadequacy of the allowance, was not, however, left untouched, as those concerned were well aware that there was no subject of grievance which would come more home to the people of England than one which turned upon a deficiency either in the quantity or quality of the food supplied to the exiles. Montholon's letter was clamant on the subject; and Santini intimated, that the Emperor must sometimes have gone without a meal altogether, had he (Santini) not been successful with his gun.

The true state of the case was this:—The British Government had determined that Napoleon's table should be provided for at the rate of a general of the first rank, together with his military family. The expense of such an establishment was, by the regulations furnished to Sir Hudson Lowe, dated 15th April, and 22d November, 1816, supposed to reach to £8000 a-year, with permission, however, to extend it as far as £12,000, should he think it necessary. The expense could not, in Sir Hudson Lowe's opinion, be kept within £8000; and indeed it was instantly extended by him to £12,000, paid in monthly instalments to the purveyor, Mr. Balcombe, by whom it was expended in support of the establishment at Longwood. If, however, even £12,000, the sum fixed as a probable ultimatum, should, in the governor's opinion, be found, from dearth, high price of provisions, or otherwise, practically insufficient to meet and answer the expense of a general's family, calculated on a liberal scale, Sir Hudson Lowe had liberty from Government to extend the purveyor's allowance without limitation. But if, on the other hand, the French should desire to add to their housekeeping any thing which the governor should think superfluous, in reference to the rank assigned to the principal person, they were themselves to be at the charge of such extraordinary expenditure.

It is apprehended that the British Government could not be expected to do more for Napoleon's liberal maintenance, than to give the governor an unlimited order to provide for it, upon the scale applicable to the rank of a general officer of the first rate. But yet the result, as the matter was managed, was not so honourable to

Great Britain, as the intentions of the Government really designed. The fact is, that virtues as well as vices have their day of fashion in England; and at the conclusion of the peace, when the nation were cloyed with victory, men began, like epicures after a feast, to wrangle about the reckoning. Every one felt the influence of the *Quart d'heure de Rabelais*. It ascended into the Houses of Parliament, and economy was the general theme of the day. There can be no doubt that a judicious restriction upon expenditure is the only permanent source of national wealth; but, like all other virtues, parsimony may be carried to an extreme, and there are situations in which it has all the meanness of avarice. The waste of a few pounds of meat, of a hundred billets of wood, of a few bottles of wine, ought not to have been made the shadow of a question between Britain and Napoleon; and it would have been better to have winked at and given way to the prodigality of a family, which had no motives of economy on their own part, than to be called upon to discuss such petty domestic details in the great council of the nation, sitting as judges betwixt England and her prisoner. A brief answer to those who might in that case have charged the government with prodigality, might have been found in referring the censors to the immense sums saved by the detention of Napoleon in St. Helena. It is something of a different scale of expense, which is requisite to maintain a score of persons even in the most extravagant manner, and to support an army of three hundred thousand men.

But although such disputes arose, we think, from the governor mistaking the meaning of the British ministers, and descending, if he really did so, to details about the quality of salt or sugar to be used in the kitchen at Longwood, there is no reason to entertain the belief that the prisoners had any actual restriction to complain of, though it might not always happen that articles of the first quality could be procured at St. Helena so easily as at Paris. The East India Company sent out the supplies to the purveyor, and they consisted of every luxury which could be imagined; so that delicacies very unusual in St. Helena could, during Napoleon's residence, be obtained there for any one who chose to be at the expense. The wine was (generally speaking) excellent in quality, and of the first price;[243] and although there was rather too much said and thought about the quantity consumed, yet it was furnished, as we shall hereafter see, in a quantity far beyond the limits of ordinary conviviality. Indeed, though the French officers, while hunting for grievances, made complaints of their treatment at table, and circulated, in such books as that of Santini, the grossest scandal on that subject, yet when called on as men of honour to give their opinion, they did justice to the governor in this respect.

In a letter of General Bertrand to the governor, he expresses himself thus:—"Be assured that we are well persuaded of the good intentions of the governor, to supply us with every thing necessary, and that as to provisions there will never be any complaints, or if there are, they will be made against the government, not against the governor, upon whom the matter does not depend." He adds, "that such were the sentiments of the Emperor. That indeed they had been under some difficulties when the plate was broken up, but that ever since then they had been well supplied, and had no complaint whatever to make." Such is the evidence of Count Bertrand, when deliberately writing to the governor through his military secretary.

But we have also the opinion of the Ex-Emperor himself, transmitted by Dr. O'Meara, who was at that time, as already noticed, in the habit of sending to the governor such scraps of information as he heard in conversation at Longwood:

"*5th June, 1817.*

"He (Buonaparte) observed that Santini's was a foolish production, exaggerated, full of *coglionerie*, and some lies: Truths there were in it, but exaggerated. That there never had existed that actual want described by him; that there had been enough to eat supplied, but not enough to keep a proper table; that there had been enough of wine for them; that there certainly had been sometimes a deficiency of necessary articles, but that this might be accounted for

---

[243] The claret, for example, was that of Carbonel, at £6 per dozen without duty. Each domestic of superior rank was allowed a bottle of this wine, which is as choice, as dear certainly, as could be brought to the table of sovereigns. The labourers and soldiers had each, daily, a bottle of Teneriffe wine of excellent quality.—S.

by accidents; that he believed frequent purchases had been made, at the camp, of bread and other provisions, which might also have occasionally arisen from the same cause. He added, he was convinced some Englishman had written it, and not Santini."

There is something to the same purpose in Dr. O'Meara's printed book,[244] but not so particular. What makes Napoleon's confutation of Santini's work the more amusing, is, that according to General Gourgaud's communication to the British Government, Napoleon was himself the author of the whole, or greater part, of the work in question. The difference between the prisoner and governor, so far as it really existed, may have had its rise in the original dispute; for a table, which suited the rank of a general, must have been considerably inferior to one kept for an emperor; and while the former was what the governor was directed to maintain, the latter was what Napoleon conceived himself entitled to expect.

The permission given to Buonaparte, and which indeed could not be well refused, to purchase from his own funds what additional articles he desired beyond those supplied by the British Government, afforded peculiar facilities to the French, which they did not fail to make use of. Napoleon's money had been temporarily taken into custody when he left the Bellerophon, with a view to prevent his having the means of facilitating his escape by bribery. The permitting him to draw upon the Continent for money, would have been in a great measure restoring to him the golden key before which prison-gates give way, and also tending to afford him the means of secret correspondence with those friends abroad, who might aid him to arrange a scheme of flight.

Indeed, the advantages of this species of correspondence were of such evident importance, that Napoleon, through General Montholon, made the following proposal, which was sent to Lord Bathurst by the governor, 8th September, 1816:—

"The Emperor," he said, "was desirous to enter into arrangements for paying the *whole* of his expenses, providing any house here, or in England, or on the continent of Europe, to be

---

[244] Voice, &c., vol. ii., p. 76.

fixed on with the governor's consent, or even at his own choice, were appointed to transact his money-matters; under assurance from him, General Buonaparte, that all letters sent through his hands would be solely on pecuniary affairs. But provided always, that such letters should pass *sealed and unopened* to their direction."

It is probable that Napoleon concluded, from the ferment which was at that time taking place in Parliament on the subject of economy, that the English nation was on the point of bankruptcy, and did not doubt that an offer, which promised to relieve them of £12,000 a-year, would be eagerly caught at by Sir Hudson Lowe, or the British Ministry. But the governor saw the peril of a measure, which, in its immediate and direct tendency, went to place funds to any amount at the command of the Ex-Emperor, and might, more indirectly, lead the way to private correspondence of every kind. Napoleon, indeed, had offered to plight his word, that the communication should not be used for any other than pecuniary purposes; but Sir Hudson liked not the security. On his part, the governor tendered a proposal, that the letters to the bankers should be visible only to himself, and to Lord Bathurst, the secretary for the colonial department, and pledged his word that they would observe the most inviolable secrecy on the subject of the contents; but this arrangement did not answer Napoleon's purposes, and the arrangement was altogether dropped.

It was about the same time that Sir Hudson Lowe was desirous to keep the expense of the establishment within £12,000. A conference on this subject was held betwixt General Montholon, who took charge of the department of the household, and Major Gorrequer, belonging to Sir Hudson's staff, who acted on the part of the governor. It appears that Sir Hudson had either misapprehended the instructions of the government, and deemed himself rigidly bound to limit the expenses of Longwood within £12,000 yearly, not adverting that he had an option to extend it beyond that sum; or else that he considered the surplus above £1000 per month, to consist of such articles of extra expenditure as the French might, in a free interpretation of his instructions, be required to pay for themselves, as being beyond the limits of a general-officer's table, provided upon the most liberal plan. General

Montholon stated, that the family could not be provided, even after many reductions, at a cheaper rate than £15,194, and that this was the *minimum of minimums*, the least possible sum. He offered, that the Emperor would draw for the sum wanted, providing he was permitted to send a sealed letter to the banking-house. This, Major Gorrequer said, could not be allowed. Count Montholon then declared, that as the Emperor was not permitted by the British Government to have access to his funds in Europe, he had no other means left than to dispose of his property here; and that if the Emperor was obliged to defray those expenses of the establishment, which went beyond the allowance made by Britain, he must dispose of his plate.

This proposal was too rashly assented to by Sir Hudson Lowe, whose instructions of 22d November empowered him to have prevented a circumstance so glaringly calculated to accredit all that had ever been said or written respecting the mean and sordid manner in which the late Emperor of France was treated. Napoleon had an opportunity, at the sacrifice of a parcel of old silver plate, to amuse his own moments of languor, by laughing at and turning into ridicule the inconsistent qualities of the English nation—at one time sending him a house and furniture to the value of £60,000 or £70,000; at another, obliging him to sell his plate, and discharge his servants; and all for the sake of a few bottles of wine, or pounds of meat. Sir Hudson Lowe ought not to have exposed his country to such a charge; and, even if his instructions seemed inexplicit on the subject, he ought, on his own interpretation of them, to have paid the extra expense, without giving room to such general scandal as was sure to arise from Napoleon's disposing of his plate.

But if the governor took too narrow a view of his duty upon this occasion, what are we to say of the poor conduct of Napoleon, who, while he had specie in his strong-box to have defrayed three times the sum wanted to defray the alleged balance, yet preferred making the paltry sale alluded to, that he might appear before Europe *in formâ pauperis*, and set up a claim to compassion as a man driven to such extremity as to be obliged to part with the plate from his table, in order to be enabled to cover it with the necessary food! He was well aware that little compassion would have been paid to him, had he been possessed of ready money sufficient to supply any deficiencies in the tolerably ample allowance paid by England; and that it was only the idea of his poverty, proved, as it seemed, by a step, which even private individuals only take in a case of necessity, which made his case appear strong and clamant. The feeling of compassion must have given place to one of a very different kind, had the actual circumstances of the case been fully and fairly known.

The communications of General Gourgaud, upon parting with Sir Hudson Lowe, put the governor in possession of the curious fact, that the breaking up of the plate[245] was a mere trick, resorted to on account of the impression it was calculated to produce in England and Europe; for that at the time they had at Longwood plenty of money. Sir Hudson Lowe conjectured, that General Gourgaud alluded to the sale of some stock belonging to Las Cases, the value of which that devoted adherent had placed at Napoleon's disposal; but General Gourgaud replied, "No, no; before that transaction they had received 240,000 francs, chiefly in Spanish doubloons." He further said, that it was Prince Eugene who lodged the money in the hands of the bankers. In London, General Gourgaud made the same communication. We copy the words in which it is reported by Sir Hudson Lowe to Lord Bathurst:—

"General Gourgaud stated himself to have been aware of General Buonaparte having received a considerable sum of money in Spanish doubloons, viz. £10,000, at the very time he disposed of his plate; but, on being pressed by me as to the persons privy to that transaction, he contented himself with assuring me, that the mode of its transmission was one purely accidental; that it could never again occur; and that, such being the case, he trusted that I should not press a discovery, which, while it betrayed its author, could have no effect, either as it regarded the punishment of the offenders, or the prevention of a similar act in future. The actual possession of

---

[245] "Sept. 19.—The Emperor examined a large basket-full of broken plate, which was to be sent next day to the town. This was to be for the future the indispensable complement for our monthly subsistence, in consequence of the late reductions of the governor. When the moment had come for breaking up this plate, the servants could not, without the greatest reluctance, bring themselves to apply the hammer to these objects of their veneration. This act upset all their ideas; it was to them a sacrilege, a desolation! Some of them shed tears on the occasion!!"—Las Cases, tom. iii., p. 184.

money was, moreover, not likely, in his view of the subject, to afford any additional means of corrupting the fidelity of those whom it might be advisable to seduce; as it was well known, that any draught, whatever might be its amount, drawn by General Buonaparte on Prince Eugene, or on certain other members of his family, would be scrupulously honoured."

He further stated, that it was Napoleon's policy to make a *moyen*, a fund for execution of his plans, by placing sums of money at his, General Gourgaud's command, and that he had sustained ill-treatment on the part of Napoleon, and much importunity on that of Bertrand, because he declined lending himself to facilitate secret correspondence.

Whatever sympathy Buonaparte may claim for his other distresses at St. Helena, it was made plain from this important disclosure, that want of funds could be none of them; and it is no less so, that the trick of selling the plate can now prove nothing, excepting that Napoleon's system was a deceptive one; and that evidence of any sort, arising either from his word or actions, is to be received with caution, when there is an apparent point to be carried by it.

INSTRUCTIONS TO THE GOVERNOR

When Sir Hudson Lowe's report reached England, that the excess of the expenditure at Longwood, about twelve thousand pounds, had been defrayed by Napoleon himself, it did not meet the approbation of the Ministry; who again laid before the governor the distinction which he was to draw betwixt expenses necessary to maintain the table and household of a general officer, and such as might be of a nature different from, and exceeding those attendant on the household of a person of that rank; which last, and those alone, the French might be called on to defray. The order is dated 24th Oct. 1817.

"As I observe from the statement contained in your despatch, No. 84, that the expense of General Buonaparte's establishment exceeds £12,000 per annum, and that the excess beyond that sum has, up to the date of that despatch, been defrayed from his own funds, I deem it necessary again to call your attention to that part of my despatch, No. 15, of the 22d November last, in which, in limiting the expense to £12,000 a-year, I still left you at liberty to incur a farther expenditure, should you consider it to be necessary for the comfort of General Buonaparte; and to repeat, that, *if you should consider the sum of £12,000 a-year not to be adequate to maintain such an establishment as would be requisite for a general officer of distinction, you will have no difficulty in making what you deem to be a requisite addition*. But, on the other hand, if the expenses which General Buonaparte has himself defrayed are beyond what, on a liberal construction, might be proper for a general officer of distinction, you will permit them, as heretofore, to be defrayed from his own funds."

These positive and reiterated instructions serve to show that there was never a wish on the part of Britain to deal harshly, or even closely with Napoleon; as the avowals of General Gourgaud prove, on the other hand, that if the governor was too rigid on the subject of expense, the prisoner possessed means sufficient to have saved him from any possible consequences of self-denial, which might have accrued from being compelled to live at so low a rate as twelve thousand pounds a-year.

The subject of the residence of Napoleon continued to furnish great subjects of complaint and commotion. We have recorded our opinion, that, from the beginning, Plantation-house, as the best residence in the island, ought to have been set apart for his use. If, however, this was objected to, the building a new house from the foundation, even with the indifferent means which the island affords, would have been far more respectable, and perhaps as economical, as constructing a great wooden frame in London, and transporting it to St. Helena, where it arrived, with the furniture destined for it, in May, 1816. It was not, however, a complete *parapluie* house, as such structures have been called, but only the materials for constructing such a one; capable of being erected separately, or, at Napoleon's choice, of being employed for making large and commodious additions to the mansion which he already occupied. It became a matter of courtesy to inquire whether it would best answer Napoleon's idea of convenience that an entirely new edifice should be constructed, or whether that end would be better attained by suffering the former building to remain, and constructing the new one in the form of an addition to it. We have recounted an interview betwixt Napoleon and the governor, in the words of the former, as delivered to O'Meara. The present we give as furnished by Sir Hudson, in a despatch to Lord Bathurst, dated 17th May, 1816:—

INTERVIEW WITH SIR H. LOWE

"It becoming necessary to come to some decision in respect to the house and furniture which had been sent from England for the accommodation of General Buonaparte and his followers, I resolved on waiting upon him, communicating to him the arrival of the various materials, and asking his sentiments with respect to their appropriation, before I made any disposition of them. I previously called on General Bertrand, to ask if he thought General Buonaparte would be at leisure to receive me; and on his reply, which was in the affirmative, I proceeded to Longwood-house, where, having met Count Las Cases, I begged he would be the bearer of my message to the general, acquainting him with my being there, if his convenience admitted of being visited by me. I received a reply, saying, 'The Emperor would see me.'

"I passed through his outer dining-room into his drawing-room. He was alone, standing with his hat under his arm, in the manner in which he usually presents himself when he assumes his imperial dignity. He remained silent, expecting I would address him. Finding him not disposed to commence, I began in the following words:—'Sir, you will probably have seen by our English newspapers, as well, perhaps, as heard through other channels, of the intention of the British Government to send out hither for your accommodation the materials for the construction of a house, with every necessary furniture. These articles have now for the first time arrived. In the meantime, Government has received information of the building prepared for your reception at this place, and I have instructions for appropriating the articles as may seem best, whether for making a new building, or adding to the conveniences of your present one. Before making any disposition on the subject, I waited to know whether you had any desires to communicate to me regarding it.' He stood as before, and made no reply.

"Observing his silence continue, I again commenced by saying, 'I have conceived, sir, that possibly the addition of two or three good rooms (*deux ou trois salons*) to your present house, with other improvements to it, might add to your convenience in less time than by constructing a new building.' He then commenced, but spoke with such rapidity, such intemperance, and so much warmth, that it is difficult to repeat every word he used. Without apparently having lent an ear to what I said, he began—'I do not at all understand the conduct of your government towards me. Do they desire to kill me? And do you come here to be my executioner, as well as my gaoler?—Posterity will judge of the manner in which I have been treated. The misfortunes which I suffer will recoil upon your nation. No, sir; never will I suffer any person to enter into the interior of my house, or penetrate into my bed-chamber, as you have given orders. When I heard of your arrival in this island, I believed that, as being an officer of the army, you would be possessed of a more polite character than an admiral, who is a navy-officer, and might have more harsh manners. I have no reason to complain of his heart. But you, sir—in what manner do you treat me? It is an insult to invite me to dinner by the name of General Buonaparte. I am not General Buonaparte—I am the Emperor Napoleon. I ask you again—have you come hither to be my gaoler—my hangman?' Whilst speaking in this manner, his right arm moved backward and forward; his person stood fixed; his eyes and countenance exhibiting every thing which could be supposed in a person who meant to intimidate or irritate.

"I suffered him to proceed throughout, not without a strong feeling of restraint on myself, until he was really out of breath, when, on his stopping, I said, 'Sir, I am not come here to be insulted, but to treat of an affair which regards you more than me. If you are not disposed to talk upon the subject'——

"'I have no intention to insult you, sir,' he replied; 'but in what sort of manner have you treated me? is it in a soldierlike fashion?'

"I answered, 'Sir, I am a soldier according to the fashion of my own country, to do my duty to her accordingly, and not according to the fashion of foreigners. Besides, if you conceive you have any reason to complain of me, you have only to put your accusation upon paper, and I will send it to England by the first opportunity.'

"'To what good purpose?' he said; 'my complaints will not be more public there than here.'

"'I will cause them be published,' I answered, 'in all the gazettes of the continent, if you desire it. I do my duty, and every thing else is indifferent to me.'

"Then, adverting for the first time to the matter which had brought me to him, he said, 'Your government has made me no official communication of the arrival of this house. Is it to be constructed where I please, or where you may fix it to be?'

"'I am now come, sir, for the express purpose of announcing it to you. I have no difficulty in replying to the other point: If there is any particular spot, which you might have thought of to erect it upon, I will examine it, and have it erected there, if I see no objection to it. If I see any objection to it, I will acquaint you with it. It was to combine this matter in some degree of concert with you that I am now come.'

"'Then you had better speak to the grand maréchal about it, and settle it with him.'

"'I prefer, sir, addressing you upon it. I find so many *mésintelligences* happen, when I adopt the medium of other persons (particularly as in the instance of the orders which you mention I had given for forcing an entrance into your private apartments,) that I find it more satisfactory to address yourself.'

"He made no particular reply to this, walked about for a moment, and then, working himself up apparently to say something which he thought would appal me with extraordinary surprise or dread, he said—'Do you wish me, sir, to tell you the truth? Yes, sir, I ask you if you desire me to tell you the truth? I believe that you have received orders to kill me—yes, to kill me—yes, sir, I believe that you have received orders to stick at nothing—nothing.' He then looked at me, as if expecting a reply. My answer was—'You were pleased to remark, sir, in our last interview, that you had miscalculated the spirit of the English people. Give me leave to say, you at present calculate as erroneously the spirit of an English soldier.'

"Our interview here terminated; and, as if neither of us had any thing more to say, we mutually separated."

Sir Hudson received a letter in reply to his account of this strange and violent scene, in which his forbearance and firmness are approved of. But we quote it, chiefly because it marks the intention of the British Government with respect to Buonaparte, and shows the consideration which they had for his peculiar condition, and the extent of forbearance which it was their desire should be extended towards him by the governor of St. Helena:

"There is a wide distinction between the conduct which you ought to hold towards General Buonaparte, and towards those who have chosen to follow his fortunes, by accompanying him to St. Helena.

"It would be a want of generosity not to make great allowance for the intemperate language into which the former may at times be betrayed. The height from whence he has been precipitated, and all the circumstances which have attended his fall, are sufficient to overset a mind less irritable than his; and it is to be apprehended that he can find little consolation in his reflections, either in the means by which he obtained his power, or his manner of exercising it. So long, therefore, as his violence is confined to words, it must be borne with—always understanding, and giving him to understand, that any wilful transgression, on his part, of the rules which you may think it necessary to prescribe for the security of his person, will place you under the necessity of adopting a system of restraint, which it will be most painful to you to inflict.

"With respect to his followers, they stand in a very different situation; they cannot be too frequently reminded, that their continuance in the island is an act of indulgence on the part of the British Government; and you will inform them that you have received strict instructions to remove them from the person of General Buonaparte, and to transport them out of the island, if they shall not conduct themselves with that respect which your situation demands, and with that strict attention to your regulations which is the indispensable condition on which their residence in the island is permitted."

LONGWOOD

The stormy dispute, which took place on the 16th May, 1816,[246] left every thing unsettled with respect to the house; and indeed it may be conjectured, without injustice, that Napoleon preferred the old and inconvenient mansion, with the right to complain of it as a grievance, to the new and commodious one, the possession of which must have shut his lips upon one fertile subject of misrepresentation. Repeated and equally nugatory discussions on the subject took place during the course of two or three years, all which time Napoleon complained of the want of the promised house, and the governor, on his side, alleged, there was no getting Napoleon to express a fixed opinion on the situation or the plan, or to say whether he would prefer a thorough repair of the old house, occupying M. Bertrand's apartments in the mean while, until the

---

[246] "As I was waiting in the antechamber with the military secretary, I could hear, from the Emperor's tone of voice, that he was irritated. The audience was a very long, and a very clamorous one. On the governor's departure, I went to the garden, whither the Emperor had sent for me. 'Well, Las Cases,' said he, 'we have had a violent scene. I have been thrown quite out of temper! They have now sent me worse than a gaoler! Sir Hudson Lowe is a downright executioner; I received him to-day with my stormy countenance, my head inclined, and my ears pricked up. We looked most furiously at each other. My anger must have been powerfully excited, for I felt a vibration in the calf of my left leg. This is always a sure sign with me; and I have not felt it for a long time before.'"—Las Cases, tom. ii., p. 286.

work should be accomplished. Sometimes Napoleon spoke of changing the situation of the house, but he never, according to Sir Hudson Lowe's averment, intimated any specific wish upon that subject, nor would condescend to say distinctly in what place it should be erected. Napoleon on his part maintained that he was confined for three years in an unhealthy barn, during which time the governor was perpetually talking about a house which had never been commenced. While the blame is thus reciprocally retorted, the impartial historian can only say, that had Sir Hudson Lowe delayed willingly the building of the house, he must have exposed himself to severe censure from his government in consequence, since his despatches were daily urging the task. There was nothing which the governor could place against this serious risk, except the malicious purpose of distressing Napoleon. On the other hand, in submitting to indifferent accommodation, rather than communicate with a man whom he seemed to hold in abhorrence, Napoleon only acted upon his general system, of which this was a part, and sacrificed his convenience, as he afterwards did his health, rather than bend his mind to comply with the regulations of his place of captivity. Mr. Ellis, an unprejudiced witness, declares that the original house seemed to him commodious and well furnished.

The fate of the new house was singular enough. It was at last erected, and is said to be a large and comfortable edifice. But it happened, that the plan directed the building to be surrounded, as is common in England, with something like a sunk ditch, surrounded by cast-iron railing of an ornamental character. No sooner had Napoleon seen these preparations, than the idea of a fortification and a dungeon entered into his head; nor was it possible to convince him that the rails and sunk fence were not intended as additional means of securing his person. When Sir Hudson Lowe learned the objection which had been started, he ordered the ground to be levelled, and the palisade removed. But before this was accomplished, Napoleon's health was too much broken to permit of his being removed, so that he died under the same roof which received him after his temporary residence at Briars.

Another subject of complaint, which Napoleon greatly insisted upon, was, that the governor of St. Helena had not been placed there merely as a ministerial person, to see duly executed the instructions which he should receive from Britain, but as a legislator, himself possessing and exercising the power to alter the regulations under which his prisoner was to be confined, to recall them, to suspend them, and finally, to replace them. To this it must be answered, that in such a situation, where the governor, holding so important a charge, was at so great a distance from the original source of his power, some discretionary authority must necessarily be lodged in him, since cases must occur where he was to act on the event as it arose, and it was indispensable that he should possess the power to do so. It must also be remembered, that different constructions might possibly be given to the instructions from the Secretary of State; and it would, in that case, have been equally anomalous and inconvenient should the governor not have had it in his power to adopt that explanation which circumstances demanded, and not less so if he had been obliged to litigate the point with his prisoner, and, as a mere ministerial person must have done, wait till a commentary on the disputed article should arrive from England.

It is a different question, and on which we are far from having so clear an opinion, whether Sir Hudson Lowe, in every case, exercised this high privilege with sound discretion. It would be unjust to condemn him unheard, who has never fairly been put upon his defence, and the evidence against whom is, we must again say, of a very suspicious nature. Still it appears, that alterations of the existing regulations were, as far as we have information, more frequent than necessity, the best if not the only apology for varying the manner of such proceedings, seems to have authorised.

For example, one of the heaviest of Napoleon's complaints is made against the restriction of the limits within which he might take exercise without the company of a British officer, which, instead of extending to twelve miles in circumference, were contracted to two-thirds of that space. Every thing in this world is relative, and we can conceive the loss of one-third of his exercising ground to have been, at this moment, a more sincere subject of distress to Napoleon, than the loss of a kingdom while he yet governed Europe. The apology alleged for this was the disposition which Napoleon seemed to show to cultivate the acquaintance of the inhabitants of St. Helena, more than it was advisable that he should have the opportunity of doing. We can easily conceive this to be true; for not only might Napoleon be disposed, from policy, to make friends among the better classes by his irresistible conciliation of manners, and of the lower class by familiarity and largesses; but he must also be supposed, with the feelings natural to humanity in distress, to seek some little variety from the monotony of existence, some little resumption of connexion with the human race, from which, his few followers excepted, he was in a manner excluded. But this aptitude to mingle with such society as chance threw within his reach, in his very limited range, might perhaps have been indulged without the possibility of his making any bad use of it, especially since no one could enter these grounds without passes and orders. The limits were shortly after restored by Sir Hudson Lowe to their original extent, Napoleon having declared that unless this were the case, he would not consent to take exercise, or observe the usual means of keeping himself in health.

The injunction requiring that Buonaparte should daily be seen by an orderly officer, was, under Sir Hudson Lowe's authority, as it had been under that of Sir George Cockburn, the subject of Buonaparte's most violent opposition. He affected to apprehend that it was to be enforced by positive violence, and carried this so far as to load fire-arms, with the idea of resisting by force any attempt of an orderly officer to insist upon performing this part of his duty. He alludes resentfully to the circumstance in his angry interview with Sir Hudson Lowe upon the 16th May, 1816. Yet, of all unpleasant regulations to which a prisoner is subjected by his captivity, that appears the least objectionable, which, assuring us from space to space that the person of the prisoner is secure, enables us, in the interval, to leave him a much greater share of personal freedom than otherwise could be permitted, because the shortness of each interval does not allow him time to use it in escape. Nevertheless, Sir Hudson Lowe, as already hinted, was content in this case to yield to the violent threats of Napoleon, and rather suffer the duty to be exercised imperfectly and by chance, than run the risk of his prisoner perishing in the affray which his obstinacy threatened. Perhaps the governor may be in this case rather censured as having given up a point impressed upon him by his original instructions, than blamed for executing them too strictly against the remarkable person who was his prisoner. We cannot but repeat the opinion we have been led to form, that, could Buonaparte's bodily presence have been exactly ascertained from time to time, his rambles through the whole of the island might have been permitted, even without the presence of a military officer.

This regulation was another circumstance, of which Napoleon most heavily complained. He regarded the company of such attendant as a mark of his defeat and imprisonment, and resolved, therefore, rather to submit to remain within the limits of the grounds of Longwood, narrow as they were, than, by stirring without them, to expose himself to the necessity of admitting the company of this odious guardian. It may be thought, that in thus judging, Napoleon did not adopt the most philosophical or even the wisest opinion. Misfortune in war is no disgrace; and to be prisoner, has been the lot before now both of kings and emperors. The orderly officers, also, who were ready to accompany Napoleon in his ride, might be often men of information and accomplishment; and their society and conversation could not but have added some variety to days so little diversified as those spent by Napoleon.

The prisoner, however, was incapable of deriving amusement from any such source. It might be as well expected that the occupant of a dungeon should amuse himself with botanizing in the ditches which moat it round. Napoleon could not forget what he had been and what he was, and plainly confessed by his conduct that he was contented rather to die, than to appear in public wearing the badge of his fate, like one who was sitting down resigned to it.

While so averse to this regulation, Napoleon had not taken the proper mode of escaping from its influence. Sir George Cockburn, upon his remonstrance after his first arrival, had granted to him a dispensation from the attendance of an orderly officer, at least in his immediate company or vicinity. This privilege was suddenly withdrawn while the admiral was yet upon the island, and both Napoleon and the various St. Helena authors, Las Cases in particular, make the most bitter complaints on the tantalizing conduct of Sir George Cockburn, who gave an indulgence, as it would seem, only with the cruel view of recalling it the next morning. The truth is here told, but not the whole truth. Napoleon had engaged to the admiral, that, in consideration of this indulgence, he would not enter into any intercourse with any of the inhabitants whom he might meet during the time of his excursion. He chose to break through his promise the very first time that he rode out alone, or only with his suite; and hence Sir George Cockburn, considering faith as broken with him, recalled the permission altogether. It was not, therefore, with a good grace, that Napoleon complained of the want of inclination on the part of the governor, to restore an indulgence to him, which he had almost instantly made a use of that was contrary to his express engagement. The truth is, that the Ex-Emperor had his own peculiar manner of viewing his own case. He considered every degree of leniency, which was at any time exercised, as a restoration of some small portion of that liberty, of which he conceived himself to be deprived illegally and tyrannically; and scrupled no more to employ what he got in endeavouring to attain a farther degree of freedom, than the prisoner whose hand is extricated from fetters would hesitate to employ it in freeing his feet. There can be no doubt, that if by means of such a privilege as riding without the attendance of an officer, he could have arranged or facilitated any mode of final escape, he would not have hesitated to use it to that effect.

But, on the other hand, such being his way of thinking, and hardly disguised, it put the governor strongly on his guard against granting any relaxation of the vigilance necessary for effectually confining him. Indulgences of this nature are, so far as they go, a species of confidence reposed in the captive by the humanity of his keeper, and cannot, in perfect good faith, be used to purposes, which must lead to the disgrace, or perhaps the ruin, of the party who grants them. If, therefore, Napoleon showed himself determined to hold a closer and more frequent intercourse with the natives of St. Helena, and the strangers who visited the island, than Sir Hudson Lowe approved, it only remained for the latter to take care that such interviews should not occur without a witness, by adhering to the restrictions, which required that a British officer should attend upon the more distant excursions of the hard-ruled captive.

GOURGAUD—LONGWOOD

It is to be remarked, that this intercourse with the inhabitants, and others who visited St. Helena, was no imaginary danger, but actually existed to a considerable extent, and for purposes calculated to alarm Sir Hudson Lowe's watchfulness, and to transgress in a most material respect his instructions from government. The disclosures of General Gourgaud are on these points decisive.

That officer "had no difficulty in avowing, that there has always existed a free and uninterrupted communication betwixt the inhabitants of Longwood and the country, without the knowledge or intervention of the governor; and that this has been made use of, not only for the purpose of receiving and transmitting letters, but for that of transmitting pamphlets, money, and other articles, of which the party in Longwood might from time to time have been in want; and that the correspondence was for the most part carried on direct with Great Britain. That the persons employed in it were those Englishmen who from time to time visit St. Helena, to all of whom the attendants and servants of Buonaparte have free access, and who, generally speaking, are willing, many of them without reward, and others for very small pecuniary considerations, to convey to Europe any letter or packet intrusted to their charge. It would appear also, that the captains and others on board the merchant ships touching at the island, whether belonging to the East India Company, or to other persons, are considered at Longwood as being peculiarly open to the seduction of Buonaparte's talents; so much so, that the inhabitants of Longwood have regarded it as a matter of small difficulty to procure a passage on board one of these ships for General Buonaparte, if escape should be at any time his object."

In corroboration of what is above stated, of the free communication betwixt St. Helena and Europe, occurs the whimsical story told by Dr. Antommarchi, of a number of copies of Dr. O'Meara's book being smuggled ashore at St. Helena, under the disguise of tracts distributed by a religious society. Another instance is mentioned by Count Las Cases, who, when removed from Longwood, and debarred from personally communicating with his master, felt considerable difficulty in discovering a mode of conveying to him a diamond necklace of great value, which had been intrusted to his keeping, and which Napoleon might want after his departure. He addressed at hazard the first decent-looking person he saw going to Longwood, and conjured him in the most pathetic manner, to take charge of the packet. The stranger slackened his pace without speaking, and pointed to his coat-pocket. Las Cases dropt in the packet; and the jewels, thus consigned to the faith of an unknown person, reached their owner in safety.[247]

It is honourable to humanity, that distress of almost any kind, but especially that which affects the imagination by exciting the memory of fallen greatness, should find assistants even among those who were enemies to that greatness when in prosperity.

But it was the duty of the governor to take heed, that neither overstrained notions of romantic compassion and generosity, nor the temptation of worse motives, should lead to any combination which might frustrate his diligence; and Napoleon having at once avarice and the excess of generosity to solicit in his favour, the governor naturally secluded him as much as he could from those individuals who might be liable to be gained over to his interest by such powerful seductions.

Upon the 7th January, 1818, the Government of Britain intimated their approbation of the enlargement of Napoleon's bounds of exercise to the ordinary limits which had been for a time restricted; and, in order to preserve for him the opportunity of keeping up society with such of the people of the island as he might desire to receive on business, or as visitors, the following regulation was adopted:—

"Respecting the intercourse with the inhabitants, I see no material objection to the placing it upon the footing recently suggested by Count Bertrand, as it is one which he represents would be more consonant to General Buonaparte's wishes. The count's proposition is, that a list of a given number of persons, resident in the island, should be made out who shall be at once admitted to

---

[247] Las Cases, tom. i., p. 61.

Longwood on the general's own invitation, without a previous application being made to your excellency on each invitation. You will, therefore, consider yourself at liberty to accede to the suggestions of Count Bertrand; and you will for this purpose direct him to present to you for your approbation, a list of persons, not exceeding fifty in number, resident in the island, who may be admitted to Longwood at reasonable hours, without any other pass than the invitation of General Buonaparte, it being understood that they are on each occasion to deliver in the invitation as a voucher, with their names, at the barrier. In giving your approbation to the list, you will, as far as is consistent with your duty, consult the wishes of General Buonaparte; but you will let it be clearly understood, that you reserve to yourself a discretionary power of erasing from the list, at any time, any of those individuals, to whom you may have found it inexpedient to continue such extraordinary facility of access; and you will take special care, that a report be always made to you by the orderly officer, of the several persons admitted to Longwood upon General Buonaparte's invitation."

We have touched upon these various subjects of grievance, not as being the only causes of dispute, or rather of violent discord, which existed betwixt the Ex-Emperor of France and the governor of St. Helena, for there were many others. It is not in our purpose, however, nor even in our power, to give a detailed or exact history of these particular quarrels, but merely to mark—as our duty, in this a very painful one, demands—what was the character and general scope of the debate which was so violently conducted on both sides. Of course it follows, that a species of open war having been declared betwixt the parties, every one of the various points of discussion which must necessarily have arisen betwixt Sir Hudson Lowe and Napoleon, or through their respective attendants and followers, was turned into matter of offence on the one side or the other, and as such warmly contested. It is thus, that, when two armies approach each other, the most peaceful situations and positions lose their ordinary character, and become the subjects of attack and defence. Every circumstance, whether of business or of etiquette, which occurred at St. Helena, was certain to occasion some dispute betwixt Napoleon and Sir Hudson Lowe, the progress and termination of which seldom passed without an aggravation of mutual hostilities. It is beneath the dignity of history to trace these *tracasseries*; and beyond possibility, unless for one present on the spot, and possessed of all the minute information attending each subject of quarrel, to judge which had the right or the wrong.

It would be, indeed, easy for us, standing aloof and remote from these agitating struggles, to pass a sweeping condemnation on the one party or the other, or perhaps upon each of them; and to show that reason and temper on either side would have led to a very different course of proceeding on both, had it been permitted by those human infirmities to which, unhappily, those who have power or pretensions are more liable than the common class, who never possessed the one, and make no claim to the other.

Neither would it be difficult for us to conceive a governor of St. Helena, in the abstract, who, treating the reviling and reproaches with which he was on all occasions loaded by Buonaparte, as the idle chidings of a storm, which must howl around whatever it meets in its course, would, with patience and equanimity, have suffered the tempest to expend its rage, and die away in weakness, the sooner that it found itself unresisted. We can conceive such a person wrapping himself up in his own virtue, and, while he discharged to his country the duty she had intrusted to him, striving, at the same time, by such acts of indulgence as might be the more gratifying because the less expected, or perhaps merited, to melt down the sullenness which the hardship of his situation naturally imposed on the prisoner. We can even conceive that a man of such rare temper might have found means, in some happy moment, of re-establishing a tolerable and ostensible good understanding, if not a heartfelt cordiality, which, could it have existed, would so much have lessened the vexations and troubles, both of the captive and of the governor. All this is very easily conceived. But in order to form the idea of such a man, we must suppose him, in the case in question, stoically impassive to insults of the grossest kind, insults poured on him before he had done any thing which could deserve them, and expressed in a manner which plainly intimated the determination of Napoleon to place himself at once on the most hostile terms with him. This must have required the most uncommon share of calmness and candour. It is more natural that such a functionary as the governor of St. Helena—feeling the impulse of ill usage from a quarter where no regular satisfaction could be had—if he did not use the power which he held for the time, to the actual annoyance and vexation of the party by whom he had been deliberately insulted, should be apt at least to become indifferent how much, or how little, his prisoner was affected by the measures which he adopted, and to go forward with the necessary means of confining the person, without being so solicitous as he might otherwise have been, to spare the feelings. An officer, termed to his face a liar, a brigand, an assassin, a robber, a hangman, has few terms to keep with him by whom he has been loaded with such unworthy epithets; and who, in using them, may be considered as having declared mortal war, and disclaimed the courtesy, while he defied the power, of the person to whom he addressed them.

In the same manner, judging with the coolness of a third party, we should be inclined to say, that the immediate attendants and followers of Napoleon might have here served their master more effectually, by endeavouring to accommodate the subjects of dispute with Sir Hudson Lowe, than by aggravating and carrying them still farther by their own subordinate discussions with the governor and his aides-de-camp, and thus heating their master's passions by their own. But while that was the line of conduct to be desired, it is impossible to deny that another was more naturally to be expected. Generals Bertrand, Montholon, and Gourgaud, were all soldiers of high reputation, who rising to fame under Napoleon's eye, had seen their own laurels flourish along with his. In the hour of adversity, they had most laudably and honourably followed him, and were now sharing with him the years of solitude and exile. It was not, therefore, to be wondered at, that they, wearied of their own restrained and solitary condition, enraged, too, at every thing which appeared to add to the calamitous condition of their fallen master, should be more disposed to increase the angry spirit which manifested itself on both sides, than, by interposing their mediation, to endeavour to compose jars which might well render Napoleon's state more irritable and uncomfortable, but could not, in any point of view, tend to his comfort, peace, or even respectability.

But perhaps we might have been best entitled to hope, from the high part which Napoleon had played in the world, from the extent of his genius, and the natural pride arising from the consciousness of talent, some indifference towards objects of mere form and ceremony, some confidence in the genuine character of his own natural elevation, and a noble contempt of the change which fortune could make on circumstances around him. We might have hoped that one whose mental superiority over the rest of his species was so undeniable, would have been the last to seek with eagerness to retain the frippery and feathers of which the wind of adverse fortune had stripped him, or to be tenacious of that etiquette, which now, if yielded to him at all, could only have been given by compassion. We might have thought the conqueror in so many bloody conflicts, would, even upon provocation, have thought it beneath him to enter on a war of words with the governor of an islet in the Atlantic, where foul language could be the only weapon on either side, and held it a yet greater derogation, so far to lay aside his high character, as to be the first to engage in so ignoble a conflict. It might, we should have supposed, have been anticipated by such a person, not only that calm and patient endurance of inevitable misfortunes is the noblest means of surmounting them, but that, even with a view to his liberty, such conduct would have been most advisable, because most politic. The people of Europe, and especially of Britain, would have been much sooner apt to unite in the wish to see him removed from confinement, had he borne himself with philosophical calmness, than seeing him, as they did, still evincing within his narrow sphere the restless and intriguing temper which had so long disturbed the world, and which now showed itself so engrained in his constitution, as to lead him on to the unworthy species of warfare which we have just described. But the loftiest and proudest beings of mere humanity are like the image which the Assyrian monarch beheld in his dream—blended of various metals, uniting that which is vile with those which are most precious; that which is frail, weak, and unsubstantial, with what is most perdurable and strong. Napoleon, like many an emperor and hero before him, sunk under his own passions after having vanquished nations; and became, in his exile, the prey of petty spleen, which racked him almost to frenzy, and induced him to hazard his health, or perhaps even to throw away his life, rather than submit with dignified patience to that which his misfortunes had rendered unavoidable.

Chapter XCVI

Napoleon's Domestic Habits—Manner in which he spent the day—his Dress—Nature of the Fragments of Memoirs he dictated to Gourgaud and Montholon—His admiration of Ossian—He prefers Racine and Corneille to Voltaire—Dislike of Tacitus—His Vindication of the Character of Cæsar—His Behaviour towards the Persons of his Household—Amusements and Exercises—His Character of Sir Pulteney Malcolm—Degree of his Intercourse with the Islanders, and with Visitors to the Island—Interview with Captain Basil Hall—with Lord Amherst and the Gentlemen attached to the Chinese Embassy.

DOMESTIC HABITS

The unpleasant and discreditable disputes, of which we have given some account in the last chapter, form, unhappily, the most marked events of Napoleon's latter life. For the five years and seven months that he remained in the island of St. Helena, few circumstances occurred to vary the melancholy tenor of his existence, excepting those which affected his temper or his health. Of the general causes influencing the former, we have given some account; the latter we shall hereafter allude to. Our present object is a short and general view of his personal and domestic habits while in this melancholy and secluded habitation.

Napoleon's life, until his health began to give way, was of the most regular and monotonous character. Having become a very indifferent sleeper, perhaps from his custom of assigning, during the active part of his life, no precise time for repose, his hours of rising were uncertain, depending upon the rest which he had enjoyed during the earlier part of the night. It followed from this irregularity, that during the day time he occasionally fell asleep, for a few minutes, upon his couch or arm-chair. At times, his favourite valet-de-chambre, Marchand, read to him while in bed until he was composed to rest, the best remedy, perhaps, for that course of "thick-coming fancies," which must so oft have disturbed the repose of one in circumstances so singular and so melancholy. So soon as Napoleon arose from bed, he either began to dictate to one of his generals, (Montholon or Gourgaud generally,) and placed upon record such passages of his remarkable life as he desired to preserve; or, if the weather and his inclination suited, he went out for an hour or two on horseback. He sometimes breakfasted in his own apartment, sometimes with his suite, generally about ten o'clock, and almost always *à la fourchette*. The fore part of the day he usually devoted to reading, or dictating to one or other of his suite, and about two or three o'clock received such visitors as had permission to wait upon him. An airing in the carriage or on horseback generally succeeded to this species of levee, on which occasions he was attended by all his suite. Their horses, supplied from the Cape of Good Hope, were of a good race and handsome appearance. On returning from his airings, he again resumed the book, or caused his amanuensis take up the pen until dinner-time, which was about eight o'clock at night. He preferred plain food, and eat plentifully, and with an apparent appetite. A very few glasses of claret, scarce amounting to an English pint in all, and chiefly drank during the time of dinner, completed his meal. Sometimes he drank champagne; but his constitutional sobriety was such, that a large glass of that more generous wine immediately brought a degree of colour to his cheek. No man appears to have been in a less degree than Napoleon, subject to the influence of those appetites which man has in common with the lower range of nature. He never took more than two meals a day, and concluded each with a small cup of coffee. After dinner, chess, cards, a volume of light literature, read aloud for the benefit of his suite, or general conversation, in which the ladies of his suite occasionally joined, served to consume the evening till ten or eleven, about which time he retired to his apartment, and went immediately to bed.

We may add to this brief account of Napoleon's domestic habits, that he was very attentive to the duties of the toilet. He usually appeared in the morning in a white night-gown, with loose trousers and stockings joined in one, a chequered red Madras handkerchief round his head, and his shirt-collar open. When dressed, he wore a green uniform, very plainly made, and without ornament, similar to that which, by its simplicity, used to mark the sovereign among the splendid dresses of the Tuileries, white waistcoat, and white or nankeen breeches, with silk stockings, and shoes with gold buckles, a black stock, a triangular cocked hat, of the kind to be seen in all the caricatures, with a very small tri-coloured cockade. He usually wore, when in full dress, the riband and grand cross of the Legion of Honour.[248]

HIS MEMOIRS

Such were the personal habits of Napoleon, on which there is little for the imagination to dwell, after it has once received the general idea. The circumstance of the large portion of his time employed in dictation, alone interests our curiosity, and makes us anxious to know with what he could have found means to occupy so many pages, and so many hours. The fragments upon military subjects, dictated from time to time to Generals Gourgaud and Montholon, are not voluminous enough to account for the leisure expended in this manner; and even when we add to them the number of pamphlets and works issuing from St. Helena, we shall still find room to suppose either that manuscripts remain which have not yet seen the light, or that Napoleon was a slow composer, and fastidious in the choice of his language. The last conjecture seems most probable, as the French are particularly scrupulous in the punctilios of composition, and Napoleon, emperor as he had been, must have known that he would receive no mercy from the critics upon that particular.

The avowed works themselves, fragments as they are, are extremely interesting in a military point of view; and those in which the campaigns of Italy are described, contain many most invaluable lessons on the art of war. Their political value is by no means so considerable. Gourgaud seems to have formed a true estimation of

---

[248] Las Cases, tom. ii., pp. 1-7.

them, when, in answer to Baron Sturmer's inquiries, whether Napoleon was writing his history, he expressed himself thus:—"He writes disjointed fragments, which he will never finish. When asked why he will not put history in possession of the exact fact, he answers, it is better to leave something to be guessed at than to tell too much. It would also seem, that not considering his extraordinary destinies as entirely accomplished, he is unwilling to detail plans which have not been executed, and which he may one day resume with more success." To these reasons for leaving blanks and imperfections in his proposed history, should be added the danger which a faithful and unreserved narrative must have entailed upon many of the actors in the scenes from which he was lifting the veil. It is no doubt true, that Napoleon seems systematically to have painted his enemies, more especially such as had been once his adherents, in the most odious colours, and particularly in such as seemed likely to render them most obnoxious to the ruling powers; but the same principle induced him to spare his friends, and to afford no handle against them for their past efforts in his favour, and no motive for taking from them the power of rendering him farther service, if they should be in a capacity to do so.

These considerations operated as a check upon the pen of the historian; and it may be truly said, that no man who has written so much of his own life, and that consisting of such singular and important events, has told so little of himself which was not known before from other sources. But the present is not the less valuable; for there is sometimes as much information derived from the silence as from the assertions of him who aspires to be his own biographer; and an apology for, or vindication of, the course of a remarkable life, however partially written, perhaps conveys the most information to the reader, next to that candid confession of faults and errors, which is so very seldom to be obtained in autobiography.

Napoleon's Memoirs, together with the labour apparently bestowed upon his controversial pamphlets written against Sir Hudson Lowe, seem to have furnished the most important part of his occupation whilst at St. Helena, and probably also of his amusement. It was not to be expected that in sickness and calamity he could apply himself to study, even if his youth had furnished him with more stores to work upon. It must be remembered that his whole education had been received at the military school of Brienne, where indeed he displayed a strong taste for the sciences. But the studies of mathematics and algebra were so early connected and carried on with a view to the military purposes in which he employed them, that it may be questioned whether he retained any relish for prosecuting his scientific pursuits in the character of an inquirer into abstract truths. The practical results had been so long his motive, so long his object, that he ceased to enjoy the use of the theoretical means, when there was no siege to be formed, no complicated manœuvres to be arranged, no great military purpose to be gained by the display of his skill—but when all was to begin and end with the discussion of a problem.

That Napoleon had a natural turn for belles lettres is unquestionable; but his leisure never permitted him to cultivate it, or to refine his taste or judgment on such subjects. The recommendation which, in 1784, described him as fit to be sent to the Military School at Paris, observes, that he is tolerably acquainted with history and geography, but rather deficient in the ornamented branches, and in the Latin language.[249] At seventeen years of age, he joined the regiment of La Fère, and thus ended all the opportunities afforded him of regular education. He read, however, very extensively; but, like all young persons, with little discrimination, and more to amuse himself than for the purpose of instruction. Before he had arrived at that more advanced period when youths of such talent as his, and especially when gifted with such a powerful memory, usually think of arranging and classifying the information which they have collected during their earlier course of miscellaneous reading, the tumults of Corsica, and subsequently the siege of Toulon, carried him into those scenes of war and business which were his element during the rest of his life, and down to the period we now speak of.

The want of information which we have noticed, he supplied, as most able men do, by the assistance derived from conversing with persons possessing knowledge, and capable of communicating it. No one was ever more dexterous than Napoleon at extracting from

---

[249] See *ante*, vol. ii., *note*.

individuals the kind of information which each was best qualified to impart; and in many cases, while in the act of doing so, he contrived to conceal his own ignorance, even of that which he was anxiously wishing to know. But although in this manner he might acquire facts and results, it was impossible to make himself master, on such easy terms, of general principles, and the connexion betwixt them and the conclusions which they lead to.

OSSIAN

It was no less certain, that though in this manner Napoleon could obtain by discoursing with others the insulated portions of information which he was desirous of acquiring, and though the knowledge so acquired served his immediate purpose in public life, these were not habits which could induce him to resume those lighter subjects of study so interesting and delightful in youth, but which an advanced age is unwilling to undertake, and slow to profit by. He had, therefore, never corrected his taste in the belles lettres, but retained his admiration for Ossian, and other books which had fascinated his early attention. The declamatory tone, redundancy of expression, and exaggerated character of the poetry ascribed to the Celtic bard, suit the taste of very young persons; but Napoleon continued to retain his relish for them to the end of his life; and, in some of his proclamations and bulletins, we can trace the hyperbolical and bombastic expressions which pass upon us in youth for the sublime, but are rejected as taste and reason become refined and improved. There was indeed this apology for Napoleon's lingering fondness for Ossian, that the Italian translation, by Cesarotti, is said to be one of the most beautiful specimens of the Tuscan language. The work was almost constantly beside him.

Historical, philosophical, or moral works, seem more rarely to have been resorted to for the amusement of Longwood. We have, indeed, been informed, that the only books of this description for which Napoleon showed a decided partiality, were those of Machiavel and Montesquieu, which he did not perhaps consider as fit themes of public recitation; Tacitus, who holds the mirror so close to the features of sovereigns, he is said always to have held in aversion, and seldom to have mentioned without terms of censure or dislike. Thus will the patient sometimes loathe the sight of the most wholesome medicine. The French novels of the day were sometimes tried as a resource; but the habits of order and decency which Napoleon observed, rendered their levities and indelicacies unfitted for such society.

There remained another department of literature, from which the party at Longwood derived frequent resources. The drama occupied a considerable part of those readings with which Napoleon used to while away the tedious hours of his imprisonment. This was an indication that he still retained the national taste of France, where few neglect to attend the spectacle, in one form or another, during the space betwixt dinner and the reunion of society in the evening. Next to seeing his ancient favourite Talma, was to Napoleon the reading some of those chef-d'œuvres to which he had seen and heard him give life and personification. He is himself said to have read with taste and effect, which agrees with the traditions that represent him as having been early attached to theatrical representations.[250] It was in the discussions following these readings, which Las Cases has preserved with so much zeal, that Buonaparte displayed his powers of conversation, and expressed his peculiar habits and opinions.

Corneille[251] and Racine[252] stood much higher in his estimation than Voltaire. There seems a good reason for this. They wrote their immortal works for the meridian of a court, and at the command of the most monarchical of monarchs, Louis XIV. The productions,

---

[250] "Plays occupied our attention for the future; tragedies in particular. Napoleon is uncommonly fond of analyzing them, which he does in a singular mode of reasoning, and with a great deal of taste. He remembers an immense quantity of poetry, which he learned when he was eighteen years old, at which time, he says, he knew more than he does at present."—Las Cases, tom. i., p. 249.

[251] "Tragedy fires the soul, elevates the heart, and is calculated to generate heroes. Considered under this point of view, perhaps, France owes to Corneille a part of her great actions; and, had he lived in my time, I would have made him a prince."—Napoleon, tom. i., p. 250.

[252] "Napoleon is delighted with Racine, in whom he finds an abundance of beauties. He thinks but little of Voltaire, who, he says, is full of bombast and tinsel; always incorrect, unacquainted either with men or things, with truth or the sublimity of the passions of mankind."—Las Cases, tom. i., p. 249.

therefore, contain nothing that can wound the ear of the most sensitive sovereign. In the King of Denmark's phrase, they "have no offence in them."

With Voltaire it is different. The strong and searching spirit, which afterwards caused the French Revolution, was abroad at this time, and though unaware of the extent to which it might lead, the philosopher of Ferney was not the less its proselyte. There were many passages, therefore, in his works, which could not but be instantly applied to the changes and convulsions of the period during which Napoleon had lived, to the despotic character of his government, and to the plans of freedom which had sunk under the influence of his sword. On this account Voltaire, whose compositions recalled painful comparisons and recollections, was no favourite with Napoleon. The *Mahomet*[253] of that author he particularly disliked, avowing, at the same time, his respect for the Oriental impostor, whom he accused the poet of traducing and misrepresenting. Perhaps he secretly acknowledged a certain degree of resemblance between his own career and that of the youthful camel-driver, who, rising from a mean origin in his native tribe, became at once the conqueror and the legislator of so many nations. Perhaps, too, he remembered his own proclamations while in Egypt, in the assumed character of a Moslem, which he was wont to term by the true phrase of *Charlatanerie*, but adding, that it was charlatanerie of a high and elevated character.

The character of Cæsar was another which Napoleon always strove to vindicate. The French general could not be indifferent to the Roman leader, who, like himself, having at first risen into notice by his victories over the enemies of the republic, had, also like himself, ended the struggles between the patricians and plebeians of

---

[253] "Voltaire, in the character and conduct of his hero, has departed both from nature and history. He has degraded Mahomet, by making him descend to the lowest intrigues. He has represented a great man who changed the face of the world, acting like a scoundrel, worthy of the gallows. He has no less absurdly travestied the character of Omar, which he has drawn like that of a cut-throat in a melo-drama. Voltaire committed a fundamental error in attributing to intrigue that which was solely the result of opinion. Those who have wrought great changes in the world, never succeeded by gaining over chiefs: but always by exciting the multitude. The first is the resource of intrigue, and produces only secondary results: the second is the resort of genius, and transforms the face of the universe."—Napoleon, *Las Cases*, tom. ii., p. 80.

ancient Rome, by reducing both parties equally under his own absolute dominion; who would have proclaimed himself their sovereign, even by the proscribed title of king, had he not been prevented by conspiracy; and who, when he had conquered his country, thought of nothing so much as extending an empire, already much too large, over the distant regions of Scythia and Parthia. The points of personal difference, indeed, were considerable; for neither did Napoleon indulge in the gross debauchery and sensuality imputed to Cæsar, nor can we attribute to him the Roman's powers as an author, or the gentle and forgiving character which distinguished him as a man.

CONDUCT TOWARDS HIS HOUSEHOLD

Yet, although Napoleon had something vindictive in his temper, which he sometimes indulged when Cæsar would have scorned to do so, his intercourse with his familiar friends was of a character the most amiable. It is true, indeed, that, determined, as he expressed himself to be Emperor within Longwood and its little demesne, he exacted from his followers the same marks of severe etiquette which distinguished the Court of the Tuileries; yet, in other respects, he permitted them to carry their freedom in disputing his sentiments, or replying to his arguments, almost beyond the bounds of ordinary decorum. He seemed to make a distinction between their duty towards him as subjects, and their privileges as friends. All remained uncovered and standing in his presence, and even the person who played at chess with him sometimes continued for hours without sitting down. But their verbal intercourse of language and sentiments was that of free men, conversing with a superior, indeed, but not with a despot. Captain Maitland mentions a dispute betwixt Napoleon and General Bertrand. The latter had adopted a ridiculous idea that £30,000 a-year, or some such extravagant sum, was spent in maintaining the grounds and establishment at Blenheim. Napoleon's turn for calculation easily detected the improbability. Bertrand insisted upon his assertion, on which Buonaparte said with quickness, *"Bah! c'est impossible."*—"Oh!" said Bertrand, much offended, "if you are to reply in that manner, there is an end of all argument;" and for some time would not converse with him. Buonaparte, so far from taking umbrage, did all he could to soothe him and restore him to good-humour, which was not very difficult to effect.[254]

But although Napoleon tolerated freedoms of this kind to a considerable extent, yet he still kept in his own hands the royal privilege of starting the topic of conversation, and conducting it as he should think proper; so that, in some respects, it seemed that, having lost all the substantial enjoyment of power, he had become more attached than ever to the observance of its monotonous, wearisome, unprofitable ceremonial. Yet there might be a reason for this, besides the gratification of his own pertinacious temper. The gentlemen who inhabited Longwood had followed him from the purest motives, and there was no reason to suppose that their purpose would waver, or their respect diminish. Still their mutual situation compelled the deposed sovereign, and his late subjects, into such close familiarity, as might perhaps beget, if not contempt, at least an inconvenient degree of freedom betwixt the parties, the very possibility of which he might conceive it as well to exclude by a strict barrier of etiquette.

AMUSEMENTS

We return to Napoleon's habits of amusement. Music was not one of the number. Though born an Italian, and possessing something of a musical ear, so far, at least, as was necessary to enable him to hum a song, it was probably entirely without cultivation.[255] He appears to have had none of the fanaticism for music which characterises the Italians; and it is well known that in Italy he put a stop to the cruel methods which had been used in that country to complete their concerts.

---

[254] Narrative, p. 234.
[255] "The sound of bells produced upon Napoleon a singular effect. When we were at Malmaison, and while walking in the avenue leading to Ruel, how often has the booming of the village bell broken off the most interesting conversations. He stopped, lest the moving of our feet might cause the loss of a tone in the sounds which charmed him. The influence, indeed, was so powerful, that his voice trembled with emotion while he said—'That recalls to me the first years I passed at Brienne.'"—Bourrienne, tom. iii., p. 222.

Neither was Napoleon, as we have heard Denon reluctantly admit, a judge or an admirer of painting. He had some pretence to understand sculpture; and there was one painting in the Museum, before which he used to pause, terming it his own; nor would he permit it to be ransomed for a very large sum by its proprietor the Duke of Modena.[256] But he valued it, not on account of its merits, though a masterpiece of art, but because he had himself been the means of securing it to the Museum at a great sacrifice. The other paintings in that immense collection, however great their excellence, he seldom paid much attention to. He also shocked admirers of painting by the contempt he showed for the durability of the art. Being informed that a first-rate picture would not last above five or six hundred years, he exclaimed, "Bah! a fine immortality!" Yet by using Denon's advice, and that of other sçavans, Napoleon sustained a high reputation as an encourager of the arts. His medals have been particularly and deservedly admired.

In respect of personal exercise at St. Helena, he walked occasionally, and while strong, did not shun steep, rough, and dangerous paths. But although there is some game on the island, he did not avail himself of the pleasure of shooting. It does not indeed appear that he was ever much attached to field sports, although, when Emperor, he replaced the hunting establishment upon a scale still more magnificent, as well as better regulated, than formerly. It is supposed he partook of this princely pastime, as it has been called, rather out of a love of magnificent display than any real attachment to the sport. We may here mention, in his own words, the danger in which he was once placed at a boar hunt. The picture will remind the amateur of the pieces of Rubens and Schneider.

"Upon one occasion at Marli," said the Emperor, "at a boar-hunt, I kept my ground with Soult and Berthier against three enormous wild-boars, who charged us up to the bayonet's point. All the hunting party fled: 'twas a complete military rout. We killed the three animals dead; but I had a scratch from mine, and had nigh lost my finger" (on which a deep scar was still visible.) "But the jest was to see the number of men, surrounded with their dogs, concealing themselves behind the three heroes, and crying at top of their

---

[256] See *ante*, vol. ii.

throats—'to the Emperor's assistance! save the Emperor! help the Emperor!'—and so forth; but not one coming forward."[257]

While on the subject of Napoleon's exercises, we may mention another danger which he incurred by following an amusement more common in England than in France. He chose at one time to undertake the task of driving a calash, six in hand, which he overturned, and had a severe and dangerous fall. Josephine and others were in the vehicle.[258] The English reader cannot fail to recollect that a similar accident happened to Cromwell, who, because, as the historian says, he could manage three nations, took upon him to suppose that he could drive six fiery horses, of which he had just received a present; and, being as unsuccessful as Napoleon in later days, overturned the carriage, to the great damage of the Secretary Thurlow, whom he had placed inside, and to his own double risk, both from the fall, and from the explosion of a pistol, which he carried privately about his person. Buonaparte's sole observation, after his own accident, was, "I believe every man should confine himself to his own trade."

SOCIETY AT LONGWOOD

The chief resource of Napoleon at St. Helena, as we have already said, was society and conversation, and those held chiefly with the gentlemen of his own suite. This need not have been the case, had he been able in the present instance to command that temper which had not failed him under great misfortunes, but seemed now to give way under a series of petty quarrels and mortifications.

The governor and the staff belonging to him were of course excluded from the society of Longwood, by the terms on which Napoleon stood with Sir Hudson Lowe. The officers of the regiments which lay in the island might most probably have afforded some well-informed men, who, having been engaged in the recent war, would have occasionally supplied amusing society to the

---

[257] Las Cases, tom. ii., p. 325.
[258] Las Cases, tom. ii., p. 324.

Emperor and his suite. But they did not in general frequent Longwood. Dr. O'Meara observes, that the governor had exerted his influence to prevent the officers from cultivating the acquaintance of the French; which Sir Hudson Lowe repels as a calumny, confuted by the declarations of the officers of the 53d themselves. But admitting that no intimations were used of set purpose to keep asunder the British officers from the French prisoners, such estrangement naturally followed from the unwillingness of military men to go where they were sure to hear not only their commanding officer for the time, but also their country and its ministers, treated with the grossest expressions of disrespect, while there was no mode of calling the person who used them either to account or to explanation.

The rank and character of Sir Pulteney Malcolm, who commanded the squadron upon the station, set him above the feelings which might influence inferior officers, whether of the army or navy. He visited Napoleon frequently, and was eulogised by him in a description, which (though we, who have the advantage of seeing in the features of Sir Pulteney those of an honoured friend, can vouch for its being just) may have been painted the more willingly, because it gave the artist an opportunity of discharging his spleen, while contrasting the appearance of the admiral with that of the governor, in a manner most unfavourable to the latter. Nevertheless we transcribe it, to prove that Buonaparte could occasionally do justice, and see desert even in a Briton.

"He said he had seen the new admiral. 'Ah! there is a man with a countenance really pleasing, open, frank, and sincere. There is the face of an Englishman. His countenance bespeaks his heart, and I am sure he is a good man: I never yet beheld a man of whom I so immediately formed a good opinion, as of that fine soldier-like old man. He carries his head erect, and speaks out openly and boldly what he thinks, without being afraid to look you in the face at the time. His physiognomy would make every person desirous of a further acquaintance, and render the most suspicious confident in him.'"[259]

---

[259] O'Meara, vol. i., p. 65.

Sir Pulteney Malcolm was also much recommended to Napoleon's favourable judgment by the circumstance of having nothing to do with the restraints imposed upon his person, and possessing the power neither of altering or abating any of the restrictions he complained of. He was fortunate, too, in being able, by the calmness of his temper, to turn aside the violent language of Buonaparte, without either granting the justice of his complaints or giving him displeasure by direct contradiction. "Does your Government mean," said Napoleon, one day to the English admiral, "to detain me upon this rock until my death's day?"—"I am sorry to say, sir," answered Sir Pulteney, "that such I apprehend is their purpose."—"Then the term of my life will soon arrive," said Napoleon. "I hope not, sir," answered the admiral; "I hope you will survive to record your great actions, which are so numerous that the task will ensure you a term of long life." Napoleon bowed, and was gratified, probably both as a hero and as an author. Nevertheless, before Sir Pulteney Malcolm left the island, and while he was endeavouring to justify the governor against some of the harsh and extravagant charges in which Napoleon was wont to indulge, the latter began to appeal from his judgment as being too much of an Englishman to be an impartial judge. They parted, however, on the best terms, and Napoleon often afterwards expressed the pleasure which he had received from the society of Sir Pulteney Malcolm.

The colonists of St. Helena did not, it may be well supposed, furnish many individuals, sufficiently qualified, by rank and education, to be admitted into the society of the exile. They, too, lay under the same awkward circumstances, which prevented the British officers from holding intercourse with Longwood and its inhabitants. The governor, should he be displeased at the too frequent attentions of any individual, or should he conceive any suspicion arising out of such an intercourse, had the power, and, in the opinion of the colonists, might not want the inclination, to make his resentment severely felt. Mr. Balcomb, however, who held the situation of purveyor, with one or two other inhabitants of the island, sometimes visited at Longwood. The general intercourse between the French prisoners and the colonists was carried on by means of the French domestics, who had the privilege of visiting James' Town as often as they pleased, and whose doing so could infer no disadvantageous suspicions. But the society of Longwood gained no advantage by the intercourse with James' Town, although unquestionably the facility of foreign communication was considerably increased to the exiles. Their correspondence was chiefly maintained by the way of Bahia; and it is certain they succeeded in sending many letters to Europe, although they are believed to have been less fortunate in receiving answers.

It was to be expected, that some accession to the society of Longwood might have accrued, from the residence of three gentlemen of rank (two of them, we believe, having ladies and a family) the commissioners of Austria, Russia, and France. But here also ceremonial interposed one of those bars, which are effectual, or otherwise, according to the opinion of those betwixt whom they are erected. The commissioners of the allied powers had requested to be presented to Napoleon. On their wish being announced, he peremptorily declined to receive them in their official capacity, disclaiming the right which the princes of Europe had to interfere with and countenance the custody of his person. On the other hand, the commissioners, finding their public function disowned, refused to hold any communication with Longwood in their private capacity; and thus there were excluded from this solitary spot three persons, whose manners and habits, as foreigners, might have assorted tolerably with those of the exile and his attendants.

The society of St. Helena receives a great temporary increase at the seasons when vessels touch there on their way to India, or on their return to Europe. Of course, every officer and every passenger on such occasions was desirous to see a person so celebrated as Napoleon; and there might sometimes occur individuals among them whom he too might have pleasure in receiving. The regulation of these visits to Longwood seems to have been one of the few parts of the general system of which Napoleon made no complaints. He had a natural reluctance to gratify the idle curiosity of strangers, and the regulations protected him effectually against their intrusion. Such persons as desired to wait upon Napoleon were obliged to apply, in the first place, to the governor, by whom their names were transmitted to General Bertrand, as grand maréchal of the household, who communicated Napoleon's reply, if favourable, and assigned an hour at which he was to receive their visit.

Upon such occasions, Napoleon was particularly anxious that the etiquette of an imperial court should be observed, while the visitors, on the contrary, were strictly enjoined by the governor not to go beyond the civilities due to a general of rank. If, therefore, as sometimes happened, the introduction took place in the open air, the French part of the company attendant on Buonaparte remained uncovered, while the English replaced their hats after the first salutation. Napoleon saw the incongruity of this, and laid his orders on his attendants to imitate the English in this particular point. It is said, that they did not obey without scruples and murmurs.

Those visitors who were permitted to pay their respects at Longwood, were chiefly either persons of distinguished birth, officers of rank in the army and navy, persons of philosophical inquiry (to whom he was very partial,) or travellers from foreign regions, who could repay, by some information, the pleasure which they received from being admitted to the presence of a man so remarkable. Of these interviews, some who enjoyed the benefit of them have published an account; and the memoranda of others we have seen in manuscript. All agree in extolling the extreme good grace, propriety, and appearance of benevolence, with which Napoleon clothed himself whilst holding these levees; and which scarce left the spectators permission to believe that, when surprised by a fit of passion, or when choosing to assume one for the purpose of effect, he could appear the rude, abrupt, and savage despot, which other accounts described him. His questions were uniformly introduced with great tact, so as to put the person interrogated at his ease, by leading to some subject with which he was acquainted, while, at the same time, they induced him to produce any stock of new or curious information which he possessed.

CAPTAIN BASIL HALL

The Journal of Captain Basil Hall of the Royal Navy, well-known by his character both in his profession and in literature, affords a pleasing example of what we have been endeavouring to express, and displays at the same time the powerful extent of Buonaparte's memory. He recognised the name of Captain Hall instantly, from having seen his father, Sir James Hall, Bart. when he was at the Military Academy of Brienne, to which visit Sir James had been led by the love of science, by which he was always distinguished. Buonaparte explained the cause of his recollecting a private individual, after the intervention of such momentous events as he had himself been concerned in. "It is not," he said, "surprising. Your father was the first Englishman that I ever saw; and I have recollected him all my life on that account." He was afterwards minute in his inquiries respecting the Royal Society of Edinburgh, of which Sir James Hall was long President. He then came to the very interesting subject of the newly-discovered island of Loo-Choo; and Captain Hall gives an account of the nature of the interrogations which he underwent, which we will not risk spoiling by an attempt at condensing it.

"Having settled where the island lay, he cross-questioned me about the inhabitants with a closeness—I may call it a severity of investigation—which far exceeds every thing I have met with in any other instance. His questions were not by any means put at random, but each one had some definite reference to that which preceded it, or was about to follow. I felt in a short time so completely exposed to his view, that it would have been impossible to have concealed or qualified the smallest particular. Such, indeed, was the rapidity of his apprehension of the subjects which interested him, and the astonishing ease with which he arranged and generalized the few points of information I gave him, that he sometimes outstripped my narrative, saw the conclusion I was coming to before I spoke it, and fairly robbed me of my story.

"Several circumstances, however, respecting the Loo-Choo people, surprised even him a good deal; and I had the satisfaction of seeing him more than once completely perplexed, and unable to account for the phenomena which I related. Nothing struck him go much as their having no arms. '*Point d'armes!*' he exclaimed, '*c'est à dire point de canons—ils ont des fusils?*' Not even muskets, I replied. '*Eh bien donc—des lances, ou, au moins, des arcs et des flèches?*' I told him they had neither one nor other. '*Ni poignards?*' cried he, with increasing vehemence.—'No, none.'—'*Mais!*' said Buonaparte, clenching his fist, and raising his voice to a loud pitch, '*Mais! sans armes, comment se bat-on?*'

"I could only reply, that as far as we had been able to discover, they had never had any wars, but remained in a state of internal and external peace. 'No wars!' cried he, with a scornful and incredulous expression, as if the existence of any people under the sun without wars was a monstrous anomaly.

"In like manner, but without being so much moved, he seemed to discredit the account I gave him of their having no money, and of their setting no value upon our silver or gold coins. After hearing these facts stated, he mused for some time, muttering to himself, in a low tone, 'Not know the use of money—are careless about gold and silver.' Then looking up, he asked, sharply, 'How then did you contrive to pay these strangest of all people for the bullocks and other good things which they seem to have sent on board in such quantities?' When I informed him that we could not prevail upon the people of Loo-Choo to receive payment of any kind, he expressed great surprise at their liberality, and made me repeat to him twice, the list of things with which we were supplied by these hospitable islanders."

The conversation proceeded with equal spirit, in which it is singular to remark the acuteness of Napoleon, in seizing upon the most remarkable and interesting facts, notwithstanding the hurry of a casual conversation. The low state of the priesthood in Loo-Choo was a subject which he dwelt on without coming to any satisfactory explanation. Captain Hall illustrated the ignorance of the people of Loo-Choo with respect to all the world, save Japan and China, by saying they knew nothing of Europe at all—knew nothing of France and England—and never had even heard of his Majesty; at which last proof of their absolute seclusion from the world, Napoleon laughed heartily. During the whole interview, Napoleon waited with the utmost patience until his questions were replied to, inquired with earnestness into every subject of interest, and made naturally a most favourable impression on his visitor.

"Buonaparte," says the acute traveller, "struck me as differing considerably from the pictures and busts I had seen of him. His face and figure looked much broader and more square, larger, indeed, in every way, than any representation I had met with. His corpulency, at this time universally reported to be excessive, was by no means remarkable. His flesh looked, on the contrary, firm and muscular. There was not the least trace of colour in his cheeks; in fact, his skin was more like marble than ordinary flesh. Not the smallest trace of a wrinkle was discernible on his brow, nor an approach to a furrow on any part of his countenance. His health and spirits, judging from appearances, were excellent; though at this period it was generally believed in England, that he was fast sinking under a complication of diseases, and that his spirits were entirely gone. His manner of speaking was rather slow than otherwise, and perfectly distinct: he waited with great patience and kindness for my answers to his questions, and a reference to Count Bertrand was necessary only once during the whole conversation. The brilliant and sometimes dazzling expression of his eye could not be overlooked. It was not, however, a permanent lustre, for it was only remarkable when he was excited by some point of particular interest. It is impossible to imagine an expression of more entire mildness, I may almost call it of benignity and kindliness, than that which played over his features during the whole interview. If, therefore, he were at this time out of health and in low spirits, his power of self-command must have been even more extraordinary than is generally supposed; for his whole deportment, his conversation, and the expression of his countenance, indicated a frame in perfect health, and a mind at ease."[260]

The date of this meeting was 13th August, 1817.

LORD AMHERST

In the above interview, Buonaparte played a natural part. Upon another remarkable occasion, 1st July, 1817, when he received Lord Amherst and the gentlemen composing and attached to the embassy, then returning from China, his behaviour and conversation

---

[260] Captain Hall's Voyage to the Eastern Seas, vol. i., ch. vii., pp. 302, 319.

were of a much more studied, constrained, and empirical character. He had obviously a part to play, a statement to make, and propositions to announce, not certainly with the view that the seed he had sowed might fall into barren ground, but that it might be retained, gathered up, and carried back to Britain, there to take root in public credulity, and bear fruit sevenfold. He rushed at once into a tide of politics, declaring that the Russian ascendency was to be the destruction of Europe; yet, in the same moment, proclaimed the French and English to be the only effective troops deserving notice for their discipline and moral qualities. Presently after, he struck the English out of the field on account of the smallness of the army, and insisted that, by trusting to our military forces, we were endangering our naval ascendency. He then entered upon a favourite topic—the extreme negligence of Lord Castlereagh in failing to stipulate, or rather extort, a commercial treaty from France, and to wring out of Portugal reimbursement of our expenses. He seemed to consider this as sacrificing the interest and welfare of his country, and stated it as such with a confidence which was calculated to impress upon the hearers that he was completely serious in the extravagant doctrines which he announced.

He failed, of course, to make any impression on Lord Amherst, or on Mr. Henry Ellis, third commissioner of the embassy, to whom a large portion of this violent tirade was addressed, and who has permitted us to have the perusal of his private journal, which is much more full on the subject of this interview than the account given in the printed narrative of the embassy which appeared in 1817.[261]

Having stated Lord Castlereagh's supposed errors towards the state, Napoleon was not silent upon his own injuries. It was chiefly in his conversation with Lord Amherst that he dwelt with great bitterness on Sir Hudson Lowe's conduct to him in various respects; but totally failed in producing the conviction which he aimed at. It seemed, on the contrary, to the ambassador and his attendants, that there never, perhaps, was a prisoner of importance upon whose personal liberty fewer actual restraints had been imposed, than on

---

[261] See Appendix, No. IV., for one of the best and most authentic accounts of Napoleon's conversation and mode of reasoning.

that of the late Sovereign of France. Mr. Ellis, after personal inspection, was induced to regard his complaints concerning provisions and wine as totally undeserving of consideration, and to regret that real or pretended anger should have induced so great a man to countenance such petty misrepresentations. The house at Longwood, considered as a residence for a sovereign, Mr. Ellis allowed to be small and inadequate; but, on the other hand, regarded as the residence of a person of rank living in retirement, being the view taken in England of the prisoner's condition, it was, in his opinion, both convenient and respectable. Reviewing, also, the extent of his limits, Mr. Ellis observes that greater personal liberty, consistent with any pretension to security, could not be granted to an individual supposed to be under any restraint at all. His intercourse with others, he observes, was certainly under immediate surveillance, no one being permitted to enter Longwood, or its domains, without a pass from the governor; but this pass, he affirms, was readily granted, and had never formed any check upon such visitors as Napoleon desired to see. The restraint upon his correspondence is admitted as disagreeable and distressing to his feelings, but is considered as a "necessary consequence of that which he now is, and had formerly been." "Two motives," said Mr. Ellis, "may, I think, be assigned for Buonaparte's unreasonable complaints: The first, and principal, is to keep alive public interest in Europe, but chiefly in England, where he flatters himself that he has a party; and the second, I think, may be traced to the personal character and habits of Buonaparte, who finds an occupation in the petty intrigues by which these complaints are brought forward, and an unworthy gratification in the *tracasseries* and annoyance which they produce on the spot."

The sagacity of Mr. Ellis was not deceived; for General Gourgaud, among other points of information, mentions the interest which Buonaparte had taken in the interview with the embassy which returned to Britain from China, and conceived that his arguments had made a strong impression upon them. The publication of Mr. Ellis's account of the embassy dispelled that dream, and gave rise to proportional disappointment at St. Helena.

Having now given some account of the general circumstances attending Buonaparte's residence in St. Helena, while he enjoyed a considerable portion of health, of his mode of living, his studies and amusements, and having quoted two remarkable instances of his intercourse with strangers of observation and intelligence, we have to resume, in the next chapter, the melancholy particulars of his decline of health, and the few and unimportant incidents which occurred betwixt the commencement of his sickness and its final termination.

Chapter XCVII

Napoleon's Illness—viz. Cancer in the Stomach—Removal of Las Cases—Montholon's Complaints brought forward by Lord Holland—and replied to by Lord Bathurst—Effect of the failure of Lord Holland's motion—Removal of Dr. O'Meara from his attendance on Buonaparte—who refuses to permit the visits of any other English Physician—Two Priests sent to St. Helena at his desire—Dr. Antommarchi—Continued Disputes with Sir Hudson Lowe—Plans for Effecting Buonaparte's Escape—Scheme of a Smuggler to approach St. Helena in a Submarine Vessel—Seizure of the Vessel—Letter expressing the King of England's interest in the Illness of Napoleon—Consent of the latter to admit the visits of Dr. Arnott—Napoleon employs himself in making his Will—and gives other directions connected with his Decease—Extreme Unction administered to him—His Death, on 5th May, 1821—Anatomization of the Body—His Funeral.

ILLNESS

Reports had been long current concerning the decline of Buonaparte's health, even before the battle of Waterloo; and many were disposed to impute his failure in that decisive campaign, less to the superiority of his enemies than to the decrease of his own habits of activity. There seems no room for such a conclusion: The rapid manner in which he concentrated his army upon Charleroi, ought to have silenced such a report for ever. He was subject occasionally to slight fits of sleepiness, such as are incident to most men, especially after the age of forty, who sleep ill, rise early, and work hard. When he landed at St. Helena, so far did he seem from showing any appearance of declining health, that one of the British grenadiers, who saw him, exclaimed, with his national oath, "They told us he was growing old;—he has forty good campaigns in his belly yet, d—n him!" A speech which the French gentlemen envied, as it ought, they said, to have belonged to one of the Old Guard. We have mentioned Captain Hall's account of his apparent state of health in summer 1817; that of Mr. Ellis, about the same period, is similar, and he expresses his belief that Buonaparte was never more able to undergo the fatigues of a campaign than at the moment he saw him. Yet at this time, viz. July, 1817, Napoleon was alleging the decline of his health as a reason for obtaining more indulgence, while, on the other hand, he refused to take the exercise judged necessary to preserve his constitution, unless a relaxation of superintendence should be granted to him. It is probable, however, that he himself felt, even at that period, the symptoms of that internal malady which consumed his life. It is now well known to have been the cruel complaint of which his father died, a cancer, namely, in the stomach, of which he had repeatedly expressed his apprehensions, both in Russia and elsewhere. The progress of this disease, however, is slow and insidious, if indeed it had actually commenced so early as 1817. Gourgaud, at a much later period, avowed himself a complete disbeliever in his illness. He allowed, indeed, that he was in low spirits to such an extent as to talk of destroying himself and his attached followers, by shutting himself and them up in a small apartment with burning charcoal—an easy death, which Berthollet the chemist had, it seems, recommended. Nevertheless, "on the subject of General Buonaparte's health, General Gourgaud stated, that the English were much imposed upon; for that he was not, as far as bodily health was concerned, in any degree materially altered, and that the representations upon this subject had little, if any, truth in them. Dr. O'Meara was certainly the dupe of that influence which General Buonaparte always exercises over those with whom he has frequent intercourse, and though he (General Gourgaud) individually had only reason *de se louer de Mr. O'Meara,* yet his intimate knowledge of General Buonaparte enabled him confidently to assert, that his state of health was not at all worse than it had been for some time previous to his arrival at St. Helena."

Yet, as before hinted, notwithstanding the disbelief of friends and foes, it seems probable that the dreadful disease of which Napoleon died, was already seizing upon the vitals, though its character was not decisively announced by external symptoms. Dr. Arnott, surgeon to the 20th regiment, who attended on Napoleon's death-bed, has made the following observations upon this important subject:

"We are given to understand, from great authority,[262] that this affection of the stomach cannot be produced without a considerable predisposition of the parts to disease. I will not venture an opinion: but it is somewhat remarkable, that he often said that his father died of scirrhus of the pylorus; that the body was examined after death, and the fact ascertained. His faithful followers, Count and Countess Bertrand, and Count Montholon, have repeatedly declared the same to me.

"If, then, it should be admitted that a previous disposition of the parts to this disease did exist, might not the depressing passions of the mind act as an exciting cause? It is more than probable that Napoleon Buonaparte's mental sufferings in St. Helena were very poignant. By a man of such unbounded ambition, and who once aimed at universal dominion, captivity must have been severely felt.

"The climate of St. Helena I consider healthy. The air is pure and temperate, and Europeans enjoy their health, and retain the vigour of their constitution, as in their native country."

Dr. Arnott proceeds to state, that notwithstanding this general assertion, dysentery, and other acute diseases of the abdominal viscera, prevailed among the troops. This he imputes to the carelessness and intemperance of the English soldiers, and the fatigue of the working parties; as the officers, who had little night duty, retained their health and strength as in Europe.

"I can therefore safely assert," continues the physician, "that any one of temperate habits who is not exposed to much bodily exertion, night air, and atmospherical changes, as a soldier must be,

---

[262] "See Dr. Baillie's inestimable book on Morbid Anatomy, pp. 141, 142."—S.

may have as much immunity from disease in St. Helena as in Europe; and I may therefore farther assert, that the disease of which Napoleon Buonaparte died was *not* the effect of climate."

In support of Dr. Arnott's statement, it may be observed, that of Napoleon's numerous family of nearly fifty persons, English servants included, only one died during all their five years' residence on the island;[263] and that person (Cipriani, the major-domo) had contracted the illness which carried him off, being a species of consumption, before he left Europe.

Dr. Arnott, to whose opinion we are induced to give great weight, both from the excellence of his character and his having the best opportunities of information, states that the scirrhus, or cancer of the stomach, is an obscure disease; the symptoms which announce it being common to, and characteristic of, other diseases in the same region; yet he early conceived that some morbid alteration of the structure of the stomach had taken place, especially after he learned that his patient's father had died of scirrhus of the pylorus. He believed, as already hinted, that the disease was in its incipient state, even so far back as the end of the year 1817, when the patient was affected with pain in the stomach, nausea, and vomiting, especially after taking food; which symptoms never left him from that period, but increased progressively till the day of his death.

From this period, therefore, Napoleon was in a situation which, considering his great actions, and the height of his former fortunes, deserved the compassion of his most bitter enemies, and the sympathy of all who were disposed to take a moral lesson from the most extraordinary vicissitude of human affairs which history has ever presented. Nor can we doubt that such reflections might have eventually led to much relaxation in the severity with which the prisoner was watched, and, it may be, at length to his entire emancipation. But to attain this end, it would have been necessary that Napoleon's conduct, while under restrictions, should have been of a very different character from that which he thought it most politic, or felt it most natural, to adopt. First, to obtain the sympathy

---

[263] See, for a detailed account of the establishment at Longwood, Appendix, No. V.

and privileges due to an invalid, he ought to have permitted the visits of some medical person, whose report might be held as completely impartial. This could not be the case with that of Dr. O'Meara, engaged as he was in the prisoner's intimate and even secret service, and on the worst terms with the governor; and Napoleon's positive rejection of all other assistance seemed to countenance the belief, however unjust, that he was either feigning indisposition, or making use of some slight symptoms of it to obtain a relaxation of the governor's vigilance. Nor was it to be supposed that Dr. Antommarchi's evidence, being that of an individual entirely dependent on Napoleon, could be considered as more authentic, till corroborated by some indifferent, and, at the same time, competent medical authority.

Secondly, It is to be remembered, that the fundamental reason on which Napoleon's confinement was vindicated, was, that his liberty was inconsistent with the tranquillity of Europe. To prove the contrary, it would have been necessary that the Ex-Emperor should have evinced a desire to retreat from political disputes, and shown symptoms of having laid aside or forgotten those ambitious projects which had so long convulsed Europe. Compassion, and the admiration of great talents, might then have led the states of Europe to confide in the resigned dispositions of one, whom age, infirmities, and sufferings, appeared to incline to dedicate the remainder of his days to ease and retirement, and in whom they might seem a sure guarantee for his pacific intentions. But so far were such feelings from being exhibited, that every thing which emanated from St. Helena showed that the Ex-Emperor nourished all his former plans, and vindicated all his former actions. He was not satisfied that the world should adopt the opinion that his ambition was allayed, and his pretensions to empire relinquished. On the contrary, his efforts, and those of the works into which he breathed his spirit, went to prove, if they proved any thing, that he never entertained ambition of a culpable character—that his claims of sovereignty were grounded upon national law and justice—that he had a right to entertain them formerly, and that he was disposed and entitled to assert them still. He was at pains to let the world know that he was not altered in the slightest degree, was neither ashamed of his projects, nor had renounced them; but, if restored to Europe, that he would be in all respects the same person, with the same claims, and little diminished activity, as when he landed at Cannes to recover the empire of France.

This mode of pleading his cause had the inevitable consequence of confirming all those who had deemed restrictions on his freedom to be necessary in the outset (and these were the great majority of Europe,) in the belief that the same reasons existed for continuing the restraint, which had originally caused it to be imposed. We are unwilling to revert again to the hackneyed simile of the imprisoned lion; but certainly, if the royal animal which Don Quixotte desired to set at liberty, had, instead of demeaning himself peaceably and with urbanity, been roaring, ramping, and tearing the bars of his cage, it may be questioned whether the Great Redresser of Wrongs himself would have advocated his freedom.

LAS CASES

In November 1816, Napoleon sustained a loss to which he must have been not a little sensible, in the removal of Count Las Cases from his society. The devoted attachment of the Count to his person could not be doubted, and his age and situation as a civilian, made him less apt to enter into those feuds and quarrels, which sometimes, notwithstanding their general attachment to Napoleon, seemed to have arisen among the military officers of the household of Longwood. He was of a literary turn, and qualified to converse upon general topics, both of history and science. He had been an emigrant, and understanding all the manœuvres and intrigues of the ancient noblesse, had many narrations which Napoleon was not unwilling to listen to. Above all, he received and recorded every thing which was said by Napoleon, with undoubting faith and unwearied assiduity. And, like the author of one of the most entertaining books in the English language (Boswell's Life of Johnson,) Count Las Cases thought nothing trivial that could illustrate his subject. Like Boswell, too, his veneration for his principal was so deep, that he seems to have lost, in some cases, the exact perception of right and wrong, in his determination to consider Napoleon as always in the right. But his attachment, if to a certain degree tending to blind his judgment, came warm from his heart. The count gave a substantial mark, also, of his sincerity, in dedicating to his master's service a sum of £4000, or thereabout, his whole private fortune, which was vested in the English funds.[264]

For our misfortune, as also for his own, since he must have considered his separation from Buonaparte as such, Count Las Cases had been tempted into a line of conduct inconsistent with the engagement he had come under with the other attendants of the Ex-Emperor, not to hold secret communication beyond the verge of the island. The opportunity of a servant of his own returning to England, induced him to confide to the domestic's charge a letter, written upon a piece of white silk, that it might be the more readily concealed, which was stitched into the lad's clothes. It was addressed to Prince Lucien Buonaparte. As this was a direct transgression, in a most material point, of the conditions which Count Las Cases had promised to observe, he was dismissed from the island and sent to the Cape of Good Hope, and from thence to Europe.[265] His Journal remained for some time in the hands of Sir Hudson Lowe; but, as we had formerly occasion to mention, alterations and additions were afterwards made, which, in general, are more vituperative of the governor, than the manuscript as it originally stood when the Count left St. Helena. The abridgement of the Count's stay at the island was much to be regretted, as his Journal forms the best record, not only of Napoleon's real thoughts, but of the opinions which he desired should be received as such. Unquestionably, the separation from this devoted follower added greatly to the disconsolate situation of the Exile of Longwood; but it is impossible to suppress the remark, that, when a gentleman attached to Napoleon's suite found himself at liberty thus to break through a plighted engagement in his chief's behalf, it sufficiently vindicated Sir Hudson Lowe for putting little faith in the professions made to him, and declining to relax any reasonable degree of vigilance which the safe custody of his prisoner seemed to demand.

The complaints of Napoleon and his followers produced, as they ought to have done, an inquiry into the personal treatment of

---

[264] Las Cases, tom. iii., p. 359.
[265] Las Cases, tom. iv., p. 281.

the Ex-Emperor, in the British Parliament; when the general reasoning which we have hinted at, joined to the exposure which ministers afforded of the exaggerated representations that had been made in the statements which had come from St. Helena, were found greatly to preponderate over the arguments of Napoleon's compassionate and accomplished advocate, Lord Holland.

LORD HOLLAND'S MOTION

The question came before the House of Lords, on 18th March, 1817.[266] Lord Holland, in a speech of great good sense and moderation, disowned all attempts at persuading the House, that the general line of policy adopted with respect to Napoleon should be changed. It had been adopted in contradiction to his (Lord Holland's) sentiments, but it had been confirmed by Parliament, and he did not hope to obtain a reversal of their judgment. But, if the confining Napoleon was, as had been alleged, a measure of necessity, it followed that necessity must limit what necessity had created, and of course that the prisoner should be treated with no unnecessary harshness. His lordship did not presume to state the reports which had reached him as absolute matters of fact, but only as rumours which demanded an inquiry, where the honour of the country was so nearly concerned. Most of the allegations on which Lord Holland grounded his motion, were contained in a paper of complaints sent by General Montholon. The particulars noticed in this remonstrance were circumstances which have been already adverted to, but may be here briefly noticed, as well as the answers by the British Government.

First, the restrictions upon the exercising ground formerly allowed to Napoleon, was alleged as a grievance. The climate of St. Helena, Lord Holland admitted, was good, but his lordship complained that the upper part of the island, where Longwood was situated, was damp and unhealthy. The inconvenience of the house was also complained of.

---

[266] See Parl. Debates, vol. xxxv., p. 1137.

Lord Bathurst, the colonial secretary of state, replied to this charge, that the general accounts of Longwood described it as healthy. It had been the usual country residence of the lieutenant-governor, which went far to show that the site could not be ineligible. The situation had been preferred by Napoleon himself, who was so impatient to take possession of it, that he even wished to have pitched a tent there till the house could be cleared for his reception. The restriction of the bounds of exercise, he explained to have been caused by Napoleon's evincing some disposition to tamper with the inhabitants. He still had a circuit of eight miles, within which he might range unattended and uncontrolled. If he wished to go farther, he was at liberty to traverse the island, upon permitting an orderly officer to join his suite. His refusal to take exercise on such terms, was not the fault of the British Government; and if Napoleon's health suffered in consequence, it was the result not of the regulations, which were reasonable and indispensable, but of his own wilfulness in refusing to comply with them.

The second class of exceptions taken by Lord Holland, was against what he considered as the harsh and iniquitous restrictions upon the exile's communication with Europe. He was not, his lordship stated, permitted to obtain books, or to subscribe for journals and newspapers. All intercourse by letter was interdicted to the distinguished prisoner, even with his wife, his child, and his nearest and dearest relatives. He was not allowed to write under seal to the Prince Regent.

Upon these several topics Lord Bathurst answered, that a list of books, the value of which amounted to £1400 or £1500 (which General Montholon termed a few books,) had been sent by Napoleon to Britain; that the commissioners put this list into the hands of an eminent French bookseller, who had supplied as many as could be obtained in London and Paris, but several of them, chiefly works on military matters, could not be procured. The volumes which could be procured, had been sent, with an apology for the omission of those which were not to be gotten; but the residents of Longwood had not admitted the excuse. Respecting the permission of a free subscription by Napoleon to journals, Lord Bathurst deemed it his duty to place some restriction upon that species of indulgence, attempts having been detected to establish a correspondence with Napoleon through the medium of newspapers. On the subject of intercourse with Europe by letter, Lord Bathurst stated that it was not interdicted, unless by the condition that Sir Hudson Lowe should previously be permitted to read the letter, whether of business or otherwise. This right, Lord Bathurst stated, had been exercised only by the governor in person, and with strict delicacy and feeling; and he repelled, with the most flat contradiction, the assertions of Montholon, that the governor of St. Helena had broken open and detained letters, under pretence that they did not come through the channel of the English minister. Lord Bathurst said, that General Montholon had been challenged by Sir Hudson Lowe to produce a single instance of such tyranny having been permitted, but that the French general had remained silent, the assertion being absolutely false. All the letters which the relatives of Napoleon were disposed to send through his, Lord Bathurst's office, he said, should be instantly forwarded, but it was a necessary preliminary that such should be written. Now, a letter from his brother Joseph, which was received in October last, and instantly forwarded, was the only one from any of his family or relatives which had reached the office. His lordship then adverted to the regulation which enacted, that even a letter to the Prince Regent must pass through the governor of St. Helena's hands in an open state. Lord Bathurst explained that the regulation gave the governor no authority or option as to transmitting the letter, which he was directed to forward instantly. The rule only required that Sir Hudson Lowe should be privy to the contents, in order, that, if it should contain any impeachment of his conduct, his defence or apology might reach London as soon as the accusation. This, his lordship remarked, was necessary, in order that no time might be lost in redressing a complaint of a grave character, or in repelling any frivolous and unsubstantial charge. He added, that should any sealed letter be addressed to the Prince Regent by Napoleon, he, Lord Bathurst, would have no hesitation to open it, if the governor had not previously done so. He should conceive it to be his duty to forward it instantly as addressed, whenever he was acquainted with the contents; but being in his department responsible for the acts of the sovereign, he would feel it his duty to make himself previously acquainted with the nature of the communication.

Thirdly, Lord Holland touched on the inadequacy of the sum allowed for the maintenance of Napoleon, and on the unworthiness of making that personage contribute to bear his own charges. The ministers, his lordship stated, having placed him in a situation where great expense was necessary, turned round upon him, and insisted that he should himself be in a great measure at the charge of supporting it.

Lord Bathurst replied by stating the facts with which the reader is already acquainted. He mentioned, that the sum of £8000 had been fixed upon as adequate, after the heavy expenses of the first year; and that it was increased to £12,000 on the remonstrance of Sir Hudson Lowe. This allowance, he said, was the same given to the governor, who had to bear the cost of frequent entertainments. It did not appear to government, that the family of Napoleon, which was to be maintained on the footing of that becoming a general officer of distinction, ought to cost more than that of Sir Hudson Lowe, who actually held that condition, with the necessity of discharging the expenses of his staff, and all other incumbent disbursements. He gave some details on the subject of the provisions and the cellar, from which it appeared, that, besides the inferior species of wine, the table of Napoleon was supplied at the rate of two bottles daily of those of a superior quality for each individual.

Lord Holland concluded with stating, that although Queen Mary could be no otherwise regarded than as the bitterest enemy of the illustrious Elizabeth, yet the greatest stain upon the memory of the latter sovereign was not the unjust, for *unjust* it was not, but the harsh and ungenerous treatment of Mary. He reminded the House, that it would not be considered by posterity, whether Buonaparte had been justly punished for his crimes, but whether Great Britain had acted in that generous manner which became a great country. He then moved for the production of such papers and correspondence betwixt St. Helena and the British Government, as should seem best fitted to throw light on the personal treatment of Napoleon.

It may be observed, that in the candid and liberal manner in which Lord Holland stated the case, he was led into a comparison unfavourable to his own argument. To have rendered the case of Mary (the justice of which his lordship admitted, in questioning its generosity) parallel to that of Napoleon, two remarkable circumstances were wanting. First, Mary, far from being at war with Queen Elizabeth, was ostensibly on the most friendly terms with that sovereign when she took refuge in England; secondly, the British Ministry testified no design to finish Napoleon's confinement by cutting off his head.

Lord Darnley, who had concurred with Lord Holland in desiring an inquiry, now considered the reports alluded to as totally refuted by the candid and able statement of Lord Bathurst, and was not of opinion that Lord Holland should press the motion farther. The Marquis of Buckingham's opinion was founded on the broad ground of Napoleon's delinquencies towards Europe, and England in particular. He was of opinion, that every degree of restraint necessary to prevent his escape, should be imposed and enforced. The severe and close durance to which General Buonaparte was subjected, was not, his lordship said, dictated by motives of revenge, but of security. It was a piece of political justice which we owed to Europe, and the defeat of which would never be forgotten in this or in any other state of the civilized world.

The motion of Lord Holland does not appear to have been seconded, and was negatived without a division.

There can be no doubt that the failure of this effort in the British Senate had a deep effect on Napoleon's spirits, and may, perhaps, have aggravated that tendency to disease in the stomach, which was suspected to have already taken place. Nothing is better known, though perhaps few things are more difficult to be satisfactorily explained, than the mysterious connexion betwixt distress of mind and the action of the digestive powers. Violent sickness is produced on many persons by extreme and sudden affliction, and almost every one feels the stomach more or less affected by that which powerfully and painfully occupies the mind. And here we may add, that Lord Holland's kindness and compassion for so great a man, under such severe circumstances, were shown by a variety of delicate attentions on his part and that of his lady, and that the supplies of books and other articles sent by them through the Foreign Office, where every facility was afforded for the conveyance, continued from time to time to give Napoleon assurance of their sympathy. But though he gratefully felt their attentions, his distress of body, and perhaps of mind, assumed a character incapable of receiving consolation.

This unhappy state was kept up and prolonged by the extent to which Buonaparte indulged in determined opposition to the various regulations respecting the custody of his person; on which subject every thing which occurred occasioned a struggle against the authority of Sir Hudson Lowe, or a new effort to obtain the Imperial distinctions which he considered as due to his rank.

The last point seems to have been carried to the length of childish extravagance. It was necessary, for example, that Dr. O'Meara should report to the governor of the island the state of the prisoner's health, which began to give room for serious apprehension. Napoleon insisted, that when this bulletin was rendered in writing, O'Meara, whom he considered as in his own service, should give him the title of Emperor. It was in vain that the Doctor remonstrated, pleading that the instructions of Government, as well as the orders of Lieutenant-General Lowe, prohibited him from using this forbidden epithet; and it was with difficulty that he at last prevailed that the word Personage or Patient might be substituted for the offensive phrase of *General Buonaparte*. Had this ingenious device not been resorted to, there could have been no communication with the Government on the subject of Napoleon's health.

The physician of Napoleon had till now enjoyed an easy office. His health was naturally sound; and, like many persons who enjoy the same inestimable advantage, the Ex-Emperor doubted of the healing powers of medicines which he never needed to use. Abstinence was his chief resource against stomach complaints, when these began to assail him, and the bath was frequently resorted to when the pangs became more acute. He also held it expedient to change the character of his way of living, when he felt affected with illness. If it had been sedentary, he rode hard and took violent exercise; and if, on the contrary, he had been taking more exercise than usual, he was accustomed to lay it aside for prolonged repose. But more recently he had not the wish to mount on horseback, or take exercise at all.

About the 25th of September, 1817, Napoleon's health seems to have been seriously affected. He complained much of nausea, his legs swelled, and there were other unfavourable symptoms, which induced his physician to tell him that he was of a temperament which required much activity; that constant exertion of mind and body was indispensable; and that without exercise he must soon lose his health. He immediately declared, that while exposed to the challenge of sentinels, he never would take exercise, however necessary. Dr. O'Meara proposed calling in the assistance of Dr. Baxter, a medical gentleman of eminence on Sir Hudson Lowe's staff. "He could but say the same as you do," said Napoleon, "and recommend my riding abroad; nevertheless, as long as the present system continues, I will never stir out." At another time he expressed the same resolution, and his determination to take no medicines. Dr. O'Meara replied, that, if the disease should not be encountered by remedies in due time, it would terminate fatally. His answer was remarkable: "I will have at least the consolation that my death will be an eternal dishonour to the English nation, who sent me to this climate to die under the hands of * * * *." The physician again represented, that, by neglecting to take medicine, he would accelerate his own death. "That which is written is written," said Napoleon, looking up. "Our days are reckoned."[267]

This deplorable and desperate course seems to have been adopted partly to spite Sir Hudson Lowe, partly in the reckless feelings of despondency inspired by his situation, and in some degree, perhaps, was the effect of the disease itself, which must necessarily have disinclined him to motion. Napoleon might also hope, that, by thus threatening to injure his health by forbearing exercise, he might extort the governor's acquiescence in some points which were disputed betwixt them. When the governor sent to offer

---

[267] Voice, &c., vol. ii., p. 256.

him some extension of his riding ground, and Dr. O'Meara wished him to profit by the permission, he replied, that he should be insulted by the challenge of the sentinels, and that he did not choose to submit to the caprice of the governor, who, granting an indulgence one day, might recall it the next. On such grounds as these—which, after all, amounted just to this, that being a prisoner, and one of great importance, he was placed under a system of vigilance, rendered more necessary by the constant intrigues carried on for his escape—did he feel himself at liberty to neglect those precautions of exercise and medicine, which were necessary for the preservation of his health. His conduct on such occasions can scarce be termed worthy of his powerful mind; it resembled too much that of the froward child, who refuses its food, or its physic, because it is contradicted.

REMOVAL OF O'MEARA

The removal of Dr. O'Meara from Napoleon's person, which was considered by him as a great injury, was the next important incident in the monotony of his life. It seems, from quotations given elsewhere in this volume, that Dr. O'Meara had been for some time a confident of Sir Hudson Lowe, and was recommended by him to ministers as a person by whose means he could learn what passed in the family of Napoleon. But in process of time, Dr. O'Meara, growing, perhaps, more intimate with the prisoner, became unwilling to supply the governor with the information of which he had been formerly profuse, and a quarrel took place betwixt him and Sir Hudson Lowe. In describing the scenes which passed between him and the governor, we have already said that Dr. O'Meara writes with a degree of personal animosity, which is unfavourable to his own credit. But his departure from St. Helena was occasioned by a warmer mark of the interest which he took in Napoleon's fortunes, than could be inferred from his merely refusing to inform Sir Hudson of what was said at Longwood.

Dr. O'Meara seems not only to have taken the part of Napoleon in his controversies with the governor, but also to have engaged deeply in forwarding a secret correspondence with a Mr.

Holmes, the Ex-Emperor's agent in London. This appears to have been clearly proved by a letter received from the agent, relating to large remittances of money to St. Helena, by the connivance of the physician.[268] Under such suspicions, Dr. O'Meara was withdrawn by the governor's mandate from attending on the person of Napoleon, and sent back to England. Napoleon had never obeyed his medical injunctions, but he complained severely when he was recalled from his household; expressing his belief that the depriving him of the medical attendant, whose prescriptions he had never followed, was a direct and bold step in the plan contrived for murdering him. It is probable, however, he regretted Dr. O'Meara's secret services more than those which were professional.

Sir Hudson Lowe again offered the assistance of Dr. Baxter, but this was construed at Longwood into an additional offence. It was even treated as an offer big with suspicion. The governor tried, it was said, to palm his own private physician upon the Emperor, doubtless that he might hold his life more effectually in his power. On the other hand, the British ministers were anxious that every thing should be done which could prevent complaints on this head. "You cannot better fulfil the wishes of his Majesty's Government" (says one of Lord Bathurst's despatches to the Governor) "than by giving effect to any measure which you may consider calculated to prevent any just ground of dissatisfaction on the part of General Buonaparte, on account of any real or supposed inadequacy of medical attendance."

Dr. Stokoe, surgeon on board the Conqueror, was next called in to visit at Longwood. But differences arose betwixt him and the governor, and after a few visits his attendance on Napoleon was discharged.

After this period, the prisoner expressed his determination, whatever might be the extremity of his case, not to permit the visits of an English physician; and a commission was sent to Italy to obtain a medical man of reputation from some of the seminaries in

---

[268] The letter alluded to is quoted at full length in the Quarterly Review, vol. xxviii., p. 224 to p. 226. It was received after Dr. O'Meara's dismission; which therefore, must have been occasioned only by the suspicion of what was afterwards proved.—S.

that country. At the same time, Napoleon signified a desire to have the company of a Catholic priest. The proposition for this purpose came through his uncle, Cardinal Fesch, to the Papal government, and readily received the assent of the British ministry. It would appear that this mission had been thought by his Holiness to resemble, in some degree, those sent into foreign and misbelieving countries; for two churchmen were despatched to St. Helena instead of one.

The senior priest, Father Bonavita, was an elderly man, subject to the infirmities belonging to his period of life, and broken by a residence of twenty-six years in Mexico. His speech had been affected by a paralytic stroke. His recommendation to the office which he now undertook, was his having been father confessor to Napoleon's mother. His companion was a young abbé, called Vignali.[269] Both were pious, good men, well qualified, doubtless, to give Napoleon the comfort which their Church holds out to those who receive its tenets, but not so much as to reclaim wanderers, or confirm those who might doubt the doctrines of the Church.

RELIGIOUS OPINIONS

Argument or controversy, however, were not necessary. Napoleon had declared his resolution to die in the faith of his fathers. He was neither an infidel, he said, nor a philosopher. If we doubt whether a person who had conducted himself towards the Pope in the way which history records of Napoleon, and who had at one time been excommunicated, (if, indeed, the ban was yet removed,) could be sincere in his general professions of Catholicism, we must at least acquit the Exile of the charge of deliberate atheism. On various occasions, he expressed, with deep feelings of devotion, his conviction of the existence of the Deity, the great truth upon which the whole system of religion rests; and this at a time when the detestable doctrines of atheism and materialism

---

[269] "As member of the College of the Propaganda, he could not go alone. Missions in which the line is to be crossed, must be composed of at least two missionaries; and the Abbé Vignali, who had some notions of medicine, was attached to Bonavita. Princess Pauline gave her cook; Madame Mère one of her valets; and thus a little colony was formed."—*Antommarchi*, vol. i., p. 9.

were generally current in France. Immediately after his elevation to the dignity of First Consul, he meditated the restoration of religion; and thus, in a mixture of feeling and of policy, expressed himself upon the subject to Thibaudeau, then a counsellor of state. Having combated for a long time the systems of modern philosophers upon different kinds of worship, upon deism, natural religion, and so forth, he proceeded. "Last Sunday evening, in the general silence of nature, I was walking in these grounds (of Malmaison.) The sound of the church-bell of Ruel fell upon my ear, and renewed all the impressions of my youth. I was profoundly affected, such is the power of early habit and associations; and I considered, if such was the case with me, what must not be the effect of such recollections upon the more simple and credulous vulgar? Let your philosophers answer that. The people must have a religion." He went on to state the terms on which he would negotiate with the Pope, and added, "They will say I am a Papist—I am no such thing. I was a Mahomedan in Egypt. I will be a Catholic here, for the good of the people. I do not believe in forms of religion, but in the existence of a God!" He extended his hands towards heaven—"Who is it that has created all above and around us?"[270] This sublime passage proves, that Napoleon (unfortunate in having proceeded no farther towards the Christian shrine) had at least crossed the threshold of the temple, and believed in and worshipped the Great Father of the Universe.

The missionaries were received at St. Helena with civility, and the rites of mass were occasionally performed at Longwood. Both the clergymen were quiet, unobtrusive characters, confining themselves to their religious duties, and showing neither the abilities, nor the active and intriguing spirit which Protestants are apt to impute to the Catholic priesthood.

The same vessel which arrived at St. Helena on the 18th September, in 1819, with these physicians for the mind, brought with them Dr. F. Antommarchi, anatomic pro-sector (that is, assistant to a professor of anatomy) to the Hospital of St. Marie Neuve at Florence, attached to the University of Pisa, who was designed to supply the place about the prisoner's person, occupied

---

[270] Mémoire sur le Consulat, 1799 et 1804.—S.

by Dr. O'Meara, and after him provisionally by Dr. Stokoe. He continued to hold the office till Napoleon's death, and his Account of his Last Moments, a work in two volumes, though less interesting, and showing far less acuteness than that of Las Cases, or of O'Meara, is yet useful and entertaining, as relating to the last days of so extraordinary a person. Dr. Antommarchi seems to have been acceptable to Napoleon, and the rather that he was a native of Corsica. He brought also news from his family. The Princess Pauline Borghese had offered to come to attend him. "Let her remain where she is," said Napoleon; "I would not have her witness the degrading state which I am reduced to, and the insults to which I am subjected."

It is needless to resume the subject of these alleged insults. They consisted in the precautions which Sir Hudson Lowe deemed himself obliged to take for the security of his prisoner; particularly in requiring that a British officer should be regularly made assured of his being at Longwood, and that an officer, not under the rank of captain, should attend him on the excursions which he proposed to make through the island. On these subjects, Napoleon had made his mind up to a species of passive resistance; and had, as we have seen, already expressed himself determined to take no exercise, however indispensable to his health, unless the regulations of his confinement were entirely dispensed with, or modified according to his own pleasure. This was an argument *ad misericordiam*, which must have given the governor great distress and uneasiness; since, if the health of the prisoner should fail, even though it was through his own wilfulness, Sir Hudson could not expect that his conduct would escape censure. At the same time, if he yielded to this species of compulsory argument, it might be carried to an extent altogether inconsistent with the safe custody of the captive. His vigilance was also sharpened by constant reports of plots for the liberation of Napoleon; and the sums of money which he and his family had at their command, rendered it dangerous to trust to the natural securities of the island. It is remarkable, too, that, in demanding, as a matter of right, freedom from the restrictions of which he complained, Napoleon never proposed any concessions on his part, by offer of his parole or otherwise, which might tend to give any additional moral assurance, in place of those limitations which he desired to have removed. Yet, to accommodate himself, in some degree to his prisoner's obstinacy, Sir Hudson Lowe was content that the British officer, whose duty it was to report on the presence of Napoleon at Longwood, should only be required to satisfy himself of it by such indirect opportunities as his walking in the garden, or appearing at the window, permitted him to enjoy, and on such occasions he was enjoined to keep his own person concealed. In this way, there were days which passed without any regular report on this most important point, for which Sir Hudson Lowe would have been highly responsible if an escape had been effected. We beg to refer to Dr. Antommarchi's work for instances of the peculiar and grossly indelicate opportunities, which, to compound between the necessity of the case and the obstinacy of Napoleon, his attendants took to make his person visible when he was not aware of it.[271]

PLANS OF ESCAPE

Schemes for Napoleon's escape were not wanting. A Colonel Latapie, distinguished as a partisan officer, was said to be at the head of an attempt to carry him off from St. Helena, which was to be undertaken by a band of desperadoes from America. But Napoleon said, he knew too well the character of such adventurers to hope to profit by them. Government had other information of attempts to be made from America, but none of them seem to have proceeded to any serious length.

It was different with the undertaking of Johnstone, a smuggler of an uncommonly resolute character, and whose life had been a tissue of desperate risks. He had made a memorable escape from Newgate, and had afterwards piloted Lord Nelson's vessel to the attack of Copenhagen, when the ordinary masters of the fleet, and pilots, declined the task. Johnstone was also said to have meditated a bold attempt to carry off Buonaparte on a former occasion, when he trusted himself on the water for the purpose of visiting Flushing.[272]

---

[271] Antommarchi, vol. ii., p. 71.
[272] Such at least was the report. The attempt was to have been made by Johnstone and his desperate associates in a boat, which they were to row across the Scheldt towards Flushing,

And now he certainly engaged in a plot to deliver Napoleon from St. Helena, of a very singular kind. A submarine vessel—that is, a ship capable of being sunk under water for a certain time, and of being raised again at pleasure by disengaging certain weights, was to be the means of effecting this enterprise. It was thought that, by sinking the vessel during the daytime, she might escape the notice of the British cruizers, and being raised at night, might approach the guarded rock without discovery. The vessel was actually begun in one of the building-yards upon the Thames; but the peculiarity of her construction having occasioned suspicions, she was seized by the British Government.

These, and others which we could name, were very perilous and wild attempts, yet calculated to keep vigilance alive; for in every case in which great natural difficulties had been surmounted by such enterprises, it has been because these difficulties have been too much relied upon. But while such precarious means of escape were presented from time to time, the chance upon which Napoleon secretly relied for release from his present situation was vanishing from his eyes.

His case was mentioned in the House of Commons, but incidentally only, on the 12th July 1819.[273] The subject was introduced into a debate on finance, when Mr. C. H. Hutchinson pointed out the yearly expense of detaining Napoleon at St. Helena, which he stated to amount to half-a-million sterling, as a useless expenditure of public money. In this statement, he received no countenance from any one except Mr. Joseph Hume. It was answered by the Chancellor of the Exchequer; and the expense was declared not to exceed a fifth-part of the sum alleged. The leading members of Opposition seemed to take no interest in the question; and it was believed at St. Helena, that Napoleon's disappointment in

---

just when Napoleon was proceeding thither. They were to board the imperial barge, throw every one save Napoleon into the sea, and, removing him to their own light row-boat, were to pull out and deliver him up to the British squadron, then cruizing off the island. It is added, that Napoleon took the alarm from seeing a boat rowing very swiftly towards him, and, ordering his crew to pull harder, or give way, as it is called, the smuggler, instead of running athwart the barge, fell astern, and the opportunity was lost. We do not know that there is any good authority for this story.—S.

[273] Parl. Debates, vol. xl., p. 1559.

the hopes which he had entertained of their strong and overpowering interposition in his behalf, first led to his mental depression and total abandonment of hope.

The complexion of the times, indeed, had become such as to strengthen every reason which existed for detaining him in captivity. The state of England, owing to the discontent and sufferings of the manufacturing districts—and more especially that of Italy, convulsed by the short-lived revolutions of Naples and Savoy—rendered the safe custody of Napoleon a matter of more deep import than it had been at any time since his fall. What the effect of his name might have produced in that moment of general commotion, cannot be estimated, but the consequences of his escape must have been most formidable.

The British Ministry, aware of the power of such a spirit to work among the troubled elements, anxiously enjoined additional vigilance to the governor of St. Helena:

"The overthrow of the Neapolitan government, the revolutionary spirit which more or less prevails over all Italy, and the doubtful state of France itself, must excite his attention, and clearly show that a crisis is fast approaching, if not already arrived, when his escape would be productive of important consequences. That his partisans are active, cannot be doubted; and if he be ever willing to hazard the attempt, he will never allow such an opportunity to escape. You will, therefore, exert all your attention in watching his proceedings, and call upon the admiral to use his utmost vigilance, as upon the navy so much must ultimately depend."[274]

INCREASED ILLNESS

The alarm was natural, but there was no real cause for apprehension. Politics and war were never more to know the powerful influence of Napoleon Buonaparte. His lost hopes aggravating the progress of the cruel disease, which had its source in

---

[274] Despatches to Sir Hudson Lowe, 30th September 1820.—S.

the stomach, it now affected the whole frame, and undermined the strength of the constitution. Death was now finally to terminate the fretful and degrading discussions, by which he inflicted, and from which he received, so much pain, and to open the gates of a prison, for which Hope herself could scarce present another key. The symptoms of disorganisation in the digestive powers became more and more apparent, and his reluctance to take any medicine, as if from an instinctive persuasion that the power of physic was in vain, continued as obstinate as ever. On one of the many disputes which he maintained on this subject, he answered Antommarchi's reasoning thus:—"Doctor, no physicking. We are, as I already told you, a machine made to live. We are organised for that purpose, and such is our nature. Do not counteract the living principle. Let it alone—leave it the liberty of defending itself—it will do better than your drugs. Our body is a watch, that is intended to go for a given time. The watchmaker cannot open it; and must, on handling it, grope his way blindfolded and at random. For once that he assists and relieves it by dint of tormenting it with his crooked instruments, he injures it ten times, and at last destroys it."[275] This was on the 14th of October, 1820.

As the Ex-Emperor's health grew weaker, it cannot be thought extraordinary that his mind became more and more depressed. In lack of other means of amusing himself, he had been somewhat interested in the construction of a pond and fountain in the garden of Longwood, which was stocked with small fishes. A mixture of copperas in the mastick employed in cementing the basin, had affected the water. The creatures which had been in a good measure the object of Napoleon's attention, began to sicken and to die. He was deeply affected by the circumstance, and, in language strongly resembling the beautiful verses of Moore, expressed his sense of the fatality which seemed to attach itself to him. "Every thing I love—every thing that belongs to me," he exclaimed, "is immediately struck.[276] Heaven and mankind unite to afflict me."[277] At other times he lamented his decay of energy. The

---

[275] Antommarchi, vol. i., p. 339.
[276] Antommarchi, vol. i., p. 363.
[277] "'Twas ever thus—from childhood's hour I've seen my fondest hopes decay; I never loved a tree or flower, But was the first to fade away."

bed, he said, was now a place of luxury, which he would not exchange for all the thrones in the universe. The eyes, which formerly were so vigilant, could now scarcely be opened. He recollected that he used to dictate to four or five secretaries at once. "But then," he said, "I was Napoleon—now I am no longer any thing—my strength, my faculties, forsake me—I no longer live, I only exist."[278] Often he remained silent for many hours, suffering, as may be supposed, much pain, and immersed in profound melancholy.

About the 22d January, 1821, Napoleon appeared to resume some energy, and to make some attempt to conquer his disease by exercise. He mounted his horse, and galloped, for the last time, five or six miles around the limits of Longwood, but nature was overcome by the effort. He complained that his strength was sinking under him rapidly.[279]

The governor had already transmitted to Britain accounts of Napoleon's decay of health, without having it, however, in his power to ascertain how far it was real, or how far the appearances were assumed. The patient would neither receive the visit of any English surgeon or physician, nor would he authorise the communication of Dr. Antommarchi with Sir Hudson Lowe. The governor was obliged to state accounts of the prisoner's declining health as reports, the reality of which he had no means of ascertaining. The generous feelings of the great personage at the head of the British Government were naturally deeply interested in the fate of the prisoner, and prompted him, by every means in his power, and especially by expressions of his own sympathy, to extend such hope and comfort to Napoleon as he could be supposed to receive, under the necessity of his continued captivity. The following

---

[278] Antommarchi, vol. i., p. 371.

[279] "He repeated the attempt three or four times, and with as little success. 'I now see,' said he, with a tone of affliction, 'that my strength forsakes me. Nature no longer answers, as formerly, to the appeals of my will; violent shocks are no longer suited to my debilitated frame: but I shall attain the end I propose by moderate exercise.' On the following day, the Emperor was labouring under profound depression of spirits;—he still felt persuaded that exercise would save him. 'Sire,' said Montholon, 'perhaps the see-saw would do your Majesty good?'—'True, I will try: have one arranged.' This was immediately done; but this motion produced no favourable effect, and he gave it up."—Antommarchi, vol. i., p. 393.

is Lord Bathurst's despatch to Sir Hudson Lowe on this interesting subject, dated 16th February, 1821:—

"I am aware how difficult it is to make any communication to the General which will not be liable to misrepresentation; and yet, if he be really ill, he may derive some consolation by knowing, that the repeated accounts which have of late been transmitted of his declining health, have not been received with indifference. You will, therefore, communicate to General Buonaparte the great interest which his Majesty has taken in the recent accounts of his indisposition, and the anxiety which his Majesty feels to afford him every relief of which his situation admits. You will assure General Buonaparte that there is no alleviation which can be derived from additional medical assistance, nor any arrangement consistent with the safe custody of his person at St. Helena, (and his Majesty cannot now hold out any expectation of his removal,) which his Majesty is not most ready and desirous to afford. You will not only repeat the offer which has already been more than once made, of such further medical assistance as the island of St. Helena affords, but you will give him the option of procuring the attendance of any of the medical gentlemen who are at the Cape, where there is one, at least, of considerable eminence in his profession; and in case of any wish being expressed by the General to receive such assistance, you will consider yourself authorised to make a communication to the Cape, and take such other measures as may be necessary to secure the immediate attendance of the person whom the General may name."

Napoleon had not the satisfaction to know the interest which his Majesty took in his illness, which would probably have afforded him some gleam of consolation. The tenor of the letter might, perhaps, have induced him to think, that his own system of pertinacious contest with the authorities under whose charge he was placed, had been so far injudicious, as to lead to doubts of the reality of the disorder under which he was dying; and had therefore been one great cause of intercepting the sympathy, and perhaps the relief, which must otherwise have extended itself to a situation so well deserving of commiseration.

LAST ILLNESS

Towards the end of March the disease assumed a character still more formidable, and Dr. Antommarchi became desirous of obtaining a consultation with some of the English medical men. The Emperor's aversion to their assistance had been increased by a well-meant offer of the governor, announcing that a physician of eminence had arrived at the island, whom he therefore placed at General Buonaparte's devotion.[280] This proposal, like every other advance on the part of Sir Hudson Lowe, had been received as a meditated injury; "He wants to deceive Europe by false bulletins," said Napoleon; "I will not see any one who is in communication with him."[281] To refuse seeing every physician but his own, was certainly an option which ought to have been left in Napoleon's choice, and it was so left accordingly. But in thus obstinately declining to see an impartial medical man, whose report must have been conclusive respecting his state of health, Napoleon unquestionably strengthened the belief, that his case was not so desperate as it proved to be.

At length the Ex-Emperor consented that Dr. Antommarchi should consult with Dr. Arnott, surgeon of the 20th regiment.[282] But the united opinion of the medical gentlemen could not overcome the aversion of Napoleon to medicine, or shake the belief which he reposed in the gloomy doctrines of fatalism. "Quod scriptum scriptum," he replied in the language of a Moslem; "All that is to happen is written down. Our hour is marked, and it is not in our power to claim a moment longer of life than Fate has predestined for us."[283]

---

[280] Dr. Shortt, physician to the forces; who, at this time, replaced Dr. Baxter as principal medical officer at St. Helena, and to whom we have been obliged for much valuable information.—S.

[281] Antommarchi, vol. ii., p. 59.

[282] "I seized a moment, when the Emperor was more tranquil, to hazard a few words about the necessity of a consultation.—'A consultation! what would be the use of it? You all work in the dark. No! I will have none of them.' The Emperor was warm, and I therefore did not insist for the moment, but waited until he was more calm, when I again pressed the subject. 'You persist,' said he, with a tone of kindness, 'consult with the physician of the island that you consider the most skilful. I accordingly applied to Dr. Arnott."—Antommarchi, vol. ii., p. 59.

[283] Antommarchi, vol. ii., p. 65.

Dr. Antommarchi finally prevailed in obtaining admittance for Dr. Arnott into the apartment and presence of the patient, who complained chiefly of his stomach, of the disposition to vomit, and deficiency of the digestive powers. He saw him, for the first time on 2d April, 1821, and continued his visits regularly. Napoleon expressed his opinion that his liver was affected. Dr. Arnott's observations led him to think, that though the action of the liver might be imperfect, the seat of the disease was to be looked for elsewhere. And here it is to be remarked, that Napoleon, when Dr. Antommarchi expressed doubts on the state of his stomach, had repelled them with sharpness, though his own private belief was, that he was afflicted with the disease of his father. Thus, with a capricious inconsistency, natural enough to a sick bed, he communicated to some of his retinue his sense of what disease afflicted him, though, afraid perhaps of some course of medicine being proposed, he did not desire that his surgeon should know his suspicions.[284] From the 15th to the 24th of April, Napoleon was engaged from time to time in making his testamentary bequests, of which we shall have occasion to make some mention hereafter, as illustrative of his peculiar character and sentiments. On the day last mentioned, he was greatly exhausted by the fatigue of writing, and showed symptoms of over-excitation. Among these may be safely included, a plan which he spoke of for reconciling all religious dissensions in France, which he said he had designed to carry into effect.

As the strength of the patient gradually sunk, the symptoms of his disease became less equivocal, until, on the 27th April, the ejection of a dark-coloured fluid gave farther insight into the nature of the malady. Dr. Antommarchi persevered in attributing it to climate, which was flattering the wish of the patient, who desired to lay his death upon his confinement at St. Helena; while Dr. Arnott expressed his belief that the disease was the same which cut off his father in the pure air of Montpellier. Dr. Antommarchi, as usually happens to the reporter of a debate, silenced his antagonist in the argument, although Dr. Arnott had by this time obtained the patient's own authority for the assertion. Upon the 28th of April,

---

[284] Madame Bertrand mentioned to Dr. Shortt that Napoleon conceived himself dying of cancer in the stomach, which she considered as a mere whim.—S.

Napoleon gave instructions to Antommarchi, that after his death his body should be opened, but that no English medical man should touch him, unless in the case of assistance being absolutely necessary, in which case he gave Antommarchi leave to call in that of Dr. Arnott. He directed that his heart should be conveyed to Parma, to Maria Louisa; and requested anxiously that his stomach should be particularly examined, and the report transmitted to his son. "The vomitings," he said, "which succeed one another without interruption, lead me to suppose that the stomach is, of all my organs, the most diseased; and I am inclined to believe that it is attacked with the same disorder which killed my father—I mean a scirrhus in the pylorus." On the 2d May, the patient returned to the same interesting subject, reminded Antommarchi of his anxiety that the stomach should be carefully examined. "The physicians of Montpellier had announced that the scirrhus in the pylorus would be hereditary in my family. Their report is, I believe, in the hands of Louis. Ask for it, and compare it with your own observations, that I may save my son from the sufferings I now experience."

DEATH

During the 3d May, it was seen that the life of Napoleon was drawing evidently to a close; and his followers, and particularly his physician, became desirous to call in more medical assistance;—that of Dr. Shortt, physician to the forces, and of Dr. Mitchell, surgeon of the flagship, was referred to. Dr. Shortt, however, thought it proper to assert the dignity belonging to his profession, and refused (being under the same roof with the patient,) to give an opinion on a case of so much importance in itself, and attended with so much obscurity, unless he were permitted to see and examine him. The officers of Napoleon's household excused themselves, by professing that the Emperor's strict commands had been laid on them, that no English physician, Dr. Arnott excepted, should approach his dying bed. They said, that even when he was speechless they would be unable to brook his eye, should he turn it upon them in reproof for their disobedience.

About two o'clock of the same day, the priest Vignali administered the sacrament of extreme unction. Some days before, Napoleon had explained to him the manner in which he desired his body should be laid out in state, in an apartment lighted by torches, or what Catholics call *une chambre ardente*. "I am neither," he said, in the same phrase which we have formerly quoted, "a philosopher nor a physician. I believe in God, and am of the religion of my father. It is not every body who can be an atheist. I was born a Catholic, and will fulfil all the duties of the Catholic Church, and receive the assistance which it administers." He then turned to Dr. Antommarchi, whom he seems to have suspected of heterodoxy, which the doctor, however, disowned. "How can you carry it so far?" he said. "Can you not believe in God, whose existence every thing proclaims, and in whom the greatest minds have believed?"[285]

As if to mark a closing point of resemblance betwixt Cromwell and Napoleon, a dreadful tempest arose on the 4th May, which preceded the day that was to close the mortal existence of this extraordinary man. A willow, which had been the Exile's favourite, and under which he had often enjoyed the fresh breeze, was torn up by the hurricane; and almost all the trees about Longwood shared the same fate.

The 5th of May came amid wind and rain. Napoleon's passing spirit was deliriously engaged in a strife more terrible than that of the elements around. The words *"tête d'armée,"* the last which escaped his lips, intimated that his thoughts were watching the current of a heady fight. About eleven minutes before six in the evening, Napoleon, after a struggle which indicated the original strength of his constitution, breathed his last.

The officers of Napoleon's household were disposed to have the body anatomized in secret. But Sir Hudson Lowe had too deep a sense of the responsibility under which he and his country stood, to permit this to take place. He declared, that even if he were reduced to make use of force, he would insure the presence of English physicians at the dissection.

---

[285] Antommarchi, vol. ii., p. 120.

Generals Bertrand and Montholon, with Marchand, the valet-de-chambre of the deceased, were present at the operation, which took place on the 6th of May. It was also witnessed by Sir Thomas Reade, and some British staff-officers. Drs. Thomas Shortt, Archibald Arnott, Charles Mitchell, Matthew Livingstone, and Francis Burton, all of them medical men, were also present. The cause of death was sufficiently evident. A large ulcer occupied almost the whole of the stomach. It was only the strong adhesion of the diseased parts of that organ to the concave surface of the lobe of the liver, which, being over the ulcer, had prolonged the patient's life by preventing the escape of the contents of the stomach into the cavity of the abdomen. All the other parts of the viscera were found in a tolerably healthy state. The report was signed by the British medical gentlemen present. Dr. Antommarchi was about to add his attestation, when, according to information which we consider as correct, General Bertrand interdicted his doing so, because the report was drawn up as relating to the body of *General Buonaparte*. Dr. Antommarchi's own account does not, we believe, greatly differ from that of the British professional persons, though he has drawn conclusions from it which are apparently inconsistent with the patient's own conviction, and the ghastly evidence of the anatomical operation. He continued to insist that his late patron had not died of the cancer which we have described, or, in medical language, of scirrhus of the pylorus, but of a *chronic gastro hepatitis*, a disease he stated to be endemic in the island of St. Helena; although we do not observe it asserted or proved that the hospital of the island, at any time, produced a single case like that of the deceased captive.

The gentlemen of Napoleon's suite were desirous that his heart should be preserved and given to their custody. But Sir Hudson Lowe did not feel himself at liberty to permit this upon his own authority. He agreed, however, that the heart should be placed in a silver vase, filled with spirits, and interred along with the body; so that, in case his instructions from home should so permit, it might be afterwards disinhumed and sent to Europe.

The place of interment became the next subject of discussion. On this subject Napoleon had been inconsistent. His testamentary disposition expressed a wish that his remains should be deposited on the banks of the Seine; a request which he could not for an instant suppose would be complied with, and which appears to have been made solely for the sake of producing effect. The reflection of an instant would have been sufficient to call to recollection, that he would not, while in power, have allowed Louis XVIII. a grave in the land of his fathers; nor *did* he permit the remains of the Duc D'Enghien any other interment than that assigned to the poorest outcast, who is huddled to earth on the spot on which he dies. But neither did the agitated state of the public mind, now general through Italy, recommend the measure.

FUNERAL

A grave for the Emperor of France, within the limits of the rocky island to which his last years were limited, was the alternative that remained; and sensible that this was likely to be the case, he had himself indicated the spot where he wished to lie. It was a small secluded recess, called Slane's, or Haines' Valley, where a fountain arose, at which his Chinese domestics used to fill the silver pitchers which they carried to Longwood for Napoleon's use. The spot had more of verdure and shade than any in the neighbourhood; and the illustrious Exile was often accustomed to repose under the beautiful weeping willows which overhung the spring. The body, after lying in state in his small bed-room, during which time it was visited by every person of condition in the island, was, on the 8th May, carried to the place of interment. The pall which covered the coffin was the military cloak which Napoleon had worn at the battle of Marengo. The members of his late household attended as mourners, and were followed by the governor, the admiral, and all the civil and military authorities of the island. All the troops were under arms upon the solemn occasion. As the road did not permit a near approach of the hearse to the place of sepulture, a party of British grenadiers had the honour to bear the coffin to the grave. The prayers were recited by the priest, Abbé Vignali. Minute guns were fired from the admiral's ship. The coffin was then let down into the grave, under a discharge of three successive volleys of artillery, from fifteen pieces of cannon. A large stone was then lowered down on the grave, and covered the moderate space now sufficient for the man for whom Europe was once too little.

CONCLUSION

CONCLUSION

Arrived at the conclusion of this momentous narrative, the reader may be disposed to pause a moment to reflect on the character of that wonderful person, on whom Fortune showered so many favours in the beginning and through the middle of his career, to overwhelm its close with such deep and unwonted afflictions.

The external appearance of Napoleon was not imposing at the first glance, his stature being only five feet six inches English. His person, thin in youth, and somewhat corpulent in age, was rather delicate than robust in outward appearance, but cast in the mould most capable of enduring privation and fatigue. He rode ungracefully, and without the command of his horse which distinguishes a perfect cavalier; so that he showed to disadvantage when riding beside such a horseman as Murat. But he was fearless, sat firm in his seat, rode with rapidity, and was capable of enduring the exercise for a longer time than most men. We have already mentioned his indifference to the quality of his food, and his power of enduring abstinence. A morsel of food, and a flask of wine hung at his saddle-bow, used, in his earlier campaigns, to support him for days. In his latter wars, he more frequently used a carriage; not, as has been surmised, from any particular illness, but from feeling in a frame so constantly in exercise the premature effects of age.

The countenance of Napoleon is familiar to almost every one from description, and the portraits which are found every where. The dark-brown hair bore little marks of the attentions of the toilet. The shape of the countenance approached more than is usual in the human race to a square. His eyes were grey and full of expression, the pupils rather large, and the eyebrows not very strongly marked.

The brow and upper part of the countenance was rather of a stern character. His nose and mouth were beautifully formed. The upper lip was very short. The teeth were indifferent, but were little shown in speaking.[286] His smile possessed uncommon sweetness, and is stated to have been irresistible. The complexion was a clear olive, otherwise in general colourless. The prevailing character of his countenance was grave, even to melancholy, but without any signs of severity or violence. After death, the placidity and dignity of expression which continued to occupy the features, rendered them eminently beautiful, and the admiration of all who looked on them.

Such was Napoleon's exterior. His personal and private character was decidedly amiable, excepting in one particular. His temper, when he received, or thought he received, provocation, especially if of a personal character, was warm and vindictive. He was, however, placable in the case even of his enemies, providing that they submitted to his mercy; but he had not that species of generosity which respects the sincerity of a manly and fair opponent. On the other hand, no one was a more liberal rewarder of the attachment of his friends. He was an excellent husband, a kind relation, and, unless when state policy intervened, a most affectionate brother. General Gourgaud, whose communications were not in every case to Napoleon's advantage, states him to have been the best of masters, labouring to assist all his domestics wherever it lay in his power, giving them the highest credit for such talents as they actually possessed, and imputing, in some instances, good qualities to such as had them not.

There was gentleness, and even softness, in his character. He was affected when he rode over the fields of battle, which his ambition had strewed with the dead and the dying, and seemed not only desirous to relieve the victims—issuing for that purpose directions, which too often were not, and could not be, obeyed—but showed himself subject to the influence of that more acute and imaginative species of sympathy, which is termed sensibility. He mentions a circumstance which indicates a deep sense of feeling. As he passed over a field of battle in Italy, with some of his generals, he saw a houseless dog lying on the body of his slain master. The

---

[286] When at St. Helena, he was much troubled with toothache and scurvy in the gums.—S.

creature came towards them, then returned to the dead body, moaned over it pitifully, and seemed to ask their assistance. "Whether it were the feeling of the moment," continued Napoleon, "the scene, the hour, or the circumstance itself, I was never so deeply affected by any thing which I have seen upon a field of battle. That man, I thought, has perhaps had a house, friends, comrades, and here he lies deserted by every one but his dog. How mysterious are the impressions to which we are subject! I was in the habit, without emotion, of ordering battles which must decide the fate of a campaign, and could look with a dry eye on the execution of manœuvres which must be attended with much loss; and here I was moved—nay, painfully affected—by the cries and the grief of a dog. It is certain that at that moment I should have been more accessible to a suppliant enemy, and could better understand the conduct of Achilles in restoring the body of Hector to the tears of Priam."[287] The anecdote at once shows that Napoleon possessed a heart amenable to humane feelings, and that they were usually in total subjection to the stern precepts of military stoicism. It was his common and expressive phrase, that the heart of a politician should be in his head; but his feelings sometimes surprised him in a gentler mood.

A calculator by nature and by habit, Napoleon was fond of order, and a friend to that moral conduct in which order is best exemplified. The libels of the day have made some scandalous averments to the contrary, but without adequate foundation. Napoleon respected himself too much, and understood the value of public opinion too well, to have plunged into general or vague debauchery.

Considering his natural disposition, then, it may be assumed that if Napoleon had continued in the vale of private life, and no strong temptation of passion or revenge had crossed his path, he must have been generally regarded as one whose friendship was every way desirable, and whose enmity it was not safe to incur.

But the opportunity afforded by the times, and the elasticity of his own great talents, both military and political, raised him with

---

[287] Las Cases, tom. i., part ii., p. 5.

unexampled celerity to a sphere of great power, and at least equal temptation. Ere we consider the use which he made of his ascendency, let us briefly review the causes by which it was accomplished.

The consequences of the Revolution, however fatal to private families, were the means of filling the camps of the nation with armies of a description which Europe had never seen before, and it is to be hoped, will never witness again. There was neither safety, honour, nor almost subsistence, in any other profession than the military; and accordingly it became the refuge of the best and bravest of the youth of France, until the army ceased to consist, as in most nations, of the miserable and disorderly class of the community, but was levied in the body and bosom of the state, and composed of the flower of France, whether as regarded health, moral qualities, or elevation of mind. With such men, the generals of the republic achieved many and great victories, but without being able to ensure corresponding advantages. This may have been in a great measure occasioned by the dependence in which these leaders were held by the various administrators of the republic at home—a dependence accounted for by the necessity of having recourse to those in power at Paris, for the means of paying and supporting their armies. From the time that Napoleon passed the Alps, he inverted this state of things; and made the newly conquered countries not only maintain the army by means of contributions and confiscations, but even contribute to support the government. Thus war, which had hitherto been a burden to the republic, became in his hands a source of public revenue; while the youthful general, contributing to the income of the state, on which his predecessors had been dependent, was enabled to assert the freedom at which he speedily aimed, and correspond with the Directory upon a footing approaching to equality. His talents as a soldier, and situation as a victorious general, soon raised him from equality to pre-eminence.

These talents applied not less to the general arrangements of the campaign, than to the dispositions for actual battle. In each of these great departments of war, Napoleon was not merely a pupil of the most approved masters of the art—he was an improver, an innovator, and an inventor.

In strategie, he applied upon a gigantic scale the principles upon which Frederick of Prussia had acted, and gained a capital or a kingdom, when Frederick would have won a town or a province. His system was, of course, that of assembling the greatest possible force of his own upon the vulnerable point of the enemy's position, paralyzing, perhaps, two parts of their army, while he cut the third to pieces, and then following up his position by destroying the remainder in detail. For this purpose, he taught generals to divide their armies upon the march, with a view to celerity of movement and facility of supply, and to unite them at the moment of contest, where an attack would be most feebly resisted, because least expected. For this, also, he first threw aside all species of baggage which could possibly be dispensed with—supplied the want of magazines by the contributions exacted from the country, or collected from individuals by a regular system of marauding—discontinued the use of tents, and trusted to bivouacking with his soldiers, where hamlets could not be found, and there was no time to erect huts. His system was ruinous in point of lives, for even the military hospitals were often dispensed with; but although Moreau termed Napoleon a conqueror at the rate of ten thousand men a-day, yet the sacrifice for a length of time uniformly attained the object for which it was designed. The enemy who had remained in their extensive cantonments, distracted by the reports of various columns moving in different directions, were surprised and defeated by the united force of the French, which had formed a junction where and when it was least expected. It was not till they had acquired the art of withdrawing from his attack so soon as made, that the allies learned to defeat the efforts of his movable columns.

Napoleon was not less original as a tactician than as a strategist. His manœuvres on the field of battle had the promptness and decision of the thunderbolt. In the actual shock of conflict, as in the preparations which he made for bringing it on, his object was to amuse the enemy upon many points, while he oppressed one by an unexpected force of numbers. The breaking through the line, the turning of a flank, which had been his object from the commencement of the fight, lay usually disguised under a great number of previous demonstrations, and was not attempted until both the moral and physical force of the enemy was impaired by the length of the combat. It was at this period that he brought up his guards, who, impatient of inactivity, had been held in readiness for hours, and now, springing forward like wolf-dogs from the leash, had the glorious task, in which they rarely failed, of deciding the long-sustained contest. It may be added, as further characteristic of his tactics, that he preferred employing the order of the column to that of the line; perhaps on account of the faith which he might rest in the extreme valour of the French officers by whom the column was headed.

The interest which Napoleon preserved in the French soldier's affection by a frequent distribution of prizes and distinctions, as well as by his familiar notice of their persons, and attention to their wants, joined to his possession of absolute and independent command, rendered it no difficult matter for him to secure their support in the revolution of the eighteenth Brumaire, and in placing him at the head of affairs. Most part of the nation were heartily tired by this time of the continually unsettled state of the government, and the various changes which it had experienced, from the visionary speculations of the Girondists, the brutal and bloody ferocity of the Jacobins, and the sordid and undecided versatility and imbecility of the Directory; and the people in general desired a settled form of government, which, if less free, should be more stable in duration, and better calculated to assure to individuals the protection of property and of personal freedom, than those which had followed the downfall of the monarchy. A successful general, of a character more timid, or conscience more tender, than that of Napoleon, might have attempted the restoration of the Bourbons. But Napoleon foresaw the difficulties which would occur by an attempt to reconcile the recall of the emigrants to the assurance of the national sales, and aptly concluded, that the parties which tore France to pieces would be most readily amalgamated together under the authority of one, who was in a great measure a stranger to them all.

Arrived at the possession of supreme power, a height that dazzles and confounds so many, Napoleon seemed only to occupy the station for which he was born, to which his peculiar powers adapted him, and his brilliant career of success gave him, under all circumstances, an irresistible claim. He continued, therefore, with a calm mind and enlightened wisdom, to consider the means of rendering his power stable, of destroying the republican impulse, and establishing a monarchy, of which he destined himself to be the monarch. To most men the attempt to revive, in favour of a military adventurer, a form of government, which had been rejected by what seemed the voice of the nation with universal acclaim, would have appeared an act of desperation. The partisans of the Republic were able statesmen, and men of superior talent, accustomed also to rule the fierce democracy, and organise those intrigues which had overthrown crown and altar; and it was hardly to be supposed that such men would, were it but for shame's sake, have seen their ten years' labour at once swept away by the sword of a young though successful general.

But Napoleon knew himself and them; and felt the confidence, that those who had been associates in the power acquired by former revolutions, must be now content to sink into the instruments of his advancement, and the subordinate agents of his authority, contented with such a share of spoil as that with which the lion rewards the jackall.

To the kingdom at large, upon every new stride towards power, he showed the certificate of superior efficacy, guaranteed by the most signal success; and he assumed the empire of France under the proud title, *Detur dignissimo*. Neither did his actions up to this point encourage any one to challenge the defects or flaws of his title. In practice, his government was brilliant abroad, and, with few exceptions, liberal and moderate at home. The abominable murder of the Duc d'Enghien showed the vindictive spirit of a savage; but, in general, the public actions of Napoleon, at the commencement of his career, were highly laudable. The battle of Marengo, with its consequences—the softening of civil discord, the reconciliation with the Church of Rome, the recall of the great body of the emigrants, and the revivification of National Jurisprudence—were all events calculated to flatter the imagination, and even gain the affections, of the people.

But, with a dexterity peculiar to himself, Napoleon proceeded, while abolishing the Republic, to press into his service those very democratical principles which had given rise to the Revolution, and encouraged the attempt to found a commonwealth. His sagacity had not failed to observe, that the popular objections to the ancient government were founded less upon any objection to the royal authority in itself, than a dislike, amounting to detestation, of the privileges which it allotted to the nobles and to the clergy, who held, from birth and office, the right to fill the superior ranks in every profession, and barred the competition of all others, however above them in merit. When, therefore, Napoleon constructed his new form of monarchical government, he wisely considered that he was not, like hereditary monarchs, tied down to any particular rules arising out of ancient usage, but, being himself creator of the power which he wielded, he was at liberty to model it according to his own pleasure. He had been raised also so easily to the throne, by the general acknowledgment of his merits, that he had not needed the assistance of a party of his own; consequently, being unfettered by previous engagements, and by the necessity of gratifying old partisans, or acquiring new ones, his conduct was in a very unusual degree free and unlimited.

Having, therefore, attained the summit of human power, he proceeded, advisedly and deliberately, to lay the foundation of his throne on that democratic principle which had opened his own career, and which was the throwing open to merit, though without farther title, the road to success in every department of the state. This was the secret key of Napoleon's policy; and he was so well aided in the use of it, by acute perception of character, as well as by good nature and good feeling (both of which, in his cooler moments, he possessed,) that he never, through all his vicissitudes, lost an opportunity of conciliating and pleasing the multitude by evincing a well-timed attention to distinguish and reward talent.[288] To this his conversation perpetually alluded; and for this he claims, and is entitled to, the highest praise. We have little hesitation in repeating, that it was thus opening a full career to talent of every kind, which was the key-stone of his reputation, and the main foundation of his power. Unhappily, his love of merit, and

---

[288] See Appendix, No. VI.

disposition to reward it, were not founded exclusively upon a patriotic attention to the public welfare, far less on a purely benevolent desire to reward what was praiseworthy; but upon a principle of selfish policy, to which must be ascribed a great part of his success, no small portion of his misfortunes, and almost all his political crimes.

We have quoted elsewhere the description given of the Emperor by his brother Lucien, in a moment probably of spleen, but which has been nevertheless confirmed by almost all the persons habitually conversant with Napoleon at whom we have had an opportunity of making inquiries. "His conduct," said his brother, "is entirely regulated by his policy, and his policy is altogether founded upon egotism." No man, perhaps, ever possessed (under the restrictions to be presently mentioned) so intense a proportion of that selfish principle which is so common to humanity. It was planted by nature in his heart, and nourished by the half monastic, half military education, which so early separated him from social ties; it was encouraged by the consciousness of possessing talents which rendered him no mate for the ordinary men among whom his lot seemed cast; and became a confirmed habit, by the desolate condition in which he stood at his first outset in life, without friend, protector, or patron. The praise, the promotion he received, were given to his genius, not to his person; and he who was conscious of having forced his own way, had little to bind him in gratitude or kindness to those who only made room for him because they durst not oppose him. His ambition was a modification of selfishness, sublime indeed in its effects and consequences, but yet, when strictly analyzed, leaving little but egotism in the crucible.

Our readers are not, however, to suppose, that the selfishness of Napoleon was of that ordinary and odious character, which makes men miserly, oppressive, and fraudulent in private life; or which, under milder features, limits their exertions to such enterprises as may contribute to their own individual profit, and closes the heart against feelings of patriotism, or of social benevolence. Napoleon's egotism and love of self was of a far nobler and more elevated kind, though founded on similar motives—just as the wings of the eagle, who soars into the regions of the sun, move on the same principles with those which cannot bear the dunghill fowl over the pales of the poultry-yard.

To explain our meaning, we may add that Napoleon loved France, for France was his own. He studied to confer benefits upon her, for the profit redounded to her emperor, whether she received amended institutions, or enlarged territories. He represented, as he boasted, the People as well as the Sovereign of France; he engrossed in his own person her immunities, her greatness, her glory, and was bound to conduct himself so as to exalt at the same time the emperor and the empire. Still, however, the sovereign and the state might be, and at length actually were, separated; and the egotistical character of Buonaparte could, after that separation, find amusement and interest in the petty scale of Elba, to which his exertions were then limited.[289] Like the magic tent in the Arabian Tales, his faculties could expand to enclose half a world, with all its cares and destinies, or could accommodate themselves to the concerns of a petty rock in the Mediterranean, and his own conveniences when he retreated to its precincts. We believe that while France acknowledged Napoleon as emperor, he would cheerfully have laid down his life for her benefit; but we greatly doubt, if, by merely raising his finger, he could have made her happy under the Bourbons, whether (unless the merit of the action had redounded to his own personal fame) that finger would have been lifted. In a word, his feelings of self-interest were the central point of a circle, the circumference of which may be extended or contracted at pleasure, but the centre itself remains fixed and unchanged.

It is needless to inquire how far this solicitous, and we must add, enlightened attention to his own interest, facilitated Buonaparte's ascent to the supreme power. We daily witness individuals, possessed of a very moderate proportion of parts, who, by intently applying themselves to the prosecution of some particular object, without being drawn aside by the calls of pleasure, the seductions of indolence, or other interruptions, succeed ultimately in attaining the object of their wishes. When, therefore, we conceive the powerful mind of Napoleon, animated by an

---

[289] See *ante*.

unbounded vivacity of imagination, and an unconquerable tenacity of purpose, moving forward, without deviation or repose, to the accomplishment of its purpose, which was nothing less than to acquire the dominion of the whole world, we cannot be surprised at the immense height to which he raised himself.

But the egotism which governed his actions,—subject always to the exercise of his excellent sense, and the cultivation of his interest in the public opinion—if in a great measure it favoured the success of his various enterprises, did him in the end much more evil than good; as it instigated his most desperate enterprises, and was the source of his most inexcusable actions.

Moderate politicians will agree, that after the imperial system was substituted for the republican, the chief magistrate ought to have assumed and exerted a considerable strength of authority, in order to maintain that re-establishment of civil order, that protection of the existing state of things, which was necessary to terminate the wild and changeful recurrence of perpetual revolutions. Had Napoleon stopped here, his conduct would have been unblameable and unblamed, unless by the more devoted followers of the House of Bourbon, against whom Providence appeared to most men to have closed the gate of restoration. But his principles of egotism would not be satisfied until he had totally destroyed every vestige of those free institutions which had been acquired by the perils, the blood, the tears of the Revolution, and reduced France, save for the influence of public opinion, to the condition of Constantinople, or of Algiers. If it was a merit to raise up the throne, it was natural that he who did so should himself occupy it; since in ceding it to the Bourbons he must have betrayed those at whose hands he accepted power; but to plunder the nation of their privileges as free-born men, was the act of a parricide. The nation lost, under his successive encroachments, what liberty the ancient government had left them, and all those rights which had been acquired by the Revolution. Political franchises, individual interests, the property of municipalities, the progress of education, of science, of mind and sentiment, all were usurped by the government. France was one immense army, under the absolute authority of a military commander, subject to no control nor responsibility. In that nation so lately agitated by the nightly assembly of thousands of political clubs, no class of citizens under any supposable circumstances, had the right of uniting in the expression of their opinions. Neither in the manners nor in the laws, did there remain any popular means of resisting the errors or abuses of the administration. France resembled the political carcass of Constantinople, without the insubordination of the Pachas, the underhand resistance of the Ulemas, and the frequent and clamorous mutinies of the Janizaries.[290]

Whilst Napoleon destroyed successively every barrier of public liberty—while he built new state prisons, and established a high police, which filled France with spies and jailors—while he took the charge of the press so exclusively into his own hand—his policy at once, and his egotism, led him to undertake those immense public works, of greater or less utility or ornament as the chance might be, but which were sure to be set down as monuments of the Emperor's splendour. The name given him by the working classes, of the General Undertaker, was by no means ill bestowed; but in what an incalculably greater degree do such works succeed, when raised by the skill and industry of those who propose to improve their capital by the adventure, than when double the expense is employed at the arbitrary will of a despotic sovereign! Yet it had been well if bridges, roads, harbours, and public works, had been the only compensation which Napoleon offered to the people of France for the liberties he took from them. But he poured out to them, and shared with them, to drown all painful and degrading recollections, the intoxicating and fatal draught of military glory and universal domination. To lay the whole universe prostrate at the foot of France, while France, the nation of Camps, should herself have no higher rank than the first of her own Emperor's slaves, was the gigantic project, at which he laboured with such tenacious assiduity. It was the Sisyphæan stone which he rolled so high up the hill, that at length he was crushed under its precipitate recoil.

The main objects of that immense enterprise were such as had been undertaken while his spirit of ambition was at its height; and no one dared, even in his councils, to interfere with the resolutions

---

[290] Histoire de la Guerre de la Péninsule, par Le Général Foy.—S.

which he adopted. Had these been less eminently successful, it is possible he might have paused, and perhaps might have preferred the tranquil pursuit of a course which might have rendered one kingdom free and happy, to the subjugation of all Europe. But Napoleon's career of constant and uninterrupted success under the most disadvantageous circumstances, together with his implied belief in his Destiny, conspired, with the extravagant sense of his own importance, to impress him with an idea that he was not "in the roll of common men,"[291] and induced him to venture on the most desperate undertakings, as if animated less by the result of reason than by an internal assurance of success. After great miscarriages, he is said sometimes to have shown a corresponding depression; and thence he resigned four times the charge of his army when he found his situation embarrassing, as if no longer feeling confidence in his own mind, or conceiving he was deserted for the moment by his guardian genius. There were similar alternations, too, according to General Gourgaud's account, in his conversation. At times, he would speak like a deity,[292] at others, in the style of a very ordinary person.

To the egotism of Napoleon, we may also trace the general train of deception which marked his public policy, and, when speaking upon subjects in which his own character was implicated, his private conversation.

In his public capacity, he had so completely prostituted the liberty of the press, that France could know nothing whatever but through Napoleon's own bulletins. The battle of Trafalgar was not hinted at till several months after it had been fought, and then it was totally misrepresented; and so deep and dark was the mantle which covered the events in which the people were most interested, that, on the very evening when the battle of Montmartre was fought, the *Moniteur*, the chief organ of public intelligence, was occupied in a commentary on *nosographie*, and a criticism on a drama on the subject of the chaste Susannah.[293] The hiding the truth is only one step to

---

[291] "And all the courses of my life do show, I am not in the roll of common men."—*Henry IV.*, act iii., sc. 2.
[292] "For *deity*, read *great man*, and Gourgaud's account is perfectly correct."—Joseph Buonaparte, *Erreurs de Bourrienne*, tom. i., p. 233.
[293] Memorable Events at Paris, p. 93.

the invention of falsehood, and, as a periodical publisher of news, Napoleon became so eminent for both, that, to "lie like a bulletin," became an adopted expression, not likely soon to lose ground in the French language, and the more disgraceful to Napoleon, that he is well known to have written those official documents in most instances himself.

Even this deceptive system, this plan of alternately keeping the nation in ignorance, or abusing it by falsehood, intimated a sense of respect for public opinion. Men love darkness, because their deeds are evil. Napoleon dared not have submitted to the public an undisguised statement of his perfidious and treacherous attacks upon Spain, than which a more gross breach of general good faith and existing treaties could scarce have been conceived. Nor would he have chosen to plead at the public bar, the policy of his continental system, adopted in total ignorance of the maxims of political economy, and the consequences of which were, first, to cause general distress, and then to encourage universal resistance against the French yoke throughout the whole continent of Europe. Nor is it more likely that, could the public have had the power of forming a previous judgment upon the probable event of the Russian campaign, that rash enterprise would ever have had an existence. In silencing the voice of the wise and good, the able and patriotic, and communicating only with such counsellors as were the echoes of his own inclinations, Napoleon, like Lear,

"Kill'd his physician, and the fee bestow'd Upon the foul disease."

This was the more injurious, as Napoleon's knowledge of the politics, interests, and character of foreign courts was, excepting in the case of Italy, exceedingly imperfect. The peace of Amiens might have remained uninterrupted, and the essential good understanding betwixt France and Sweden need never have been broken, if Napoleon could, or would, have understood the free constitution of England, which permits every man to print or publish what he may choose; or if he could have been convinced that the institutions of Sweden did not permit their government to place their fleets and armies at the disposal of a foreign power, or to sink the ancient kingdom of the Goths into a secondary and vassal government.

Self-love, so sensitive as that of Napoleon, shunned especially the touch of ridicule. The gibes of the English papers, the caricatures of the London print-shops, were the petty stings which instigated, in a great measure, the breach of the peace of Amiens. The laughter-loving Frenchmen were interdicted the use of satire, which, all-licensed during the times of the republic, had, even under the monarchy, been only punished with a short and easy confinement in the Bastile. During the time of the consulate, Napoleon was informed that a comic opera, something on the plan of the English farce of *High Life Below Stairs*, had been composed by Monsieur Dupaty, and brought forward on the stage, and that, in this audacious performance, three valets mimicked the manners, and even the dress of the three Consuls, and especially his own. He ordered that the actors should be exposed at the Grève, in the dresses they had dared to assume, which should be there stripped from their backs by the executioner; and he commanded that the author should be sent to St. Domingo, and placed, as a person under requisition, at the disposal of the commander-in-chief. The sentence was not executed, for the offence had not existed, at least to the extent alleged;[294] but the intention shows Napoleon's ideas of the liberty of the stage, and intimates what would have been the fate of the author of the *Beggar's Opera*, had he written for the French Opera Comique.

But no light, which reason or information could supply, was able to guide the intensity of a selfish ambition, which made Napoleon desire that the whole administration of the whole world should not only remotely, but even directly and immediately, depend on his own pleasure. When he distributed kingdoms to his brothers, it was under the express understanding that they were to follow in every thing the course of politics which he should dictate; and after all, he seemed only to create dependent states for the purpose of resuming them. The oppressions, which, in the name of France, he imposed upon Holland, were the direct, and, in all probability, the calculated means of dethroning his brother Louis; and he had

---

[294] Thibaudaud, Mémoires sur le Consulat, p. 148.—S.

thoughts of removing Joseph from Spain, when he saw of what a fair and goodly realm he had pronounced him king. In his wild and insatiable extravagance of administering in person the government of every realm which he conquered, he brought his powerful mind to the level of that of the spoiled child, who will not be satisfied without holding in its own hand whatever has caught its eye. The system, grounded on ambition so inordinate, carried with it in its excess the principles of its own ruin. The runner who will never stop for repose must at last fall down with fatigue. Had Napoleon succeeded both in Spain and Russia, he would not have rested, until he had found elsewhere the disasters of Baylen and of Moscow.

The consequences of the unjustifiable aggressions of the French Emperor were an unlimited extent of slaughter, fire, and human misery, all arising from the ambition of one man, who, never giving the least sign of having repented the unbounded mischief, seemed, on the contrary, to justify and take pride in the ravage which he had occasioned. This ambition, equally insatiable and incurable, justified Europe in securing his person, as if it had been that of a lunatic, whose misguided rage was not directed against an individual, but against the civilized world; which, wellnigh overcome by him, and escaping with difficulty, had a natural right to be guaranteed against repetition of the frantic exploits of a being who seemed guided by more than human passion, and capable of employing in execution of his purpose more than human strength.

The same egotism, the same spirit of self-deception, which marked Napoleon during his long and awful career of success, followed him into adversity. He framed apologies for the use of his little company of followers, as he had formerly manufactured bulletins for the Great Nation. Those to whom these excuses were addressed, Las Cases and the other gentlemen of Napoleon's suite, being too much devoted to him, and too generous to dispute, after his fall, doctrines which it would have been dangerous to controvert during his power, received whatever he said as truths delivered by a prophet, and set down doubtless to the score of inspiration what could by no effort be reconciled to truth. The horrid evils which afflicted Europe during the years of his success, were represented to others, and perhaps to his own mind, as consequences which the

Emperor neither wished nor contemplated, but which were necessarily and unalterably attached to the execution of the great plans which the Man of Destiny had been called upon earth to perform, resembling in so far the lurid and fear-inspiring train pursuing the rapid course of a brilliant comet, which the laws of the universe have projected through the pathless firmament.

Some crimes he committed of a different character, which seem to have sprung, not like the general evils of war, from the execution of great and calculated plans of a political or military kind, but must have had their source in a temper naturally passionate and vindictive. The Duc d'Enghien's murder was at the head of this list; a gratuitous act of treachery and cruelty, which, being undeniable, led Napoleon to be believed capable of other crimes of a secret and bloody character—of the murder of Pichegru and of Wright—of the spiriting away of Mr. Windham, who was never afterwards heard of—and of other actions of similar atrocity. We pause before charging him with any of those which have not been distinctly proved. For while it is certain that he had a love of personal vengeance—proper, it is said, to his country—it is equally evident, that, vehement by temperament, he was lenient and calm by policy; and that, if he had indulged the former disposition, the security with which he might have done so, together with the ready agency of his fatal police, would have made his rage resemble that of one of the Roman emperors. He was made sensible, too late, of the general odium drawn upon him by the murder of the Duc d'Enghien, and does not seem to have been disposed to incur farther risks of popular hatred in prosecution of his individual resentment. The records of his police, however, and the persecutions experienced by those whom Napoleon considered as his personal enemies, show that, by starts at least, nature resumed her bent, and that he, upon whom there was no restraint, save his respect for public opinion, gave way occasionally to the temptation of avenging his private injuries. He remarked it as a weakness in the character of his favourite Cæsar, that he suffered his enemies to remain in possession of the power to injure him; and Antommarchi, the reporter of the observation, admitted, that when he looked on the person before him, he could not but acknowledge that *he* was unlikely to fall into such an error.[295]

When Napoleon laid aside reserve, and spoke what were probably his true sentiments, he endeavoured to justify those acts of his government which transgressed the rules of justice and morality, by political necessity, and reasons of state; or, in other words, by the pressure of his own interest. This, however, was a plea, the full benefit of which he reserved to vindicate his own actions, never permitting it to be used by any other sovereign. He considered *himself* privileged in transgressing the law of nations, when his interests required it; but pleaded as warmly upon the validity of public law, when alleging it had been infringed by other states, as if he himself had in all instances respected its doctrines as inviolable.

But although Napoleon thus at times referred to state necessity as the ultimate source of actions otherwise unjustifiable, he more frequently endeavoured to disguise his errors by denial, or excuse them by apologies which had no foundation. He avers in his Will,[296] that by the confession of the Duc d'Enghien, the Comte d'Artois maintained sixty assassins against his life;[297] and that for this reason the Duc d'Enghien was tried, convicted, and put to death. The examination of the duke bears no such confession, but, on the contrary, an express denial of the whole of the alleged system; nor was there the slightest attempt made to contradict him by other testimony. He bequeathed, in like manner, a legacy to a villain[298] who had attempted the assassination of the Duke of Wellington; the assassin, according to his strange argument, having as good a right to kill his rival and victor, as the English had to detain him prisoner at St. Helena. This clause in the last will of a dying man, is not striking from its atrocity merely, but from the inaccuracy of the

---

[295] Antommarchi, vol. i., p. 249.
[296] See Appendix, No. VII.
[297] The precise words of the Will seem to bear, that it was the *Comte d'Artois'* confession which established this charge. But no such confession was ever made; neither, if made, could it have been known to Napoleon at the time of the trial; nor, if known, could it have constituted evidence against the party accused, who was no accessary to the fact alleged. The assertion is utterly false in either case, but under the latter interpretation, it is also irrelevant. The Duc d'Enghien might be affected by his own confession, certainly not by that of his kinsman.—S.
[298] Cantillon. See Fourth Codicil to Will, Appendix, No. VII.

moral reasoning which it exhibits. Napoleon has drawn a parallel betwixt two cases, which must be therefore both right or both wrong. If both were wrong, why reward the ruffian with a legacy? but if both were right, why complain of the British Government for detaining him at St. Helena?

But, indeed, the whole character of Napoleon's autobiography marks his desire to divide mankind into two classes—his friends and his enemies;—the former of whom are to be praised and vindicated; the latter to be vilified, censured, and condemned, without any regard to truth, justice, or consistency. To take a gross example, he stoutly affirmed, that the treasures which were removed from Paris in April 1814, and carried to Orleans, were seized and divided by the ministers of the allied powers—Talleyrand, Metternich, Hardenberg, and Castlereagh; and that the money thus seized included the marriage-portion of the Empress Maria Louisa.[299] Had this story been true, it would have presented Napoleon with a very simple means of avenging himself upon Lord Castlereagh, by putting the British public in possession of the secret.

It is no less remarkable, that Napoleon, though himself a soldier, and a distinguished one, could never allow a tribute of candid praise to the troops and generals by whom he was successively opposed. In mentioning his victories, he frequently bestows commendation upon the valour and conduct of the vanquished. This was an additional and more delicate mode of praising himself and his own troops by whom these enemies were overthrown. But he never allows any merit to those by whom he was defeated in turn. He professes never to have seen the Prussian troops behave well save at Jena, or the Russians save at Austerlitz. Those armies of the same nations, which he both saw and felt in the campaigns of 1812 and 1813, and before whom he made such disastrous retreats as those of Moscow and Leipsic, were, according to his expressions, mere *canaille*.

---

[299] See Dr. O'Meara's Voice from St. Helena, who seems himself to have been startled at the enormity of the fiction. What makes it yet more extravagant is, that Napoleon's Will disposes of a part of that very treasure, as if it were still in the hands of Maria Louisa.—S.

In the same manner, when he details an action in which he triumphed, he is sure to boast, like the old Grecian (very justly perhaps,) that in this Fortune had no share; while his defeats are entirely and exclusively attributed to the rage of the elements, the combination of some most extraordinary and unexpected circumstances, the failure of some of his lieutenants or maréchals, or, finally, the obstinacy of the general opposed, who, by mere dint of stupidity, blundered into success through circumstances which should have ensured his ruin.

In a word, from one end of Napoleon's works to the other, he has scarcely allowed himself to be guilty of a single fault or a single folly, excepting of that kind, which, arising from an over confidence and generosity, men secretly claim as merits, while they affect to give them up as matters of censure. If we credit his own word, we must believe him to have been a faultless and impeccable being. If we do not, we must set him down as one that, where his own reputation was concerned, told his story with a total disregard to candour and truth.

Perhaps it was a consequence of the same indifference to truth, which induced Napoleon to receive into his favour those French officers who broke their parole by escape from England. This, he alleged, he did, by way of retaliation, the British Government having, as he pretended, followed a similar line of conduct. The defence is false, in point of fact; but if it were true, it forms no apology for a sovereign and a general countenancing a breach of honour in a gentleman and a soldier. The French officers who liberated themselves by such means, were not the less dishonoured men, and unfit to bear command in the army of France, though they could have pointed with truth to similar examples of infamy in England.

But the most extraordinary instance of Napoleon's deceptive system, and of his determination, at all events, to place himself under the most favourable light to the beholders, is his attempt to represent himself as the friend and protector of liberal and free principles. He had destroyed every vestige of liberty in France—he had persecuted as ideologists all who cherished its memory—he had boasted himself the restorer of monarchical government—the war between the Constitutionalists and him, covered, after the return from Elba, by a hollow truce, had been renewed, and the Liberalists had expelled him from the capital—he had left in his Testament, the appellation of *traitor* with La Fayette, one of their earliest, most devoted, and most sincere chiefs—yet, notwithstanding all this constant opposition to the party which professes most to be guided by them, he has ventured to represent himself as a friend of liberal ideas! He has done so, and he has been believed.

There is but one explanation of this. The friends of revolution are upon principle the enemies of ancient and established governments—Napoleon became the opponent of the established powers from circumstances; not because he disputed the character of their government, but because they would not admit him into their circle; and though there was not, and could not be, any real connexion betwixt his system and that of the Liberalists, yet both had the same opponents, and each loved in the other the enemy of their enemies. It was the business of Napoleon in his latter days, to procure, if professions could gain it, the sympathy and good opinion of any or every class of politicians; while, on the contrary, it could not be indifferent to those to whom he made advances, to number among their disciples, even in the twelfth hour, the name of Napoleon. It resembled what sometimes happens in the Catholic Church, when a wealthy and powerful sinner on his death-bed receives the absolution of the Church on easy terms, and dies after a life spent in licentious courses, wrapt up in the mantle, and girded with the cord, of some order of unusual strictness. Napoleon, living a despot and a conqueror, has had his memory consecrated and held up to admiration by men, who term themselves emphatically the friends of freedom.

The faults of Buonaparte, we conclude as we commenced, were rather those of the sovereign and politician, than of the individual. Wisely is it written, that "if we say we have no sin we deceive ourselves, and the truth is not in us." It was the inordinate force of ambition which made him the scourge of Europe; it was his efforts to disguise that selfish principle, that made him combine fraud with force, and establish a regular system for deceiving those whom he could not subdue. Had his natural disposition been coldly cruel, like that of Octavius, or had he given way to the warmth of his temper, like other despots, his private history, as well as that of his campaigns, must have been written in letters of blood. If, instead of asserting that he never committed a crime, he had limited his self-eulogy to asserting, that in attaining and wielding supreme power, he had resisted the temptation to commit many, he could not have been contradicted. And this is no small praise.

His system of government was false in the extreme. It comprehended the slavery of France, and aimed at the subjugation of the world. But to the former he did much to requite them for the jewel of which he robbed them. He gave them a regular government, schools, institutions, courts of justice, and a code of laws. In Italy, his rule was equally splendid and beneficial. The good effects which arose to other countries from his reign and character, begin also to be felt, though unquestionably they are not of the kind which he intended to produce. His invasions, tending to reconcile the discords which existed in many states between the governors and governed, by teaching them to unite together against a common enemy, have gone far to loosen the feudal yoke, to enlighten the mind both of prince and people, and have led to many admirable results, which will not be the less durably advantageous, that they have arisen, are arising slowly, and without contest.

In closing the Life of Napoleon Buonaparte, we are called upon to observe, that he was a man tried in the two extremities, of the most exalted power and the most ineffable calamity, and if he occasionally appeared presumptuous when supported by the armed force of half a world, or unreasonably querulous when imprisoned within the narrow limits of St. Helena, it is scarce within the capacity of those whose steps have never led them beyond the middle path of life, to estimate either the strength of the temptations to which he yielded, or the force of mind which he opposed to those which he was able to resist.

APPENDIX

No. I

REMARKS ON THE CAMPAIGN OF 1815, BY CAPTAIN JOHN W. PRINGLE, OF THE ROYAL ENGINEERS

The following observations were hastily made, at a time when much public interest was excited by the various accounts of the campaign of 1815, edited by several individuals, all claiming the peculiar distinction of having been dictated by Napoleon, or written under his immediate direction. With some slight exceptions, and occasional anecdotes, they nearly correspond, as far as relates to the military details.[300] The 9th volume of the Memoirs of Napoleon, published by O'Meara, is perhaps the original from which the greatest part of the other productions are derived. It is now generally acknowledged to have been, to a certain extent, composed by Buonaparte.

These works have had one particular object—the defence of an unfortunate and great man. The individual, however, is always held up to view; the actions are softened or strengthened to suit this

---

[300] Liv. ix., Mémoires Historiques de Napoleon. London, Sir R. Philips, 1820.—Montholon, Mémoires de Napoleon; Colburn, London, 1823.—Las Cases; London, 2 vols.—Gourgaud, War of 1815; London, 1824.—Many passages in these works will be found quite parallel; for instance, Montholon, vol. ii., pp. 272-289, with Liv. ix., p. 43. Grouchy, p. 4, designates these works from St. Helena, as containing, "des instructions et des ordres supposés; des mouvements imaginaires," &c. &c.; also, "des assertions erronnées, des hypothèses faites après coup;" see also p. 26. P. 22, he says, with justice, of these authors: "Des individus qui se persuadent que l'auréole de gloire d'un grand homme, en les éclairant un moment, les à transformé en d'irrécusables autorités, et ne voyant pas qu'un éclat d'emprunt qui ne se refléchit sur aucun fait d'armes connus, sur aucuns services éminens, ne sert qu'à mieux faire ressortir la présomptueuse impéritie des jugements qu'ils prononcent."

purpose, and in the extension of this design, the reputation of his own officers, and a strict adherence to facts, are occasionally sacrificed. The military features of the campaign have remained unanswered; whilst the wounded honour and fame of his generals have called for some counter-statements, which throw curious light on the whole campaign, and on the machinery of a system which so long alarmed the world. These last are little known in Britain.

Whoever has perused the mass of military works by French officers, most of them ably written, and many artfully composed, must feel how much they tend to encourage a peculiar feeling of national superiority in young minds, in a country where only their own military works are read. In these works they never find a French army beaten in the field, without some plausible reason; or, as Las Cases terms it [vol. ii., p. 15,] "a concurrence of unheard-of fatalities," to account for it. Upon the minds of young soldiers, this has an effect of the most powerful description.

Great care appears to have been taken in these various works, to meet the accusations of military men respecting the disposition and employment of the French army. Where a fault is admitted, the error is at least transferred from Buonaparte to the incapacity or remissness of his generals. The talents and honour of the British commanders are rated at a low state; their success attributed more to chance than to military skill, and the important result of the battle, less to the courage of the British troops, than to the opportune arrival of the Prussians, whom they allege to have saved the British army from destruction. What are now termed liberal ideas, seem to have made it a fashion to assert, and give credence to these accounts; and it is no uncommon occurrence to meet with Englishmen who doubt the glory and success of their countrymen on that eventful day. A wounded spirit of faction has contributed to this feeling, and in the indulgence of its own gratification, and under the mask of patriotism, endeavoured to throw a doubt over the military achievements of our countrymen, eagerly laid hold of any faults or failures, palliating, at the same time, those of their enemies, and often giving that implicit belief to the garbled accounts of the French, which they deny to the simple and manly dispatch of a British general.

There does appear in this a decay of that national feeling, and jealousy of our country's honour, the mainspring of all great actions, which other nations, our rivals, cling to with renewed ardour. No man could persuade a Frenchman that it was British valour which has conquered in almost every battle from Cressy, down to Waterloo; and it is impossible to forget that national pride, so honourable to the French name, which could make their unfortunate emigrants even forget for a while their own distresses, in the glory which crowned the arms of the Republicans at that Revolution which drove them from their homes.

The British works on the campaign, with one exception [Batty,] are incomplete productions, written by persons unacquainted with military affairs, and hastily composed of rude materials, collected from imperfect sources.[301]

Whoever has endeavoured to analyse the accounts of modern actions, and to separate in them what can be proved to be facts, from what is affirmed to be so, or to compare the private accounts (too often indiscreetly published) with the official documents, and the information procured from proper sources, will not be surprised to find in these home-made accounts of this campaign, fulsome praises lavished on individuals and regiments;[302] tales of charges, which one would imagine must have annihilated whole corps, and yet find not more than fifty or sixty men killed and wounded in a whole regiment.[303]

Our officers, whatever their corps may be, should be above the idea of vain boasting or exaggeration. It is much that we can claim, during a long period of eight years, the praise of having

---

[301] The best account of the campaign is by an anonymous author, C. de W., published at Stutgard, 1817, and is attributed to Baron Muffling. It does honour to its illustrious author, from its candour and manliness, though he naturally wishes to give more effect to the Prussian attack on the 18th, than was actually the case; that is, he brings them into action, with their whole force, considerably too early in the day.

[302] It is well remarked, in Liv. ix., p. 150,—"Ces détails en appartient plus à l'histoire de chaque régiment qu'à l'histoire générale de la bataille."

[303] Rogniat, p. 147, speaking of charges, says,—"S'ils marchent, à la baïonette, ce n'est qu'un simulacre d'attaque: ils ne la croisent jamais avec celle d'un ennemi qu'ils craignent d'aborder, parcequ'ils se sentent sans défence contre ses coups, et l'un de deux partis prend la fuite avant d'en venir aux mains."—Such is the case in all charges.

successfully contended with troops of the first military power in Europe; while our soldiers have disputed the palm of valour; and our officers, with less trumpeted claims than their boasted marshals, have shown as great military skill; and our armies, in the moment of victory, a spirit of humanity and moderation, not frequently evinced by their antagonists.

In the following observations, it is not pretended that any new matter can be given on a subject already so much discussed; still some facts and considerations are treated of, which have not been perhaps fully or fairly appreciated. Many charges of blame have been brought forward against the generals of the allied forces; and superior talent in profiting by their mistakes, has been attributed to their opponents, which might well be accounted for, as arising from the situations in which they were relatively placed. In order to judge, for instance, of the credit given to Napoleon, of having surprised their armies in their cantonments, it is necessary to be aware of the state of both countries (France and Belgium,) and the objects, besides the mere watching of the frontiers, to which the attention of the allied commanders was necessarily directed previous to the commencement of the war, and whilst it may be supposed as still in some measure doubtful.

France, as is well known, is, on the Belgian frontier, studded with fortresses; Belgium, on the contrary, is now defenceless. The numerous fortresses in the Low Countries, so celebrated in our former wars, had been dismantled in the reign of the Emperor Joseph; and their destruction completed by the French when they got possession of the country at the battle of Fleurus, 1794, with the exception of Antwerp, Ostend, and Nieuport, which they had kept up on account of their marine importance. These circumstances placed the two parties in very different situations, both for security and for facility of preparing and carrying into execution the measures either for attack or defence.

The French had maintained their own celebrated triple line of fortresses; extending, on that part of the frontier, from Dunkirk to Philipville, and which had been put into a state of defence during the war in the preceding year [Liv. ix., p. 36;]—these gave every facility for the concentration and formation of troops—for affording a supply of artillery, and every requisite for taking the field, and for concealing their movements—particularly from the French organisation of their national guards, which enabled the latter immediately to take the garrison duties, or relieve and occupy the outposts along the frontiers;—such was the relative situation of the frontiers at the period of Napoleon's return from Elba.

The necessity of re-establishing the principal fortresses on the Belgian frontier, which commanded the sluices and inundation of the country, had indeed already been evident; and decided upon whilst Napoleon was yet in Elba. A committee of British engineers had been employed in examining the country for that purpose, but only the general plans and reports had been prepared, when Buonaparte's sudden return and rapid advance upon Paris, and the probability of a speedy renewal of the war, called for expeditious and immediate means of defence. The declaration of the Congress of Vienna, of the 13th March, reached Paris on the same day he arrived there, which must have convinced him he would not be allowed quietly to repossess his throne.

It may be well supposed, that the general impression in Belgium was, that he would lose no time to endeavour to regain a country which he considered as almost part of France; important to him from the resources it would have afforded, and perhaps still more so, as it would deprive his enemies of so convenient a base of operations, for the preparation of the means for attacking France. The discontent in Belgium, and the Prussian provinces on the Rhine, also amongst the Saxon troops who had served in his army, was known.—[Liv. ix., pp. 58-61.]—The mutinous spirit of these troops appeared to be in concert with the movements of the French forces on the frontiers; so much so, that they were disarmed and sent to the rear.—[Muffling, p. 5.]—In the former, the discontent was particularly favoured by the number of French officers and soldiers, who had been discharged as aliens from the French army, in which they had served nearly since the Revolution, and now gave themselves little care to conceal their real sentiments and attachments. The flight of Louis from Lisle, through Flanders, added to this feeling in Belgium—such appeared to be the prevailing spirit. The force the British had to keep it in check, and resist an invasion, amounted only to 6000 or 7000 men, under the orders of Sir Thomas Graham, consisting chiefly of second battalions, hastily collected, a great portion of our best troops not having yet returned from America. There were also in Belgium the German Legion, together with 8000 to 10,000 men of the new Hanoverian levies. The organisation of the Belgian troops had been just commenced, so that the force of the Prince of Orange might amount to about 20,000 men.

The Prussian General Kleist, who commanded on the Rhine and Meuse, had 30,000 men, afterwards augmented to 50,000, which, however, included the Saxons.—[Muffling, pp. 1-5.]

These generals had immediately agreed to act in concert; but from what we have mentioned, had Napoleon concentrated 36,000 men at Lisle on the 1st April, which he says was possible for him to have done—[Montholon, vol. ii., p. 281; Liv. ix., p. 58]—and advanced into Belgium, it is certainly probable he might have obtained the most important results; for the Prince of Orange, who had united his troops at Ath, Mons, and Tournay, was not strong enough to have covered Brussels, and must have either fallen back on Antwerp, or formed a junction with the Prussian General Kleist. The intelligence of Napoleon having landed at Cannes on the 1st March, reached Brussels on the 9th. Preparations were immediately made for the defence of the country. The British troops under General Clinton concentrated, with their allies, near Ath, Mons, and Tournay; and these places, with Ypres, Ghent, and Oudenarde were ordered to be put in a state of defence consistently with the exigence of the moment. To effect this, every use was made of what remained of the old fortifications. New works were added, and advantage was taken of the great system of defence in that country, which is generally under the level of some canal, or the sea, and consequently capable of being inundated. The sluices which commanded the inundations were covered by strong redoubts.

The inundation of the country near the sea, admits of being made in two ways. The canals or rivers are drains for the fresh water of the country to the sea. The sluice gates are opened for its egress at low water, and shut to prevent the ingress of the salt water at the return of the tide. It is evident, therefore, that we could have laid the country under water, and so covered their fortresses on two or three sides, which would prevent the necessity of their having large garrisons to defend them.[304] But salt-water inundation ruins the soil for several years, and it was determined only to employ it as a last resource; and in the meantime the sluice-gates were merely kept shut to prevent the egress of the fresh water, which in that wet season soon accumulated; and the fresh water inundation only destroyed the crops of one season.

About 20,000 labourers, called in by requisitions on the country, were daily employed on the works, in addition to the working parties furnished by the troops. The necessary artillery and stores were supplied from England and Holland. Troops arrived daily, and were immediately moved to the frontiers, where, from the movements that were constantly taking place, it is probable that exaggerated accounts were transmitted to the enemy. By these vigorous and prompt measures, confidence became restored—the panic amongst the people of Belgium was removed—they saw that their country was not to be given up without a severe struggle—it fixed the wavering, and silenced the disaffected. In less than a month, most of the frontier places were safe from a coup-de-main.

The Duke of Wellington had arrived at Brussels from Vienna early in April, and immediately inspected the frontier and the fortresses; after which, he agreed on a plan of operations with the Prussians, by which they concentrated their troops along the Sambre and Meuse, occupying Charleroi, Namur, and Liege, so as to be in communication with his left. The Prussians had repaired the works round Cologne, which assured their communications with Prussia, and gave them a tête-du-pont on the Rhine. The small fortress of Juliers afforded them the command of the Roer on the same line, and they held Maestricht on the Lower Meuse. It was important to occupy Liege and Namur, though their fortifications had been destroyed. They afforded a facility to act rapidly on either side of the Meuse, and a choice of the strong positions along the banks of that

---

[304] The salt-water inundation could be raised at Ghent, so as to place the Great Square five feet under water.

river. The disaffection in the provinces on the Rhine, which had been recently added to Prussia, was considered even greater than in Belgium. The fortress of Luxembourg was the great key which Prussia possessed for their preservation; and her interest would have led her to make that her depôt and base of operations for the invasion of France; but besides being so far distant from Brussels, that armies occupying such distant points could not act in concert, the roads in that part of the country, between the Meuse and the Moselle, were in a state almost impracticable for artillery, and for the general communication of an army. On the other hand, the roads and communications to cross the Rhine at Cologne are good, the town itself could be put in a state of defence, and have become the best and safest line of communication. Reference to the map will elucidate these observations, and show that the cantonments of the Prussians, along the Sambre and Meuse, enabled them to act in concert with our army; to cover their line of communication with Prussia; and to move rapidly into the provinces of the Moselle, in the event of the enemy advancing from Metz.[305]

The Russians were to have come into the line at Mayence, but they did not reach the Rhine until June, and then only the first corps; so that, for the present, a gap existed from the Prussian left at Dinant, to the Austro-Bavarian right at Manheim.

It was an important object to cover Brussels; and it is to be considered, that this city forms, as it were, a centre to a large portion of the French frontier, extending about seventy miles from the Lys to the Meuse, viz. from Menin to Philipville or Givet; that it is about fifty miles distant from these extreme points; and that it was necessary to guard the entry from France by Tournay, Mons, and Charleroi; and also to prevent Ghent, a very important place, from being attacked from Lisle. The protection of all these distant points, with the difficulty of subsisting troops, particularly cavalry and artillery, are sufficient causes to explain why the armies were not more united in their cantonments.[306] Buonaparte appears to have

---

[305] Such, however, could only be a desultory attack, for the chaussée by Charleroi and Givet was the nearest entry from France on this side. The country from this to Mayence was then nearly impracticable for large armies. Good roads have since been made through it.
[306] Buonaparte blames the allied generals for not having formed a camp in front of Brussels, as he alleges might have been done in the beginning of May. The wet season, and

attached much importance to the occupation of Brussels, as appears by the bulletins found ready printed in his baggage, which was captured. It was, therefore, of much importance, in every point of view, to prevent even a temporary occupation of this city, and this could only be done by risking an action in front of it. The Duke of Wellington and Marshal Blucher had also separate views in preserving their lines of operation—the one by Cologne with Prussia; the other with England, by Brussels, which neither was disposed willingly to abandon. This probably may have been the cause why Quatre-Bras and Ligny were chosen as positions covering both.

It is evident, that an army placed in cantonments, so as to meet all these objects, could only be concentrated in a position covering the city, by the troops in advance being able to keep the enemy in check, so as to afford time for that concentration, which was certainly accomplished. The positions on the different roads of approach from the French frontier had been attentively reconnoitred; that of Mont St. Jean, or Waterloo, very particularly; and no precaution appears to have been omitted, by which an offensive movement of the enemy was to be encountered.

Some movements were observed on the French frontier between Lisle and Berguer, as if preparing for offensive operations, about the end of March, at which period the troops, cantoned near Menin, had orders, after making due resistance, and destroying the bridge on the Lys, to fall back on Courtrai, their point of assembling; and then, after such a resistance as would not compromise their safety in retreat, to endeavour to ascertain the object of the enemy's movements, and give time for the troops to assemble. They were to retire on Oudenarde and Ghent, opening the sluices, and extending the inundation. About the beginning of

---

difficulty of subsisting so large a body of troops, is some reason against it. Besides which, Buonaparte might have made demonstrations in front, and sent 20,000 men from his garrisons to ravage Ghent and the country beyond the Scheldt, and cut off our communications with Ostend. In 1814, when the Prussians were concentrated near Brussels, this had been done with effect from Lisle. Though little advantage might have resulted to the enemy from such a measure, much blame would have been attached for not taking precautions against it. To cover Brussels, the capital of the country, was certainly of great importance; and had that been the only object, a camp in its front would have certainly been the best means of effecting it.

May similar movements were also observed, but less was then to be apprehended, since, by the advanced state of the works at Tournay, the tête-du-pont at Oudenarde and Ghent, we then commanded the Scheldt, and could have assumed the offensive.

Great credit is undoubtedly due to Napoleon, for the mode in which he concealed his movements, and the rapidity with which he concentrated his army. The forced marches he was obliged to make, appear, however, to have paralysed his subsequent movements, from the fatigue his troops underwent. The numerous French fortresses favoured his plans in a very great degree, by affording him the means of employing the garrison and national guards to occupy the advanced posts along the frontier, and opportunity afterwards to make demonstrations across the frontiers near Lisle, whilst he assembled his army on the Sambre.—[Liv. ix., pp. 68-85; Montholon, vol. ii., p. 153.] They were also somewhat favoured by the circumstance, that hostilities were not actually commenced, which prevented our advanced posts (even if they suspected a change in the troops opposed to them) from obliging the enemy to show himself, or, by bringing on a skirmish, to obtain from prisoners intelligence of their movements. He had another advantage of powerful consequence. The army he commanded were mostly old soldiers of the same nation, under a single chief. The allied armies were composed of different nations, a great portion young levies, and under two generals, each of such reputation, as not likely to yield great deference to the other.[307]

On the night of the 14th June, the French army bivouacked in three divisions, as near the frontier as possible, without being observed by the Prussians; the left at Ham-sur-heure, the centre at Beaumont, where the headquarters were established, and the right at Philipville.[308]

At three o'clock, A.M., on the 15th June, the French army crossed the frontier in three columns, directed on Marchiennes,

---

[307] Buonaparte himself has remarked,—"L'unité de commandement est la chose la plus importante dans la guerre."
[308] Buonaparte, Liv. ix., p. 69, rates his force at 122,400 men, and 350 guns. Muffling, p. 17, at 130,000. Other accounts make it smaller, and Batty, 127,400, with 350 guns.

Charleroi, and Chatelet. The Prussian out-posts were quickly driven in; they, however, maintained their ground obstinately at three points, until eleven o'clock, when General Ziethen took up a position at Gilly and Gosselies, in order to check the advance of the enemy, and then retired slowly on Fleurus, agreeably to the orders of Maréchal Blucher, to allow time for the concentration of his army.[309] The bridge at Charleroi not having been completely destroyed, was quickly repaired by the enemy. Upon Ziethen's abandoning the chaussée, which leads to Brussels through Quatre-Bras, Marshal Ney, who commanded the left of the French army, was ordered to advance by this road upon Gosselies, and found at Frasnes part of the Duke of Wellington's army, composed of Nassau troops, under the command of Prince Bernard of Saxe Weimar, who, after some skirmishing, maintained his position.[310] The French army was formed, on the night of the 15th, in three columns, the left at Gosselies, the centre near Gilly, and the right at Chatelet. Two corps of the Prussian army occupied the position at Sombref on the same night, where they were joined by the first corps, and occupied St. Amand, Bry, and Ligny; so that, notwithstanding all the exertions of the French, at a moment where time was of such importance, they had only been able to advance about fifteen English miles during the day, with nearly fifteen hours of daylight.[311] The corps of Ziethen had suffered considerably, but he had effected his orders: so that Maréchal Blucher was enabled to assemble three corps of his army, 80,000 men, in position early on the 15th, and his fourth corps was on its march to join him that evening.

---

[309] Grouchy, p. 59, speaks of the rapidity with which Blucher assembled his army. It is also adverted to by several French military writers.

[310] Ney might probably have driven back these troops, and occupied the important position at Quatre-Bras; but hearing a heavy cannonade on his right flank, where Ziethen had taken up his position, he thought it necessary to halt, and detach a division in the direction of Fleurus. This brings forward a remarkable case, as he was severely censured by Napoleon for not having literally followed his orders, and pushed on to Quatre-Bras. This was done in the presence of Maréchal Grouchy,—(see Grouchy's Observations)—who gives it as a reason (pp. 32, 33, 61,) for acting in the manner he did on the 18th, and not moving to his left to support Napoleon at Waterloo.

[311] Rogniat, p. 341, says that a great portion of the French army only reached Charleroi late on the 15th, and Fleurus at 11 A.M. on the 16th.—See Grouchy, p. 36.

The Duke of Wellington seems to have expected an attack by the Mons chaussée,[312] and on his first receiving information of the enemy's movements, merely ordered his troops to hold themselves in readiness; this was on the evening of the 15th of June, at six o'clock. Having obtained farther intelligence about eleven o'clock, which confirmed the real attack of the enemy to be along the Sambre, orders were immediately given for the troops to march upon Quatre-Bras; a false movement of the English general to his right, at that period, could not have been easily remedied in time to have fought in front of Brussels, and to have effected his junction with the Prussians; and in such a case, as Maréchal Blucher only fought at Ligny on the expectation of being supported by the Duke of Wellington, it is probable that that action would not have taken place. He had, however, a safe retreat on Bulow's corps and Maestricht, as had the Duke of Wellington on Ghent and Antwerp, or else the plan afterwards adopted of concentrating at Waterloo and Wavres, could not have been easily executed. It is, indeed, a matter of surprise, that Buonaparte did not make a more important demonstration on the side of Lisle and Mons. The Duke, in deciding on these movements, was under the necessity of acting on the intelligence given by spies or deserters, which can only be so far depended on, as it is confirmed by reports from the outposts, who may be themselves deceived.[313] What was true at their departure, may be entirely changed at their arrival with the information; and whatever may have been the case formerly, few or no instances occur at present of a person in the confidence of the cabinet, particularly of a military officer, betraying the confidence placed in him.

The Duke of Wellington arrived at Quatre-Bras on the 16th, at an early hour, and immediately proceeded to Bry, to concert measures with Marshal Blucher, for arranging the most efficient plan of support. It appeared at that time, that the whole French attack would be directed against the Prussians, as considerable masses of the enemy were in movement in their front. Blucher was at this time

---

[312] Official Despatch; Muffling, pp. 8, 10, 18.
[313] Muffling, p. 17. Yet a story is told of Fouché, who is said to have sent intelligence of Buonaparte's movements to Lord Wellington. The courier was attacked and waylaid, as supposed by Fouché's contrivance, so that he had an excuse ready for both parties.

at the wind-mill of Bry, about five English miles from Quatre-Bras. [Muffling, p. 10.] The Duke proposed to advance upon Frasnes and Gosselies, which would have been a decided movement, as acting on the French communications, and immediately in rear of their left flank; but as the troops could not be ready to advance from Quatre-Bras before four o'clock, the attack must have been too late, and in the meantime the Prussians would have to sustain the attack of nearly the whole French army. Maréchal Blucher, therefore, judged it more desirable, that the Duke should form a junction with the Prussian right, by marching direct by the chaussée from Quatre-Bras to Bry.[314]

The object of the enemy on the 16th, as may be seen by the general orders of Napoleon, communicated by Soult to Ney and Grouchy, was to turn the Prussian right, by driving the British from Quatre-Bras, and then to march down the chaussée upon the Bry, and thus separate the armies. [Batty, p. 150.] For this purpose, Ney was detached with 43,000 men. [Liv. ix., p. 103.] On reference to the above orders, it appears that not much resistance was expected in getting possession both of Sombref and Quatre-Bras.[315] Ney has been accused of delaying to attack, but reference to those orders will show that Ney had not been commanded to attack[316] until two o'clock P.M., in consequence of the allies having assembled in force at Quatre-Bras. The plan was excellent, and if Ney had been successful, would have led to important results. After obtaining possession of Quatre-Bras, he was to have detached part of his forces to attack the Prussian right flank in rear of St. Amand, whilst Buonaparte was making the chief attack on that village, the strongest in the position, and at the same time keeping the whole Prussian line engaged. Half of Ney's force was left in reserve near Frasnes, to be in readiness either to support the attacks on Quatre-Bras or St.

---

[314] Muffling, p. 64, allows that the position at Ligny was too much extended to the left, but the object of this was to have a line of communication with the Meuse and Cologne; a fault alluded to as arising from having two armies, and two chiefs, with different objects in view.
[315] Grouchy, p. 47; Gourgaud, Liv. ix., p. 102.
[316] It is hardly to be supposed that an officer of Ney's bold and enterprising character, with so much at stake, would have hesitated to attack at Quatre-Bras, if he had had his troops in readiness; but it appears that he could not have had time to move to that point at the early hour stated by Buonaparte. Ney had, also, too much experience of the nature of the troops he was opposed to, to act rashly.

Amand, and in the event of both succeeding, to turn the Prussian right, by marching direct on Wagnele or Bry.[317]

The village of St. Amand was well defended; it formed the strength of the Prussian right, and from the intersection of several gardens and hedges, was very capable of defence; although so much in advance of the rest of the Prussian position. The face of the country in front of this position possesses no remarkable features; the slopes towards the stream are gentle, and of easy access. After a continued attack for two hours, the enemy had only obtained possession of half the village of St. Amand, and a severe attack was made upon Ligny, which was taken and retaken several times.[318] At this time Buonaparte sent for the corps of reserve left by Ney at Frasnes; before, however, it reached St. Amand, in consequence of the check they had sustained at Quatre-Bras, it was countermarched, and from this circumstance became of little use either to Buonaparte or Ney. Buonaparte having observed the masses of troops which Blucher had brought up behind St. Amand (and probably in consequence of the corps above mentioned being necessary at Quatre-Bras,)[319] appears to have changed the disposition of his reserves, who were marching upon St. Amand, and moved them towards the right, to attack the Prussian centre at Ligny, which they succeeded in forcing, and so obtained possession of that village.[320] A large body of French cavalry, and another of infantry, then pushed forward to the height between Bry and Sombref, immediately in the rear of Ligny, and quite in the heart of the Prussian position, where they were attacked by Blucher at the head of his cavalry; this attempt to re-establish the action failed, and the Prussian cavalry were driven back upon the infantry.[321] It was now nine o'clock, about dark, which prevented the French from advancing farther, and they contented themselves with the occupation of Ligny. The Prussians

---

[317] The French did not attack until three P.M., the different corps not being arrived to make the necessary arrangements at an earlier hour.—Grouchy, p. 36; Rogniat, p. 341.
[318] Ney's Letter to the Duc d'Otranto. Paris, 1815.—Muffling, p. 14.
[319] Muffling, pp. 15-64.—Blucher had employed his reserves to support his right at St. Amand, and was not prepared for this change of attack. Muffling, however, considers, that, instead of his cavalry, had he moved his infantry from St. Amand to retake Ligny, he would have succeeded and gained the action.
[320] Grouchy, p. 10, shows how little decisive the battle was. "La bataille de Ligny n'a fini que vers la neuf heure de soir, seulement alors la retraite des Prussiens a été présumée."
[321] Here it was that Blucher was so nearly falling into the hands of the French cavalry.

did not evacuate Bry before three o'clock A.M. on the 17th.[322] In the course of the night, the Prussians fell back on Tilly and Gembloux. The loss of the Prussians, according to their own account, amounted to 14,000 men, and fifteen pieces of artillery. The French official account in the *Moniteur* to 15,000.[323] The French acknowledge to have lost 7000. It is evident that Buonaparte, in changing the point of attack from the Prussian right at St. Amand, to the centre at Ligny, in a manner forced the Prussians, if defeated, to retreat upon the British army, and give up their own line of operations; but still, at that hour in the evening, when the situation of the armies is considered, the change of attack appears to be the only hope he had of obtaining even a partial success; under such circumstances, it was perhaps the best course he could pursue.[324]

It is not easy to conceive that a defeat, in any case, would have been such as to prevent their junction, since each army had such considerable reinforcements moving up, and close upon them; but even in an extreme case, they could each have retired on their fortresses, and formed intrenched camps of perfect security, with every means of repairing the losses they sustained.[325]

The force of the enemy, at the time the Duke of Wellington left Quatre-Bras to communicate with Blucher, appeared to be so

---

[322] Grouchy, p. 11, says, that, even on the 17th, it was supposed the Prussians had retired upon Namur, so feebly were they followed; the light cavalry of General Pajot pursued them in this direction on the 17th, captured a few guns, which, with some stragglers, as are found in all armies, was his whole success.

[323] The St. Helena productions raise the amount to 20,000 men, 40 guns, standards, &c. See Grouchy, pp. 48, 49.—Montholon says they lost 60,000.—Liv. x., 148, says, that the Prussian army was reduced to 40,000 men by the loss they had sustained; 30,000 men killed and wounded, and 20,000 men, who had disbanded and ravaged the banks of the Meuse, and by the detachments sent to cover their retreat, and that of the baggage, in the direction of Namur.

[324] The intention of the allied maréchals to remain together, whatever might be the issue, is known. Lord Wellington had ordered the inundations of Antwerp to be effected to their utmost extent. The fortresses were to have been abandoned to their own strength, and had the events of the 16th been such as to necessitate a retreat, and give up Brussels, Maestricht is probably the point on which both armies would have retired.

[325] Had earlier or more positive information of the enemy's plans been received by Lord Wellington, and the troops put in movement on the evening of the 15th, the combinations of the two allied chiefs would have been perfect. Nothing more is necessary to show how well their plans had been laid, but which were not carried into full effect, by one of those accidental occurrences which no human foresight can prevent.

weak, that no serious attack was at that time to be apprehended; but on his return to that position, about three o'clock, he found they had assembled a large force at Frasnes, and were preparing for an attack, which was made about half-past three o'clock by two columns of infantry, and nearly all their cavalry, supported by a heavy fire of artillery. The force at that time under his orders, was 17,000 infantry and 2000 cavalry, of which about 4500 were British infantry, the rest Hanoverians, and Belgians, and Nassau troops.[326] They at first obtained some success, driving back the Belgian and Brunswick cavalry; their cavalry penetrated amongst our infantry before they had quite time to form squares, and forced a part to retire into the adjoining wood; they were, however, repulsed. At this period of the action, the third British division, under General Alten, arrived about four o'clock, soon after the action had commenced. They consisted of about 6300 men, and were composed of British, King's German legion, and Hanoverians. They had some difficulty in maintaining their ground, and one regiment lost a colour.[327] They succeeded, however, in repelling the enemy from the advanced points he had gained at the farm of Gemincourt and village of Pierremont.

Ney still, however, occupied part of the wood of Bossu, which extends from Quatre-Bras, on the right of the road towards Frasnes, to the distance of about a mile. This favoured an attack on the right of our position, which he accordingly made, after having been repulsed on the left. At this moment the division of General Cooke [Guards,] 4000 strong, arrived from Enghien, and materially assisted to repel this attack, which, after considerable exertions, was done, and the enemy driven back upon Frasnes, in much confusion. This affair was severely contested, and though the enemy were repulsed, the loss on each side was nearly equal, owing to the superiority of the French in artillery. The loss, however, inflicted on the French by

---

[326] Liv. ix., p. 103. Buonaparte says, that Ney attacked with 16,000 infantry, 3000 cavalry, and 44 guns, leaving 16,000 infantry, 4500 cavalry, and 64 guns, in reserve at Frasnes.

[327] This belonged to the 69th regiment, not to the 42d, as Liv. ix. states, p. 104, and was almost the only one captured during the whole war. It may here be remarked, that if the French had carried one quarter the number of eagles with their regiments that we have of colours, a much larger proportion would now be found at Whitehall. A weak battalion of English infantry always carries two large colours, very heavy and inconvenient, whilst a French eagle, about the size of a blackbird, was only given to a regiment composed of several battalions, which was easily secured in case of defeat.

the fire of musketry, which their attacking columns were exposed to, was very considerable, and counterbalanced the advantage they derived from their artillery. It required great exertions to maintain the important post of Quatre-Bras, in the present relative situations of the two armies. It is certain that, if Ney had advanced as rapidly as Buonaparte says he might have done, he would have obtained his object. Ney, however, in his letter, contradicts the possibility of his having done so, which seems to be confirmed by Soult's letter to him, dated at 2 o'clock P.M., where he tells him, that Grouchy is to attack Bry with the 3d and 4th corps, at half-past 2 P.M. [Batty, App.]; that he is to attack the corps in his front, and afterwards to assist Grouchy; but that if he (Ney) defeats the troops in his front first, Grouchy would be ordered to assist his operations. It is most probable that the corps left at Frasnes, which Ney complains was taken away without his knowledge, was destined to assist either attack as might be found necessary.

Even had Ney got possession of Quatre-Bras at an early hour, he would scarcely have been able to detach any sufficient force against the Prussians, seeing, as he must have done, or at least ought to have calculated, that the British forces were arriving rapidly on the point which we suppose him to have occupied. The British could have still retreated on Waterloo, and been concentrated on the 17th at that position; and there was nothing to prevent the Prussians retreating on Wavre, as they afterwards did. Though Buonaparte says [Liv. ix., p. 209,] that on the 15th every thing had succeeded as he wished, and that the Duke of Wellington had manœuvred as he would have wished him to do; yet one corps of the Prussian army had so far kept him in check, that he was not able to reach Fleurus; and on the 16th, could not commence the attack until three hours after mid-day. He did not gain possession of Quatre-Bras until the forenoon of the 17th. He had sustained a severe check with one part of his army, and gained an indecisive action with the other; the loss of the allies not exceeding his own, whilst they had the advantage of retiring leisurely on their resources and reinforcements, and by the retreat, gave up no place or position now of consequence to the pursuing enemy. The result of the operations of the 16th produced no important consequences to the French. The celebrated engineer, General Rogniat, does not hesitate to term it an indecisive action.

The success of the British in repelling the attack of Quatre-Bras, tended to make them meet the renewed attack at Waterloo with more confidence, and probably had a contrary effect on the enemy; whilst the manner in which the Prussian corps of Thielman received the attack of Grouchy on the 18th, who had superior forces, showed how little the confidence of the Prussians had been shaken by the action at Ligny. It may be observed, that the forces engaged at Ligny were nearly equal, even deducting D'Erlon's corps, which was left at Frasnes, as not engaged. The French passed the frontiers with about 125,000 men—Blucher had 80,000—and at *the close* of the day, Lord Wellington had 30,000.[328] The commanders of the allied armies appear not to have overrated what was to be expected from their troops, which was not exactly the case with their opponents.

The outline of the operations, and the strategie on the part of Napoleon to separate the two armies, was no doubt finely conceived, and, as we have seen, was nearly successful; yet it is presumed, that, had it been so, even to the extent Buonaparte could hope or expect, the allies had still a safe retreat, and sufficient resources. On all sides, it was a calculation of hours. It is hardly possible to know the point an enterprising enemy means to attack, especially on so extended a line; and here the assailant has the advantage. Fault has been found with the Duke of Wellington for having no artillery and very few cavalry upon the 16th. No portion of either were with the reserve at Brussels, which is remarkable, particularly as regards the artillery.[329]

The spirited manner in which the allied maréchals adhered to their plans of defence previously agreed on, and extricated

---

[328] Liv. ix., p. 60. Buonaparte remarks, that the numbers of the allied army must not be rated at their numerical force. "Parceque l'armée des alliés étoit composée de troups plus ou moins bonnes. Un Anglois pourrait être compté pour un Français; et deux Hollandais, Prussiens, ou hommes de la confédération, pour un Français. Les armées ennemies étoient cantonnées sous le commandement de deux Généraux différents, et formées de deux nations divisées d'intérêts et de sentiments." His army, on the contrary, was under one chief, the idol of his soldiers, who were of the best description—veterans who had fought in the brilliant campaign of 1813-14, and draughts from the numerous garrisons who had since entered France from Antwerp, Hamburg, Magdeburg, Dantzic, Mayence, Alexandria, Mantua, &c., with the numerous prisoners from England. Liv. ix., p. 201.

[329] Three brigades of iron eighteen-pounders were preparing at Brussels, but not in a state of forwardness to be sent to Waterloo.

themselves from the difficulties which they found themselves placed in, by the sudden and vigorous attack they had to sustain, and which their distinct commands tended rather to increase, must command admiration; and since war is only a great game, where the movements are influenced by many events which occur during their execution and progress—events which human calculation cannot foresee—it becomes easy to criticise when the operations are passed, when all the data on which they rested, or might have rested, are known; but to form a good plan of attack, or a campaign—to act with decision and firmness, and with a "coup d'œil," so as immediately to profit by the changes which incessantly take place, can be said of very few men of the many who have ever arrived at the command of an army.

On the morning of the 17th, the British troops remained in possession of Quatre-Bras, where the rest of the army had joined the Duke of Wellington, who was prepared to maintain that position against the French army, had the Prussians remained in the position of Ligny, so as to give him support.

Maréchal Blucher had sent an aide-de-camp to inform the duke of his retreat, who was unfortunately killed; and it was not until seven o'clock on the 17th, that Lord Wellington learned the direction which the Prussians had taken. A patrol sent at daylight to communicate with the Prussians, advanced beyond Bry and Sombref, which confirmed how little of the Prussian position had been occupied by the French. The Prussians had fallen back very leisurely on Wavre, their rear-guard occupying Bry, which they did not evacuate before three o'clock on the morning of the 17th. Buonaparte, in deceiving the French people, by the accounts he gave of the defeat of the Prussians at Ligny, seems almost to have deceived himself. He must have known that the action was not a decisive one—that the enemy had retired in excellent order—that he had not been able to pursue them—and that his own loss must have considerably weakened his army, whilst the Prussians were falling back upon their reinforcements—and, above all, that Maréchal Blucher commanded them. The Prussian army was concentrated at Wavre at an early hour, and communication took place between the Duke of Wellington and Blucher, by which a junction of the army was arranged for the succeeding day at Waterloo.[330] The retrograde movement of the Prussians rendered a corresponding one necessary on the part of the British, which was performed in the most leisurely manner, the duke allowing the men time to finish their cooking. About ten o'clock, the whole army retired, in three columns, by Genappe and Nivelles, towards a position at Waterloo—a rear-guard was left to occupy the ground, so as to conceal the movement from the enemy, who, about mid-day, deployed their troops in columns of attack, as if expecting to find the English army in position there. They immediately followed up the retreat with cavalry and light-artillery. An affair of cavalry occurred at Genappe, where the 7th hussars attacked a French regiment of lancers without success; upon which the heavy cavalry were brought up by the Marquis of Anglesea, who checked the enemy's advance by a vigorous and decisive charge.

As the troops arrived in position in front of Mont Saint Jean, they took up the ground they were to maintain, which was effected early in the evening. The weather began to be very severe at this period. The whole French army, under Buonaparte, with the exception of two corps under Grouchy (32,000 men, and 108 guns,) took up a position immediately in front; and after some cannonading, both armies remained opposite to each other during the night, the rain falling in torrents. The duke had already communicated with Maréchal Blucher, who promised to come to his support with the whole of his army, on the morning of the 18th. It was consequently decided upon to cover Brussels (the preservation of which was of such importance, in every point of view, to the King of the Netherlands,) by maintaining the position of Mont St. Jean. The intention of the allied chiefs, if they were not attacked on the 18th, was to have attacked the enemy on the 19th.

Since we are now arrived at the position of Mont St. Jean, it may be necessary to offer a few remarks as regards the position itself, which has been considered as a bad one by some writers,[331] and some loose allusions to its defects thrown out; but more

---

[330] Muffling, p. 20, says, "that Blucher only asked for time to distribute food and cartridges to his men."
[331] Montholon, vii., p. 134; Liv. ix., pp. 123-207; Gourgaud, p. 131.

particularly fixing upon its not affording a secure retreat, in the event of the enemy's attack having proved successful. Previous, however, to entering into any disquisition as to the merits of the position of Mont St. Jean, it may be well to consider a few of the conditions that are judged essential in a greater or less degree, for every position taken up by an army. The first requisite is, that the ground in front, within cannon-shot, should be well seen; and every point of approach with musket-shot, well discovered.—2d, That the ground which is occupied should admit of a free communication for troops and guns, from right to left, and from front to rear, in order to move supports wherever they may be wanted; also that, by the sinuosities of the ground, or other cover, such movements may be made unseen by the enemy.—3d, That your flanks rest on some support, secure from being turned—And, lastly, that your retreat be ensured in the event of your position being forced or turned.

The site of the position of Mont St. Jean, and the features of the ground round it, have been so often and well described, that we may conclude it to be familiar to most people; and hence the possession of these necessary conditions will be already evident. The easy slope from our front into the valley, from whence it rises in an ascent equally gentle and regular, to the opposite heights, on which the enemy were posted at the distance of about a mile, or a mile and a half, gave it, in an eminent degree, the condition stated in the first remark. The two chaussées, running nearly perpendicular to our line—the valley immediately in rear of our first line, and parallel to it, with two country roads passing in the same direction; also the openness of the country—gave the position the requisites mentioned in the second. The same valley afforded cover for the support of the first line; also for its artillery, and spare ammunition-waggons; whilst the second line and reserves, placed on and behind the next ridge, and about 500 or 600 yards in rear of the first, were unseen from the enemy's position, although certainly so far exposed, that many of his shot and shells, which passed over the first line, ricocheted into the second, and amongst the reserves. The fourth requisite, as far as regards the security of the flanks, was completely obtained, by the occupation of the village of Braine la Leude on its right, which would have been intrenched, but for an accidental misunderstanding of orders; and La Haye and Ohain on the left; also by both flanks being thrown back on the forest of Soignies.

That our retreat in case of a reverse, was sufficiently provided for, we trust, notwithstanding the criticism above noticed, to establish in a satisfactory manner. Our position was sufficiently in advance of the entrance of the chaussée into the forest, to give a free approach from every part of the field to that point; which the unenclosed state of the country afforded the troops every means of profiting by. Had our first position been forced, the village of Mont St. Jean, at the junction of the two chaussées, afforded an excellent centre of support for a second, which the enemy would have had equal difficulty in carrying;—besides which there is another farm house and wood immediately behind Mont St. Jean, and in front of the entrance of the forest; which would have enabled us to keep open that entrance. By occupying these points, we might have at any time effected a retreat; and with sufficient leisure to have allowed all the guns, that were in a state to be moved, to file off into the forest. Undoubtedly, had our centre been broken by the last attack of the enemy [about half-past seven,] a considerable part of our artillery must have been left behind, a number of guns disabled, and many men and horses killed and wounded; these must have fallen into the enemy's hands; also the brigades at the points attacked, which were placed rather in front of the infantry, and remained until the last, firing grape-shot into the enemy's columns. The men and horses would have saved themselves with the infantry, and soon found a fresh equipment in the fortresses. The troops at Hougomont would have been cut off had that attack succeeded, but their retreat was open, either upon the corps of 16,000 men left at Halle to cover Brussels, or upon Braine la Leude, which was occupied by a brigade of infantry, who had strengthened their post; between which and our right flank a brigade of cavalry kept a communication open. From Braine la Leude there is a very good road through the forest by Alemberg to Brussels, by which the troops and artillery of our right flank could have effected their retreat. If we now suppose, that the enemy, instead of our right centre, had broken our left centre by the great attack made on it at three o'clock, Ohain afforded nearly the same advantage to the left of our army that Braine la Leude would have done on the right. A road leads from it through the forest to Brussels; or that wing might have retired on the Prussians at Wavre; so that, had either of these two grand attacks succeeded, the retreat into the defiles of the forest need not have been precipitated. It is no fault of our troops to take alarm and lose confidence, because they find themselves turned or partially beaten. Of this many instances might be given. The best proof, however, is, that the enemy can scarcely claim having made a few hundred prisoners during the whole of the last war. No success on the part of the enemy, which they had a right to calculate on, could have then precipitated us into the forest in total disorder. The attacks we sustained to the last on the 18th, were as determined and severe as can be conceived. Still, to the last, a part of the reserve and the cavalry had not suffered much; whereas the French cavalry (heavy) had all been engaged before five o'clock, and were not in a state, from the severe losses they had sustained, to take advantage of a victory.[332]

But suppose we had been driven into the wood in a state of deroute, similar to what the French were, the forest did not keep us hermetically sealed up, as an impenetrable marsh did the defeated troops at Austerlitz. The remains of our shattered battalions would have gained the forest, and found themselves in security. It consists of tall trees without underwood, passable almost any where for men and horses. The troops could, therefore, have gained the chaussée through it, and when we at last came to confine ourselves to the defence of the entrance to the forest, every person, the least experienced in war, knows the extreme difficulty in forcing infantry from a wood which cannot be turned. A few regiments, with or without artillery, would have kept the whole French army in check, even if they had been as fresh as the day they crossed the frontiers.[333] Indeed, the forest in our rear gave us so evident an

---

[332] See Liv. ix., p. 196. "Ainsi à cinq heures après midi, l'armée se trouva sans avoir une reserve de cavalerie. Si, à huit heures et demi, cette reserve eut existée," &c. &c. It is singular how great soldiers, in reporting military actions, will contradict each other. Napoleon ascribes the loss of the battle in great measure to his cavalry being so soon and generally engaged, that he had not a reserve left to protect his retreat. General Foy, on the contrary, affirms, that it was not the French, but the British cavalry, which was annihilated at Waterloo.—*Guerre de la Péninsule*, p. 116. *Note.*

[333] On the 16th, at Quatre-Bras, the 33d regiment (British,) and afterwards two battalions of the Guards, when obliged to give way to an attack of the enemy, and pursued by the

advantage, that it is difficult to believe that an observation to the contrary was made by Napoleon. Could he quite forget his own retreat? It little availed him to have two fine chaussées, and an open country in his rear; his materiel was all abandoned, and not even a single battalion kept together.

The two farms in front of the position of Mont St. Jean, gave its principal strength. That of Hougomont, with its gardens and enclosures, could contain a force sufficient to make it a most important post. La Haye Sainte was too small for that purpose; otherwise its situation in the Genappe chaussée, in the centre of the position, rendered it better adapted for that purpose. These farms lay on the slope of the valley, about 1500 yards apart, in front of our line; so that no column of the enemy could pass between them, without being exposed to a flank fire. Indeed, without these posts, the ground gave us little advantage over our enemy, except the loss he must be necessarily exposed to in advancing in column upon a line already fixed.

From these observations it will appear that our retreat was well secured, and that the advantages of the position for a field of battle were very considerable; so that there was little risk but that it would have been successfully defended, even if the Prussians had by "some fatality" been prevented from forming a junction. The difficulties of the roads, from the severe rains, detained them from joining us at least double the time that was calculated upon. We had therefore to sustain the attack of a superior army so much longer; yet they were not able to make any impression. Every attack had been most successfully repulsed; and we may safely infer that, even if the Prussians had not joined in time, we would still have been able to maintain our position, and repulse the enemy, but might have been perhaps unable, as was the case at Talavera, to profit by this advantage, or to follow up our success.[334]

French cavalry, saved themselves in the wood of Bossu, formed along the skirts of it, and repelled the enemy with severe loss.

[334] The armies were now placed under their favourite commanders, as the military of both nations had long wished; and on an arena which may be considered as fair a one as could well have offered in the chances of war. The British troops, however, were not composed of our best regiments, at least our infantry, nor equal to that army which had been in the

The morning of the 18th, and part of the forenoon, were passed by the enemy in a state of supineness, for which it was difficult to account. The rain had certainly retarded his movements, more particularly that of bringing his artillery into position; yet it was observed that this had been accomplished at an early hour. In Grouchy's publication, we find a reason which may have caused this delay; namely, that Napoleon's ammunition had been so much exhausted in the preceding actions, that there was only a sufficiency with the army for an action of eight hours. Buonaparte states [Liv. ix.] that it was necessary to wait until the ground was sufficiently dried, to enable the cavalry and artillery to manœuvre [Montholon, tom. ii., p. 136;] however, in such a soil, a few hours could make very little difference, particularly as a drizzling rain continued all the morning, and indeed after the action had commenced. The heavy fall of rain on the night of the 17th to 18th, was no doubt more disadvantageous to the enemy than to the troops under Lord Wellington; the latter were in position, and had few movements to make; whilst the enemy's columns, and particularly his cavalry, were much fatigued and impeded by the state of the ground, which, with the trampled corn, caused them to advance more slowly, and kept them longer under fire. On the other hand, the same causes delayed the Prussians in their junction, which they had promised to effect at eleven o'clock, and obliged Lord Wellington to maintain the position alone, nearly eight hours longer than had been calculated upon.

About twelve o'clock, the enemy commenced the action by an attack upon Hougomont, with several columns, preceded by numerous light troops, who, after severe skirmishing, drove the Nassau troops from the wood in its front, and established themselves in it. This attack was supported by the constant fire of a numerous artillery. A battalion of the Guards occupied the house and gardens, with the other enclosures, which afforded great

---

preceding year in the south of France. Many of the most efficient regiments had been sent to America; first a brigade from Bourdeaux to Washington; another to Canada: and afterwards a force from Portsmouth to New Orleans. None of those returned in time for Waterloo, though they were *on their way.*—Liv. ix., p. 208. It has been shown how the French army was composed.

facilities for defence; and after a severe contest, and immense loss, the enemy were repulsed, and a great part of the wood regained.[335]

During the early part of the day, the action was almost entirely confined to this part of the line, except a galling fire of artillery along the centre, which was vigorously returned by our guns. This fire gradually extended towards the left, and some demonstrations of an attack of cavalry were made by the enemy. As the troops were drawn up on the slope of the hill, they suffered most severely from the enemy's artillery. In order to remedy this, Lord Wellington moved them back about 150 or 200 yards, to the reverse slope of the hill, to shelter them from the direct fire of the guns; our artillery in consequence remained in advance, that they might see into the valley. This movement was made between one and two o'clock by the duke in person; it was general along the front or centre of the position, on the height to the right of La Haye Sainte.

It is by no means improbable, that the enemy considered this movement as the commencement of a retreat, since a considerable portion of our troops were withdrawn from his sight, and determined in consequence to attack our left centre, in order to get possession of the buildings, called Ferme de M. St. Jean, or of the village itself, which commanded the point of junction of the two chaussées. The attacking columns advanced on the Genappe chaussée, and by the side of it; they consisted of four columns of infantry (D'Erlon's corps, which was not engaged on the 16th,) thirty pieces of artillery, and a large body of cuirassiers (Milhaud's.) On the left of this attack, the French cavalry took the lead of the infantry, and had advanced considerably, when the Duke of

---

[335] Buonaparte, liv. ix., 142, says, that he saw with pleasure that the English guards were placed on our right, as they were our best troops, which rendered his premeditated attack on our left more easy. Our guards are not, as is the case in other armies, the élite of our army; they are not selected, as in other services, from the best soldiers in other regiments, but are recruited exactly as troops of the line, except that they are required to be somewhat taller. It may be here remarked, the great superiority in *appearance*, that the French and other troops possessed over ours at the close of the war. The mode of recruiting accounts for this. Even our militia were much superior in this point of view to the troops of the line, and most of the best men were obtained from them. Our recruits were in general composed of the population of large cities, or of manufacturing towns, certainly not the best specimens of our population; the military service is not in any estimation amongst our peasantry, whilst the French army was composed of the picked men of thirty millions, and other nations in proportion.

Wellington ordered the heavy cavalry (Life Guards) to charge them as they ascended the position near La Haye Sainte. They were driven back on their own position, where the chaussée, being cut into the rising ground, leaves steep banks on either side. In this confined space they fought at swords' length for some minutes, until the enemy brought down some light artillery from the heights, when the British cavalry retired to their own position. The loss of the cuirassiers did not appear great. They seemed immediately to reform their ranks, and soon after advanced to attack our infantry, who were formed into squares to receive them, being then unsupported by cavalry. The columns of infantry in the mean time, pushed forward on *our* left of the Genappe chaussée, beyond La Haye Sainte, which they did not attempt in this attack to take. A Belgian brigade of infantry, formed in front, gave way, and these columns crowned the position. When Sir Thomas Picton moved up the brigade of General Pack from the second line (the 92d regiment in front,) which opened a fire on the column just as it gained the height, and advanced upon it. When within thirty yards, the column began to hesitate; at this moment a brigade of heavy cavalry (the 1st and 2d dragoons) wheeled round the 92d regiment, and took the column in flank; a total rout ensued; the French, throwing down their arms, ran into our position to save themselves from being cut down by the cavalry; many were killed, and two eagles, with 2000 prisoners, taken. But the cavalry pursued their success too far, and being fired upon by one of the other columns, and at the same time, when in confusion, being attacked by some French cavalry who had been sent to support the attack, the British were obliged to retire with considerable loss. In this attack the enemy had brought forward several pieces of artillery, which were captured by our cavalry; the horses in the guns were killed, and we were obliged to abandon the guns. General Ponsonby, who commanded the cavalry, was killed. The gallant Sir Thomas Picton also fell, leading on his division to repel this attack.[336] The number of occurrences which crowded on the attention, rendered it impossible for any individual to see the whole action, and in the midst of noise, bustle, and

---

[336] Rogniat, p. 231, blames both generals for the too early employment of their cavalry. In the case here mentioned, he says, the success was "contre toute probabilité," as the cavalry charged unbroken infantry. The head of the attacking columns had, however, been already shaken by the charge of the 92d regiment, which took place nearly at the moment the cavalry charged.

personal danger, it is difficult to note the exact time in which the event happens.[337]

It is only afterwards, in discussing the chances and merits of each, that such questions become of interest, which may in some measure account for the discrepancy of the statements of officers present, as to the time and circumstances of some of the principal events. From this period, half-past two, until the end of the action, the British cavalry were scarcely engaged, but remained in readiness in the second line.[338] After the French cuirassiers had re-formed, and were strongly reinforced,[339] they again advanced upon our position, and made several desperate attacks upon our infantry, who immediately formed into squares, and maintained themselves with the most determined courage and coolness. Some time previous to this, about three o'clock, an attack was made upon La Haye Sainte, which is merely a small farm-house; it was occupied by two companies of the German Legion. The enemy had advanced beyond it, so that the communication was cut off for some time, and it could not be reinforced. The troops having expended their ammunition, the post was carried. A continued fire was kept up at this point, and the enemy was soon afterwards obliged to abandon it, without being able to avail himself of it as a point of support for his attacking columns. The house was too small for a sufficient number of troops to maintain themselves so close to our position, under such a heavy fire.

The French cavalry, in the attack on the centre of our line above mentioned, were not supported by infantry. They came on, however, with the greatest courage, close to the squares of our infantry; the artillery, which was somewhat in advance, kept up a well-directed fire upon them as they advanced, but on their nearer approach, the gunners were obliged to retire into the squares, so that the guns were actually in possession of the enemy's cavalry, who could not, however, keep possession of them, or even spike them, if they had the means, in consequence of the heavy fire of musketry to

---

[337] Muffling, p. 26, observes, "La fumée étoit si épaisse que personne ne voyoit l'ensemble de l'action."
[338] Liv. ix., p. 209. Buonaparte says, "L'infanterie Anglaise a été ferme et solide. La cavalerie pouvait mieux faire."
[339] Rogniat, p. 231, says they amounted to 12,000, including other heavy cavalry.

which they were exposed. The French accounts say, that several squares were broken, and standards taken, which is decidedly false; on the contrary, the small squares constantly repulsed the cavalry, whom they generally allowed to advance close to their bayonets before they fired. They were driven back with loss on all points, and the artillerymen immediately resumed their guns in the most prompt manner, and opened a severe and destructive fire of grape-shot on them as they retired.[340]

After the failure of the first attack, the French had little or no chance of success by renewing it; but the officers, perhaps ashamed of the failure of such boasted troops, endeavoured repeatedly to bring them back to charge the squares; but they could only be brought to pass between them, and round them. They even penetrated to our second line, where they cut down some stragglers and artillery-drivers, who were with the limbers and ammunition-waggons. They charged the Belgian squares in the second line, with no better success, and upon some heavy Dutch cavalry showing themselves, they soon retired.

If the enemy supposed us in retreat, then such an attack of cavalry might have led to the most important results; but by remaining so uselessly in our position, and passing and repassing our squares of infantry, they suffered severely by their fire; so much so, that before the end of the action, when they might have been of great use, either in the attack, or in covering the retreat, they were nearly destroyed.[341] The only advantage which appeared to result

---

[340] The cavalry came up to one of the squares at a trot, and appeared to be hanging back, as if expecting our fire; they closed round two sides of it, having a front of seventy or eighty men, and came so close to one angle, that they appeared to try to reach over the bayonets with their swords. The squares were generally formed four deep, rounded at the angles: on the approach of the cavalry, two files fired, the others reserving their fire; the cavalry then turned, and it is not easy to believe how few fell,—only one officer and two men; no doubt many were wounded, but did not fall from their horses. Many squares fired at the distance of thirty paces, with no other effect. In fact, our troops fired too high, which must have been noticed by the most casual observer.

[341] It has been said, that if the enemy had brought up infantry and light artillery, our squares must have given way. This would no doubt have been preferable: but then our reserve and cavalry would have been moved forward to check the cavalry, and the squares would have probably repelled the attack of the infantry. The enemy had tried to bring guns with the attacking columns, on our left, early in the day; the consequence was, that the horses were killed before they had advanced far, so that they could not follow the movements of the

from their remaining in our position, was preventing the fire of our guns on the columns which afterwards formed near La Belle Alliance, in order to debouche for a new attack. The galling fire of the infantry, however, forcing the French cavalry at length to retire into the hollow ground, to cover themselves, the artillerymen were again at their guns, and, being in advance of the squares, saw completely into the valley, and by their well-directed fire, seemed to make gaps in them as they re-formed to repeat this useless expenditure of lives. Had Buonaparte been nearer the front, he surely would have prevented this useless sacrifice of his best troops. Indeed, the attack of cavalry at this period, is only to be accounted for by supposing the British army to be in retreat. He had had no time to avail himself of his powerful artillery to make an impression on that part of the line he meant to attack, as had always been his custom, otherwise it was not availing himself of the superiority he possessed; and it was treating his enemy with a contempt, which, from what he had experienced at Quatre-Bras, could not be justified.[342] He allows, in Liv. ix., p. 156, that this charge was made too soon,[343] but that it was necessary to support it, and that the cuirassiers of Kellerman, 3000 in number, were consequently ordered forward to maintain the position. And at p. 196 and 157, Liv. ix., he allows that the grenadiers-à-cheval, and dragoons of the guard, which were in reserve, advanced without orders; that he sent to recall them, but, as they were already engaged, any retrograde movement would then have been dangerous. Thus, every attack of the enemy had been repulsed, and a severe loss inflicted. The influence this must have had on the "morale" of each army, was much in favour of the British, and the probability of success on the part of the enemy was consequently diminished from that period.

The enemy now seemed to concentrate their artillery, particularly on the left of the Genappe chaussée, in front of La Belle

---

infantry, and were left behind. A similar attempt was made in the south of France, in the attack of Lord Hill's corps on the Nive; the guns were harnessed, so as to allow them to fire as they advanced, but the horses were soon killed or disabled, and the guns were abandoned when the attack was repulsed.

[342] This was what Marmont had done at the Aripiles, at the battle of Salamanca, and for which he suffered so severely.

[343] Muffling, p. 27, says, after this attack, which he states to be at four o'clock, "La bataille avoit été très sanglante, mais il n'y avoit point de danger pour l'armée Anglaise." He says it was then five o'clock.

Alliance, and commenced a heavy fire (a large proportion of his guns were twelve-pounders) on that part of our line extending from behind La Haye Sainte towards Hougomont. Our infantry sheltered themselves by lying down behind the ridge of the rising ground, and bore it with the most heroic patience. Several of our guns had been disabled, and many artillerymen killed and wounded, so that this fire was scarcely returned; but when the new point of attack was no longer doubtful, two brigades were brought from Lord Hill's corps on the right, and were of most essential service.

It may here be proper to consider the situation of the Prussian army, and the assistance they had rendered up to this time, about six o'clock.

The British army had sustained several severe attacks, which had been all repulsed, and no advantage of any consequence had been gained by the enemy. They had possessed part of the wood and garden of Hougomont, and La Haye Sainte, which latter they were unable to occupy. Not a square had been broken, shaken, or obliged to retire. Our infantry continued to display the same obstinacy, the same cool, calculating confidence in themselves, in their commander, and in their officers, which had covered them with glory in the long and arduous war in the Peninsula. From the limited extent of the field of battle, and the tremendous fire their columns were exposed to, the loss of the enemy could not have been less than 15,000 killed and wounded. Two eagles, and 2000 prisoners, had been taken, and their cavalry nearly destroyed. We still occupied nearly the same position as we did in the morning, but our loss had been severe, perhaps not less than 10,000 killed and wounded. Our ranks were further thinned by the numbers of men who carried off the wounded, part of whom never returned to the field. The number of Belgian and Hanoverian troops, many of whom were young levies, that crowded to the rear, was very considerable, besides the number of our own dismounted dragoons, together with a proportion of our infantry, some of whom, as will always be found in the best armies, were glad to escape from the field. These thronged the road leading to Brussels, in a manner that none but an eyewitness could have believed, so that perhaps the actual force under the Duke of Wellington at this time, half-past six, did not amount to more than 34,000 men.[344] We had at an early hour been in communication with some patroles of Prussian cavalry on our extreme left. A Prussian corps, under Bulow, had marched from Wavre at an early hour to manœuvre on the right and rear of the French army, but a large proportion of the Prussian army were still on the heights above Wavre, after the action had commenced at Waterloo.[345] The state of the roads, and the immense train of artillery they carried, detained Bulow's corps for a remarkably long time; they had not more than twelve or fourteen miles to march. At one o'clock,[346] the advanced guard of this corps was discovered by the French; about two o'clock the patroles of Bulow's corps were discovered from part of our position. The French detached some light cavalry to observe them, which was the only diversion that had taken place up to this time. At half-past four, Blucher had joined in person Bulow's corps, at which time two brigades of infantry and some cavalry were detached to act on the right of the French. [Muffling, p. 30.] He was so far from the right of the French, that his fire of artillery was too distant to produce any effect, and was chiefly intended to give us notice of his arrival. [Muffling, p. 31.] It was certainly past five o'clock before the fire of the Prussian artillery (Bulow's corps) was observed from our position, and it soon seemed to cease altogether. It appears that they had advanced, and obtained some success, but were afterwards driven back to a considerable distance by the French, who sent a corps under General Lobau to keep them in check.[347] About half-past six, the first Prussian corps came into communication with our extreme left near Ohain.

The effective state of the several armies may be considered to be as follows:

---

[344] See Muffling, p. 32, who makes the number amount to 10,000, and there is little doubt but that he is correct. A regiment of allied cavalry, whose uniform resembled the French, having fled to Brussels, an alarm spread that the enemy were at the gates. Numbers of those who had quitted the field of battle, and, let the truth be spoken, Englishmen too, fled from the town, and never halted until they reached Antwerp. This fact is too well attested to be doubted.
[345] Muffling, p. 29. At four o'clock, he says, "Il n'avoit pas encore paru un homme de cette armée."
[346] See Soult's letter to Grouchy, dated from the field of battle, at one o'clock.
[347] Liv. ix., p. 175. Buonaparte says it was seven o'clock when Lobau repulsed them.

The army under the Duke of Wellington amounted, at the commencement of the campaign, to 75,000 men, including every description of force,[348] of which nearly 40,000 were English, or the King's German Legion. Our loss at Quatre-Bras amounted to 4500 killed and wounded, which reduced the army to 70,500 men; of these about 54,000 were actually engaged at Waterloo; about 32,000 were composed of British troops, or the King's German Legion, including cavalry, infantry, and artillery; the remainder, under Prince Frederick, took no part in the action, but covered the approach to Brussels from Nievelles, and were stationed in the neighbourhood of Halle. The French force has been variously stated, and it is not easy to form a very accurate statement of their strength. Batty gives it at 127,000; that is the number which crossed the frontiers. Liv. ix., p. 69, it is given at 122,000. Gourgaud reduces it to 115,000; of these, 21,000 were cavalry, and they had 350 guns. Let us, however, take the statement in Liv. ix., and say,

		122,000
Deduct left at Charleroi, Liv. ix., 92,[349]	5,300	
Loss at Quatre-Bras and Ligny, Liv. ix., 100 and 106,	10,350	
Left at Ligny (Grouchy, p. 8,) Liv. ix., 193; this is stated at 3000,	3,200	
With Grouchy (Grouchy, p. 8,)	32,000	
		50,850
Engaged at Waterloo,		71,150

This number, however, is certainly underrated; and there is little doubt but Buonaparte had upwards of 75,000 men under his immediate command on the 18th June.[350]

Buonaparte, liv. ix., 162, 117, states the Prussian force concentrated at Wavre to be 75,000 men. Grouchy, p. 9, makes it

---

[348] Of these, about 12,700 were cavalry.
[349] Liv. ix., p. 193. This force is stated "4 à 5000 hommes."
[350] Muffling, p. 58, mentions, that Buonaparte stated to some general officer on the morning of the 18th, that he had 75,000 men, and the English only 50,000. Liv. ix., p. 193, by taking Buonaparte's own account in this part of the book, upon calculation it will be seen that he there allows that he had upwards of 74,000.

95,000. It is, however, generally understood that they had not above 70,000 with the army at Wavre.

It may be necessary here to refer to the operations of the corps under Grouchy, who were detached in pursuit of the Prussians. It appears, that at twelve o'clock on the 17th, Buonaparte was ignorant of the direction the Prussian army had taken.—[Grouchy, p. 13.]—It was generally supposed that it was towards Namur. At that hour, Buonaparte ordered Grouchy, with 32,000 men, to follow them. As the troops were much scattered, it was three o'clock before they were in movement, and they did not arrive at Gembloux before the night of the 17th, when Grouchy informed Buonaparte of the direction the Prussian army had taken. He discovered the rear-guard of the Prussians near Wavre about twelve o'clock on the 18th, and at two o'clock he attacked Wavre, which was obstinately defended by General Thielman, and succeeded in obtaining possession of a part of the village. By the gallant defence of this post by General Thielman, Grouchy was induced to believe that the whole Prussian army was before him. Blucher, however, had detached Bulow's corps (4th) at an early hour upon Chapelle-Lambert, to act on the rear of the French army. The movement of this corps was, however, much delayed by a fire which happened at Wavre, and by the bad state of the roads; so that they had great difficulty in bringing up the numerous artillery they carried with this corps, which prevented them from attacking the enemy before half-past four o'clock.[351]

The 2d Prussian corps marched upon Chapelle-Lambert and Lasne; and at a later period of the day[352] the 1st corps moved in the direction of Ohain. The 3d corps was also to have supported the 4th and 2d corps. Blucher was not aware of the large force under Grouchy, who attacked the 3d corps as it was preparing to leave Wavre, and obliged it to take up a position on the Dyle, between Limale and Wavre, where he afterwards ordered it to maintain itself as well as it could.

---

[351] See Muffling, pp. 22, 31, 62. Gourgaud, pp. 98 and 99, says it was half-past four when General Dumont informed Buonaparte of their arrival.
[352] Liv. ix., pp. 168, 169, Buonaparte makes Bulow's attack after sunset.

The British army, at this eventful period of the day, amounted to about 34,000 men (allowing 10,000 killed and wounded, and 10,000 more who had left the field,) 18,000 of whom are English.—[Muffling, p. 32.]—The enemy may have had about 45,000 immediately opposed to us, allowing 20,000 killed, wounded, and taken prisoners; and 10,000 men detached to act against the Prussians.

The assistance of the Prussians had been expected at an early hour,[353] which had induced Lord Wellington to accept a battle; so that the British army had to bear the whole brunt of the action for a much longer period than was calculated. Lord Wellington, however, showed no anxiety as to the result. The corps of Lord Hill, several Belgian battalions, and a considerable portion of the cavalry, had been little engaged. He knew the troops he had under his command, and seemed confident of being able to maintain his position, even if the Prussians did not arrive before night. The army was not aware of their approach, nor did he think it necessary to animate their exertions by this intelligence. Buonaparte, on the contrary, thought proper to revive the drooping spirits of his troops, even of his guards, who had not yet been engaged, by sending his aide-de-camp Labédoyère to inform them, as they were about to advance,[354] that Grouchy had joined their right flank, and even deceived Ney himself by this false intelligence.

The above detail has been entered into for the purpose of showing the state of the armies towards the close of the day. Buonaparte was now aware of the powerful diversion the Prussians were about to make, but at the same time seems to have imagined that Grouchy would be able to paralyse their movements. He therefore resolved to make a last desperate effort to break the centre of the British army, and carry their position before the attack of the Prussians could take effect.

The imperial guard had been kept in reserve, and had been for some time formed on the heights extending from La Belle Alliance,

---

[353] Muffling, p. 62, says, it was hoped the Prussian army could have attacked at two o'clock, but that it was half-past four before a cannon was fired by them.
[354] Liv. ix., p. 167, Ney's letter.

towards Hougomont, which supported their left flank. They had not yet been engaged.

About seven o'clock they advanced in two columns,[355] leaving four battalions in reserve. They were commanded by Ney, who led them on. At the same time, they pushed on some light troops in the direction of La Haye. The advance of these columns of the guards was supported by a heavy fire of artillery. Our infantry, who had been posted on the reverse of the hill, to be sheltered from the fire of the guns, were instantly moved forward by Lord Wellington. General Maitland's brigade of guards, and General Adam's brigade (52d and 71st regiments, and 95th rifles,) met this formidable attack. They were flanked by two brigades of artillery, who kept up a destructive fire on the advancing columns. Our troops waited for their approach with their characteristic coolness, until they were within a short distance of our line, when they opened a well-directed fire upon them. The line was formed four deep. The men fired independently, retiring a few paces to load, and then advanced and fired, so that their fire never ceased for a moment. The French, headed by their gallant leader, still advanced, notwithstanding the severe loss they sustained by this fire, which apparently seemed to check their movement. They were now within about fifty yards of our line, when they attempted to deploy, in order to return the fire. Our line appeared to be closing round them. They could not, however, deploy under such a fire; and from the moment they ceased to advance, their chance of success was over. They now formed a confused mass, and at last gave way, retiring in the utmost confusion. They were immediately pursued by the light troops of General Adam's brigade. This decided the battle. The enemy had now exhausted his means of attack. He had still, however, the four battalions of the old guard in reserve. Lord Wellington immediately ordered the whole line to advance to attack their position. The enemy were already attempting a retreat. These battalions formed a square to cover the retreat of the flying columns, flanked by a few guns, and supported by some light cavalry (red lancers.)

The first Prussian corps had now joined our extreme left. They had obtained possession of the village of La Haye, driving out

---

[355] See Lord Wellington's dispatches.

the French light troops who occupied it. Bulow, with the fourth corps, had some time previous to this made an unsuccessful attack upon the village of Planchenot, in the rear of the enemy's right wing, and being joined by the second corps, (Pirch's) was again advancing to attack it.[356] In the meantime, the square of the Old Guard maintained itself, the guns on its flank firing upon our light cavalry, who now advanced, and threatened to turn their flank. Our light troops were close on their front, and our whole line advancing, when this body, the "élite," and now the only hope of the enemy to cover their retreat, and save their army, gave way, and mixed in the general confusion and rout, abandoning their cannon and all their materiel. It was now nearly dark. Bulow, upon being joined by Pirch's corps, again attacked Planchenot, which he turned; and then the enemy abandoned it. He immediately advanced towards the Genappe chausée, and closed round the right of the French—[Liv. ix., p. 169]—driving the enemy before him, and augmenting their confusion. His troops came into the high-road, or chausée, near Maison du Roi, and Blucher and Wellington having met about the same time near La Belle Alliance, it was resolved to pursue the enemy, and give him no time to rally. The loss of the Prussians on the 18th did not exceed 800 men. The brunt of the action was chiefly sustained by the troops of the British and King's German Legion, as their loss will show. In stating this, it must be allowed, that much support was afforded by the other contingents; but they were chiefly raw levies, newly raised, who could not be depended upon in a situation of importance. Some behaved ill, as is publicly known. None were in the first line, except the Nassau troops at Hougomont, and some on our extreme left. They were placed in the second line, and in the valley behind the first line, and on the right, at Braine la Leude. They had generally been formed with the British brigades of the different divisions (in the manner Lord Wellington found so advantageous with the Portuguese troops,) but these arrangements had just been made. The different brigades in a division had not any knowledge of, or confidence in, each other. Many battalions, particularly some Belgian troops, in the rear of the first line, stood with firmness against the French cavalry, and drove them back. They suffered more severely, perhaps, than the first line,

---

[356] Gneisnau says, it was half-past seven o'clock before Pirch's corps arrived.—See Blucher's dispatches.

from the fire of the enemy's artillery, and at the close of the action, advanced in support of the first line with great steadiness and regularity.

The Prussians, who had made only a short march during the day, pursued the enemy with such vigour, that they were unable to rally a single battalion. The British army halted on the field of battle. They once attempted to make a show of resistance at Genappe, where, perhaps, if they had had a chief to direct them, they might have maintained themselves until daylight, the situation of the village being strong; this might have given them the means of saving at least the semblance of an army. The second Prussian corps was afterwards detached to intercept Grouchy, who was not aware of the result of the battle until twelve o'clock next day. He had succeeded in obtaining some advantage over General Thielman, and got possession of Wavre. He immediately retreated towards Namur, where his rear-guard maintained themselves against all the efforts of the Prussians, who suffered severely in their attempt to take the place. This served to cover his retreat, which he executed with great ability, keeping in a parallel line to Blucher, and having rallied many of the fugitives, he brought his army without loss to Paris. He had been considered as lost, and his army made prisoners; this belief was a great cause of the resignation of Buonaparte; otherwise, with this army he could have mustered 70,000 or 80,000 men; with the fortifications and resources of Paris, which was sufficiently secure against a coup-de-main, it is not likely he would have so easily submitted without another struggle, after the brilliant defensive campaign he had made the preceding year. The great central depôts of Paris and Lyons gave him great advantages, as is well shown in the introductory chapter, Liv. ix., p. 181. There are always some turns of fortune in the events of war; he might at least have made terms. The southern and eastern parts of France were certainly in his favour; he and his army had been well received there only a few weeks before. That army, and a great part of the population, would still have been glad to make sacrifices to endeavour to re-establish the sullied lustre of his arms. At least the honour of falling sword in hand was in his power.

The time of the arrival and co-operation of the Prussians has been variously stated.[357] The above account is perhaps as near the truth as can be. The French writers make it at an early hour, to account more satisfactorily for their defeat. The Prussians also make it somewhat earlier than was actually the case, in order to participate more largely in the honours of the day. Their powerful assistance has been acknowledged to its full extent. They completed the destruction of the French army, after they had failed in all their attacks against the British, which continued upwards of seven hours, after their cavalry had been destroyed, their Imperial Guards driven back, and eagles and prisoners taken, and when their means of further attack may be considered as exhausted. The British army had suffered severely, and was not in a state to have taken great advantage of the retreat of the French. But its safety was never for a moment compromised, and no calculation could justify the idea, that we would have been so easily defeated and driven from our position, but that the enemy would have been so much crippled, that he could not have taken much advantage of our reverses. Even in such a case, the arrival of the Prussians must have obliged him to have retired. Muffling has observed, that the bold movement of Blucher on the 18th has not been sufficiently appreciated.[358] It was bold and masterly. Even when he was told that Grouchy was in his rear with a large force, his plans were not shaken, though this might have somewhat retarded his movements. The skilful veteran knew that it was on the field of Waterloo where the fate of the day was to be decided, and if even Grouchy had attacked Bulow's corps, there was nothing to prevent the first and second corps from joining the British army by Ohain. Grouchy could only, at farthest, have checked the third and fourth corps. There cannot be a moment's doubt of the anxiety and exertions of the Prussians to assist on the 18th. The cordiality and friendship of the Prussians have been felt and acknowledged by every officer who has had occasion to visit

---

[357] Liv. ix. says it was eleven o'clock when the Prussians joined. Gourgaud and Montholon copy this. The letter from Soult to Grouchy, dated half-past one o'clock, stating that they were informed by a prisoner of Bulow's march, and that they thought they discovered his advanced posts at that hour, completely contradicts this.—Liv. ix.

[358] Muffling, p. 61. "Il ne s'agit pas de savoir ce qu'un général ordinaire auroit fait; mais une nouvelle de cette nature auroit pu entraîner le général le plus distingué à prendre des précautions, ou la résolution de changer l'offensive vigoureuse en simple démonstration."

Prussia subsequently;—this has been particularly the case with the military.

This short campaign of "Hours" was a joint operation. The honours must be shared. On the 16th, the Prussians fought at Ligny under the promise of our co-operation, which could not, however, be given to the extent it was wished or hoped. On the 18th, Lord Wellington fought at Waterloo, on the promise of the early assistance of the Prussians, which, though unavoidably delayed, was at last given with an effect, which perhaps had never before been witnessed. The finest army France ever saw, commanded by the greatest and ablest of her chiefs, ceased to exist, and in a moment the destiny of Europe was changed.

No. II

BUONAPARTE'S PROTEST

"I hereby solemnly protest, in the face of Heaven and of men, against the violence done me, and against the violation of my most sacred rights, in forcibly disposing of my person and my liberty.

"I came voluntarily on board of the Bellerophon; I am not a prisoner—I am the guest of England. I came on board even at the instigation of the captain, who told me he had orders from the Government to receive me and my suite, and conduct me to England, if agreeable to me. I presented myself with good faith, to put myself under the protection of the English laws. As soon as I was on board the Bellerophon, I was under shelter of the British people. If the Government, in giving orders to the captain of the Bellerophon to receive me as well as my suite, only intended to lay a snare for me, it has forfeited its honour, and disgraced its flag. If this act be consummated, the English will in vain boast to Europe, their integrity, their laws, and their liberty. British good faith will be lost in the hospitality of the Bellerophon. I appeal to history; it will say that an enemy, who for twenty years waged war against the English people, came voluntarily, in his misfortunes, to seek an asylum under their laws. What more brilliant proof could he give of his esteem and his confidence? But what return did England make for so much magnanimity?—They feigned to stretch forth a friendly hand to that enemy; and when he delivered himself up in good faith, they sacrificed him.

(Signed) "Napoleon.

"On board the Bellerophon, 4th August, 1815."

We have already, in the text, completely refuted the pretence, that Buonaparte was ensnared on board the Bellerophon. Every expression of Captain Maitland went to disown any authority to treat with Napoleon, or grant him conditions of any kind; nor could he say more when his private opinion was demanded, than that he had no reason to suppose that Napoleon would be ill received in England. This was in presence of Captain Sartorius and Captain Gambier, both of whom Captain Maitland appealed to in support of his statement. We do not, however, feel it too much, on the present occasion, to copy the letters which passed betwixt Lord Keith, on the one hand, and Captain Maitland, Captain Sartorius, and Captain Gambier, on the other.

"Tonnant, at anchor under Berryhead,
7th August, 1815.

"Sir,—Count Las Cases having this morning stated to me, that he understood from you, when he was on board the Bellerophon in Basque roads, on a mission from General Buonaparte, that you were authorised to receive the General and his suite on board the ship you command, for conveyance to England; and that you assured him, at the same time, that both the General and his suite would be well received there; you are to report, for my information, such observations as you may consider it necessary to make upon these assertions. I am, Sir, &c.

"Keith, Admiral.

"Captain Maitland, Bellerophon."

"H. M. S. Bellerophon,
Plymouth Sound, 8th August, 1815.

"My Lord,—I have to acknowledge the receipt of your lordship's letter of yesterday's date, informing me that Count Las Cases had stated to you, that he had understood from me, when he was on board the Bellerophon in Basque roads, on a mission from General Buonaparte, that I was authorised to receive the General and his suite on board the ship I command, for a conveyance to England; and that I assured him, at the same time, that both the General and his suite would be well received there; and directing me to report, for your lordship's information, such observations as I may consider it necessary to make upon these assertions. I shall, in consequence, state, to the best of my recollection, the whole of the transaction that took place between Count Las Cases and me, on the 14th of July, respecting the embarkation of Napoleon Buonaparte, for the veracity of which I beg to refer your lordship to Captain Sartorius as to what was said in the morning, and to that officer and Captain Gambier (the Myrmidon having joined me in the afternoon) as to what passed in the evening.

"Your lordship being informed already of the flag of truce that came out to me on the 10th of July, as well as of every thing that occurred on that occasion, I shall confine myself to the transactions of the 14th of the same month.

"Early in the morning of that day, the officer of the watch informed me, a schooner, bearing a flag of truce, was approaching. On her joining the ship, about seven A. M., the Count Las Cases and General Lallemand came on board; when, on being shown into the cabin, Las Cases asked me if any answer had been returned to the letter sent by me to Sir Henry Hotham, respecting Napoleon Buonaparte being allowed to pass for America, either in the frigates or in a neutral vessel. I informed him no answer had been returned, though I hourly expected, in consequence of those despatches, Sir Henry Hotham would arrive; and, as I had told Monsieur Las Cases, when last on board, that I should send my boat in when the answer came, it was quite unnecessary to have sent out a flag of truce on that account; there, for the time, the conversation terminated. On their coming on board, I had made the signal for the captain of the Slaney, being desirous of having a witness to all that might pass.

"After breakfast (during which Captain Sartorius came on board) we retired to the after-cabin, when M. Las Cases began on the same subject, and said, 'The Emperor was so anxious to stop the farther effusion of blood, that he would go to America in any way the English Government would sanction, either in a neutral, a disarmed frigate, or an English ship of war.' To which I replied, 'I have no authority to permit any of those measures; but if he chooses to come on board the ship I command, I think, under the orders I am acting with, I may venture to receive him, and carry him to England; but if I do so, I can in no way be answerable for the reception he may meet with'—(this I repeated several times)—when Las Cases said, 'I have little doubt, under those circumstances, that you will see the Emperor on board the Bellerophon.' After some more general conversation, and the above being frequently repeated, M. Las Cases and General Lallemand took their leave; and I assure your lordship, that I never in any way entered into conditions with respect to the reception General Buonaparte was to meet with; nor was it at that time finally arranged that he was to come on board the Bellerophon. In the course of conversation, Las Cases asked me, whether I thought Buonaparte would be well received in England? to which I gave the only answer I could do in my situation—'That I did not at all know what was the intention of the British Government; but I had no reason to suppose he would not be well received.' It is here worthy of remark, that when Las Cases came on board, he assured me that Buonaparte was then at Rochefort, and that it would be necessary for him to go there to report the conversation that had passed between us (this I can prove by the testimony of Captain Sartorius, and the first lieutenant of this ship, to whom I spoke of it at the time,) which statement was not fact; Buonaparte never having quitted isle d'Aix, or the frigates, after the 3d.

"I was therefore much surprised at seeing M. Las Cases on board again before seven o'clock the same evening; and one of the first questions I put to him was, whether he had been at Rochefort? He answered, that, on returning to isle d'Aix, he found that Napoleon had arrived there.

"M. Las Cases then presented to me the letter Count Bertrand wrote concerning Buonaparte's intention to come on board the ship (a copy of which has been transmitted to your lordship by Sir Henry Hotham,) and it was not till then agreed upon that I should receive him; when either M. Las Cases or General Gourgaud (I am not positive which, as I was employed writing my own dispatches) wrote to Bertrand to inform him of it. While paper was preparing to write the letter, I said again to M. Las Cases, 'You will recollect I have no authority for making conditions of any sort.' Nor has M. Las Cases ever started such an idea till the day before yesterday. That it was not the feeling of Buonaparte, or the rest of his people, I will give strong proof, drawn from the conversations they have held with me.

"As I never heard the subject mentioned till two days ago, I shall not detail every conversation that has passed, but confine myself to that period. The night that the squadron anchored at the back of Berryhead, Buonaparte sent for me about ten P.M., and said he was informed by Bertrand that I had received orders to remove him to the Northumberland, and wished to know if that was the case; on being told that it was, he requested that I would write a letter to Bertrand, stating I had such orders, that it might not appear he went of his own accord, but that he had been forced to do so. I told him I could have no objection, and wrote a letter to that effect, which your lordship afterwards sanctioned, and desired me, if he required it, to give him a copy of the order.

"After having arranged that matter, I was going to withdraw, when he requested me to remain, as he had something more to say. He then began complaining of his treatment in being forced to go to St. Helena; among other things he observed, 'They say I made no conditions—certainly I made no conditions; how could a private man (*un particulier*) make conditions with a nation? I wanted nothing from them but hospitality, or (as the ancients would express it) air and water. I threw myself on the generosity of the English nation: I claimed a place *sur leurs foyers*, and my only wish was to purchase a small estate, and end my life in tranquillity.' After more of the same sort of conversation, I left him for the night.

"On the morning he removed from the Bellerophon to the Northumberland, he sent for me again, and said, 'I have sent for you to express my gratitude for your conduct to me, while I have been on board the ship you command. My reception in England has been very different from what I expected; but you throughout have behaved like a man of honour; and I request you will accept my thanks, as well as convey them to the officers and ship's company of the Bellerophon.' Soon afterwards, Montholon came to me from Buonaparte; but, to understand what passed between him and me, I must revert to a conversation that I had with Madame Bertrand on the passage from Rochefort.

"It is not necessary to state how the conversation commenced, as it does not apply to the present transaction; but she informed me that it was Buonaparte's intention to present me with a box containing his picture set with diamonds. I answered, 'I hope not, for I cannot receive it.'—'Then you will offend him very much,' she said.—'If that is the case,' I replied, 'I request you will take measures to prevent its being offered, as it is absolutely impossible I can accept of it; and I wish to spare him the mortification, and myself the pain, of a refusal.' There the matter dropped, and I heard no more of it, till about half an hour before Buonaparte quitted the Bellerophon, when Montholon came to me, and said he was desired by Buonaparte to express the high sense he entertained of my conduct throughout the whole of the transaction;—that it had been his intention to present me with a box containing his portrait, but that he understood I was determined not to accept it. I said, 'Placed as I was, I felt it impossible to receive a present from him, though I was highly flattered at the testimony he had borne to the uprightness of my conduct throughout.' Montholon added, 'One of the greatest causes of chagrin he feels in not being admitted to an interview with the Prince Regent is, that he had determined to ask as a favour, your being promoted to the rank of rear-admiral.' To which I replied, 'That would have been quite impossible, but I do not the less feel the kindness of the intention.' I then said, 'I am hurt that Las Cases should say I held forth any assurances as to the reception Buonaparte was to meet with in England.'—'Oh!' said he, 'Las Cases is disappointed in his expectations; and as he negotiated the affair, he attributes the Emperor's situation to himself: but I can assure you that he (Buonaparte) feels convinced you have acted like a man of honour throughout.'

"As your lordship overheard part of a conversation which took place between Las Cases and me on the quarterdeck of the Bellerophon, I shall not detail it; but on that occasion, I positively denied having promised any thing as to the reception of Buonaparte and his suite; and I believe your lordship was of opinion he could not make out the statement to you. It is extremely unpleasant for me to be under the necessity of entering into a detail of this sort; but the unhandsome representation Las Cases has made to your lordship of my conduct, has obliged me to produce proofs of the light in which the transaction was viewed by Buonaparte as well as his attendants.

"I again repeat that Captains Gambier and Sartorius can verify the principal part of what I have stated, as far as concerns the charge made against me by Count Las Cases.—I have the honour to be your lordship's, &c.

"Frederick L. Maitland.

"To the Right Hon.
Viscount Keith, G.C.B., &c. &c."

*"Slaney, in Plymouth Sound,
15th August, 1815.*

"My Lord,—I have read Captain Maitland's letter to your lordship, of the 8th instant, containing his observations upon the assertions made on the preceding day by Count Las Cases; and I most fully attest the correctness of the statement he has made, so far as relates to the conversations that took place in my presence.—I have the honour to be your lordship's, &c.

"G. R. Sartorius,
Capt. of H. M. S. Slaney.

"To the Right Hon.
Viscount Keith, G.C.B., &c. &c."

It happened that Captain Gambier's attestation to the above statement was not in Captain Maitland's possession; but having obtained a copy of it from the kindness of Mr. Meike, secretary to Lord Keith, we can supply this additional piece of evidence to a proof already so distinct in itself.

"I have read the preceding letter" [that of Captain Maitland,] "and most fully attest the correctness of what Captain Maitland has said, so far as relates to what occurred in my presence on the evening of the 14th of July.

(Signed) "Robert Gambier,
"Captain of H. M. Ship Myrmidon."

No. III

States of Thermometer, as taken at *Deadwood*, island of St. Helena, during twelve calendar months, viz. from 1st Sept. 1820, to 31st Aug. 1821, inclusive.—This condensed view of the different states of the Thermometer was kept at Deadwood, which is just one short mile from Longwood, and therefore expresses the exact temperature of the climate in which he lived—milder, and more equable, certainly, than most in the known world. In point of moisture, Dr. Shortt is not of opinion that St. Helena differs materially from any other tropical island of the same extent. His account of the general state of health among the troops has been already referred to.

Months.		Thermometer.			Remarks	
		Maximum.	Medium.	Minimum.		
Sept.	1820,	66	64	62	Wind blowing from S.E.	
Oct.	do.	68	65	62	Do.	Do.
Nov.	do.	72	66	61	Generally S.E. 6 days from N.W.	
Dec.	do.	72	66	61	Wind from S.E.	
Jan.	1821,	76	70	68	Do.	Do.
Feb.	do.	76	70	67	Do.	Do.
March	do.	76	71	67	Do.	Do.
April	do.	74	70	66	Do.	Do.
May	do.	72	68	64	Do.	Do.
June	do.	70	65	57	Generally S.E. 1 day westerly.	
July	do.	71	66	57	Do.	Do.
Aug.	do.	68	64	62	Wind from S.E.	

(Certified) by Thomas Shortt,
Physician to H.M. Forces, and
Principal Medical Officer at St. Helena.

No. IV

INTERVIEW BETWIXT NAPOLEON BUONAPARTE AND HENRY ELLIS, ESQ., THIRD COMMISSIONER OF LORD AMHERST'S EMBASSY TO CHINA

Although, like others, I was familiar with the details of Buonaparte's present situation, and might, therefore, be supposed to have become saturated with those sentiments of surprise, which such an extraordinary reverse of fortune was calculated to excite—I must confess that I could boast but little self-possession on entering the presence of a man, who had been at once the terror and wonder of the civilized world. The absence of attendants, and the other circumstances of high station, did not seem to me to have affected his individual greatness; however elevated his rank had been, his actions had been still beyond it. Even the mighty weapons which he had wielded were light to his gigantic strength; the splendour of a court, the pomp, discipline, and number of his armies, sufficient to have constituted the personal greatness of an hereditary monarch, scarcely added to the effect produced by the tremendous, but unfortunately ill-directed, energies of his mind. Their absence, therefore, did not diminish the influence of his individuality. I do not know that I ever before felt myself in the presence of a mind differing from mine, not in degree, but in nature; and could have had but little disposition to gratify curiosity by inquiries into the motives which had guided his conduct in the eventful transactions of his life. I came prepared to listen and recollect, not to question or speculate. Lord Amherst having presented me, Napoleon began by saying, that my name was not unknown to him; that he understood I had been at Constantinople, and had a faint recollection of some person of my name having been employed in Russia. I, in reply, said that I had been at Constantinople in my way to Persia. "Yes," says he, "it was I who showed you the way to that country? *Eh bien, comment se porte mon ami le Shah?* What have the Russians been doing lately in that quarter?" On my informing him that the result of the last war had been the cession of all the territory in the military occupation of their troops—he said, "Yes, Russia is the power now most to be dreaded; Alexander may have whatever army he pleases. Unlike the French and English, the subjects of the Russian empire improve their condition by becoming soldiers. If I called on a Frenchman to quit his country, I required him to abandon his happiness. The Russian, on the contrary, is a slave while a peasant, and becomes free and respectable when a soldier. A Frenchman, leaving his country, always changes for the worse, while Germany, France, and Italy, are all superior to the native country of the Russians. Their immense bodies of Cossacks are also formidable; their mode of travelling resembles the Bedouins of the desert. They advance with confidence into the most unknown regions." He then related the following instance of the extraordinary powers of vision possessed by the Arabs. When in Egypt, he took up his glass to examine an Arab, who was still at some distance. Before Buonaparte had, with the assistance of the instrument, ascertained his appearance, a Bedouin standing near him, had so completely made him out, as to distinguish the dress of the tribe to which he belonged.

"Russia," continued he, "has still her designs upon Constantinople. To obtain my consent to his projects upon Turkey, was the great wish of the Emperor Alexander, but in vain; I told him I would never allow the Greek cross to be added to the crown of the Czars. Austria would unite with Russia against Turkey, on condition of being allowed to retain the provinces contiguous to her frontier. France and England are the only powers interested in opposing their schemes; I always felt this, and always supported the Turks, although I hated them as barbarians. If Russia," he added, "organises Poland, she will be irresistible." Napoleon here took a rapid view of the military character of the nations of Europe, and, without reference to what he had just said respecting the Russians, declared the French and English were the only troops deserving notice for their discipline and moral qualities. "The Austrian and Prussian," he said, "were much inferior: in fact, real strength and efficiency were confined to the English and French." The remainder of his harangue (for his habit of not waiting for, or indeed listening to replies, renders conversation an inapplicable term) was employed upon the present state of England, which he considered was most calamitous, and as produced by the impolicy of mixing with continental affairs. The dominion of the seas, and the maintenance of a monopoly of commerce, he considered as the only true foundation of our national prosperity. "Whatever might be the bravery of our troops, their limited number would for ever prevent us from becoming a great military power. *Vous avez toujours vôtre bravoure des siècles, mais avec quarante cinq mille, vous ne serez jamais, puissance militaire.* In sacrificing maritime affairs, we were acting like Francis I. at the battle of Pavia, whose general had made an excellent disposition of his army, and had placed forty-five pieces of cannon (an unheard of battery at that time) in a situation that must have secured the victory: Francis, however, his grand sabre à la main, placed himself at the head of his gendarmerie and household troops, between the battery and the enemy, and thereby lost the advantage his superiority of artillery gave him; thus," said he, "seduced by a temporary success, you are masking the only battery you possess, your naval pre-eminence. While that remains, you may blockade all Europe. I well know the effect of blockade. With two small wooden machines, you distress a line of coast, and place a country in the situation of a body rubbed over with oil, and thus deprived of the natural perspiration. I," says he, "am now suffering in my face from this obstruction to perspiration, and blockade has the same effect upon a nation. What have you gained by the war? You have gained possession of my person, and had an opportunity of exhibiting an example of ungenerousness. By placing the Bourbons on the throne, you have disturbed the legitimacy of kings, for I am the natural sovereign of France. You conceived that none but Napoleon could shut the ports of Europe against you, but now every petty sovereign insults you with prohibitory regulations upon your commerce.—*L'Angleterre est déchue depuis qu'elle s'est mêlée des affaires du continent.*—You should have been aware of the advance I had made towards the improvement of manufacture throughout my empire, and secured the repayment of your expenses during the war, by a forced extension of your trade. Who placed the King of Portugal on his throne? Was it not England? Had you not, therefore, a right to be reimbursed? and that reimbursement might have been found in the exclusive trade to the Brazils for five years. This demand was reasonable, and could not, therefore, have been refused." I observed, that such a proceeding would not have been consonant with our political system, and that the King of Portugal, aware of this, would have resisted, the more especially as, when placed on the throne, he no longer wanted our assistance. "The demand should have been made in the first instance," said he, "when you might have asked anything; but it is now too late; and you have only to blame your ministers, who have totally neglected the interests of England. Russia, Austria, Prussia, have all been gainers; England alone has been a loser. You have even neglected that poor kingdom of Hanover. Why not have added three or four millions to its population? Lord Castlereagh got among the monarchs, became a courtier, and thought more of their aggrandisement, than of the claims of his country. Your good fortunes, *et mes fautes, mes imprudences*, have brought about a state of things which even Pitt never dared to dream of; and what is the result? your people are starving, and your country is convulsed with riots. The situation of England is most curious. She has gained all, and yet she is ruined. Believe the opinion of a man accustomed to consider political subjects; England should look wholly to commerce, and naval affairs; she never can be a continental power, and in the attempt must be ruined. Maintain the empire of the seas, and you may send your ambassadors to the courts of Europe, and ask what you please. The sovereigns are aware of your present distressed situation, and insult you." He repeated, "Forty-five thousand men will never make you a military power; it is not in the genius of your nation. None but the very dregs of the nation enlist in your army; the profession is not liked." He would not listen to an observation respecting the great channel of supply from the militia to the line, which he seemed to confound with the volunteers.

Napoleon continued his observations by saying, "The suspension of the habeas corpus would not prove a remedy for the riots; people must have food; the stagnation of commerce diminishes your exports, and your manufacturers are starving. It is absurd to describe the evils as temporary. Wellesley is right in that, the distress is general, and must be lasting. Stopping the evils by suspending the habeas corpus, is applying topical remedies when the disease is in the system; topical remedies will only remove topical eruption; the complaint extends over the whole body.—There is not a man of ability in the cabinet. Lord Chatham understood the true interests of England, when he said, 'If we are just for twenty-four hours, we must be ruined.' Immense extension of commerce, combined with reductions and reforms, could alone have prevented the present crisis in England. For his part, he wished that all was tranquil and settled, as that was his only chance of being released. A large army," he remarked, "was moreover inconsistent with our free constitution, to which we were, with reason, so much attached." I remarked, that the superior importance to England of maritime concerns was fully acknowledged by our ministers, and that they would heartily rejoice in being enabled to withdraw the British contingent in France (to which he seemed to have alluded); that the actual distress in England arose from the system of public credit, by which the war had been supported, and the consequences of which were in their nature lasting; that these consequences had been anticipated, and were not, it was to be hoped, irremediable. "Yes," said Napoleon, "your resources are great; but your ruin, from persisting in your present policy, is certain. Your ministers have affected generosity, and have ruined the country. In this generosity you have departed from the system of your ancestors, who never concluded a peace without gaining, or attempting to gain, some advantage; they were steady merchants, who filled their purses; but you have set up for gentlemen, and are ruined. Although the peace, on the termination of the American war, was honourable to France, for she compelled England to acknowledge the independence of America, the treaty in 1783 was fatal to French commerce; and how do you suppose that came to be concluded? The French ministers were fully aware of its injurious consequences, but England threatened war, and they had no money to defray the expenses." I understood Buonaparte to say, that this account was supported by memoirs in the Bureau des Affaires Etrangères.

During the conversation, which, notwithstanding the variety of topics started, if not discussed, did not occupy more than half an hour, there were frequent repetitions of particular expressions, such as "*L'Angleterre est déchue; avec 45,000 hommes vous ne serez jamais puissance continentale.*" Buonaparte never listened to any reply naturally arising from his observations, but continued his own view of the subject he was discussing; he seemed little studious in arrangement, but poured out his ideas with a rapidity of language almost equal to the rapidity of their succession in the mind. His style upon political subjects is so epigrammatic and tranchant, that in a man whose actions had not been correspondent, it would look like charlatanerie. Buonaparte must be allowed to be eloquent, and possesses that species of oratory well adapted for a popular assembly, or for influencing persons already prepared to look up to him. Upon the former, his point would produce impression; and a sort of oracular confidence, in which he abounds, would command the conviction of the latter. His manner, on the whole, was pleasing, and had a mixture of simplicity and conscious superiority which I never before witnessed. The expression of his countenance is more intellectual than commanding; and his person, so far from being overgrown with corpulency, seems fully equal to the endurance of the greatest exertion. I should say that he was as fit as ever to go through a campaign, and that, considering his age, he was not unusually corpulent. I have omitted to mention an illustration made use of by Buonaparte, in speaking of the conduct of the English ministers at the Congress. "You were," said he, "like the dog in the fable, who dropt the piece of meat in the water, while looking at his own image. You had the commerce of the world, and you took no precautions to retain it. Nothing but a great extension of commerce could have enabled you to bear your immense taxes, and you made no effort to obtain it." Buonaparte miscalls English names and words more than any foreigner I ever before heard, who had pretensions to a knowledge of the language; and notwithstanding his reading, and the attention he has probably paid to the subject, he seems little acquainted with the nature of our domestic policy. His plans, like his practice, are all despotic, and are formed without adverting to constitutional restrictions.

In his conversation with Lord Amherst, he dwelt much upon his present situation, and expressed himself with great and unjustifiable bitterness respecting Sir H. Lowe. Lord Bathurst's speech had evidently annoyed him, and he expressed disappointment at the countenance such language and treatment received from Lords Sidmouth and Liverpool, with whom he affected to consider himself as having been formerly on terms of amicable intercourse. He said such a man as Lord Cornwallis ought to have been placed in Sir H. Lowe's situation. It is difficult to conceive any complaints more unreasonable than those made by

Buonaparte of Sir H. Lowe's conduct. There perhaps never was a prisoner so much requiring to be watched and guarded, to whom so much liberty and range for exercise was allowed. With an officer he may go over any part of the island; wholly unobserved, his limits extend four miles—partially observed, eight—and overlooked, twelve. At night, the sentinels certainly close round Longwood itself. The house is small, but well furnished; and altogether as commodious as the circumstances under which it was procured would admit. I can only account for his petulance and unfounded complaints, from one of two motives—either he wishes by their means to keep alive interest in Europe, and more especially in England, where he flatters himself he has a party; or his troubled mind finds an occupation in the tracasseries which his present conduct gives to the governor. If the latter be the case, it is in vain for any governor to unite being on good terms with him to the performance of his duty. Buonaparte, in concluding the observations which he thought proper to address to me, made a motion with his hand to Lord Amherst for the introduction of Captain Maxwell and the gentlemen of the embassy. They entered, accompanied by Generals Bertrand, Montholon, and Gourgaud. A circle under the direction of the grand marshal was formed, and Lord Amherst having presented Captain Maxwell, Buonaparte said, "I have heard of you before—you took one of my frigates, the Pauline; *vous êtes un méchant*; well, your government can say nothing about your losing the ship, for you have taken one for them before." He observed of Lord Amherst's son, that he must resemble his mother, and good-humouredly asked him what he had brought from China, whether a bonnet or a mandarin? He inquired of Mr. M'Leod, the surgeon of the Alceste, how long he had served, and if he had been wounded? repeating the question in English. On Mr. Abel being introduced as naturalist, he inquired if he knew Sir Joseph Banks, saying that his name had always been a passport, and that, even during the war, his requests had always been attended to. He wished to know if Mr. Abel was a member of the Royal Society, or was a candidate for that honour. Buonaparte appeared to be under some erroneous impression respecting a son of Sir J. Banks having gone on an expedition to the coast of Africa. Mr. Cook's name led him naturally to inquire whether he was a descendant of the celebrated Cook, the navigator, adding, "he was indeed a great man." Dr. Lynn having been presented as a physician, was asked at what university he had studied? "At Edinburgh," being the reply.—"Ah! you are a Brunonian in practice; and do you bleed and give as much mercury as our St. Helena doctors?" To Mr. Griffiths, the chaplain, (whom he called *Aumonier,*) he put some questions respecting the state of religion in China; he was answered, a kind of Polytheism. Not seeming to understand this word spoken in English, Bertrand explained, *Pluralité de Dieux*. "Ah, *Pluralité de Dieux!* Do they believe," he resumed, "in the immortality of the soul?"—"They seem to have some idea of a future state," was the reply. He then asked to what university he belonged? and jokingly said to Lord Amherst, "you must get him a good living when you go home;" adding, "I wish you may be a prebendary." He then inquired of Mr. Hayne, how and where he had been educated? On being told that he had been educated at home by his father, he immediately turned away; and having now said something to each, he dismissed us.

No. V

MEMORANDUM OF THE ESTABLISHMENT AT LONGWOOD

General Buonaparte,	1
Followers.	
General and Madame Bertrand,	2
Children of ditto,	3
General and Madame Montholon,	2
Children of ditto,	2
General Gourgaud,	1
Count Las Cases,	1
Monsieur Las Cases, his son,	1
Captain Prowtowski,	1
Foreign Servants to General Buonaparte,	12
Marchand,	
Santini,	
Lepage,	
Aby,	
Cipriani,	
Rosseau,	
Noverraz,	
Pierron,	
Archambaud, 1,	
Archambaud, 2,	
Gentilini,	
1 female cook,	
Bernard, wife, and son, foreign servants to General Bertrand,	3
1 French female servant to General Montholon,	1

English Attendants.

1 English gardener,	1
English soldiers (servants,)	12
1 boy, a soldier's son,	1
1 English maid-servant to General Bertrand,	1
2 English female servants to General Montholon,	2
Black servants,	3

British Officers attached to the Establishment.

Captain Poppleton, captain of the guard,	1
Dr. O'Meara, surgeon,	1
Servants,	3
Total,	55

29th August, 1816.

Of these persons, General Gourgaud, Madame Montholon and her children, Count Las Cases and his son, Prowtowski and Santini, returned to Europe at different periods.

Cipriani, the maître d'hôtel, died on the island.

The Abbé Bonavita, surgeon Antommarchi, the priest, Vignali, and two cooks, were sent out to St. Helena in 1819.

The abbé returned to Europe in 1821, having left St. Helena in the month of March of that year.

Something happened to three of the servants, Pierron, Aby, and Archambaud, which cannot be now precisely ascertained. It is thought, however, that Pierron was sent away in consequence of some quarrel about a female servant; Aby (probably) died, and one of the Archambauds went to America.

General Bertrand's family in France, and the relations of his wife in England (the Jerninghams,) were employed to send them out several servants, whose names cannot be ascertained.

EXTRAIT DU JOURNAL MANUSCRIT DE M. DE LAS CASES

Dec. 1815.—Depuis nôtre départ de Plomouth, depuis nôtre débarquement dans l'île, jusqu'à nôtre translation à Longwood, la maison de l'Empereur, bien que composée de onze personnes, avait cessée d'exister.

Personnes composant le Service de l'Empereur:—

Marchand		Prem. valet de chambre.
St. Denis	Chambre	Valet de chambre.
Noverraz		Id.
Santini		Huissier.
Cipriani		Maître d'hôtel.
Pierron	Bouche	Officier.
Lepage		Cusinier.
Rosseau		Argentier.
Archambault, ainé		Piqueur.
Archambault, cadet	Livrée	Id.
Gentilini		Valet de pied.

Dès que nous fumes tous réunis à Longwood, l'Empereur voulut régulariser tout ce qui étoit autour de lui, et chercha à employer chacun de nous suivant la pente de son esprit, conservant au grand maréchal le commandement et la surveillance de tout en grand. Il confia à M. de Montholon tous les détails domestiques. Il donna à Monsieur Gourgaud la direction de l'écurie, et me reserva le détail des meubles, avec la régularisation des objets qui nous seroient fournis. Cette dernière partie me sembloit tellement en contraste avec les détails domestiques, et je trouvois que l'unité sur ce point devoit être si avantageux au bien commun, que je me prêtai le plus que je pus à m'en faire dépouiller; ce qui ne fut pas difficile.

No. VI

INTERVIEW BETWEEN BUONAPARTE AND THE WIDOW OF THEOBALD WOLFE TONE

In vindication of what we have said in the text respecting the ready access afforded by Napoleon, when Emperor, we may refer to the following interesting extract from the Memoirs of Theobald Wolfe Tone, already quoted. It is the account given by his widow of an interview with the Emperor; and it is only necessary to add, by way of introduction, that Mrs. Tone, having received a pension from the French government after her husband's catastrophe, became desirous, in addition, to have her son admitted into the military school at St. Cyr. Being discountenanced in her pretensions by the minister-at-war, she was advised to present her memorial to the Emperor himself. The following is a very pleasing account of the scene that took place betwixt them, in which we give Napoleon full credit for acting from his feelings of generosity towards the widow and orphan of a man who had died in his service:—

"Very soon the carriage with the Emperor and Empress drove into the circle; the horses were changed as quick as thought, but I stept up and presented the book and memorial. He took them, and handing the book to his *écuyer*, opened the paper. I have said it commenced by recalling Tone to his memory. When he began, he said 'Tone!' with an expressive accent—'I remember well,' (*Je m'en souviens bien.*) He read it all through, and two or three times stopped, looked at me, and bowed in reading it. When he had finished, he said to me, 'Now, speak to me of yourself,' (*Maintenant, parlez moi de vous.*) I hesitated, for I was not prepared for that question, and took small interest in the subject. He proceeded. 'Have you a pension?' I said I had. 'Is it sufficient? Do you want any extraordinary succour?' By this time I had recovered myself, and said, 'That his Majesty's goodness left me no personal want; that all my cares, all my interest in life, were centered in my child, whom I now gave up to his Majesty's service.' He answered, 'Be tranquil then on his account—

be perfectly tranquil concerning him,' (*Soyez donc tranquille sur son compte—soyez parfaitement tranquille sur lui.*) I perceived a little half smile when I said 'my child' (*mon énfant.*) I should have said 'my son.' I knew it, but forgot.—He had stopped so long, that a crowd had gathered, and were crushing on, crying *Vive l'Empereur!* They drove in the guard, and there came a horse very close to me. I was frightened, and retiring; but he called to stay where I was—'*Restez, restez là.*' Whether it was for my safety, or that he wanted to say more, I cannot tell; but more it was impossible to say, for the noise. I was close to the carriage door, and the guards on horseback close behind me, and indeed I was trembling. He saluted the people, and directed that two Napoleons a-piece should be given to the old women, and women with little children, who were holding out their hands. He then drove on, and, in going, nodded to me two or three times with affectionate familiarity, saying, 'Your *child* shall be well naturalized,' (*Vôtre enfant sera bien naturalisé,*) with a playful emphasis on the words *vôtre enfant.*"

The youth was admitted to the cavalry school of St. Cyr, and the following is an account of Napoleon visiting that seminary:—

"The Emperor frequently visited the school of infantry at St. Cyr, reviewed the cadets, and gave them cold collations in the park. But he had never visited the school of cavalry since its establishment, of which we were very jealous, and did all in our power to attract him. Whenever he hunted, the cadets were in grand parade on the parterre, crying, '*Vive l'Empereur,*' with all their young energies; he held his hat raised as he passed them; but that was all we could gain. Wise people whispered that he never would go whilst they were so evidently expecting him; that he liked to keep them always on the alert; it was good for discipline. The general took another plan, and once allowed no sign of life about the castle when the Emperor passed—it was like a deserted place. But it did not take neither; he passed, as if there was no castle there. It was *désesperant.* When, lo! the next day but one after I had spoken to him, he suddenly gallopped into the court of the castle, and the cry of the sentinel, '*L'Empereur!*' was the first notice they had of it. He examined into every thing. All were in undress, all at work, and this was what he wanted. In the military schools, the cadets got ammunition-bread, and lived like well fed soldiers; but there was great outcry in the circles of Paris against the bread of the school of St. Germains. Ladies complained that their sons were poisoned by it; the Emperor thought it was all nicety, and said no man was fit to be an officer who could not eat ammunition-bread. However, being there, he asked for a loaf, which was brought, and he saw it was villanous trash, composed of pease, beans, rye, potatoes, and every thing that would make flour or meal, instead of good brown wheaten flour. He tore the loaf in two in a rage, and dashed it against the wall, and there it stuck like a piece of mortar, to the great annoyance of those whose duty it was to have attended to this. He ordered the baker to be called, and made him look at it *sticking*. The man was in great terror first at the Emperor's anger; but, taking heart, he begged his Majesty not to take his contract from him, and he would give good bread in future; at which the Emperor broke into a royal and imperial passion, and threatened to send him to the galleys; but, suddenly turning round, he said, 'Yes, he would allow him to keep his contract, on condition that, as long as it lasted, he should furnish the school with good white household bread, (*pain de ménage,*) such as was sold in the baker's shops in Paris;—that he might choose that, or lose his contract;' and the baker thankfully promised to furnish good white bread in future, at the same price."

No. VII

BUONAPARTE'S LAST WILL AND TESTAMENT

Napoleon,

This 15th April, 1821, at Longwood, Island of St. Helena. This is my Testament, or Act of my last Will.

I.

1. I die in the apostolical Roman religion, in the bosom of which I was born, more than fifty years since. 2. It is my wish that my ashes may repose on the banks of the Seine, in the midst of the French people, whom I have loved so well. 3. I have always had reason to be pleased with my dearest wife, Marie Louise. I retain for her, to my last moment, the most tender sentiments—I beseech her to watch, in order to preserve my son from the snares which yet environ his infancy. 4. I recommend to my son never to forget that he was born a French prince, and never to allow himself to become an instrument in the hands of the triumvirs who oppress the nations of Europe; he ought never to fight against France, or to injure her in any manner; he ought to adopt my motto—"*Every thing for the French people.*" 5. I die prematurely, assassinated by the English oligarchy and its * * *. The English nation will not be slow in avenging me. 6. The two unfortunate results of the invasions of France, when she had still so many resources, are to be attributed to the treason of Marmont, Augereau, Talleyrand, and La Fayette. I forgive them—may the posterity of France forgive them like me! 7. I thank my good and most excellent mother—the Cardinal—my brothers Joseph, Lucien, Jerome—Pauline, Caroline, Julie, Hortense, Catarine, Eugène, for the interest which they have continued to feel for me. I pardon Louis for the libel which he published in 1820: It is replete with false assertions and falsified documents. 8. I disavow the "Manuscript of St. Helena," and other works, under the title of Maxims, Sayings, &c., which persons have been pleased to publish

for the last six years. These are not the rules which have guided my life. I caused the Duc d'Enghien to be arrested and tried, because that step was essential to the safety, interest, and honour of the French people, when the Count d'Artois was maintaining, by his confession, sixty assassins at Paris. Under similar circumstances, I would act in the same way.

II.

1. I bequeath to my son, the boxes, orders, and other articles; such as my plate, field-bed, saddles, spurs, chapel plate, books, linen, which I have been accustomed to wear and use, according to the list annexed (A.) It is my wish that this slight bequest may be dear to him, as recalling the memory of a father, of whom the universe will discourse to him. 2. I bequeath to Lady Holland the antique cameo which Pope Pius VI. gave me at Tolentino. 3. I bequeath to Count Montholon two millions of francs, as a proof of my satisfaction with the filial attentions which he has paid to me during six years, and as an indemnity for the losses which his residence at St. Helena has occasioned. 4. I bequeath to Count Bertrand five hundred thousand francs. 5. I bequeath to Marchand, my first valet-de-chambre, four hundred thousand francs. The services which he has rendered to me are those of a friend; it is my wish that he should marry the widow, sister, or daughter of an officer of my old guard. 6. Item, To St. Denis, one hundred thousand francs. 7. Item, To Novarre, one hundred thousand francs. 8. Item, To Pieron, one hundred thousand francs. 9. Item, To Archambaud, fifty thousand francs. 10. Item, To Cursor, twenty-five thousand francs. 11. Item, to Chandellier, item. 12. Item, to the Abbé Vignali, one hundred thousand francs. It is my wish that he should build his house near the Ponte nuovo di Costino. 13. Item, To Count Las Cases, one hundred thousand francs. 14. Item, To Count Lavalette, one hundred thousand francs. 15. Item, To Larrey, surgeon-in-chief, one hundred thousand francs.—He is the most virtuous man I have known. 16. Item, To General Brayher, one hundred thousand francs. 17. Item, To General Le Fevre Deshouettes, one hundred thousand francs. 18. Item, To General Drouot, one hundred thousand francs. 19. Item, To General Cambrone, one hundred thousand francs. 20. Item, To

the children of General Mouton Duvernet, one hundred thousand francs. 21. Item, To the children of the brave Labédoyère, one hundred thousand francs. 22. Item, To the children of General Girard, killed at Ligny, one hundred thousand francs. 23. Item, To the children of General Marchand, one hundred thousand francs. 24. Item, To the children of the virtuous General Travost, one hundred thousand francs. 25. Item, To General Lallemand the elder, one hundred thousand francs. 26. Item, To Count Real, one hundred thousand francs. 27. Item, To Costa de Basilica, in Corsica, one hundred thousand francs. 28. Item, To General Clausel, one hundred thousand francs. 29. Item, To Baron de Menevalle, one hundred thousand francs. 30. Item, To Arnault, the author of Marius, one hundred thousand francs. 31. Item, To Colonel Marbot, one hundred thousand francs.—I engage him to continue to write in defence of the glory of the French armies, and to confound their calumniators and apostates. 32. Item, To Baron Bignon, one hundred thousand francs.—I engage him to write the history of French diplomacy, from 1792 to 1815. 33. Item, To Poggi di Talavo, one hundred thousand francs. 34. Item, To surgeon Emmery, one hundred thousand francs. 35. These sums will be raised from the six millions which I deposited on leaving Paris in 1815; and from the interest, at the rate of five per cent., since July 1815. The account will be settled with the banker by Counts Montholon, Bertrand, and Marchand. 36. Whatever that deposit may produce beyond the sum of five million six hundred thousand francs, which have been above disposed of, shall be distributed as a gratuity amongst the wounded at the battle of Waterloo, and amongst the officers and soldiers of the battalion of the Isle of Elba, according to a scale to be determined upon by Montholon, Bertrand, Drouot, Cambrone, and the surgeon Larrey. 37. These legacies, in case of death, shall be paid to the widows and children, and in default of such, shall revert to the bulk of my property.

III.

1. My private domain being my property, of which no French law deprives me, that I am aware of, an account of it will be required from the Baron de la Bouillerie, the treasurer thereof; it ought to

amount to more than 200,000,000 of francs; namely, 1. The portfolio containing the savings which I made during fourteen years out of my civil list, which amounted to more than 12,000,000 per annum, if my memory be good. 2. The produce of this portfolio. 3. The furniture of my palaces, such as it was in 1814, including the palaces of Rome, Florence, and Turin. All this furniture was purchased with moneys accruing from the civil list. 4. The proceeds of my houses in the kingdom of Italy, such as money, plate, jewels, furniture, equipages; the accounts will be rendered by Prince Eugene, and the steward of the crown, Campagnoni.

Napoleon

2. I bequeath my private domain, one half to the surviving officers and soldiers of the French army who have fought since 1792 to 1815, for the glory and the independence of the nation. The distribution shall be made in proportion to their appointments upon active service. One half to the towns and districts of Alsace, of Lorraine, of Franche Compté, of Burgundy, of the isle of France, of Champagne Forest, Dauphiné, which may have suffered by either of the invasions. There shall be previously deducted from this sum, one million for the town of Brienne, and one million for that of Meri. I appoint Counts Montholon, Bertrand, and Marchand, the executors of my will.

This present will, wholly written with my own hand, is signed, and sealed with my own arms.

(L. S.)

Napoleon.

List (A.)

Affixed to my Will.

Longwood, Island of St. Helena, this 15th April 1821.

I.

1. The consecrated vessels which have been in use at my chapel at Longwood. 2. I enjoin the Abbé Vignali to preserve them, and to deliver them to my son, when he shall reach the age of sixteen years.

II.

1. My arms, that is to say, my sword, that which I wore at Austerlitz, the sabre of Sobieski, my dagger, my broad sword, my hanger, my two pair of Versailles pistols. 2. My gold travelling box, that of which I made use on the morning of Ulm and of Austerlitz, of Jena, of Eylau, of Friedland, of the island of Lobau, of Moscow, of Monmirail. In this point of view, it is my wish that it may be precious in the eyes of my son. (It has been deposited with Count Bertrand since 1814.) 3. I charge Count Bertrand with the care of preserving these objects, and of conveying them to my son, when he shall attain the age of sixteen years.

III.

1. Three small mahogany boxes, containing, the first, thirty-three snuff-boxes, or comfit-boxes; the second, twelve boxes, with the Imperial arms, two small eye-glasses, and four boxes found on the table of Louis XVIII., in the Tuileries, on the 20th of March, 1815; the third, three snuff-boxes, ornamented with silver medals, according to the custom of the Emperor; and sundry articles for the use of the toilet, according to the lists numbered I., II., III. 2. My field-beds, which I used in all my campaigns. 3. My field telescope. 4. My dressing-box, one of each of my uniforms, a dozen of shirts, and a complete set of each of my dresses, and generally of every thing used in my toilet. 5. My wash-hand stand. 6. A small clock which is in my chamber at Longwood. 7. My two watches, and the chain of the Empress's hair. 8. I charge Marchand, my principal valet-de-chambre, to take care of these articles, and to convey them to my son, when he shall attain the age of sixteen years.

IV.

1. My cabinet of medals. 2. My plate, and my Sevres china, which I used at St. Helena. (List B and C.) 3. I charge Count Montholon to take care of these articles, and to convey them to my son, when he shall attain the age of sixteen years.

V.

1. My three saddles and bridles, my spurs, which I used at St. Helena. 2. My fowling-pieces, to the number of five. 3. I charge my huntsman, Novarre, to take care of these articles, and to convey them to my son, when he shall attain the age of sixteen years.

VI.

1. Four hundred volumes, selected from those in my library, which I have been accustomed to use the most. 2. I charge St. Denis to take care of them, and to convey them to my son, when he shall attain the age of sixteen years.

List (A.)

1. None of the articles which have been used by me shall be sold: the residue shall be divided amongst the executors of my will and my brothers. 2. Marchand shall preserve my hair, and cause a bracelet to be made of it, with a gold clasp, to be sent to the Empress Marie Louise, to my mother, and to each of my brothers, sisters, nephews, nieces, the cardinal, and one of larger size for my son. 3. Marchand will send one pair of my gold shoe-buckles to Prince Joseph. 4. A small pair of gold knee-buckles to Prince Lucien. 5. A gold collar-clasp to Prince Jerome.

List (A.)

Inventory of my Effects, which Marchand will take care of, and convey to my Son.

1. My silver dressing-box, that which is on my table, furnished with all its utensils, razors, &c. 2. My alarm-clock: it is the alarm-clock of Frederick II. which I took at Potsdam (in box No. III.) 3.

My two watches, with the chain of the Empress's hair, and a chain of my own hair for the other watch: Marchand will get it made at Paris. 4. My two seals (one French,) contained in box No. III. 5. The small gold clock which is now in my bed-chamber. 6. My washstand, its water-jug and foot-bath, &c. 7. My night-table, that which I used in France, and my silver-gilt bidet. 8. My two iron bedsteads, my mattresses, and my coverlets if they can be preserved. 9. My three silver decanters, which held my eau de vie, which my chasseurs carried in the field. 10. My French telescope. 11. My spurs, two pair. 12. Three mahogany boxes, No. I., II., III., containing my snuff-boxes, and other articles. 13. A silver-gilt perfuming-pan.

Body Linen.

6 shirts, 6 handkerchiefs, 6 cravats, 6 napkins, 6 pair of silk stockings, 6 black stocks, 6 pair of under stockings, 2 pair of cambric sheets, 2 pillow cases, 2 dressing gowns, 2 pair of night drawers, 1 pair of braces, 4 pair of white kerseymere breeches and vests, 6 madras, 6 flannel waistcoats, 6 pair of drawers, 6 pair of gaiters, 1 small box filled with my snuff, [1 gold neck-buckle, 1 pair gold knee-buckles, 1 pair gold shoe-buckles, contained in the little box, No. III.]

Clothes.

1 Uniform of the chasseurs, 1 ditto grenadiers, 1 ditto national guards, 2 hats, 1 green-and-grey great coat, 1 blue cloak (that which I had at Marengo,) 1 sable green pelisse, 2 pair of shoes, 2 pair of boots, 2 pair of slippers, 6 belts.

Napoleon.

List (B.)

Inventory of the Effects which I left in possession of Monsieur the Count de Turenne.

1. Sabre of Sobieski. It is by mistake inserted in List A. It is the sabre which the Emperor wore at Aboukir, which is in the hands

of the Count Bertrand. 1 grand collar of the legion of honour, 1 sword, of silver gilt, 1 consular sword, 1 sword, of steel, 1 velvet belt, 1 collar of the golden fleece, 1 small travelling box of steel, 1 ditto of silver, 1 handle of an antique sabre, 1 hat of Henry IV., and a cap, the lace of the Emperor, 1 small cabinet of medals, 2 turkey carpets, 2 mantles, of crimson velvet, embroidered, with vests and small-clothes.

I give to my son	the sabre of Sobieski.
Do.	the collar of the legion of honour.
Do.	the sword, silver gilt.
Do.	the consular sword.
Do.	the steel sword.
Do.	the collar of the golden fleece.
Do.	the hat of Henry IV. and the cap.
Do.	the golden dressing-box for the teeth, which is in the hands of the dentist.

To the Empress Marie Louise, my lace.

To Madame, the silver night-lamp.

To the Cardinal, the small steel travelling-box.

To Prince Eugene, the wax candlestick, silver gilt.

To the Princess Pauline, the small travelling-box.

To the Queen of Naples, a small Turkey carpet.

To the Queen Hortense, a small Turkey carpet.

To Prince Jerome, the handle of the antique sabre.

To Prince Joseph, an embroidered mantle, vest, and small-clothes.

To Prince Lucien, an embroidered mantle, vest, and small-clothes.

April 16th, 1821. Longwood.

This is a Codicil to my Will.

1. It is my wish that my ashes may repose on the banks of the Seine, in the midst of the French people, whom I loved so well. 2. I bequeath to Counts Bertrand, Montholon, and to Marchand, the money, jewels, plate, china, furniture, books, arms, and generally

every thing that belongs to me in the island of St. Helena. This codicil, entirely written with my own hand, is signed, and sealed with my own arms.

(L. S.)

Napoleon.

This 24th April, 1821. Longwood.

This is my Codicil or Note of my last Will.

Out of the settlement of my civil list of Italy, such as money, jewels, plate, linen, equipages, of which the Viceroy is the depositary, and which belonged to me, I dispose of two millions, which I bequeath to my most faithful servants. I hope that, without acting upon the credit of any account, my son, Eugene Napoleon, will pay them faithfully. He cannot forget the forty millions which I gave him in Italy, and in the distribution of the inheritance of his mother.

1. Out of these two millions, I bequeath to Count Bertrand, 300,000 francs, of which he will deposit 100,000 in the treasurer's chest, to be disposed of according to my dispositions, in payment of legacies of conscience. 2. To Count Montholon, 200,000 francs, of which he will deposit 100,000 in the chest, for the same purpose as above mentioned. 3. To Count Las Cases, 200,000, of which he will deposit 100,000 in the chest, for the same purpose as above mentioned. 4. To Marchand, 100,000, of which he will deposit 50,000 in the chest, for the same purpose as above mentioned. 5. To Count Lavalette, 100,000. 6. To General Hogendorf, of Holland, my aide-de-camp, who has retired to the Brazils, 100,000. 7. To my aide-de-camp, Corbineau, 50,000. 8. To my aide-de-camp, General Caffarelli, 50,000 francs. 9. To my aide-de-camp, Dejean, 50,000. 10. To Percy, surgeon-in-chief at Waterloo, 50,000. 11. 50,000, that is to say, 10,000 to Pieron, my maître d'hôtel; 10,000 to St. Denis, my head chasseur; 10,000 to Novarre; 10,000 to Cursor, my clerk of the kitchen; 10,000 to Archambaud, my overseer. 12. To Baron Mainevalle, 50,000. 13. To the Duke d'Istria, son of Bessières,

50,000 francs. 14. To the daughter of Duroc, 50,000 francs. 15. To the children of Labédoyère, 50,000. 16. To the children of Mouton Duvernet, 50,000. 17. To the children of the brave and virtuous General Travost, 50,000. 18. To the children of Chartrand, 50,000. 19. To General Cambrone, 50,000. 20. To General Lefevre Desnouettes, 50,000. 21. To be distributed amongst such proscribed persons as wander in foreign countries, whether they may be French, or Italian, or Belgians, or Dutch, or Spanish, or inhabitants of the departments of the Rhine, at the disposal of my executors, 100,000. 22. To be distributed amongst those who suffered amputation, or were severely wounded at Ligny, or Waterloo, who may be still living, according to lists drawn up by my executors, to whom shall be added, Cambrone, Larrey, Percy, and Emmery. The guard shall be paid double; those of the island of Elba, quadruple; 200,000 francs.

This codicil is written entirely with my own hand, signed, and sealed with my arms.

Napoleon.

This 24th of April, 1821, at Longwood.

This is a third Codicil to my Will of the 16th of April.

1. Amongst the diamonds of the crown which were delivered up in 1814, there were some to the value of five or six hundred thousand francs, not belonging to it, but which formed part of my private property; repossession shall be obtained of them, in order to discharge my legacies. 2. I had in the hands of the banker Torlonia, at Rome, bills of exchange to the amount of two or three hundred thousand francs, the produce of my revenues of the island of Elba, since 1815. The Sieur De La Perouse, although no longer my treasurer, and not invested with any character, possessed himself of this sum. He shall be compelled to restore it. 3. I bequeath to the Duke of Istria three hundred thousand francs, of which only one hundred thousand francs shall be reversible to his widow, should the duke be dead at the payment of the legacy. It is my wish, should there be no inconvenience in it, that the duke may marry Duroc's

daughter. 4. I bequeath to the Duchess of Frioul, the daughter of Duroc, two hundred thousand francs: should she be dead at the payment of this legacy, none of it shall be given to the mother. 5. I bequeath to General Rigaud (to him who was proscribed,) one hundred thousand francs. 6. I bequeath to Boisnod, the intendant commissary, one hundred thousand francs. 7. I bequeath to the children of General Letort, who was killed in the campaign of 1815, one hundred thousand francs. 8. These eight hundred thousand francs of legacies shall be considered as if inserted at the end of Article xxxvi. of my testament, which will make the legacies which I have disposed of, by my will, amount to the sum of six million four hundred thousand francs, without comprising the donations which I have made by my second codicil.

This is written with my own hand, signed, and sealed with my arms.

(L. S.)

Napoleon.

[On the outside, nearly at the centre, is written:]

This is my third codicil to my will, entirely written with my own hand, signed, and sealed with my arms.

[The words are intermixed with the signatures of Bertrand, Montholon, Marchand, Vignali, with their respective seals, and a piece of green silk runs through the centre. On the upper left corner are the following directions:]

To be opened the same day, and immediately after the opening of my will.

Napoleon.

[With some fragments of the signatures of the above-named witnesses.]

This 24th April, 1821. Longwood.

This is a fourth Codicil to my Testament.

By the dispositions which we have heretofore made, we have not fulfilled all our obligations; which has decided us to make this fourth codicil.

1. We bequeath to the son or grandson of Baron Dutheil, lieutenant-general of artillery, and formerly lord of St. André, who commanded the school of Auxonne before the Revolution, the sum of one hundred thousand francs, as a memento of gratitude for the care which that brave general took of us when we were lieutenant and captain under his orders.

2. Item. To the son or grandson of General Dugomier, who commanded in chief the army of Toulon, the sum of one hundred thousand francs. We under his orders directed that siege, and commanded the artillery; it is a testimonial of remembrance for the marks of esteem, of affection, and of friendship, which that brave and intrepid general gave us.

3. Item. We bequeath one hundred thousand francs to the son or grandson of the deputy of the Convention, Gasparin, representative of the people at the army of Toulon, for having protected and sanctioned with his authority, the plan which we had given, which procured the capture of that city, and which was contrary to that sent by the Committee of Public Safety. Gasparin placed us, by his protection, under shelter from the persecution and ignorance of the general officers who commanded the army before the arrival of my friend Dugomier.

4. Item. We bequeath one hundred thousand francs to the widow, son, or grandson, of our aide-de-camp, Muiron, killed at our side at Arcola, covering us with his body.

5. Item. Ten thousand francs to the subaltern officer Cantillon, who has undergone a trial, upon the charge of having endeavoured to assassinate Lord Wellington, of which he was

pronounced innocent. Cantillon had as much right to assassinate that *oligarchist*, as the latter had to send me to perish upon the rock of St. Helena. Wellington, who proposed this outrage, attempted to justify himself by pleading the interest of Great Britain. Cantillon, if he had really assassinated that lord, would have excused himself, and have been justified by the same motives, the interest of France, to get rid of a general, who, moreover, had violated the capitulation of Paris, and by that had rendered himself responsible for the blood of the martyrs Ney, Labédoyère, &c.; and for the crime of having pillaged the museums, contrary to the text of the treaties.

6. These four hundred thousand francs shall be added to the six million four hundred thousand of which we have disposed, and will make our legacies amount to six million eight hundred and ten thousand francs; these four hundred and ten thousand are to be considered as forming part of our testament, article 36; and to follow in every thing the same course as the other legacies.

7. The nine thousand pounds sterling which we gave to Count and Countess Montholon, should, if they have been paid, be deducted and carried to the account of the legacies which we have given to him by our testament. If they have not been paid, our notes of hand shall be annulled.

8. In consideration of the legacy given by our will to Count Montholon, the pension of twenty thousand francs granted to his wife, is annulled. Count Montholon is charged to pay it to her.

9. The administration of such an inheritance, until its final liquidation, requiring expenses of offices, of journeys, of missions, of consultations, and of law-suits, we expect that our testamentary executors shall retain three per cent upon all the legacies, as well upon the six million eight hundred thousand francs, as upon the sums contained in the codicils, and upon the two millions of the private domain.

10. The amount of the same thus retained, shall be deposited in the hands of a treasurer, and disbursed by drafts from our testamentary executors.

11. If the sums arising from the aforesaid deductions be not sufficient to defray the expenses, provision shall be made to that effect, at the expense of the three testamentary executors and the treasurer, each in proportion to the legacy which we have bequeathed to them in our will and codicils.

12. Should the sums arising from the before-mentioned subtractions be more than necessary, the surplus shall be divided amongst our three testamentary executors and the treasurer, in the proportion of their respective legacies.

13. We nominate Count Las Cases, and in default of him, his son, and in default of the latter, General Drouot, to be treasurer.

This present codicil is entirely written with our hand, signed, and sealed with our arms.

Napoleon

This 24th of April, 1821. Longwood.

This is my Codicil or Act of my last Will.

Upon the funds remitted in gold to the Empress Maria Louise, my very dear and well-beloved spouse, at Orleans, in 1814, she remains in my debt two millions, of which I dispose by the present codicil, for the purpose of recompensing my most faithful servants, whom moreover I recommend to the protection of my dear Marie Louise.

1. I recommend to the empress to cause the income of thirty thousand francs, which Count Bertrand possessed in the duchy of Parma, and upon the Mont Napoleon at Milan, to be restored to him, as well as the arrears due.

2. I make the same recommendation to her with regard to the Duke of Istria, Duroc's daughter, and others of my servants who have continued faithful to me, and who are always dear to me. She knows them.

3. Out of the above-mentioned two millions, I bequeath three hundred thousand francs to Count Bertrand, of which he will lodge one hundred thousand in the treasurer's chest, to be employed in legacies of conscience, according to my dispositions.

4. I bequeath two hundred thousand to Count Montholon, of which he will lodge one hundred thousand in the treasurer's chest, for the same purpose as above-mentioned.

5. Item, Two hundred thousand to Count Las Cases, of which he will lodge one hundred thousand in the treasurer's chest, for the same purpose as above-mentioned.

6. Item, To Marchand, one hundred thousand, of which he will place fifty thousand in the treasurer's chest, for the same purpose as above-mentioned.

7. To Jean Jerome Levie, the mayor of Ajaccio at the commencement of the Revolution, or to his widow, children, or grand-children, one hundred thousand francs.

8. To Duroc's daughter, one hundred thousand.

9. To the son of Bessières, Duke of Istria, one hundred thousand.

10. To General Drouot, one hundred thousand.

11. To Count Lavalette, one hundred thousand.

12. Item, One hundred thousand; that is to say, twenty-five thousand to Piéron, my maître d'hôtel; twenty-five thousand to Novarre, my huntsman; twenty-five thousand to St. Denis, the keeper of my books; twenty-five thousand to Santini, my former door-keeper.

13. Item, One hundred thousand; that is to say, forty thousand to Planta, my orderly officer; twenty thousand to Hebert, lately housekeeper of Rambouillet, and who belonged to my

chamber in Egypt; twenty thousand to Lavigné, who was lately keeper of one of my stables, and who was my jockey in Egypt; twenty thousand to Jeanet Dervieux, who was overseer of the stables, and served in Egypt with me.

14. Two hundred thousand francs shall be distributed in alms to the inhabitants of Brienne-le-Chateau, who have suffered most.

15. The three hundred thousand francs remaining, shall be distributed to the officers and soldiers of my guard at the island of Elba, who may be now alive, or to their widows or children, in proportion to their appointments; and according to an estimate which shall be fixed by my testamentary executors. Those who have suffered amputation, or have been severely wounded, shall receive double: The estimate of it to be fixed by Larrey and Emmery.

This codicil is written entirely with my own hand, signed, and sealed with my arms.

  Napoleon.

[On the back of the codicil is written:]

This is my codicil, or act of my last will—the execution of which I recommend to my dearest wife, the Empress Marie Louise.

  (L. S.)

  Napoleon.

[Attested by the following witnesses, whose seals are respectively affixed:]

    Montholon,
    Bertrand,   A piece of green silk.
    Marchand,
    Vignali.

6th Codicil.

Monsieur Lafitte, I remitted to you, in 1815, at the moment of my departure from Paris, a sum of near six millions, for which you have given me a receipt and duplicate. I have cancelled one of the receipts, and I charge Count Montholon to present you with the other receipt, in order that you may pay to him, after my death, the said sum, with interest at the rate of five per cent. from the 1st of July, 1815, deducting the payments which you have been instructed to make by virtue of my orders.

It is my wish that the settlement of your account may be agreed upon between you, Count Montholon, Count Bertrand, and the Sieur Marchand; and this settlement being made, I give you, by these presents, a complete and absolute discharge from the said sum.

I also, at that time, placed in your hands a box, containing my cabinet of medals. I beg you will give it to Count Montholon.

This letter having no other object, I pray God, Monsieur Lafitte, to have you in his holy and good keeping.

Napoleon.

Longwood, Island of St. Helena,
the 25th April, 1821.

7th Codicil.

Monsieur le Baron Labouillerie, treasurer of my private domain, I beg you to deliver the account and the balance, after my death, to Count Montholon, whom I have charged with the execution of my will.

This letter having no other object, I pray God, Monsieur le Baron Labouillerie, to have you in his holy and good keeping.

Napoleon.

*Longwood, Island of St. Helena,
the 25th April, 1821.*

THE END

www.ingramcontent.com/pod-product-compliance
Lightning Source LLC
Chambersburg PA
CBHW060309230426
43663CB00009B/1646